The Lovecraft Lexicon

Other Titles From New Falcon Publications

Cosmic Trigger: The Final Secret of the Illuminati
Prometheus Rising
 By Robert Anton Wilson
Undoing Yourself With Energized Meditation
Secrets of Western Tantra
 By Christopher S. Hyatt, Ph.D.
Rebels & Devils: The Psychology of Liberation
 Edited by Christopher S. Hyatt, Ph.D. with contributions by
 Wm. S. Burroughs, Timothy Leary, Robert Anton Wilson et al.
Pacts With the Devil: A Chronicle of Sex, Blasphemy & Liberation
Urban Voodoo: A Beginner's Guide to Afro-Caribbean Magic
 By S. Jason Black and Christopher S. Hyatt, Ph.D.
Taboo: Sex, Religion & Magick
 By Christopher S. Hyatt, Ph.D., Lon Milo DuQuette, et al.
The Pathworkings of Aleister Crowley
 By Aleister Crowley
Info-Psychology
 By Timothy Leary, Ph.D.
The Chaos Magick Audio CDs
PysberMagick: Advanced Ideas in Chaos Magick
 By Peter J. Carroll
Condensed Chaos: An Introduction to Chaos Magick
The Pseudonomicon
 By Phil Hine
The Infernal Texts: NOX & Liber Koth
 By Stephen Sennitt
The Complete Golden Dawn System of Magic (New, Expanded Edition)
The Golden Dawn Audio CDs
The World of Enochian Magic (CD)
 By Israel Regardie
Astrology & Consciousness: The Wheel of Light
 By Rio Olesky
Beyond Duality: The Art of Transcendence
 By Laurence Galian
Astrology & Consciousness
 By Rio Olesky
Zen Without Zen Masters
 By Camden Benares
Astrology, Aleister & Aeon
 By Charles Kipp

Please visit our website at http://www.newfalcon.com

The Lovecraft Lexicon

A Reader's Guide to Persons, Places and Things in the Tales of H.P. Lovecraft

Anthony B. Pearsall

NEW FALCON PUBLICATIONS
TEMPE, ARIZONA, U.S.A.

International Standard Book Number: 1-56184-129-3
Library of Congress Catalog Card Number: 97-65816

First Edition 2005

Cover Art and portrait of H.P. Lovecraft
by Linda Joyce Franks

With our deepest appreciation to Frater Vince Grubb
for his excellent editing and suggestions

The paper used in this publication meets the minimum requirements of the American National Standard for Permanence of Paper for Printed Library Materials Z39.48-1984

Address all inquiries to:
NEW FALCON PUBLICATIONS
1739 East Broadway Road #1-277
Tempe, AZ 85282 U.S.A.

(or)
320 East Charleston Blvd. #204-286
Las Vegas, NV 89104 U.S.A.

website: http://www.newfalcon.com
email: info@newfalcon.com

Now I ride with the mocking and friendly ghouls on the night-wind, and play by day among the catacombs.
— H.P. Lovecraft, in *The Outsider*

This book is affectionately dedicated to

Professor Robert Brainard Pearsall,

my father,

and to

Professor Marilyn M. Pearsall,

my mother,

as inadequate recompense

for many debts of long standing.

TABLE OF CONTENTS

Howard Phillips Lovecraft
1890–1937

INTRODUCTION

No one can deny that the most attractive figures in literature are always those around whom a world of lies and legend has been woven, those half mythical artists whose real characters become cloaked forever under a veil of the bizarre.
— Dylan Thomas

It all began for me with a used book I had picked up somewhere, as a 12-year-old: a copy of the 1965 Lancer Books edition of selected H.P. Lovecraft tales, *The Colour Out of Space*, a paperback edition whose cheaply-bound, sun-burned pages were already brownish, brittle, and crumbling apart, like poor Nahum Gardner and his wife at the end of the title story. After more than thirty years the opening sentence of that tale—"West of Arkham the hills rise wild, and there are valleys with deep woods that no axe has ever cut"—is still somehow entrancing to me whenever I read it, and at this point I have read it quite often. *The Call of Cthulhu* was in the collection too, and *The Picture in the House*; and by the time I finished reading the book I had become a Lovecraft fan, apparently for life. By now, after the massive and prolonged over-exposure to Lovecraft's work that will be confirmed by the remainder of these pages, my continued enjoyment of many of the tales, and my ability to find redeeming qualities even in the ones I don't much care for, are a testament to the skill with which he could write, and the creative vision that he could so often employ. If you've picked up this book and read this far, chances are you are a Lovecraft enthusiast as well. So, together, let us enter—to mock the master for a moment—some "eldritch and unnamable elder horrors of hideous nighted abysses and Cyclopean towers of mystery under a leering gibbous moon."

The following work grew from a passing thought a number of years ago, that the modern reader of many of the tales of H.P. Lovecraft might well be confused by some of the historical, geographical, literary, and mythological references—many of them quite obscure—with which he salted and peppered his tales. Likewise it can be a real task even to get and keep straight all of the matters he invented, and the many characters, some real and some fictitious, who appear in one story or another. So with the vague idea of an encyclopedic reference to every person, place, and thing (or "Thing!") in the tales, *The Lovecraft Lexicon* was born. This is the book I would have liked to have at hand when I was first reading all the tales.

Its composition has proceeded fitfully, with many and long interruptions, as time permitted between professional and family commitments over the years. But now I would like finally to put the book before the public. It does not, after all, contain an entry for *every* person, place and thing. In some few instances—for example, the names of Providence or Boston or Innsmouth streets where Our Hero walks for a few blocks, or the over-long recital of Cairo tourist attractions in the boring "travelogue" section of *Under the Pyramids*—exhaustion, boredom, or an attack of critical judgment led me to choose deliberate omissions. But such are very rare. The nature of the work and the manner of its writing must doubtlessly mean that there are also some surviving accidental omissions and inaccuracies, despite my care; or that some topics could well have been "covered" better, since I could not hope to develop equal mastery of all the material that the book touches upon. For all such faults, I take full responsibility, and apologize in advance to the gentle reader.

I should state quite clearly that this is a reference book, a compilation, and does not pretend to be more. The dictionary format does not lend itself to footnotes, and moreover I make no pretense of significant critical insights or deep and scholarly inquiries. My debts are to the researchers and authors who did the spadework before me, and whom I have acknowledged as well in "A Note On Sources," below. Beyond their writings, the sources of the book are various standard reference works, and a sort of knack for remembering historical or literary trivia which may be my own nearest point of personal resemblance to Lovecraft, who could so well remember such small facts, and then bring them artfully into play.

The heart of this Lexicon is in its explanatory entries, which (if they have any particular goal) are intended to help readers now and in the future to in some measure *know what Lovecraft knew*, insofar as his tales are concerned. But since I have no plans to write about H.P. Lovecraft ever again, I shall use this introduction to present some facts and impressions concerning him.

Howard Phillips Lovecraft was born in the city of Providence, Rhode Island (in his day, a community of around 120,000 inhabitants), on August 20, 1890. He was fated to be an only child. On the Lovecraft side, he was the great-grandson of a carpenter who had emigrated from

England by way of Canada, and the grandson of a harness-maker. His father, Winfield Scott Lovecraft (1853–98), born and raised in Rochester, New York, succeeded in getting a bit of education and escaping the small-tradesman class as a moderately successful man of business, perhaps for some time a "commercial traveler" (manufacturer's representative) for a Providence silverware company with a national clientele. Lovecraft's mother, Sarah Susan ("Susie") Phillips (1857–1921), was the daughter of a wealthy capitalist of old Rhode Island settler stock. There was no particular tradition of artistic skill or intellectual achievement on either side of the family; however, serious books and artwork were abundant in the home environment. The boy Lovecraft was an absurdly precocious reader who showed early signs of genius; and from a very young age, he enjoyed inventing and writing stories of various kinds.

Lovecraft's father became incurably insane in 1893 while in Chicago on a business trip, with the onset of severely delusional thinking, paranoia, and violent rages. He was committed to a Providence insane asylum and remained there, his condition steadily worsening, until his death in 1898. It is believed by scholars that his madness and early death were long-term ("tertiary") effects of untreated or unsuccessfully treated syphilis, a widespread venereal disease which was still rather poorly understood in the late 19th century, and which remained very difficult to cure before the development of specific antibiotics in the 1940s. It killed a lot of people other than Mr. Lovecraft, who presumably got his case from a prostitute or mistress in his bachelor years, perhaps as long as 15–20 years before the insanity cropped up. How much H.P. Lovecraft himself was ever aware of such details of his father's situation remains uncertain.

As a result of this domestic catastrophe the small boy and his mother went to live with her parents in 1893 (Lovecraft's grandmother would die soon after, in 1896), in their small mansion on Angell Street in the College Hill district of Providence, the very house in which Lovecraft had been born. During his life Lovecraft had an occasional habit of alluding offhandedly to his background and personal formation as if it were not too terribly dissimilar from that of the offspring of generations of dukes. To this day, some writers rather carelessly refer to his "aristocratic lineage" as though such a thing existed. But as we have seen, Lovecraft's commercial-traveler father was the son of a man who made and sold bridles and horse-collars for an honest living up in Rochester, while in dull reality his mother's family belonged to the solid American upper middle-class, at best to a municipal-level "commercial aristocracy," and all because of the dogged moneymaking efforts of a classic American one-generation success story, Lovecraft's grandfather Whipple. As things fell out, "one generation" also described the family's length of stay in that commercial aristocracy.

Whipple V. Phillips (1833–1904) was an ambitious and intelligent Rhode Islander who had worked hard, taken risks, and made his small fortune in business, light manufacturing, and real estate; finally attaining the status of a minor tycoon in a minor city, with time and money to enjoy the good life. The good life included trips to Europe; the small mansion with elegant grounds and a stable of horses, in the city's best neighborhood; expensive home furnishings, books, and paintings; and the opportunity for this successful former country boy, rural storekeeper, and on-the-make entrepreneur to raise his own daughters as Victorian ladies. He was by all accounts a very kindly, encouraging, even indulgent presence in his grandson Howard's life, a better-than-good replacement for the vanished and vaguely shameful father whom in adult years Lovecraft could only barely remember. (Significantly, in the 1926 story "The Silver Key"—written after the deaths of Lovecraft's mother and Whipple Phillips—the troubled Randolph Carter, Lovecraft's principal fictional alter-ego, "would often awake calling for his mother and grandfather, both in their graves....")

Curiously, H.P. Lovecraft's basic familial triangle, or sequence—the wise and powerful grandfather with not much time to live; the weak, clinging, less intelligent and increasingly useless daughter/mother in the middle; and the mentally precocious, unusual grandson whose relationship with his formidable grandfather was as son to father and student to teacher—is precisely recreated, albeit in a horribly sinister way, in the characters of Old Whateley, Lavinia Whateley, and Wilbur Whateley in *The Dunwich Horror.*

The future author grew up surrounded by much older relatives, and some even older books—including a splendid collection of bound volumes of 18th century English journals, and other books of the same era, which lay in a windowless attic store-room of the mansion and furnished his favorite reading material even before his tenth year—a child who combined some ordinary childish pursuits with a zest for the sort of books few children could ever have managed. While growing up (and forever afterwards) he read enormously and omnivorously. Although he was certainly a "town boy" as the current phrase was, in his childhood the Rhode Island countryside began only a short walk from his front door on Angell Street, so that he came by an early appreciation of New England rural scenes.

In 1904 Whipple Phillips died suddenly in the midst of severe financial reverses, and most of his wealth vanished in a chaos of debts and failed speculations. The mansion was sold. A small remnant of the fortune provided much, if not most, of Lovecraft's income—a very slender income at best—for the rest of his life. Meanwhile, the teenage Lovecraft and his mother moved into a rented duplex unit a few blocks away at 598 Angell Street, where they would live together in a few rooms for the next fifteen years.

He attended, but never graduated from, the local public high school. An apparent nervous breakdown was the principal cause of his withdrawal from school before his senior year.

> ...I had to drop out of school for a greater or lesser period & take a complete rest free from all responsibilities; & when I was 18 suffered such a breakdown that I had to forego college. In those days I could hardly bear to see or speak to anyone, & liked to shut out the world by pulling down dark shades & using artificial light.

Ironically Lovecraft, whose high-flown language and diverse learning were so striking, never earned a high-school diploma; he would never spend a day in college, nor would he ever train for (or work in) any profession or business other than freelance writing and story-editing or ghostwriting. American public high schools were far better places to receive a classical education in Lovecraft's day, before mass enrollment became the rule (only a minority of people "went on" to high school then) and a century of grade inflation and dumbing down of the curriculum had occurred. But the fact remains that Lovecraft's hoard of knowledge, as his ex-wife wrote, "was far greater than that of many a university student," and it was for the most part self-acquired by reading hard books on many subjects.

During his early manhood, roughly between the years 1908 and 1913, Lovecraft lived more reclusively than ever before or afterward, reading constantly, and pursuing his hobbies of astronomy and chemistry. Although he was not a total recluse, his life was a solitary and inward one, his days and nights spent in self-imposed isolation in the rented rooms he shared with his mother. He did not go to college, he did not go to work, and to a large extent he did not even go out of the house.

Lovecraft's cash inheritance from his grandfather, supplemented by whatever he got by the death of his mother when he was 31, was both too small and too large. Too small because it was not enough to provide the benefits of real wealth: property, travel, financial assurance; not even enough, as events would prove, to last him through a lifetime of low-budget living. On the other hand it was too large because, for a number of years, including his late teens and early twenties when a middle-class man was expected to complete his education and learn a profession or trade, the sum he and his mother had been left was sufficient to permit him to delude himself that some cash would always be there for him, without effort: because for the moment, there it was! Less than four months before he died—he did not know that he had so little time, and that his financial worries were soon to come at an abrupt end—he wrote to a friend:

> I made the mistake in youth of not realising that literary endeavour does not always mean an income. I ought to have trained myself for some routine clerical work…affording a dependable stipend yet leaving my mind free enough for a certain amount of creative activity—but in the absence of immediate need I was too damned a fool to look ahead. I seemed to think that sufficient money for ordinary needs was something which everyone had as a matter of course—and if I ran short, I "could always sell a story or poem or something." Well—my calculations were inaccurate!

"And so Lovecraft condemned himself to a life of ever-increasing poverty," Lovecraft biographer S.T. Joshi comments on this sad confession. By the time he first made a serious effort to find a job, he was 34, with no training or experience, and not desirable to employers as a new hire; and by the time he *really* needed a job—because his inheritance had almost vanished—the Great Depression had crushed the economy, the U.S. unemployment rate approached 25%, and better candidates for hiring than he were fruitlessly pounding the pavements or riding the rails, desperate for any job paying the "$10 a week" he felt was the least he could live on. It seems that his mother and aunts were seriously at fault simply for not pushing him out of the nest, or at least convincing him that, as a young man, he would have to prepare for work—something they should have been able to realize. One presumes that if Lovecraft's father or his grandfather, who were successful businessmen first and foremost, had been around to counsel him in his teens, they would certainly have done a much better job of explaining the economic facts of life to the young man. But they were no longer available, and his womenfolk did not do so, or not well enough.

At the same time, the thing he could do better than almost anyone else—writing—he always resisted treating as a paying proposition, although he became increasingly dependent on whatever income it did provide. He argued the principle that his writing should be a gentlemanly, amateur pursuit, indulged in primarily for his own pleasure, secondly perhaps for the entertainment of his circle of friends to whom he might show his work, thirdly, if at all, for filthy lucre. This is fine for a writer who has a real fortune already in the bank, as did his early fantasy-writing idol Lord Dunsany; but for Lovecraft—who lacked such a fortune or even some "routine clerical work…affording a dependable stipend"—it was a policy of financial doom.

So we see him growing mortally discouraged by a handful of rejections, such as come the way of any long-time professional in the magazine-writing trade, to the point where he almost quits writing fiction. We see him taking months to write a superb, book-length tale, *The Case of Charles Dexter Ward,* and then letting the manuscript sit in a drawer until he died, even after a major publisher had invited him to send in a novel for consideration. We see him taking a few months to research and write a lengthy, certainly very competent, essay or monograph, *Supernatural Horror in Literature,* all in order that a friend of his could publish it for free in an amateur journal mailed to a few hundred fellow-amateur subscribers. We see him writing a travelogue in 18th century English about the city of Quebec, which he apparently never even showed to anyone else—and it was the longest thing he ever wrote, and it took him several more months of time. All the while he was drifting into penury. One of the "fussy" members of the Boston Art Club, in *Pickman's Model*, suggests that the sinister artist Pickman is "bound down the toboggan of reverse evolution," and this pseudo-Darwinian concept appears in other tales—but the only reverse evolution that really mattered in Lovecraft's life was his own, from a rich child in a mansion in 1897 to a poor man in a rented room forty years later.

Some may argue that really pursuing writing as a commercial venture, as did the numerous professional writers he came to know, could have spelled his artistic ruination; since none of his contemporaries and friends ever amounted to much, or to nearly as much as he did, in terms of their works' lasting value. One may answer with the names of Shakespeare, Dostoyevsky, Twain, Wilde. Or that early idol of Lovecraft's, Samuel Johnson, who so famously and unfairly grunted: "No man but a blockhead ever wrote except for money."

The poorer Lovecraft grew, the more of a self-proclaimed "socialist" he became. To his credit, he steadily rejected Soviet-style class warfare and its cruelty, even in the 1930s when many Western intellectuals or demi-intellectuals, including some of his younger friends, had responded to false signs of "capitalism's impending collapse" by making the fashionable turn toward a Moscow that was then presided over by the monstrous Josef Stalin. Lovecraft's socialism would not have been recognized by many socialists of the time: as one friend wrote, tongue in cheek:

> The embroideries contributed by Lovecraft included adequate provisions for indigent gentlemen and scholars, baronial largesse for the peasantry, liberal endowments for those desiring to practice the arts and sciences, a stiff educational test for voters, and the gradual substitution of an aristocracy of intellect for an aristocracy of wealth.

Naturally, Lovecraft (or "HPL" as he shall be called in the main part of this book) dressed up his "socialist" vision in loftier terms, but at root his utopia has a common root with those of many other published utopias; being the dream of a solitary man, objectively unsuccessful in his own society, furiously scribbling the plans for a radically-reorganized world where the philistine, money-hungry bourgeoisie that ignored him would be eliminated as a class, and intellectual men of his own type would wisely be put in charge. Phrased more brutally: as Lovecraft had dreamed in the past of being the traditional type of property-owning aristocrat in a caste society, who could pursue his interests without working, now he dreamed of a future with nationalized industries, social welfare, and strict government control of the economy—in which he could be a new type of aristocrat, an "aristocrat of intellect," who could still pursue his interests without working—or rather, in which pursuing his interests would now be deemed work, and paid accordingly from the common fund. Although some have praised Lovecraft, the fanatically, even outrageously, arch-conservative polemicist of as late as the mid-1920s, the only member of the King George III branch of the Republican Party, for his "socially conscious" turn of mind in the radical 1930s, the daydream was fundamentally a self-serving and narcissistic one; and Lovecraft provides an example of how close together political opposite extremes can really be.

Readers who wish to get some picture of the Lovecraftian utopia, but who are of no mind to wade through his non-fiction writing of the period, may find it expressed pretty well in the description of the society of the non-human and pre-human "Great Race" in the 1935 tale *The Shadow Out of Time*: "...a sort of fascistic socialism, with major resources rationally distributed, and power delegated to a small governing board elected by the votes of all those able to pass certain educational and psychological tests." The Great Race is even more of a Lovecraftian utopia than could be possible in a human society since its members never need to sleep, and they have no sex, only reproducing by spores.

With this digression concluded we may return to the chronology of Lovecraft's life.

Beginning in 1914, he became heavily involved in the cause of "amateur journalism," a pastime for many non-professional writers in that period; and we can be sure that the world "amateur" was an especially pleasing word to him. With a swarm of idiosyncratic "little magazines," privately printed or self-printed, and distributed to other hobbyists, the amateur journalism movement provided Lovecraft with the initial publishing outlets for his early tales, poems, and essays; with new friends who shared his love of words; and with his earliest fans. For some years Lovecraft was one of the zealous leaders of amateur journalism, as a writer, a critic, and an elected official of the two national membership organizations. He even published his own "little magazine," on the typically erratic schedule of amateurdom. (It was called *The Conservative*.) Although as a writer he would eventually grow beyond amateurdom and the frog-pond organizational politics that went along with it, it is not difficult to believe the words he wrote in a convention speech made in 1921: "...what Amateur Journalism has given me is—life itself."

In 1919 Lovecraft's mother, that over-sheltered, over-sheltering specimen of Victorian maidenhood, whose conduct had grown increasingly peculiar as the years went by, became permanently deranged. Her symptoms included erratic and disoriented public behavior, weeping spells, and delusions; it might now be labeled as severe anxiety and depression, at the very least. A lady who knew both Lovecraft and his mother in this period recollected many years later:

> Although of a younger generation, I knew Howard's mother better than I knew Howard who even as a young boy was strange and rather a recluse, who kept by himself and hid from other children, because, as his mother said, he could not bear to have people look upon his awful face. She would talk of his looks (it seemed to be an obsession with her) which would not have attracted any particular attention if he had been normal as were the other children in the community....
>
> I met her often on the Butler Avenue [streetcars], and one day after many urgent invitations I went to call on her. She was considered then to be getting rather odd. My call was pleasant enough but the house had a strange and shut-up air and the atmosphere seemed weird and Mrs. Lovecraft talked continuously of her unfortunate son who was so hideous that he hid from everyone and did not like to walk the streets where people could gaze at him.
>
> When I protested that she was exaggerating and that he should not feel that way, she looked at me with a rather pitiful look as though I did not understand about it. I remember that I was glad to get out in the fresh air and the sunshine and that I did not repeat my visit. Surely it was an environment suited for the writing of horror stories but an unfortunate one for a growing youth....
>
> After a time one did not meet Mrs. Lovecraft very often.... Sometimes when going around the corner to mail a letter on an early summer evening, one would see a dark figure fluttering about the shrubbery of her house, and I discovered that it was Mrs. Lovecraft.
>
> I remember the aunts who came to the little house on Angell Street often, as I recollect, quiet, determined little New England women, quite different from Mrs. Lovecraft, although Mrs. Lovecraft was a very determined person herself. I remember Mrs. Lovecraft spoke to me about weird

and fantastic creatures that rushed out from behind buildings and from corners at dark, and that she shivered and looked about apprehensively as she told her story.

After being sent in 1919 to the same Providence insane asylum where her husband had died many years before, Sarah Susan Philipps Lovecraft perished there as well in 1921, from complications following gall-bladder surgery. As soon as the gates of the madhouse had closed behind his mother in 1919, one of Lovecraft's formidable aunts moved into the Angell Street duplex, to look after the grown man as his mother had done earlier.

Lovecraft biographer S.T. Joshi suggests that Lovecraft's mother had "finally cracked under the strain of financial worries," which is very plausible. Her husband and her father were both long dead, her only child was a 28-year-old eccentric (with a "hideous" face, to boot) who had never held a job, finished high school, or even had a girlfriend, and who still lived with her; and the inheritance that had to support them both was too small. In this analysis her accumulated sorrows and cares simply grew too great to bear. For Lovecraft's part, it seems that he put his own feelings into one of his fictional characters, the semi-autobiographical figure of Edward Derby in *The Thing on the Doorstep* (1933), when he wrote:

> Edward's mother died when he was thirty-four, and for months he felt incapacitated by some odd psychological malady…. Afterward he seemed to feel a sort of grotesque exhilaration, as if of partial escape from some unseen bondage. He began to mingle….

A future good friend who met Lovecraft early enough to have seen him both at and away from his mother's side, in 1916, had this to say:

> It has always seemed to me that Lovecraft's fundamental instincts were entirely normal. Removed from the repressive sick-room atmosphere of his home and the attendance of his mother or his aunts, he blossomed out astonishingly. Furthermore, he had a real knack for making himself liked.

One of Lovecraft's friends and fans from his amateur journalism organization, with whom he "began to mingle" beginning in the fateful year of 1921, was Sonia Greene (1883–1972), a warmhearted, generous, and hard-working Russian-Jewish immigrant, seven years his senior. She was born Sonia Simyonovna Shifirkin in the modest village of Ichnya, some one hundred miles northeast of Kiev, now in the nation of Ukraine. When she was nine years old she came to New York, part of the great wave of Jewish emigration from the Russian Empire to the United States in the years roughly between 1890 and 1914. Denied the chance for sustained formal education by the circumstances of her life—at 13 she was sent out to work as an apprentice to a milliner (*i.e.*, a designer, maker and seller of expensive ladies' hats, which in those days were often elaborate constructions using several materials), at 15 she married her first husband, at 17 she was already a mother, and at 33 a widow—Sonia was nonetheless a thoughtful and reasonably well-read person, as devoted to books, music, the fine arts, and intellectual self-improvement as her busy professional life in the New York City garment industry permitted her to be. When the tall brunette met H.P. Lovecraft at an amateur journalism convention in Boston, in the summer of 1921, she was still glamorous in her late thirties, outgoing and energetic, immaculately groomed and fashionably attired. The gaunt intellectual New Englander seems to have intrigued her immediately.

One of Lovecraft's best friends, Alfred Galpin (1901–83), left a wonderful sketch of an indomitable female who still had Russia and the spirit of the "great Russian soul" in her bones, for good or ill:

> When she dropped in on my reserved and bookish student life at Madison [in 1921 or 1922, while Galpin was an undergraduate at the University of Wisconsin], I felt like an English sparrow transfixed by a cobra. Junoesque and commanding, with superb dark eyes and hair, she was too regal to be a Dostoievsky character and seemed rather a heroine from some of the most martial pages of *War and Peace*. Proclaiming the glory of the free and enlightened human personality, she declared herself a person unique in depth and intensity and urged me to Write, to Do, to Create.

A mutual friend, who knew both Lovecraft and Sonia well, wrote after her death that she was "one of the most beautiful women I have ever met, and the kindest."

Sonia was a woman who knew how to make things happen, and the story of her personal journey, even more unusual a century ago, from a teenage mother in a bad marriage to a prosperous and independent businesswoman in the prime of her life, would be interesting in itself if only we knew much more about it than we do, which is really almost nothing. At any rate, when Sonia first met Lovecraft she was employed as a saleswoman and workshop manager for an elegant New York women's apparel company, and she must have been good at it: the "close to $10,000 a year" salary that she mentions in her memoir of Lovecraft was well beyond what most *men* could earn in a year during the 1920s, while for women of that era such compensation was almost unheard of. (As S.T. Joshi notes, this sum was "probably at least five to ten times as much as Lovecraft ever made in any given year of his entire career.") In her spare time she pursued a new hobby in amateur journalism, with an eager spirit if not much ability—for Sonia's grade-school and night-

school English, while fluent and idiomatic, was never up to the requirements of literary writing.

She also pursued H.P. Lovecraft with what seems to have been her
typical combination of boldness, energy, and determination. By this time,
although he was over thirty years old, Lovecraft as far as we know had
never had a relationship with a woman, gone on a date, or even been
kissed, except by his mother and aunts and then only while he was still a
small child. Perhaps it should have always remained that way; but
Sonia's attractions and attentions wore down his considerable inhibitions.
To the extent the old familiar phrase was ever true of any couple, it was
true of this one: She chased him until he caught her.

This grew. Early in 1924 they were secretly married after a covert
courtship, apparently to the intense surprise of everyone who knew them.
(Upon hearing the news, "I had a feeling of faintness at the pit of my
stomach and became very pale," reminisced a New York friend of Lovecraft's who also knew Sonia.) Setting aside the pronounced difference in
their backgrounds and characters, in the 1920s the marriage of any non-
Jew with a Jew—even a Jew as "assimilated" as Sonia—was still a rare
event, unlike now. And H.P. Lovecraft, whose devotion to his native
place of College Hill, Providence, was well-nigh fanatical, even moved
to Sonia's large apartment at 259 Parkside Avenue, Brooklyn, New
York.

At the outset of the marriage, Lovecraft seems to have sincerely
hoped, and tried, to obtain a salaried job and be a reasonably ideal husband. Had he found success in New York, congenial employment with
good pay, maybe the whole thing could have worked, or at least taken
longer to fail. Unfortunately, as a man in his mid-30s with no career
training or employment history, and with stiffly "aristocratic" and old-
fashioned modes of speech, dress, and bearing (never stiffer, alas, than
when meeting strangers!) that did not seem to impress prospective employers in America's bustling metropolis, Lovecraft never did find viable
work in New York City. Eventually he became discouraged and quit
looking. Meanwhile Sonia's Manhattan employer went out of business
and to keep supporting them both, she had to accept work out of town,
turning their marriage into a long-distance or commuter relationship.

Lovecraft at first had enjoyed the sights of New York—focusing on
architectural antiquities as was his custom, but also taking some pleasure
in the "Cyclopean" high-rise skyline—and using the opportunity to
spend much time (before long, more time than he did with his wife) with
old cronies from amateur journalism who lived in New York. But the
mass of the people of the metropolis were, on the whole, not so pleasing
to his eyes and ears. A yelping anti-Semite and racist since at least his

early teens, Lovecraft in 1924–26 found himself stuck in the one city with substantially more Jews—a quarter of New York's population, then—and more immigrants than any other city in America at the time, a melting-pot stew that was seasoned with a hearty helping of "negroes." On top of all his other troubles and his chronic homesickness, it was more than he could bear, and he began to crack.

As Sonia wrote later:

> ...when he saw the crowds in the subway, on the streets, and in the parks, he actually hated them and suffered through that hate....
>
> ...whenever he would meet crowds of people—in the subway, or, at the noon hour, on the sidewalks in Broadway, or crowds, wherever he happened to find them, and these were usually the workers of minority races—he would become livid with anger and rage.

His private letters from this period provide many ugly examples—sometimes amazingly ugly examples—of feverish race-hatred and racial paranoia aimed at the "non-Nordic" people he saw whenever he stepped outside, or for that matter whenever he looked across the kitchen table. Regrettably, many of these letters have survived to harm his posthumous reputation. Even for an admiring biographer it is easy to grow a little impatient with the object of admiration when perusing these outpourings, after most of a century has gone by and attitudes have changed so much. It seems simply disappointing in a man who was so capable of grand-scale thinking in many other directions.

Lovecraft's ingrained prejudices against "inferior" groups and the dreaded "race-mixing," were clearly exaggerated many times over—in an historically familiar pattern—by his own fish-out-of-water feelings of social alienation in Brooklyn and Manhattan, by his personal economic failures (the most desperate racists being almost inevitably the people only one or two steps above the hated minority on the socioeconomic ladder), and by his yearning for the white man's town he had left behind, beloved Providence.

Of course it is only fair to put his racial animosities into historical perspective. Lovecraft's New York-era letters home bordered on racial monomania; he never wrote so virulently before or afterwards. But he clung to the white-supremacist, anti-Semitic, nativist ideas that were current and popular in the New England of his youth, in a more mild-mannered form, for most or all of his life. Although in his last years he grew much more tolerant of, for example, French-Canadians and even Jews—which is a good thing to say—some deeply-rooted prejudices never altered. For example, S.T. Joshi advises that: "To the end of his life Lovecraft retained a belief in the *biological* (as opposed to the cultural) inferiority of blacks, and maintained that a strict color line must be preserved in order to prevent miscegenation"—the latter word meaning the cross-breeding of the two races; a terrifying, infuriating idea to white racists before, during, and after Lovecraft's life.

He grew up, after all, in the noonday of Social Darwinism, ethnic nationalism, and academically-approved ethnocentrism. The idea that all of history had been a movement toward white rule over the whole world was a popular idea, promoted in best-selling books, praised in daily newspapers. The overt and antagonistic racism that has since become taboo in American society, was then the norm; tolerance was abnormal, "diversity" not considered of value by anyone. (To give only one example where thousands could be provided: the hallowed English science-fiction master, iconoclastic social commentator, and popular historian H.G. Wells (1866–1946), wrote when Lovecraft was a boy that the (white) nation which "most resolutely picks over, educates, sterilizes, exports or poisons its 'People of the Abyss' [the poor or criminal under-class]" would prevail over its rivals in the long run, and that as far as the rest of the world went, "the swarms of black and brown, and dirty-white, and yellow people...will have to go.... [It is] their portion to die and disappear."—*Anticipations of the Reaction of Mechanical and Scientific Progress Upon Human Life and Thought*, 1901).

For whatever psychological reason, Lovecraft drank deep at the well of such thinking when he was young and most impressionable, and could never entirely walk away from it. Indeed, two of the reasons he enjoyed visiting the southern states so much, besides the warm climate which was very agreeable to him, were his lifelong admiration for the Lost Cause of the southern Confederate states, and his opinion that with the strict racial segregation then in force, and the low number of immigrants compared to the northeast, southern cities hadn't fallen from grace and still preserved their Anglo-Saxonism intact. The hatred of "change" was very strong in him to the end of his life.

I cannot praise thy marriage-choices, son. Lovecraft certainly must have read these words from Milton's *Samson Agonistes* at some point in life, and they would have been apt words for him. All students of Lovecraft have probably wondered at some point how *this* man wound up married to *this* woman, who was a Jew—if a fairly progressive and unobservant one—and an immigrant from eastern Europe who had learned English as a second language. To a woman, moreover, who was a hustling and independent entrepreneur unlike any other female he had ever known. The answer was that both of the partners deceived themselves. Like many another woman before and since, Sonia deceived herself that she could change her mate—for the better, as she saw it. Lovecraft deceived himself that he could thrive as a married man in New York, that he could be more of a modernist man, and that Sonia was or could be—as he told her when she reminded him of her personal membership in group(s) that he despised—"no longer [one of] these mongrels.... *You are now Mrs. H.P. Lovecraft of 598 Angell Street, Providence, Rhode Island!*"

Sadly, if predictably, the marriage proved unsuccessful, and it ended for all practical purposes in the spring of 1926, although a legal divorce petition was not filed until some time afterward. (Gradually the two fell out of touch, and Sonia, by then remarried—to a very romantic Jewish man!—and living in California, did not learn of her ex-husband's death until eight years after the fact.) On April 17, 1926 Lovecraft boarded a train in New York, alone, and joyously returned to his native place. "He was without question the happiest man I ever saw," wrote an old friend who visited Lovecraft during his first few days back on College Hill. Except for sightseeing vacations in the eastern United States and Canada during the subsequent years, he would never leave Providence again.

Sonia's last-ditch attempt to save her marriage makes painful reading. After Lovecraft had moved back to Providence—a middling city at best, which she in all likelihood privately considered to be narrow, provincial, and small-townish—she came for a visit. In conference with Lovecraft's aunts, Lillian and Annie, both widows in nearly the same financial situation as their nephew, she made what must have seemed like a reasonable proposal:

> I suggested that I would take [rent] a large house, secure a good maid, pay all the expenses and have the two aunts live with us at no expense to them, or at least they would live better at no greater expense. H.P. and I actually negotiated the rental of such a house with the option to buy if we found we liked it. H.P. was to use one side of it as his study and library, and I would use the other side as a business venture of my own. At this time the aunts gently but firmly informed me that neither they nor Howard could afford to have Howard's wife work for a living in Providence. That was that. I now knew where we all stood. Pride preferred to suffer in silence; both theirs and mine.
>
> After getting Howard well settled in Providence I returned to N.Y....

Put aside the fact that "Howard" actually had few friends or connections in Providence and that very few of the hard-working and hard-headed locals would have known or cared what he and his wife might do. By 1926, more than twenty years after Whipple V. Phillip's self-made fortune had evaporated, his family's elite position in local society appears to have been only the last illusion remaining to the aunts. The fact is that hardly anyone in town noticed when H.P. Lovecraft left Providence in 1924, and hardly anyone noticed when he came back in 1926.

For that matter, hardly anyone there would notice when he died eleven years later; his burial at Swan Point Cemetery was attended by only seven people, two of them family members. Ironically, a funeral in New York City would have attracted far more mourners.

Apparently it would even have been all right for "Howard's wife" to work for a living outside of Providence, and discreetly send him funds: it was the appearance of things, which meant everything. S.T. Joshi correctly observes that "the 1920s in New England were a time when standards of propriety meant more than an income, and the aunts were simply adhering to the codes of behaviour by which they had led their entire lives." Assessed more negatively, the remnant of social status—based on the money their dead father used to possess—that they clung to among their surviving friends (Lovecraft's wife's job would scarcely have mattered to anyone else) meant more to them than the chance of preserving their nephew's marriage to the only woman who had ever given him the time of day. In any case, as hard as Sonia tried to get and stay on the good side of the aunts, they seem never to have been pleased about their Howard's marriage to—of all things!—a Jewess and career woman from New York, not even a real American. (Tellingly, it took him until six days after the surprise wedding to tell his aunts about the event, and then he did so by mail with a painfully long-winded series of explanations, never including that word "love.") But they can be faulted the least; they were simply dinosaurs behaving like dinosaurs.

But what about a 36-year-old man content to let his elderly aunts negotiate the continuance or non-continuance of his wedded life? S.T. Joshi, usually willing to give Lovecraft the benefit of a doubt, properly labels much of Lovecraft's conduct in the marriage as shabby, as well as "thoughtless, spineless, emotionally remote, and financially incompetent." But what about Sonia, who was old enough to know better? As previously mentioned, she had let wishful thinking about a makeover of her prospective husband's personality and views overrule her better judgment. And while Lovecraft later wrote that their break-up was based principally on financial issues or fundamental differences in temperament, Sonia allowed herself to be more specific in a letter to a mutual friend, many years later: "I did *not* leave him on account of [his inadequacies concerning money], but chiefly on account of his harping hatred of [Jews]. This and this alone was the reason"—suggesting that at least in Sonia's own mind, the worm may finally have turned.

But H.P. Lovecraft is—with reason—not famous as a philanthropist, original philosopher, astute economist, or innovative political theorist, despite his reams of private writing on society, philosophy, economics, and politics. Much less is he famous as a great romantic. He is famous as a very significant author in his chosen genre of fiction, and to that much happier subject we now return. In the early 1920s he began to write professionally. During that final pre-television era which was the first half of the 20th century, the newsstands and mailboxes of America were laden with the so-called "pulp magazines"—collections of short stories and serialized novels, cheaply printed on wood-pulp paper with garish eye-catching covers, typically devoted to a genre of popular fiction such as romance, adventure, crime and detection, humor, the Wild West, or the like. Lovecraft himself had been a devoted reader of such journals for years. For an author such as Lovecraft whose gifts lay in the direction of fantasy, supernatural horror, and an offbeat style of science fiction, there were also pulp-fiction "markets," and he broke into them—including the foremost of all the shock pulps, the now-legendary *Weird Tales*, where from 1923 onwards the byline "H.P. Lovecraft" first began to garner some public attention.

A critical discussion of Lovecraft's work is not called for in a biographical sketch such as this one. Suffice it to say here that in such masterpieces as *The Colour Out of Space, The Festival, The Rats in the Walls, The Call of Cthulhu, The Shadow Over Innsmouth, At the Mountains of Madness*, and *The Shadow Out of Time*, Lovecraft earned his title as America's finest author of the fantastic after the hallowed master Edgar Allan Poe; and that he is credited with significant advances in the writing and plotting of fantasy, horror, and science fiction.

Worth mentioning, however, is the typical Lovecraftian protagonist who appears again and again in the tales, either equipped with a name or as a nameless narrator. The critic T.E.D. Klein, in his splendid introduction to the current Arkham House edition of *Dagon and Other Macabre Tales*, has described him as nervous, high-born, hypersensitive, scholarly, reclusive, easily unbalanced. These men leave the impression of observers, at best investigators, rather than actors in events. This passive trait is in some degree a reflection of Lovecraft's own personality and behavior, but also it turns out to be a deliberate policy, as Lovecraft explained:

> I believe that—because of the foundation of most weird concepts in dream-phenomena—the best weird tales are those in which the narrator or central figure remains (as in actual dreams) largely passive, & witnesses or experiences a stream of bizarre events which—as the case may be—flows past him, just touches him, or engulfs him utterly.

Writing for the pulps was an uncertain way to make a living even in the economic good times of the 1920s, and was only occasionally the road to even the steady middle-class prosperity that the average pulp-fiction writer might have hopefully aspired to as wealth. Certainly it was not one for an author who consistently averred that he wrote primarily to please himself, and who was usually willing to drop writing-for-money whenever some personal project appeared more attractive, or whenever a letter to a friend, or some editing/ghostwriting job (for which he was chronically underpaid), called upon his attention. Lovecraft was such an author—his self-image as a refined gentleman of aristocratic background, even though poor in money, kept him from ever becoming more prolific—or saved him from the danger of becoming a mere hack writer, depending on one's point of view. What is clear is that, like his "God of fiction," Edgar Allan Poe, Lovecraft was not the man to get rich from writing; he was paid nothing for his amateur-press publications, and the going rate of about a penny a word by the pulp magazines, sometimes less. In one notorious instance he was paid an absurd $25 by a pulp magazine (not *Weird Tales*, which always treated him better) for *The Colour Out of Space*, the most perfect tale he ever wrote in his own opinion and that of many readers: and he had to badger the publisher for seven months before he finally got the $25.

In her memoir of their relationship, written long after Lovecraft's death and after she had heard or read some details about his last years, the survivor-type Sonia summed up with half-contemptuous, half-despairing, very practical bluntness: "Had he been less proud [not] to write for money he need not have starved himself to death."

Indeed, as the 1920s turned into the 1930s, and American prosperity slid into the hard years of the Great Depression, Lovecraft's life and work began drawing to a close, a bit early. If not precisely "starving to death," he was poor in the so-called "shabby genteel" way—always more shabby than genteel as time rolls along—eking out the money for essentials (principally rent, writing paper, postage stamps, and his very meager meals) with intermittent magazine sales, freelance editing, and the drawing-down of that ever-dwindling small inheritance. He may have begun to grow tired of writing stories, seemingly discouraged as his longer and more thought-inspiring later tales engendered much confusion and criticism, and editorial rejections that soured him on his own efforts; his production-rate declined markedly.

But he increased the duration and distance of his ultra-budget holidays of inter-city bus rides, all-day urban walks, YMCA cots or friends' couches, and persisted with his tremendous output of personal letters and postcards to correspondents around the country who respected or even idolized him. In these years, he finally mellowed in some—although hardly all, and even the "mellowing" was comparative—of his previous prejudices and crotchets, rejected some of the opinions he had cherished in earlier days, and achieved a more mature appreciation of the world and at least some of its people.

A word-sketch of the mature Lovecraft in the early 1930s, written by his friend E. Hoffman Price (1898–1989), will serve to depict his appearance and character better than many more words of second-hand impressions could do:

> My first sight of HPL was in the lobby of a third class hotel on St. Charles Street, in New Orleans, early in June of 1932. He wore a baggy and threadbare suit, snuff-colored, and neatly patched in several places... The eyes I saw were dark brown, animated, intense, and entirely normal, without any of the weirdness I had expected.
>
> For the rest, he carried himself with enough of a slouch to make me underestimate his height as well as the breadth of his shoulders. His face was narrow, longish, with long chin and jaw. He walked with a quick step. His speech was quick and inclined to jerkiness. It was as though his body was hard put to it to keep up with the agility of his mind....
>
> He was not pompous, he was not pretentious—quite the contrary. He merely had a knack of using formal and academic diction for the most casual remark. We had not walked a block before I realized that no other way of speech could be truly natural for HPL. Had he used locutions less stilted, and taken to speaking as others did, that would have been the affectation...
>
> [Although Lovecraft did not drink alcohol][H]is taste for coffee simplified that refreshment problem. Rather than "taste"—passion. He drank cup after cup, and I made pot after pot. Into each cup he stirred four heaping spoonsful of sugar. For twenty-eight consecutive hours during which we chatted at a giddy tempo, he drank coffee.
>
> He had an enormous enthusiasm for new experience: of sight, of sound, of word pattern, of idea pattern. I have met in all my time [Price was in his fifties when he wrote these words] only one or two others who approached him in what I call "mental greed." A glutton for words, ideas, thoughts. He elaborated, combined, distilled, and at a machine gun tempo.
>
> He neither smoked nor drank, and, judging from all his conversation and letters, women did not exist as far as he was concerned. But excepting these, his tastes and interests approached the universal....

Lovecraft's gluttony for "words, ideas, thoughts" led to the breadth of historical, geographical, literary, and scientific references which have partly motivated the composition of this Lexicon. Likewise, his own "knack of using formal and academic diction for the most casual remark," and inability to speak "as others did," go a long way to explain why direct dialogue is so often absent from his tales, and why what dialogue there is, is always so unconvincing.

A longtime friend and correspondent, Frank Belknap Long (1901–94), wrote with some awe of the pattern of their many meetings, frequently as part of a circle of bookish buddies ready for some combative intellectual chat. Clearly Lovecraft was the leader in these gatherings. What a professor he might have made!

> Almost invariably...Howard did most of the talking, at least for the first ten or fifteen minutes. He would sink into an easy chair...and words would flow from him in a continuous stream.
>
> He never seemed to experience the slightest necessity to pause between words. There was no groping about for just the right term, no matter how recondite his conversation became. When the need for some metaphysical hair-splitting arose, it was easy to visualize scissors honed to a surgical sharpness snipping away in the recesses of his mind.

For ordinary human-interest purposes it may also be mentioned that Lovecraft loved cats, loathed the smell and taste of seafood, enjoyed Italian food and spicy *chili con carne* or Indian-style "curry" concoctions, never went out in public without wearing a jacket and tie (far more typical behavior in that era than now, it is true), was an atheist from childhood who believed in a blind, impersonal, and purposeless cosmos with no guiding power and no afterlife, preferred to do his writing late at night, and suffered abnormally in cold temperatures for some medical reason which cannot now be determined—a fact which he used as a starting-point for his 1926 horror tale *Cool Air*:

> You ask me to explain why I am afraid of a draught of cool air; why I shiver more than others upon entering a cold room, and seem nauseated and repelled when the chill of evening creeps through the heat of a mild autumn day.

He was extremely fond of ice cream and sweets—on one special outing with two friends in an ice-cream parlor he consumed two and a half quarts of ice cream at one sitting, and he told his wife that the only reason he drank tea at all was because he liked the lemon and the sugar so well—had no interest in sports or games and apparently no interest in sex, relished long walks, went to the movies now and then, and would sometimes mail a friend a handwritten letter sixty or seventy pages long.

He was also, famously, a dreamer, a producer of frequent and vivid dreams which he could remember in detail the next day. Lovecraft told friends that he tended to dream more in the wintertime, and that most of his dreams were actually innocuous recreations of the scenes and people of his childhood. "But the real scenes frequently merge into unknown and fantastic realms, & include landscapes & architectural vistas which could scarcely be on this planet. At times I also have historical dreams—with a setting in various remote periods. Occasionally—but not often, a dream of mine forms a usable fictional plot." L. Sprague de Camp wrote that:

> During his last years, Lovecraft dreamed of climbing with a group of men in medieval costume over the roofs of an old city, in pursuit of "a Thing of primal evil"; of approaching a street car to find that its crew had conical faces ending in a red tentacle; of meeting an evil clergyman in a garret full of books; of being visited by a troop of sinister black-magicians in dinner jackets; of revisiting his former home at 598 Angell Street, finding it in moldering decay and hearing dragging footsteps from his former room; of being attacked by insects that pierced his brain, giving him visions of life on other worlds....

All his life Lovecraft was addicted to making dogmatic judgments and pronouncements on such varied topics as: what was good or bad art; what a gentleman "could" and "could never" do; science; religion; the existence of God; American foreign policy; economics; education; how much better things used to be; proper English usage; issues in anthropology or philosophy, or other areas of higher learning; domestic animals; warfare; architecture; the hierarchy of the races; the menace of racial mongrelization; the Jewish problem; the Negro problem; the immigrant problem; socialism, fascism, and the creation of an ideal society with aspects of both; to name but a few! Since his early preferences were sometimes replaced by later ones, often to be just as dogmatically asserted, there is something in Lovecraft's corpus of preserved opinions to infuriate just about everybody. Readers of Lovecraft biographies will find this statement confirmed.

In this regard it is instructive to consider some contrasting passages from his personal correspondence. In 1923, as a 33-year-old man who had barely spent a couple of nights in his life away from home and the coddling care of his mother and aunts, he wrote these quite ferocious words in separate letters to friends:

> ...shall we ever be such women as to prefer the emasculate piping of an [international] arbitrator to the lusty battle-cry of a blue-eyed, blond-bearded warrior? The one sound power in the world is the power of a hairy muscular right arm!

And:

> I am naturally a Nordic—a chalk-white, bulky Teutonic killer of the Scandinavian or North-German forests—a Viking—a berserk killer—a predatory rover of the blood of Hengist and Horsa [two leaders of the Anglo-Saxon conquest of the future "England" in the 5th century A.D.]—a conquerer of Celts and mongrels and founder of Empires—a son of the thunders and the arctic winds, and brother to the frosts and the auroras—a drinker of foemen's blood from new-picked skulls....

The natural-born killer and "predatory rover"—who was brown-eyed, more gaunt than "bulky," and who regarded beards and mustaches with lifelong distaste—had flopped in attempting to become a mere National Guard recruit half-a-dozen years earlier, when the United States entered World War I. Rejected for enlistment in Providence through the intervention of his hysterical mother, the typewriter-fighter who had spent the previous two and a half years baying for German blood was content to take that "no" for a final answer, although he could easily have gone to Canada, or with some more difficulty even to his cherished England—or for that matter to any other American city—and gotten into the so-called "war to preserve civilization" from there, had he not perhaps been secretly relieved to simply stay at home writing essays about it. Later, the drinker of foemen's blood, etc., would prove too squeamish to remove dead mice from his own mousetraps, preferring to throw away the entire trap instead. And the Nordic son of the arctic winds and brother to the frosts recounted in a letter to another friend, in 1932:

> I can't write decently under 73°[Fahrenheit] or 74°. From there down to freezing the effect of a falling temperature is simply increasing discomfort and sluggishness; but after that it begins to be painful to breathe. I can't go out at all under +20°, since the effects are varied and disastrous. First my lungs and throat get sore, and then I become sick at the stomach and lose anything I've eaten. My heart also pounds and palpitates. At about 17° or 16° my muscular and nervous coordination gets all shot to hell, and I have to flounder and stagger around like a drunken man. When I try to walk ahead, I feel as if I were trying to swim through some viscous, hampering medium of resistance. Finally, at 15° or 14°, I lose consciousness.

Biographers point to some unknown physical cause for Lovecraft's abnormal sensitivity to cold. In the winter of 1926–27, after Lovecraft and Sonia had separated, she visited him in Providence. Sonia, with her childhood experience of brutal Ukrainian winters, was prone to enjoy the comparatively milder New England variety:

> ...as I loved the cold weather I'd persuade H.P. to join me on some interesting exploration jaunt. But as he could not stand the severe cold I actually had to help him up the hill, walking beside him with an arm around his waist, with the other holding his arm. Ordinarily I would have hailed a taxi but there was none in sight and I did not dare leave him to go search for one. When we got home I quickly removed his shoes and began rubbing his numb feet. He was half unconscious as he lay on the bed. After "thawing" out his hands and feet I gave him some hot tea with lemon and plenty of sugar. He was very grateful for my attendance.

The picture of the collapsing Nordic-Teutonic iceman being half-carried up through the snows of little College Hill—assuming that that was "the hill" in question—by a shorter and older Jewish woman, is priceless in itself, but beyond the inherent humor of the situation these disconnected passages illustrate some significant truths about Lovecraft's character. He was consistently inconsistent, an incarnation of the clichéd phrase "a bundle of contradictions"; and he often enjoyed writing for dramatic effect more than in sober and boring realism—whether the purpose was to blow off steam, to be provocative, to express some sweeping opinion or feeling that had momentarily aroused his passions, or sometimes maybe just because he liked the way the words would look on the page. He was a writer, after all. And so, ironically, the worst things that can be written about him come not from anything that anyone ever experienced at his hands; but rather from the Mountains of Madness of his own gigantic correspondence, the absurd or vainglorious or bitter or cynical words to be found here and there among the millions of words he wrote and mailed in decades of letter-writing, or the frequently obnoxious essays he published in early amateur journalism days. His bark could be loud, but his bite didn't exist.

Rather, Sonia's rescue operation—after all she had already been through with this impossible man—and also Lovecraft's voluble gratitude for it, point up two facts on which all witnesses seem to agree. First, that Lovecraft was really a lovable person. He inspired in many quite intelligent and self-sufficient friends and correspondents (some of whom would never meet him in person) an obvious respect and affection, even love, so that they were frequently eager to help him as well as they could. On the other side of the coin, he seems to have had no real enemies. Secondly, Lovecraft was courteous and gentleman-like in his conduct with everyone he met; despite the bloodthirsty or racist rhetoric in some of his essays and letters, he was personally one of the mildest of men, harmless and kind. Even his agreement to go outside for a "jaunt" with the snow-bunny Sonia, on a freezing day when he must have realized he would be in danger of trouble on a long walk, speaks for his good nature, his habitual desire to be accommodating and not to disappoint.

In the letters or memoirs they have left behind, Lovecraft's bygone array of friends and acquaintances unite in telling us that he was unfailingly "gentle," "polite," "honest," "kindly," "patient," "thoughtful," and also one who would scarcely show any irritation, let alone say or do anything unpleasant, to the dimmest or most personally uncongenial person he might encounter in life's winding way. In some ways his life manifested a constant struggle between the chilly racist snob he felt called to be by virtue of his "unmixed English" familial heritage and his exaggerated sense of an aristocratic background—such important things they were to him!—and the good-natured, curious, and courteous person he was by nature and inclination.

It is thought-provoking that an author who achieved such marvelous and unsettling effects of time-stretching, of space-bending, and of "cosmic horror" lurking under the surface of life, and a man always so interested in the latest science and in intellectual progress, could in daily life be so reactionary and petty about such a complex of topics, combining some of the worst features of an early-20th century race-baiter, a late-19th century crank, and a mid-18th century hanging judge. He addressed this problem himself, in 1929. Essentially he saw himself as a man of two minds:

> I am, you see, a sort of hybrid betwixt the past and the future—archaic in my personal tastes, emotions, and interests, but so much of a scientific realist in philosophy that I cannot abide any intellectual point of view short of the most advanced.

At times in his last years Lovecraft seems to have thought himself a failure, "a total loss." This is a sad irony, almost hard to imagine, when one considers the millions of Lovecraft books sold and the translations into many languages, the movie and television "versions," the legions of fans, the critical studies, the memorial plaque on a wall at Brown University, and in our historical moment, the websites and the "Cthulhu Mythos"-inspired fantasy role-playing games; but that all happened years after his death.

In 1935, with his inherited capital almost gone, feeling profoundly discouraged as a writer, and deep in middle age with its typical sense of declining powers and of ambivalence, he wrote to a younger pen-pal who had complained to him of feeling "hopeless, useless, incompetent, and generally miserable":

> In actual fact, there are few total losses and never-was's which discourage and exasperate me more than [me]. I know of few persons whose attainments fall more consistently short of their aspirations, or who in general have less to live for. Every aptitude which I wish I had, I lack. Everything which I wish I could formulate & express, I have failed to formulate & express. Everything which I value, I have either lost or am likely to lose. Within a decade, unless I can find some job paying at least $10.00 per week, I shall have to take the cyanide route through inability to keep around me the books, pictures, furniture, & other familiar objects which constitute my only remaining reason for keeping alive. And so far as solitude is concerned, I probably capture all medals…. The reason I have been more "melancholy" than usual in the last few years is that I am coming to distrust more & more the value of the material I produce. Adverse criticism has of late vastly undermined my confidence in my literary powers.

There is some exaggeration of his misery going on here (doubtless to cheer up his younger friend, by the comparison), particularly concerning his "solitude"—he had numerous friends and admirers who barely left him alone, although not many lived in Providence. Moreover, he went on to make the essential point that despite all his accumulated sorrows, he was living as happily as he could manage in every way, through books, travel, and all his other normal enjoyments, and being stoical about whatever he could not affect—in the approved manner of ancient philosophers. Having said all of which, his words are poignant and clearly come from his heart, and if he indeed was not unduly depressed by a sense of failure, he might still have been elated by a powerful sense of achievement, which was missing. If he could but have lived another thirty-odd years, to see himself famous, to have enough money to buy a colonial-era house or to afford so much as a sightseeing vacation to Europe, to (not least) come back with renewed interest to writing, and to see the fantasy-fiction world catch up with him! But he did not.

Early in 1937 some nagging and increasingly severe internal pains, which he had characteristically ignored and failed to see a doctor about, were diagnosed as symptoms of cancer of the small intestine, already in an advanced and terminal phase. He was only 46 years old. S.T. Joshi interestingly suggests that Lovecraft's miserable eating habits—which were certainly those of a penny-pinching and ascetic bachelor who tended to make a virtue of self-denial, except where his sweet tooth was concerned (the years of barely-adequate meals built around coffee, doughnuts, and the cheapest canned foods, often eaten cold from the can)—could have caused or contributed both to the relatively rare form of cancer and to the kidney disease that was also discovered. Only days after the diagnosis, Lovecraft was moved to the Jane Brown Memorial Hospital in Providence, where he died a few days later on March 15, 1937. He was buried alongside his parents; fans put a headstone on his grave forty years later.

H.P. Lovecraft's sudden passing went all but unnoticed in the great world outside of friendship and fandom. At the time of his death he was little known—"unknown" is more the right word—except to his personal friends, and the passionate but not terribly numerous readers of one category of pulp magazines. He never had a book published in his lifetime. Loyal friends and devoted fans managed to keep some or all of his tales in print one way or another, for the next few decades. Then the fantasy-friendly 1960s arrived and the long dead Lovecraft finally became an overnight success, whose mere name is now enough to suggest an entire genre of fantasy-writing, and whose works have been translated, published, discussed and, above all, enjoyed throughout the civilized world.

During his adult life HPL had quite a number of male friends, generically "the boys"—with whom he exchanged long letters, took long conversation-filled walks, and spent long hours chatting or debating about many topics of mutual interest. For the most part "the boys" were fellow-writers or at least intelligent men intelligently interested in books and ideas, and with a tiny handful of exceptions they are only remembered today because of their personal connections with Lovecraft. With the boys he shared the easy, undemanding pleasures of male friendship, full of juvenile nicknames and in-jokes, labored jocularity and jesting (rather tiresome to read very much of, frankly), politely combative arguments about issues neither party could ever affect or disputed matters that neither party could ever prove, low emotional investment, and a clubby no-girls ethos, more typical of his day than our own.

But except for his mother and his stiff-necked aunts, and an isolated female pen-pal now and again, there was really no woman in Lovecraft's life except for Sonia—nor was there ever another woman in his life like Sonia—who for several years tried her best to make an impossible relationship work. A Jewish woman who meekly tolerated her new gentile husband's request that henceforth whenever they had company "he would appreciate it if there were 'Aryans' in the majority," must have had a lot of love to give. Fittingly Sonia shall have the last word, written presciently in 1948:

> I believe he loved me as much as it was possible for a temperament like his to love. He'd never mention the word love. He would say instead, "My dear, you don't know how much I appreciate you." I tried to understand him and was grateful for any crumbs from his lips that fell my way.
>
> More than any one else at that time, I believe, I felt or sensed that a great genius, though dormant as yet, existed in H.P.
>
> I am afraid that my optimism and my excessive self-assurance misled me, and perhaps him too. I had always admired great intellectuality perhaps more than anything else in the world (perhaps, too, because I lacked so much of it myself) and had hoped to lift H.P. out of his abysmal depths of loneliness...
>
> I do not believe it to be an exaggeration to say that Howard had the mind, taste and personality of a much greater artist and genius than that with which he had been accredited [*sic*] in his lifetime.
>
> As the years pass, I am quite sure that he will be to the generations of readers yet unborn a legendary and mysterious figure. The irony of fate lies in the great misfortune that Lovecraft passed away before he could have enjoyed the fruits of his labor, both the financial reward as well as the celebrity.
>
> And even though I am not his widow, I bow my head in sorrow and reverence at the untimely passing of a gentle soul and a great genius. May the God in whom he so little believed rest his soul in peace.

A NOTE ON SOURCES

The serious study of Howard Phillips Lovecraft now and forever must necessarily begin with *H.P. Lovecraft: A Life* (West Warwick, R.I., 1996) by Mr. S.T. Joshi, A.B., A.M. of Brown University. This brilliant book of some 650 tightly-written, densely-footnoted pages deserves some sort of monument for comprehensiveness in a one-volume literary biography, and might qualify as the greatest work of its kind that any minor literary figure has ever been posthumously blessed with. I am indebted to it for many, many facts and critical insights, presented in an incisive and masterly style. Mr. Joshi is without a doubt the world's foremost expert on Lovecraft's life and works, and his total command of the subject stands revealed on every page.

The earlier major life-study, *Lovecraft: A Biography* (Garden City, N.Y., 1975), by the late L. Sprague de Camp, a respected and prolific science-fiction/fantasy and science-nonfiction author, is no rival to Joshi's masterpiece in any significant way and should be considered as superseded by it. On the other hand it is a much faster "read," wryly entertaining with some perceptive observations, and covers the basic story with reasonable accuracy. His working-writer's pained and persistent critique of Lovecraft's gentleman-amateur ethos, or posturing—for which he had little patience—will probably appeal to some and irritate others. De Camp's biography often reads like a brief for the prosecution regarding Lovecraft's conduct of his life, while Joshi's book usually seems like a brief for the defense. I have gained from reading them both, although one is clearly better than the other.

I have drawn from or gained knowledge from some small editions published by the Necronomicon Press of West Warwick, Rhode Island, namely *Autobiographical Writings* (S.T. Joshi, ed.) (1992); *History of the Necronomicon, by H.P. Lovecraft* (1980); *Off the Ancient Track: A Lovecraftian Guide to New-England & Adjacent New-York,* by Jason Eckhardt (rev. ed., 1994); *The Private Life of H.P. Lovecraft,* by Sonia H. [Greene] [Lovecraft] Davis (S.T. Joshi, ed.) (1985); *The Chronology out of Time: Dates in the Fiction of H.P. Lovecraft,* by Peter Cannon (2nd ed., 1997).

I am generally indebted to various works by Lovecraft experts (in no particular order) Peter Cannon, Dirk W. Mosig, Donald R. Burleson, Philip A. Shreffler, Darrell Schweitzer, and Barton L. St. Armand, which I consulted at the very beginning of this labor.

I also gladly mention *Schnitzler's Century: The Making of Middle-Class Culture 1815–1914* (New York, 2002), by Peter Gay, Sterling Professor Emeritus of History, Yale University, which helped me very much in understanding the ordinary mental furniture of Lovecraft and his family. To learn more about Lovecraft's revered master, people can do much worse than to read *Edgar A. Poe: Mournful and Never-ending Remembrance* (New York, 1991) by Professor Kenneth Silverman at New York University.

I am grateful to my kinfolk Dr. Cornelia Pearsall, of Smith College; Dr. Sarah Pearsall, of Northwestern University; Dr. John Rogers, of Yale University; and Dr. Peter Kail, of Oxford University, for their prompt assistance in clearing up some refinedly academic points.

I am also grateful to New Falcon Publications and especially Mr. Nicholas Tharcher, for his optimistic patience during the seven years that elapsed for him between signing a contract and receiving a final manuscript.

I am extraordinarily indebted to my wife, Pauline Stone Pearsall, for her steady encouragement and other assistance. This project would probably never have come to fruition without her.

Lovecraft wrote volumes of fiction, poetry, and personal letters. For purposes of this book, some line needed to be drawn, and I chose to draw it around the canonical fifty-two principal tales, four "early tales," and three "fragments" contained in the following standard editions, published by Arkham House Publishers, Inc., Sauk City, Wisconsin: *Dagon and other Macabre Tales* (Corrected Seventh Printing), *The Dunwich Horror and Others* (Corrected Ninth Printing), and *At the Mountains of Madness* (Corrected Seventh Printing). The chosen texts, with the years of their composition and the name-abbreviations used in this book, are listed below in "Chronology of Selected Tales." This universe omits, except for isolated references, Lovecraft's poetic productions and the tales which he worked on for his "revision" clients, his thousands of letters, and the ever-expanding body of tales written by other authors in imitation of, homage to, and/or expansion of his so-called "Cthulhu Mythos." It also omits, quite arbitrarily, the "early tale" *Poetry and the Gods*, a saccharine Grecian-fantasia pageant, written in collaboration with a lady amateur: a tale which strives to be Olympian and only achieves Limp. Some background material has also been drawn from the very useful and interesting *Miscellaneous Writings: H.P. Lovecraft* (S.T. Joshi, ed.) (Sauk City, Wis., 1995).

H.P. Lovecraft never came within a thousand miles of California, but that is where I had to write this Lexicon. On one solitary occasion I was able to visit Providence for a day and to make my way along what could be called the "Lovecraft Trail," including the site of his boyhood home on Angell Street; his 1904–24 home at 598 Angell Street a few blocks away; his later home at 10 Barnes Street; and his last residence, the

"Lewis Mumford House"; as well as Brown University, Prospect Terrace, Benefit Street and the "Shunned House," and the venerable graveyard of St. John's Church. My personal tour wound up a mile or two away at Swan Point Cemetery, where Lovecraft's remains have spent most of a century returning to the New England soil he loved so much. Standing only six feet away from my subject—six feet of earth, that is—and studying his tombstone in that green and peaceful place, I promised myself that I would one day finish this Lexicon, and a few years later I did.

CHRONOLOGY OF SELECTED TALES

Title (Abbreviation)	Year
The Beast in the Cave (BC)	1905
The Alchemist (TA)	1908
The Tomb (TT)	1917
Dagon (DA)	1917
Polaris (PO)	1918
Beyond the Wall of Sleep (BWS)	1919
The Transition of Juan Romero (TJR)	1919
The White Ship (WS)	1919
The Doom That Came to Sarnath (DCS)	1919
The Statement of Randolph Carter (SRC)	1919
The Terrible Old Man (TOM)	1920
The Tree (TR)	1920
The Cats of Ulthar (CU)	1920
The Temple (TE)	1920
Facts Concerning the Late Arthur Jermyn and His Family (AJ)	1920
The Street (TS)	1920
Celephaïs (CE)	1920
From Beyond (FB)	1920
The Picture in the House (PH)	1920
The Nameless City (NC)	1921
The Quest of Iranon (QI)	1921
The Moon-Bog (MB)	1921
The Outsider (TO)	1921
The Other Gods (OG)	1921
The Music of Erich Zann (MEZ)	1921
Herbert West—Reanimator (HW)	1921–22
Hypnos (HY)	1922
The Hound (TH)	1922
The Lurking Fear (LF)	1922
The Rats in the Walls (RW)	1923
The Unnamable (TU)	1923
The Festival (TF)	1923
Under the Pyramids (UP)	1924
The Shunned House (SH)	1924
The Horror at Red Hook (HRH)	1925
He (HE)	1925
In the Vault (IV)	1925

Cool Air (CA)	*1926*
The Call of Cthulhu (CC)	*1926*
Pickman's Model (PM)	*1926*
The Silver Key (SK)	*1926*
The Strange High House in the Mist (SHH)	*1926*
The Dream-Quest of Unknown Kadath (DQ)	*1926–27*
The Case of Charles Dexter Ward (CDW)	*1927*
The Colour Out of Space (COS)	*1927*
The Dunwich Horror (DH)	*1928*
The Whisperer in Darkness (WD)	*1930*
At the Mountains of Madness (MM)	*1931*
The Shadow Over Innsmouth (SOI)	*1931*
The Dreams in the Witch House (DWH)	*1932*
Through the Gates of the Silver Key (TGSK)[1]	*1932–33*
The Thing on the Doorstep (TD)	*1933*
The Evil Clergyman (EC)	*1933*
The Shadow Out of Time (SOT)	*1934–35*
The Haunter of the Dark (HD)	*1935*
In the Walls of Eryx (WE)[2]	*1936*

[1] with E. Hoffman Price
[2] with Kenneth J. Sterling

Abbreviations of Selected Tales Referenced in the Lexicon (Alphabetical)

AJ	*Facts Concerning the Late Arthur Jermyn and His Family*
BC	*The Beast in the Cave*
BWS	*Beyond the Wall of Sleep*
CA	*Cool Air*
CC	*The Call of Cthulhu*
CDW	*The Case of Charles Dexter Ward*
CE	*Celephaïs*
COS	*The Colour Out of Space*
CU	*The Cats of Ulthar*
DA	*Dagon*
DCS	*The Doom That Came to Sarnath*
DH	*The Dunwich Horror*
DQ	*The Dream-Quest of Unknown Kadath*
DWH	*The Dreams in the Witch House*
EC	*The Evil Clergyman*
FB	*From Beyond*
HD	*The Haunter of the Dark*
HE	*He*
HRH	*The Horror at Red Hook*
HW	*Herbert West—Reanimator*
HY	*Hypnos*
IV	*In the Vault*
LF	*The Lurking Fear*
MB	*The Moon-Bog*
MEZ	*The Music of Erich Zann*
MM	*At the Mountains of Madness*
NC	*The Nameless City*
OG	*The Other Gods*
PH	*The Picture in the House*
PM	*Pickman's Model*
PO	*Polaris*
QI	*The Quest of Iranon*
RW	*The Rats in the Walls*
SH	*The Shunned House*
SHH	*The Strange High House in the Mist*

SK	*The Silver Key*
SOI	*The Shadow Over Innsmouth*
SOT	*The Shadow Out of Time*
SRC	*The Statement of Randolph Carter*
TA	*The Alchemist*
TD	*The Thing on the Doorstep*
TE	*The Temple*
TF	*The Festival*
TGSK	*Through the Gates of the Silver Key*
TH	*The Hound*
TJR	*The Transition of Juan Romero*
TO	*The Outsider*
TOM	*The Terrible Old Man*
TR	*The Tree*
TS	*The Street*
TT	*The Tomb*
TU	*The Unnamable*
UP	*Under the Pyramids*
WD	*The Whisperer in Darkness*
WE	*In the Walls of Eryx*
WS	*The White Ship*

THE LEXICON

A

ABBADON (NC): Having witnessed unimaginable horrors in the caverns far below the Nameless City, and without so much as a torch to light his way back to the surface, the fear-maddened narrator somehow survives to tell the tale, not knowing "what Abbadon guided me back to life, where I must always remember and shiver in the night-wind till oblivion—or worse—claims me."

Abbadon appears in the Bible, in Chapter 9 of the Book of Revelations. At Armageddon, the fifth angel will open "the bottomless pit" and set free a swarm of monstrous, scorpion-tailed, horse-sized, partly-manlike "locusts" whose power will be to hurt men for five months. "And they [the locusts] had a king over them, which is the angel of the bottomless pit, whose name in the Hebrew tongue is Abbadon, but in the Greek tongue his name is Appolyon." (Revelations 9:11, in the King James Version: the 17th century literary classic which HPL would naturally have preferred to any other English translation.) Abbadon means "destruction" in Hebrew; the Greek word "Appolyon" means "the destroyer"; by whatever name, he is a demon. Metaphorically the narrator credits some "Abbadon" for helping him back from miles below the ground in total darkness—the bottomless pit—while he was half-insane with terror.

ABBOTT'S DISTIL-HOUSE (CDW): On a winter morning in 1771 the naked body of a huge and muscular man is inexplicably found "on the jams of ice around the southern piers of the Great Bridge, where the Long Dock stretched out beside Abbott's distil-house." A distil-house is an obsolete word for a distillery, a place for the production of liquor or cider. It may be noted without further repetition that the frequent references to real colonial-era people, shops, activities and local institutions found in *The Case of Charles Dexter Ward* owe much to HPL's frequent reading of the 1912 book *Providence in Colonial Times* by Gertrude S. Kimball; it is still a useful reference work.

ABDUL REIS EL DROGMAN (UP): "A shaven, peculiarly hollow-voiced, and relatively cleanly fellow who looked like a pharaoh," writes Houdini; "like King Khephren," he later specifies, referring to one of the pyramid-building Egyptian pharaohs of the Old Kingdom. Other than that, he is an excellent and personally impressive guide to local antiquities whom Houdini and his wife employ on their visit to Cairo in 1910. By means of a phony quarrel with another native, Ali Ziz, he tricks Houdini into visiting the Great Pyramid at midnight with a crowd of Egyptians. He then supervises the process of seizing and binding Houdini and lowering him into the black shafts beneath the pyramid, by means of a concealed shaft. Houdini helpfully explains that *reis* in Arabic is "a name for any person in authority," while *el Drogman* means the Guide.

ACHERON (LF): The nameless narrator hopes at one point to find "a slight guarantee of mental and physical safety in this Acheron of multi-form diabolism." Acheron (pronounced "Ack-uh-ron," more or less), a Greek word, was the name of one of the five rivers that flow through Hades, the Greek and Roman underworld of the dead; it means "woeful."

ACROPOLIS (CC, CDW): Generically, an acropolis (the classical Greek word meaning the point of the city), was the highest land inside the walls of a number of ancient Greek cities, typically the site of a city's central monuments and fortifications. The most famous example, then and now, is the Acropolis of Athens. In *The Call of Cthulhu* the area of R'lyeh which has risen above sea level—only a fraction of what still must lie beneath the Pacific—is described as an acropolis. In *The Case of Charles Dexter Ward*, it is said in a letter from Count Ferenczy/Edward Hutchinson to Joseph Curwen, dated March 7, 1928: "Laste monthe M. got me ye Sarcophagus [burial container] of ye Five Sphinxes from ye Acropolis where He whome I call'd up say'd it wou'd be, and I have hadde 3 Talkes with *What was therein inhum'd*."

ADAMS, STANLEY (WD): Name given by "a lean, sandy and rustic-looking" man, with a "queerly thick droning voice," to the railway express clerk on train number 5508 of the B&M rail line, at the Keene, New Hampshire station on July 18, 1928. His voice had a dizzying effect on the clerk. Apparently a human agent of the Mi-Go, who mesmerized the clerk long enough to remove a box carrying a certain carved black stone which Henry W. Akeley had attempted to ship to Professor Wilmarth, in Arkham.

ADIRONDACKS (CDW): A range of forested hills or low mountains in northern New York state; at some point between the spring of 1920 and April, 1923, Charles Dexter Ward seeks out "a small village in the Adirondacks whence reports of certain odd ceremonial practices had come."

AFRASIAB (NC): This is the name of an important character—the war-like King of Turan—in the *Shahnameh*, the epic poem of the legendary pre-Islamic kings of Persia or Iran, composed by the poet Firdousi

(d. circa 1025). The *Shahnameh* is the classic of Iranian literature. In *The Nameless City*, the tremendously well-read nameless narrator, while descending into the black depths of caverns under the Nameless City, "muttered of Afrasiab and the daemons that floated with him down the Oxus." Thereby hang many tales.

To begins with, the Oxus River was the name in classical times of the river now called Amu Darya, which rises in the Pamir plateau of western central Asia, and flows in a generally northwestern direction to the inland Aral Sea. For most of its course it forms the border of the current nations of Turkmenistan and Uzbekistan. In the *Shahnameh*, King Afrasiab is at one point stuck on a boat floating down the Oxus with a number of demons, who are fortunately asleep; if they awaken, they will devour him according to the nature of demons.

There is no indication that HPL ever read the *Shahnameh*. On the other hand, he certainly read Edgar Allan Poe's semi-comic tale *The Premature Burial*, which ends:

> There are moments when, even to the sober eye of Reason, the world of our sad Humanity may assume the semblance of a Hell—but the imagination of man is no Carathis, to explore with impunity every cavern. Alas! the grim legion of sepulchral terrors cannot be regarded as altogether fanciful—but, like the Demons in whose company Afrasiab made his voyage down the Oxus, they must sleep, or they will devour us—they must be suffered to slumber, or we perish.

HPL had also read *History of the Caliph Vathek* by William Beckford (1760–1844). This fabulously wealthy and equally hedonistic and eccentric Englishman—by most accounts the richest subject in Great Britain during the late 18th century, with wealth inherited from his father—wrote the scandalous and gorgeous "Oriental-Gothic horror novel" at the tender age of 22; it was published in 1784, in some ways about 200 years before its time. In *Vathek*, "Carathis" is an evil witch, who is also the mother of the title character, a fabulously wealthy and hedonistic caliph or ruler. At the end of *Vathek* several main characters find themselves dead and in the Muslim hell, including Carathis. Before she clearly understands that she is there for an eternity of suffering, Carathis:

> ...eagerly entered the dome of Soliman and, without regarding in the least the groans of the prophet, undauntedly removed the covers of the vases, and violently seized on the talismans. Then, with a voice more loud than had hitherto been heard in these mansions, she compelled the Dives to disclose to her the most secret treasures, the most profound stores, which the Afrit himself had not seen. She passed by rapid descents known only to Eblis and his most favored potentates, and thus penetrated the very entrails

of the earth, where breathes the Sansar, or icy wind of death. Nothing appalled her dauntless soul.

AFRICA, OBSERVATIONS ON THE SEVERAL PARTS OF (AJ): A book published prior to 1765 by Sir Wade Jermyn, explorer of the vast Congo River region of central Africa, in which he hypothesized "a prehistoric white Congolese civilization."

AGRICOLA (CDW): One of the authors whose books are to be found in the scientific library of Joseph Curwen's home in 18th century Providence. Georgius Agricola (the Latinized version of Georg Bauer, or as we would say in English, George Farmer) (1494–1555), a native of Saxony in eastern Germany, was a physician and alchemist. He was also an expert in mineralogy and geology; his great work, *De Re Metallica* (1556), was the preeminent book on mining and metallurgy for almost two centuries.

AI (DCS): A winding river in the land of Mnar, by whose banks "a dark shepherd folk…with fleecy flocks" built their cities of Thraa, Ilarnek, and Kadatheron.

AIOLOS (TE): On the night that the delegation arrives in Tegea from Syracuse to take delivery of Musides' new statue of Tyché, a violent storm of wind hits the district, and as "the wind shrieked more horribly…both the Syracusans and the Arcadians prayed to Aiolos." Aiolos, more commonly spelled Aeolus, was the Greek god of the winds.

AIRA (QI): Aira is the "far city" that the minstrel Iranon "recalls only dimly but seeks to find again," a frequent theme in HPL's "Dunsanian" fantasies. In Iranon's memories, Aira is a city of beryl and marble, full of palaces with golden domes and painted walls, blue pools and crystal fountains. In this city there flow two rivers, the big Nithra and the "tiny Kra," which latter river however features a waterfall. In Aira, Iranon remembers, his father was the king, he was the Prince of Aira, and his mother sang and rocked him to sleep in a window beneath the moonbeams. At the end of his life, Iranon realizes that Aira was only a delusion.

AKARIEL, GATE OF (WS): Huge carved gateway to the city of Thalarion, by the stone pier.

AKELEY, GEORGE GOODENOUGH (WD): Son of Henry W. Akeley. In 1928 he lives at "176 Pleasant Street" in San Diego, California, or in other words about as far from his dismal ancestral home in the lonely hills of Vermont as he could travel without getting on a boat or learning Spanish! On a couple of occasions Henry Akeley writes about a plan to leave his farm and move to his son's house out in California for safety, but in a Lovecraftian manner, can never tear himself away from the old homeplace until it is too late and he realizes that "they" will never let him go. On a 1928 vacation in rural Vermont, prior to writing this tale, HPL spent some time with a man who had the wonderful name of Arthur Goodenough, and was introduced to a local farmer with some artistic interests, a certain Bert G. Akley.

Lovecraft was a friend by correspondence of a few Californians, and seems to have wished at times to cross the continent and visit the place; but in a state where, then and now, a building fifty years old is considered a rather old building, how impossible he would have found it to dwell for long. The sprawling, raw, and ethnically heterogeneous metropolis of Los Angeles would have inspired him with the most horror of all. It is an apt symbol of their differences that his ex-wife Sonia chose to spend the last years of her life there, dying in 1972 in a private rest home in Sunland, California, a suburb of Los Angeles, at the age of eighty-nine: eighty years after a little girl from Europe had stepped off a ship in New York harbor.

AKELEY, HENRY WENTWORTH (WD): Owner of a lonely but well-appointed farm and farmhouse, in his family for six generations, south of the village of Townshend, Windham County, Vermont. Fifty-seven years old in the spring of 1928, he comes from a long line of "jurists, administrators, and gentleman-agriculturalists." He attended the University of Vermont and excelled at mathematics, astronomy, biology, anthropology, and folklore. He is a dedicated investigator of the peculiar winged creatures said by legend to lurk in some of Vermont's remote hilly areas. On May 1, 1915, succeeds in secretly recording an apparent dialogue between a human voice and the voice of an unidentified alien being. Subsequently has covertly recorded many other such conversations taking place in the wild hills by night, which indicate the speakers' familiarity with much of Earth's oldest lore. Also takes photographs of alien footprints, lairs, etc. He also discovers a black stone with peculiar markings at an apparent worship site.

Early in 1928, begins corresponding with Miskatonic University professor Albert Wilmarth, and reveals some of his discoveries. On May 5, 1928, for example, he writes of "evidence that monstrous things…live in the woods on the high hills which nobody visits." Akeley comes under increasing nocturnal harassment by the aliens and their human agents, which he resists with gunfire and fierce guard dogs. Before Wilmarth can visit him in person later that year, Akeley has disappeared. It is indicated that his brain, at least, has been preserved by the Mi-Go for their own purposes. This is certainly indicated when some kind of creature in a voluminous dressing-gown and leg-wrappings, posing as Henry Akeley, while displaying for the trusting and deceived Dr. Wilmarth the brain-cylinders on a shelf, says pointedly: "Don't bother that fresh, shiny cylinder joined to the two testing-instruments—the one with my name on it." Later that night, Wilmarth hears what seems to be that brain in that cylinder pleading with two of the Mi-Go to let Wilmarth leave unharmed. While making his subsequent escape, Wilmarth finds three things fitted with "ingenious metal clamps to attach...to organic developments of which I dare not form any conjecture. I hope—devoutly hope—that they were the waxen products of some master artist, despite what my inmost fears tell me." These three things—"perfect to the last, subtle detail of microscopic resemblance—or identity—were the face and hands of Henry Wentworth Akeley."

HPL may have been one of the most prolific personal correspondents of all time—he mailed an estimated 100,000 letters in his lifetime, sometimes five, ten, or up to forty pages long—and in *The Whisperer in Darkness* he successfully crafted a story in which the protagonist is known only by way of his long letters, which also contain most of the story's action.

AKLO LANGUAGE (HD, DH): An ancient, secret writing-system in which certain powerful spells have been recorded. Robert Blake, in *The Haunter of the Dark*, used Aklo to translate a mysterious book that he found in the deserted Starry Wisdom church on Federal Hill, Providence. In *The Dunwich Horror*, Wilbur Whateley learned Aklo to perform a "Sabaoth" ceremony. HPL borrowed the Aklo language concept from Arthur Machen's moody horror story *The White People*, which he considered to be the "second-best" weird tale of their time. In Machen's tale a little English girl being trained in the occult writes in her diary:

> I must not write down the real names of the days and months which I found out a year ago, nor the way to make the Aklo letters, or the Chian language, or the great beautiful Circles, nor the Mao Games, nor the chief songs.

AKMANS (WE): They are creatures on Venus, described as a kind of vermin, "slimy," "wriggling," small and carnivorous, idly crushed underfoot by the Venusians whenever they become a nuisance. "Akman" is thought to be derived from the name of Forrest Ackerman, a contemporary science-fiction critic whom HPL disliked.

AKURION (DCS): A grey rock which "reared high above the lake by the shore" of Sarnath city. On the night of Sarnath's doom, this rock was completely submerged by the rising lake waters, an indication of the height of the waters which drown the city.

ALBERTUS MAGNUS (CDW, EC): "Albert the Great," a German Dominican scholar and a saint of the Catholic Church (1206–80). Known to the Church as the *Doctor Universalis* for his comprehensive learning, which included whatever his age knew of physics, astronomy, chemistry, and biology, as well as all facets of philosophy and metaphysics. He was the instructor of the young St. Thomas Aquinas, who went on to become the Church's greatest theologian and philosopher. Albertus Magnus' writings were voluminous, and his fame for centuries after his death was immense. Albertus Magnus' proto-scientific works or purported works were standard references for classical alchemists, therefore some of these titles appear in the libraries of Joseph Curwen and of "the Evil Clergyman."

ALCHEMY (TA, HE, CDW, EC): More than a naïve attempt to transmute base metals into gold or discover the "philosopher's stone" whose touch would bring eternal youth, medieval and renaissance-era alchemy was a complex thought-system incorporating both physical science and spiritual lore, combining what the men of distant times understood about chemistry, physics, and astronomy, with theology, astrology, magic, and speculative metaphysics. Historically, alchemy may have originated in ancient Egypt or ancient China—or both; for centuries its center was the great city of Alexandria on the coast of Egypt, and the main practitioners were Greek. The conquering Arabs took up the study of alchemy in the 8th century A.D. By the 12th century, after the early Crusades, Arabic texts were being brought to Europe and translated, beginning the western European obsession with the old art of alchemy, which after some centuries gave birth to the new science of chemistry. HPL, a fervent chemistry hobbyist in his youth, was fond of the historical subject of alchemy and made use of it in certain stories, alluding meaningfully to the titles of many old alchemical texts.

The title of *The Alchemist* is self-explanatory, and the books in the collection of *The Evil Clergyman* make it quite clear that his interests are more alchemical than theological. Joseph Curwen in *The Case of Charles Dexter Ward* is feared by his 18th century Providence neighbors as "a 'chymist'—by which they meant an alchemist." Since he continues to look like a healthy 35-year-old man even after his chronological age exceeds one hundred years, it seems as though he had already found some alchemical means of preserving youth. (The same being true of his old Salem cohorts Simon Orne and Edward Hutchinson, who were born in the seventeenth century and are still alive under different names in the twentieth.) A third man to find life prolonged through unnatural stretches of time—a fantasy of special interest to the time-obsessive HPL—is the Squire in *He*, who provides this 18th century bombast on the subject:

He [referring to his purported ancestor, but really meaning himself] had not been at Oxford for nothing, nor talked to no account with an ancient chymist and astrologer in Paris. He was, in fine, made sensible that all the world is but the smoke of our intellects; past the bidding of the vulgar, but by the wise to be puffed out and drawn in like any cloud of fine Virginia tobacco. What we want, we may make around us, and what we don't want, we may sweep away.

ALERT (CC): A steam yacht employed in the South Pacific island freight trade, she is heavily armed with brass cannon. Her home port is Dunedin, New Zealand. The crew consists of "queer and evil-looking...Kanakas [Pacific islanders] and half-castes [half-breeds]." In Dunedin, this unpopular crew of sailors is remembered for holding frequent private meetings, and making night excursions to the nearby forests, as well as at least one trip to some hills inland, when "faint drumming and red flame" were noted by the city's residents. On the "alert" for Cthulhu, the *Alert* leaves Dunedin on March 1, 1925. On March 22, the *Alert* encounters the off-course schooner *Emma* at latitude 49°34′ South, longitude 128° 34′ West, far out in the South Pacific. The *Alert* orders the *Emma* to turn back, and when the *Emma*'s captain refuses, the crew of the *Alert* opens fire on the other ship. The *Emma*'s crew manages to board and seize the *Alert*, killing her entire crew in a desperate hand-to-hand fight. Since their own ship was sinking from battle damage, the surviving sailors transfer to the *Alert* to continue their voyage. On April 12, the *Alert* is found drifting with one living man aboard (Second Mate Johansen), at latitude 34° 21′ South, longitude 152° 17′ West, by the freighter *Vigilant*, and towed to Sidney, Australia, arriving on April 18. Francis W. Thurston later sees the *Alert* moored at Circular Quay in Sidney Cove, but learns nothing from it.

ALEXANDER, COSMO (CDW): A non-fictitious 18th century Scottish portraitist (1724–72) who resided at Newport, Rhode Island during the 1760s, and was an early teacher of the more famous American painter Gilbert Stuart, who was born nearby in 1755. In HPL's tale, Alexander paints a portrait of Joseph Curwen in 1765, which Charles Dexter Ward rediscovers in 1919.

ALGOL (BWS): Algol is a binary star in the constellation Perseus, whose larger component revolves about and regularly eclipses the smaller, brighter orb, causing variations in brightness as seen from Earth. Algol's name comes from the Arabic *al-Ghul*, "the Ghoul," symbolizing the "eating" of one star by the other. In the confusing denouement to this early tale, the appearance of a nova in the sky near Algol indicates that the extraterrestrial being which had lodged in the body of Joe Slater has achieved its liberation, and revenge on its cosmic enemy.

ALHAZRED, ABDUL (TF, TH, NC, CC, MM, CDW): One of HPL's most familiar and, so to speak, most beloved fictional creations, the "mad Arab" of the 8th century A.D. who wrote the *Necronomicon*, based on older sources. The name Abdul is a common one among Arabs; in "Alhazred" some see an allusion to "Hazard", a name in HPL's family tree, although perhaps it is a pun on "all-has-read" for a book-loving little boy. The name was one of HPL's youthful imagined alter-egos, coined by "some kindly elder," as HPL wrote in later years, during the child's enthusiasm for tales from the *Arabian Nights* when he was five years old or thereabouts.

In the mock-historic squib, "A History of the Necronomicon" (1936), HPL called Abdul Alhazred:

> a mad poet of Sanaa, in Yemen, who is said to have flourished during the period of the Ommiade [Ummayad] Caliphs, circa *a.d.* 700. He visited the ruins of Babylon and the subterranean secrets of Memphis and spent ten years in the great southern desert of Arabia—the Roba El Khaliyeh [Rub' al-Khali] or "empty space".... Of this desert many strange and unbeliev-able marvels are told by those who pretend to have penetrated it. In his last years Alhazred dwelt in Damascus, where the Necronomicon (*Al Azif*) was written, and of his final death or disappearance (*a.d.* 738) many terrible and conflicting things are told. He is said by Ebn Khallikan (twelfth century biographer) to have been seized by an invisible monster in broad daylight and devoured horribly.... Of his madness many things are told. He claimed to have seen the fabulous Irem, or City of Pillars, and to have found beneath the ruins of a certain nameless desert town the shocking annals and secrets of a race older than mankind. He was only an indifferent Moslem, worshipping unknown Entities whom he called Yog-Sothoth and Cthulhu.

Abdul Alhazred makes his first appearance in *The Nameless City*, in which he is quoted without any reference to the *Necronomicon*. That book, and Alhazred's authorship of it, are both mentioned for the first time in *The Hound*.

ALI ZIZ (UP): A Cairo street-Arab who provokes a loud quarrel and tussle with Houdini's guide, Abdul Reis el Drogman, bringing about the midnight "fight of honor" on the apex of the Great Pyramid to which Houdini is invited. The entire affair, of course, has been a "set-up" to lure Houdini to his doom in the catacombs of the "older Egypt."

"ALLEN, DR." (CDW): A mysterious, sandy-haired individual wearing dark glasses, with a "thin and scholarly aspect" and a hollow voice. Seen with Charles Dexter Ward in Pawtuxet, but later "disappears"; Dr. Allen turns out to have been the disguise of the revenant wizard Joseph Curwen.

ALLEN, ZADOK (SOI): A lean and ingratiating 96-year-old human resident of Innsmouth, Massachusetts, and the town drunk. Born in Innsmouth circa 1831, as a boy he watches strange doings by night out on Devil Reef, as he stands in his home's cupola and looks over the harbor with his father's telescope. In 1846 he tells Selectman Mowry, a town leader, about what he has seen. Soon afterwards, he witnesses the massacre of about half of the townsfolk by the sea-creatures and their human allies, led by Captain Obed Marsh. Allen's father left the house with his musket that night to try to find Mowry and organize some kind of resistance, but was never seen again. Zadok served in the Civil War, but then returned to Innsmouth. By the time of the story's modern events, he has taken the First and Second Oaths of Dagon, and therefore has some protection; for example, he notes that he cannot be slain unless a jury of fellow-Dagonites finds that he has deliberately given away secrets. In 1927, he meets the visiting narrator by chance and tells him the town's hideous secret history, after his tongue has been loosened with a bottle of bootleg liquor. At the end of his long account, he realizes that he has been observed talking to the young traveler, screams and runs away. He is never seen again, even after the federal government's secret raid on Innsmouth.

The name "Zadok," thought to stem from a Hebrew word for "right-eous," is given for seven different men in the Old Testament. The most prominent was Zadok the son of Ahitub, who was appointed as a priest in the Temple by King David. Due to his loyalty in all circumstances to David and his successor King Solomon, he was named high priest by the latter monarch, and his descendants were given special prominence in the Temple even centuries later. The name of such a hero of ancient Israel naturally attained popularity as a boy's name in New England two or three centuries ago, when the Puritan tradition favored Old Testament names for children.

At one point in his narrative, Zadok Allen talks about the helplessness of Matt Eliot and the community's clergymen, then makes several allusions to evil powers mentioned in the Bible:

> Wrath o' Jehovy—I was a mighty little critter [creature], but I heerd what I heerd an' seen what I seen—Dagon an' Ashtoreth—Belial an' Beelzebub—Golden Caff an' the idols of Canaan an' the Philistines—Babylonish abominations—*Mene, mene, tekel, upharsin!*

Besides the "wrath of Jehovah" which is obvious enough, "Dagon" was a god of the pagan Philistines, who were among the principal enemies of the Hebrews, and who worshipped their gods in the form of idols. Belial was Satan, Beelzebub a demon. Ashtoreth was the Hebrew pronunciation of "Astarte," the love-goddess of the Phoenicians and also the Babylonians (as "Ishtar"), regarded as an evil spirit by the children of Israel. The "Golden Caff" is a reference to the golden idol in the shape of a calf which the Israelites set up to worship after their flight from Egypt, provoking the wrath and the harsh punishment of God, through His faithful servant Moses (the story is in the Bible, in the 32nd chapter of the Book of Exodus). The Canaanites, Philistines, and Babylonians, all contemporaries of the ancient Israelites or Hebrews, worshipped the idols of multiple gods and goddesses and were violently and repeatedly denounced for it by the Hebrew prophets and chroniclers.

The phrase *Mene, mene, tekel, upharsin!*, which Zadok Allen repeats a couple of pages later, is seemingly uttered to indicate an opinion on Zadok's part that the judgment of God must have been against the normal humans of Innsmouth. It is found in the Bible, Daniel 5:25–28, a passage in which the prophet Daniel interprets some words written by a ghostly hand on the wall of the banquet chamber of the proud Babylonian king, Belshazzar:

> 25. And this is the writing that was written, MENE, MENE, TEKEL, UPHARSIN. 26. This is the interpretation of the thing: MENE; God hath numbered thy kingdom, and finished it. 27. TEKEL; Thou art weighed in the balances, and art found wanting. 28. PERES; Thy kingdom is divided, and given to the Medes and the Persians.... 30. In that night was Belshazzar the king of the Chaldeans slain.

Old Zadok, like some of HPL's other decrepit rustics, speaks in the extreme and archaic Yankee dialect that HPL took pains to revive in print. (During HPL's formative years and for long afterwards, it was the standard practice of writers to phonetically reproduce the twisted English pronunciation of their fictional characters, particularly those of a foreign or differently-pigmented breed or a lower social class or both; Irish rogue with a brogue, Scottish crone, Cockney scamp, Uncle Remus on the Georgia plantation, Chinese coolie ["Me velly solly!"], and so on.) It has been suggested that HPL derived much of this arcane lingo straight from the 19th century dialect-poems of James Russell Lowell (1819–91), collected as *The Biglow Papers* (1848), a collection of satires on political or social issues of the day. Lowell, a Massachusetts native who became a Harvard professor and an influential magazine editor, claimed that the dialect of these poems was that which he had heard spoken by ordinary workmen during his childhood, "when an Irish laborer was as rare as a Yankee laborer is now." In this connection a quote from one of HPL's letters, from 1929, is quite amusing: "As for Yankee farmers—oddly enough, I haven't noticed the majority speak any differently from myself.... If I were to say, 'Mornin', Zeke, haow ye be?' to anybody along the road...I fancy I'd receive an icy stare in return—or perhaps a puzzled inquiry as to what theatrical troupe I had wandered out of!"

ALOS (PO): "A true man and a patriot," commander of the forces of Olathoë on the plateau of Sarkis, in Lomar, a city under attack by the fierce Inutos 26,000 years ago. Alos appoints his friend, the nameless narrator, to solitary sentinel-duty in the all-important watchtower of Thapnen, although the friend is "given to strange faintings" and is physically exhausted.

ANCHESTER (RW); Fictitious English village three miles away from the fictitious Exham Priory, for which place the people of Anchester held "an almost unbelievable fear and hatred," a morbid dislike which extended to the castle's hereditary owners, the narrator's family. The village is overrun by an army of rats three months after Exham Priory became deserted, in the early 17th century. During all or part of the period of Roman imperial rule in Britain (from the 1st to 5th centuries A.D.), it is said (in the tale) that the future site of Anchester was the permanent encampment of the "third Augustan legion," a Roman army unit which would have consisted of several thousand troops. As HPL would have known well, the "-chester" ending in an English place-name indicates the original Latin *castrum*, a Roman camp (for example, in the names of the non-fictitious English cities of Winchester and Manchester).

ANDERSON (WE): Aircraft pilot employed by the Crystal Company on Venus. He makes an aerial map of the land route followed by Kenton J. Stanfield, whom he had earlier warned about the danger of mirage-plants. Later, he flies Repair Plane FG-7 to the Eryx site with a demolition team, and then flies back to Terra Nova in Scout Plane FR-58 with a cargo of the giant crystal and the remains of Stanfield and Frederick Dwight.

ANDERSON, DOCTOR (BWS): Scottish astronomer who discovered a "marvelous" new star, *Nova Persei*, on February 22, 1901.

ANDROS, GOVERNOR (SH, PM, SHH): Sir Edmond Andros (1637–1714) was the appointed British royal governor of the colony of New York (1674–81) and of the "Dominion of New England"—a monstrous entity which included not only the colonies of New England proper, but New York and "the Jerseys" as well (1686–89). His overbearing and oppressive conduct in office led the colonials in Boston to arrest him and ship him back to England. His royal favor held good, and he was later appointed governor of Virginia—a less fractious, more royalist community than that of New England—from 1692–97. In *The Shunned House* it is mentioned that the Roulet family's unpopularity with English colonists stemmed from something more than simple ethnic dislike, or the baneful influence of land disputes involving other French settlers "which not even Governor Andros could quell." Some formerly "splendid dark-oak panelling" in Pickman's secret studio, in *Pickman's Model*, reminds Thurber of "the times of Andros..."

ANGAROLA (PM, CC): The references in these tales to the artist called "Angarola" or "Angarola of Chicago," someone who could draw a weird scene with the best, are to Anthony Angarola (1893–1929). He was a talented illustrator who lived in Chicago for part of the 1920s and also taught for four years at the Kansas City Art Institute. Angarola won a prestigious Guggenheim Fellowship in Fine Arts for advanced study in New York City in 1928, but died unexpectedly the next year when his artistic career might have been on the brink of greater things and wider fame. As fate would have it, he is now probably best-known for having been mentioned in these two tales. In a letter written to a friend after learning of Angarola's untimely death, HPL noted that the artist had wished to illustrate his tale *The Outsider* for its magazine publication, but the publisher had already given the contract to another artist.

ANGELL, COLONEL (SH): Israel Angell (1740–1832), an historical figure who commanded Rhode Island soldiers against British forces during the Revolutionary War. As of 1780, the fictitious William Harris is a captain in Angell's command, in New Jersey.

These time-and-place indications make historical sense. On June 23, 1780, strong British forces advanced on the town of Springfield, New Jersey, George Washington's temporary headquarters, from their own base in Elizabethtown (now Elizabeth), on the coast. General Washington had already left the area, leaving General Nathanael Greene in command, with Colonel Angell and his Rhode Islanders holding a defensive line in the vicinity of the Rahway River, facing the British columns attempting to break through to Springfield. Colonel Angell's troops, along with New Jersey militiamen, brought the British advance to a halt and inflicted heavy losses. The invaders were forced to retire to Elizabethtown, and fighting in New Jersey was generally at an end for the remainder of the war. HPL indicates William Harris' courage and good health by associating him with this "famous victory" by Rhode Island warriors. HPL visited Elizabeth, New Jersey, shortly before beginning this tale.

ANGELL, GEORGE GAMMELL (CC): Professor emeritus (*i.e.,* retired) of Semitic Languages, at Brown University, Providence. He lives on Williams Street in Providence. He dies very suddenly one day during the winter of 1927–28, shortly after he is "jostled" by a "negro sailor" while walking home from the Newport ferry. We are meant to suspect some poisoning or other form of covert assassination, by a Cthulhu-cultist. He was a widower without children; his executor and sole heir is his grand-nephew Francis W. Thurston, of Boston. At the 1908 annual convention of the American Archaeological Society (a fictitious organi-zation) in St. Louis, Missouri, Professor Angell meets Inspector J. Legrasse of the New Orleans police department, and gets his first inkling of the existence of the Cthulhu cult. Throughout the month of March, 1925, Angell studies the bizarre dreams of the Providence artist Henry A. Wilcox. He also employs a "clipping service" (a business which, for a fee, would have its professional readers sift through a large number of newspapers from many places, clipping out and sending to clients items relevant to their designated interest), to locate worldwide press accounts of occurrences of "panic, mania, and eccentricity" during that fateful month.

> Here was a nocturnal suicide in London, where a lone sleeper had leaped from a window after a shocking cry. Here likewise a rambling letter to the editor of a paper in South America, where a fanatic deduces a dire future from visions he has seen. A despatch from California describes a theoso-phist colony as donning white robes *en masse* for some "glorious fulfill-ment" which never arises, while items from India speak guardedly of seri-ous native unrest toward the end of March. Voodoo orgies multiply in Hayti [Haiti], and African outposts report ominous mutterings. American officers in the Philippines find certain tribes bothersome about this time, and New York policemen are mobbed by hysterical Levantines on the night of March 22–23.... And so numerous are the recorded troubles in insane asylums that only a miracle can have stopped the medical fraternity from noting strange parallelisms.

It seems quite likely that HPL, in basing this story in his own every-day home of Providence, derived the professor's name from his own beloved Angell Street, and from "Gamwell", his Aunt Annie's surname by marriage. Annie Phillips Gamwell's husband E.F. Gamwell, a former newspaperman, was for a time an English instructor at Brown University, where fictional George Gammell Angell held his professorship. Seen only in the narrator's hindsight, the late Professor Angell is a worthy if especially luckless member of HPL's fraternity of intrepid academic investigators.

ANGELL STREET, PROVIDENCE (SH): A lovely residential avenue in the historic College Hill section, bearing the name of a prominent local clan from colonial times. HPL was born in his grandfather Whipple Phillips' big house at 454 Angell Street (demolished in 1961), and lived there between the ages of 3 and 14 years, leaving him with eternal memories of a wealthy Victorian-era home with fifteen rooms, nearly half a dozen servants, and a stable of carriage horses. HPL's wife Sonia later recalled being shown the "large, rambling, three-story mansion" with its "beautiful, spacious grounds and huge stables" while on a tour of the neighborhood with HPL and his aunt Annie Gamwell. Soon after his grandfather's death in 1904, catastrophic financial reverses forced the quick sale of the old home. HPL and his mother were compelled to move into a rented duplex-unit three blocks away at 598 Angell Street, where he lived until he got married and moved to New York City in 1924. More than twenty years after moving out, HPL still harbored fantasies about repurchasing the old Phillips mansion from its later owners—it eventually was converted to a medical office-building—and restoring it to the appearance it had when he last lived there in 1904.

In *The Shunned House*, it is mentioned that Archer Harris built a hideous "French-roofed" mansion on Angell Street in 1876. This can only be a reference to the "Hamilton House," a mansion built in 1896 at 276 Angell Street, and still standing. Its French-style architecture clashes architecturally with the traditional New England houses around it, and therefore HPL detested it.

ÅNGSTROM (CC): A sailor on the *Emma* with a Swedish name; he survives the sea-battle with the Cthulhu-cultists in March, 1925, and continues the voyage with his fellow-survivors on the *Alert*. One of the eight men who land on the risen city of R'lyeh. He is "swept up by the flabby claws" of Cthulhu along with two other unfortunate sailors, and presumably crushed or else eaten as a tender morsel by Cthulhu, who has, after all, been fasting in his house for millions of years.

ANTARCTICA (MM, HD): The great frozen southern continent, near the center of which lies the South Pole. The Scott vs. Amundsen "race to the Pole," an event which included the tragic deaths of Captain R.F. Scott and several of his companions in 1912, took place during Lovecraft's youth and seized the world's imagination—as did numerous other fortunate or unfortunate polar expeditions in the era. HPL read widely on the subject of Antarctica as a boy and, during his later years, Antarctica remained one of the last nearly-uncharted places on Earth, a place where mountain ranges higher than the Himalayas, and the undiscovered remains of a vast prehistoric city, could at least be conjectured in the void. In *The Haunter of the Dark*, Robert Blake learned that the Shining Trapezohedron, a "window on all time and space," was "treasured and placed in its curious box by the crinoid things of Antarctica"—plainly, the builders of that prehistoric city—eons before the first human beings.

The long tale *At the Mountains of Madness* showcased Lovecraft's book-learning about Antarctica and polar exploration, before veering off into brilliant fantasy.

ANTHROPOLOGISTS OF THE MI-GO (WD): In his first letter to Dr. Albert N. Wilmarth of Miskatonic University, dated May 5, 1928, Henry W. Akeley tells him:

> I might say, with all proper modesty, that the subject of anthropology and folklore is by no means strange to me. I took a good deal of it at college, and am familiar with most of the standard authorities such as Tylor, Lubbock, Frazer, Quatrefages, Murray, Osborn, Keith, Boule, G. Elliott Smith, and so on. It is no news to me that tales of hidden races are as old as mankind.

This is quite a mouthful. Sir Edward Burnett Tylor (1832–1917), author of the trailblazing book *Anthropology* (1881) was Professor of Anthropology at Oxford University from 1896–1909. His work centered on primitive religions, particularly animism. Sir John Lubbock (1834–1913), who lived in the last era when a dedicated amateur scientist could combine a busy career as a banker and Member of Parliament with significant contributions to anthropology and entomology (the study of insects), authored the popular 1865 textbook *Prehistoric Times*, which remained in use for many years. For Sir James Frazer, *see* separate entry. Professor Jean Louis Armand de Quatrefages de Breau (1810–92), was for many years the Chairman of Anthropology and Ethnography at the *Musée d' Histoire Naturelle* (Museum of Natural History) in Paris. His works on these subjects, translated into different languages, had wide circulation. For Margaret Murray, see separate entry. The spectacular academic career of Henry Fairfield Osborn (1857–1935), an American, included stints as a professor at Princeton University (Comparative Anatomy) and Columbia (Biology and Zoology); from 1908–33 he was president of the American Museum of Natural History and simultaneously did years of service as a consulting paleontologist and geologist for the U.S. Geological Survey. He also published several popular books on evolution and numerous technical articles on paleontology. Sir Arthur Keith, M.D. (1866–1955), primarily an anatomist and physiologist, also authored *The Antiquity of Man* (1915), a popular study on primitive humans or pre-humans, based on analysis of fossil bones from Europe and northern Africa. Marcellin Boule (1861–1942), an important French paleontologist in his day, published a popular book on Neanderthal Man (*Homo sapiens neandertalensis*) in 1913, which portrayed these mysterious, robust, Ice Age cousins of *Homo sapiens sapiens* (the readers of this Lexicon) as "dullwitted, brutish, and apelike." The stereotype of Neanderthal Man as a knuckle-dragging semi-ape persists although modern science has discredited it. G. Elliott Smith was a prominent English anthropologist and Egyptologist of the early 20th century, author of books both technical (*Archaeological Survey of Nubia*) and popular (*Elephants and Ethnographers*).

ANZIQUES (PH): Referred to in the tale as a cannibal tribe in Africa, described in the book *Regnum Congo* by Filippo Pigafetta, based on the tales of the explorer Duarte Lopez. An engraving of an Anzique butcher shop, with its neat arrangement of human heads and limbs, arouses an unseemly interest in the book's Yankee owner. The "country" of the tribe in question, a district on the lower reaches of the Congo River, was called something similar to "Anziko," hence the derivation of "Anziques."

ARABIA (NC, SOT, SK): HPL had an early and intense childhood interest in the fantasy "Arabia" of the "Arabian Nights" and similar exotic tales; it was in this era that an adult playfully dubbed him "Abdul Alhazred." As a somewhat older writer, HPL remained interested in the creative fantasy possibilities of lost cities in Arabian deserts; characteristically, his vision extended to before the dawn of mankind. The Nameless City, in the tale of the same name, was abandoned by its inhabitants countless ages before Egypt or Babylon came to be; it lies in a "parched and terrible valley" in the remotest part of the Arabian peninsula, and the desert tribes are careful to avoid the vicinity entirely. The city's "proportions and dimensions" are somehow "wrong," a typical Lovecraftian theme. In the tale of *The Shadow Out of Time*, Professor Wingate Peaslee travels to Arabia in 1911 and makes a mysterious camel-journey across the desert, for an unknown purpose. An admirer since childhood of the refined civilization of the medieval Arab kingdoms, HPL frequently provides his truth-seekers with crumbling Arabic-language texts.

ARAN, PEAK OF (CE, DQ): Snow-capped Mount Aran rises from the shore by the city of Celephaïs; on its lower slopes grow ginkgo trees, which sway in the soft breezes from the wide Cerenarian Sea.

ARCADIA (TR): A region of central Greece, which is the locale for this tale set in classical Greek times.

ARCTURUS (BWS, TGSK): Arcturus or "Alpha Bootis," an orange giant sun in the constellation of Bootes, the Herdsman, is the brightest star in the northern hemisphere and the fourth-brightest of all visible stars; it was the first star (in 1635), to be seen in daylight with a telescope. It is mentioned in the Bible, when God challenges Job: "Canst thou guide Arcturus and his sons?" (Job 38:32) It is mentioned in the works of Homer, Hippocrates, Lord Byron, and Alexander Pope, to name only a few. In *Beyond the Wall of Sleep*, the nameless narrator's "brother of light" telepathically tells him that in the past: "You and I have drifted to the worlds that reel about the red Arcturus...." In *Through the Gates of the Silver Key*, Randolph Carter once encounters one of the pre-human entities "which had dwelt in primal Hyperborea and worshipped black, plastic Tsathoggua after flying down from Kythanil, the double planet that once revolved around Arcturus...."

ARDOIS-BONNOT (CC): A fictitious painter of fantastic subjects, who exhibits a "blasphemous" painting entitled *Dream Landscape* at the Paris art exhibit of Spring, 1926. This was further circumstantial evidence of the global epidemic of mental reactions to the reawakening of Cthulhu a year earlier, in March, 1925.

ARKHAM (MM): One of the two ships carrying the Miskatonic University Expedition to Antarctica; her captain is J.B. Douglas. After departing from Boston on September 2, 1930, the vessels sail through the Panama Canal, and put in at Samoa and at Hobart, New Zealand, on their way south. Icebergs are sighted at latitude 62° South, and the explorers cross the Antarctic Circle "with appropriately quaint ceremonies," on October 20. (Seasons are reversed from the northern hemisphere in Antarctica, so of course the expedition is aiming for the brief Antarctic summer.) On October 26, the voyagers catch sight of the Admiralty Range of mountains on the Antarctic coast. Next they round Cape Adare, proceed along the east coast of Victoria Land, pass Franklin Island on November 7, and the next afternoon make landfall in McMurdo Sound. The expeditionary gear is unloaded on Ross Island, but the headquarters remains on board the *Arkham*, which is moored in the lee of Mount Erebus, perhaps because the large and powerful radio transmitter on the ship is the only link between the expedition and the outside world. On January 28, 1931, the survivors of the land expedition return to the base camp at McMurdo Sound, and depart from Antarctica aboard the *Arkham* and her sister ship *Miskatonic* five days later.

ARKHAM (PH, HW, TF, SK, SHH, COS, DH, WD, MM, SOI, DWH, TGSK, TD, SOT): Fictitious city in Essex County, Massachusetts, several miles north of Boston. The city was founded in the 17th century on the banks of the Miskatonic River and it is the home of Miskatonic University, whose library, science and anthropology departments, and medical school feature in various tales. Arkham took part in the "Salem" witchcraft terror of 1692, when Keziah Mason was jailed, but escaped in an inexplicable way. Some of the leading families of Dunwich migrated there from Arkham at that time. A typhoid epidemic struck the city in

1904 while Herbert West was finishing his course at the Miskatonic medical school. During the 1920s, Walter Gilman studied at the university and lived in the Witch House, Keziah Mason's former dwelling. His tale mentions movie theaters and cafés in the town. The white Anglo-Saxon Protestant well-to-do of Arkham inhabit fine houses along Miskatonic Avenue, High Street, and Saltonstall Street, but there is also a sizeable working-class population, which seems to be largely Catholic in religion and Polish, Italian, or French-Canadian in ethnicity; a typical social picture in New England cities of the early 20th century. Arkham's smaller neighbors include Kingsport and Innsmouth. A "queer turbaned man" exchanged some gold bullion for cash at the First National Bank in Arkham in October, 1930.

HPL's Arkham is a heavily fictionalized doublet of Danvers (formerly Salem), Massachusetts, center of the witchcraft mania of 1692; with a strong admixture of New England college towns such as New Haven, Connecticut (Yale) and Cambridge, Massachusetts (Harvard).

ARKHAM *ADVERTISER* **and** *GAZETTE* (DH, MM, COS): Local newspapers. The *Advertiser* prints a humorously-written news wire item from near Dunwich on September 12, 1928, which Dr. Armitage correctly understands to mean that the Horror is on the loose. In 1930–31, the *Advertiser* has the "exclusive" on news stories radioed from the Miskatonic University Expedition in Antarctica. In 1917, both the Arkham *Advertiser* and the Boston *Globe* print "flamboyant Sunday stories" about Wilbur Whateley's physical precocity, Old Whateley's reputed practice of black magic, and "the weirdness of the whole [Dunwich] region." It may also have been in the *Advertiser*—the newspaper name is not stated—in which Walter Gilman reads of the disappearance of little Ladislas Wolejko from the street called Orne's Gangway, in Arkham, and of the reported sighting of a huge "negro" in robes, a tame rat, a raggedly-dressed old woman, and a young white man wearing pajamas, at the entrance to the Gangway at around midnight on the night of the boy's disappearance.

The Arkham *Gazette* covers the fall of the meteorite on the Nahum Gardner farm in June, 1882, and the subsequent investigation of the object by science professors from Miskatonic University. Perhaps counting on the newspaper's continued interest as a result, Gardner took some bizarrely-colored saxifrage blossoms from his farm to Arkham the next month, to show to the editor. But that gentleman only wrote a humor-piece ridiculing country people. A month later, the *Gazette* did print a paragraph about a traveling salesman's account of passing a farm that seemed to glow in the dark, one recent night in the Miskatonic Valley.

Neighbors reading the article understand that the stranger had seen the Gardner place.

ARKHAM SANITARIUM (TD): The hospital where Daniel Upton "put six bullets through the head of my best friend," Edward P. Derby, who had been committed there for schizophrenic behavior, but who was soon to be released. After the shooting, Upton is confined in the same institution.

ARMINGTON (IV): The "lodgekeeper" of the Peck Valley Cemetery. On Good Friday, April 15, 1881, he answers the door at about midnight when the injured undertaker George Birch clawed on the wood panels, helps Birch into a bed, and sends his son Edwin to fetch Dr. Davis, the town physician.

ARMITAGE, DR. HENRY (DH): Probably born circa 1855, Dr. Armitage holds a master of arts degree from Miskatonic University, a Ph.D. from Princeton, and a D.Litt. from Johns Hopkins University in Baltimore. In the 1920s he is the "old, white-bearded" chief librarian at Miskatonic. A "scholarly correspondent" of Wilbur Whateley, he visits him at his Dunwich farm in 1925 and departs "pale and puzzled." In 1928 he again meets Whateley, when that youth visits Miskatonic University to consult the library's copy of the *Necronomicon*, an attempt which Armitage prevents. Armitage begins to investigate Whateley's background, and later witnesses Whateley expire and evaporate after being mauled to death by the campus guard-dog. In the following weeks he deciphers Wilbur Whateley's encrypted diary, and finally drives to Dunwich with two university colleagues on September 14, 1928, after bizarre and hideous killings begin to occur in the area. Dr. Armitage takes the lead role in rallying the terrified farmers, cornering the Horror, and pronouncing the counter-spell that drives it from our planet.

ARRUDA, CAPTAIN MANUEL (CDW): In this tale, the captain of the merchant ship *Fortaleza* from Barcelona, which voyages from Cairo, Egypt, to Providence, Rhode Island, in 1769–70. In January 1770, the vessel is seized by a British coast-guard ship, H.M.S. *Cygnet*, while trying to secretly enter Rhode Island's waters. But the *Fortaleza* is released because the ship's peculiar cargo consists of ancient mummies, which are not contraband. Captain Arruda sails away to Boston, where the mummies were presumably unloaded somewhere and brought to their purchaser, Joseph Curwen. In real life, Manuel Arruda was the name of a door-to-door produce salesman who worked in HPL's Providence neighborhood in the 1920s.

ART CLUB (PM): The painter Richard Upton Pickman is a member of this elite Boston club, as is "Thurber," the narrator of *Pickman's Model*.

The Boston Art Club—presumably the one referred to in the tale—was a real organization, founded in 1854. It was the earliest private-membership art club in the United States, and one of the first such societies to promote American artists and to showcase their work alongside the best available examples from Europe. During HPL's youth, the Art Club was still in the forefront of such artistic movements as the "Hudson River School," luminism, and impressionism. However, the club did not stay current with modern art, suffered a fatal decline in membership, and ceased to exist in about 1950.

ARTEPHOUS or ARTEPHIUS (CDW): A semi-legendary medieval alchemist who was said to have died in the year 1119, at the age of a thousand years or so. It was specified by some chroniclers that he was the same person as the ancient writer Appolonius of Tyana, known to have been born in the 1st century A.D. One of the books attributed to Artephius was *De vita propaganda*, "On prolonging life," which the author begins by claiming that he is writing it at the age of 125. Joseph Curwen's 18th century Providence library contained works of "Artephous"; their significance in the light of Curwen's unnaturally long life is obvious.

ARTHUR, MR. (TJR): Superintendent of the great Norton Mine, where the well-bred English narrator—an Oxford University man and former British army officer in India, from the few clues he drops—and the illiterate Mexican peasant Juan Romero work together as common laborers in 1894. He "often discussed the singularity [unusual nature] of the local geological formations.... He considered the auriferous [gold-containing] cavities the result of the action of water, and believed the last of them would soon be opened." When a dynamite operation opens the cavern which seems bottomless, the superintendent "did not reproach" the workers who refuse to continue examining it. "Instead, he pondered deeply, and made many plans for the following day." The next day the cavern has vanished, seemingly transformed into solid rock: "The Superintendent abandoned his attempts [to locate it]; but a perplexed look occasionally steals over his countenance as he sits thinking at his desk." For purposes of this tale, Mr. Arthur represents scientific or technical knowledge, and its limitations.

ASA and **HANNAH** (CDW): "Old Asa and stout Hannah" are a black couple in Providence, presumably husband and wife, who are "much esteemed for occasional washing, housecleaning, and furnace tending services." In 1919, they are the tenants in the house in Olney Court,

Stampers' Hill, which Joseph Curwen built for himself in the 1760s. Charles Dexter Ward finds Curwen's portrait and his secret papers hidden in this house. In 1927 Hannah, hired at the Ward mansion to help with spring cleaning, mentions that the young man has been in her house often lately, performing "curious delving in the cellar," but that he seemed more worried than in the past—"which grieved her very much, since she had watched him grow up from birth."

ASHLEY, PROFESSOR FERDINAND C. (SOT): A member of the Department of Ancient History at Miskatonic University in 1934. He accompanies Dr. Nathanael Peaslee and others to Western Australia in order to investigate the colossal stone ruins found in the Great Sandy Desert.

ASHMODEI, ASTAROTH (HRH): Names of demons from European witchcraft and previously from the Middle East, used along with other such names in the conjurations of the Brooklyn-based cultists. It is said that HPL researched the spellcasting stage-business of this minor tale in the prosaic *Encyclopedia Britannica*.

ASPINWALL, ERNEST B., ESQ. (SK, TGSK): "Esq." stands for Esquire, the courtesy title for American attorneys, and this ten-years-older cousin of Randolph Carter is a Chicago lawyer. Red-faced, stout, and side-whiskered, he is the sort of reactionary bigot who calls a Hindu sage "a damned nigger" to his face. Moreover, he lives in Chicago, a city that HPL regarded negatively for its lack of any colonial-era structures or past. At a conference held in Etienne-Laurent de Marigny's New Orleans home to settle the matter of the missing Carter's estate, Aspinwall is discourteous, abrasive, and very infuriated by "Swami Chandraputra's" cosmic explanations for Carter's absence. He pulls the mask from the face of the purported Hindu sage, and drops dead of fright at what he sees beneath the mask.

ATAL (CU, OG, DQ): Atal is the innkeeper's son in the town of Ulthar; on the night that the evil cat-killing couple are slain, he is the small boy who observes all the town's cats "pacing very slowly and solemnly around [their] cottage, two abreast, as in performance of some sacred rite of beasts." He receives a piece of candy for telling his story to the village elders. In *The Other Gods*, the observant small boy has grown to be a young priest in Ulthar, the disciple of the sage Barzai the Wise, with whom he scales the mountain of Hatheg-Kla. After the sage's sudden and disturbing disappearance, Atal awakens later to find himself lying in the snow on the lower slopes of the mountain. In *The Dream-Quest of Unknown Kadath*, Randolph Carter encounters Atal when he is a 300-

year-old patriarch in Ulthar's "Temple of the Elder Ones." Carter consults Atal to help locate the stronghold of earth's gods in unknown Kadath. Although he at first tries to dissuade Carter from making the attempt, Atal becomes more talkative when plied with "moon wine," suggests that Carter seek his goal on the mountain called Ngranek, and then falls asleep.

ATHIB (CE): The captain of a galley who takes Kuranes as a passenger from the harbor of Celephaïs, over the Cerenarian Sea, and through the sky to Serannian in the clouds. When Kuranes finds the city he had seen in a childhood dream after forty years of dream-searching, he also finds Athib, "who had agreed to carry him so long ago," "sitting on the same chest of spices he had sat upon before, and Athib seemed not to realize any time had passed."

ATHOK (QI): Shoemaker in the city of Teloth; Iranon is ordered to apprentice himself to Athok if he wishes to remain in that city another day, but prefers to leave instead.

ATLAANÂT (TGSK): Randolph Carter observes the Shapes dreaming together to open the Ultimate Gate for him, but he understands what is going on:

> He had seen such things on earth—in India, where the combined, projected will of a circle of adepts can make a thought take tangible substance, and in hoary Atlaanât, of which few men speak.

ATLANTIS (TT, SHH): German submarine U-29 comes to rest on the ocean floor in what may have been the lost city of Atlantis, under the North Atlantic Ocean at estimated latitude 20° North, longitude 35° West, or some 1200 miles off the coast of northwest Africa. U-29 has been drifting powerlessly while slowly sinking to the bottom, in August, 1917, but seems drawn as if by external power until she settles in the middle of the drowned city. It is full of marble buildings, in a narrow valley, with numerous temples and villas on the slopes above. There is also a titanic and well-preserved temple, with façade carvings of "phenomenal perfection, largely Hellenic in idea, yet strangely individual...of terrible antiquity, as though it were the remotest rather than the immediate ancestor of Greek art." Normal laws of science seem to be suspended in this place, as the submarine, her captain, and many dolphins can exist at that depth without being crushed by water pressure, while flames can be seen and music can be heard from within the temple itself. In *The Strange High House in the Mist,* while talking to the occupant of the Strange High House, Thomas Olney hears some stories about the battles of the Kings of Atlantis against dreadful foes from the deep.

ATWOOD, PROFESSOR (MM): Professor of physics and meteorology at Miskatonic University, and a leading member of the Miskatonic University Expedition to Antarctica, 1930–31. He is a licensed airplane pilot, able to navigate on long cross-country flights with compass and sextant (still useful flight skills at that time). He is a skillful builder of aircraft shelters, windbreaks, and reinforcing structures for big tents, using heavy blocks of congealed snow as his construction material. He accompanies Professor Lake on the sub-party that leaves the main group. He makes the surveying measurements that show the height of the mountains they discover to be an incredible 30,000–40,000 feet above sea level. He supervises the snow-banking of the tents, the dog corral, and the aircraft shelters, is found dead with the rest of Lake's group on January 25, 1931, and is buried at their site.

ATYS (RW): Name of a pagan god whose cult was imported to ancient Rome from Phrygia in Asia Minor (modern Turkey). As Mr. de la Poer mentions, the Atys-cult became intertwined with that of Cybele, a Greco-Roman earth deity whose followers celebrated her with wild and orgiastic rites. (Left unmentioned is that Cybele, the Great Goddess or Magna Mater, raised her son-lover Atys from the dead after he castrated himself in remorse for betraying her.) Atys was worshipped especially at the beginning of spring, in connection with the death and rebirth of vegetation. The word "ATYS" is found carved on the walls in the lowest grotto beneath Exham Priory, the one which dates to the time of Roman Britain; and Mr. de la Poer mutters her name in his final madness. The "Catullus" in whose writings Mr. de la Poer remembered having seen Atys' name is the famed Roman lyric poet, a contemporary of the emperor Caesar Augustus in the 1st century A.D.

AUCKLAND, NEW ZEALAND (CC): Home port of the two-masted sailing schooner *Emma*, which encounters a shipload of Cthulhu-cultists in the South Pacific Ocean in March, 1925. Second Mate Johansen, of the *Emma*, lived with his wife on West Street in Auckland. Francis W. Thurston visits Auckland while investigating his uncle George G. Angell's notes on Cthulhu, but only learns there that Johansen had returned from the 1925 voyage with his hair turned white, and had shortly afterwards retired to his native Oslo, Norway.

AYLESBURY, MASSACHUSETTS (DH): Nearest normal (although also fictitious) town to Dunwich, in north central Massachusetts. Aylesbury is the location of the local probate court, where following Wilbur

Whateley's death on the campus of Miskatonic University, litigation over the ownership of his farm is "still in progress among the innumerable Whateleys, decayed and undecayed, of the upper Miskatonic Valley." The five state troopers who hunted for the Horror (without knowing it) in Cold Spring Glen during September, 1928, and who were never seen again, came from the Aylesbury post of the Massachusetts State Police. There is a real Aylesbury, in Buckinghamshire, England, and presumably HPL borrowed its name for his New England Aylesbury.

AYLESBURY *TRANSCRIPT* (DH): A most unenterprising local newspaper. When someone from nearby Dunwich telephones to report that an invisible monster has smashed a farmhouse, wiped out an entire herd of cattle overnight, and knocked down trees, the editor merely "concocts a humorous paragraph" about the story, puts the gag-item on the Associated Press news wire (so that it is eventually read about by Dr. Armitage of Miskatonic University), and stays home.

AZATHOTH (AZ, DQ, DWH, HD, WD): Azathoth is the "daemon-sultan" who gnaws hungrily in the central void, the epicenter of ultimate Chaos. Around his throne, musicians with thin flutes play mindless, monotonous rhythms, and all manner of strange beings disport themselves. In *The Dreams in the Witch House*, Keziah Mason seeks to have Walter Gilman sign the "book of Azathoth," a name Gilman remembers seeing in the *Necronomicon*. Nyarlathotep is said to be Azathoth's deputy. Edward Derby, of *The Thing on the Doorstep*, caused a sensation with *Azathoth and Other Horrors*, a book of poetry published when he was only eighteen. In *The Whisperer in Darkness*, there is a startling revelation; Professor Wilmarth, while talking with the alien organism that is disguised as Henry Akeley, is "told of the monstrous nuclear chaos beyond angled space which the *Necronomicon* had mercifully cloaked under the name of Azathoth." In *The Haunter of the Dark*, in his last moments, Robert Blake's "frenzied jottings" include the exclamation: "Azathoth have mercy!"

It has been suggested that the name "Azathoth" came to HPL's conscious or subconscious mind as a combination of "Azoth," an alchemical term for mercury (or alternately "Aza" as a form of "Assur," the principal god of the ancient Assyrians), and "Thoth," the Egyptian god who was the patron of writing and learning. In the absence of firm evidence, it seems just as possible and does not multiply complications as much, to surmise that Azathoth occurred to him as a slight change from "Anathoth," the name of a town a few miles from Jerusalem, which is mentioned as such more than a dozen times in the Old Testament, and in two other places as a Hebrew clan name in the tribe of Benjamin and the name of one of the "chiefs of the people" at the time of the restoration of the Temple at Jerusalem in the 5th century B.C.

In 1922, HPL toyed with the idea of writing a novel, whose theme was to be "imagination is the great refuge"; the working title was *Azathoth*, like Edward Derby's book of verse. Nothing came of this short-lived project except for a fragment of only a few hundred words, found in HPL's personal papers after his death. The theme is similar to that of some other "Dunsanian" tales, about a man who escapes in personal visions from the dullness and sterility of his waking life.

B

B-67 (WD): "Now [reach] for the cylinder with the label 'B-67' pasted on it," instructs the thing disguised as Henry Akeley. When Dr. Wilmarth has duly taken the small metal cylinder from its shelf and attached it to the "faculty machines," the voice-machine proclaims the contents to be the brain of a human being whose body is being kept alive under Round Hill, and who originally met the Mi-Go in the Himalayas. Owing to the mechanical, metallic, and lifeless tones of the voice machine, no judgments can be made about the speaker's origin, but he certainly speaks English in an educated manner:

> I am, of course, one of the men who have become allied with the outside beings visiting our planet...and [I] have helped them in various ways. In return they have given me experiences such as few men have ever had.
>
> Do you realise what it means when I say I have been on thirty-seven different celestial bodies—planets, dark stars, and less definable objects—including eight outside our galaxy and two outside the curved cosmos of space and time? All this has not harmed me in the least. My brain has been removed from my body by fissions so adroit that it would be crude to call the operation surgery...and one's body never ages when the brain is out of it. The brain, I may add, is virtually immortal with its mechanical faculties and a limited nourishment supplied by occasional changes of the preserving fluid.

BABCOCK, RESOLVED (SOI): Reverend Resolved Babcock is the pastor of the Baptist church in Innsmouth in the 1840s. He "disappears" prior to the 1846 massacre, presumably murdered, or even sacrificed to the Deep Ones.

BABSON, EUNICE (TD): Servant in the Arkham home of Edward Derby and Asenath Waite Derby. From Asenath's hometown of Innsmouth, Babson is "a swarthy young wench who had marked anomalies of feature and seemed to exude a perpetual odour of fish." One is meant to understand that she has "the Innsmouth look," the product of mixed marriage between human beings and fish-things, accounting for the characteristic Innsmouth stench of fish as well. Edward Derby fires her and sends her away after he murders Asenath, as he thinks.

BABYLON (CC, MM): In *At the Mountains of Madness*, Professor Dyer compares a stone ramp that winds around the inside of a tower in the ancient city to "those once climbing outside the monstrous towers or ziggurats of antique Babylon." The ziggurats of the ancient city of Babylon (in modern Iraq; it was a city and sometimes an empire, of legendary wealth and power, from the 3rd millennium B.C. to the 3rd century B.C.) were high brick towers built for the worship of the gods, ascended by circular ramps around the outside of the structure. In *The Call of Cthulhu*, Henry A. Wilcox says paradoxically that the dream-inspired clay tablet he has just made is new, "for I made it last night in a dream of strange cities, and dreams are older…than garden-girdled Babylon." The "Hanging Gardens of Babylon"—splendid terraces of plantings—were considered as one of the "Seven Wonders of the World" in ancient times. Babylon is mentioned many times in the Bible, eventually as a symbol of worldly power, riches, and overweening pride. Later in the tale, R'lyeh is called "this dripping Babylon of elder daemons."

BACON, ROGER (CDW): Roger Bacon (c. 1220–1292), was a brilliant Franciscan monk or "friar" in medieval England. Educated at the universities of Oxford and Paris, Bacon was renowned for his learning and intelligence, being a skillful philosopher and an enthusiastic student of alchemy, optics, astronomy, and scientific experiments. He was particularly interested in the transmutation of metals, and may have been the first European to produce and use the explosive mineral compound known as gunpowder. Bacon is now ranked as one of the fathers of modern Western science. He is mentioned in this tale as an esoteric authority, and Joseph Curwen owned his book *Thesaurus Chemicus*; Charles Dexter Ward tells Dr. Willett that "the papers of his ancestor [Joseph Curwen] had contained some remarkable secrets of early scientific knowledge…of an apparent scope comparable only to the discoveries of Friar Bacon and perhaps surpassing even those."

BAHARNA (DQ): A port city in Dreamland, on the isle of Oriab. Baharna's seagoing merchants wear silken robes and travel to Dylath-Leen to trade in sweet-smelling resins, delicate Baharnian ceramics, and figures carved from the black lava stone of Mount Ngranek. In return they take away Ulthar wool, iridescent fabrics from Hatheg, and ivory carvings from Parg. Baharna is apparently a ten-day sailing voyage over the Southern Sea from Dylath-Leen. It is a mighty city in appearance, with wharves made from the semi-precious mineral called porphyry; streets of steps, overarched by bridges and overhanging buildings, ascend the terraced hillside behind the harbor. A large canal passes through the city to reach the inland Lake Yath. There are two impressive lighthouses in the harbor, the beacons of Thon and Thal. Randolph Carter makes the voyage to Baharna and spends some time here gathering information about Ngranek, before hiring a riding-zebra and traveling to the mountain.

BAILEY (WE): Apparently an employee of the Venus Crystal Company, perhaps a dead one. "Recalling what happened to Bailey three years ago," writes Kenton Stanfield in his journal, "I fell into a momentary panic," as he came under the effects of some mirage-plants.

BALLYLOUGH (MB): Fictitious town or village in County Meath, Ireland, close to Denis Barry's ancestral castle "Kilderry". After learning of Barry's plan to drain the ancient bog by the castle, the people of Ballylough, hitherto well-disposed to him, refuse to work there any longer, forcing him to import construction workers from Northern Ireland. The Bally-prefix is common in Irish place-names, "-lough" means "lake" in the Irish language, and there have been real Ballyloughs. One was counted among the old "townlands" of County Down, and Ballylough was also the name of one of the "great houses" of the ruling Anglo-Irish aristocracy, constructed in the 18th century at Bushmills, County Antrim. Perhaps HPL came across the name in the course of reading history.

BANOF, VALLEY OF (PO): A misty valley near Olathoë, visible from the high tower of Thapnen.

BAPTIST CHURCH (SOI, HD, SHH, CDW): While he believed in no religion, HPL seemed to take some small special pleasure in "needling" the Baptist sect of Christianity. His family was mainly of the Baptist persuasion, and by HPL's own account, he was sent at the age of 5 to attend the "infant class" of the Sunday school at First Baptist Church, in Providence. (Located at 75 North Main Street, First Baptist is said to be the oldest Baptist congregation in the United States, and its 18th century meeting-house is one of the architectural treasures of the city.) According to HPL, even at that very young age he proved to be such a precocious skeptic and "pestiferous questioner" of the hapless lady teacher, "that I was permitted to discontinue attendance." This incident, or something like it, may not actually have happened until HPL's twelfth year, which seems more likely but less charming. HPL and his erstwhile Sunday-school teacher might both have been surprised by some of the changes at First Baptist a century later; for example, on the "millennium" New Year's Eve, part of the evening entertainment program at the church was a selection of American popular songs performed by the Providence Gay Men's Chorus. On one occasion, while taking some out-of-town visitors on a walking tour of downtown Providence, HPL led them up to the organ loft of First Baptist Church and tried to play the then-popular comic song "Yes, We Have No Bananas" on the instrument.

In *The Shadow Over Innsmouth*, the Congregationalist parson was driven out of town by Obed Marsh's followers in the 1840s, and the Methodist pastor simply quit his job and moved away, but the Baptist minister Resolved Babcock is singled out for the presumed unpleasant fate of being sacrificed to the fish-things on Devil Reef. In *The Haunter of the Dark,* the sinister Starry Wisdom cult purchases an abandoned Baptist church to convert into its temple. And in *The Strange High House in the Mist*, while Thomas Olney is reveling with his new friends Nodens and the mer-creatures, his dull wife and dull children, left at home, say their evening prayers to "the bland proper god of the Baptists." For what it is worth, in *The Case of Charles Dexter Ward* the monstrously evil Joseph Curwen passes as a Congregationalist, but he weds his unfortunate wife Eliza Tillinghast in a ceremony at her home Baptist church, another thumbing of the Lovecraft nose.

BARNABAS (CDW): Apparently a grave-robber employed by Simon/ Jedediah Orne (by then masquerading as "Josef Nadek" in Prague), mentioned by him in a letter to Joseph Curwen dated February 11, 1928.

BARNARD, DR. (BWS): One of the "alienists" (psychiatrists) in a New York state hospital for the criminally insane, where the murderer Joe Slater is confined during the winter of 1900–01. Dr. Barnard carefully observes the patient and succeeds in convincing him to put on his own leather restraining-harness each night at bedtime, for his own good. On one occasion the doctor notices in the pale blue eyes of the normally-idiotic Slater "a certain gleam of peculiar quality; and in the flaccid lips an all but imperceptible tightening, as if of intelligent determination."

BARNARD, THOMAS (CDW): Described as a pastor at Salem, Massachusetts, in 1771, Reverend Thomas Barnard is plainly a man of some local authority. Letters to him and to some other Salemites that year, sent by Providence citizens who are investigating Joseph Curwen, bring about the "quiet removal to parts unknown" of Curwen's Salem friend Jedediah Orne.

BARNES STREET (CDW): Upon his return from the two-year "New York Exile" during his marriage, HPL moved into a rented room at 10 Barnes Street in Providence in April, 1926, and lived there until May, 1933. His aunt Lillian lived in another rental unit upstairs. In a letter to his good friend Frank Belknap Long, HPL commented: "I have a fine large ground-floor room (a former dining-room with fireplace) and kitchenette alcove in a spacious brown Victorian wooden house of the 1880 period—a house, curiously enough, built by some friends of my own family, now long dead." HPL was willing to share his address with Dr.

Marinus B. Willett, who sends a letter from 10 Barnes Street to Charles Dexter Ward's father on April 12, 1928. This house is also just around the corner from the "Halsey Mansion" at 140 Prospect Street, the model for the fictitious Ward family home.

BARRY, DENIS (MB): Wealthy Irish-American son of an immigrant from "Kilderry," County Meath, Ireland, and a friend of the tale's narrator. An early fictional analog to Mr. de la Poer/Delapore in *The Rats in the Walls*, Barry returns to Ireland to purchase and restore the crumbling castle of his ancestors, certainly a Lovecraftian motif. "For all his love of Ireland, America had not left him untouched, and he hated the beautiful wasted space where peat might be cut and land opened up." With remorseless American efficiency, Barry becomes determined to drain the large bog which adjoins his castle grounds, despite the fearful protests of the local people, who all turn against him as a result. Because of the refusal of the natives to work for him, he hires workers and staff from Northern Ireland, perhaps Protestant "Ulstermen," who are presumably more hardheaded and less "superstitious." In Greek classical style, his *hubris* or overweening pride brought about his own downfall—and at the hands of what appear to be Greek gods! On the night when the Northern Irish staff disappear into the bog and (apparently) reemerge only as toads, the narrator in his castle chamber "began to hear the shrieks in the castle far below me. Soon those shrieks had attained a magnitude and quality which cannot be written of, and which make me faint as I think of them. All I can say is that they came from something I had thought of as a friend." Later he seems to see a "vague contorted shadow" struggling in the air above the bog, "a blasphemous effigy of him who had been Dennis Barry."

The Moon-Bog was written for a party for amateur journalists in a Boston apartment on St. Patrick's Day; each party guest had to compose and read a short story with an "Irish" theme. Caring relatively little about Ireland, HPL recalled the Irish legends about ancient colonists from distant and exotic places, and found a way to quickly turn from the frogs-and-bogs Irish background scenery to the Greek classical religion he knew so well. But someone else's story won the prize at the party.

BARZAI THE WISE (OG, DQ): Barzai is a sage in Ulthar, learned in the Pnakotic Manuscripts and the Seven Cryptical Books of Hsan. He is lacking in "common superstition," being the son of a landgrave who dwelt in an ancient castle, a great aristocrat. (The unusual English word "landgrave" is a translation of the German *Landgraf*, a count controlling a large territory.) It is Barzai who advises the elders of Ulthar to pass the law mandating death for anyone who harms a cat. Barzai knew much about earth's gods, and is determined to see their faces as they dance on the peak of Hatheg-Kla. With his disciple Atal, he climbs the great mountain, eagerly rushing ahead of his younger companion as they approach the summit. He sees earth's gods. He sees more, namely "the other gods" who protect earth's gods. From farther down the mountain, Atal helplessly hears his master's last scream: "Merciful gods of earth, *I am falling into the sky!*"

BASALT PILLARS OF THE WEST (WS, DQ): Like the Pillars of Hercules (the ancient name for the Straits of Gibraltar which separate the Mediterranean Sea from the Atlantic Ocean), the Basalt Pillars of the West represent the end of the known world in Dreamland. (Basalt is a dark rock of volcanic origin. It sometimes forms in the shape of tall pillars during lava flows.) Venturing through the Basalt Pillars after a 31-day voyage from Sona-Nyl, Basil Elton and the White Ship's crew see them shrouded in mist, their tops invisible. Then the ship is caught in a powerful current and borne irresistibly over a mighty waterfall, "wherein the oceans of the world drop down to abysmal nothingness." But in *The Dream-Quest of Unknown Kadath*, when the moon-beasts' galley, carrying the kidnapped Randolph Carter, travels the same way, the ship reaches the edge of the cataract and flies off into the sky, sailing through space to the moon.

BAUDELAIRE, CHARLES (HY, HW, TH): A major French poet, Charles Baudelaire (1821–67) was also an astute and elegant critic and essayist, and the great translator and promoter of the works of Edgar Allan Poe in France. HPL begins the minor tale *Hypnos* with a quote from Baudelaire:

> Apropos of sleep, that sinister adventure of all our nights, we may say that men go to bed daily with an audacity that would be incomprehensible if we did not know that it is the result of ignorance of the danger.

A sentiment that was sure to appeal to the nightmare-ridden dreamer in Providence! But in the hackwork that is *Herbert West—Reanimator*, Baudelaire's image is crudely employed as a type of perverse addiction to the fiendishly abnormal; in a ridiculous passage, Dr. West is called "a fastidious Baudelaire of physical experiment." The criminal aesthetes of *The Hound* find that Baudelaire and the so-called Decadent poets (a poetic movement of the late 19th century) "were soon exhausted of thrills," and so they turn to high-class grave-robbing instead.

HPL and Charles Baudelaire make an odd couple in literary history, although they were both great admirers of Poe. By contrast to HPL's life-long policy of ascetic living, physical self-denial, and puritanical abstaining from vice, the passionate, turbulent French artist enjoyed or endured a frantic love-life and many quarrels, drank too much, became addicted to opium and hashish, and died of the venereal disease syphilis. Several of Baudelaire's poems in his famous 1857 collection *Les Fleurs du Mal* ("The Flowers of Evil"), while artistically meritorious and quite tame by modern standards, deal frankly with sexuality, prostitution, and related themes, and landed him in a French criminal court on charges of obscenity. (HPL enjoyed the beautiful poetry of *Les Fleurs du Mal*, regardless of the controversial subject-matter.) A recent biographer of Baudelaire notes that "for several generations [his works] remained a byword for depravity, morbidity, and obscenity," and it is in this light that Lovecraft alludes to him in *Herbert West—Reanimator*.

BAYONNE (SK): An actual ancient city in the "Basque country" of far southwestern France, in the *departement* of Pyrénées Atlantiques. Randolph Carter and his fellow Foreign Legion soldier de Marigny visit the city while on leave from World War I trench combat, and explore the tunnels beneath it.

BEACON HILL (PM): Pickman shows Thurber a "disgusting canvas" with a painting of "a vast cross-section of Beacon Hill," showing "ant-like armies" of ghouls passing through networks of tunnels. Beacon Hill is a socially prestigious district of the city of Boston.

BEARDSLEY, AUBREY (HRH): For Thomas Malone, "daily life had...come to be a phantasmagoria of macabre shadow-studies ["studies" is used here in the sense of the word that means "drawings"]; [sometimes] glittering and leering with concealed rottenness as in Beardsley's best manner...."

Aubrey Beardsley (1872–98), English artist, was, according to one indulgent old source:

> A wonderfully precocious boy all his life, with the frank merriment, enthusiasm and exuberance of a lad. He was unable to withstand the desire to do clever, mischievous things and to shock people of narrow opinions, and his ignoble and vicious works were more the result of his Puck-like mischief and eccentricity of habit than of any evil disposition. During his short life he carried the art of black and white [illustration] farther than any man since Albrecht Dürer [the Renaissance-era German master].

The bourgeoisie were never easier to shock than in the last years of the 19th century, and the "mischievous" boy-genius Beardsley was responsible for illustrations in limited private editions of the ancient Greek comedy *Lysistrata* and Oscar Wilde's play *Salome* (to mention only two) that were certainly considered shocking and obscene in their day, and to some extent might still be so perceived. He also harbored a strong religious impulse, and converted to Catholicism not long before his death.

BECHER (CDW): One of the authors whose works are found in Joseph Curwen's private library in Providence. Johann Joachim Becher (1635–1682), a German, was a chemist/alchemist who wrote on a number of topics. In trying to ascertain the nature of fire, Becher came up with the theory of "phlogiston"—a hypothetical substance present in all matter, whose release appeared as fire. Becher's proposed explanation was completely incorrect, but modern historians of science point to it as the first example of a scientific hypothesis—an explanation of a natural phenomenon that could be objectively tested in the laboratory.

BELIAL (TH): Belial is a name sometimes used in the Bible for Satan or the Devil, and is familiar in literature. Etymologically it is related to the word *Bel* or *Baal*, a principal pagan god worshipped by the heathen neighbors of the Hebrews.

BELLOWS FALLS (WD): A small town in southern Vermont on the upper Connecticut River. It is not very many miles away from Townshend, the village outside of which HPL located Henry Akeley's farm. Bellows Falls was an unlucky place for Akeley. He travels here on July 19, 1928, to ship the "black stone" by railway express to Professor Wilmarth in Arkham for inspection. The stone is, however, pursued to Keene, New Hampshire, by Akeley's antagonists, and mysteriously "lost in transit." In mid-August, Wilmarth receives a telegram sent by "Akely" from the telegraph office in Bellows Falls; it is a trick designed to lull his suspicions. On Tuesday, September 4, Wilmarth receives a typewritten letter from Akeley, telling "what they want to do to me," and postmarked in Bellows Falls. So was the typed letter of September 6 which Wilmarth receives two days later, with its curiously altered writing style and its new, wholly conciliatory attitude toward the star-spawn.

BELLOY-EN-SANTERRE (SK): A small French village located northeast of Paris, approximately halfway between Amiens and Cambrai. It was in the area of some of the heaviest combat on the Western Front during World War I, 1914–18. In this tale, Belloy-en-Santerre is the place where Randolph Carter is severely wounded in 1916, while fighting the Germans as a member of the French Foreign Legion. After his disappearance many years later, one of the peculiar things that people remember about Carter is that in 1897, he had turned pale with shock at the casual mention of this little-known and unimportant village by some traveler returned from France.

HPL must certainly have been thinking of Alan Seeger (1888–1916) at this point. A young American poet and Harvard graduate, Seeger did enlist in the Foreign Legion and was killed in action while fighting for France at Belloy-en-Santerre, an event that was much reported in propaganda and the press in the United States, which had not yet entered the war against Germany. In the months before his death, Seeger wrote his most well-known poem, with the opening line, "I have a rendezvous with Death."

BENEFIT STREET (SH, CDW): An old street in Providence—civic tourism officials now bill its central mile as "the most impressive concentration of original Colonial homes in America." HPL provides some of the street's early history in *The Shunned House*. The actual "Shunned House," known as the "Stephen Harris house" from the name of its original owner, is still to be seen at 135 Benefit Street, a few blocks from the Brown University campus and only about a mile from HPL's old haunts on Angell Street; it was built in 1764. It was empty at the time that HPL wrote this tale, and considered to be a "spooky place," although in earlier years HPL's widowed aunt Lillian had lived in rented rooms there, having moved out of 161 Benefit Street following her husband's death. By coincidence, HPL's own remains were readied for burial only a few doors down from the Shunned House, at 187 Benefit Street, which in 1937 was a funeral home. As HPL notes in the tale, Edgar Allan Poe must often have walked along Benefit Street and past the Shunned House when he was unsuccessfully courting the Providence poet Sarah Helen Whitman (during 1848–49), who lived at Number 88.

The Shunned House relies on a bit of local lore as its inspiration. The house was said to have been built on the site of a very early colonial-era graveyard, in which the bones of a French married couple had been inadvertently left behind when all the other remains were disinterred and moved to permit the extension and development of Benefit Street in the 18th century. Mrs. Stephen Harris, the wife of the first owner, was said to have gone mad after the deaths of her children from sickness, and to have screamed—from the window of the upstairs room where her family confined her—in French, a language she had purportedly never studied. So did poor "Rhoby Harris" in *The Shunned House*.

Charles Dexter Ward does research at Shepley Library, which is also on Benefit Street. It is there that he reviews Joseph Curwen's 18th-century business account books, and made "dark comparisons between the large number of Guinea [West African] blacks he imported until 1766, and the disturbingly small number for whom he could produce bills of sale" to other slave owners or to slave dealers.

BENEVOLENT STREET (FB): Crawford Tillinghast lives in an "ancient, lonely" house on this real street in the vicinity of Brown University.

BENNETT, GEORGE (LF): A "faithful and muscular man," one of a pair of trusted assistants who had assisted the fainting-prone narrator in other "ghastly explorations." In late August, 1921, Bennett accompanies the nameless narrator for a night in Jan Martense's old bedchamber in the long-abandoned Martense mansion. He shares the ancient bed, sleeping on the side closest to the window. While the narrator sleeps between his two bodyguards, Bennett disappears forever, presumably the prey of the mysterious man-eaters that are troubling the region.

BETHMOORA (WD): Bethmoora, alluded to without additional explanation, was a mythical city imagined by HPL's early fantasy-writing idol, Lord Dunsany, in a tale of the same name.

BHOLES (DQ, TGSK): In the Vale of Pnath, a vast subterranean world of eternal darkness, the bholes "crawl and burrow nastily" among giant heaps of bones. Bholes are enormous creatures, at least twenty-five feet long and slimy to the touch; however, nobody has ever seen a bhole to describe it, because the Vale is pitch-black. Randolph Carter, deposited and left in the Vale by a night-gaunt, narrowly escapes an approaching bhole with the aid of a rope-ladder lowered by ghouls from the cliffs above. In *Through the Gates of the Silver Key*, it is mentioned that there are bholes on the planet Yaddith: "bleached" and "viscous" creatures hundreds of feet long, whom the surface-dwellers must constantly fight to keep down in their burrows. Seers have revealed that, one day, the bholes will win and conquer the surface of Yaddith. When Randolph Carter in-the-body-of-Zkauba has "brought the planet-angle to the right aeon" for directing his light-beam envelope to Earth in 1928, Yaddith is in its own future, "a dead world dominated by triumphant bholes." When he has made the adjustment, "he could see that he floated free in space—the metal building from which he had started having decayed ages before. Below him the ground was festering with gigantic bholes; and even as he looked, one reared up several hundred feet and leveled a bleached, viscous end at him."

BICKNELL, THOMAS W. (SH): Mentioned in the tale as a Providence antiquarian with whom the narrator's uncle, Whipple Phillips, occasionally debated on topics of local history. The real Thomas William Bicknell (1834–1925) was a native of Barrington, Rhode Island, but by 1875 he had moved to Boston, where he became one of the founders (1879) of the American Library Association. From 1913 he was retired in

Providence, where he published *History and Genealogy of the Bicknell Family and Collateral Lines* (a sumptuous example of New England ancestor worship, typical of its era in American history), and his life-work *History of the State of Rhode Island and Providence Plantations.*

BIG CYPRESS SWAMP (SRC): A large swamp, presumably in the southern United States, which Randolph Carter and his South Carolina friend Harley Warren visit late one night in December, 1919, to investigate a tomb in a very old, abandoned graveyard deep in the marshes. One part of the swamp was within walking distance of a public highway called the "Gainsville Pike," along which a witness sees the two men walking that night. There is a real Big Cypress Swamp, in the Florida Everglades region about 300 miles south of Gainesville (not "Gainsville"), Florida, and perhaps HPL was thinking of it.

BIRCH, GEORGE W. (IV): The undertaker of "Peck Valley," a 19th century New England farming community. A bachelor without relatives, Birch is "bungling and thick-fibered...calloused and primitive," and woefully lacking in imagination. He goes bankrupt in 1876, despite his thefts of clothing and valuables from the bodies of the dead entrusted to his care, and his skimping on the quality of the coffins he builds. Moreover, he is often half-drunk and even more careless. His professional shortcomings climax following the very cold winter of 1880–81, when the ground froze solid in December and compelled the storage of nine coffined corpses in the cemetery's "receiving tomb" or waiting area. After the spring thaw, in April, 1881, Birch begins transferring the caskets to newly-dug graves. On April 15, Good Friday, the day he prepared graves for Darius Peck and Matthew Fenner, he accidentally locks himself in with eight of the cadavers. He constructs a tower of coffins to climb out through the transom, but has his Achilles' tendons—the ligaments in the backs of the ankles—severed by some means, and has to crawl to safety when he reaches the outside. He spends the rest of his life lame, drunk, strangely fearful, and in another line of work.

BISHOP, MAMIE (DH): A local gossip, Mamie is the "common-law wife" (that is, publicly cohabiting as a spouse, but without a marriage license or ceremony) of Dunwich farmer Earl Sawyer. A friend of Lavinia Whateley, she visits Lavinia and the infant Wilbur Whateley in 1913, during the first month of Wilbur's life. In 1926 she hears Lavinia speak of feeling afraid of Wilbur.

BISHOP, SETH (DH): Dunwich farmer. His farm is the closest to that of Old Whateley, and the first to be "visited" when the Horror breaks loose. All of his cattle are maimed, drained of blood, or carried off on the night of September 9, 1928. On September 15, the Horror emerges from its lair in Cold Spring Glen, demolishes the Seth Bishop house and barn, and devours Mr. Bishop, his "housekeeper" Sally Sawyer, and her son Chauncey.

BISHOP, SILAS (DH): Dunwich farmer, one of the "undecayed [that is, not sunken to degeneracy] Bishops." (The ancestors of the Dunwich-area Bishops had settled in Dunwich as fugitives from the witchcraft mania in Salem in 1692—like the Whateleys—and like that family had also come to consist of many branches. There was, in historical fact, a Bishop family in 17th century Salem, and in 1923 HPL toured a Salem farmhouse built by one of the clan in 1636.) Silas was searching for a lost heifer in the twilight of Halloween, 1913, when he saw Wilbur Whateley—then a mere eight months old—"running sturdily" up Sentinel Hill ahead of his mother Lavinia. Both mother and son appeared to Bishop's surprised eyes to be completely naked, except that the little boy may have been wearing a "fringed belt" and "pair of dark trousers." In fact, Silas Bishop had seen Wilbur Whateley's non-human lower body.

BIXBY, HANNAH (IV); A woman buried in the Peck Valley cemetery, whose remains her survivors had arranged to have exhumed and reburied in their new town. To their chagrin, and the embarrassment of the incompetent undertaker George Birch, a certain Judge Capwell's body was found buried in Hannah Bixby's grave instead.

BLACK MAN (CDW, DWH, DQ): In European folklore, Satan or his emissary frequently appeared at meetings of witches' covens in the form of "a black man"—not an African, but a man of "normal" features and black color, symbolic of darkness and evil. Cotton Mather, in *The Wonders of the Invisible World* (1693) mentions "the Black Man (as the Witches call the Devil; and they generally say he resembles an Indian)." An old English proverb goes so far as to remind us that even *The devil is not so black as he is painted.* In *The Case of Charles Dexter Ward*, young Ward learns that in Salem in 1692, a certain woman named Hepzibah Lawson had testified to Judge Hathorne that "fortie Witches and the Blacke Man were wont to meet in the Woodes behind Mr. Hutchinson's house." Additionally, in about 1771, Simon/Jedediah Orne writes a letter to Joseph Curwen which includes the request: "I am desirous you will Acquaint me with what ye Blacke Man learnt from Sylvanus Cocidius in ye Vault, under ye Roman Wall..." Nyarlathotep, whom *The Dreams in the Witch House* seems to suggest is the real "Black Man" of the witches, is described as a tall and perfectly black man in appearance, without Negroid features. Some modern-day Arkhamites who glimpse him by night do the natural thing, however, and call him "a huge negro." In *The*

Dream-Quest of Unknown Kadath, Nyarlathotep appears again in the guise of a black pharaoh with "Egyptian" features, surrounded by gigantic slaves who are, by contrast, "true black men of earth's dreamland."

BLACK PRINCE, LIMOGES, HAUTE VIENNE COVEN (CDW): One night between 1766–71, the hidden Ezra Weeden overheard a dialogue in which Joseph Curwen seemed to be questioning some "alternately raging and sullen" person in French:

> ...about the Black Prince's massacre at Limoges in 1370...whether the order to slay was given because of the Sign of the Goat found under the altar in the ancient Roman crypt below the Cathedral, or whether the Dark Man of the Haute Vienne Coven had spoken the Three Words.

The "Black Prince" was Edward of Woodstock (1330–76), Prince of Wales, the oldest son of King Edward III of England. The Black Prince was a model soldier-prince of the turbulent 14th century, who spent most of his life in France and Spain, fighting near-constant wars and ruling a vast region in Aquitaine, southwestern France. Limoges was already an ancient city, founded by the Romans in 10 B.C.; it was part of Prince Edward's French domain, and he had granted it a number of benefits. Nonetheless, the citizens rose up against his rule in 1370, having conspired against him with the French king Charles V. On capturing the city after a siege, he ordered the death of every man, woman and child—and some 3000 inhabitants were slain by his foot soldiers. The reason typically suggested for this notorious crime is the prince's rage and frustration, perhaps combined with a declining mental and physical condition—he had only a few more years to live: since earlier in his career he had been a tough but not extraordinarily bloodthirsty commander for the time and place.

The "Haute Vienne Coven" seems like a mistake. The region around Limoges was traditionally called Limousin; this became the name of the French royal province, and would have been the term used in the 14th century. "Haute Vienne," which refers to the upper Vienne river, is the name of the French *departement* or administrative district of which Limoges is now the capital. The *departement Haute Vienne* was created after the French Revolution, when the new republican authorities decided to break up and rationalize the old, haphazard patchwork of provinces large and small, replacing them all with *departements* of approximately equal size, frequently named after local mountain ranges or rivers—such as the upper Vienne, in this case. The point is that in the 14th century a coven in Limoges would have been called the coven of Limoges or perhaps the Limousin coven, but not "Haute Vienne," a regional term that would not come into use for another four centuries.

BLACK STONE (WD): "A great black stone with unknown hieroglyph-ics half worn away," which Henry Akeley found in the woods of Round Hill, east of his farmhouse. The stone was small enough to be portable and to be placed on Akeley's study desk, in front of a bust of the poet John Milton. The stone, measuring one foot by two feet, has an irregu-larly carved surface; irregular to human eyes, that is, but perhaps regular to other kinds of eyes. "What outlandish geometrical principles had guided its cutting, I could not even begin to guess." A couple of the unknown symbols are recognizable as ideographs found in the *Necro-nomicon*. On Wednesday, July 18, 1928, Akeley takes the stone to Bellows Falls and ships it to Professor Wilmarth by railroad. However, an agent of the Mi-Go hypnotizes the railway express clerk in Keene, New Hampshire, and apparently recovers and absconds with the stone in its parcel.

BLACK WINGED ONES (CC): According to the rabble of Cthulhu-cultists who are arrested while conducting a human-sacrifice ritual with kidnap victims in a Louisiana bayou on November 1, 1907, the ten or so kidnapped Cajun women and children whom the police found dead and "curiously marred" were actually killed by "Black Winged Ones which had come...from their immemorial meeting place in the haunted wood." The investigators can obtain no more information from their prisoners about these Black Winged Ones.

BLACKWOOD, ALGERNON (CC): HPL once wrote of the famed English fantasy-author (1869–1951): "Blackwood has absolutely no [literary] style except by accident now and then." Despite this sniping, he enjoyed reading Blackwood's tales, and actually described his story *The Willows* as the best "supernatural horror" tale of its time, and years later as probably "the greatest weird tale ever written" and "perhaps the most devastating piece of supernaturally hideous suggestion which I have beheld in a decade." *The Call of Cthulhu* begins with a passage from an Algernon Blackwood novel (*The Centaur*, 1911) that sets the tone for all that follows, indeed for the entire Lovecraft Mythos:

> Of such great powers or beings there may be conceivably a survival...a survival of a hugely remote period when...consciousness was manifested, perhaps, in shapes and forms long since withdrawn before the tide of advancing humanity...forms of which poetry and legend alone have caught a flying memory and called them gods, monsters, mythical beings of all sorts and kinds.

BLAESUS, TITUS SEMPRONIUS (SOT): One of the captive minds encountered by Professor Nathaniel Peaslee during his sojourn with the Great Race; a Roman who "had been a quaestor in Sulla's time." A *quaestor* was a junior magistrate in Rome; the quaestorship was an appointed office which was often the first to be held by young men ambitious for a career in government and politics. Lucius Cornelius Sulla (138–78 B.C.), a successful Roman general, prevailed in a civil war and became "dictator" of Rome in 82 B.C. During his two-year dictatorship there were murderous and extensive purges of Sulla's political opponents and their families, one of the bloodiest and most long-term destructive episodes in the last century of the Roman republic. In Sulla's time there were a maximum of 20 state quaestors.

BLAIR: *See* "Cryptographers of Dunwich."

BLAKE, ROBERT HARRISON (HD): A character who is thinly based on a young pen-pal who would grow up to become the successful and prolific horror, suspense and science-fiction writer Robert Bloch (1917–94), whose name always has to be followed with the words: "the author of the novel on which the classic Hitchcock film *Psycho* was based." In 1935 Bloch was a mere teenage tale-spinner, and one of HPL's admiring fan-correspondents. Blake/Bloch's contemporary address (620 E. Knapp Street, Milwaukee) was even used in the tale. The in-joke twitting becomes more funny when the narrator refers to the doomed young man's "abnormal imagination and unbalanced emotions" and "excessive imagination and neurotic imbalance." Bloch lived long enough to write the foreword to a collection of his youthful correspondence with the master, published in 1993. In this tale, young Robert Blake from Wisconsin, author of such tales as *The Burrower Beneath*, *The Stairs in the Crypt*, *Shaggai*, *In the Vale of Pnath*, and *The Feaster From the Stars*, takes an apartment in Providence, becomes fascinated by the church he can see off in the distance on Federal Hill, and breaks into the abandoned place through its cellar. Inside he discovers occult books and pictures of the old Starry Wisdom congregation, the bones of 19th century reporter Edwin M. Lillibridge, and the Shining Trapezohedron. His curiosity leads inevitably to his frightful death.

BLANDOT (MEZ): An elderly, partially paralyzed man, the landlord of the miserable tenement in the Rue d'Auseil where the narrator and Erich Zann both reside.

BLASTED HEATH (COS): In Shakespeare's tragedy *Macbeth,* this is the name given to a wasteland where the Three Witches meet Macbeth and his comrade-in-arms Banquo. In HPL's tale, it is the local name for the "five acres of grey desolation" that is centered on the ruins of the old Nahum Gardner farm, many miles west of Arkham, "at the bottom of a spacious valley" that is soon to be flooded to create Arkham's new reservoir. The Shakespearean connection is made explicit when the nameless narrator—although the phrase seemed "odd and theatrical" when he heard it in Arkham—actually saw the desolated area he felt: "No other name could fit such a thing, or any other thing fit such a name. It was as if the post [i.e., Shakespeare] had coined the phrase from having seen this one particular region." To the narrator, the blasted heath is like "a great spot eaten by acid," with no vegetation, only a "fine grey dust or ash" blown hither and thither by the wind. So the blasted heath has remained for decades; but the local people claim that it is still growing around its circumference at the rate of about an inch per year.

BNAZIC DESERT (QI, DCS): The well-documented record of HPL's life and travels—mostly limited to the eastern seaboard of the United States and Canada, and no further west than the Mississippi River—indicates that he never saw a desert in real life. But he used their mysterious and picturesque qualities in some of his fiction. The Bnazic Desert is referred to in these two early "Dunsanian" tales. In doomed Sarnath, the king and his noblemen feast on the tender "heels of camels" imported from here. In his old age, Iranon wanders even into the lands beyond the Bnazic Desert.

BOERHAVE (CDW): Doctor Herman Boerhaave or Boerhave (1668–1738) was a Dutch surgeon and professor of medicine, credited with pioneering post-mortem examinations to discover causes of death, and the use of thermometers to assess patients' conditions. Books by Boerhave are among the works on Joseph Curwen's Providence library shelves in the mid-18th century. One of them could have been *Elementa Chemiae*, Boerhave's very popular chemistry textbook, published in 1724.

BOHM (TT): A sailor on the German submarine U-29 in 1917. On June 19, he is one of the crewmen who become unfit for duty, being "dazed and stupid," having been troubled by nightmares on the previous night. On June 20, he becomes violently insane, and the captain orders that "drastic steps" be taken: in other words, Bohm's summary execution.

BOKRUG (DCS): The water-lizard god worshipped by the toadlike creatures who dwelt in Ib, in the land of Mnar, before the invading founders of the imperial city Sarnath exterminated them. Bokrug's idol of green stone was the only thing preserved from the destruction of Ib. It is placed in the temple of Sarnath, but it disappears on the night of that day, and the Sarnath high priest Taran-Ish is found dead the next morning in front of his altar. During the following centuries, the priests of Sarnath regularly perform a secret ritual "in detestation of Bokrug." After Sarnath is drowned and wiped off the face of the earth on the night of its thousandth anniversary, the people of Mnar rediscover the Bokrug idol in the rushes by the lake shore. They take it to the city of Ilarnek and enshrine it there.

BOLTON (HW, RW, COS): Fictitious industrial city in Massachusetts, seemingly up the Miskatonic River from Arkham. It is the home of the large "Bolton Worsted Mills," the largest in the valley. ("Worsted" is the name of a specific type of cloth fabric.) Bolton, perhaps, is an analog for the old textile-mill town of Lawrence, Massachusetts, a city which lies more or less where Bolton might have.

Dr. Herbert West and his comrade set up as doctors in general practice in this "neighboring town" after graduating from Miskatonic University's medical school in 1904. They rent a rundown clinic and house on Pond Street, close to the "potter's field" (charity graveyard), from whence they frequently carried home fresh corpses for their experiments. It is also in this clinic that they experiment with the corpses of Buck "The Harlem Smoke" Robinson, and the Midwestern business traveler Robert Leavitt. The two men reside in Bolton for ten years, until the outbreak of World War I in 1914.

Mr. de la Poer of *The Rats in the Walls*, although a native of Virginia by birth, makes his life and his great fortune as a Bolton manufacturer, where he "merged into the greyness of Massachusetts business life." Bolton also turns up indirectly in *The Colour Out of Space*, again as a manufacturing center: a "timid windmill salesman" from Bolton, driving his horse and buggy through a farming district one night in May, 1883, notices all the vegetation around Nahum Gardner's farm glowing with a "dim but distinct luminosity," and also the furtive stirring of a detached luminescence in the farmyard.

There has been critical comment on HPL's "inexplicable" interest in Bolton, which in real life is the name of a small village in central Massachusetts, northeast of Worcester. Neither in size nor in location does the real Bolton correspond to the Bolton of fiction. So although one of HPL's friends mentioned this rural community to him in a 1920 letter (and the fictitious, big Bolton appeared for the first time in *Herbert West—Reanimator*, later that year), it seems as though HPL could have borrowed nothing from the real place but its name, if that. As a name for a center of production of mechanical pieces and of textiles, "Bolton" may have resonated in HPL's mind with the thoughts of metal *bolts* and *bolts* of cloth. Moreover, like Dunwich and like so many genuine Massachusetts place-names, Bolton also had an English counterpart: in this case, Bolton, Lancashire, a large factory town in England's West Midlands industrial area. In 1920, more than half of the English Bolton's labor force toiled in its textile mills. Perhaps HPL read about this town somewhere.

BORCHGREVINK, CARSTEN E. (MM): Norwegian polar explorer (1864–1934), a member of the first expedition to set foot on the shore of Antarctica (1894). He led the 1898–1900 British expedition which became the first to "winter over" on the frozen continent, when that meant being cut off from all communication with the outside world for several months of icy darkness. HPL once wrote that this expedition, contemporary with his own youth, "greatly stimulated" his childhood interest in Antarctica. He saluted Borchgrevink's achievements with a mention of the explorer in this tale.

BORELLUS (CDW, EC): A French physician and chemist (1620–71), real name Pierre Borel. A long passage attributed to Borellus, dealing with the possibility of reconstituting the dead and bringing them back to life from their "essential Saltes," lies at the heart of Joseph Curwen's skullduggery. However, it appears that the passage is actually derived from a similar flight of fancy in Cotton Mather's book *Magnalia Christi Americana*, which HPL is known to have read. In *The Evil Clergyman*, the presence of a book by Borellus on the table helps to suggest the wicked cleric's erudition in alchemy.

BOSTON (HW, TU, COS, PM, CC, CDW, PH, SOT): The capital of Massachusetts and the metropolis of New England. Dr. Herbert West and his comrade return from World War I and open a medical practice in Boston, where the suave mad scientist swiftly builds up a "fashionable clientele." In an appropriately Lovecraftian manner, they move into "a venerable house of much elegance" across the street from a colonial-era graveyard, "for purely symbolic and fantastically aesthetic reasons" since the remains in the old burying-ground are too old for West's use. Below their house the two men locate a hidden sub-cellar which shares a common wall with "a secret chamber beneath the tomb of the Averills," the name of a (non-fictitious) leading Boston family long ago. A Lovecraftian bonanza of concealed caverns! Through this common wall come the "tomb-legions" that finally deanimate the Reanimator. In *The Unnamable*, the narrator comments that his friend Joel Manton, although now living in Arkham, was "born and bred in Boston...sharing New England's self-satisfied deafness to the delicate overtones of life."

A Boston newspaper sends a reporter to cover the landing of a meteorite at Nahum Gardner's farm in 1883, in *The Colour Out of Space*; and the nameless narrator who passes through the old Gardner farm while surveying for a new reservoir in the 1920s, also comes from Boston. Francis W. Thurston, narrator of *The Call of Cthulhu*, is a Bostonian.

Pickman's Model takes place entirely in Boston, with the climax occurring in an ancient house in the part of the city called "North End." Charles Dexter Ward, having attained the age of 21 and come into an inheritance, departs from the White Star Line pier at Charlestown harbor for an ocean journey to Liverpool in June, 1923, the beginning of his three years of travel and study in London, Paris, Prague, and Transylvania. In *The Shadow Out of Time*, the telephone call summoning Professor Nathaniel Wingate Peaslee's physician, Dr. Wilson, to Peaslee's house on September 27, 1913, is later traced to a public phone-booth at North Station, in Boston.

BOSTON *GLOBE* (DH): A real newspaper, still in existence. The *Globe* in 1917 prints articles about the weird back-country village of Dunwich, and Old Whateley's peculiar household there.

BOSWORTH (PM): Apparently one of the Boston art-fanciers who "dropped" Richard Upton Pickman from their acquaintance-list as his paintings grew more morbid and horrid. Thurber lumps him in contemptuously with the "fussy old women like Dr. Reid or Joe Minot."

BOTTLES, SPIRITS IN (TOM): In the Terrible Old Man's cottage home in Kingsport are "many peculiar bottles, in each a small piece of lead suspended pendulum-wise from a string." He talks to the bottles, addressing various ones as "Jack," "Scar-Face," "Long Tom," "Peters," "Mate Ellis" and presumably others as well. The pendulums vibrate as if to answer him. In a pinch, the bottle-spirits (of some of his old shipmates?) seems capable of doing more than that, as evidenced by the marks as of many boot-heels and cutlass strokes on the bodies of the three would-be robbers.

BOUDREAU (MM): A Miskatonic University graduate student and a member of the Antarctic expedition. He goes with the sub-party under Professors Lake and Atwood. He and his fellow-searchers, Mills and Fowler, find the cluster of thirteen winged, star-headed Old Ones frozen and preserved in a subterranean cavern. Other members of the expedition find his dead body along with those of other members of the Lake-Atwood sub-party on January 25, 1931.

BOULE (WD): *See* "Anthropologists of the Mi-Go."

BOWEN, PROFESSOR ENOCH (HD): A fictitious 19th century resident of Providence. He returns from travels in Egypt in May, 1844. In July of the same year he purchases the "old Free-Will [Baptist] Church" on Federal Hill in the city, and establishes the Starry Wisdom cult there. He apparently brought the Shining Trapezohedron back with him from

Egypt. There is no description of Professor Bowen's subsequent activities, although it is obviously likely that he stayed active in the leadership of Starry Wisdom for the rest of his days. There is a Bowen Street in HPL's Providence neighborhood; Bowen was once a common family-name in old Providence.

BOWEN, HANNAH (SH): Domestic servant in the William Harris household, in 1763–64; she dies of a wasting illness in June of the latter year. Mehitabel Pierce is hired as her replacement. The actual "Shunned House" is near the corner of Benefit Street and Bowen Street in Providence.

BOWEN, DR. JABEZ (CDW): A non-fictitious early apothecary (pharmacist), who moved to Providence from nearby Rehoboth, Massachusetts, in the mid-18th century, opening a shop called *The Unicorn and Mortar*. Joseph Curwen "incessantly" purchases drugs, acids, or rare metals from him. Despite, or because of, his large sales to Curwen, Dr. Bowen joins the secret committee of prominent men formed in 1770 to investigate and deal with the sinister old suspected alchemist. In January, 1771, Dr. Bowen performs an autopsy on a naked, muscular man found frozen in the ice by the Great Bridge—an escaped victim of Curwen's revival experiments, although none of the citizens know that—and determines that the huge man's digestive organs had never been used. Despite his advanced age, Dr. Bowen volunteers as one of the raiders of Curwen's Pawtuxet lair on the night of April 12, 1771, carrying his surgical kit instead of a weapon. He is a member of the main assault party led by Captain Abraham Whipple, and later he is—deliberately, no doubt—the only doctor to treat the wounded or injured survivors of the raid.

BOYLE (CDW): No doubt a reference to Robert Boyle (1627–91), an Anglo-Irish aristocrat and pioneer of mathematics-based science, widely considered to be the "father of modern chemistry" for having been first to define a chemical "element" as "a material that cannot be further simplified or broken down into another substance by any chemical or physical process." His name also lives on in "Boyle's Law," the standard equation he developed for deriving the relation between the pressure and the volume of a trapped gas. It is no surprise that the works of this great early chemist and physicist would be among those on Joseph Curwen's bookshelves in the 18th century.

BOYLE, DR. E.M. (SOT): A psychologist in Perth, Australia, circa 1934, he is shown some photographs of curious stoneworks in the Great Sandy Desert by the mining engineer R.B.F. Mackenzie. He makes a mental association between the pictures and some articles on the subject of dreams, written by Dr. Nathaniel Peaslee. After first putting Peaslee and Mackenzie in contact, he also helps to arrange the Australian end of the subsequent expedition, which he also joins. Dr. Boyle is "elderly, pleasant, and intelligent."

BRAN (WD): Dropping this name in *The Whisperer in Darkness*, HPL tipped his hat to his pen-friend Robert E. Howard, of Texas (whom HPL sometimes called "Two-Gun Bob"), one of the hardest-working and most successful authors for adventure pulp-magazines, the creator of "Conan the Barbarian." "Bran," which was really the name of a pagan deity worshipped in ancient Britain, is instead a reference to "Bran Mak Morn," a sword-wielding, death-dealing, ancient Scottish warrior in a series of tales by Howard.

BRATTLEBORO (WD): A regional center in southern Vermont, with a current population of about 10,000, at the gateway to the Mi-Go country of Windham County; HPL spent a couple of weeks enjoying the Brattleboro area as a tourist and houseguest in June, 1928.

In late June, 1928, Henry Akeley drives his car to Brattleboro to ship a mysterious phonograph recording to Professor Wilmarth at Miskatonic University. Starting in mid-July, Wilmarth has to mail his letters to Akeley in care of the Brattleboro post office, because of the danger of the interception and theft of home mail by Akeley's mysterious antagonists. In one late letter Akeley tells Wilmarth that he had just gotten a letter from his enemies—"[the] R.F.D. man brought it from Brattleboro." ("R.F.D." meant "Rural Free Delivery," the postal department which serviced remote farming regions.) Akeley also travels to Brattleboro several times to replenish his force of savage guard-dogs. On Wednesday, September 12, 1928, Professor Wilmarth takes the 8:07 a.m. local train from Arkham down to Boston, changes to a train from Boston west to Greenfield, Massachusetts, and finally to a northbound train which arrives in Brattleboro at 1:08 p.m.—a journey which the interested reader may imitate today by driving on Massachusetts State Highway 2 from Boston to Greenfield, and then proceeding north along Interstate 91. Wilmarth/Lovecraft complimented Brattleboro as being "like the older New England cities which one remembers from boyhood...something in the collection of roofs and steeples and chimneys and brick walls formed contours touching deep viol-strings of ancestral emotion." Mr. Noyes picks up Wilmarth at the Brattleboro train station, and drives him through the village of Newfane to the remote Akeley farm. After escaping on the same night, Wilmarth bravely remains in Brattleboro for a week, making inquiries.

BRATTLEBORO *REFORMER* (WD): A real newspaper. HPL's friend Vrest Orton, whom he visited in Brattleboro in the summer of 1928, sometimes contributed articles to it. In the tale, the *Reformer* reprints one of Professor Wilmarth's lengthy pieces on history and mythology, and dismisses the legends of strange creatures lurking in Vermont's hill country, in its April 23, 1928 edition. Henry Akeley reads the article and begins a fateful correspondence with its author.

BREWSTER, SQUIRE (TT): A wealthy "maker of local history" in the somewhere-near-Boston area where Jervas Dudley lived; the Squire was buried in a local cemetery in 1711. After a night spent alone in the cemetery many years later, Jervas avers that Goodman Simpson, the undertaker, had stolen the squire's silver-buckled shoes, silken hose, and satin knee-breeches before the burial service, and furthermore that the unfortunate squire had revived briefly in his coffin after being buried.

BRIDEN, WILLIAM (CC): Sailor on the *Emma*, who transfers to the captured *Alert* with the rest of his surviving shipmates and goes ashore at R'lyeh with the crew. He and Second Mate Johansen are the only men to get back to the *Alert* alive. As the ship steams away from R'lyeh, Briden looks back at the pursuing Cthulhu, and instantly goes mad. He dies on the ship as it drifts through the South Pacific "of exhaustion or exposure," on a date that is not certain but more than a week before the *Alert* is spotted by the freighter *Vigilant*.

BRIGHTHOLME, VISCOUNT (AJ): A viscount is a high title of rank in the British aristocratic hierarchy, just below an earl. In 1815, a daughter of the fictitious Viscount Brightholme marries Sir Robert Jermyn.

BRINTON, SIR WILLIAM (RW): A London-based archaeologist whose "excavations in the Troad" (*i.e.*, in the district of the ancient city of Troy, now in western Turkey), have made him famous. He is one of the team of experts who accompany Mr. de la Poer and Captain Norrys into the subterranean reaches of Exham Priory on August 8, 1923. Brinton works out how to tilt back the Roman altar in the Priory's sub-cellar, revealing the stairway that leads downward to the caves. Of the seven men who make the descent, he is the only one to fully retain his composure when light enables them to get a first glimpse of the horror they have uncovered. He translates the ritual text found carved in the "Roman" ruin in the grotto, locates a vault with empty prisoner-cells beneath it, and a crypt with cases of human bones and carved funerary inscriptions in Latin, Greek, and Phrygian—a Phrygian priest is mentioned in the tale as having served in the pagan sanctuary at the site during Roman-British times.

BRISTOL HIGHLANDS (SHH): A resort community where the Thomas Olney family buys a bungalow and takes summer vacations after their one summer at Kingsport, Massachusetts. Bristol Highlands— "where no tall crags tower, and the neighbours are urban and modern"— is a real community, part of the town of Bristol, Rhode Island, on the shore of Narragansett Bay. In this tale it is a symbol of conventional summer-resort normality after the weirdness of Kingsport, part of the ultra-conventionality that Professor Olney always displays after his amazing night in the Strange High House.

BROWN FAMILY (SH, CDW): HPL paid due respect to one of the historical leading families of late colonial Providence. The four Brown brothers—John, Joseph, Nicholas, and Moses, "the recognized local magnates" in the latter half of the 18th century—all take part in the secret committee which investigated and tried to eradicate Joseph Curwen and his evil works. John Brown (1736–1803) was the head of the committee.

The tale mentions the merchant vessels and the commercial warehouses which were the foundation of the Browns' fortune. HPL suggests that Joseph Curwen was for a time second only to the Browns as an importer of manufactured goods from Europe to the Rhode Island colony. It is in the Brown family's warehouses that the committee recruits the raiding party of tough sailors and privateersmen who attack Curwen's farm in Pawtuxet. The firm of Nicholas Brown & Co. is given as the owner of the brig *Prudence*, a merchant ship which Captain William Harris began commanding in 1761, two years before he built what would later be termed the Shunned House, for his family's new home.

BROWN JENKIN (DWH): "Brown Jenkin" is the "familiar" (a witch's traditional non-human companion in evil) of the Arkham witch Keziah Mason. He or it appears in the Salem Gaol (an old English variant spelling of "jail", now archaic) in 1692, when the jailer "went mad and babbled of a small, white-fanged furry thing which scuttled out of Keziah's cell" at the same time the witch inexplicably disappeared. In the same year eleven eyewitnesses testify to having seen Brown Jenkin here and there in Arkham. It has the shape of a very large rat with long hair, but also a bearded, sharp-fanged, "evilly human" face, and paws like little human hands. It nurses on Keziah's blood, carries messages between Keziah and her master, the Black Man, and is said to be able to speak in all languages, with a "loathsome titter." In the 1920s, Keziah Mason and Brown Jenkin still infest the night-streets of Arkham, especially in the Witch House, where ratholes appear which metal coverings and poison traps cannot keep closed. In Keziah's company, Brown

Jenkin constantly appears in Walter Gilman's dreams, and in the other-dimensional scenes where he journeys in his dreams. It assists Keziah's attempts to involve Gilman in their rituals. At one point in the tale, Gilman realizes that the demon-rat's curious facial features were a small parody of the crone Keziah Mason's own face.

Brown Jenkin does not seem to lack a pet's loyalty. One night, Walter Gilman notices it "rubbing itself with a kind of affectionate playfulness around the ankles" of the Black Man. On a later date, as Gilman is strangling Keziah Mason to death, her familiar attempts to save her by nipping at him, and eventually it takes a bloody and conclusive revenge on the young student.

In December, 1931, some years after Walter Gilman's death, workmen demolishing the storm-damaged Witch House find, among the skeletons of scores of dead children, the bones of a "huge, diseased rat" with prehensile paws and what resembles a tiny, degraded, human skull. Wherever it first came from, Brown Jenkin's apparent final resting place is on a shelf in the Department of Comparative Anatomy at Miskatonic University.

BROWN, LUTHER (DH): In 1928, the hired boy at the George Corey farm, between Dunwich village and Cold Spring Glen. At 7:00 a.m. on September 10, he rushes back to the farmhouse in terror from his morning walk to Ten-Acre Meadow with the cattle herd, followed back in short order by the equally terrified cows. He is the first to see the giant footprints of the Horror, and he tells Mrs. Corey about what he has seen. On September 15, he receives another shock when he sees the signs of the invisible monster leaving Cold Spring Glen and crossing the bridge over Bishop's Brook.

BROWN UNIVERSITY (CDW, CC, HD): Located in central Providence, and one of the group of eight old and prestigious northeastern universities (the others being Harvard, Yale, Princeton, Dartmouth, Columbia, Cornell, and the University of Pennsylvania) which are now known as the Ivy League. Brown University was founded in 1764 as Rhode Island College, and was a familiar place to HPL and as dear to him as all the rest of Providence's old institutions. HPL might well have become a student at Brown if an apparent nervous breakdown, possibly complicated by psychosomatic ailments, had not prevented his graduation from high school.

In *The Call of Cthulhu*, retired Brown professor George G. Angell makes the critical series of discoveries and connections to reveal the existence of the Cthulhu-cult. In *The Haunter of the Dark*, Robert Blake settles in an apartment on College Street in Providence, "near the Brown

University campus and behind the marble John Hay Library." Men from a university fraternity house are witnesses to Robert Harrison Blake's shocking demise. Charles Dexter Ward is a regular patron of the John Hay and the John Carter Brown libraries, where he delves for history and lore. Joseph Manning, one of the raiders of Joseph Curwen's Pawtuxet compound in April, 1771, was historically the name of the first president of Rhode Island College, as it then was.

HPL's private papers are now among the treasures of the very John Hay Library which he treasured in life. His last home was at 66 College Street, next door to the library (although later moved to its current location at 65 Prospect Street). On HPL's 100th birthday, August 20, 1990, the city of Providence, Brown University, and private individuals came together to dedicate a bronze tablet in his memory at the library entrance. The tablet bears some lines from Sonnet XXX, *Background*, of his verse collection *Fungi From Yuggoth*:

> *I never can be tied to raw, new things,*
> *For I first saw the light in an old town,*
> *Where from my windows huddled roofs sloped down*
> *To a quaint harbor rich with visionings.*
> *Streets with carved doorways where the sunset beams*
> *Flooded old fanlights and small window-panes,*
> *And Georgian steeples topped with gilded vanes—*
> *These were the sights that shaped my childhood dreams.*

BROWN, WALTER (WD): Human agent of the Mi-Go in the southern Vermont hills. A "surly farmer who lived on a run-down hillside place near the deep woods," and is often seen "inexplicably" hanging around in the small neighboring towns of Brattleboro, Bellows Falls, Newfane, and South Londonderry. Henry Akeley believes that he had heard Walter Brown conversing with the Mi-Go in the forests at night, and that he has seen the farmer's footprints intermixed with the pad or paw impressions of the extraterrestrials, near the Brown farm. On the night of August 12, 1928, Walter Brown is apparently with the gang of Mi-Go who attempt to harass Akeley from the perimeter of his farmhouse. In one of the subsequent night-raids in August-September 1928, Akeley apparently kills Brown with one of his wild rifle-shots into the darkness, for Walter Brown is seen no more in his old haunts.

BUBASTIS (DQ): An ancient Egyptian city in the Nile's northern delta. The city was consecrated to the cat-goddess Bast, and cats were sacred and protected animals there.

BUCHAREST (CDW): The capital city of Romania. In 1928 the Romanian authorities would have summoned Count Ferenczy/Hutchinson here for "serious questioning" about his ill-reputed activities, had his castle not suddenly exploded, killing everyone inside.

BUDDAI (SOT): In the tale, a character (invented by the author) in the mythology of the Australian aborigines. In HPL's description, Buddai is "a gigantic old man who lies asleep for ages underground, and who will some day awake and eat up the world"—which sounds comparable to the Cthulhu legend. It is said that the aborigines connect the Buddai-myth to the enormous and very old carved stones which Nathaniel Peaslee investigates in the Great Sandy Desert. (The non-fictitious Australian aboriginal chief deity, Baiame, is or was often depicted as a sleepy old man, but he is a force for good.)

BULWER (DA, WD): In *Dagon*, the narrator describes the "faces and forms" of the creatures carved on the monolith risen from the ocean depths as "grotesque beyond the imagination of a Poe or a Bulwer." Poe remains well-known! But "Bulwer" much less so.

Edward George Earle Bulwer (later Bulwer-Lytton) (1803–73), first Baron Lytton of Knebworth, was a rich and well-connected Cambridge graduate, who combined a highly successful career in the service of the British government and parliament with a second profession as an acclaimed novelist and playwright. Among his lushly rhetorical historical novels was *The Last Days of Pompeii* (1834), a Roman-era melodrama whose popularity lasted into the 20th century. A serious student of magic and the occult, including alchemy and the Rosicrucian movement, Bulwer also wrote some excellent tales of the supernatural—now all but forgotten—which HPL was presumably referring to.

BUO, ARCH-ANCIENT (TGSK): One of the leading minds on planet Yaddith. When Zkauba the wizard is tormented by his "possession" by the alien mind of Randolph Carter, he consults with Buo and other sages.

BUOPOTHS (DQ): Shy, lumbering animals who live in the woods by the river Oukranos.

BURROUGHS, GEORGE (CDW): Charles Dexter Ward reviews some (fictitious) Salem witch trial records which indicate that, on August 8, 1692, a witness testified to the court that Reverend George Burroughs was the "Mr. G.B." who put the Devil's Mark on several persons at a meeting of the Salem coven, including "Simon O. and Joseph C.," whom we understand to be Simon Orne and Joseph Curwen. Lovecraft must have read this passage by Cotton Mather in his book *The Wonders of the Invisible World* (1692):

This G.B. Was Indicted for Witch-craft, and in the prosecution of the Charge against him, he was Accused by five or six of the Bewitched, as the Author of their Miseries; he was Accused by Eight of the Confessing Witches, as being an head Actor at some of their Hellish Rendezvouzes, and one who had the promise of being a King in Satan's Kingdom, now going to be Erected.... And now upon the Tryal of one of the Bewitched Persons, [she] testified, that in her Agonies, a little black Hair'd Man came to her, saying his Name was B. and bidding her set her hand to [sign] a Book which he shewed unto her; and bragged that he was a *Conjurer,* above the ordinary Rank of Witches; That he often Persecuted her with the offer of that Book, saying, *She should be well, and need fear nobody, if she would but Sign it;* But he inflicted cruel Pains and Hurts upon her, because of her denying so to do.

The underlying historical facts are that during the 1692 Salem witchcraft investigation, several dozen people from neighboring Andover were accused of sorcery and jailed, pending their trials. A number of these Andover prisoners provided confessions alleging a vast regional conspiracy of up to 500 witches and warlocks, a conspiracy with the goal of "pulling down the Kingdom of Christ and setting up the Kingdom of Satan" in the Massachusetts colony. Many of the confessing prisoners apparently stated that the leader at large coven meetings was a former Christian minister—in fact, a former pastor of the Salem Village church, George Burroughs. There was testimony that he, as leader of all the witches, blew a trumpet to summon coven meetings, and so forth. This spectacular conspiracy-story, which in the hysterical atmosphere of that time and place only needed to be mentioned to be believed by most, led to Burroughs' swift arrest, witchcraft trial, and sentence of death. On August 19, 1692, with Reverend Cotton Mather in attendance from Boston, Burroughs was hanged for a witch alongside three other men and one woman. The condemned ex-minister spoke movingly to the crowd from the scaffold, and recited the Lord's Prayer in a loud voice and without any errors. (This last detail was of definite importance, for according to popular belief no witch could utter this most important of Christian prayers without making at least one mistake.) Cotton Mather, perhaps especially incensed because Burroughs had once been a fellow-clergyman, was very hostile concerning him.

BUTLER STREET STATION (HRH): The New York Police Department precinct headquarters (not far from HPL's abode when he lived at 169 Clinton Street in 1925) with responsibility for the Red Hook district of Brooklyn. NYPD detective Thomas F. Malone is assigned to Butler Street.

C

(de) C FAMILY (TA): In the manner often encountered in the short stories of Edgar Allan Poe, a fictitious noble family whose "identity" is denoted with a first initial instead of a last name. The "de Cs" are members of the most ancient French aristocracy, with a pedigree dating back into the so-called Dark Ages. Their ruined chateau (castle), although it is centuries old, is still less old than their known family line. At some point during the 13th century, the contemporary "Count de C" was named Henri and was 32 years old; his little boy was named Godfrey. Mistakenly believing that a wicked old alchemist who lived in the neighborhood, Michel Mauvais ("Michael the Evil"), had murdered Godfrey, the count impulsively killed the wizard. Moments later Michel's son Charles killed Count Henri in return (apparently with an instantaneous poison thrown into his face), and also cursed the de C family with the curse that no future count would ever grow older than 32. Godfrey died of a mysteriously-launched arrow at the age of 32. His son Robert was found dead at 32. Robert's son Louis drowned at 32, and so on down the centuries. After six hundred years of this suffering, Count Antoine de C is the last surviving member of the family, and about to mark—"celebrate" probably being the incorrect word—his 32nd birthday. By wandering into unknown and unsuspected caverns below the castle, he finds the wizard Charles (whose alchemical skills have given him unnaturally long life, during which he has relentlessly assassinated the Counts de C), and manages to burn him alive, thus preserving his own life.

This clumsy and melodramatic story with its atmosphere of knights and magicians, reminiscent of the plots of Gothic novels that were old-fashioned before HPL's parents were born, dates from very early in his literary career.

CACTUS MOUNTAINS (TJR): A fictitious mountain range wherein lies the Norton Mine, in a "nearly unpeopled waste" in "America's vast West," a West that HPL knew principally from adventure stories in pulp magazines, since he never went there. The references to Piute (now usually "Paiute") Indians in the area, and the very name "Cactus Mountains," naturally suggest a southwestern locality, perhaps in Arizona or southern Nevada.

CAERLEON; HEXHAM; HADRIAN'S WALL (CDW): Dr. Willett receives under circumstances of mystery and horror a parchment with writing in:

> ...the pointed Saxon minuscules [letters] of the eighth or ninth century A.D., [which] brought with them memories of an uncouth time when under a fresh Christian veneer ancient faiths and ancient rites stirred stealthily, and the pale moon of Britain looked sometimes on strange deeds in the Roman ruins of Caerleon and Hexham, and by the towers along Hadrian's Wall.

Caerleon in southeastern Wales was the site of a large Roman fortress during much of the Roman occupation of their "Britannia" province, which lasted from the 1st–5th century A.D. Hexham is a town in Northumberland, most northerly of the English counties. Like Caerleon, Hexham in Roman times was the site of a legionary fortress defending the frontier of Roman territory. Hadrian's Wall was a Roman wall built across the entire island at its narrowest part between the years 122–26, during the reign of Emperor Hadrian, separating Britannia from the unpacified areas to the north (modern Scotland). Like the Great Wall of China, Hadrian's Wall had watchtowers at regular intervals.

CAHOONE, CAPTAIN (SH): Dutee Harris' commanding officer on the ship *Vigilant* during the War of 1812. Historically, a Captain John Cahoone commanded the U.S. revenue cutter *Vigilant* at the Newport, Rhode Island station from 1812 until as late as 1832. Captain Cahoone is or was a famous man in the small world of Rhode Island nautical history, for leading the *Vigilant*'s brave nighttime boarding and capture of the British privateer *Dart* off Newport in 1813, during the War of 1812; he is regarded as a hero by the modern United States Coast Guard, descendant of the U.S. Revenue Cutter Service.

CAMORIN, GROVES OF (WS): Forests of fragrant aloe plants and sandalwood trees, located in some unspecified place, perhaps Sona-Nyl; Basil Elton compares them in his mind to the beautiful forests he believes he will find in Cathuria.

CANNIBALISM (HW, RW, PH, LF): Anthropophagism makes relatively few appearances in HPL's work, and those are principally in early stories when he made use of the built-in shock effect, before he learned to induce his shocks with far more subtle means. But the rural Yankee cannibal in *The Picture in the House* is a memorable character of "straight" horror fiction. Some of Herbert West's experimental subjects become man-eaters, as did the over-inbred Martense family of upstate New York in *The Lurking Fear*. In *The Rats in the Walls*, the searchers discover evidence of a grand-scale cannibal cult in the natural caverns beneath Exham Priory, a cult in which human beings, eventually dehumanized into quadrupedal herd animals, had been raised and slaughtered for eating for at least 2000 years.

CAPE VERDE ISLANDS (CC, CDW): The Cthulhu-cultists arrested in Louisiana in 1907 are "men of a very low, mixed-blooded, and mentally aberrant type. Most were seamen, and a sprinkling of negroes and mulattoes, largely West Indians or Brava Portuguese from the Cape Verde Islands." In HPL's lifetime, the Cape Verde Islands (now the republic of Cape Verde), a small Atlantic archipelago 300 miles west of Africa, formed a colony of Portugal, having been discovered and settled by the Portuguese in the 15th century. Portuguese colonists imported African slaves for labor, and by modern times the population of the islands had become almost entirely divided between those who were mulatto and those who were purely African. Brava is the name of one of the islands; a "Brava Portuguese" suggests one who is half-Portuguese at best. Tony Gomes, the evil-looking mulatto servant with the Portuguese surname, employed at the Pawtuxet bungalow in *The Case of Charles Dexter Ward*, is called a "Brava." Given the small size, poor agricultural conditions, and endemic poverty of these islands, emigration has been common since the 19th century, including emigration to the United States; the most recent U.S. census found about 72,000 inhabitants who claimed Cape Verdean origin.

CAPWELL, JUDGE (IV): His remains are found accidentally buried in Hannah Bixby's grave in the Peck Valley cemetery, another mistake by the incompetent and hard-drinking undertaker George Birch.

CAREW, SAM (IV): Briefly mentioned in this tale as an 18th century Providence apothecary (*i.e.,* pharmacist), a contemporary of Joseph Curwen.

CARFAX (RW): This is the name of the Delapore family's plantation, on the James River in eastern Virginia. (Some of the earliest English settlement took place along the James, as HPL was virtually certain to have been aware; therefore Carfax's location is another indication of the family's long time in America.) Mr. de la Poer (as he later renamed himself) can remember watching as a small child while Federal troops burned the Carfax mansion during the Civil War. He provides no date, but we can assume it was sometime between spring, 1864 and spring 1865. The area was heavily fought over during General Ulysses S. Grant's spring offensive of 1864, by which time Northern soldiers were looting and sometimes burning almost every plantation's "Big House" (*i.e.,* the owner's mansion) that they passed; the war itself ended in April, 1865). Lost in the fire was the envelope of family secrets that had been passed down to the eldest son in each generation, so that neither Mr. de la Poer nor his own father ever learned what message the envelope contained. Had he known it, presumably he would never have returned to England with a self-imposed mission of restoring Exham Priory from the ruins.

Although the story provides no reason why the Delapore estate in Virginia was called Carfax, it can scarcely be imagined that HPL (who in his able monograph *Supernatural Horror in Literature* called Bram Stoker's novel *Dracula* worthy of "a permanent place in English letters"), could have forgotten that the vacant manor house which Count Dracula purchased in England was named "Carfax".

CARROLL (MM): Graduate student at Miskatonic University; a member of the Miskatonic University Expedition, and a trained airplane pilot. On December 13–15, 1930, he climbs the nearly 15,000-foot-high Mount Nansen along with Professor Pabodie and another of the graduate students, Gedney. On January 6, 1931, he is part of the large group of expedition members who fly over the South Pole. He becomes a member of the Lake-Atwood sub-party. On January 22, Carroll flies Professor Lake on aerial-reconnaissance trips which discover mountains comparable in height to the Himalayas. On January 23, he participates in the excavation and study of sundry mysterious objects, including five-sided soapstone fragments. He is found dead with the rest of the Lake-Atwood group on January 25, 1931, and buried at the site.

CARTER, CHRISTOPHER (SK): Randolph Carter's great-uncle. As a child, "Randy" Carter often visits "Uncle Chris" at his farmhouse in the hills outside of Arkham. He is married to Martha Carter and employs Benijah Corey as a farm hand. He once begins to tell young Randy something about an old box with a key in it, but unfortunately Martha prevents him from finishing whatever he was going to say.

CARTER, EDMUND (TGSK): An ancestor of Randolph Carter, and a reputed sorcerer. He lives at Salem, Massachusetts during the witchcraft mania of 1692, and it was said that he escaped from Salem just in time to avoid being hanged as a witch himself. He settles in the hills near Arkham, in a "great homestead" which is only a ruin by 1928, when Randolph Carter passes it. He is later said to have practiced his magic in the "Snake-den," a cave near his farm.

CARTER, JOHN (CDW): An historical figure, the publisher of the *Providence Gazette and Country Journal* newspaper before the American

Revolution. In the tale, during the 1760s the new (founded in 1762) and struggling newspaper receives financial assistance from Joseph Curwen, during his "town booster" phase of public donations; but in 1770 Carter becomes a member of the secret committee investigating Joseph Curwen's inexplicable and possibly criminal activities. John Carter takes part in the April 12, 1771 raid on Curwen's Pawtuxet farm, assigned to Captain Hopkins' team by the riverbank.

CARTER, MARTHA (SK): Wife of Christopher Carter, and therefore Randolph Carter's great-aunt by marriage. She seems to have a disapproving attitude toward the Carter family's supernatural leanings.

CARTER, PICKMAN (TGSK): HPL puts two of his great names together! The BEING whom Randolph Carter meets in another dimension reveals to him that his descendant Pickman will "use strange means in repelling the Mongol hordes from Australia" in the year 2169.

CARTER, RANDOLPH (SRC, DQ, SK, TGSK, CDW): Born circa 1874 (on circumstantial evidence) in Boston, and raised in that city. On October 7, 1883, he has a mysterious experience while visiting his great-uncle Christopher's farm, and afterwards seems to have odd premonitions about his own future, but only as far as 1928. In 1914 he enlists in the Foreign Legion of the French army, and serves through World War I. He is badly wounded in action at Belloy-en-Santerre, France, in 1916. He makes friends with a fellow-Legionnaire, Etienne-Laurent de Marigny of New Orleans, Louisiana, and goes with him on leave to the French city of Bayonne, where de Marigny shows him "terrible secrets" in the crypts and tunnels beneath that ancient town. After the war, he loses a close friend, Harley Warren, when the two men investigate a frightful abandoned graveyard deep in a swamp in the southern United States. Another of his friends, it turns out, proves to be Dr. Marinus B. Willett of *The Case of Charles Dexter Ward*, who sees the Sign of Koth in the caverns beneath the site of Joseph Curwen's Pawtuxet farmhouse, and remembers what Randolph Carter had told him about this secret emblem. Carter is the central character in the novel-length *The Dream-Quest of Unknown Kadath*, in which he undergoes many harrowing adventures in Dreamland while attempting to find Kadath, and in the connected "Silver Key" stories, in which he "disappeared from the sight of man on the seventh of October, 1928," while his mind or spirit travels through space, time, and other dimensions, encountering many unorthodox beings and even switching bodies with the alien wizard Zkauba, on a planet called Yaddith.

   To a considerable extent Randolph Carter seems to be HPL as he might have wished to be: independently wealthy; a world traveler in the pursuit of esoteric lore and old architecture, but rooted firmly in New England; resourceful in many a tight situation. Especially poignant is the author's posting of the wealthy aesthete Randolph Carter to four years of trench warfare in the Foreign Legion, one of the world's most legendary he-man fighting outfits, particularly renowned in the adventure fiction of HPL's time. HPL himself, while attempting to enlist for the same war in 1917, was rejected on health grounds (and through his mother's strenuous intervention with the recruiters), by the much more humble Rhode Island National Guard. (Revealingly, in *The Statement of Randolph Carter*, the earliest tale in which this character appeared, Carter's friend Harley Warren refers to him as a man who couldn't even pass the physical examination to join the army, which was more or less HPL's own real situation; Randolph Carter's Foreign Legion heroics were a later inspiration.) Carter's most profound family relationship is, like HPL's, not with his own father and most certainly not with his mother, but with his grandfather, who along with his great-uncle Christopher Carter is "the only one who understands [Randolph's] mental life." This seems like a fictional encore, at least to some extent, of HPL's relationship with his adored maternal grandfather Whipple Phillips, and his favorite uncle, Dr. Franklin Chase Clark (the husband of one of his aunts), two much older men of marked intelligence, who took an encouraging interest in the boy Lovecraft's reading and intellectual pursuits.

CARTER, SIR RANDOLPH (SK): English ancestor of Randolph Carter, who "studied magic when Elizabeth was queen" (*i.e.*, during the reign of Elizabeth I of England, between the years 1558–1603).

CASEY, MR. (SOI): A government factory-inspector who visits Innsmouth in about 1925, to inspect the Marsh gold refinery. Working under the unpleasant gazes of the handful of employees, Mr. Casey finds the financial books and accounts in bad shape, "with no clear account of any kind of dealings." Stays overnight at the Gilman House hotel in central Innsmouth, becoming so frightened by the "slopping-like" voices he overhears from neighboring rooms that he sits awake all night and flees the town at dawn. We can imagine him filing a report stating that he did not need to return to Innsmouth. Mr. Casey was lucky all the same. The chatty railroad ticket agent in Newburyport who recounts the story also tells the narrator that he has heard of "more'n one business or government man that's disappeared" while visiting Innsmouth, and of another unwanted outside visitor who went mad and was now locked up in the state hospital at Danvers, Massachusetts: "They must have fixed up some awful scare for that fellow." One of the families in Lovecraft's maternal genealogy was named Casey.

CASTRO (CC): A Cthulhu-cult member, arrested during an orgiastic cult celebration and human sacrifice in a Louisiana bayou in 1907, by Inspector J. Legrasse of the New Orleans police department. He is already dead by the time of Professor Angell's 1925–26 investigations. An "aged mestizo" (a Latin-American Spanish word for a half-breed, typically part-white and part-Indian), old Castro claimed to have "sailed to strange ports and talked with the undying leaders of the cult in the mountains of China." Under police interrogation, he reveals a good deal about the cult to detectives, but refuses to discuss the Old Ones very much.

One of HPL's steadiest "revision" or ghostwriting clients, commencing in 1927, was an amazing old character named Adolphe de Castro (real name Gustav Adolphe Danziger, 1859–1959). This person was a European immigrant who had already had careers as a dentist, journalist, lawyer, and even as the U.S. Vice-Consul in Madrid. Oddly enough, he also served as one of the first Jewish rabbis in San Jose, California, when that sprawling city was still but a small town surrounded by farms and fruit groves. While still known as Danziger, de Castro was an occasional writing and publishing collaborator of Ambrose Bierce (1842–1913?) which brought HPL within one degree of separation from another American master of supernatural horror fiction. HPL described de Castro to his own friends at various times as "generous and likable," "an amiable charlatan," and "an unctuous old hypocrite," but he worked carefully to edit his client's wretched books and stories, and the connection persisted. He even took the old man on a walking tour of central Providence when de Castro turned up there for a visit in 1936, little knowing that he himself would be dead in a year while his elderly client would live on for almost a quarter-century. L. Sprague de Camp ventured to suggest that "it is probably not a coincidence that the garrulous captive cultist…is named Castro," but this can only remain a conjecture.

CATHURIA (WS, DQ): A land that no man has seen, but which many imagine to lie somewhere beyond the Basalt Pillars of the West. "It is the Land of Hope, and in it shine the perfect ideals of all that we know elsewhere"; meaning the ideal forms of everything existing in our world, the so-called "Platonic ideals" of all things. Basil Elton envisions Cathuria as the country of gods and golden cities, with pink marble temples and silver fountains, perfumed lakes with coral beds, marble and porphyry houses, gold-roofed. The chance of finding Cathuria becomes so imperative that it seems to him worth leaving the lovely land of Sona-Nyl and daring the unknown waters on the other side of the Basalt Pillars.

CATS (HRH, CU, RW, COS, DQ, CDW, HD): HPL was very fond of cats and seems to have had a special knack for communicating with them. In 1921 HPL wrote: "It is good to be a cynic—it is better to be a contented cat—and it is best not to exist at all." In the emphatic opinion of his ex-wife: "...cats were 'people' of special interest to him. I think he loved his feline brothers more than he did humanity. In fact, I may state this without apology."

Unsurprisingly, cats have an honored place in several of his tales. In *The Cats of Ulthar*, an evil old man and wife who take pleasure in trapping, torturing, and killing cats in their solitary cottage are slain by a small army of cats, and the men of Ulthar thereafter pass a law forbidding anyone to harm a cat. In *The Dream-Quest of Unknown Kadath*, Randolph Carter gives a bowl of cream to a little kitten in Ulthar, where the Ultharian cats had eaten the zoogs who were shadowing him. Later, when kidnapped to the moon, Carter is rescued and carried back to Earth by a large army of cats who have flown through space. Other cats in Dreamland also help him from time to time, and one measure of the eeriness of the northern lands where he finally travels is that no cat will live in Inganok.

Mr. de la Poer in *The Rats in the Walls* moves into the restored castle of Exham Priory and notes with delicate irony: "My household consisted of seven servants and nine cats, of which latter species I am particularly fond." One of his cats, the unfortunately named (to modern ears) Nigger-Man, a black seven-year-old, was brought along from Massachusetts, while the others were all acquired in England. Nigger-Man is so alert to the presence of the spectral rats that he is practically a story character in his own right. At the end, the dazed and wandering de la Poer sees his favorite cat "stalk unperturbed" through the horrors of the hidden caverns. "Once I saw him monstrously perched atop a mountain of bones, and wondered at the secrets that might lie behind his yellow eyes." Finally the cat "darts past me like a winged Egyptian god, straight into the illimitable gulf of the unknown. But I was far behind...." Three hours later the other investigators "found me crouching over the plump, half-eaten body of Capt. Norrys, with my own cat leaping and tearing at my throat." In his mental and spiritual atavism, he has become what even his affectionate cat instinctively loathes.

During a New York police raid in certain tunnels beneath Brooklyn, Detective Malone in *The Horror at Red Hook* is tripped up by a lean black-and-white cat, making him overturn a beaker half full of some red liquid. "The shock was severe, and to this day Malone is not certain of what he saw; but in dreams he still pictures that cat as it scuttled away with certain monstrous alterations and peculiarities." Smart cats, like

Mrs. Nahum Gardner's in *The Colour Out of Space*, depart when the psychic influences get too bad. If they can not escape, like Nig in *The Case of Charles Dexter Ward*, then they risk dying of fright (as he does) because of their heightened sensitivity.

The reference in *The Haunter of the Dark* to the "huge, friendly cats [that] sunned themselves atop a convenient shed," close by Robert Blake's Providence apartment (which was really a description of HPL's own rooms), describes a band of neighborhood felines whose daily presence helped to brighten HPL's impoverished last years. He named them the "Kappa Alpha Tau" (KAT) fraternity, with the initials standing for the Greek words *Kompson Ailuron Taxis*, the Company of Elegant Cats.

CATSKILL MOUNTAINS (BWS, LF): A real range of small, heavily-forested mountains in southeastern New York state, settled by Dutch and English colonists in the 17th century. Joe Slater, a degenerate Catskills yokel, becomes the fleshly prison for an alien intelligence in *Beyond the Wall of Sleep*. The action of *The Lurking Fear* takes place in a Catskills district of old Dutch settlements. HPL never really visited the Catskills region, although he could have done so easily enough. Of *Beyond the Wall of Sleep*, he told a friend that it had been written spontaneously after reading an account of some Catskills "degenerates" in the New York *Tribune*, in 1919, an article which mentioned a family called Slater or Slahter. The physical and moral degeneracy of isolated rural communities or clans was a familiar scare-topic in late 19th and early 20th century books and journalism.

CATULLUS (RW): Gaius Valerius Catullus (c. 84–c. 54 B.C.) was one of the great Roman lyric poets, a specialist in love poems; his works are notable for technical perfection and passionate emotion. A poem of his on a religious-mythological subject—the story of "Atys"—is alluded to in this tale.

CAVES, CAVERNS, WELLS and ABYSSES (BC, TA, TT, DA, TJR, SRC, TE, AJ, CE, NC, TO, OG, HW, TH, LF, RW, TF, UP, SH, HRH, HE, IV, CC, PM, SK, SHH, DQ, CDW, COS, WD, MM, SOI, DWH, TGSK, SOT, WE): *See* Appendix.

CELEPHAÏS (CE, DQ): A great city in Dreamland. Its ruler is King Kuranes, formerly an English dreamer. Celephaïs is in the Valley of Ooth-Nargai beyond the Tanarian hills, on the river Naraxa, where Mount Aran rises by the shores of the Cerenarian Sea. The city is carefully described as having marble walls surmounted by bronze statues (which never tarnish or discolor), and high minarets. The city gates are bronze, the streets are made of onyx, and the Temple of Nath-Horthath is constructed of turquoise. The temple is staffed by eighty priests who wear chains of orchid-flowers; they happen to be the very same priests who built the temple, ten thousand years earlier. The "Street of the Pillars" leads a person down through the city to the sea-wall, where splendid galleys await a traveler. Celephaïs' merchants deal in spices, carved jade, spun gold, and little red songbirds. The suburbs are built on low green hills full of groves and asphodel-gardens, dotted with little shrines and with cottages. King Kuranes reigns over the city from the Palace of Seventy Delights, or from his retreat outside of Celephaïs, which is built to exactly resemble a manor house in the English region of Cornwall, Kuranes' earthly home. Randolph Carter visits Celephaïs while attempting to reach Inganok. He consults with the high priest of Nath-Horthath, and with Kuranes, both of whom try to dissuade him from the difficult journey. He also gains information about Inganok from the chief cat of Celephaïs, who lives by the bazaar of the sheep-butchers!

CEMETERIES (TT, HW, SRC, TO, PO, TH, LF, TU, SH, TF, HRH, IV, PM, DQ, CDW, WE): "H.P. was particularly fond of old graveyards whose tombstones were crumbling," his ex-wife Sonia reminisced after his death. But any burying-ground would do. Alone, or with many a friend during his lifetime, HPL explored many cemeteries large and small, rural and urban, by day and by night. Naturally, burial-places are not unknown in his tales.

The Tomb is constructed around the fascination of the narrator, Jervas Dudley, with the ancient tomb of the Hyde family, in a country place near his home. In *Herbert West—Reanimator*, the boys pilfer bodies from the graveyards of Arkham, including Christchurch Cemetery, for their experiments; later they do so in Bolton as well. (The "potter's field" mentioned in this tale is an old expression in English, although now only a literary expression, for a charity graveyard for the very poor or unknown dead. It comes from the Bible, Matthew 27:7, when the chief priests of the Temple decided what to do with the tainted thirty pieces of silver they had paid Judas Iscariot—who had betrayed Jesus to them—after he had thrown the money back to them and hanged himself in remorse: "And they took counsel, and bought with them the potter's field, to bury strangers in.") Finally, West and his comrade open a Boston medical practice across the street from a very old cemetery, and find that their cellar shares a wall with an unsuspected tomb.

In *The Statement of Randolph Carter,* Carter and his friend Harley Warren journey to a wonderfully Gothic environment in a southern swamp:

> The place was an ancient cemetery; so ancient that I trembled at the manifold signs of immemorial years. It was in a deep, damp hollow, overgrown with rank grass, moss, and curious creeping weeds, and filled with a vague stench which my idle fancy associated absurdly with rotting stone. On every hand were the signs of neglect and decrepitude…noisome vapours… seemed to emanate from unheard-of catacombs, and…I could distinguish a repellent array of antique slabs, urns, cenotaphs, and mausolean facades; all crumbling, moss-grown, and moisture-stained, and partly concealed by the gross luxuriance of the unhealthy vegetation.

In *The Outsider*, a very Poe-esque fantasy, the narrator escapes from the dark castle where he has always lived, to climb through a stone trapdoor at the top of the highest tower; whereupon he is in a little tomb, through the door of which he sees "nothing less than the *solid ground*, decked and diversified by marble slabs and columns, and overshadowed by an ancient stone church," traversed by a "white gravel path": a cemetery. In *Polaris,* the narrator, who knows himself to have been a citizen of Olathoë in Lomar thousands of years ago, "vainly [strives] to shake off this unnatural dream of a house of stone and brick south of a sinister swamp and a cemetery on a low hillock…,"

The characters of *The Hound*, St. John and his friend the nameless narrator, are decadent outlaws, aesthetic grave-robbers, and they plunder many a cemetery for bodies or body parts, which they lovingly arrange in a subterranean museum-collection all their own. Their downfall comes when they raid "that terrible Holland churchyard":

> I can recall the scene in these final moments—the pale autumnal moon over the graves, casting long horrible shadows; the grotesque trees, drooping sullenly to meet the neglected grass and the crumbling slabs; the vast legions of strangely colossal bats that flew against the moon; the antique ivied church pointing a huge spectral finger at the livid sky; the phosphorescent insects that danced like death-fires under the yews in a distant corner; the odours of mould, vegetation, and less explicable things that mingled feebly with the night-wind from over far swamps and seas….

The nameless narrator of *The Lurking Fear* begins to find the real answer to the gruesome mystery of Tempest Mountain on the night when he finds himself "digging alone and idiotically in the grave of Jan Martense," in the Martense family graveyard of long ago, "where deformed trees tossed insane branches as their roots displaced unhallowed slabs and sucked venom from what lay below." The slight tale called *The Unnamable* begins engagingly with: "We were sitting on a dilapidated seventeenth-century tomb in the late afternoon of an autumn day at the old burying-ground in Arkham, and speculating about the unnamable." In fact, flat tomb-tops were among HPL's favorite places to sit for a while and chat with a friend.

The entire problem with *The Shunned House* is that it was built over the Roulet family graveyard, which had been forgotten when the remains in all the other old family plots behind Back Street/Benefit Street were exhumed and moved to North Burial Ground. Later in the tale the nameless narrator mentions raising a marble urn for his uncle's memory "in St. John's churchyard—the place that Poe loved—the hidden grove of giant willows on the hill, where tombs and headstones huddle quietly between the hoary bulk of the church and the houses and bank walls of Benefit Street."

In *The Festival*, the nameless narrator must pass through the churchyard of the church on Central Hill in Kingsport, before going into the sanctuary with the rest of the midnight procession. It is mentioned in *The Horror at Red Hook* that Robert Suydam and his innocent bride of one day, Cornelia Gerritsen, are buried side by side in Brooklyn's Greenwood Cemetery. *In the Vault* takes place entirely in and around the "receiving tomb" for the storage of bodies soon to be buried in the fictional Peck Valley Cemetery. In *Pickman's Model* there is mention of Copp's Hill Burying Ground in Boston and the Mount Auburn cemetery across the Charles River in Cambridge. In *The Dream-Quest of Unknown Kadath*, Randolph Carter encounters the ghoul that was Pickman while the latter sits on a tombstone stolen from the Granary Street Burying Ground, another historic Boston cemetery, and later Carter's ghoul-escorts take along a handy gravestone removed from the Charter Street Burying Ground in Salem, Massachusetts. After a journey through "endless burrows," Carter and his trio of ghouls emerge in "a forest of vast lichened monoliths reaching nearly as high as the eye could see and forming the modest gravestones of the gugs." It is the gugs' cemetery, where "ghouls come often, for a buried gug will feed a community for almost a year, and even with the added peril it is better to burrow for gugs than to bother with the graves of men."

Joseph Curwen's "passion for graveyards, in which he was glimpsed at all hours and under all conditions, was notorious" in 18th century Providence. Together with his cohorts Simon Orne and Edward Hutchinson, Curwen or his minions "violate graves in every part of the world" in their quest for "essential Saltes" to resurrect and question about ancient lore. Circa 1927–28, both Charles Dexter Ward and Dr. Marinus B. Willett conduct operations of exhumation or interment in Providence's North Burial Ground. It is mentioned at the end of *In the Walls of Eryx* that the remains of Frederick Dwight and Kenton J. Stanfield will be buried in the Venus Crystal Company's graveyard at Terra Nova, Venus.

CERENARIAN SEA (CE, DQ): A sea in Dreamland. By description it is a calm body of water, "gentle blue" and "billowy," much traveled by galleys and sailing ships. Kuranes takes a galley over the Cerenarian Sea, all the way to the cloud-city of Serranian. Randolph Carter walks and then boats down the river Oukranos to reach the Cerenarian; the harbor of Hlanith is at the mouth of the river, and there he boards a coastal vessel for the two-day voyage to Celephaïs. From that city he sails north across the Cerenarian Sea for 22 days to reach the land of Inganok.

CHALDAEA (NC, HRH): In *The Nameless City* the narrator pictures to himself "all the splendours of an age so distant that Chaldaea could not recall it." In *The Horror at Red Hook* the name of Lilith appears for a moment in the ocean-liner stateroom of the dead Robert Suydam and his wife, written in "Chaldee" characters.

Chaldaea, or Chaldea, was the name of a nation in southern Babylonia, or lower Mesopotamia, between the Tigris and Euphrates rivers; the location of their ancient country lies entirely within modern Iraq. The Chaldeans were a Semitic people who continually attacked the region until they became its rulers, circa 625 B.C. The English name of the Chaldeans comes from the Hebrew *kasdim*, and they are referred to a number of times in the Old Testament. In ancient times the Babylonians/Chaldeans were famous for the production of astrologers and wizards.

CHAMBERS STREET (TGSK): A real Boston street where Randolph Carter/Zkauba lived for a time.

CHANDRAPUTRA, SWAMI (TGSK): "An adept from Benares," in India. (Benares, now officially written Varanasi, on the banks of the Ganges River, is the holiest city of the Hindu religion; many Hindus even believe that to die in the sacred precinct of Varanasi will release them from the cycle of reincarnation, allowing them to enter heaven.) Swami Chandraputra appears at the 1932 meeting in the New Orleans home of Etienne-Laurent de Marigny, to discuss the disposition of the missing Randolph Carter's estate. By his account, he has been living in Boston's West End. He says he has also been corresponding by mail with de Marigny since 1930. The Swami is lean, dark, heavily bearded, with black, burning eyes, wearing loose western-style clothing, and "the turban of a high-class Brahmin." He speaks excellent, idiomatic English. His face is curiously immobile, his voice curiously hollow and metallic, and his hands curiously encased in large, white mittens. The Swami waits until the other men have had their say, then reveals in great detail what his dreams and "other sources" have told him about Carter's activities since he was missing. Ernest B. Aspinwall, the suspicious Chicago attorney who is one of Carter's cousins, figures out that the Swami's face is only a mask, and boldly pulls it off. He is the only one to see what was underneath the mask and he drops dead of fright. The "Swami," presumably the alien Zkauba's body which had been under the temporary sway of Randolph Carter's mind, begins to make rattling and buzzing sounds, and shuffles toward the tall "cosmic clock" in de Marigny's chamber. He climbs inside this "cosmic clock" (which is not otherwise explained), and vanishes completely.

CHAPMAN FARMHOUSE (HW): A deserted farmhouse beyond Meadow Hill in Arkham. As of 1904, it is still far from roads or other houses. Herbert West and his comrade fit the house out with an operating room, a laboratory, and a burial pit for failed experiments. Here they reanimate a brawny young workman, drowned only the day before, and become so frightened by his screams that they flee, upsetting an oil lamp and burning the place down by accident.

CHAPMAN'S BROOK (COS): A stream that divides the two parts of Nahum Gardner's farm and which can be crossed over a small bridge. Ammi Pierce and the men from Arkham cross Chapman's Brook to escape from the increasingly frightening phenomena taking place around the Gardner farmhouse.

CHARLES LE SORCIER (TA): Charles "the Sorcerer," loving son and apt pupil of the 13th century wizard Michel Mauvais. Charles uses his profound skills in alchemy to live an additional six hundred years in a secret chamber below the de C chateau, using the time to murder one Count de C after another. When finally uncovered by the last Count, Charles is clad in a medieval robe and skullcap, with incredibly long and thick hair and beard. Furthermore his skin is whiter than white marble, his body is skeletally lean, and his eyes are of "abysmal blackness." Somewhat like a James Bond villain, he spends a long time gloating over his revenge-plan to the Count before killing him (speaking in the so-called "Low Latin of the middle ages"; fortunately the Count understands this perfectly!), long enough for the Count to recover his wits, assess the situation—somewhat like James Bond himself—and hurl a flaming torch at Charles, which burns him to ashes.

CHARTER STREET BURIAL GROUND (DQ): An old and non-fictitious cemetery in Salem, Massachusetts, from which the ghouls stole the slate headstone of one Colonel Nehemiah Derby. The ghouls who escort Randolph Carter through the city of the Gugs carry the headstone with them as a tool for wedging open the trapdoor to Upper Dreamland, and also use it to bludgeon a ghast to death.

CHASE and WHITMARSH, DRS. (SH): Providence physicians who attended the last tenants of the Shunned House in 1860–61, finding a series of anemia deaths preceded by vampiric madness. The victims, who were Americans of no great education, babbled curses and threats in vulgar and idiomatic French. Dr. Elihu Whipple heard the story personally from these doctors before he left to serve in the Civil War.

CHASM OF NIS (LF): At one point the nameless narrator remarks: "Sometimes, in the throes of a nightmare when unseen powers whirl one over the roofs of strange dead cities toward the grinning chasm of Nis, it is a relief and even a delight to shriek wildly and throw oneself along."

In Edgar Allan Poe's very minor tale *The Valley of Unrest*, he mentioned a valley of Nis. The invented valley of Nis then appeared in an early and minor tale or parable called *Memory*, which HPL wrote in 1919, two or three years before this tale, and which begins:

> In the valley of Nis the accursed waning moon shines thinly, tearing a path for its light with feeble horns through the lethal foliage of a great upas-tree. And within the depths of the valley, where the light reaches not, move forms not meant to be beheld. Rank is the herbage on each slope, where evil vines and creeping plants crawl amidst the stones of ruined palaces, twining tightly about broken columns and strange monoliths, and heaving up marble pavements laid by forgotten hands.

CHAUCER (CE): On his triumphant ride with an escort of noble knights at the end of *Celephaïs,* Kuranes seems to "gallop back through Time" for instead of modern English scenery they perceive "only such houses and villages as Chaucer or men before him might have seen...." Geoffrey Chaucer (circa 1340–1400) was the earliest of the great English poets; his verse masterpiece *The Canterbury Tales*, about a motley crew of religious pilgrims riding through the southern English countryside while exchanging entertaining stories of all sorts, is one of the classics of world literature.

CHECKLEY, DR. JOHN (CDW): An historical personage (1680–1754) of colonial Providence, born in Boston. Educated at Oxford University in England, with a doctorate in Divinity (*i.e.*, theology), Dr. Checkley was a "famous wit" who came from Boston to Providence to serve as rector of King's Church (now St. John's), the Anglican parish, and to do missionary work with local Indians.

In the tale, he makes a social call on Joseph Curwen shortly after moving to the city, but the visit is brief; the clergyman detects "a sinister undercurrent in his host's discourse," and hastily departs. Although Dr. Checkley was never willing to repeat what he had heard, people know that he was "hideously shocked" by something, and that he never thought of Curwen without losing his customary "gay urbanity."

CHEPACHET (HRH): A formerly rural Rhode Island village (current population approximately 900), on the Chepachet River, about 25 miles northwest of central Providence. It was in this "quaint hamlet of wooden colonial houses" that Detective T.F. Malone of the New York Police Department boarded with a dairy farmer's family, trying to recuperate in those peaceful and bucolic surroundings while on psychological disability leave following a disaster in Brooklyn that killed many of his fellow police officers. HPL hiked around the Chepachet area with a friend on September 19, 1923, a few years prior to writing this tale.

CHESTERFIELD (TT): "My formerly silent tongue waxed voluble with the easy grace of a Chesterfield," writes Jervas Dudley as his mind comes more and more into communion with that of the 18th century profligate Jervas Hyde.

Philip Dormer Stanhope (1694–1773), the fourth Earl of Chesterfield, was a wealthy and witty aristocrat of 18th century England, a great conversationalist who is still known today for his frank, irreverent, and beautifully written work, *Letters to His Son*, a collection of advice to his illegitimate (therefore a "commoner") offspring on how to be popular, successful, and socially upward-mobile in elegant society, while still enjoying life. "I shall endeavour to assist your youth with all the experience that I have purchased, at the price of seven and fifty years." The famous and caustic wit Dr. Samuel Johnson, after Lord Chesterfield was safely dead, famously pronounced that the *Letters* taught "the morals of a whore, and the manners of a dancing master [*i.e.,* teacher]."

CHESUNCOOK (TD): A tiny community in one of the wildest, remotest regions of the Maine woods, at the north end of Chesuncook Lake. Even now Chesuncook is not particularly close to any other town, and in the 1920s its isolation must have been as extreme as anywhere that could be found in New England. (HPL himself never visited Chesuncook or anyplace near it, but picked it off a map as being self-evidently in the middle of nowhere.) Nonetheless Daniel Upton receives a telegram from the Chesuncook town marshal one day, saying that Edward Derby had stumbled into town from the forest, remembering only his own name and Daniel Upton's name and address. Upton makes the long drive up to Chesuncook, where Edward is in a cell at the "town farm" (a combination of jail and workhouse, to have been found in that era in many rural sections of the United States). The next day he buys Edward some new clothing in Chesuncook, and the two men return to Arkham. It develops that the coven to which Edward's wife Asenath belongs conducts its meetings somewhere in the vast, unpopulated woods beyond Chesuncook; the rites are presided over by "the Hooded Thing," in Edward's words.

CHICAGO (WE, TGSK): The Crystal Company apparently has its Earth base here; it is mentioned that a Company ship will fly the huge crystal found by Frederick Dwight from Venus back to Chicago. Ernest K. Aspinwall, Randolph Carter's odious attorney cousin, lives in Chicago. HPL never visited the Windy City, but he didn't like what he read about it, and transferred his feelings about the city's putative soullessness into print in these side-references.

CHOYNSKI (DWH): A Polish-American tenant in the Witch House in Arkham at the time that Walter Gilman also lives there.

CHRISTCHURCH CEMETERY (HW): An Arkham burial ground. Herbert West and his comrade consider stealing bodies here, but decide against it because almost all the interred corpses at Christchurch have been embalmed, totally ruling them out as reanimation subjects. Then, during the great typhoid epidemic of 1904, unembalmed bodies do pile up in the receiving tomb of the Christchurch Cemetery, but West is too busy working as an emergency doctor to get at them in time! Later, after West conducts his experiments with the body of Dr. Halsey, the night watchman at Christchurch Cemetery is clawed to death by the revenant.

CHURCHES (RW, TF, SH, HRH, DH, SOI, DWH, HD, CDW): During his thirties, HPL wrote for an amateur-journalist audience that "the environment into which I was born was that of the average American Protestant of urban, civilised type—in theory quite orthodox, but in practice very liberal. Morals rather than faith formed the real keynote." The lukewarm mainstream religion of his forebears slipped completely from his own shoulders, so that from a quite young age he was not a Christian, and from not many years afterwards he had no religion at all, a condition in which he persisted vigorously for the rest of his life.

Suitably, in HPL's tales, churches are often turned from their original purposes, their religious and benevolent associations become twisted.

In *The Festival*, the strange creatures he's met lead the narrator on a midnight procession through sleeping Kingsport. From the house on Green Lane, he and his guides proceed with many others to "a great white church," in a parody of Sunday-go-to-meeting routines in traditional New England villages of old. The crowd enters the church, walks up the aisle to the pulpit, and descends into hideous vaults through a trapdoor "which yawned loathsomely open just before the pulpit." Within this subterranean crypt, they enter a particular tomb and continue to descend. HPL's description of the church fits St. Michael's Episcopal Church on Summer Street, in Marblehead, Massachusetts, the town which inspired "Kingsport".

In *The Dunwich Horror*, the only church in the village has a significantly "broken steeple," and has been converted into Dunwich's general store.

In *The Horror at Red Hook*, a similar token of the civic degeneracy of Red Hook, Brooklyn, is "a tumbledown stone church, used Wednesdays as a dance hall, which reared its Gothic buttresses near the vilest part of the waterfront. It was nominally Catholic, but priests throughout the Brooklyn diocese denied the place all standing and authenticity, and policemen agreed with them when they listened to the noises it emitted at night." When this church is first raided by the New York police, Detective Malone notes "crudely painted panels...which depicted sacred faces with particularly worldly and sardonic expressions," as well as a "diabolical" inscription on the wall over the altar. In a later raid, the police uncover a secret crypt with a "croaking organ," a "vast arched chapel with wooden benches and a strangely-figured altar," and small prison cells lining the chapel walls. In these cells the lawmen find 17 manacled prisoners "in a state of complete idiocy."

The Starry Wisdom cult in *The Haunter of the Dark* also puts a former Christian church to unchristian uses. Their church on Federal Hill is full of bizarre paintings and statues, not to mention an alien monster in the belfry. (HPL's model for this building was St. John's Catholic Church on Federal Hill in Providence, now demolished.)

In *The Shunned House*, the narrator places an urn in his uncle's memory within the churchyard of St. John's Episcopal Church on Benefit Street, a very old graveyard that both Poe and HPL loved to visit.

In *The Shadow Over Innsmouth*, all three of Innsmouth's churches—Baptist, Methodist, Congregational—were subverted and turned to the town's Dagon-cult in the 1840s. All were "violently disavowed by their respective denominations elsewhere, and apparently [were] using the queerest kinds of ceremonials and clerical vestments. Their creeds were heterodox and mysterious, involving hints of certain marvelous transformations leading to bodily immortality—of a sort—on this earth." In another parody, this time of the stereotype of churches as places of welcome and haven for the newcomer, the narrator learns that the still-functioning Innsmouth churches are "not advisable neighborhoods for strangers," while the disused churches are all in ruins. Zadok Allen refers to "the haowlin' night arter [after] night from the churches," not all of which came from human throats.

Mr. de la Poer notes in *The Rats in the Walls* that for hundreds of years the prehistoric cannibal cult continued under the cover of a powerful but strange Catholic monastery, the original Exham Priory; meaning that the cannibal-cultists of those Anglo-Saxon and Norman dynasty times passed as Christian monks and men of religion.

Even when churches are turned to their appropriate uses, a hint of the nefarious is sometimes not far off. Robert Suydam marries Cornelia Gerritsen in the old Dutch Reformed Church, a landmark in Brooklyn's Flatbush district, but both are slain on their wedding night. Joseph Curwen, living in a time and place (18th century New England) when fairly regular church attendance was an essential condition for membership in good society, affects to worship God at the Congregational Church "on the hill" in Providence, a church he helped to erect in 1723; but in 1743 he switches to Deacon Snow's rival church across the river, continuing to make shows of piety every now and then. He marries his bride Eliza Tillinghast in the First Baptist meeting house, her "home" church, but has their daughter baptized at King's Church, the socially more prestigious Anglican parish they have joined.

Finally, Catholic churches become refuges for crowds of superstitious, working-class white ethnic residents in *The Dreams in the Witch House* (St. Stanislaus, Arkham, where people also light candles in 1931 after the bones of Brown Jenkin and many murdered children are found during the demolition of the Witch House), and *The Haunter of the Dark* (the church of Sancto Spirito, on Federal Hill in Providence; in this case HPL was certainly thinking of the Church of the Holy Ghost at 472 Atwells Avenue on Federal Hill, home of a long-established Italian-Catholic parish, "Sancto Spirito" being but the Italian equivalent of "Holy Ghost.").

CHURCHWARD, COLONEL (TGSK): In this tale, it is briefly mentioned that a certain "Colonel Churchward" had been shown the mysterious parchment Randolph Carter left behind in his 1928 disappearance, and could only declare that it was not written in the "Naacal language." HPL provides no further explanation, but Colonel James Churchward, a retired British officer, was a genuine figure from the history of occultism. A member of the Theosophical Society founded by the mystic Helena Blavatsky (1831–91), he also published in the early 1930s at least five books about the legendary, prehistoric Lost Continent of Mu (Lemuria), allegedly based on information he garnered from Mayan tablets which he alone understood how to interpret. He believed the Mayan people of southern Mexico were the descendants of colonists from Mu. According to Colonel Churchward, Mu was a huge continent whose great cities, and population of 60,000,000 people, sank beneath the Pacific Ocean in an abrupt and spectacular geological catastrophe about twelve thousand years ago. Using his "inner eye," Churchward "translated" the enigmatic writing on thousands of stone tablets and carved stone heads found in Mexico, which would be incomprehensible unless one knew "the language, the symbols, the alphabet and the cosmogony of Mu." In his vision of the past, the fabled Atlantis was but a mere colony of Mu in the Pacific, and the lore of the ancient Egyptians was likewise a remote hand-me-down of the knowledge of prehistoric Lemurian colonists. HPL kept abreast of this sort of mystical pseudo-science without placing much—or any—credence in it, and it did provide him with material for writing.

CLAPHAM-LEE, MAJOR SIR ERIC MORELAND, M.D., D.S.O.

(HW): He was not only a Canadian Army major but also a British knight; not only a medical doctor but also an awardee of the Distinguished Service Order—a high British military decoration. He was a man upon whom HPL lavished such a magnificent collection of names and titles of honor, that he deserved a longer life and a better fate. He appears in the fifth installment of the laughable serial *Herbert West—Reanimator*, a story so bad that Lovecraft biographer S.T. Joshi is probably right to consider it a tongue-in-cheek parody; a parody, that is, of a certain kind of breathless horror story to be found in the pulp magazines of that day. (Sample passage: "The phantasmal, unmentionable thing occurred.... I wonder even now if it could have been other than a daemoniac dream of delirium.") Dr. West and his ever-breathless assistant and biographer are at this point Canadian military surgeons in a field hospital at St. Eloi, Flanders (in Belgium), in late March, 1915. Major-Doctor-Sir Eric, etc., D.S.O., is dead. The "greatest surgeon in the division," he was hurrying to St. Eloi as a passenger in a biplane when it was unfortunately shot down by the German foe, but fortunately directly over Dr. West's field hospital, ensuring that the decapitated but otherwise unmarred corpse will be absolutely fresh.

It is said that he has helped West and West's comrade to get their officer commissions in the Canadian Army (historically, quite a few Americans who wished to get into World War I on the British side in the years before the United States entered the war in 1917, did so by enlisting in the Canadian Army), and that he has in the past "secretly studied the theory of reanimation to some extent under West." But: "Once a student of reanimation, this silent trunk was now gruesomely called upon to exemplify it." In the secret laboratory he has created in an otherwise-unused part of the field hospital, Dr. West "greedily seizes" Sir Eric and gets to work. The headless body is injected with "reanimating solution," the bodiless head is dumped into a vat of molten "reptile tissue." The trunk sits up and waves its arms around like a man trying to leap from a seat in a falling airplane, and the head in the vat shouts a warning to the airplane pilot. "At that instant" comes "the sudden and complete destruction of the building by German shell-fire," which only West and his comrade survive. The secret laboratory and its contents presumably are all destroyed.

However, in the future, West "used to make shuddering conjectures about the possible actions of a headless physician with the power of reanimating the dead," a unique image which can only point to Sir Eric Moreland Clapham-Lee. In 1921, a silent band of men appear at Sefton Asylum, their leader a "menacing military figure" with a waxen face and glass eyes, who talks through his briefcase. The band frees a certain cannibalistic madman—Dr. Halsey—who has been confined at Sefton for years, and departs. One night later, Dr. West receives with the mail a wooden box marked from "Eric Moreland Clapham-Lee, St. Eloi, Flanders." It goes into the incinerator without being opened, but one may suppose it contained the needless head. On the same night, Dr. West is dismembered by a posse of his past victims, commanded by "a stalking thing with a beautiful head made of wax" in the uniform of a Canadian Army officer.

CLARK AND NIGHTINGALE (CDW): Non-fictional 18th century Providence shopkeepers, at the sign of "the Frying-Pan and Fish." They did business with leading merchant Joseph Curwen.

CLARK, PARSON (PH): Around 1770, he is a rural Massachusetts "parson" or local clergyman, in the Miskatonic Valley not far from Arkham. In church services, the minister "ranted on Sundays in his big wig," as one particular local man who used to see him recollects for a passing stranger—some 126 years later! Parson Clark also used to translate some of the Latin text of Pigafetta's 16th century book *Regnum Congo* for the same local man, a simple farmer who had come to own a copy of it and was fascinated by the woodcut drawing of a cannibal butcher-shop. Apparently it was said when Parson Clark mysteriously disappeared, that he must have drowned in the pond; but we know better.

CLARK'S CORNERS (COS): Fictitious Massachusetts village, which Ammi Pierce visits in his horse-drawn sleigh during the winter of 1882–83. On his way home, he sees a strange rabbit leaping near the Gardner farm. Potter's general store in Clark's Corners is a local gathering-place, and in March, 1883, there is much talk there about the thing that Stephen Rice had seen.

CLAVE, SIR JOHN (RW): At some unstated date between the late 13th and early 17th centuries, a knight by this name was riding after dark through a lonely field near Exham Priory, when his horse trod upon some "floundering, squealing white thing." This story adds to the evil reputation of the de la Poers' family seat. At the end of the tale, we understand that the "white thing" must have been one of the de la Poer family's dehumanized, quadrupedal, human cattle, bred and raised underground for eventual consumption, and which had somehow managed to escape from the caverns under Exham Priory, only to flounder and squeal uncomprehendingly in the outside world it had never known.

CLEIS (MB): In a dream the narrator seems to perceive the final days of the ancient Greek community that once occupied the site of the bog, when he sees a pestilential epidemic, "and then a frightful avalanche of wooded slopes that covered the dead bodies in the streets and left unburied only the temple of Artemis on the high peak, where the aged moon-priestess Cleis lay cold and silent with a crown of ivory on her silver head."

Artemis was the Greek goddess of the moon and the hunt; her Roman counterpart was Diana the Huntress. The only famous "Cleis" in classical Greek literature is the daughter of the brilliant poet Sappho (c. 613–570 B.C.). She is mentioned in a famous poem which HPL may well have read, which Sappho wrote to, or about her daughter:

> *Don't ask me what to wear*
> *I have no embroidered*
> *headband from Sardis to*
> *give you, Cleis, such as*
> *I wore*
>
> *and my mother*
> *always said that in her*
> *day a purple ribbon*
> *looped in the hair was thought*
> *to be high style indeed*
>
> *but we were dark: a girl*
> *whose hair is yellower than*
> *torchlight should wear no*
> *headdress but fresh flowers*

COCIDIUS, SYLVANUS (CDW): A Renaissance-era European scholar, the author of a book owned by Joseph Curwen in the 18th century. His name also turns up in a very sinister way in a letter from Simon/Jedediah Orne to Joseph Curwen, circa 1770–71: "I am desirous you will

Acquaint me with what yᵉ Blacke Man learnt from Sylvanus Cocidius in yᵉ Vault, under yᵉ Roman Wall..."

COLD SPRING GLEN (DH): A deep, thickly-forested ravine outside of Dunwich village, where the Horror takes refuge after it breaks out of the Whateley barn. Five officers of the Massachusetts state police venture into the glen in pursuit of the unknown, against advice from the local people, and are not seen again. In an earlier part of the tale, Sally Sawyer tells Mrs. Corey, in old-time Yankee dialect: "I allus [always] says Col' Spring Glen ain't no healthy nor decent place. The whippoorwills [a type of songbird] an' fireflies there never did act like they was creaters o' Gawd [creatures of God], an' they's them as says ye kin [there are those who say you can] hear strange things a-rushin' and a-talkin' in the air down there ef [if] ye stand in the right place, atween [between] the rock falls an' Bear's Den."

This glen is a close fictional copy of a ravine outside North New Salem, Massachusetts, near the town of Athol. There is a "rock falls," and there is a so-called Bear's Den, a natural opening in the ravine's side that really becomes too narrow to proceed into after several feet, but which hints at "cyclopean gulfs"—as HPL might have written—further within. On his visit to this spot, HPL noted that the bears which might possibly live in the Bear's Den were less to be feared than what might come out from the deeper recesses to eat the bears! Caves within caves were indeed a Lovecraftian favorite.

COLLEGE STREET (HD): In this tale, Robert Blake moves into an apartment which is described in such a way as to make it clear that HPL was describing his own home. This was in an old house at 66 College Street in Providence, which had been converted to rental units. The so-called "Lewis Mumford House" was built in 1825, and by May, 1933, when HPL moved in, it was the property of Brown University. At that time the house still stood in its original location next to the John Hay Library; in 1959 it was moved several blocks to 65 Prospect Street, where it still stands. Lovecraft and his mother's sister Aunt Annie Gamwell shared a flat of five large rooms on the upper floor. HPL was overjoyed to be living in an early 19th century house; not quite colonial-era, but as close to it as he would ever get. He dwelt here until March 10, 1937, when he went to the hospital where he would die of intestinal cancer.

COLLINS, CAPTAIN (CC): Captain of the *Emma*, who is mortally wounded during the sea battle with the crew of the *Alert* on March 22, 1925. Second Mate Johansen takes command of the survivors, as the first mate was also killed in action. The fight, and the discovery of R'lyeh, take place in an exceptionally empty sector of the South Pacific Ocean, approximately 2000 miles west of Wellington Island, Chile, the nearest landfall in that direction.

COLOUR, THE (COS): "What it is, God only knows. In terms of matter I suppose the thing...would be called a gas, but this gas obeyed laws that are not of our cosmos. It was just a colour out of space—a frightful messenger from unformed realms of infinity beyond all Nature as we know it; from realms whose mere existence stuns the brain and numbs us with the black extra-cosmic gulfs it throws open before our frenzied eyes." Arriving in a meteorite that lands on Nahum Gardner's beautiful farm in March, 1882, the "colour" takes up residence in the farmyard well, and permeates soil, plants, trees, animals and eventually the human residents of the farm, whom it devours by a slow, sucking, "burning" process that reduces them to crumbling ashes, the "grey brittle death." By this means, it apparently gathers enough reserves of energy to launch itself back into space, in November, 1883. If a gas, it behaved like a gas with intelligence. In fact, the scientists and the narrator have no words for whatever it was: "it was only by analogy that they called it a colour at all." Writing in 1933, HPL stated that *The Colour Out of Space* was personally his most favorite of all his tales.

COLUMBIA (SOI): One of three ships belonging to Captain Obed Marsh of Innsmouth, circa 1840; it is a merchant vessel in the long-range East India and Pacific trade, at a time when such voyages lasted close to a year, round trip.

COMMERCIAL HOUSE (HW): Possibly a hotel that catered to visiting businessmen; itinerant salesmen in the 19th century were often called "commercial travelers." Be it whatever it was, Commercial House in Arkham had a bar, where Herbert West, his comrade, and some other medical students spent the afternoon drinking on August 15, 1904, after Dr. Halsey's public funeral.

COMMORIOM MYTH-CYCLE (WD, MM): A mythology of the prehistoric land of "Hyperborea," a mythology which was purportedly "preserved by the Atlantean high-priest Klarkash-Ton" which was HPL's nickname for his pen-friend and fantasy-writing colleague Clark Ashton Smith, of Auburn, California. Commoriom is a city mentioned in Smith's fantasy-story *The Tale of Satampra Zeiros*; it is mentioned in *At the Mountains of Madness*.

CONSTANTINE (MM): Professor Dyer compares the removal of fine old art from the Antarctic surface city of the Old Ones to their new underwater city to "the policy of Constantine the Great [who] in a similar age of decline, stripped Greece and Asia of their finest art to give his new Byzantine capital greater splendours than its own people could create." Constantine I, known as the Great (288?–337 A.D.), a Roman emperor, transferred the capital of the Empire to the older Greek city of Byzantium, which was renamed Constantinople (modern Istanbul) in 330.

CONE MOUNTAIN (LF): A small fictitious mountain in the Catskills, near which lies the shabby hamlet of the seventy-five mountain-dwelling squatters who were slaughtered by some unknown and unbelievably brutal attackers one summer night in 1921.

COPP'S HILL BURYING GROUND (PM): One of Boston's oldest cemeteries (the oldest legible epitaph dates from 1625, which predates the founding of the city itself), currently a stop on the "Freedom Trail" urban walking tour. Cotton Mather is buried here. It is a favorite background for the ghoul-paintings of Richard Upton Pickman.

COREY, BENIJAH (SK): The elderly hired man at Christopher Carter's farm outside of Arkham. He wears peculiar "heel-less" boots, and speaks in a thick, old-fashioned Yankee dialect ("Dun't ye know yer Aunt Marthy's all a-fidget over yer bein' off arter dark?"). He finds young Randolph Carter alone in the woods on an autumn evening in 1883, and hurries him back to the safety of the Carter farm, where the child is late for dinner. He dies circa 1898 when Randolph Carter is a young man. However, his distinctive boot prints are allegedly seen again on the ground during the 1928 search for the missing Randolph Carter near the old farm, although Benijah was thirty years dead by then. This stolid countryman's name probably comes from those of Benejah Place, a farmer who owned a house across the road from the house where HPL stayed during a 1926 visit to his ancestral area of Foster, Rhode Island, and of Emma Corey Phillips, one of HPL's maternal-side relatives in the same area. ("Benijah" itself is the name of an obscure Israelite in the Old Testament; part of New England's Puritan heritage was expressed in the frequent use of Old Testament Hebrew names for boys and girls.)

COREY, GEORGE (DH): Dunwich farmer; he owns a farm between Cold Spring Glen and the village. Luther Brown is his hired boy and cowherd.

COREY, HANNAH (SK): Presumably the wife of Benijah Corey; she works as the cook at the Christopher Carter farm in the 1880s. Hannah was an extremely common woman's name in old-time New England.

COREY, MRS. (DH): Wife of George Corey, and a local gossip on the party-line telephone. (From the earliest days of private telephone service, and lasting until the late 20th century in some very rural areas, a "party line" was a single telephone line shared by a number of subscribers in a less-populated area, for example along one country road. Distinct numbers or lengths of rings would identify which household an incoming call was meant for. One feature of a party line was that any subscriber could pick up his own telephone and listen, or cut into, whatever conversation someone else was already having, although good etiquette usually prevented this. Many of the Dunwichers hear the doom that came to the Seth Bishop farm over a party line.) She hears an excited story from young Luther Brown in September, 1928, and has a conversation with Sally Sawyer about it; later, she discusses events with Zebulon Whateley, before the Seth Bishop farm is annihilated by the Horror.

COREY, WESLEY (DH): One of the Dunwich men who accompany Dr. Armitage and the other Miskatonic University professors. He observes part of the climactic confrontation on Sentinel Hill, from a safe distance, through a telescope.

CORNWALL (CE, DQ): A region roughly comprising England's southwest peninsula. Cornwall is noted for a rocky, windswept beauty, and green fields watered by rains from the Atlantic, rather like the New England coastline on the other side of the ocean. In *Celephaïs* it is suggested that the man who became King Kuranes was, in his earth-life, a native of Innsmouth, Cornwall (a fictitious place) and dwelt as a boy in a Cornish castle, "Trevor Towers"—now owned by a millionaire brewer. In *The Dream Quest of Unknown Kadath*, Randolph Carter calls on King Kuranes at the elaborate reproduction of a Cornish estate that Kuranes has constructed outside of Celephaïs, complete down to Dreamland servants whom he has uniformed like an English household staff and taught to speak English with Cornish accents.

CORONA BOREALIS (HY): The narrator's friend, after one particular night, is afraid to be outside at night; and if he is, "he would often glance furtively at the sky as if hunted by some monstrous thing therein."

> He did not always glance at the same place in the sky—it seemed to be a different place at different times. On spring evenings it would be low in the northeast. In the summer it would be nearly overhead. In the autumn it would be in the northwest. In winter it would be in the east, but mostly in the small hours of the morning. Midwinter evenings seemed the least dreadful to him. Only after two years did I connect this fear with anything in particular; but then I began to see that he must be looking at a special spot on the celestial vault whose position at different times corresponded to the direction of his glance—a spot roughly marked by the constellation Corona Borealis.

age of decline, stripped Greece and Asia of their finest art to give his new Byzantine capital greater splendours than its own people could create." Constantine I, known as the Great (288?–337 A.D.), a Roman emperor, transferred the capital of the Empire to the older Greek city of Byzantium, which was renamed Constantinople (modern Istanbul) in 330.

CONE MOUNTAIN (LF): A small fictitious mountain in the Catskills, near which lies the shabby hamlet of the seventy-five mountain-dwelling squatters who were slaughtered by some unknown and unbelievably brutal attackers one summer night in 1921.

COPP'S HILL BURYING GROUND (PM): One of Boston's oldest cemeteries (the oldest legible epitaph dates from 1625, which predates the founding of the city itself), currently a stop on the "Freedom Trail" urban walking tour. Cotton Mather is buried here. It is a favorite background for the ghoul-paintings of Richard Upton Pickman.

COREY, BENIJAH (SK): The elderly hired man at Christopher Carter's farm outside of Arkham. He wears peculiar "heel-less" boots, and speaks in a thick, old-fashioned Yankee dialect ("Dun't ye know yer Aunt Marthy's all a-fidget over yer bein' off arter dark?"). He finds young Randolph Carter alone in the woods on an autumn evening in 1883, and hurries him back to the safety of the Carter farm, where the child is late for dinner. He dies circa 1898 when Randolph Carter is a young man. However, his distinctive boot prints are allegedly seen again on the ground during the 1928 search for the missing Randolph Carter near the old farm, although Benijah was thirty years dead by then. This stolid countryman's name probably comes from those of Benejah Place, a farmer who owned a house across the road from the house where HPL stayed during a 1926 visit to his ancestral area of Foster, Rhode Island, and of Emma Corey Phillips, one of HPL's maternal-side relatives in the same area. ("Benijah" itself is the name of an obscure Israelite in the Old Testament; part of New England's Puritan heritage was expressed in the frequent use of Old Testament Hebrew names for boys and girls.)

COREY, GEORGE (DH): Dunwich farmer; he owns a farm between Cold Spring Glen and the village. Luther Brown is his hired boy and cowherd.

COREY, HANNAH (SK): Presumably the wife of Benijah Corey; she works as the cook at the Christopher Carter farm in the 1880s. Hannah was an extremely common woman's name in old-time New England.

COREY, MRS. (DH): Wife of George Corey, and a local gossip on the party-line telephone. (From the earliest days of private telephone service, occasionally make social calls on the Derbys there, but less and less frequently. In the months after Upton drives Edward Derby home from Chesuncook, Maine, passers-by report the sound of someone sobbing from inside the house. Following Asenath's disappearance, Edward continues to live in the house until he is committed to Arkham Sanitarium. On the climactic night of the tale, Upton receives a mysterious phone call, later traced to the Crowninshield place. Subsequently investigators find "upheaval in a remote cellar storeroom," tracks, loose dirt, a hastily-ransacked wardrobe cabinet, clumsily-handled personal stationery, and a terrible stench over all. "The Crowninshield place" of this tale has been identified with the real "Crowninshield-Bentley House," in Salem, Massachusetts, a three-story colonial manse built in 1727 and now the property of the Peabody Essex Museum (formerly the Essex Institute), a preserver of local history.

CRYPTOGRAPHERS OF DUNWICH (DH): While trying to decipher the journal of the late Wilbur Whateley in August, 1928, Dr. Armitage, the learned librarian of Miskatonic University:

> ...fortified himself with the massed lore of cryptography; drawing upon the fullest resources of his own library, and wading night after night amidst the arcana of Trithemius' *Poligraphia*, Giambattista Porta's *De Furtivis Literarum Notis*, De Vigénère's *Traité des Chiffres*, Falconer's *Cryptomenysis Patefacta*, Davys' and Thicknesse's eighteenth-century treatises, and such fairly modern authorities as Blair, von Marten, and Klüber's *Kryptografik*.

This most impressive display of knowledge concerning centuries-old European technical writings on cryptography (from the Greek word for "hidden writing," the science of making and breaking encoded communications) can best be explained by quoting from the same source where HPL presumably borrowed it himself, namely, the "Cryptography" entry in an early 20th century edition of the *Encyclopedia Britannica*:

> John Trithemius (d. 1516), the first abbot of Spanheim, was the first important writer on cryptography. His *Polygraphia*, published in 1518, has passed through many editions, and has supplied the basis upon which subsequent writers have worked.... The next treatises of importance were those of Giovanni Battista della Porta, the Neapolitan mathematician, who wrote *De Furtivis litterarum notis*, 1563; and of Blaise de Vigénère, whose *Traité des Chiffres* appeared in Paris, 1587. Writers on the subject are John Falconer (*Cryptomenesis Patefacta*), 1685; John Davys (*An Essay on the Art of Deciphering*), 1737; Philip Thicknesse (*A Treatise on the Art of Decyphering and of Writing in Cypher*), 1772; William Blair (the writer of the comprehensive article "Cipher" in Rees's Cyclopedia), 1819; and G. von Marten (*Cours Diplomatique*), 1801 (a fourth edition of which appeared in 1851). Perhaps the best modern work on this subject is the

Kryptografik of J.L. Klüber (Tübingen, 1809) who was drawn into the investigation by inclination and official circumstances. In this work the different methods of cryptography are classified.

CTHULHU (CC, SOI, WD, DH, MM): A leading entity of the Old Ones who once ruled the earth, long ages ago. The name is properly pronounced *Khlul-hloo* or *Tluh-luh*, with a guttural intonation, according to HPL; but as he pointed out at the same time, even these are only attempts to pronounce a word that was never intended for human vocal organs:

> ...the word is supposed to represent a fumbling human attempt to catch the phonetics of an *absolutely non-human word.* The name of the hellish entity was invented by beings whose vocal organs were not like man's, hence it has no relation to the human speech equipment. The syllables were determined by a physiological equipment wholly unlike ours, *hence could never be uttered perfectly by human throats....* The actual sound—as nearly as human organs could imitate it or human letters record it—may be taken as something like *Khlul'-hloo*, with the first syllable pronounced gutturally and very thickly. The *u* is about like that in *full*; and the first syllable is not unlike *klul* in sound, hence the *h* represents the guttural thickness.

Cthulhu was a priest at the city of R'lyeh, which sank beneath the Pacific Ocean millions upon millions of years ago. His appearance, as seen by a few humans in their dreams, is awesome and fear-inspiring. Statues based on such dreams depict something as large as a tall building, "of vaguely anthropoid outline, but with an octopus-like head whose face was a mass of feelers, a scaly, rubbery-looking body, prodigious claws on hind and fore feet, and long, narrow wings behind.... [He is somehow] instinct with a fearsome and unnatural malignancy, [and] of a somewhat bloated corpulence."

A close-up view of Cthulhu on R'lyeh causes two sturdy sailors to drop dead of sheer fright. The gigantic door to Cthulhu's house opens, then "...It lumbered slobberingly into sight and gropingly squeezed Its gelatinous green immensity through the black doorway... The Thing cannot be described.... A mountain walked or stumbled.... The Thing of the idols, the green, sticky spawn of the stars...." Later, when Cthulhu is "greasily" swimming in the ocean water and the escaping *Alert* steams straight through the monster's "awful squid-head with writhing feelers," seeming to split and explode it like a foul puff-ball (with "a bursting as of an exploding bladder, a slushy nastiness as of a cloven sunfish, a stench as of a thousand unopened graves, and a sound that the chronicler would not put on paper"), the scattered debris merely recombines itself in its original form.

In *The Call of Cthulhu* it is said that he is one of the Great Old Ones that came to earth from somewhere else in the universe, unimaginable eons ago. In a dazzling feat of conception, HPL explained their long absence and peacefulness thus:

> [They] were not composed of flesh and blood. They had shape...but that shape was not made of matter. When the stars were right, They could plunge from world to world through the sky, but when the stars were wrong, They could not live. But although They no longer lived, They would never really die. They all lay in stone houses in Their great city of R'lyeh, preserved by the spells of the mighty Cthulhu for a glorious resurrection when the stars and the earth might once more be ready for them. But at that time some force from outside must serve to liberate Their bodies. The spells that preserved them intact likewise prevented Them from making an initial move, and They could only lie awake in the dark and think whilst uncounted millions of years rolled by. They knew all that was occurring in the universe, for Their mode of speech was transmitted thought. Even now they talked in their tombs. When...the first men came [to exist], the Great Old Ones spoke to the sensitive among them by the medium of their dreams; for only thus could Their language reach the fleshly minds of mammals.

HPL's Cthulhu probably owes something to *The Kraken*, a short poem by Alfred, Lord Tennyson (1809–92). In lines which HPL had certainly read, Tennyson wrote of the Kraken, a mythical, sleeping sea-monster from Norwegian folklore:

> *Below the waters of the upper deep,*
> *Far, far, beneath in the abysmal sea,*
> *His ancient, dreamless, uninvaded sleep*
> *The Kraken sleepeth; faintest sunlights flee*
> *About his shadowy sides; above him swell*
> *Huge sponges of millennial growth and height;*
> *And far away into the sickly light*
> *From many a wondrous grot and secret cell*
> *Unnumber'd and enormous polypi*
> *Winnow with giant arms the slumbering green.*
> *Thus he has lain for ages, and will lie,*
> *Battening upon huge sea-worms in his sleep,*
> *Until the latter fire shall heat the deep;*
> *Then once by men and angels to be seen,*
> *In roaring he will rise and on the surface die.*

In *At the Mountains of Madness*, readers learn a little more about Cthulhu's origins. In this story, it is suggested from wall-murals that "a land race of beings shaped like octopi and probably corresponding to the...spawn of Cthulhu" came to Earth from out of the cosmos, and began a terrible war with the winged, star-headed Old Ones. Eventually there was peace, with the lands then in the middle of the Pacific Ocean going to the invaders. "Then suddenly the lands of the Pacific sank again, taking with them the frightful stone city of R'lyeh and all the cosmic octopi...."

The Great Old Ones are also mentioned in *The Dunwich Horror*, actually in a long passage mostly about Yog-Sothoth, in the *Necronomicon*. "*Great* Cthulhu *is Their cousin, yet he can spy Them only dimly.*"

CTHULHU CULT (CC, SOI): They are the worshippers of great Cthulhu. In the legends which old Castro heard from the cult's leaders in the mountains of China, and later recounts to the New Orleans police detectives, some of the earliest of men founded the cult of the Great Old Ones "around small idols which the Great Ones showed them," idols which had originally come from outer space and are made from no mineral known on Earth. Owing to unfavorable star-alignments, the Great Old Ones stopped "living," going into suspended animation in their stone houses at R'lyeh. But they spoke to men through dreams until R'lyeh sank beneath the ocean, for the deep ocean waters are the one medium "through which not even thought can pass." But the cult preserves the memories. When the stars are right again, the cult priests will free Cthulhu from his tomb, and he will liberate the other Great Old Ones.

> The time would be easy to know, for then mankind would have become as the Great Old Ones; free and wild and beyond good and evil, with laws and morals thrown aside and all men shouting and killing and reveling in joy. Then the liberated Old Ones would teach them new ways to shout and kill and enjoy themselves, and all the earth would flame with a holocaust of ecstasy and freedom.

The cult is almost unknown outside of its own membership, who seem to be drawn mostly from poor and non-white outcasts—it must be said, the kind of people that HPL would predictably associate with an orgiastic blood-cult dedicated to the destruction of the world as we know it. It exists in widely scattered places, such as western Greenland, Louisiana swamps, a seaport in New Zealand. Castro saw and spoke with cult leaders in China, but personally believed the center of the cult to be in an Arabian lost city called Irem.

The cultists chant some words once taught to their predecessors by the Great Old Ones, in their language:

Ph'nglui mglw'nafh Cthulhu R'lyeh wgah'nagl fhtagn

Or in English:

In his house at R'lyeh dead Cthulhu waits dreaming.

The cultists also refer to a celebrated couplet in the *Necronomicon* of Abdul Alhazred: "That is not dead which can eternal lie/And with strange eons even death may die." The cult worships in orgiastic celebrations, around statuettes of Cthulhu, celebrations which can include the human sacrifice of non-members. Its reach is long and deadly: one after another, Professor George G. Angell, the sailor Johansen, and Angell's executor Francis W. Thurston, outsiders who know too much, are all marked to die: Angell, "after being jostled by a nautical-looking negro" in the streets of Providence; Johansen, after a bundle of papers falls from an attic window in Oslo, Norway, and knocks him down, and "two Lascar sailors" help him to his feet. And as Thurston writes, "I know too much, and the cult still lives."

In *The Shadow Over Innsmouth*, old Zadok Allen repeats the Cthulhu chant, and later the narrator predicts that one day the Deep Ones would rise again "for the tribute Cthulhu craved."

CULTES DES GOULES (HD, SOT): A fictitious book whose French-language title means "Ghoul Cults," purportedly written by a French aristocrat called the Comte d'Erlette. The title was invented by HPL's young pen-friend and fellow-writer Robert Bloch. In *The Haunter of the Dark*, Robert Blake finds a copy in a trove of "mildewed, disintegrating books" on a shelf in a side room of the old abandoned Starry Wisdom church. In *The Shadow Out of Time*, *Cultes des Goules* is among the books that the Great Race member inhabiting Professor Peaslee's body studies during 1908–13, and the real Professor Peaslee consults the very same volume in 1917–18, finding that his alter-ego had made marginal notes in perfect French.

CUNNINGHAM, INSPECTOR (CDW): Providence police detective assigned to investigate the cases of grave-robbery at North Burial Ground.

CURWEN, JOSEPH (CDW): Alchemist, necromancer: "a very astonishing, enigmatic, and obscurely horrible individual," as the narrator introduces him. He was born on February 28, 1662–63 (old style), at Salem Village, Massachusetts. (HPL pointedly notes that "the Curwens or Corwins of Salem needed no introduction in New England"; an historical Jonathan Corwin was one of the magistrates who rode over from Salem to Salem Village on March 1, 1692, to open up the Salem witchcraft investigations.) At 15, Curwen runs away to sea and stays away for nine years, from 1678–87, living in England for a time and making at least two voyages to Asia. He returns to the Massachusetts colony with

"English" (therefore superior to the local norm) manners and mode of dress, settles in Salem, and apparently joins the coven of Salem witches, receiving the "Devil's Mark" from a "Mr. G.B." at a coven meeting, along with his friend Simon Orne.

In March, 1692 (at the time the witchcraft investigations and trials were beginning), he leaves Salem and moves to Providence in the Rhode Island colony, where he becomes a "freeman of the city"—in other words, a legally-accepted permanent resident, a citizen. He builds a house for himself on Stampers' Hill, with a windowless attic, and goes into business as a merchant, purchasing his own wharf near Mile-End Cove. He donates to a fund to rebuild the Great Bridge in 1713, and helps financially to establish and build the Congregational Church in 1723. In the same era he purchases a farm on Pawtuxet Road, several miles outside of town, in which he dwells during the summer and which he visits often during the rest of the year.

As glimpsed by a visitor in 1746, his unique book-collection in Providence includes the Greek, Roman, and English classics, as well as "a remarkable battery of philosophical, mathematical, and scientific works including Paracelsus, Agricola, Van Helmont, Sylvius, Glauber, Boyle, Boerhaave, Becher, and Stahl." At the Pawtuxet Road farm, he keeps a host of alchemical and theological standard works, and "all the cabbalists [experts in the Kaballah or Hebrew mystical works], daemonologists, and magicians known to man," including works of Hermes Trismegistus, the *Turba Philosophorum*, Geber's *Liber Investigationis*, Artephius' *Key of Wisdom*, the Zohar, works of St. Albertus Magnus, Raymond Lully's *Ars Magna et Ultima*, Roger Bacon's *Thesaurus Chemicus*, Fludd's *Clavis Alchimiae*, Trithemius' *De Lapide Philosophico*, the *Necronomicon*, and works of Borellus.

Over the course of unnaturally long years in business as an importing and exporting merchant in Providence, Curwen obtains "a virtual monopoly of...trade in saltpetre, black pepper, and cinnamon," all highly-lucrative imported goods in that time and place. He also imports quantities of brassware, indigo (a substance used for making blue dye), cotton, woolen items, salt, rigging (ropes for sailing ships), iron, paper, and English manufactured goods. In return he is a major exporter of colony products, such as rum, cheese, horses, and candles. As part of this immense business he naturally owns his own fleet of cargo ships. He keeps his warehouse on Doubloon Street near the harbor, employing only white men as desk clerks and ship officers, but ever-shifting crews of "mongrels" from such West Indies ports as Martinique, St. Eustatius, Havana, and Port Royal. While on shore leave in Providence, it sometimes happens that sailors sent on special errands for Curwen disappear, never to be seen again; and he begins to have an increasingly difficult time finding crews for his ships. In 1758 when two English army regiments were stationed in Providence, a number of individual soldiers also disappear forever, not long after being seen in conversation with Curwen. Up until 1766 he imports large numbers of black slaves, who also seem to vanish without a trace like the sailors and the soldiers.

By 1760, Curwen is in his 68th year in Providence, and is known to be almost a century old, although somehow looking like a man of about 35 years. This phenomenon, as well as the other facts whispered about him, have made him the subject of much fear, suspicion, and hatred, despite his great wealth and his steady donations to civic and charitable causes. For example, in 1760 alone he contributes to the rebuilding of the Colony House and (as in 1713!) the Great Bridge, replaces many books that had burned in the public library fire; and donates money toward the paving of Market Parade and Town Street. A year later, in 1761, he has his old house on Stampers' Hill torn down, and builds a new and elegant one on the same site; it is still standing in the 1920s when Charles Dexter Ward visits it.

On March 3, 1763, he marries Miss Eliza Tillinghast, of Providence, the socially well-connected, 18-year-old daughter of one of his sea captains, a man without much money who is subject to Curwen's will. To both her own and the town's considerable surprise, the 100-year-old husband with the sinister reputation treats her "with extreme graciousness and consideration" after they have become man and wife. (One comes to understand that this was because of his great concern that she should be healthy and fertile so as to bear him offspring and descendants.) Their daughter Ann is duly born on May 7, 1765, and christened at King's Church; she will be one of Charles Dexter Ward's ancestors. In the same year, he has a portrait of himself painted by the artist Cosmo Alexander, on a wall-panel in the library of the Stampers' Hill home, where Charles Dexter Ward will find it about 160 years later. His civic life continues with an eloquent speech at Hetcher's Hall in 1765, against the proposed division of Providence into multiple separate communities.

In 1766–67, he ceases to import any more of those large quantities of black slaves whose apparent vanishment was such an enduring source of speculation in Providence. Readers come to understand that he no longer needs "test subjects" for his necromancy project. Instead, he begins to receive boxes and cases full of unknown contents, dropped off by ships that put in at Namquit Point (not in the Providence harbor), and for some reason do their work by night, with few if any outside witnesses. He comes to spend every possible free moment at the Pawtuxet Road place, and secret observers note sounds like interrogations, whiplashes and screams coming from within the walls. Beginning in July, 1766, more-over, he begins to astonish people by his knowledge of personal information that "only their long-dead ancestors would seem able to impart." Their long-dead ancestors are, in fact, being forced to do so.

On Friday, April 12, 1771, a raiding party organized by a secret committee of leading Providence citizens storms the Pawtuxet Road farmhouse, destroys it, and "kills" Joseph Curwen, who is buried in North Burial Ground and becomes a person who is never mentioned. He is revived on Good Friday, April 15, 1927 (after all, his initials are "J.C."!), by his great-great-great-grandson Charles Dexter Ward, whose own body he eventually takes over. Dr. Marinus B. Willett destroys him for good on Friday, April 13, 1928, by repeating the "Descending Node" invocation of the Dragon's Tail.

Curwen's evil inspiration came from a passage allegedly in the writings of the French alchemist Borellus (actually cribbed—and slightly enhanced—from Cotton Mather's mammoth tome *Magnalia Christi Americana*):

> The essential Saltes of Animals may be so prepared and preserved, that an ingenious Man may have the whole Ark of Noah in his own Studie, and raise the fine Shape of an Animal out of its Ashes at his Pleasure, and by the lyke Method from the essential Saltes of humane Dust, a Philosopher may, without any criminal Necromancy, call up the shape of any dead Ancestour from the Dust whereinto his Bodie has been incinerated.

From this concept, HPL conceived of a scheme in which evil men "were robbing the tombs of all the ages, including those of the world's wisest and greatest men," and "bartering illustrious bones with the calm calculativeness of schoolboys swapping books…" They also traffic with entities from "Outside," including Yog-Sothoth.

CYBELE (RW): Greco-Roman goddess, identified with *Magna Mater*, the Great Mother, and with wild mystery celebrations akin to the orgies of Dionysus. Exham Priory is said to have been a grand temple of Cybele in Roman-British times, thronged with worshippers and presided over by a Phrygian priest (from the region of Phrygia in Asia Minor, now southern Turkey, but then a part of the Roman Empire). As HPL notes, Cybele's worship became mixed with that of the Asiatic goddess Atys in the time of the Empire.

CYDATHRIA (QI, DCS): A country in the vicinity of Sarnath; its groves supply nuts and spices. Iranon visits the cities of Cydathria after leaving Oonai.

CYGNUS and DENEB (COS): Stars which are close enough to Earth to be visible to the naked eye. The Colour, or most of it, seems to depart in their general direction during a night in early November, 1883.

CZANEK, JOE (TOM): One of the three robbers who pay a call on the Terrible Old Man one night in his cottage in Water Street, Kingsport. Czanek is the driver of the getaway car, in which he waits on Ship Street by the back gate of the house. Described as "more than ordinarily tender-hearted," Czanek tells his cohorts Ricci and Silva not to be too hard on the old man while they rob his house. Therefore he is sad to hear the awful screams coming from inside the house as he continues to wait. Seeing a figure appear at the back gate, Czanek is disconcerted to see the Terrible Old Man, "smiling hideously"; his last recorded thought is surprise that the T.O.M.'s eyes are a remarkable yellow color. Presumably Czanek's body was one of the three unidentified corpses, slashed and mangled as if by many men, that the tide later washes up on the shore near Kingsport.

CZANEK, MARY (DWH): She is a neighbor of the Arkham laundry-worker Anastasia Wolejko. Afraid that her baby will be kidnapped for a human sacrifice on Walpurgis-night, Anastasia asks Mary to stay in the same room with it, but Mary is too frightened to do so. Like Anastasia Wolejko's, Mary Czanek's name, along with her evident social class, mark her as one of the masses of working-class immigrants from Central and Eastern Europe who flocked into the cities of New England during the late 19th and early 20th centuries, to the great distress of HPL and many other status-conscious descendants of earlier English settlers.

D

DAEMONOLATREIA (TF, DH): An old book on demonology and witchcraft written by a certain Remigius, which the narrator spots in the Kingsport house he visits on Yule eve. Dr. Armitage consults it while figuring out what to do about the Dunwich Horror. "Remigius," or Nicolas Remy, was a judge and privy counselor in the duchy of Lorraine (now a part of France), and his book was first published in Latin in the French city of Lyon in 1595; a German edition followed not many years later. But it had to wait until 1930 to appear in an English translation, under the disturbing title: *Demonolatry: Drawn from the Capital Trials of 900 Persons, More or Less, Who Within the Last Fifteen Years Have in Lorraine Paid the Penalty of Death for the Crime of Witchcraft.*

DAGON (DA, SOI): In the Bible, Dagon is referred to as a god worshipped by the Philistines (the polytheistic neighbors and enemies of the Hebrews during one phase of the long history of ancient Israel) in the form of a stone idol (*See* Judges 16:23, 1 Samuel 5:2). Archaeology has revealed that the ancient Mesopotamians and Assyrians also worshipped Dagon among other gods. His attributes nonetheless remain somewhat uncertain, although he may have been associated with storms. HPL conceived of him as "the Fish-God" and invested Dagon with the horror that he felt for seafood and all things piscine. In *Dagon*, the narrator adrift in a small open boat runs aground on land newly raised from the depths of the Pacific Ocean—a concept that seems to have swelled into R'lyeh in later tales—and finds an obelisk carved with images of fish-men; he then sees a colossal fish-man crawling up from the watery depths, and worshipping or adoring the obelisk!

In Innsmouth, it is the Deep Ones and Captain Obed Marsh who institute the worship of "deathless Father Dagon." The children of physical unions between humans and Deep Ones will never die, it is promised, but will "go back to the Mother Hydra and Father Dagon what we all come from onct [once]."

For what it is worth, a biblical reference work current in HPL's young years, *Easton's Bible Dictionary* (1897), stated that Dagon was "the fish-god, the national god of the Philistines. This idol had the body of a fish with the head and hands of a man. It was an Assyrio-Babylonian deity, the worship of which was introduced among the Philistines through

137

Chaldea. The most famous of the temples of Dagon were at Gaza and Ashdod."

DAGON, ESOTERIC ORDER OF (SOI): A secretive cult established by Captain Obed Marsh in Innsmouth, during the early 1840s, and still operating as the town religion in the 1920s. Its headquarters, at least in its early days, was in the former Masonic Hall on New Church Green (the description of this building is based on the American Legion Hall in Gloucester, Massachusetts), which was purchased from the "Calvary Commandery," a higher-level organization in Freemasonry. Described by one outsider to another as "a debased, quasi-pagan thing," the Order is feared by the uninformed as a devil-worship cult of some kind. In fact, the Esoteric Order of Dagon "formalizes" the worship of Deep Ones and Dagon, with the membership providing human sacrifices in exchange for gold and good fishing. All the survivors of the 1846 *coup d'etat* and municipal massacre have to take the first Oath of Dagon, in order to continue surviving; there are second and third oaths, linked to higher status and privileges (Zadok Allen, having once taken the second Oath of Dagon, can't be killed unless a jury finds him guilty of giving away secrets), but they are said to be horrid.

DAIKOS (PO): A city in ancient Lomar. Its fall to the invading Inutos causes a crisis of survival in the narrator's city, Olathoë.

DAMASCIUS (NC): In the darkness of the vaults beneath the Nameless City, the narrator is inspired to think of "paragraphs from the apocryphal nightmares of Damascius."

The Greek Neo-Platonist philosopher Damascius (480–550?) was the last head of the Academy, the Athenian school of philosophy founded by Plato in the 4th century B.C. In his book, *Problems and Solutions About the First Principles*, Damascius urged a wide-ranging mysticism to attain an understanding of the "first principle"—the divine reality—that unaided human reason could never achieve. His book includes much of what have been called "theosophical fantasies." Historically he is considered to have set the stage for the growth of Christian mysticism, although he personally remained a pagan.

"DANIELS" (MM): A phantom member of the Miskatonic University Expedition, only mentioned as a passenger on the exploration flight of January 6, 1931. Possibly a textual error for Danforth, or even Atwood.

DANFORTH (MM): Graduate student, member of the Miskatonic University Expedition, airplane pilot. Described by Professor Dyer as "brilliant," Danforth is a great reader of "fantastic" literature, including the works of Edgar Allan Poe. He has even read the copy of the *Necro-*

nomicon which is kept sequestered in the Miskatonic University library. He compares Mount Erebus in Antarctica to Poe's "Yaanek." Danforth is apparently on the flight over the South Pole on January 6, 1931, and he is also on the rescue flight to the Lake-Atwood camp on January 25. The next day, he joins Professor Dyer on a scouting flight across the nearby mountain range, and the exploration of the deserted, billion-year-old city they find on the other side. At the end of their quest, he sees a shoggoth and becomes "totally unstrung," hysterically chanting the names of stations on the Boston-Cambridge train line as if to compare the shoggoth to an oncoming subway train. He escapes with Professor Dyer and returns to the United States with the Expedition's other survivors.

Danforth, who was not flying the plane as he and Professor Dyer make their escape, had a chance to survey the scenery: "the terrible receding city, the cave-riddled, cube-barnacled peaks" and other suggestive sights, and glimpsed "one final horror" which may or may not have been a mirage. No good description can he give, but later he sometimes whispers:

> ...disjointed and irresponsible things about "the black pit," "the carven rim," "the proto-shoggoths," "the windowless solids with five dimensions," "the nameless cylinder," "the elder pharos," "Yog-Sothoth," "the primal white jelly," "The Colour Out of Space," "the wings," "the eyes in darkness," "the moon-ladder," "the original, the eternal, the undying," and other bizarre conceptions; but when he is fully himself he repudiates all this and attributes it to his curious and macabre reading of earlier years.

A certain Thomas Danforth, of Boston, and one Bartholomew Gedney, of Salem, were two of the associate judges during the Salem witchcraft trials of 1692; in Danforth and Gedney, two of the key graduate students on the Antarctic expedition, HPL reunited their names.

DANTE (WD): Dr. Wilmarth's host at the Akeley farmhouse, after describing the "black rivers of pitch" that flow under mysterious bridges on Yuggoth "ought to be enough to make any man a Dante or a Poe if he can keep sane long enough to tell what he has seen."

Dante Alighieri (1265–1321), of Florence, Italy, is the greatest Italian poet,;his masterpiece is *The Divine Comedy*, a 14,000-line poem in three parts, describing the narrator's guided tour of Hell, Purgatory, and Heaven, in that order. It is one of the world's literary treasures, although its theological viewpoint—that of the medieval-era Catholic church—is of course not the implicit belief-system of most modern readers. Most often read is the first section, *Inferno* or Hell. In this part the narrator descends level by level to the bottom of hell, encountering increasingly wicked categories of eternally-damned sinners at each level.

DANVERS (PM): A small non-fictitious Massachusetts city north of Boston, in Essex County; for many years it was the site of a state hospital for the insane. Thurber hyperbolically describes Pickman's "art theories and philosophic speculations wild enough to qualify him for the Danvers asylum." Danvers was known as "Salem Village" in the late 17th century (not to be confused with the still-existing nearby town of Salem), when it was the epicenter of the Salem witchcraft trials.

DARK MOUNTAIN (WD): A fictitious mountain near Henry Akeley's home in Vermont. Strange voices can be heard on its wooded western slope; Akeley manages to make sound recordings of some of these.

DAROHS (WE): A creature on Venus, possibly a large and slow-moving insect-form; darohs crash into the crystal prospector Stanfield as he walks along, splattering his leather prospecting-uniform but not disturbing him or slowing his progress.

DAVENPORT, ELI (WD): A fictitious 19th century antiquarian, whose rare monograph (a long article devoted to a single research subject) on Vermont folktales "obtained prior to 1839 among the oldest people of the state" is known to Professor Wilmarth. The folklore "hinted at a hidden race of monstrous beings which lurked somewhere among the remoter hills."

DAVIS, DR. (IV): The town doctor of Peck Valley in 1881; he is called to the cemetery's gate-lodge to treat the severely-maimed undertaker George Bush after the latter's "accident" in the receiving tomb. Later the same night, he goes to the tomb to investigate further, returns and then explains the shocking truth to Bush.

DAVYS (DH): *See* "Cryptographers of Dunwich."

DEAN'S CORNERS (DH): Fictitious village near Dunwich.

DEE, DR. JOHN (DH): The multifaceted English scholar and magician (1527–1608). A biographer described him as:

> ...one of the most celebrated and remarkable men of the Elizabethan age. Philosopher, mathematician, technologist, antiquarian, teacher and friend of powerful people, Dee was at the center of some of the major developments of the English renaissance.... But Dee was also a magician deeply immersed in the most extreme forms of occultism; he was Elizabethan England's great magus [magician].

HPL presents this famous occult scholar as the English translator of the *Necronomicon*, presumably from the earlier Latin version of Olaus Wormius. Wilbur Whateley owns a damaged and imperfect copy of the

Dee edition; it is because of the missing pages that he is compelled to visit the Miskatonic University library—and to attempt to break into it by night—to consult the Latin version it holds.

DEEP ONES (SOI): Intelligent beings who dwell at the bottom of the seas, apparently in great numbers. Apparently they are shaped somewhat like people (or people are shaped somewhat like them!), but with numerous amphibian or fish-like traits, such as gills, webbed feet, and scaly skin. They can walk about on dry land, to some extent. They worship Father Dagon and Mother Hydra, and apparently keep shoggoths. One enormous species advantage that the Deep Ones enjoy is physical immortality, unless one is "killed violent," according to Zadok Allen of Innsmouth. They are already numerous enough to wipe out the people of Earth's surface, but have chosen not to do so for the time being. Even a person with only one-eighth Deep One blood may turn into an immortal Deep One himself in time, with the necessary morphological changes, sometime during his terrestrial life.

After being attracted to Innsmouth by Captain Obed Marsh, who longs for the riches they can bring in the form of fish and gold, the Deep Ones gradually help him to seize control of the town, climaxing with their horrifying assistance in the 1846 massacre of resisting townspeople. Afterwards, Innsmouth humans are required to procreate with Deep Ones, led by Captain Marsh, who takes a Deep One wife; this leads to a situation in which the older members of the community gradually and regularly take on more and more characteristics of the Deep Ones— getting "the Innsmouth look"—until they eventually go to live on the ocean floor.

DE LA POER FAMILY (RW): An English aristocratic clan, descended from the Anglo-Norman knight Gilbert de la Poer, who in 1261 was granted Exham Priory as a family seat by King Henry III, with the title Baron of Exham. Although the family's reputation was spotless before this event, some time soon afterward the de la Poers changed into a sinister lot. "Something strange must have happened then," muses the narrator at the beginning of one of the great Lovecraftian flights of *faux*-history. In 1307 a de la Poer is referred to in an historical chronicle as "cursed of God." The family develops a hideous local reputation for cruelty, and are justly blamed for the disappearance of many a peasant or villager over the years. The worst offenders were said to be the successive barons themselves, and their direct heirs. It was believed that there is some kind of internal cult presided over by the head of the family in each generation, into which other family members—even members by marriage such as Lady Margaret Trevor—might be invited on the basis of the proper temperament. The English de la Poers come to a bloody end during the reign of King James I, in the early 17th century, when Walter, the third son of the current baron, murders his father, his five brothers and sisters, and several of the domestic servants, then emigrates to Virginia without hindrance by the royal authorities. In America, the name gradually becomes "Delapore," until the 20th century narrator changes his appellation back to "de la Poer" as part of his fateful return to his roots.

Literary history provides an insight into to the author's selection of this unusual family name. Le Poer is said to have been a name well up in the genealogy of Sarah Helen *Power* Whitman, a widow and poet who lived for a time in Providence, where the widowed Edgar Allan Poe courted her unsuccessfully in the 1840s. Poe romantically traced his name and Mrs. Whitman's maiden name to a common ancestor named le Poer. Concerning this matter, one of Poe's modern biographers has written:

> Helen traced her own father's family [the Powers] to a Sir Roger Le Poer, Norman chaplain of Henry the First [of England], a "high & mighty Baron," as she characterized him. Helen believed that in Sir Roger Le Poer, she and Poe had a single root. Actually the families were entirely unrelated.

DE LA POER, LADY MARY (RW): A daughter of the medieval English de la Poers, who in some unspecified year marries the equally-fictitious Earl of Shrewsfield. The earl and his mother murder her not long afterwards, with "both of the slayers being absolved and blessed by the priest to whom they confessed." Clearly there was something very bad about the bride.

DE LA POER, MR. (RW): Born circa 1858, at Carfax plantation on the James River in eastern Virginia, child of a Virginian father and a mother from the north. At age 7, during the Civil War, he witnesses the burning of Carfax by Federal soldiers. His parents move to the north after the war, and he grows up to be a very wealthy manufacturer in Bolton, Massachusetts. He marries, although we learn nothing about his wife, and circa 1894 has a son, Alfred Delapore. In 1904 his father dies, by which time his wife had already died. He learns from Alfred's letters home from England in 1917 of ancestral legends concerning the de la Poer family there. He purchases the ruins of Exham Priory in 1918 from the neighboring Norrys family, which had come to own them at some point after the royal seizure of the de la Poer lands following the mass murder of his own family by Walter de la Poer in the early 1600s.

He visits the bare ruined choirs of Exham Priory in December, 1921, and then spends a fortune rebuilding it and restoring it to medieval-style splendor, but "wholly new and free from old vermin and old ghosts alike," as he mistakenly supposes. He moves in on July 16, 1923, having changed his name from the Americanized "Delapore" back to the ancient de la Poer. On July 22, he notices his favorite cat's odd nocturnal behavior, its sniffing around walls as if searching for invisible rats. On subsequent nights, he witnesses increasingly strange behavior on the cat's part, consults with his late son's wartime friend Captain Norrys, and suffers bizarre nightmares of a "swineherd" in a "twilight grotto." Exploring some lower regions of Exham Priory, he and Norrys discover a Roman-era sub-cellar. On or about July 26, he and Norrys travel to London for "many days" to gather a group of experts for further delving. They return to Exham Priory on the evening of August 7, and he dreams again about the swineherd, and also about the sight of an orgiastic banquet (HPL likens it to the Feast of Trimalchio, a classical literary reference to a swinish dinner-party put on by a wealthy and vulgar man of that name, in the *Satyricon* by the Roman author Petronius). At 11:00 a.m. on August 8, Mr. de la Poer ventures into the subterranean grotto with Norrys and the team of scholars, and goes mad at what he sees, and what it reveals to him about his accursed ancestry. That afternoon in the caverns, he kills and partially devours Captain Norrys prior to being found and restrained by the other investigators. At the tale's end he is confined in a padded cell in Hanwell Asylum, as a dangerous madman.

DE LA POER, WALTER (RW): Third son of the tenth Baron Exham, a young man in the early 1600s. About two weeks after making some kind of shocking discovery, he murders his father, three brothers, two sisters, and several household servants (he is aided in this slaughter by four other servants). Then he hastens across the sea to the English colony in Virginia, "expressing only a frantic wish to exclude [Exham Priory] from his sight and memory." In England he had been known as a shy and gentle youth, and oddly enough, the mass murder of his family and the servants is "so slackly treated by the law that [he] escaped honored, unharmed, and undisguised to Virginia." Plainly the authorities were happy for the virtual extermination of the de la Poers, with their evil reputation. To other colonists in Virginia, he always appears "harassed and apprehensive"; but a fellow-colonist named Francis Harley described him as being "of unexampled [unequaled] justice, honor, and delicacy [courtesy]"— making his family slaughter even more inexplicable, of course. His family's English estate is forfeited to the crown, but he apparently does well as a colonist and becomes the progenitor of the Delapores of Carfax plantation, Virginia. At his death he leaves an envelope containing a letter explaining the family secret, to be opened and read only by the heir in each generation; but the envelope is destroyed in the burning of the

Carfax plantation house during the Civil War, so neither Mr. de la Poer nor his own father ever learned the secret.

DELAPORE, ALFRED (RW): The only child of Mr. de la Poer, he is born in 1894, perhaps in Bolton, Massachusetts. During the First World War he serves as an officer and aviator. Posted to England in 1917, he meets Captain Edward Norrys of the Royal Flying Corps, who shares with him some interesting facts and legends about the old de la Poer family history and English estate, which Alfred passes along in letters home to his father. Alfred Delapore is wounded or injured during the war and returns home as a "maimed invalid." His father cares for him personally, but he dies in 1920. The innocently-written contents of his letters from England influence his father to purchase and restore the ruined family seat of Exham Priory, to his own eventual doom.

DELAPORE, RANDOLPH (RW): One of the 19th century Delapores of Carfax plantation, Virginia; he was a scandalous older cousin of the Mr. de la Poer who eventually buys Exham Priory. Following his service with the U.S. Army in Mexico during the Mexican War (1845–48), Randolph Delapore (influenced by something or some things he had seen in Mexico?) "went among the negroes and became a voodoo priest." This behavior would have inevitably meant the social obliteration of a white man in America at any time in the 19th century and for a long time afterward; for Randolph Delapore to have taken such an extreme leap away from respectability is probably meant to hint at some hereditary taint of mad degeneracy lurking in the family, which perhaps his time in Mexico somehow brought to the forefront. It foreshadows Mr. de la Poer's horrible reversion in the caverns under Exham Priory.

DELRIO (HRH): The raid on the Red Hook cultists discovered seventeen prisoners in underground cells, including four mothers, whose "infants of disturbingly strange appearance" later died after being exposed to sunlight. "Nobody but Malone, among those who inspected them, remembered the sombre question of old Delrio: '*An sint unquam daemones incubi et succubae, et an ex tali congressu proles nasci queat?*'" "Old Delrio" was Martin Antonio del Rio, S.J. (1551–1608), a Spanish Jesuit priest and expert on demonology. His "sombre question" in the 1603 witchcraft manual *Disquisitionum Magicarum Libri Sext* ("Six Books of Disquisitions on Magic") is whether the types of demons called *incubi* and *succubae*—respectively, male and female demons who slept with human victims of the opposite sex to steal their vital force—really existed, and whether there could be offspring of such relationships. HPL had not read the book, but read about it in the *Encyclopedia Britannica*, 9th edition.

DE MARIGNY, ETIENNE-LAURENT (TGSK): The Creole (French-descended native of Louisiana) friend of Randolph Carter's in New Orleans. He was Carter's wartime comrade-in-arms in the French Foreign Legion, and his guide on a mysterious visit to the ancient French city of Bayonne. (The *Legion Étrangere* or "Foreign Legion" was then, and is still at this writing, a proud combat unit of the French army, in which non-citizens of France may enlist. In HPL's day the Legion's prestige among American adventure-story fans was at its absolute height.) In his exotically-furnished New Orleans home there takes place the 1932 meeting of Ernest Aspinwall, Ward Phillips, Swami Chandraputra, and himself, to decide what to do with the missing Carter's personal estate. De Marigny's real-life counterpart was HPL's friend in New Orleans, E. Hoffman Price (1898–1989), who was also a writer for *Weird Tales* and other pulp magazines. HPL described him as a very colorful character, a worthy model for the mysterious de Marigny:

> Price is a remarkable chap—a West-Pointer [*i.e.*, a graduate of the United States Military Academy, at West Point, New York], war veteran, Arabic student, connoisseur of Oriental rugs, amateur fencing-master, mathematician, dilettante coppersmith and iron worker, chess champion, pianist, & what not! He is dark and trim of figure, not very tall, and with a small black moustache.

When, after much correspondence, Price and HPL finally met face-to-face in New Orleans in 1932, they talked to each other for 25 (or maybe 28) hours.

DERBY, ASENATH WAITE (TD): The daughter of Ephraim Waite, who is one of the "Innsmouth Waites." After her father Ephraim's death as a raving lunatic locked in an attic, she is sent to be a boarding student at the Hall School in Kingsport, and later attends Miskatonic University, where she studies metaphysics and medieval lore. She meets and marries the bookish, unworldly Edward Derby, a match that surprises his friends. It becomes increasingly apparent during the tale that the immeasurably evil Ephraim Waite, by some occult means, transferred his persona from his old, dying body to the young, healthy body of his child Asenath, leaving her to die in the horror of his withered old man's frame (certainly explaining the raving madness in which "Ephraim" expired).

Like so many of HPL's collection of personal names for his New England characters, Asenath was one of the Old Testament names that were so popular among the early English colonists. The biblical Asenath was a woman in the Book of Genesis, whose name is thought to stem from the Egyptian language, for "belonging to [the goddess] Neit"; she was the daughter of an Egyptian priest, who married the Hebrew patriarch Joseph and became the mother of his youngest sons, Ephraim (!) and Manasseh.

DERBY, EDWARD PICKMAN (TD): Born and raised in Arkham, Massachusetts, this HPL alter-ego is described as brilliant but unworldly, over-sheltered in childhood and youth, with a disastrous marriage to a more dominant and powerful woman. Like HPL, "in self-reliance and practical affairs...[Derby] was greatly retarded because of his coddled existence" as a youth. The following description, put into the mouth of Derby's best friend Daniel Upton, are almost directly autobiographical, as HPL looked backward more than thirty years at his own childhood:

> He was the most phenomenal child scholar I have ever known, and at seven was writing verse of a sombre, fantastic, almost morbid cast which astonished the tutors surrounding him. Perhaps his private education and coddled seclusion had something to do with his premature flowering. An only child, he had organic weaknesses which startled his doting parents and caused them to keep him closely chained to their side. He was never allowed out without his nurse, and seldom had a chance to play unconstrainedly with other children. All this doubtless fostered a strange, secretive inner life in the boy, with imagination as his one avenue of freedom....
>
> In self-reliance and practical affairs, however, Derby was greatly retarded because of his coddled existence. His health had improved, but his habits of childish dependence were fostered by overcareful parents, so that he never traveled alone, made independent decisions, or assumed responsibilities. It was early seen that he would not be equal to a struggle in the business or professional arena, but the family fortune was so ample that this formed no tragedy.

The comparison only breaks down in the last sentence, for HPL's family fortune was not ample, and his lack of any work training or higher education always made a difficult situation worse. At any rate, Derby enters Miskatonic University at the age of 16 and graduates in the short span of three years, majoring in English and French literature. During his college days, he lives at home and mingles little with other Miskatonians, although this timid mama's boy envies the "daring" or "Bohemian" clique of students "whose superficial 'smart' language and meaninglessly ironic pose he aped, and whose dubious conduct he wished he dared adopt." He goes on to study books about magical lore, including the *Necronomicon*, the *Book of Eibon*, and the hideous *Unaussprechlichen Kulten*. At the age of 25, he is "prodigiously learned...and a fairly well-known poet and fantaisiste [fantasy-writer], though his lack of contacts and responsibilities had slowed down his literary growth by making his products derivative and over-bookish"—the mature HPL's assessment of his own youthful "products." His mother dies when he is 34 (HPL was

31 when this happened in his life), and Derby is laid low with grief for several months; but later "he seemed to feel a grotesque exhilaration, as if of partial escape from some unseen bondage"; both the nervous prostration and the sense of guilty relief seem like another manifest self-description by the author.

When he is 38 years old, Derby meets and marries Asenath Waite, a Miskatonic student of sinister family background. They take long trips to Europe together. Edward is sometimes observed to behave more vigorously than he did before his marriage, but in other moments voices his odd worries about "losing his identity" to his friend Upton. During the fourth year of Edward Derby's marriage, Upton is called upon to pick up and drive Derby home from the Chesuncook, Maine "town farm" where he had been placed after wandering out of the uninhabited woods in a dazed condition. During the drive, he begins to tell Upton of how Asenath's personality has been gradually taking control over his body; then, suddenly, the "Edward" mind is silenced, and what Upton begins to perceive as the "Asenath" mind snaps back into control.

In mid-September of that year, Derby travels out of town for a week, and it is suggested that he has gone to meet "a notorious cult-leader, lately expelled from England, who had established headquarters in New York." (This is probably a distant reference to Aleister Crowley (1875–1947), the famed English occultist and author on esoteric subjects such as "Magick" and the Tarot. Crowley resided in New York City during 1914–19 after his wittily provocative pronouncements on beliefs and morals, and his well-publicized magical ceremonies, had made him notorious in the sensationalistic British press as "the wickedest man in the world.") One may assume that this was an "Asenath" trip. But in mid-October, Edward, now quite back to normal, lets it be known that Asenath has abandoned him and Arkham. He does not move out of their home, the Crowninshield place, although he seems to hate and fear it. Around Christmas time, he experiences a nervous breakdown, shrieking that "it" is coming for him *again*; he is committed to Arkham Sanitarium. In late January, still in the Sanitarium, he appears to have recovered his full sanity, but to Upton it appears as though Asenath's personality has taken control of Edward's body once again. The next night Upton opens his own door in response to Edward Derby's familiar secret door-knocking signal, and takes a note written in Derby's handwriting from a Thing on the doorstep. After reading the note, he goes over to Arkham Sanitarium and puts six bullets through the head of his best friend.

This tale been labeled as semi-autobiographical in the sense of having clear parallels to HPL's life and marriage. In this view, Edward's disastrous marriage is likened to HPL's own marriage, which ended in separation after only two years. HPL seems to have been temperamentally unsuited to married life, particularly not with the kind of woman he married—his friends appear to have been as stunned when he took the plunge with Sonia Greene as Edward Derby's friends were when Derby suddenly married Asenath Waite—and some of the desperation HPL came to feel as a married man clearly found its way into this tale, written six or seven years after the couple's separation. L. Sprague de Camp suggested that "it seems reasonable to view Asenath as a composite product of Lovecraft's imagination, with touches of various women he had known, his mother, Sonia, and others." But, after all, HPL really never knew too many women.

The concept of a rotting corpse knocking at the door for admittance has old folklore roots, but may have been specifically planted in HPL's mind by the similar climax in the classic horror story *The Monkey's Paw* by W.W. Jacobs (1863–1943), a climax which HPL had called "an able melodramatic bit" in his 1926 essay *Supernatural Horror in Literature.*

DERBY, MR. (TD): The father of Edward Pickman Derby, he is a wealthy inhabitant of Arkham. After his wife's death he took his son for long vacations in Europe. He disapproved of Edward's relationship with Asenath Waite, but did not object to their marriage as a result of advice from Daniel Upton. About three years after the wedding, he died.

DERBY, COLONEL NEHEMIAH (DQ): A fictitious individual who died in 1719. His slate tombstone, stolen from Charter Street Burial Ground in Salem, Massachusetts, was carried by the three ghouls who escort Randolph Carter through the city of the gugs, and is used by them first to brain a pursuing ghast, and then to wedge open the heavy trapdoor at the top of the great tower in the gugs' city, a trapdoor which opens to the enchanted circle in the zoogs' forest in upper Dreamland.

DE RETZ, GILLES (RW): An historical serial-killer (1404–40). Gilles de Laval, seigneur de Retz (or de Rais) was a wealthy and powerful lord from the Brittany province of northwestern France, a brave warrior and a generous patron of the arts. Servants brought beautiful peasant boys, and occasionally girls, to one or another of his castles, where he would molest and then murder the children; he also practiced black magic and alchemy, or attempted to. He forgot the precise number of his victims, but there may have been over a hundred. He was finally arrested in 1440, tried by the Holy Inquisition and the local bishop for "heretical practices" and murder, then hanged as a common criminal along with two of his henchmen. His castles were found to contain bins full of children's bones, similar to the bone-bins in the caverns under Exham Priory.

Sometimes suggested as the inspiration for the French folktale of "Bluebeard," the monstrous Gilles de Retz passed into the literary parlance of future centuries as an archetype of bloodthirsty cruelty, like Nero or King Herod, before being replaced in the 20th century by more up-to-date monsters in various national governments or in private life. In HPL's tale, the French baron's negative exploits are compared to those of the aristocratic and malignant de la Poer family of Exham Priory.

D'ERLETTE, COMTE (SOT, HD): One of HPL's most frequent correspondents from 1926 until his death was August Derleth (1909–71), a fiction writer in Wisconsin. Derleth's own writings, which showed early signs of talent and which were always prolific and profitable, have not attained lasting fame. He must be credited as the driving force in getting and keeping HPL's works in print in the lean years after the HPL's death, and with collecting many of the dead man's letters from correspondents around the country. Derleth claimed remote descent from a French aristocrat named the Comte (Count) D'Erlette; that name in turn was assigned to the author of a book title HPL invented, *Cultes des Goules* or "Ghoul Cults."

DE SADE (RW): Donatien-Alphonse-François de Sade, French author (1740–1814). The product of a wealthy and ancient aristocratic family and an excellent classical education, the Marquis de Sade spent much of his adult life, including his last years, confined to prisons or insane asylums as an incorrigible pervert, sodomite, and abuser of women. During his nearly thirty years of off-and-on custody under different French governments, he amused himself by composing the works of sophisticated but vicious and incredibly violent pornography which led a future psychiatrist to coin the now-familiar word "sadism." It seems on the whole unlikely that HPL ever actually read any of de Sade's literary productions, which were not generally available in the United States at the time due to strict anti-obscenity laws, and which revolved around a single topic—unending and kaleidoscopic sexual expression—which held no interest for him whatsoever. But he knew of the Marquis de Sade from his wide reading and, like Gilles de Retz, de Sade is mentioned in this tale as a famous example of aristocratic cruelty and criminality, comparable to that of the medieval de la Poer family.

DE SITTER (DWH): *See* "Mathematicians of Arkham."

DESROCHERS (DWH): A French-Canadian (presumably, from his name) tenant in the Witch House. He lives in the room below Walter Gilman's room. He talks with Joe Mazurewicz, another tenant, about the "poor, doomed young gentleman" living upstairs. He overhears mysterious conversations, footsteps, and other sounds, all coming from the student's room, and on one occasion sees a violet light radiating from the cracks around the door into the room. He is also a witness to some later events, including Gilman's death.

DE VIGÉNÈRE (DH): *See* "Cryptographers of Dunwich."

DEVIL REEF (SOI): A long, black, ocean reef about one and a half miles out from Innsmouth harbor; its surface is covered by water at high tide but sometimes becomes visible at low tide. On the other side of the reef, the ocean floor falls away abruptly into an extremely deep, unsoundable abyss (meaning that the depth-finding method of the time, which consisted of dropping a line with a weighted end into the water and hoping to reach the lowermost depth—"sounding"—was insufficient to find the bottom of the oceanic trench); another Lovecraftian cave, only this one is vertical and submerged. Around 1840, Captain Obed Marsh began to visit Devil Reef with his followers, rowing out by night in "dories," the large rowboats used for New England fishing, which could hold up to 3–4 men. The boy Zadok Allen observes the men dropping things into the sea off Devil Reef; at first, presumably the "funny-shaped lead thingumajig" (a slang word meaning a small object of uncertain function) that Captain Marsh had acquired on a South Pacific island, and which was used to summon the Deep Ones to the surface; later on, the objects being dropped are human sacrifices. The Deep Ones begin meeting him at night on Devil Reef. In 1846, the Deep Ones gathered on the reef before swimming the short distance into Innsmouth to help Marsh and his supporters to seize power and slaughter his opponents.

By 1927 Devil Reef, or what lay in the water below, has practically become Innsmouth's sister city. Rather amusingly, harbor-to-reef swimming races are even mentioned as the townsfolk's primary form of entertainment! When the narrator is trying to escape from Innsmouth by night, he sees light-signals being flashed between Devil Reef and the cupola of the Gilman House hotel, and within a few more minutes he observes that the water had become "alive with a teeming horde of shapes swimming inward toward the town." Later, after federal authorities raid Innsmouth and confine the inhabitants, it is rumored that a U.S. Navy submarine had fired torpedoes *downward* into the abyss on the far side of the reef.

In the story's concluding pages, we learn that in that abyss is the undersea city of "many-columned" Y'ha-nthlei, a place of glowing phosphorescent palaces, and gardens of living coral. As the story ends, the narrator is vowing to "swim out to that brooding reef in the sea and dive down" to Y'ha-nthlei, "and in that lair of the Deep Ones we shall dwell amidst wonder and glory forever." Innsmouth's "Devil Reef" was probably inspired by "Black Rocks," a reef that breaks above the waterline in the harbor of Newburyport, Massachusetts.

DEVIL'S HOP-YARD (DH): "A bleak, blasted hillside" near Dunwich, where "no tree, shrub, or grass-blade will grow." There is a real place called "Devil's Hop Yard" in New England, but it is near East Haddam, Connecticut, not in Massachusetts. The reference is not to jumping; rather, it is to hop plants, a shrub-like vegetation whose fruits are picked for use in beer-brewing.

DE VERMIS MYSTERIIS (SOT, HD): "Of the Mysteries of the Worm," by a certain "Ludvig Prinn." Robert Blake finds a copy of it in the Starry Wisdom church, and Professor Peaslee's alter-ego from the Great Race studies another copy in a university library sometime between 1908–13. Nothing is said about its contents. *De Vermis Mysteriis* was a title invented by HPL and "given" to Robert Bloch, one of the youthful aspiring fantasy-writers who corresponded with him. In a story which the teenaged Bloch published in the September, 1935 issue of *Weird Tales*, the narrator is a correspondent of a "mystic dreamer" in Providence and, when he finds a copy of *De Vermis Mysteriis*, he shows it to the old mystic who reads aloud an incantation from the book— whereupon an outer-space monster appears and devours him. HPL's destruction of "Robert Blake" in *The Haunter of the Dark* was his in-joke "revenge."

DEXTER, DR. (HD): A Providence physician whose hobby is exotic folklore. After Robert Blake's death, Dexter takes the curiously-angled stone—the Shining Trapezohedron—and its adorned metal box out of the old Starry Wisdom church, and drops them from a rowboat into the deepest channel of Narragansett Bay. Like the Browns, Crawfords, Whipples, Fenners, Bowens and Tillinghasts who populate HPL's Providence-area tales, the real Dexters were a large colonial-era clan descended from the earliest English settlers of the 17th century.

DEXTER, KNIGHT (CDW): Non-fictitious proprietor of an 18th-century Providence store, "the Bay and Book." A journal entry of Joseph Curwen's for October 16, 1754, mentions selling Mr. Dexter several hundred pieces of various kinds of imported fabric, obviously for resale.

DEXTER, MERCY (SH): Older, unmarried sister of Rhoby Dexter Harris, the wife of Captain William Harris. She moves into the Harris house in 1768, after Rhoby goes mad, and manages the household from then until her death. She has a deep affection for her sister and for her sister's son, William Harris, Jr.; this probably is the explanation for her continuing to live in the peculiarly unlucky home. She hires and later fires the superstitious, gossiping servant Ann White, and replaces her with Maria Robbins. Although she was "a plain, raw-boned woman of great strength," her health steadily declines from the time she began to dwell in the house. Glimpsed in 1780, the tough, powerful Mercy Dexter has become "a stooped and pathetic figure with a hollow voice and disconcerting pallor," as the house sucks the life away from her as it has already done from others. On May 15, 1783, she "took leave of a useful, austere, and virtuous life."

DEXTER, PROFESSOR (WD): Professor of Zoology at Miskatonic University in 1928. Professor Wilmarth wishes to turn to him with some "conjectures" about the identity of the Vermont hill-creatures, but at Henry Akeley's request he does not do so.

DHO FORMULA; DHO-HNA FORMULA (DH): *See* "Yr."

D'IBERVILLE and LA SALLE (CC): Pierre le Moyne, sieur d'Iberville (1661–1706), a Frenchman on a sea expedition, discovered the mouth of the Mississippi River from the Gulf of Mexico side. Robert Cavelier, sieur de La Salle (1643–87) was one of the earliest and greatest explorers of North America. In 1682 he and a small party of French companions made the first descent of the Mississippi River from the Great Lakes to its mouth, the site of the modern city of New Orleans. The local people in the Louisiana swamps south of New Orleans speak fearfully:

> ...of a hidden lake unglimpsed by mortal sight, in which dwelt a huge, formless white polypous thing with luminous eyes; and squatters whispered that bat-winged devils flew up out of caverns in inner earth to worship it at midnight. They said it had been there before D'Iberville, before La Salle, before the Indians, and before even the wholesome beasts and birds of the woods. It was nightmare itself, and to see it was to die. But it made men dream, and so they knew enough to keep away.

DIONAEAN PLATEAU (WE): Martian region, mentioned as having great craters that could be hiding something.

DOELS (WD): They are a kind of monster that Henry Akeley discusses. HPL borrowed the word from the works of Arthur Machen, the British fantasist whose tales he admired. Not to be confused with "Bholes," creatures which were called "dholes" in old editions of HPL's works because of an early typographical error.

DOGS (TH, DH, COS, WD, MM): HPL was always a cat man. In his seriocomic essay *Cats and Dogs*, he drew a sharp contrast between cats (which he associated with aristocratic reserve, elegance, and self-sufficiency), and dogs (which were examples of lower-class crudeness and buffoonery, not to mention slavish dependence on their masters). At best, dogs could be useful beasts and harmless clowns; he "liked them in their place," he would say. But their traditional sensitivity to strange and alien presences is utilized in some of his tales. Thus, in *At the Mountains of Madness* and *The Dunwich Horror*, they instinctively hate and attack the Old Ones and Wilbur Whateley, who finally is killed by the Miskatonic University guard-dog—a huge and savage mastiff—after his pistol jams. Henry Akeley kept more and more guard-dogs to help ward off the Mi-Go. On his visit to Akeley's farm, Professor Wilmarth notices—but does not take the hint—that there is now no sign or sound of a dog, or any other living creature, at the place. In *The Colour Out of Space*, the Gardner family's three dogs all disappear in one night; some canine bones are later found at the bottom of the farmyard well. And in *The Hound*, a kind of winged hound invisibly pursues St. John and his friend.

DOLPHINS (TT): Dolphins, which occur in some Greek legends, feature prominently in this tale of rediscovered Atlantis. They cluster thickly around submarine U-29, even as it descends into ocean depths where, scientifically speaking, water pressure should have crushed them. Nor do these dolphins seem to need to rise to the surface for air, as ordinary dolphins must; U-29's commander carefully observes one that swims alongside the submerged and drifting submarine for two hours. Once U-29 settles on the ocean floor in Atlantis, the dolphin escort vanishes.

DOMBROWSKI (DWH): Landlord of the Witch House during Walter Gilman's residence there; his Polish surname is probably intended by HPL as another indication that the very old dwelling is now a cheap and undesirable place. However, he comes off in the tale as a concerned and good-natured man. After Walter Gilman's horrific death, he closes up the Witch House for good and moves to new quarters with some of his more senior tenants from the old place.

DONOVAN (CC): A sailor on the *Emma*. He survives the sea-battle with the *Alert*, and transfers to that vessel. He is, therefore, a member of the party that lands on R'lyeh and goes to explore. He walks or climbs around the inclined edges of the gigantic and slimy stone door of Cthulhu's house until it begins to open when, sailor-fashion he slides down the door-jamb and rejoins his comrades. A moment later he is swept up by Cthulhu's awful claws.

DOORS, RATTLING (HW, MEZ, SHH, HE, SOI, TH): One wonders if and how the unnerving sound of a rattling door-latch in the night may have imprinted itself in HPL's memory at an impressionable age; it is a dramatic device he returned to a number of times.

"Then came the steady rattling at the back door," declares Dr. West's comrade at a climactic point in *Herbert West—Reanimator*. "The rattling continued, growing somewhat louder," until the narrator throws open the door and Herbert West empties his revolver into the thing standing outside in the darkness. In *The Music of Erich Zann*, where an unseen visitor seems to lurk outside Zann's top-floor window, "the shutter began to rattle in a howling night-wind," and shortly thereafter "rattled more loudly, unfastened, and commenced slamming against the window," which breaks, letting in what Zann would rather have kept out. In *The Strange High House in the Mist*, Thomas Olney knows a moment of fear when, standing on the landward side of the house in question, he "heard a lock rattle and a bolt shoot, and a long creaking follow as if a heavy door were slowly and cautiously opened." The nameless narrator of *He* hears with horror "the steady, stealthy creaking of the stairs beyond the locked door...and at last the cautious, purposeful rattling of the brass latch that glowed in the feeble candlelight." In *The Shadow Over Innsmouth*, the narrator knows that his life is in imminent danger in his locked room at the Gilman House hotel when he hears the "cautious rattling" and "soft rattling" of someone trying to enter the room from the hall door or one of the side connecting doors, using a pass-key. Of related interest are the inexplicable "knock at my chamber door" and the "low, cautious scratching at the single door" to the secret underground museum, experienced by the nameless narrator of *The Hound*.

DORÉ, GUSTAVE (DA, HRH, WD) Gustave Doré (1832–83), of France, was one of the preeminent illustrators in the golden age of black and white illustration, the 19th century. His style of darkly-detailed etching lent itself perfectly to the depiction of sinister night scenes, misshapen demons, souls in torment, and otherworldly visions. As a child of six HPL was already familiar with Doré's famed illustrations for deluxe Victorian editions of such weirdly or demonically saturated classics as Dante Alighieri's *The Divine Comedy*, John Milton's *Paradise Lost*, and Coleridge's *The Rime of the Ancient Mariner*. Many years later he could still vividly recall the impression that Doré's spectacularly ominous artwork had on his developing visual imagination as a small boy.

The narrator in *Dagon*, viewing the monolith risen from the bottom of the ocean, notes that it bore "an array of bas-reliefs [picture-carvings] that would have excited the envy of a Doré." Daily life for Thomas F. Malone in *The Horror at Red Hook* had come to be "a phantasmagoria of macabre shadow-studies... [sometimes] hinting terrors behind the commonest shapes and objects as in subtler and less obvious works of Gustave Doré." Dr. Wilmarth compares his escape from Henry Akeley's farmhouse by night in an old Ford automobile as being like "a piece of delirium out of Poe or Rimbaud or the drawings of Doré."

DORIEB (WS): A demigod or god; "whom some say to be a demi-god and others a god" who is purportedly the ruler of legendary Cathuria. His palace is said to have a golden roof set up on ruby and azure pillars, and a glass floor beneath which flows the river Narg.

DOTHUR (DCS): The oil for the torches that illuminate rooms in Sarnath is said to come from this place.

DOUBLOON STREET (CDW): A real Providence waterfront street where Joseph Curwen kept his mercantile warehouse in the 18th century.

DOUGLAS, CAPTAIN J.B. (MM): Captain of the brig *Arkham*, Miskatonic University Expedition, and in overall command of the expedition's sailing element. He is "a veteran whaler in Antarctic waters."

DOYLE, MAYOR (HD): The historical Thomas Doyle (1827–1886), popular mayor of Providence during most of the period between 1864 and 1886, when he died. In the tale, a "secret committee" (shades of *The Case of Charles Dexter Ward*) calls on him in 1876 after the unexplained disappearances of six more people are linked to the Starry Wisdom cult.

DOYLE, SIR ARTHUR CONAN (TU): The prolific British author (1859–1930), famous as the creator of Sherlock Holmes and the author of scores of Holmes mystery-stories. Late in life he became a firm believer in spiritualism and communication with the souls of the dead, earning his little mention in this tale.

DREAMLAND (OG, CU, WS, CE, DQ): Although "Dreamland" as such is only to be found in *The Dream-Quest of Unknown Kadath*, various places (such as Hatheg, Hatheg-Kla, Ulthar, Celephaïs and Serranian, the coastal communities of Zar, Thalarion, Xura, and Sona-Nyl, the Basalt Pillars of the West, and the river Skai) and persons (such as Atal and Kuranes) from the earlier tales *The Other Gods*, *The Cats of Ulthar*, and *Celephaïs* are all found to be part of it. One of the concepts of Kadath is that it exists in Dreamland, although HPL contradicted that in other tales; *see* separate entry for "Kadath".

Dreamland is a kind of vast parallel world, reachable by some humans in their dreams. Randolph Carter reaches the place by "descending the seventy steps to the cavern of flame" in light slumber, then continuing down "the seven hundred steps to the Gate of Deeper Slumber" where he enters "the enchanted wood." From there his footsteps take him gradually to Nir and Ulthar, Dylath-Leen (with a side trip to the moon), Baharna and the peak of Ngranek, underground to lower Dreamland and the vale of Pnath, the peaks of Thok, and the giant twilit city of the gugs; back to upper Dreamland and Kiran, Thran, the jungles of Kled, and the city of Hlanith; then onward to Celephaïs, Inganok, Leng, Sarkomand, and ultimately Kadath. Along the way Carter encounters "men of Dreamland" but also many bizarre and fantastic entities such as zoogs, gugs, ghasts, moon-beasts, almost-humans from Leng, ghouls, night-gaunts, shantaks, and fearsome Nyarlathotep.

DRINEN (QI): A place to the east of Oonai, from whence come "dusky [dark-skinned] flute players."

DROWNE, DR. (HD): Pastor of Fourth Baptist Church in Providence; he warns against the Starry Wisdom cult in a sermon on December 29, 1844, only seven months after its founding by Enoch Bowen.

DRY GULCH (TJR): A fictitious village in the western United States, it is the closest settlement to the Norton Mine. Off-duty mine employees come here for whatever entertainment it might offer.

DUDLEY, JERVAS (TT): Narrator-protagonist of this very early tale. One of the first in a line of Lovecraftian alter-egos, he is a "dreamer," bookish and reclusive. In his solitary walks through his New England district, he becomes fixated on the ancient tomb of an extinct local family, the Hydes. He spends many a night outside that cryptic crypt (and later inside it, or so it seems to him). At this time, during his waking hours, he seems to take on the persona of an 18th-century wit and roaring boy (18th century British slang for a volatile, hard-partying and aggressive youth); a prefiguring of a similar but more sinister change in *The Case of Charles Dexter Ward*. Eventually, on a night of cataclysmic horror, he learns of his own incarnation of the 18th-century Jervas *Hyde*, his distant kinsman. Jervas Dudley is committed to an insane asylum, but his family promises that following his death he will be buried in the Hyde tomb, in an empty coffin which was found there marked "Jervas".

DUNEDIN, NEW ZEALAND (CC): A port city on New Zealand's South Island; in the tale, during 1925 it was the home port of the steam-powered yacht *Alert*, owned and operated by a mongrel crew working in the inter-island shipping trade; they are really Cthulhu-cultists. On or about March 1, 1925, *Alert* hurriedly steamed out of port. A few years later, Francis W. Thurston travels to Dunedin to pursue his inquiries into the Cthulhu-cult—taking nearly a month to get there from the U.S. east coast by train and ship, as was the case in those days—but he learns little new information.

DUNSANY, LORD (CDW, MM): In a tossed-away comment, the omniscient narrator of *The Case of Charles Dexter Ward* compares the near-obliteration of Joseph Curwen's memory in Providence after April, 1771, to "the fate of that sinful King of Runazar in Lord Dunsany's tale, whom the Gods decided must not only cease to be, but must cease ever to have been." And in *At the Mountains of Madness*, the sober geologist Professor Dyer, seeming a bit out of character, writes of Antarctica that "often the whole white world would dissolve into a gold, silver, and scarlet land of Dunsanian dreams and adventurous expectancy under the magic of the low midnight sun."

Edward John Moreton Drax Plunkett—HPL seems to have adored this sonorous set of names—the 18th Lord Dunsany (pronounced Dun-SAY-nee) (1878–1957), was a renowned author and playwright. He was born into the Protestant Anglo-Irish aristocracy of British-ruled Ireland, and educated in England at the ultra-prestigious Eton College (what Americans would term a boarding school, and the most elite one in Great Britain) and then Sandhurst, i.e., the Royal Military Academy. After some years of service as an army officer, he turned back to the life of a wealthy sportsman and man of letters in Ireland and London, and wrote distinctive fantastic tales published in books with titles like *The Gods of Pegana* and *The Book of Wonder*. These are tales of invented pantheons of gods, and of gorgeous kingdoms in various never-never lands; tales having (in Lovecraft biographer S.T. Joshi's words) the "main function [of] the evocation of beauty—beauty of language, beauty of conception, beauty of image." In his time, and particularly in the years between about 1910–30, his popularity among the British and American reading public was immense. Ironically, it is now far more difficult to find his works for sale than those of a certain American fan named H.P. Lovecraft.

HPL encountered Lord Dunsany's works in 1919 and was, in his own words, "arrested...as with an electrick [*sic* for this archaic (or "archaick"?) spelling] shock, & had not read two pages before I became a Dunsany devotee for life." He even attended a public lecture by the touring Lord Dunsany in Boston on October 20, 1919, sitting in a front-row chair "not ten feet" from his literary idol. (Public lectures and/or readings by the famous were immensely popular and important in those pre-television times, when they perhaps meant a book fan's solitary opportunity to actually see the object of his fanaticism; in their day authors from Edgar Allan Poe and Oscar Wilde, to Mark Twain and Bertrand Russell, hit the American lecture circuit, which although demanding in time and energy could also be very lucrative for both the promoters and the authors.) At the height of HPL's enthusiasm he wrote: "Dunsany stands dedicated to strange and lovely worlds of fantastic beauty. To the truly imaginative he is a talisman and a key unlocking rich store houses of dreams." It is pleasing to know that Lord Dunsany lived long enough to read some of HPL's tales in books, after World War II.

A number of HPL's early tales are described as "Dunsanian," specifically *Polaris* (actually written before his first encounter with Dunsany's writing, suggesting that when Lord Dunsany's works finally did reach HPL, the British author was pushing on an open door), *The Doom That Came to Sarnath*, *The White Ship*, *The Cats of Ulthar*, *Celephaïs*, *The Tree*, *The Other Gods*, *The Quest of Iranon*, and *Hypnos*, all written by 1922, and the novel-length *The Dream-Quest of Unknown Kadath*, finished in 1926–27 and marking HPL's effective farewell to the form, since by the middle 1920s both HPL and Lord Dunsany were growing away from the used-up "Dunsanian" mode of fantastic writing.

DUNWICH (DH): A small, fictitious village in rural north-central Massachusetts, on the upper reaches of the Miskatonic River. There are no road signs to direct travelers to Dunwich, but it may be found by taking the "wrong" fork in the road at the junction of the Aylesbury pike (highway), beyond the village of Dean's Corners. (Aylesbury and Dean's Corners never existed either.) The countryside around Dunwich is replete with steep gorges, forested and dome-shaped hills, and poor, struggling farms. Dunwich village itself is a tiny hamlet huddled between a small stream and the slopes of Round Mountain. As of 1928, most of the houses in the village are deserted ruins, and the collapsing former church contains a primitive general store, the town's only shop. (A "general store" in rural America's old days was an establishment that sold a bit of everything: canned goods, crackers, sweets, fabric, hardware, horse-equipment, candles, *et cetera*, for the local farming community.) Dunwich is said to have been founded in 1692 by families that had suddenly departed from Salem, Massachusetts during the witchcraft investigations there. The local people are "repellently decadent" as a result of prolonged inbreeding and cultural isolation; they are mostly ignorant folk, given to committing vicious, bloody, and perverted deeds. In 1917, when the United States entered World War I, the local authorities have a difficult time finding a quota of young Dunwich men who are even healthy enough for the military draft. Sentinel Hill and other nearby hills have dubious reputations as the meeting-places for witches and wizards, and even more unmentionable things; human bones found within the mysterious stone circles on the hilltops as apparent sacrifices, while unfairly blamed on the Pocumtuck Indians who once lived in the area, have been scientifically proved to be those of white people. The majority of the action in the tale *The Dunwich Horror* takes place in this dismal country neighborhood.

"Dunwich" was a composite portrait derived from HPL's sightseeing impressions on a vacation in the summer of 1928, when he visited friends in central Massachusetts, traveling mostly by rail and on foot. The landscape descriptions, which are among his best, are based on the hilly country around the villages of Wilbraham, Hampden, and Monson, several miles east of the large town of Springfield. The underlying theme of rural isolation, poverty, and dreaded "inbreeding," producing moral, mental and even physical degeneracy, was commonplace in American sociology and fiction in the early 20th century, clearly affecting HPL's own perceptions.

In an account of his 1928 visit, written for his own amusement, HPL recorded of Wilbraham that "the peasantry hereabouts are somewhat decadent, and their odd beliefs and doings would fill volumes.... Old witchcraft whispers are remembered, and people nowadays wonder why so many people in a certain part of the neighboring village of Monson go mad or kill themselves." However, Sentinel Hill and the other stone-circle-capped hills have their real-world counterparts not in this district, but farther north in Massachusetts, generally along the New Hampshire state line. HPL once visited the largest of these primitive stone constructions of uncertain purpose, "Mystery Hill" at North Salem, New Hampshire.

During the middle ages in England a seaside town called Dunwich flourished, until it was literally drowned by the slowly-advancing waters of the North Sea. Its last remaining ruins can still be seen on the east coast of England, about 120 miles northeast of central London, between the towns of Ipswich and Great Yarmouth. The eroding remains of Dunwich inspired the Victorian poet Algernon Swinburne's gloomy poem *By the North Sea*, which HPL had probably read, and figured in Arthur Machen's later horror-story *The Terror*, which HPL is known to have read. Since there was no real Dunwich in Massachusetts, he was free to borrow the name for another depressing town.

DURFEE-ARNOLD LETTERS (CDW): A collection of letters written in the 1760s, and found by young Ward in "the private collection of Melville F. Peters, Esq., of George St." in Providence. The correspondence sheds light on the marriage of Joseph Curwen and Eliza Tillinghast in 1763.

DURFEE, ELEAZAR (SH): "A school-teacher of middle age," and a tenant at the Shunned House in 1845, when he died there. During his last illness, he stared around him with glassy eyes, and attempted to bite the doctor's throat. In the tale, these peculiar circumstances are reported in the Providence *Daily Transcript and Chronicle* of October 27, 1845.

DWIGHT, FREDERICK N. (WE): An employee of the Venus Crystal Company, specified as Number B-9 in "Koenig's division." He is a veteran crystal prospector assigned to solitary, long-range missions. He has been "out" in search of crystals for approximately two months when he is lured into the invisible labyrinth. He apparently wanders in the transparent maze until exhaustion and despair lead him to kill himself by removing his breathing-mask. (The atmosphere on Venus was described in this tale as toxic enough to kill humans in as little as thirty seconds. Since HPL's lifetime it has been ascertained that it would really kill a human being in his first breath, except that the tremendous heat would have burned him to ashes first.) His corpse's sickeningly swift decomposition and devouring by scavengers is progressively witnessed by the hapless Kenton Stanfield, who has become caught in the same weird trap.

DWIGHT, WALTER C. (CDW): In the tale, he is a Providence artist with a studio at the foot of College Hill, and an "accomplished restorer of old paintings." Charles Dexter Ward hires him to uncover and restore the wood-panel portrait of Joseph Curwen, which Ward had discovered in Curwen's old house on Stampers' Hill.

DYER, PROFESSOR WILLIAM (MM, SOT): He is a geology professor at Miskatonic University. In 1930 he is the informal leader of the Miskatonic University Expedition, probably because the goal of the expedition is principally geological research; his leadership style plainly emphasizes collegial cooperation with Professors Pabodie, Atwood, and Lake, the other faculty members on the journey. Once in Antarctica and with the mission underway, he at first argues against the separation of the Lake-Atwood exploration party, but eventually gives his consent. On January 25, 1931, he leads the rescue mission to the Lake-Atwood camp, which has ceased responding to radio transmissions. On the following day, he flies over the nearby mountain range with Danforth and explores the lost city they find. He returns to the United States with the other survivors, and is the narrator of this tale, ostensibly to discourage another Antarctic expedition which is forming. In *The Shadow Out of Time* he is one of those who accompany Professor Peaslee to Western Australia to investigate reports of an ancient, buried city in the Great Sandy Desert. "Dyer" was a name in HPL's family tree.

DYLATH-LEEN (DQ): A significant port city in Dreamland. It lies on the shore of the Southern Sea, at the mouth of the river Skai. On the other side of the river is Parg, from whence come black slaves that are sold in Dylath-Leen. The city is built mostly of black basalt stone, with "dark and uninviting streets," "dismal sea-taverns," and many wharves. Its oddly-robed merchants trade with all of Dreamland. Randolph Carter visited here after Ulthar, still inquiring about the mountain Ngranek. After several days he has a few drinks with one of the merchants from the "black galleys," is rendered unconscious, and kidnapped to the moon. After being rescued by the cat army, he returns to Dylath-Leen, where he spends another fortnight warning the local merchants against further trade with the black galleys before departing on a ship bound to Oriab.

DZYAN, BOOK OF (HD): The *Stanzas of Dzyan*, purportedly translated from an ancient and secret language, form the core part of *The Secret Doctrine* (1888), a lengthy book by Helena Blavatsky (1831–91), mystic and founder of the Theosophical Society. In part, these "Stanzas" and Madame Blavatsky's accompanying commentaries, treat of the creation of worlds, the early teaching to humanity of otherworldly teachers or masters, reincarnation, the law of karma, Atlantis and Lemuria, and much else besides. *The Secret Doctrine* has had many readers in many lands over the years; interestingly, it was a favorite book of the popular singer Elvis Presley during the last five or ten years of his life. In this tale, a copy of the *Book of Dzyan* is among the rotting books discovered in the abandoned Starry Wisdom Church by Robert Blake.

E

EAGLE, BROOKLYN (HRH): The former leading newspaper of the New York City borough of Brooklyn, which ran from 1841, in an era when a then-independent Brooklyn briefly became the third-largest city in America, until 1955. The paper's most famous alumnus was Walt Whitman (1819–92), who was an *Eagle* reporter for a while in the 1840s–50s, before becoming a full-time poet. HPL was doubtless a frequent reader when he lived in Brooklyn in 1924–26. In the tale, the *Eagle* carries a quiet announcement of the Robert Suydam-Cornelia Gerritsen engagement.

EARTH'S GODS (OG, DQ): Mentioned in some of HPL's "Dunsanian" tales, the gods of earth are weak deities, fond of dancing and playing together. The Other Gods—such as Nyarlathotep—protect them from human intrusions, though.

EASTER ISLAND (SOI, HD, TGSK): A small, habitable island in the mid-Pacific Ocean, first reached by European explorers on Easter Sunday, 1722. It lies some 2,200 miles/3,450 km west of Chile, to which nation it now belongs, and is the world's most remote, inhabited place. Easter Island is famous for the *moai*, numerous monolithic stone heads which were carved from soft, dark volcanic rock found on the island, and sometimes erected as far as several miles away from the places where the rock was quarried and sculpted. The largest of the *moai* are some 40 feet tall and weigh over 50 tons; how the ancient island population of fewer than 15,000 people managed these feats of stonework and transportation with only stone tools and primitive technology is a marvel.

In *The Shadow Over Innsmouth*, Zadok Allen tells the narrator that the "island east of Otaheite," where Captain Obed Marsh first learned of the Deep Ones, had "a lot o' stone ruins older'n anybody knew anything abaout, kind o' like them on Ponape, in the Carolines, but with carvins' of faces that looked like the big statues on Easter Island." In *The Haunter of the Dark*, while prowling in the steeple of the Starry Wisdom church, Robert Blake finds a circle of seven high-backed "Gothic" chairs, "while behind them, ranging along the dark-panelled walls, were seven colossal images of crumbling, black-painted plaster, resembling more than anything else the cryptic carven megaliths of Easter Island." And in *Through the Gates of the Silver Key*, de Marigny tells the other three men present at the meeting that "the carvings on that box [which was left behind when Randolph Carter disappeared], though, do strongly suggest Easter Island images." After long interest in the *moai*, HPL saw the only genuine specimens in the United States in May, 1929, at the Smithsonian Institute in Washington, D.C.

EAST GREENWICH (SH): The Roulet family first settled in this town, which lies about fifteen miles south of the historic center of Providence, in 1686, as "Huguenots" following "the revocation of the Edict of Nantes." *Huguenot* is a French word, derived from the German *Eidgenossen*, "companions of [an] oath." The name was used during and after the 17th century to refer to Protestants in France, a mostly-Catholic country. The so-called "Edict of Nantes" (Nantes is a city in France), issued by King Henry IV in 1598, sought to bring a halt to decades of sectarian violence by allowing Protestants the right to practice their religion freely within certain limitations, although the Catholic church remained the state church and that of the ruling classes. However, a later French king revoked the Edict of Nantes in 1685, whereupon many thousands of Huguenots departed France to make new lives in Protestant countries, including England and her American colonies. "Unpopularity dogged [the Roulets] in East Greenwich," and after ten years they moved on to Providence in 1696.

EAST HIGH SCHOOL (TU): Joel Manton, the narrator, is the principal of this secondary school in Arkham.

EAST PROVIDENCE (FB): The nameless narrator mentions that he carries a concealed pistol ever since he was robbed in this part of town. In keeping with the dramatic rule that a pistol shown in the first act must be used by the last act, he saves his own life by firing a bullet into Crawford Tillinghast's weird machine.

EBLIS (HW): "I shall never forget that hideous summer sixteen years ago, when like a noxious afrite from the halls of Eblis typhoid stalked leeringly through Arkham," recalls the nameless narrator. These are terms which HPL borrowed from Arab legend, and specifically the 18th century novel *Vathek*, which he had read for the first time not long before writing this tale. "Eblis" is the Arab Moslem equivalent of the Devil, and an *afrite* (pronounced ah-FREET) is a subordinate demon and evil-doer.

EBN KHALIKAN: The non-fictitious Iraq-born Arab judge and scholar Ibn Khallikan (1211–82) dwelt in Egypt and Syria and was the author of a biographical dictionary of famous people, a valuable source of reasonably accurate historical information and quotations from older works which are now lost. According to HPL's pseudo-history of the *Necro-*

nomicon (in which he carelessly refers to the Arab as a "twelfth century biographer"), "Ebn Khalikan" wrote about Abdul Alhazred, particularly his mysterious and horrible disappearance. He did not actually do so, needless to say.

EDDY, ORRIN B. (HD): Possibly a former member of the Starry Wisdom cult, who is mentioned in the notebook of the dead newspaper reporter Edwin M. Lillibridge: "Story of Orrin B. Eddy 1857. They call it up by staring at the crystal, & have a secret language of their own." One of HPL's Providence friends for many years was a certain Clifford M. Eddy, who also published some stories in *Weird Tales*.

EFJEH-WEEDS (WE): Fast-growing, carrion-eating, ground-creeping vegetation on the planet Venus. Efjeh-weeds grow from the surrounding plain into the invisible labyrinth, to nip and devour the dead Frederick Dwight's leather garments, and then Dwight. Like "akmans," efjeh-weeds were a play on the name of Forrest J (not J., because it stood for nothing) Ackerman—"FJ-weeds"—a fantasy-fiction critic whom HPL politely detested.

EGYPT (UP, TO, BWS, CU, CDW, HD, SOT): "The East...Egypt... truly, this dark cradle of civilisation was ever the wellspring of horrors and marvels unspeakable!" So says Houdini in *Under the Pyramids*, which takes place in a travel-book Cairo and a Pharaonic dreamworld under the Pyramids of Giza. The narrator of *The Outsider*, having been rejected by mankind as a rotting corpse who shouldn't still be walking around, "plays by day among the catacombs of Nephren-Ka in the sealed and unknown valley of Hadoth by the Nile." In *Beyond the Wall of Sleep*, the nameless narrator's space-alien "brother of light" tells him that entities such as themselves "are all roamers of vast spaces and travellers in many ages. Next year I may be dwelling in the dark Egypt which you call ancient...."

Egypt is not mentioned in *The Cats of Ulthar*, but it is present all the same. The caravan of dark-skinned, wandering fortune-tellers that passes through the town of Ulthar is meant to suggest Gypsies, whose name in English is derived from "Egypt," since in the medieval popular mind that was where they had come from. (In fact they are descended from peoples of northwestern India, as demonstrated in modern times on linguistic and genetic grounds.) However, the caravan's wagons are painted with "strange figures with human bodies and the heads of cats, hawks, rams, and lions," parallel to the beast-headed pantheon of ancient Egyptian religion. The leader of the caravan wears "a head-dress with two horns and a curious disc between the horns," an emblem of Bast, the Egyptian cat-goddess. When the caravan boy Menes—itself an "Egyptian-sounding" name—curses the wicked old couple for murdering his kitten, "there seemed to form overhead the shadowy, nebulous figures of exotic things; of hybrid creatures crowned with horn-flanked discs."

In *The Case of Charles Dexter Ward*, Joseph Curwen's weird doings come to renewed public attention when he is sharply suspected as the ultimate destination of a cargo of mummies shipped from Egypt on the Spanish ship *Fortaleza*, seized as possible contraband in Rhode Island waters, but then released and sent on its way. "As if conscious of this belief, Curwen took care to speak casually on several occasions of the chemical value of the balsams found in mummies...." In fact, as this and later events make clear, he and his associates desire to resurrect the mummies for evil necromantic purposes.

In *The Haunter of the Dark*, it is mentioned that Professor Enoch Bowen came back to Providence from Egypt in May, 1844, and founded the Starry Wisdom cult the same year. We grow to understand that in Egypt this archaeologist had rediscovered the Shining Trapezohedron. That hideous object:

> ...sank with Atlantis before a Minoan fisher meshed it in his net and sold it to swarthy merchants from nighted Khem. The Pharaoh Nephren-Ka built around it a temple with a windowless crypt, and did that which caused his name to be stricken from all monuments and records. Then it slept in the ruins of that evil fane which the priests and the new Pharaoh destroyed, till the delver's spade once more brought it forth to curse mankind.

In *The Shadow Out of Time*, Professor Nathaniel Peaslee, during his mind's captivity among the Great Race, remembers meeting the mind of Khephnes, an Egyptian from the period of the 14th Dynasty (roughly 1650 B.C.).

EIBON, BOOK OF (DWH, TD, HD): Alternately known as *Liber Ivonis* in Latin, this is a book of forgotten lore invented by HPL's friend Clark Ashton Smith, mentioned in passing in these three HPL tales. "Eibon" was a Hyperborean wizard in a series of sword-and-sorcery tales written by Smith and published during the 1930s.

EINSTEIN, ALBERT (HY, CDW, DWH, WD, MM, SOT): One of the greatest physicists of all time, Albert Einstein (1879–1955) was born in Germany and lived and worked at different times in Germany, Switzerland, and lastly the United States of America. In the early 20th century he described and elaborated the very important scientific theory most often associated with his name, the "special theory of relativity." In their sophisticated fullness, Einstein's works are only to be understood by the small minority of people with advanced technical training in physics and mathematics. But in a tiny nutshell that omits as much scientific explanation as possible, the special theory of relativity proposes among other things that the maximum velocity attainable in the universe is the speed of light (which, by the way, is calculated as approximately 186,000 miles per second in a vacuum such as outer space). HPL followed Einstein's work and the "Einsteinian" revolution in physics carefully, and did his best to understand them as well as any intelligent non-specialist can. One of the necessary consequences of relativity theory is that linear time-travel, as it has often been imagined by humans, is impossible barring some further and greater quantum leap in our understanding of the universe's laws.

Albert Einstein is primarily responsible for the concept of "space-time" or the "space-time continuum," phrases which sometimes occur in HPL's writings. In scientific thinking up until the 20th century, it was assumed (as most people still vaguely think) that time was an absolute, completely separate from space, another absolute value. Rather, space and time are closely connected, with time forming "the fourth dimension" on top of three-dimensional space. Furthermore, depending on the position of the observer in the universe, time is not absolute, but is perceived relative to the viewer's position. Einstein tried to explain space-time-oriented relativity for the rest of us, with a helpful image: "If you are sitting in a chair with a pretty girl on your lap, an hour seems like a very short time. If you are sitting on a hot stove, a second seems like a very long time." Science-fiction and fantasy writers were quick enough to employ the concept that time could be moving at different rates in different worlds in "space-time"; HPL does this, for example, in discussing Randolph Carter's sojourn on Yaddith, or the awesome time-travels of the Great Race in *The Shadow Out of Time*; C.S. Lewis (1898–1963), to name only one other famous author, used the notion in *The Chronicles of Narnia* to explain why various human characters seem to be spending many years in Narnia while only a few moments have passed on earth, or why centuries of Narnian time may have elapsed within the span of one normal human lifetime.

In *The Shadow Out of Time*, Professor Peaslee of Miskatonic University notes that in 1914–15:

> My conception of *time*—my ability to distinguish between consecutiveness and simultaneousness—seemed subtly disordered; so that I formed chimerical notions about living in one age and casting one's mind all over eternity for knowledge of past and future ages....
>
> When I diffidently hinted to others about my impressions, I met with varied responses. Some persons looked uncomfortably at me, but men in the mathematics department spoke of new developments in those theories of relativity—then discussed only in learned circles—which were later to

become so famous. Dr. Albert Einstein, they said, was rapidly reducing time to the status of a mere dimension.

Charles Dexter Ward tells Dr. Willett that he is working to acquire knowledge of the utmost interest to mankind and to the world of thought: "Not even Einstein...could more profoundly revolutionise the current conception of things." In *Hypnos*, the nameless narrator writes: "One man with Oriental eyes has said that all space and time are relative...." He is undoubtedly referring to Einstein. Professor Lake in *At the Mountains of Madness* sends word to the base camp that his discovery of evidence of incredibly old life-forms: "Will mean to biology what Einstein has meant to mathematics and physics." In *The Whisperer in Darkness* the creature disguised as Henry W. Akeley, while talking about the prodigious powers of the fungi from Yuggoth, tells Professor Wilmarth: "Do you know that Einstein is wrong, that certain objects and forces *can* move with a velocity greater than that of light? With proper aid I expect to go backward and forward in time, and actually *see* and *feel* the earth of remote past and future epochs."

This harangue reminds one of a letter to a friend in the early 1930s, in which HPL mentioned his earliest engagement with the concept of the passage of time. According to the letter, he was only four years old:

> ...when I saw newspapers bearing the heavily-inked date-line TUESDAY, JANUARY 1, 1895. *1895!!* To me the symbol *1894* had represented an eternity—the eternity of *the present* as distinguished from such things as 1066 or 1492 or 1642 or 1776—& the idea of personally outliving that eternity was absorbingly impressive to me.... I shall never forget the sensation I derived from the idea of *moving through time* (if forward, why not backward?) which that '95 date-line gave me.

It also reminds one of a unique private game he mentions playing with his surviving aunt during 1935, when the 45-year-old bachelor and the 69-year-old widow were cutting expenses by living as roommates:

> ...imagining the calendar turned back to 1898 or 1900 or 1902 or so, & conversing as one actually would in that period...mentioning the shops, plays, songs, car [*i.e.*, streetcar] lines, news, sights, surroundings, & daily activities then flourishing, & excluding all anachronistic idioms & allusions.

ELAGABALUS (HW): This historical figure was a teenage Syrian princeling and pagan priest who, by a strange twist of fate, became the emperor of Rome in 218 A.D, with the official Roman name of Marcus Aurelius Antoninus. The 18th century English historian Edward Gibbon, in his classic *The Decline and Fall of the Roman Empire*, presented a priceless summary of Elagabalus' brief reign, a description HPL must certainly have read:

> Elagabalus...corrupted by his youth, his country, and his fortune, abandoned himself to the grossest pleasures with ungoverned fury, and soon found disgust and satiety in the midst of his enjoyments. The inflammatory powers of art were summoned to his aid; the confused multitude of women, of wines, and of dishes, and the studied variety of attitudes and sauces, served to revive his languid appetites. New terms and new inventions in these sciences, the only ones cultivated and patronized by the monarch, signalized his reign, and transmitted his infamy to succeeding times. A capricious prodigality supplied the want of taste and elegance.... To confound the order of seasons and climates, to sport with the passions and prejudices of his subjects, and to subvert every law of nature and decency, were in the number of his most delicious amusements. A long train of concubines, and a rapid succession of wives...were insufficient to satisfy the impotence of his passions. The master of the Roman world affected to copy the dress and manners of the female sex, preferred the distaff to the scepter, and dishonored the principal dignities of the empire by distributing them among his numerous [male] lovers, one of whom was publicly invested with the title and authority of the emperor's, or, as he more properly styled himself, the empress's husband.

In the year 222, following a palace revolt, this accidental and unworthy emperor was hacked to death and his body thrown into the Tiber River amid general rejoicing. The narrator of HPL's tale hyperbolically compares his friend Herbert West to "a languid Elagabalus of the tomb."

ELLERY, PROFESSOR (DWH): Chemistry professor at Miskatonic University. Analyzes the spiky metal object brought to him by Walter Gilman—who brought it back with him from some extra-dimensional "dream"—and finds that it consists of the elemental metals platinum, iron, and tellurium, together with "three other apparent elements of high atomic weight which chemistry was powerless to classify." He puts the mystery-object on display in the university museum.

ELIOT (PM): The silent listener of Thurber's narrative in this tale. Apparently he is a Boston gentleman and familiar with the local artistic circle. Famous real Boston Eliots include Charles W. Eliot (1834–1926), President of Harvard from 1869–1909, who is credited with the institutional changes that made it the preeminent American university; and the Reverend John Eliot (1604–90), a Puritan missionary to the Indians who lived in the forests west of early colonial Boston.

ELIOT, MATT (SOI): Captain Obed Marsh's first mate on the barque *Sumatra Queen* in the East Indies and Pacific trade during the 1830s. To a certain extent he corresponds to First Mate Starbuck in *Moby Dick*,

Herman Melville's classic novel set on a 19th century whaling ship: as Captain Marsh, Ahab-like in his demonic intensity, becomes more and more obsessed with raising the Deep Ones, Eliot becomes the voice of humanity, and of failed opposition. Matt Eliot, according to Zadok Allen, "was agin' [against] folks doin' any heathen things." Eliot told the Innsmouthers about "an island east of Otaheite [Tahiti] whar they was [where there were] a lot of stone ruins older'n anybody knew anything abaout," and a nearby volcanic island with once-submerged ruins that had "picters [pictures] of awful monsters all over them." Captain Marsh and Eliot wondered why the islanders in this place had plenty of fish and gold, when the tribes on neighboring islands did not. As Marsh wormed the secret of the Deep Ones from the tribal chief Walakea, Eliot "didn't like this business at all, an' wanted Obed shud [wanted Obed to] keep away from the island," but his protests were of no use. Later, after 1838, when Marsh had begun promoting the new worship in Innsmouth, Matt Eliot went into total opposition: "tried to line up the folks on his side, an' had long talks with the preachers—no use." When the Esoteric Order of Dagon was established in the early 1840s, and purchased the old Masonic Hall as its meetinghouse, Eliot (a Freemason himself) opposed the sale, "but he dropped aout of sight jest then." Presumably he was murdered, perhaps even dropped into the sea as a human sacrifice to the Deep Ones, an ironic fate.

ELIOT, T.S. (CDW): After finding horror on top of horror in the caverns under the Pawtuxet bungalow, on April 6, 1928, Dr. Marinus B. Willett tries to drive away some fearful thoughts by thinking of something else, "and repeated the Lord's Prayer to himself; eventually trailing into a mnemonic hodge-podge like the modernistic *Waste Land* of Mr. T.S. Eliot."

Thomas Stearns Eliot (1888–1965), was a poet and critic of the highest order, and the winner of the 1948 Nobel Prize for Literature. He was one of the main figures of the movement from traditional to "modern" (unrhyming, unmetrical, not formally structured) poetry, a shift that HPL resented and mocked. Eliot's most famous poem is probably *The Waste Land* (1922), a lengthy patchwork of seemingly random recollections, images and thoughts or fragmentary thoughts, that summed up what HPL despised about poetical modernism; at the time he described the poem in his "little magazine" *The Conservative* as a "practically meaningless collection of phrases, learned allusions, quotations, slang, and scraps in general." That Dr. Willett's disjointed and hysterical "hodge-podge" is compared to *The Waste Land* is no accident—and no compliment!

ELLIOTT SMITH, G. (WD): *See* "Anthropologists of the Mi-Go."

ELLIS ISLAND (HRH): From 1892–1943, a span which took in the period of massive immigration from southern and eastern Europe during 1890–1914, Ellis Island was the immigration gateway in New York harbor. Tens of millions of modern Americans can trace their ancestry to immigrants who successfully passed through Ellis Island, having convinced federal immigration authorities that they should be admitted to the United States, rather than being rejected on health or moral grounds. In this tale, it is noted that Robert Suydam's collection of Red Hook friends "coincided almost perfectly with the worst of the organized cliques which smuggled ashore certain nameless and unclassified Asian dregs wisely turned back by Ellis Island."

ELIZA (SOI): A merchant brig owned by the Gilman family of Innsmouth, and lost at sea with a crew of local sailors prior to 1838. This disaster helped to contribute to the economic crisis in town that helped incline some people toward Obed Marsh's preaching.

ELM MOUNTAIN (SK): A low mountain west of Arkham on the way to the ruins of the old Carter homestead; after Randolph Carter's disappearance on October 7, 1928, his car is found halfway up Elm Mountain. Investigators find a small box inside the car, with frightening carvings on the outside, and a queer parchment marked with unknown characters.

ELTDOWN SHARDS (SOT): A fictitious reference invented by Richard F. Searight (1902–75), an HPL correspondent in the 1930s, who published some undistinguished stories of his own in science-fiction pulps, including one in *Weird Tales* (*The Sealed Casket*, 1935). "Shards" are fragments of pottery or stone; in another, unpublished writing, HPL made it clear that the Eltdown Shards were baked clay. There is no clue as to the location of "Eltdown," assuming it is a place-name and not a personal name. A "-down" ending suggests southern England, and the so-called Piltdown Man "discovery" in southern England (*see* "Piltdown Man") might have produced this similar name for an incredibly ancient set of texts.

ELTON, BASIL (WS, DQ): He is the keeper of the North Point lighthouse near Kingsport. His father and grandfather had the same job. After seeing the mysterious White Ship passing by on many nights, he answers the call of her bearded captain and comes aboard. They sail into a "mysterious South" passing Zar, Thalarion, and Xura, and anchoring in Sona-Nyl, the Land of Fancy. After a certain time has elapsed, Elton induces the captain to sail on in quest of legendary Cathuria, through the Basalt Pillars of the West. When the ship falls over the world's-end waterfall instead, Elton awakens to find himself on the platform of the lighthouse, with the light out, and a ship breaking up on the rocks below. Later he finds a single spar (a pole or length of wood used to support a sail on a ship) of perfect whiteness. In *The Dream-Quest of Unknown Kadath*, Randolph Carter—having been kidnapped aboard the black galley at Dylath-Leen—while passing the same lands on the Southern Sea, recollects being told by them of "a fellow-dreamer of earth—a lighthouse keeper in ancient Kingsport."

ELWOOD, FRANK (DWH): A student at Miskatonic University, "the one fellow-student whose poverty forced him to room in this squalid and unpopular house." In early April he comes up to Walter Gilman's garret to seek help in working out a difficult mathematical problem; he discovers that Gilman is not in the room, although his shoes and clothing are. On April 22, with his dreams growing increasingly intense and horrific, Gilman calls on Elwood to discuss his own worries. The sympathetic Elwood proposes that Gilman move into his room for a while. For the next few days Gilman enjoys undisturbed sleep, and the two students visit local museums to gather opinions about the "spiky image" that Gilman had found in his old bed after a dream. On the night of April 28, Elwood and Gilman stay up late discussing the latter's mathematical studies as well as Keziah Mason and witchcraft lore. That night, while Elwood sleeps heavily, Keziah Mason comes to his room for Gilman. Walter Gilman spends the afternoon of the 29th alone in Elwood's room, and the two young men stay awake all night, skipping classes to sleep during the next day. The next night, Walpurgis-night, Elwood sleeps while Gilman experiences another dream-horror. On the morning of May 1, having been discovered deaf and in a state of shock, Gilman is placed on a couch in Elwood's room. Frank Elwood witnesses Gilman's horrible death, suffers a complete nervous breakdown, and withdraws from the university. He returns to Miskatonic in the fall, and graduates in June of the next year. He had left Arkham before 1931, when the Witch House is demolished and terrible things are found within its attic walls; but later he hears the news and suffers much mental anguish.

ELYSIUM (TR): After the death of Kalos, Musides makes for him a marble sepulchre with carvings that display "all the splendours of Elysium." Elysium, or the Elysian Fields, was in Greek mythology the locale of the heavenly afterlife granted to especially virtuous mortals, a place of eternal beauty, peace, and contentment.

EMMA (CC): A two-masted schooner, whose home port is Auckland, New Zealand. Sets sail for Callao, Peru, on February 20, 1925, with a crew of eleven men. Her officers are Captain Collins, First Mate Green, and Second Mate Johansen, a Norwegian; her sailors are William Briden,

Donovan, Guerrera, Ångstrom, Rodriguez, Parker, Hawkins, and one other whose name is not given. Blown far south of her correct course by a great storm on March 1; on March 22, meets the *Alert* at latitude 49° 51′ South, longitude 128° 34′ West, and is ordered to turn back. On the refusal of Captain Collins to do so, the *Alert* opens fire with its small cannons, and in the ensuing desperate sea-fight Collins, Green, the unnamed sailor, and the entire crew of the *Alert* are killed. With holes below her waterline, the *Emma* is abandoned and sinks. Her crew (Johansen and the seven other sailors) transfers to the *Alert*.

ENGLAND (TH, RW, EC, HY, CE, AJ, DQ, TS, CDW): HPL's family name stemmed from Devon, or Devonshire, in southwestern England; his father was the child of English immigrant parents. Few men who never saw England in their lives could have loved it as much as HPL did. As a product of (in his words) "unmixed Anglo-Saxon stock," in HPL's heart he was always a dual-national, a scion of the historic and picturesque England that he knew only from books and movies. Once, when sightseeing at the monument to Massachusetts militiamen who fell in the battle of Concord at the opening of the Revolutionary War, as he wrote to a friend, HPL "drew myself up and cried in a loud voice: 'So perish all enemies and traitors to His lawful Majesty, King George the Third!'" The period of his most extreme and affected anglophilia was probably over by the time he turned thirty, but something of it always remained.

His ex-wife Sonia wrote of him:

> H.P. never called himself an American; he insisted that he was an Englishman. Not only *that*, he regarded himself as a displaced Englishman, although he had never been in England. Apropos of this, he could describe very thoroughly every part of London, Stonehenge, Stratford-upon-Avon, and many other places in England.... He thought the [American] Revolution was a great mistake.

Not many genuine Englishmen, perhaps, could have (or would have), excelled HPL's digressive tribute from *The Dream-Quest of Unknown Kadath*; although, by the late 1920s when it was written, the author's vision of England was already scarcely less unreal than his vision of Dreamland:

> It seems that [Kuranes] could no more find content in [Celephaïs and Serranian], but had formed a mighty longing for the English cliffs and downlands of his boyhood, where in little dreaming villages England's old songs hover at evening behind lattice windows, and where grey church towers peep lovely through the verdure of distant valleys.... For though Kuranes was a monarch in the land of dream, with all its imagined pomps and marvels...he would gladly have resigned forever the whole of his power and luxury and freedom for one blessed day in that pure and quiet

England, that ancient, beloved England which had moulded his being and of which he must always be immutably a part.

HPL set five of his early tales in a stylized version of England, including *The Rats in the Walls* and *Arthur Jermyn*, with their plausible accumulations of English pseudo-history and "color." Additionally, in *The Case of Charles Dexter Ward*, Ward travels to England in 1923, where he finds lodgings on Great Russell Street in London and spends months doing research in the library of the British Museum and in a small laboratory he assembles in his rented rooms. Later, the mysterious revived person known only as "No. 118" leaves Dr. Willett a note, written with a common lead pencil on cheap lined paper, but the words are inscribed with:

> ...the pointed Saxon minuscules [letters] of the eighth or ninth century A.D., and brought with them memories of an uncouth time when under a fresh Christian veneer ancient faiths and ancient rites stirred stealthily, and the pale moon of Britain looked sometimes on strange deeds in the Roman ruins of Caerleon and Hexham, and by the towers along Hadrian's Wall.

Although HPL went everywhere in the universe in his imagination, he did not go to many places on earth. He traveled as far north as the Canadian city of Quebec, as far south as the Florida Keys, and no farther west than the Mississippi River—most of his travel was limited to the Atlantic seaboard. Europe he would never see at all.

EREBUS, MOUNT (TF, MM): A mountain on the east coast of Ross Island, Antarctica, discovered and named in 1841 by the Scottish explorer Sir James Ross. It is an active volcano, 12,448 feet high, and was first summited in 1908 by members of Sir Ernest Shackleford's expedition. In *The Festival*, the nameless narrator, underground beneath Kingsport, sees what he calls "that unhallowed Erebus of titan toadstools, leprous fire, and slimy water...." In *At the Mountains of Madness*, graduate student Danforth identifies it with Edgar Allan Poe's poetic "Mount Yaanek," a peak said, in Poe's poem, to lie "in the realms of the boreal pole."

ERYX, or the ERYCINIAN HIGHLAND (WE): A high and "very extensive" plateau on Venus, aerially surveyed by a certain Matsugawa twenty-two years after earthlings had landed on Venus, and fifty years before the events of this tale. The Venusians placed the invisible labyrinth and its crystal bait in the middle of this plateau.

There may be an earthly mythological explanation for the name of this fictional Venusian setting. One of the most famous shrines and pilgrimage-destinations in the Roman Empire was the temple of *Venus Erycina*, or "Venus of Eryx." (Venus being the Roman name for the same love-goddess the Greeks called Aphrodite.) Eryx, the modern Erice, was a Greek-founded city in the northeast corner of the island of Sicily, where the temple lay. It seems likely that HPL, with his excellent amateur knowledge of Greco-Roman mythology and culture, thought of this reference when he set out to co-author a science-fiction tale set on the planet Venus, the surface of which was at that time completely unknown to science. The ruins of the renowned temple were excavated during the year 1936; some news account of the preparations for this archaeological expedition may have assisted his memory. The tale was written in January, 1936.

ESQUIMAUX (ESKIMOS) (CC, PO, DQ): In *The Call of Cthulhu*, it is stated that a Professor Channing Webb encountered a degenerate, "devil-worshipping" Eskimo tribe in western Greenland in 1860; further description makes it clear that they were Cthulhu-cultists. In *Polaris*, the squat, yellow-skinned invaders of the northern land of Lomar are called "Inutos," which sounds suspiciously like "Inuits," the name the tribal people of the Arctic call themselves. ("Eskimo" is said to derive ulti-mately from an Algonquian word for "eaters of raw meat.") In *The Dream-Quest of Unknown Kadath*, while looking at the round window-less houses of moonbeasts on the surface of the moon, Randolph Carter is reminded of the huts of the "Esquimaux."

EUCLID (CC, MM, DWH): Euclid (ca. 3rd century B.C.) was one of the greatest of the ancient Greek mathematicians. His book, *The Elements,* described the fundamental principles of plane geometry in a logical and sequential fashion, which became the prototype for introductory geome-try textbooks forevermore. In *The Call of Cthulhu*, the Providence artist Henry A. Wilcox told Francis Wayland Thurston that "the *geometry* of the dream-place he saw was abnormal, non-Euclidean, and loathsomely redolent of spheres and dimensions apart from ours." To Professor Dyer's eyes, the lost city's architecture in *At the Mountains of Madness* exhibits "geometrical forms for which an Euclid could barely find a name." In *The Dreams in the Witch House*, it is mentioned that Walter Gilman's curriculum at Miskatonic University included the study of something called "non-Euclidean calculus." Non-Euclidean geometry, at any rate, was pioneered by leading mathematicians in the late 19th cen-tury; it is a very complicated subject.

EVIL CLERGYMAN (EC): Clergymen in the unbelieving HPL's tales are normally hapless or misinformed, but not evil. However the subject of this late story-fragment (which is nothing more or less than a descrip-tion of one of Lovecraft's own dreams as recounted to a friend in a per-sonal letter of 1933, and not printed anywhere until after his death), apparently a renegade English priest, is a practitioner of magic and alchemy. The narrator provides an unusually vivid description of this person's appearance:

> ...a thin, dark man of medium height attired in the clerical garb of the Anglican church [presumably meaning a black suit with a white shirt-collar]. He was apparently about thirty years old, with a sallow, olive complexion and fairly good features, but an abnormally high forehead. His black hair was well cut and neatly brushed, and he was clean-shaven though blue-chinned with a heavy growth of beard. He wore rimless spectacles with steel bows. His build and lower facial features were like other clergymen I had seen, but he had a vastly higher forehead, and was darker and more intelligent-looking—also more subtly and concealedly *evil*-looking.

On the bookshelves of the clergyman's garret rooms, which seem to be in an English seaport town, the narrator spies not only theological and classical works, but treatises on magic, some of which he can identify and some of which are in "strange alphabets whose titles I could not decipher." The narrator seems to see the images of this man being visited and denounced by a group of other churchmen including a bishop, and then on being left alone again, getting ready to hang himself—when *the truly terrible thing happens*, as HPL might have written in a regular tale. At the beginning of this dream a man, who is apparently the master of the place, shows the narrator the room with a few cryptic words:

> Yes, *he* lived here—but I don't advise your doing anything. Your curiosity makes you irresponsible. *We* never come here at night, and it's only because of *his* will that we keep it this way. You know what *he* did. That abominable society took charge at last, and we don't know where *he* is buried. There was no way the law or anything else could reach the society.

All in all, it could have made an interesting tale if HPL had ever expanded on his dream-recollection.

EXETER (SH): A rural Rhode Island village about thirty miles southwest of Providence, as the crow flies.

EXHAM PRIORY (RW): The English family seat of the de la Poers, three miles west of Ancaster village. It has been abandoned in the 17th century and forfeited to the royal government; by the time of the modern events in the tale, it belongs to the Norrys family who live nearby. The building is in ruins when it is purchased by Mr. de la Poer from America in 1918. But apparently much was left for architectural analysis. It had "peculiarly composite architecture...involving Gothic towers resting on a Saxon or Romanesque substructure, whose foundation in turn was of a still earlier order or blend of orders—Roman, and even Druidic or native

Cymric...." Some of this makes little sense—"Druidic" architecture, for example—but the point is that towers from perhaps the 13th or 14th century are resting on a substructure that is several centuries older, and the foundation under the substructure is anywhere from 1500 years old on up. The foundation merged on one side with "the solid limestone of the precipice from whose brink the priory overlooked a desolate valley." The priory's highly composite style reflects its unnaturally long history. It "stood on the site of a prehistoric temple...which must have been contemporary with Stonehenge." That temple's "indescribable rites" were later transferred intact to a Roman temple of Cybele on the same site, and later still, "certain among the Saxons [the Germanic tribesmen who invaded England after the Romans left in the 5th century] added to what remained of the temple." It is further said that "about 1000 A.D., the place is mentioned in a chronicle as being a substantial stone priory [monastery], housing a strange and powerful monastic order," naturally under the cover of Christian worship. The monastic order apparently declined, for there was "no impediment" when the priory was granted to the perfectly respectable knight Gilbert de la Poer in 1261, as his family's estate. He and his descendants constructed their castle over the old substructure and foundations.

Local folklore was full of hideous stories about Exham Priory, including "the dramatic epic of the rats," a starving multitude of which burst forth from the castle three months after its abandonment in the early 1600s, devouring animals and people alike in the surrounding countryside.

Eventually, Mr. de la Poer, along with Captain Norrys and several academic experts, descend to the lowest level of Exham Priory—a subcellar with a Roman altar and carvings—and find yet another level below it: a vast cavern-complex hollowed out of the supposedly "solid limestone" of the cliff, containing structures from various ages of English history; pens wherein, during a period lasting for centuries, a degraded race of quadruped humans were kept and fattened for eating; and huge piles of countless thousands of human bones, the former feeding-grounds of those rats. "And now," Mr. de la Poer laments in 1923, "workmen have blown up Exham Priory, and are busy obliterating the traces of its foundations."

There is no Exham, but HPL was probably thinking of several place names in southwestern England, in that very county of Devon in which he credibly believed that the Lovecrafts and Lovecrofts of his father's ancestry had dwelled. These include the Exe (pronounced "X") River, and some prominent places that the Exe flows through in its 55-mile course: Exmoor with its prehistoric earthworks and bleak highlands, the ancient cathedral town of Exeter (once a Roman legionary fort called *Isca Dumnoniorum*), and the small port of Exmouth where the river enters the sea. (Exeter was, in fact, the last Roman civil and military outpost to the west in its province of Britannia—beyond this point tribal Britons were left to their own devices in a region probably deemed too rocky and rugged to be worth the effort of pacification.) To add the frequent English place-name ending "-ham" to the ancient Devonian prefix of "Ex-" would have been a small matter for the author. This location also makes sense in light of the mention of "Lady Margaret Trevor from Cornwall, wife of Geoffrey [de la Poer]," whose evil deeds after marrying into the family made her "the daemon heroine of a particularly horrible old ballad not yet extinct near the Welsh border." Cornwall is the next English county to the west of Devonshire, nor indeed is Wales very far from either place. HPL also mentioned in a letter to a friend that *The Rats in the Walls* had a "south-of-England locale." (HPL's interest in southwestern England was shown again in *The Evil Clergyman*, where one of the local people speaks to the nameless narrator in a dialect recognizably that of Somerset or Devon, England's so-called "West Country.")

F

FALCONER (DH): *See* "Cryptographers of Dunwich."

FALONA (DCS): A country that is distant from Sarnath. Its adventurous men are blond and blue-eyed, no kin to the swarthy shepherds of Mnar. Only the Aryans from Falona are courageous enough to explore the site of the vanished city of Sarnath.

FARNOTH-FLIES (WE): A disgusting Venusian fly that swarms about and devours carrion meat, such as the corpse of the crystal prospector Frederick Dwight. By 1936, when this story was written, HPL felt that he had received a few too many rejection letters and editorial quibbles from the editor of *Weird Tales* magazine, *Farnsworth* Wright.

FARR, FRED (DH): Dunwich farmer, and a member of the group that follows Dr. Armitage and his colleagues from a safe distance. When Curtis Whateley collapses after looking through the telescope, Fred Farr helps to pick him up and stretch him out comfortably.

FEDERAL HILL (HD): A hill in Providence; it is about two miles away, and clearly visible, from HPL's last home at 66 College Street. In his time, Federal Hill was largely inhabited by Italian-Americans, who replaced the earlier Irish-American residents beginning in the later 19th century. From the windows of his apartment, HPL could see the brooding hulk of St. John's Catholic Church on Atwells Avenue, Federal Hill, which he dubbed "the old Free-Will [Baptist] Church," the place which became the home of Starry Wisdom. The church was built in 1871, and torn down in the 1990s; its site is now occupied by St. John's Park.

FEDERAL HILL BOYS (HD): Providence street gang whose members threaten the leaders of the Starry Wisdom cult in May, 1877.

FEENEY, FRANCIS X. (HD): An individual who joined the Starry Wisdom cult in 1849, but who returned to the Catholic fold in time to make a deathbed confession to a certain Father O'Malley. "Feeney" is an Irish name, and his first and middle names were in honor of St. Francis Xavier.

FENNER FAMILY (CDW): The closest neighbors of Joseph Curwen's Pawtuxet Road farmhouse outside of 18th century Providence. The family consists of Mr. and Mrs. Fenner and at least two children, Luke and his younger brother Arthur. The Curwen place is "distantly visible" from the Fenner farm. After the April, 1771 raid on Curwen's lair, Luke Fenner wrote letters to a relation in Connecticut about what he saw and heard. Charles Dexter Ward finds these letters in New London, Connecticut, in 1918–19; they give him a clearer picture of the events of that night. Historically, the Fenners were a prominent clan in colonial Rhode Island; one Arthur Fenner (1745–1805) was the governor of the state of Rhode Island from 1790 until his death; his son James (1771–1846) also served the state as governor and U.S. senator; and there is a Fenner Street in central Providence.

FENNER, MATT (IV): A little old man in Peck Valley, who was kind to George Birch during Birch's 1875–76 bankruptcy proceedings. When Fenner died some years later, the still-grateful Birch built him the best casket he knew how to make, assigning a "reject" casket to the deceased Asaph Sawyer.

FENTON, DR. (BWS): An "alienist" (psychiatrist) at the state mental hospital in New York where Joe Slater is an inmate, after Slater has been found not guilty of murder by reason of insanity. He is the superior of the nameless narrator, who is a "humble" intern at the facility. Following the narrator's experience with the dying Slater on February 21, 1901—in which his cosmic "brother of light" makes contact with him by means of the so-called "telepathic 'radio'"—old Dr. Fenton put the entire story down to his "excited imagination": "he listened with great kindness and patience…but afterward gave me a nerve-powder [presumably a tranquilizer] and arranged for the half-year's vacation on which I departed the next week." Fenton vows "on his professional honour that Joe Slater was but a low-grade paranoiac, whose fantastic notions must have come from the crude hereditary folk-tales which circulate in even the most decadent of communities."

FERENCZY, COUNT (CDW): The master of a Transylvanian castle east of the town of Rakus, in a part of Hungary that was transferred to the nation of Romania after the First World War. "Ferenczy" pronounced somewhat like "Fair-REN-zy", is a typical Hungarian surname. Charles Dexter Ward spends fifteen months in 1925–26 as a guest of this purported nobleman. The castle was appropriately situated on a mountain crag surrounded by dark forests, and was shunned by the country folk. The count was said to have peculiar manners, and to be of a "disquieting" age. Later, he becomes a correspondent of the mysterious "Dr. Allen," and ultimately is revealed to Edward Hutchinson, Joseph Curwen's friend and fellow-wizard from 17th century Massachusetts.

The count's long career is ended in 1928 by an inexplicable "titan explosion" which wipes out Castle Ferenczy and all of its inhabitants.

FLANDERS (HW): Dr. Herbert West and his comrade, while serving as surgeons with a Canadian Army division in World War I, are stationed in Flanders in 1915; typically for the nameless narrator's eternal-follower status with West, he is somehow a mere first lieutenant while West outranks him by two entire officer grades as a major, although they graduated from medical school in the same class and have practiced medicine together in the same clinic ever since. Be that as it may, Flanders is the name of an ancient region of northwestern Europe. Over its long history, Flanders has had varying sizes and compositions, but in modern times the name has generally referred to the western districts of Belgium. During 1914–18 (the years of the First World War, or, as many called it at the time, the Great War), Flanders was the scene of unending and costly trench-warfare between German and (mostly) British Empire forces including Canadian troops. With thousands of battle casualties each month, there was more work than military surgeons could handle.

FLATBUSH (HRH): A district of the borough of Brooklyn in New York City, originally settled by 17th century Dutch farmers. Robert Suydam, the last survivor of an old Dutch colonial family, lives here in a rundown mansion surrounded by the early 20th century metropolis. It is in the Dutch Reformed Church in Flatbush that he marries Miss Cornelia Gerritsen, from the Bayside district of Brooklyn.

HPL lived at 259 Parkside Avenue in Flatbush during part of his brief marriage and "New York Exile," and he visited most or all of the colonial Dutch and English antiquities in the vicinity, including the church in question.

FLEUR-DE-LYS BUILDING (CC): A building on Thomas Street, Providence, where the young artist Henry Wilcox lives circa 1925. The real building that HPL had in mind actually stands at 7 Thomas Street, and was constructed in 1885 in a garish French Provincial style that clashes with the neighboring colonial architecture. HPL hated the place as an intrusion, and called it the "Fleur-de-Lys Building" in this tale because of some ornamental carvings of the French national symbol over the front door.

FLUDD (CDW): Robert Fludd (1574–1637), a non-fictitious English Rosicrucian, Kabbalist, and all-around mystic. One of his books, *Clavis Alchimiae* ("The Key to Alchemy"), is in Joseph Curwen's 18th century library.

FOGG, EKBERG and JANAT (WE): Scientists who theorize that the Venusian "man-lizards" converse with one another by the motions of their four pectoral tentacles.

FORT, CHARLES (WD): American author (1874–1932). His self-appointed lifework was to compile newspaper and other printed accounts of strange experiences and inexplicable phenomena around the world (such as, for example, shellfish falling from the skies over Worcester, England, one day in 1881). His books were best-sellers. HPL enjoyed reading Fort's collections of oddities.

FOMALHAUT (DQ): A star of the first magnitude in the constellation *Piscis Australis*, visible in the Southern Hemisphere.

FOWLER (MM): Graduate student at Miskatonic University, member of the Miskatonic University Expedition. He becomes a member of the Lake-Atwood exploration party. Fowler makes the important discovery of fossilized footprints of the Old Ones in an Archaean-era slate formation, proving that the creatures had existed over 600 million years ago. He is found dead with the rest of the group on January 25, 1931.

FOWLER, GOODY (SK): A Puritan-era witch, whose crumbling farmhouse "with its little evil windows and great roof sloping nearly to the ground on the north side" is still to be seen in the early 20th century near the old Carter homestead outside of Arkham. "Goody" was short for "Goodwife," and was the standard term of informal address for married or mature women in the New England Puritan culture.

FRANCE (TA, MEZ, SH, TGSK, CDW): HPL located two stories in France, including one of his own most favorite tales, the Poe-esque *The Music of Erich Zann*. In *The Alchemist*, one of his juvenile works, set in a *chateau* somewhere in the French countryside, he made creative use of the possibilities of those Gothic-fiction standbys, a ruinous castle and an immemorially-cursed family line; he would come back to these themes in *The Rats in the Walls*. *The Music of Erich Zann* contains evocative descriptions of a dreamlike French city, and of the strange street where the narrator lives, the Rue d'Auseil. In addition, *The Shunned House* combines a traditional French werewolf story with the New England history of French Huguenot (Protestant Christians) refugee immigration. The shrieking of mad Rhoby Harris, who when sane had understood little or no French, "in a coarse and idiomatic form of the language," is a shocking touch derived from Providence legend. The Boston-bred Randolph Carter comes close to making the ultimate sacrifice for France, joining the Foreign Legion in 1914 and being almost mortally wounded in a 1916 battle near the northern village of Belloy-en-Santerre, as mentioned in *Through the Gates of the Silver Key*. During one military leave, he visits mysterious caverns under the French city of Bayonne. Charles Dexter Ward spends the middle of 1924 in Paris, giving an address in the Rue St. Jacques in letters to his parents. He visits the *Bibliotheque Nationale* (the French national library), and searches the rare manuscripts in the library of an "unnamed private collector."

FRAZER, SIR JAMES G. (CC): A British professor, anthropologist and folklorist at Cambridge University (1854–1941). He was the author of a fundamental text in anthropology, *The Golden Bough: A Study in Magic and Religion* (1890). HPL enjoyed browsing in this book, in which Frazer synthesized and compared an enormous amount of data about cult and magical practices from many places and centuries.

FREEBORN, PROFESSOR TYLER M. (SOT): This anthropology professor at Miskatonic University accompanied Professor Peaslee to Western Australia in 1935. On the incredibly ancient stone blocks dug out of the desert, Professor Freeborn found "traces of symbols which fitted darkly into certain Papuan and Polynesian legends of infinite antiquity."

FREUD, SIGMUND (BWS): The famous "father of psychoanalysis" (1856–1939). He is famous, among other reasons, for the "dream analysis" of mentally troubled patients, looking for keys to their nervous disorders or derangements in the coded messages of their dreams. HPL took a reserved but intelligent interest in the new science of psychiatry, an interest to which the fate of his parents might have added some impetus. He leads off this tale with some speculation about dreams, a subject close to his heart:

> Whilst the greater number of our nocturnal visions are perhaps no more than faint and fantastic reflections of our waking experiences—Freud to the contrary with his puerile symbolism—there are still a certain remainder whose immundane [non-worldly] and ethereal character permits of no ordinary interpretation....

FRYE, ELMER and SELINA (DH): A Dunwich farmer and his wife. Their farm lies on the eastern side of Cold Spring Glen, wherein the Horror takes refuge. At about 2 a.m. on September 11, 1928, the Fryes are awakened by loud noises outside their house, which turn into the sounds of their barn being torn down, and their cattle slaughtered, by some unknown force. After the sounds end, Mrs. Frye gets on the party-line telephone and tells their neighbor. On the night of September 12, the Fryes notice excitement among their dogs, and detect "vague sounds and stenches from afar." At 3 a.m. on the 13th, all the phones on the party line ring at once, and a voice is heard on each telephone, shrieking "Help, oh, my Gawd!"; then silence. After sunrise, a group of men went to the crushed farmhouse and found that "the Elmer Fryes had been erased from Dunwich." They are the first human casualties.

FUSELI, HENRY (COS, PM): Swiss-born English painter (1741–1825). According to a standard reference, Fuseli was "one of the most exotic, original and sensual of painters, although not one of the greatest." Much of his work belongs to the Romantic movement in art; some paintings (such as *The Nightmare*) have very sinister overtones. "I don't have to tell you why a Fuseli [painting] really brings a shiver while a cheap ghost-story frontispiece merely makes us laugh," says Thurber to Eliot in *Pickman's Model*.

G

GATE OF THE CARAVANS (DQ): It is found in the northern quarter of the city of Inganok, "where are the taverns of the yak-merchants and the onyx-miners." Randolph Carter comes here to speak with some miners, and the next day hires a yak and sets off through this gate on his northbound journey to Kadath.

GATE OF DEEPER SLUMBER (DQ): Seven hundred steps down from the Cavern of Flame, at the entrance to Dreamland. From here, one passes into the enchanted wood.

GALVEZ, JOSEPH D. (CC): New Orleans policeman who participates in the 1907 raid on Cthulhu-cultists one night in a Louisiana bayou. An "excitable Spaniard," Galvez thinks that he heard antiphonal (answering) responses to the outcries of the cult members, responses which were coming from someplace deeper in the swamp, where the police did not venture. He hints at a sound like "the faint beating of great wings, and of a glimpse of shining eyes and a mountainous white bulk" beyond the trees. He gives this information to Francis W. Thurston during an interview in the mid-1920s.

GARDEN OF THE GODS (MM): After cresting the mountain pass in their airplane, Professor Dyer and the graduate student Danforth see the ruins of the vast city of the Old Ones, and naturally experience a few moments of cognitive dissonance. "Of course we must have had some natural theory in the back of our heads to steady our faculties for the moment. Probably we thought of such things as the grotesquely weathered stones of the Garden of the Gods in Colorado...." The Garden of the Gods, near the city of Colorado Springs, is an area where erosion of sandstone hills and ridges has created large and unusual rock formations, many of which have received fanciful nicknames.

GARDNER, NABBY (COS): Nahum Gardner's wife and the mother of his three sons. She keeps five cats as household pets, and is a friend to her farm neighbor, Mrs. Ammi Pierce. Either because of her gender, or because (like any farm wife) she spent more time close to home and the barnyard well than did the menfolk laboring out in the fields, she is the first member of the family to succumb to the Colour; she also suffered more when all the neighbors began to shun the Gardner home. In any

184

case, by May of 1883, she sees tree branches moving at night, although there is no wind; and in June she becomes completely insane, screaming "about things in the air which she could not describe. In her raving there was not a single specific noun, but only verbs and pronouns. Things moved and changed and fluttered...she was being drained of something...nothing was ever still in the night...walls and windows shifted." Nahum Gardner allows her to wander around the house until her expression begins to frighten their children—"Thaddeus nearly fainted at the way she made faces at him"—thereafter he keeps her locked up in the attic. In July she ceases to speak, and crawls on all fours; her husband believes she has begun to glow in the dark. September brings bouts of wild screaming, including "dialogue" with Thaddeus, who has also gone mad and been locked in the adjoining attic chamber. In November, Ammi Pierce goes up to investigate Nabby's cell, where he sees in a corner "something dark" that makes the tough farmer scream: "a blasphemous monstrosity" that "very slowly and perceptibly moved as it continued to crumble." When Ammi leaves the room, he has mercifully made sure that "no moving object was left."

GARDNER, NAHUM (COS): This tale was Lovecraft's "Book of Job," in the opinion of critic John T. Gatto; a reference to Job, the pious and wealthy man who loses his fortune, family, and good health as a test from God in one of the books of the Old Testament. Nahum Gardner is a "lean, genial" Yankee farmer, about fifty years old in 1882, and the owner of a flourishing farm in the hills west of Arkham, Massachusetts, with "a trim white house amidst fertile gardens and orchards." He is the husband of Nabby Gardner, and father of three healthy sons: Zenas, Thaddeus, and Merwin. In the spring of 1882, he briefly becomes a "local celebrity" after a meteorite falls in his barnyard, and journalists and Miskatonic University professors come to see it. That summer, Gardner ("Gardener"?) works hard on his farm, but feels unusually tired. His autumn fruit harvest is beautifully colored, but inedible; he understands that the meteorite somehow poisoned the low-lying soil. By the winter, the formerly "genial" Nahum has become "taciturn and brooding"; he notices the snow tracks of squirrels, rabbits, and foxes around his farm, professing to see "something not quite right about their nature and arrangement." Along with the rest of the family, he begins to manifest a habit of stealthy "listening," which increases the local talk about their increasing strangeness. In April, 1883, at the start of another growing season, he plows and sows his ten-acre pasture and the upland lot, but leaves the low ground around the farmhouse alone, hoping that a fallow year might draw the "poison" from the soil. In May he reads an article in the Arkham *Gazette* about how his own farm glows in the dark. In the summer his wife and horses all go mad; he locks up the former, shoots the latter. By September, with the farm vegetation turning grey and crumbling into dust, Nahum and his sons are in bad shape. He has become "calloused to strange and unpleasant things." The Gardner men drink their tainted well-water:

> as listlessly and mechanically as they ate their meagre [*sic*] and ill-cooked meals and did their thankless and monotonous tasks through the aimless days. There was something of stolid resignation about them all, as if they walked half in another world between lines of nameless guards to a certain and familiar doom.

When son Thaddeus goes mad in September, Nahum confines the boy in an attic room next to Nabby Gardner's makeshift cell. His livestock begin to turn grey and brittle to the touch, his dogs all vanish in one night. On October 19, he staggers into the house of his neighbor, Ammi Pierce, to announce the death of Thaddeus. Early on October 22, he bursts into the Pierce kitchen to tell his neighbors of Merwin's sudden disappearance. One day in mid-November, Ammi Pierce visits and finds that Zenas Gardner has also vanished, and Nahum has finally lost his sanity, only babbling inanely in response to Pierce's questions: "the hapless farmer's mind was proof [armored] against further sorrow." While Ammi Pierce is upstairs in the attic putting the crumbling thing that was once Nabby Gardner out of her misery, he hears sounds of thumping and "suction" from downstairs, and returns to find his old friend Nahum crumbling away into brittle grey pieces, but still able to murmur: "...jest a colour...an' it burns an' sucks...it comes from some place whar things ain't as they is here...one o' them professors said so... he was right." A moment later Ammi Pierce covers Nahum Gardner's ash-like remains with a prosaic red-checked tablecloth. "It must all be a judgment of some sort," Nahum Gardner once says, "although he could not fancy what for, since he had always walked uprightly in the Lord's ways as far as he knew."

"Nahum" is a name originally from the Old Testament; he is the seventh of the Minor Prophets. Thereby may hang a tale. Although he was a convinced atheist, HPL knew the Bible well as a work of literature; unlike most of the faithful, he had actually *read* the Bible from beginning to end. On occasion, he demonstrated his familiarity with the so-called King James Version, the early 17th-century Bible translation that is one of the masterpieces of the English language. In this very tale, HPL compares phenomena experienced by Ammi Pierce and the other searchers during the Colour's departure from earth to the spiritual fire that came down on the Apostles' heads at Pentecost (an incident found in the New Testament at Acts 2:3). The short Book of Nahum in the Old Testament,

which deals with the fall of the Assyrian imperial city of Nineveh, opens
with the following intriguing passages in the King James Version:

> The Lord is slow to anger, and great in power, and will not at all acquit the
> wicked; *the Lord hath his way in the whirlwind and the storm*, and the
> clouds are the dust of his feet.... The mountains quake at him, and the hills
> melt, *and the earth is burned at his presence, yea, the world, and all that
> dwell therein.* (Nahum 1:3, 5; emphasis added.)

The Colour burns the Gardner farm and the people and other creatures
on it, as Nahum Gardner came finally to realize: "...the colour...it
burns...cold an' wet, but it burns..." The Colour departs from the earth
through a hole in the clouds of the night sky, in a "mounting wind," that
"shrieked and howled, and lashed the fields and distorted woods in a mad
cosmic frenzy."

GARDNER, MERWIN (COS): "Mernie," the youngest son of Nahum
and Nabby Gardner. Described as "little," his favorite playmate was his
older brother Thaddeus. In September, 1883, Merwin and his brothers
did not return to school after the summer vacation. When Thaddeus and
Nabby Gardner had both been locked in the attic, it seems to Merwin as
if their back-and-forth screaming is a conversation in some mutual language. He goes into violent hysterics upon Thaddeus' death in October.
Later still, the child suffers his own nervous collapse and begins screaming at everything. On the night of October 21 he walks outside to the well
with a lantern and a pail, to draw some water, and never returns. Some
melted and twisted metal fragments, the remnants of his lantern and pail,
are found near the well. Later his bones are found at the bottom of it.
"Merwin" is simply an English surname in origin (like Howard and
Whipple, respectively the first names of the author and his grandfather);
HPL's reason, if any, for choosing it as the youngest Gardner child's
given name is apparently unknown.

GARDNER, THADDEUS (COS): "Thad," the middle son of the
Gardner family. An "especially sensitive youth," he is fifteen years old in
the fateful spring of 1883, when he swears that he can see the trees
around the farmhouse swaying on windless nights. At school, Thaddeus
suffers the most of the three brothers from all the gossip about the weird
goings-on at his family's farm. He nearly faints at the faces his mad
mother Nabby begins making at him, and goes mad himself in September, 1883, after going out to the well for some water: "shrieking and
waving his arms, and sometimes lapsing into an inane titter or a whisper
about 'the moving colours down there'" in the well. After he begins to
run into things and hurt himself, the compassionate Nahum confines him
in an attic room next to Nabby's cell. He dies on or about October 19, of

the "crumbling away," and Nahum buries his remains in the family cemetery behind the farmhouse.

The biblical Thaddeus was certainly one of the most obscure of the Twelve Apostles. The popularity of his name in 19th century America was undoubtedly due to the renown of Thaddeus Kosciusko (1746–1817), a Polish soldier of fortune whose devotion to the cause of liberty led him in 1777 to volunteer himself for service in the American Revolution. As one of the very few men in the Continental Army with solid training as a professional military officer in Europe, General Kosciusko provided significant help in the winning of the Revolutionary War. He later fought in unsuccessful wars for the independence of his native Poland, one of the romantic lost causes of the era. In Polish the name is spelled *Tadeusz*; Thaddeus is the accepted English version.

GARDNER, ZENAS (COS): The eldest son of the Gardner family, "a big boy, full of life"; he lasted the longest of Nahum's wife and children. When the roses, zinnias and hollyhocks bloomed around the farmhouse in the summer of 1883, Zenas perceives them to be such "blasphemous-looking things" that he chops them all down. By October he is reduced to sitting and staring into space. At some point in late October or early November, he goes to the well for some water, and is not seen again. Zenas Gardner's "mainly skeletal" remains are found like those of Merwin, when the well-bottom is eventually searched. His name is found in the Epistle of St. Paul to Titus, 3:13—"Bring Zenas the lawyer and Apollos on their journey diligently, that nothing be wanting unto them"—in which the apostle apparently directs that these two believers be brought to him at the city of Nicopolis. Zenas Gardner shares his unusual first name with Zenas Low, one of the 18th century menservants of the William Harris household in *The Shunned House*.

GAY (TT): The narrator begins to scribble witty remarks on the fly-leaves of his books "which brought up suggestions of Gay [and] Prior." John Gay (1685–1732) was a leading English poet and dramatist of his day. His best-known work, a satirical musical play dealing with London's criminal underworld and called *The Beggar's Opera*, reappeared in modernized form in Germany in the 20th century as the Brecht/Weill classic *The Three-Penny Opera* with the criminal anti-hero Macheath (also known as "Mack the Knife" in the Hollywood version).

GEBER'S *LIBER INVESTIGATIONIS* (CDW): An ancient alchemy text, whose Latin title as presented by HPL means "Book of Investigation," or "Book of Inquiry". "Geber" was the medieval European version of the name of the brilliant Arab chemist/metallurgist Abu Musa Jabir ibn Hayyan, who was born at Tarsus (in modern southeastern Turkey) early in the 8th century, and later dwelled in Damascus. Of the hundreds of treatises once attributed to Geber, many or most were probably written by other hands after the sage's death, including some as late as the 14th century in Europe. His actual work centered on chemical processes and the attempted transmutation of metals, in the course of which he discovered nitric acid and red oxide of mercury. His best-known book is entitled in a Latin translation: *De Alchemia: traditio summa perfectionis in duos libros divisa. Item: Liber investigationis magisterii eiusdem*; it has been called "the oldest surviving chemistry textbook" and (with his other extant works) "the most important means by which the Arabic chemical knowledge became available to the alchemists of medieval Christendom." Joseph Curwen owns a copy in his 18th century Providence library.

GEDNEY (MM): Graduate student and member of the Miskatonic University Expedition. On December 13–15, 1930, he climbs Mount Nansen along with Professor Pabodie and the graduate student Carroll. He flies over the South Pole on January 6, 1931. He goes along with the Lake-Atwood group, and is acting foreman of the excavation team on January 23, when the drill opens up the subterranean cave full of specimens, the event which sends him shouting back to the camp to alert everyone. His body is *not* found on January 25 with those of the rest of the Lake-Atwood group, leading to the stunned conjecture that Gedney might have gone insane and somehow killed all the other men and the sled dogs, by himself. But Professor Dyer, and the graduate student Danforth, find Gedney's carefully-wrapped, hard-frozen body in a place in the abandoned city of the Old Ones, along with the body of a sled dog; ironically, they had been brought thither as scientific specimens by the revived Old Ones. Professor Dyer must leave the bodies where he finds them: "They have a strange and titanic mausoleum, and I hope the end of this planet will find them still undisturbed."

GEDNEY, JUDGE (CDW): The historical Bartholomew Gedney (1640–1697) was one of the associate judges of the Salem witchcraft trials. In this tale, it is mentioned that he presided over the August 8, 1692 examination of Amity How, who reveals that "Joseph C." and "Simon O." received the Devil's Mark from George Burroughs at a coven meeting one night. Charles Dexter Ward finds the record of this hearing during his 1919 researches in Essex County, Massachusetts.

GEOFFREY, JUSTIN (TD): A "notorious Baudelairean poet...who wrote *The People Of The Monolith* and died screaming in a madhouse in 1926 after a visit to a sinister, ill-regarded village in Hungary." Edward Derby is a "close correspondent" of this too-daring poet. ("Justin

Geoffrey" and the title of his book were fictional creations of Robert E. Howard, HPL's friend and close correspondent.)

GEOMETRY (NC, CC, MM, DWH, SH, TGSK, TD, HD, EC): History records that HPL was an excellent geometry student in high school. It is no surprise to find effective allusions to geometry at key moments of certain tales, always associated with the inhuman or unearthly, beginning with *The Nameless City*, in which the nameless narrator observes that: "There were certain *proportions* and *dimensions* in the ruins that I did not like."

In *The Call of Cthulhu*, the sculptor Henry A. Wilcox tells Francis W. Thurston of the place he had seen in dreams in early 1925, "the damp Cyclopean city of slimy green stone—whose *geometry*, he oddly said, was *all wrong*—." The sailor Johansen saw the same thing in person:

> Without knowing what futurism [a school of modern art and architecture which was influential at the time] is like, Johansen achieved something very close to it when he spoke of the city; for instead of describing any definite structure or building, he dwells only on broad impressions of vast angles and stone surfaces.... I mention his talk about *angles* because it suggests something Wilcox had told me of his awful dreams. He had said that the *geometry* of the dream-place he saw was abnormal, non-Euclidean, and loathsomely redolent of spheres and dimensions apart from ours.

Later Johansen's written narrative suggests to Thurston that "the very sun of heaven seemed distorted when viewed through the polarising miasma," and brings up again "those crazily elusive angles of carven rock where a second glance shewed [*sic*] concavity after the first shewed convexity." Then the eight sailors blunder into the "immense carved door" of Cthulhu's house:

> ...they all felt it was a door because of the ornate lintel, threshold, and jambs around it, though they could not decide whether it lay flat like a trap-door or slantwise like an outside cellar door. As Wilcox would have said, the geometry of the place was all wrong. One could not be sure whether the sea and the ground were horizontal, hence the relative position of every-thing else seemed phantasmally variable....
>
> ...Then Donovan felt over it delicately around the edge, pressing each point separately as he went. He climbed interminably along the grotesque stone moulding—that is, one would call it climbing if the thing was not after all horizontal—and the men wondered how any door in the universe could be so vast. Then, very softly and slowly, the acre-great panel began to give inward at the top; and they saw that it was balanced. Donovan slid or somehow propelled himself down or along the jamb and rejoined his fellows, and everyone watched the queer recession of the monstrously carven portal. In this phantasy of prismatic distortion it moved anoma-

lously in a diagonal way, so that all the rules of matter and perspective seemed upset.

As the three surviving sailors run away from Cthulhu, R'lyeh's geometry plays one more trick on them: "Parker slipped as [they] were plunging frenziedly over endless vistas of green-crusted rock to the boat, and Johansen swears he was swallowed up by an angle of masonry which shouldn't have been there; an angle which was acute, but behaved as if it were obtuse."

The geometry element is very strong in *At the Mountains of Madness*, when Professor Dyer and the graduate student Danforth approach and explore the lost city of the Old Ones in Antarctica. On the flight to the great mountains, Professor Dyer sees an amazingly vivid "mirage" in the air ahead:

> The effect was that of a Cyclopean city of no architecture known to man or to human imagination, with vast aggregations of night-black masonry embodying monstrous perversions of geometrical laws.... There were truncated cones, sometimes terraced or fluted, surmounted by tall cylindrical shafts here and there bulbously enlarged and often capped with tiers of thinnish scalloped discs; multitudinous rectangular slabs or circular plates or five-pointed stars with each one overlapping the one beneath. There were composite cones and pyramids either alone or surmounting cylinders or cubes or flatter truncated cones and pyramids, and occasional needle-like spires in curious clusters of five.

Not long afterwards, in the air again, Professor Dyer notices the "regular cube and rampart formations" on the mountain slopes. His first glimpse of the lost city reveals "an endless labyrinth of colossal, regular, and geometrically eurhythmic stone masses...this Cyclopean maze of squared, curved, and angled blocks...." The general shape of the buildings "tended to be conical, pyramidal, or terraced; though there were many perfect cylinders, perfect cubes, clusters of cubes, and other rectangular forms...." The city, when they investigate it on foot, offers to their view "geometrical forms for which an Euclid could scarcely find a name—cones of all degrees of irregularity and truncation; terraces of every sort of provocative disproportion; shafts with odd bulbous enlargements; broken columns in curious groups; and five-pointed or five-ridged arrangements of mad grotesqueness." After a time, naturally: "The Cyclopean massiveness and giganticism of everything around us became curiously oppressive; and there was something vaguely but deeply inhuman in all the contours, dimensions, proportions, decorations, and constructional nuances of the blasphemously archaic stonework." After his return from Antarctica, Danforth, who made the mistake of looking backward as their airplane was fleeing the city again, nervously mentions (among other things): "the windowless solids with five dimensions."

In 1692 when Keziah Mason, the witch of *The Dreams in the Witch House*, was in jail in Salem, she inexplicably escaped from her cell: "and not even Cotton Mather could explain the curves and angles smeared on the grey stone walls with some red, sticky fluid." But before that, while "under pressure":

> She had told Judge Hathorne of lines and curves that could be made to point out all directions leading through the walls of space to other spaces beyond, and had implied that such lines and curves were frequently used at certain midnight meetings.... Then she had drawn those devices on the wall of her cell and vanished.

Walter Gilman, studying Keziah Mason, "rowed out twice to the ill-regarded island in the river, and made a sketch of the singular angles described by the moss-grown rows of grey standing stones...." He lives in the "eastern attic room" which was once Keziah Mason's in the Witch House.

> Gilman's room was of good size but queerly irregular shape; the north wall slanting perceptibly inward from the outer to the inner end, while the low ceiling slanted gently downward in the same direction.... The loft above the ceiling—which must have had a slanting floor was...inaccessible.
>
> As time wore along, his absorption in the irregular wall and ceiling of his room increased; for he began to read into the odd angles a mathematical significance which seemed to offer vague clues regarding their purpose. Old Keziah, he reflected, might have had excellent reasons for living in a room with peculiar angles; for was it not through certain angles that she claimed to have gone outside the boundaries of the world of space we know?
>
> The touch of brain-fever and the dreams began early in February. For some time, apparently, the curious angles of Gilman's room had been having a strange, almost hypnotic effect on him; and as the bleak winter advanced he had found himself staring more and more intently at the corner where the down-slanting ceiling met the inward-slanting wall.

Gradually the dreams—which Gilman supposes are "a result, jointly, of his studies in mathematics and in folklore"—begin:

> Gilman's dreams consisted largely in plunges through limitless abysses of inexplicably coloured twilight and bafflingly disordered sound.... The

abysses were by no means vacant, being crowded with indescribably angled masses of alien-hued substance, some of which appeared organic while others seemed inorganic....

All the objects—organic and inorganic alike—were totally beyond description or even comprehension. Gilman sometimes compared the inorganic masses to prisms, labyrinths, clusters of cubes and planes, and Cyclopean buildings; and the organic things struck him variously as groups of bubbles, octopi, centipedes, living Hindoo idols, and intricate Arabesques....

Later still when Gilman's dreams have become "atrocious," he sees more of the abysses full of inexplicable shapes, including two which pay special attention to him and which we understand to be Keziah Mason and Brown Jenkin:

In the deeper dreams everything was likewise more distinct [than before] and Gilman felt that the twilight abysses around him were those of the fourth dimension. ...Two of the less irrelevantly moving things—a rather large congeries [*i.e.*, collection or assortment] of iridescent, prolately spheroidal bubbles and a very much smaller polyhedron of unknown colours and rapidly shifting surface angles—seemed to take notice of him and follow him about or float ahead as he changed position among the titan prisms, labyrinths, cube-and-plane clusters, and quasi-buildings....

During the night of April 19–20 the new development occurred. Gilman was half-involuntarily moving about in the twilight abysses with the bubble-mass and the small polyhedron floating ahead, when he noticed the peculiarly regular angles formed by the edges of some gigantic neighboring prism-clusters. In another second he was out of the abyss and standing tremulously on a rocky hillside bathed in intense, diffused green light....

Then he saw the two shapes laboriously crawling toward him—the old woman and the little furry thing. The crone strained up to her knees and managed to cross her arms in a singular fashion, while Brown Jenkin pointed in a certain direction with a horribly anthropoid fore paw which it raised with evident difficulty. Spurred by an impulse he did not originate, Gilman dragged himself forward along a course determined by the angle of the old woman's arms and the direction of the small monstrosity's paw, and before he had shuffled three steps he was back in the twilight abysses. Geometrical shapes seethed around him, and he fell dizzily and interminably. At last he woke in his bed in the crazily angled garret of the eldritch old house.

By a rather frequent technique in HPL's tales, these events had been clearly foreshadowed for the reader by a description of Gilman's growing prowess in mathematics classes, his "comprehension of fourth-dimensional and other problems that had floored all the rest of the class," and his "intuitive knack for solving Riemannian equations." (Georg F.B.

Riemann (1826–66), a German mathematics professor, pioneered non-Euclidean geometry with equations and processes to represent "elliptic space," as opposed to the ancient elements of Euclidean plane geometry. This and other work was of the highest importance for the progress of 20th century physics, including the development of the theory of relativity.) In particular, there is mention of a classroom discussion of "possible freakish curvatures in space" during which Gilman expressed the "sober theory that a man might—given mathematical knowledge admittedly beyond all likelihood of human acquirement—step deliberately from the earth to any other celestial body which might lie at one of an infinity of specific points in the cosmic pattern."

The nameless narrator of *The Evil Clergyman*, when seeing the Evil Clergyman for the first time, perceives that: "Everything was shadowy pantomime, as if seen at a vast distance through an intervening haze—although on the other hand the newcomer and all subsequent comers loomed large and close, as if both near and distant, according to some abnormal geometry."

In *The Shunned House* it is mentioned that Etienne Roulet, patriarch of the ill-regarded family that moved to Providence in 1696, was "less adept at agriculture than at reading queer books and drawing queer diagrams...."

The Haunter of the Dark develops around a mysterious object so otherworldly that it is only described by its geometrical shape—the Shining Trapezohedron. It is described as:

> ...an egg-shaped or irregularly spherical object some four inches through.... The four-inch seeming sphere turned out to be a nearly black, red-striated polyhedron with many irregular flat surfaces; either a very remarkable crystal of some sort, or an artificial object of carved and highly polished mineral matter.

As he approaches the Ultimate Gate in *Through the Gates of the Silver Key*, Randolph Carter finds himself among "great masses of towering stone, carven into alien and incomprehensible designs and disposed according to the laws of some unknown, inverse geometry." The cloaked and mitred Shapes sit on their "quasi-hexagonal" pedestals, which form "an oddly curved line (neither semicircle nor ellipse, parabola nor hyperbola)...."

After a few years of marriage to Asenath, Edward Derby tells his friend Daniel Upton, among other things, "of complex angles that lead through invisible walls to other regions of space and time.... He would now and then back up certain crazy hints by exhibiting objects which utterly nonplussed me—elusively colored and bafflingly textured objects like nothing ever heard of on earth, whose insane curves and surfaces answered no conceivable purpose and followed no conceivable geometry. These things, he said, came 'from outside'; and his wife knew how to get them."

GERRITSEN, CORNELIA (HRH): "A young woman of excellent position, and distantly related to the elderly bridegroom-elect" and a good old-fashioned Dutch name, who agrees to marry the much-older Robert Suydam after he has cleaned up his person, home, and life. Their engagement is announced in the Brooklyn *Eagle* (the now-defunct principal newspaper of the New York borough of Brooklyn—Walt Whitman was once a writer for it), and the marriage ceremony occurs at the old Dutch Reformed Church in Flatbush, Brooklyn. The newlywed couple departs for their European honeymoon the same evening, on an ocean liner owned by the famous Cunard Line. That night, she and Mr. Suydam are found in their cabin, strangled to death, "but the clawmarks on Mrs. Suydam's throat could not have come from her husband's or any other human hand." The bizarre group of sailors who come aboard the liner to remove Suydam's body, also drain his wife's corpse of all its blood; the blood probably figured in the occult ceremony later witnessed by Detective Malone in the catacomb under Red Hook. Cornelia Gerritsen Suydam's body is buried in Greenwood Cemetery, a notable Brooklyn burial ground.

GHASTS (DQ): Ghasts are creatures that live In the Vaults of Zin in lower Dreamland. They die when exposed to bright light, but can survive in the permanent dim twilight of their domain. Ghasts are about the size of small horses, with hard, sharp hooves; but they move by hopping on their hind legs, like kangaroos. They have humanoid faces but no fore-heads or noses. Ghasts are scabrous and venomous, eat people, ghouls, gugs, and one another, and converse among themselves in "coughing gutturals." One ghast pursues Randolph Carter and his ghoulish escort through the city of the gugs and up the stairs of the great tower, but is bludgeoned with a tombstone by a ghoul on the stairs.

GHOULS (TO, PM, DQ, TH): HPL conceived of ghouls as doglike and manlike creatures circulating between Dreamland and the world we know. His ghouls are dynamic corpse-eaters, sturdy, resourceful, and even versatile in their way. The narrator of *The Outsider* finds a place in their ranks at the end: "Now I ride with the mocking and friendly ghouls on the night-wind, and play by day among the catacombs." In *Pickman's Model*, the artist draws them amidst familiar Massachusetts scenery in paintings with cynical titles like *Ghoul Feeding, The Lesson, Subway Accident*, and the scandalous *Holmes, Lowell, and Longfellow Lie Buried in Mount Auburn* (a reference to the hallowed New England cultural fig-ures Oliver Wendell Holmes, James Russell Lowell, and Henry Wads-worth Longfellow, and to Mount Auburn cemetery in Cambridge, Massa-chusetts; the implication is that they are really *not* buried there, because ghouls ate their remains). As painted by Pickman, ghouls are "seldom completely human, but often approach humanity in varying degree... roughly bipedal...forward slumping, and [of] a vaguely canine cast." They feel "rubbery" to the touch. Mr. Thurber speaks of pointed ears, bloodshot eyes, flat noses, drooling lips, scaly claws, half-hoofed feet, and the mold-caked body of an excavating beast. Pickman's paintings and talk suggest that ghouls inhabit the ancient cellars and tunnels under old Boston—the "North End"—and that they sometimes leap through windows at night and kill sleeping people with a bite to the neck. But mostly they eat the dead in graveyards.

In *The Dream-Quest of Unknown Kadath,* by way of a lesson in rela-tive goods and bads, Randolph Carter has to contend with creatures so alien and so hostile that the ghouls become sympathetic characters, and his own private army. Carter was Pickman's friend in Boston, and he has learned from Pickman some conversational Ghoulish, so to speak; it is a "meeping," "glibbering" tongue. He finds the ghouls on the peaks of Thok, in the subterranean Vale of Pnath; from thence they travel to and from the waking world, using graveyards as their portals. We learn that ghouls are fast-moving and enjoy superhuman physical strength and endurance. At Pickman's command the ghouls give Carter much help. Three ghouls lead him through the Gug city to the enchanted wood. Later, Carter leads an army of ghouls against the rock of the moonbeasts, and flies with them all to Kadath, where they magically disappear, perhaps to his partial relief:

> "For a ghoul is a ghoul, and at best an unpleasant companion for man."

GIANTS' CAUSEWAY (DQ, MM): In *The Dream-Quest of Unknown Kadath*, it is said that Dylath-Leen, with its "thin angular towers" of basalt rock, "looks in the distance like a bit of the Giants' Causeway." In *At The Mountains of Madness*, Professor Dyer, the expedition's geologist, mentions that "igneous formations often have strange regularities— like the famous Giants' Causeway in Ireland—but this stupendous [mountain] range was above all else non-volcanic in evident structure."

Igneous—the word comes from *ignis*, Latin for "fire"—rock is the very common variety formed by the cooling of molten matter from beneath the earth's surface, often called lava. A causeway is a low bridge across a body of water. Giants' Causeway on the northern coast of Ireland is the relic of a vast lava flow millions of years ago, in which the lava cooled and cracked into thousands of similarly shaped columns in the sea, so close together as to give the fanciful impression of a "causeway."

GIBBOUS MOON (DA, DCS, TJR, CC, SOT): This phrase occurs in a few tales and has probably puzzled a large number of people, since it is not commonly encountered outside of astronomy, or literature. A gibbous moon is a moon that is convex or "bulging" to the eye, being more than half but less than completely illuminated. Naturally this visual phenomenon occurs during both the waxing and waning phases of the moon. (The odd word "gibbous" was adapted into medieval English from a Latin word for "hunchback" or "hump.")

In *Dagon,* the nameless narrator has his horrid experience during a night illuminated by "the waning and fantastically gibbous moon." Even after his rescue, he still seems to see the horror he glimpsed then, "especially when the moon is gibbous and waning." It is told of the non-human builders of the grey stone city of Ib in *The Doom That Came to Sarnath* that "they worshipped a sea-green stone idol chiselled in the likeness of Bokrug, the great water-lizard; before which they danced horribly when the moon was gibbous." It is on another night lit by a gibbous moon, on the 1000th anniversary of the destruction of Ib, that Sarnath is destroyed. Later the people of Mnar continue Bokrug's cult worship "beneath the gibbous moon." Part of the disorienting weirdness of R'lyeh in *The Call of Cthulhu* is that the daylight sky above the city appears "gibbous" to the disoriented sailors who have landed there. And in *The Shadow Out of Time,* Professor Peaslee specifies that his hideous adventure in the prehistoric ruins on the night of July 17–18, 1935, took place when "the moon, slightly past full, shone from a clear sky, and drenched the ancient sands with a white, leprous radiance which seemed to me somehow infinitely evil."

The mention of a gibbous moon attempting to shine through the clouds in *The Transition of Juan Romero* is chiefly of interest for HPL's own footnote, which reads:

> AUTHOR'S NOTE: Here is a lesson in scientific accuracy for fiction writers. I have just looked up the moon's phases for October, 1894, to find when a gibbous moon was visible at 2 a.m., and have changed the dates to fit!!

GIFFORD, JONATHAN (LF): Resident of Albany, New York; friend and correspondent of Jan Martense from the nearby Catskill Mountains. Alarmed by the cessation of Martense's letters, Gifford visits the Martense mansion on September 20, 1763, only to be put off with the story that Jan had been killed by a bolt of lightning. Very suspicious, Gifford digs up Jan Martense's grave a week later, and finds that his friend's skull was crushed with a blunt instrument. He returns to Albany and makes his discovery public, an event which completes the social ruin and isolation of the Martense family.

GILMAN FAMILY (SOI, TD): One of the "very retiring" (*i.e.*, very private and reserved) socially-superior families of Innsmouth; like the Waites, the Marshes, and the Eliots, the Gilmans live in big houses along Washington Street with well-tended lawns and gardens—and like those other families, they also have members who are never seen in public. Innsmouth's economic decline in the early 19th century was attributable in part to the loss at sea of two Gilman-owned merchant ships, the *Eliza* and the *Ranger*, with crews of irreplaceable local men. A certain Hiram Gilman was one of the younger townsfolk who were apparently kidnapped and sacrificed to the Deep Ones prior to the 1846 events in Innsmouth. In *The Thing on the Doorstep*, Edward Derby tells his friend that the Gilmans of Innsmouth—his wife Asenath's hometown—"whisper about the way that [her father Ephraim Waite] shrieked—like a frightened child" when he was locked up in a madhouse. This bit of detail rings very falsely when compared to the very detailed portrait of Innsmouth in *The Shadow Over Innsmouth*; as depicted in the latter story, residents like the Gilmans would seem unlikely ever to have "opened up" in such a way to any outsider, let alone a visiting dupe such as Edward Derby. The entire Innsmouth connection in *The Thing on the Doorstep* doesn't make much sense, in fact.

GILMAN HOUSE (SOI): The only hotel in Innsmouth, Massachusetts. Strangers unfortunate enough to have to spend a night in the town, such as the government inspector Mr. Casey, have no other choice. Unwelcome visitors have been known to disappear from this hotel. The bus from Newburyport stops outside the hotel, in Town Square. Gilman House is five stories tall, with flaking yellow paint and a half-legible sign. The narrator of *The Shadow Over Innsmouth* stays in Room 428—large enough, but with no sink or bathroom—for the price of one dollar a night. The furniture is sparse and cheap, the bed a simple iron frame with mattress, the antique lavatory located at the end of the hall. A fanatical budget-traveler by economic necessity and personal preference, HPL was more than familiar with the kind of fourth-rate hotel room he describes here.

GILMAN, WALTER (DWH): Miskatonic University undergraduate from Haverhill, Massachusetts (a non-fictitious town). He deliberately rents Keziah Mason's old attic garret in the Witch House. At Miskatonic, he studies higher mathematics, physics, folklore, and their possible interconnection. He suffers from a chronic fever while experiencing dreams of growing vividness and complexity and enjoying heightened abilities in mathematics and physics. The dreams involve Keziah Mason, Brown Jenkin, a "Black Man," and journeys into spaces lying outside our own dimension. As Walpurgis Night (April 30) draws near, his dreams seem more and more real, and during the daytime he feels himself "drawn" toward certain parts of the sky. He seeks help on a number of occasions from his fellow-student and fellow-lodger Frank Elwood. On Walpurgis Night, in some fourth-dimensional place, Gilman tries unsuccessfully to halt the sacrifice of the kidnapped infant Ladislas Wolejko, killing Keziah Mason in the process. On the next morning he is found on the floor of his room, with his eardrums ruptured as if by some tremendous sound (a sound nobody else heard, however). That afternoon, as Gilman lies resting under blankets, Brown Jenkin makes a surprise attack from below. Gilman dies badly, "emitting sounds of veritably inhuman nature, as if racked by some torment beyond description," while "writhing under the bedclothes." When the covers are pulled back, the doctor and witnesses see that there was "a virtual tunnel through his body—something had eaten his heart out."

GLANVILL, JOSEPH (TF, TJR): An Oxford University graduate (1636–80) who became an English royal chaplain. As an early Fellow of the Royal Society (still the most prominent and revered British scientific organization), Glanvill defended the scientific or experimental methods of research against mere dogmatic learning. He was a firm believer in the spirit world, which he felt should be the subject of scientific study; therefore, some consider him to be the "father" of psychical research in the modern sense. The narrator of *The Festival* notices Glanvill's book *Saducismus Triumphatus* (first published posthumously in 1681; *see* separate entry) in the house on Green Lane in Kingsport, Massachusetts.

The nameless narrator of *The Transition of Juan Romero* cites a passage in Glanvill's works which Edgar Allan Poe used as the introduction to his famous tale *A Descent into the Maelstrom*:

> —the vastness, profundity, and unsearchableness of His works, *which have a depth in them greater than the well of Democritus.*

A Descent into the Maelstrom is a story of a Norwegian fisherman whose small boat is caught in a famous tidal whirlpool, the Moskoe-Strom or "Maelstrom." As the whirlpool gains in force and speed, it takes on the proportions of a funnel with the bottom at the ocean floor, hundreds of feet down. Democritus of Abdera (c. 460–c. 370 B.C.) was one of the more important Greek philosophers, one who concentrated on the explanation for the physical world we live in. In that ancient era, he denied the creation myths of his society, and reasoned or intuited that space was a "Void" of infinite size in which floated innumerable particles—the atoms—too tiny for our senses to perceive, but which, by their motions and connections, had formed the heavenly bodies, the earth, and everything on it. Atoms—therefore matter—could not be destroyed, only changed from one form to another over time. In essence, the ancient philosopher had forecast modern atomic theory. One aspect of his reasoning was that this explanation required no supernatural explanation for the world's creation; Democritus was perhaps the first philosophical materialist. The infinite Void proposed by Democritus to be our physical universe was discussed in figurative language as "the well of Democritus" by Glanvill, presumably since a well dug deep in the earth is also a "void" of great depth, and this phrase of his is interpreted as referring to the greatest possible attainment of human knowledge. To Glanvill, as a Christian theologian, the greatness of God's works exceeded the limit of what man could know by his own intellect. Immanuel Kant (1724–1804), one of the greatest of modern philosophers, used the phrase "the well of Democritus" in a different context but in the same sense as Glanvill, in his major work *The Critique of Pure Reason*.

GNAI-KAH (DCS): One of the gods in Sarnath's pantheon.

GNOPHKEHS (PO, DQ): In *Polaris*, this is the name of the hairy, long-armed, cannibal tribesmen whom the Lomarians' ancestors defeated to conquer Lomar. General Alos uses this old history to try to rally his men of Olathoë against the Inuto invaders. HPL may have completely forgotten about this sequence of events several years later when he wrote *The Dream-Quest of Unknown Kadath,* in which an elderly zoog tells

Randolph Carter about the time when "the hairy cannibal Gnophkehs overcame many-templed Olathoë and slew all the heroes of the land of Lomar."

GNORRI (SK, TGSK): Under the twilight seas by Ilek-Vad, the "bearded and finny" Gnorri build their "singular labyrinths."

GOMES, TONY (CDW): "A villainous-looking Portuguese half-caste [*i.e.,* half-white and half-something-else] from the South Main St. waterfront who acted as a servant" to Charles Dexter Ward and "Dr. Allen" in their bungalow. A mulatto, he speaks little English. When the spurious "Charles Dexter Ward" is taken to the mental asylum on March 8, 1928, he pays off Gomes, who resists all subsequent questioning by other people. Later on, detectives are unable to find the sinister mulatto for additional questioning. Gomes is also referred to as a "Brava," *i.e.,* a man from the Cape Verde Islands; for an explanation of which, *see* "Cape Verde Islands."

GOOD FRIDAY (IV, CDW): This most important day for all Christians, the anniversary of the day on which Jesus Christ was crucified in Jerusalem and then buried in a tomb to await his resurrection, is the sardonically-chosen date for two events: George Birch's 1881 entrapment in the receiving tomb at Peck Valley cemetery; and Charles Dexter Ward's alchemical resurrection of his evil ancestor Joseph Curwen in 1927.

"GORGO, MORMO, THOUSAND-FACED MOON" (HRH): The background to this phrase is really one of the most interesting features of a generally mediocre-or-worse tale, *The Horror at Red Hook*. On the wall of the combination "dance-hall church" in a Brooklyn slum, New York police detective Thomas F. Malone spies "a Greek inscription on the wall above the pulpit; an ancient incantation which he had once stumbled upon in Dublin college days," and which he shudders to see again and in such a place. Much later, in the most terrible of circumstances, he hears the Greek incantation repeated by a repellent throng of worshippers (HPL provides stage-directions or sound-effects):

> O friend and companion of night, thou who rejoicest in the baying of dogs (*here a hideous howl burst forth*) and spilt blood (*here nameless sounds vied with morbid shriekings*), who wanderest in the midst of shades among the tombs (*here a whistling sigh occurred*), who longest for blood and bringest terror to mortals (*short, sharp cries from myriad throats*), Gorgo (*repeated in response*), Mormo (*repeated with ecstasy*), thousand-faced moon (*sighs and flute notes*), look favourably on our sacrifices!

At the end of the story we learn that, despite the apparent elimination of the wicked cult, another New York Police Department officer has just overheard an old crone teaching a little slum-boy this incantation; in the best horror-movie style, the evil lives on....

Over the years many readers have probably assumed that HPL made up what seems like some patched-together "magic" gibberish; but that is not the case. To begin with, "Mormo" was the name of a child-killing female demon in ancient Greek mythology, an attendant of the sinister female deity Hecate. Mormo long survived in Greek folk tradition as someone to threaten naughty children with, a frightful sprite who would bite them by night.

Gorgo is simply the Greek word for a "gorgon," one of the snake-haired females of Greek legend whose glance would turn a human being into stone—Medusa being the best-known gorgon. Their relationship with Hecate is indistinct but exists. There is an alternate possibility, namely that what was intended in the ritual was Gorgo as a diminutive of "Demogorgon," a Late Latin name for a major but unclearly-defined demonic entity, perhaps a combination of the Latin word *daemon* with the Greek *gorgo*, which as has been mentioned means "gorgon." "Daemogorgon" and "Demogorgon" occur in English in Spenser's poem *The Faerie Queen* (1590) and Milton's *Paradise Lost* (1667). In the thoroughly Greek context of the chant (see below), however, the evocation of the power of the frightful gorgon seems more likely.

The incantation itself is both genuine and ancient, dating back to at least the 3rd century A.D., and in its complete form in a different translation it reads as follows:

> Come infernal, terrestrial, and heavenly Bombo [Hecate], goddess of the broad roadways, of the crossroads, thou who goest to and fro at night, torch in hand, enemy of the day. Friend and lover of darkness, thou who dost rejoice when the dogs are howling and warm blood is spilled, thou who art walking amidst the phantoms and in the place of tombs, thou whose thirst is blood, thou who dost strike chill and fear in mortal hearts, Gorgo, Mormo, Moon of a thousand forms, cast a propitious eye on our sacrifice!

Hecate, a multi-faceted goddess who was permanently associated with night and the underworld, was also the goddess of crossroads and tombs, said to walk abroad in the darkness with two hounds, and to welcome blood sacrifices. Naturally, Hecate has also been associated with magic from ancient times until our own times, making a witchlike appearance, for example, in Shakespeare's tragedy *Macbeth*.

The ancient text has come down to us by curiously indirect means. In the 1840s a researcher going through the library of an old Greek monastery discovered an ancient manuscript copy of a long-lost book: *Philosophumena* (Philosophical Remarks), also known as *Kata pason aireson elegchos* (A Refutation of All Heresies). The historical author of this lengthy and comprehensive work was the important early Christian theologian Saint Hippolytus of Rome, who died as a martyr circa 236. Book IV of this compendium deals principally with astrology and the false tricks of magicians, both of which Saint Hippolytus condemned. His thorough descriptions have preserved a number of otherwise-forgotten rituals or fraudulent practices, like ancient insects caught in amber. In Book IV, Chapter 36, the churchman wrote of how a fraudulent sorcerer could produce the illusion of a "fiery demon" such as Hecate by previously drawing her figure on a blank wall using a phosphorescent substance that would burn luminously if fire were applied to it. Then, on a moonless night, he would bring his "dupes" to this wall, persuade them that Hecate would come when he invoked her, then have them cover their heads and hide their faces while he recited the above incantation. In the meantime, an accomplice with a torch or lamp would bring flame against the chemical drawing, so that "a fiery Hecate seems to fly through the air" when the sorcerer told the clients to open their eyes again. *Philosophumena* was published for the first time in 1851. Lovecraft does not seem to have read the work itself (although Book IV's denial of astrology and exposure of ancient spiritualistic frauds would have been near and dear to his heart), but rather to have copied the incantation from the *Encyclopedia Britannica.*

GOYA, FRANCISCO (TH, PM): One of the most famous European artists, a Spaniard (1746–1828) known for his frequent use of "grotesque" or violent subjects for his art. In *The Hound,* the decadent aesthete St. John owns a set of etchings which Goya allegedly drew, but dared not acknowledge: the collection is bound in human skin! In *Pickman's Model*, Pickman's ghoul-paintings are compared to Goya's most shocking efforts. "I don't believe anybody since Goya could put so much of sheer hell into a set of features or a twist of expression."

GRANARY BURYING GROUND (DQ): An historic Boston graveyard, next to the Park Street Church. It is the last resting-place of revolutionary patriots John Hancock and Samuel Adams, as well as the victims of the "Boston Massacre" by British soldiers before the American Revolution. The ghoul who once was Pickman is sitting on a tombstone robbed from this place when Randolph Carter meets him in lower Dreamland.

GRAVES, REVEREND JOHN (CDW): The minister at King's Church, Providence, an Anglican parish where Joseph and Eliza Curwen became members following their marriage. Their only child, Ann, is christened here in May, 1765. The entry recording this event is erased from the parish record book several years later. Ward only finds it by consulting a duplicate parish register which Reverend Graves, a loyalist, took away with him at the outbreak of the American Revolution, and which in the 1920s was still in the possession of one of the minister's descendants.

GREAT OLD ONES (CC, DH, MM, SOT, SOI): *See* "Old Ones."

GREAT RACE (SOT): The name the narrator gives to the time-traveling, non-human entities who inhabit Earth during part of its early eons. The Great Race "kidnap" minds from many different epochs, planets, and intelligent species, for research by transferring one of their own race's mind into the subject's body, while the subject's mind is housed in the vacated body of the Great Race member. To speak of the Great Race's outer forms is misleading, as they can and do change them at will; whenever the planet they inhabit is doomed (or at any other time they choose), they are able to transfer their minds *en masse* into the bodies of some other species on the same or a different planet, leaving the unfortunate beings they have displaced to perish "in the horror of unfamiliar shapes." When seen by Nathanael Peaslee, at an epoch he supposed to be some 150,000,000 years earlier on Earth, the bodies the Great Race inhabited "represented no surviving—or even scientifically known—line of terrestrial evolution." They are enormous and cone-shaped, about ten feet high and ten feet wide at their snail-like base; made of a semi-elastic substance with surface ridges. "From their apexes projected four flexible, cylindrical members, each a foot thick, and of a ridgy substance like the cones themselves." At the end of two of these tentacles are enormous, lobster-like claws. On the third are "four red, trumpet-like appendages." On the fourth is a yellowish globe, two feet in diameter, with three eyes ranged about its circumference. Their "blood" is a greenish ichor. They have the senses of sight and hearing, as well as many other senses which humans do not have.

Of the Great Race's society, HPL writes much. Their government is a "loosely-knit nation or league," managed by the principles of "fascistic socialism," the author's personal and eccentric political creed by the time he wrote this tale in the 1930s. Reproduction was by spores, but since the normal life span was 4000–5000 years, there was little reproduction at all. The culture was thoroughly mechanized and industrial, and the abundant leisure time which HPL (like many other utopianists) imagined would be the product of such a society was spent in strenuous intellectual pursuits; again, part of HPL's own vision of the good life that could be possible for the educated elite under the type of society he now envisioned. The Great Race had known some civil wars, and also warfare with "reptilian or octopodic invaders, or against the winged, star-headed

Old Ones" (familiar concepts to readers of *The Call of Cthulhu* or *At the Mountains of Madness*). At the time of Professor Peaslee's sojourn, the Great Race continued to maintain an enormous army for defense against certain unspeakable entities lurking in subterranean "elder ruins" beneath carefully-sealed trapdoors. He also learns that the Great Race has come to earth from a distant planet they called Yith, by a mental migration in which they displaced the minds of an earth-dwelling species, took over their bodies, and dispatched the displaced minds back to their abandoned bodies on doomed Yith. And, as they enjoyed an enviable ability to travel through time via mind transfers, the Great Race already knew its own future; its minds would next migrate to the civilization of intelligent beetles which would exist on earth after mankind's disappearance, and then go on "to another stopping-place in the bodies of the bulbous vegetable entities of Mercury."

GREEN, DANIEL (CDW): One day in January, 1771, people around Weybosset Point on the Providence waterfront see a "great, white thing" plunging frantically through the snow banks. The next morning "a giant, muscular body, stark naked, was found on the jams of ice around the southern piers of the Great Bridge." Older folk think that the mysterious corpse much resembles the blacksmith Daniel Green, who had been dead for about fifty years. He was the great-grandfather of a certain Aaron Hoppin, an employee of Joseph Curwen. An autopsy reveals that the huge man's skin has a bizarre, coarse, loosely-knit texture, and that his digestive organs have never been used! Tracks in the snow indicate that the dead man had escaped from the Curwen farm on Pawtuxet Road. A secret search of Daniel Green's grave in the North Burying Ground reveals that it has been robbed of its contents. We understand that Joseph Curwen has reconstituted Daniel Green from his "essential Saltes." It is mentioned in the tale that Curwen sometimes keeps his employees under control by letting them know that somehow he knows their darkest family secrets from long ago. This must have been by the resurrection and interrogation of their deceased ancestors, such as Aaron Coppin's progenitor Daniel Green.

GREEN, FIRST MATE (CC): Officer on the *Emma*; killed in the sea-battle with the crew of the *Alert*.

GREEN, JAMES (CDW): An 18th century shopkeeper, whose store was at the "Sign of the Elephant" in the Cheapside district of old Providence. In the tale, he buys most of his stock from Joseph Curwen.

GREENE, GENERAL NATHANAEL (SH): Nathanael Greene (1742–86), a Rhode Islander and one of the heroes of the Revolutionary War, was the commander of the "Army of Observation" surrounding British-held Boston at the start of the conflict. General Greene's home is still preserved as an historical monument at 50 Taft Street, Coventry, Rhode Island. Historically, Greene also was the local commander when Colonel Angell's Rhode Island volunteers fought an important battle against British forces at Springfield, New Jersey, in 1780.

In 1775, the 16-year-old William Harris manages to enlist in Greene's command, despite his feeble health after a youth spent in the Shunned House.

GREEN LANE (TF): "Now I was eager to knock at the door of my people, the seventh house on the left in Green Lane." There the narrator discovers an old man and woman, who invite him to join a mysterious procession through the night streets of Kingsport. Comparison of the fictional streets and landmarks mentioned in the tale's "Kingsport" with the real streets of Marblehead, Massachusetts, suggest that the real-life house HPL seems to have had in mind was the so-called Bowen House located at 1 Mugford Street in Marblehead, an old residence which shares a "jutting second story" and a "low stone doorstep" with its fictional counterpart.

GREEN RIVER (BC): This real river runs near the entrance of Mammoth Cave in Edmonson County, Kentucky, some 25 miles northeast of the city of Bowling Green.

GREENWICH VILLAGE (HE): Famous district in the lower portion of Manhattan, long ago a farming village north of the young New York City; it was swallowed up by the growing metropolis in the early 19th century, and its area is now defined from north to south by 14th Street and Houston Street, from east to west by Washington Square and the Hudson River. Greenwich Village still preserves narrow, winding streets and some distinctive Colonial or Federal period structures. It has long been a stronghold of New York's intellectual or indescribable classes. HPL, who grew to hate so much about modern New York City during his 1924–26 sojourn, nonetheless enjoyed prowling through the quaint side-streets of the Village indulging his passion for old architecture, especially by night. During one of these walks, on August 29, 1924, he found "the little back court off Perry Street" where the nameless narrator finds himself at the conclusion of *He*. By his own account, he wrote the tale itself on the morning of August 11, 1925 in a public park called Scott Park, across the Hudson River in Elizabeth, New Jersey, after a solitary all-night walk through Greenwich Village and down to the Battery at the tip of lower Manhattan, where he would have boarded a ferry boat.

In *He*, the narrator (speaking for HPL) said of Greenwich Village that "the archaic lanes and houses and unexpected bits of square and court had indeed delighted me, and when I found the poets and artists to be loud-voiced pretenders...whose lives are a denial of all that pure beauty which is poetry and art, I stayed on for love of these venerable things." Later, "The Squire" shows the narrator a vision of Greenwich Village and Manhattan in the distant future, worth noting:

> ...a hellish black city of giant stone terraces with impious pyramids flung savagely to the moon, and devil-lights burning from unnumbered windows. And swarming loathsomely on aërial galleries I saw the yellow, squint-eyed people of that city, robed horribly in orange and red, and dancing insanely to the pounding of fevered kettle-drums, the clatter of obscene crotala, and the maniacal moaning of muted horns...the blasphemous domdaniel of cacophony...the shrieking fulfillment of all the horror which that corpse-city had ever stirred in my soul....

New York, New York, it's a wonderful town! For every reader who has ever wondered, "crotala" were a kind of wooden hand-clapper akin to castanets, used in ancient Greece and elsewhere; one consisted of a length of flexible wood, flat on one side and rounded on the other, and split halfway along its length, so that by shaking it, a clattering sound could be made. They were associated especially with the wild ritual celebrations called Bacchanalia. *Brewer's Dictionary of Phrase and Fable* (1894) defined the very rare word "Dom-Daniel" as "the abode of evil spirits, gnomes and enchanters," and Roget's *Thesaurus* of 1922 lists "Domdaniel" as a synonym for Hell. Domdaniel has an alternate or secondary meaning as a place where the head of a coven or school of witches meets with his followers, and in that sense HPL might have found the word in the "Arabian" epic poem *Thalaba: The Destroyer* by the sometime Poet Laureate of England, Robert Southey (1774–1843); in Lord Byron's attack on Southey in the satirical poem *English Bards and Scotch Reviewers*; or even in Nathaniel Hawthorne's Salem novel *The House of the Seven Gables*, to name a few likely sources.

HPL's likening of always-lively New York to a "corpse-city" is puzzling until one recalls the theory he expounded during and after his time there, namely that New York City was only the "corpse" of the pleasant Anglo-Dutch town it had been a century or two earlier (when he might have enjoyed living there)—before the descendants of the "Nordic" old settlers, already swarmed by the Irish in the mid-19th century and afterward, were finally swamped by wave after wave of what the "gentleman from Providence" was once pleased to describe as "Italo-Semitico-Mongoloid trash." The image of the "corpse-city" builds on a passage earlier in the tale, in which the nameless narrator, HPL's mouthpiece, states that New York "is not a sentient perpetuation of Old New York as London is of Old London and Paris of Old Paris, but...is in fact quite dead, its sprawling body imperfectly embalmed and infested with queer animate things which have nothing to do with it as it was in life." Of course, the expert had never been to London or to Paris.

GREENWOOD CEMETERY (HRH): A large, famous graveyard in Brooklyn, New York—opened in the early 19th century—slightly west of Prospect Park, and two miles down Parkside Avenue from HPL's first New York home at 259 Parkside Avenue where he lived from 1924–25. In the tale, historic Greenwood Cemetery is mentioned as the last resting-place of Robert Suydam and his luckless bride, Cornelia Gerritsen. It is only a couple of miles away from the Red Hook district, and very characteristically was one of the places HPL enjoyed visiting while he lived in New York City.

GREEK GODS (HY, MB, TT): As a child and a young man, HPL drank deeply of the wine of Greek mythology, and later drew on this familiarity in his fiction. In *Hypnos*, the Greek god of sleep (who bears that name) is invoked, and the two artists Kalos and Musides compete to create the better statue of the goddess Tyche. *The Moon-Bog* features a return of what seem like Greek minor deities to a threatened Irish bog, where the ruins of an ancient Hellenistic temple still stand. In *The Temple,* the Atlantean ruins that Captain von Altburg-Ehrenstein observes, including "the temple" itself, make him think they could be the remotest precursors of classical Greek design. HPL once wrote:

> When about seven or eight I was a genuine pagan, so intoxicated with the beauty of Greece that I acquired a half-sincere belief in the old gods and Nature-spirits. I have in literal truth built altars to Pan, Apollo, Diana, and Athena, and have watched for dryads and satyrs in the woods and fields at dusk.

GREGORY (FB): A faithful old manservant employed by Crawford Tillinghast. He disappears from this sphere along with the other domestic servants, and at the same time, eaten by the things From Beyond.

GUERRERA (CC): A sailor on the *Emma* who survives the sea-battle with the *Alert* and transfers to that vessel. He goes ashore on R'lyeh with the other sailors. He is swept up by Cthulhu's flabby claws as the monster emerges from his "house," and is seen no more.

GUGS (DQ): Monstrous creatures of Dreamland. They are hairy and gigantic, so large that a single dead gug can feed a community of ghouls for almost a year. Their tombstones are immense monoliths, reaching almost as high as the eye can see in the twilight of their underground kingdom. The gug city is surrounded by enormous stone walls, and the gugs dwell there in circular towers with thirty-foot-high doorways. For all their great size, gugs are somewhat afraid of ghouls and will run away from them. Gugs have barrel-shaped heads with two pink eyes (jutting two inches out from either side of the face). Their mouths contain huge fangs and open sideways. A gug's paw is about two and a half feet wide. They have no voices, but communicate with one another by facial expressions. To make up for this, they have incredibly keen hearing and can move without making a sound. Gugs formally dwelt in upper Dreamland, where mortal dreamers were their favorite food. But because of some abominable crime, the gugs were condemned by earth's gods to live in lower Dreamland, never to leave. Now they feed on ghasts which they hunt in the Vaults of Zin. A great tower in their city leads directly to upper Dreamland through a trapdoor in the topmost ceiling, a portal which no gug would dare to pass through because of the curse. Randolph Carter and his three-ghoul escort travel through the city and up the tower, passing into the enchanted wood through that trapdoor.

GUNNARSSEN (MM): A sailor on the Miskatonic University Expedition. Along with the mechanic Sherman, and another sailor named Larson, he initially remains with the reserve airplane at the McMurdo Sound depot. On the night of January 24, 1931, he flies to the Dyer base camp in the reserve craft.

H

HADOTH (TO, CDW, UP): Apparently a secret, sealed-off valley of ancient Egyptian tombs somewhere near the river Nile. Joseph Curwen and his friends sometimes end letters with the phrase "Nephren-Ka nai Hadoth."

HADRIAN'S WALL (CDW): *See* "Caerleon; Hexham; Hadrian's Wall."

HAECKEL, ERNST (HW): German biologist and author (1834–1919), whose popular-science books, translated into English, had a strong influence on HPL's way of thinking. The offspring of a conservative Lutheran family, Haeckel became Germany's foremost contemporary promoter of Darwinian evolutionary theory, as well as a convinced atheist and materialist. In books with titles like *Die Welträtsel* ("The Riddle of the World"), Haeckel combined the mild-mannered English naturalist's mildly-expressed theories with the wild enthusiasm characteristic of German philosophizing in his time, to produce a volatile mixture of "social Darwinism," materialism, and what a later day would call racism; his works became foundation stones of "Nazi biology." Haeckel, as one historian has observed, was tall, blond, active and muscular, and "could have modeled for the perfect Aryan." As he grew older, he:

> continued to be fascinated with the differences between the various races, integrating his views of the moral and intellectual characteristics of those races into his grand, flamboyant schemes of the evolution of life. The blond, blue-eyed, Aryan German of athletic build and vigorous temperament was to Haeckel obviously morally, mentally, physically, and, indeed, evolutionarily superior to other types.... During and after [World War I], Haeckel's thoughts on racial differences and social causes turned more and more to eugenics...; the practice of deliberately encouraging superior "types" to reproduce while severely discouraging reproduction by inferior groups. Coupled with his strongly nationalistic romanticism, and powered by his undeniable gift for stirring the emotions with his words, Haeckel's doctrines had tremendous appeal to many Germans.

They appealed to a goodly number of non-Germans as well, including HPL, whose overarching notions of atheism and race-relations broadly corresponded with those laid down in Haeckel's books. HPL tipped his hat to the master in one tale, when Herbert West's comrade notes that they both "[held] with Haeckel that all life is a chemical and physical process and that the so-called 'soul' is a myth." HPL would go on to refer to Ernst Haeckel a good deal more in letters and non-fiction writing during his life.

HALI, LAKE OF (WD): In this tale "the Lake of Hali" is referred to in a long letter from Henry Akeley to Dr. Wilmarth, which mentions a number of frightening "names and terms" in the course of describing all the things that Akeley has learned from his studies related to the Mi-Go and the confessions of a human who had become a "spy" for the aliens and who later killed himself. The name "Hali" appeared in the tale *An Inhabitant of Carcosa* by Ambrose Bierce (1842–1913?), in his 1891 short story collection *Tales of Soldiers and Civilians.* There, Hali is apparently a dead sage whose thoughts on different kinds of death the narrator is "pondering" at the beginning of the tale.

HALL SCHOOL (TD): A girls' boarding school in Kingsport, Massachusetts, which Asenath Waite attends after the death of her father Ephraim; technically, the orphaned minor girl is made a legal ward of the school's principal, as desired by Ephraim Waite in his will. A classmate from Asenath's Hall School days—the daughter of one of Daniel Upton's friends—recalls unnerving things about the girl. The teenaged Asenath "posed as a magician" among the other schoolgirls, claiming to be able to cause a storm to occur. She had hypnotic powers, and could give other girls the feeling of momentarily "exchanged personality"—the sense of being in Asenath's body, looking out. Much worse, there were "times when she displayed snatches of knowledge and language very singular—and shocking—for a young girl; when she would frighten her schoolmates with leers and winks of an inexplicable kind, and would seem to extract an obscene and zestful irony from her present situation." In what is for HPL an almost unbelievably suggestive passage—nothing else even approaches it in any of his other tales—we are given to understand that the "present situation" was that of a wicked old man inhabiting Asenath's body, and enjoying the experience of living in a dormitory of innocent teenage girls as much as such a wicked old man might be expected to do.

HALSEY, DR. ALLAN (HW): Dean of the Miskatonic University medical school, circa 1900. "Learned and benevolent," Dr. Halsey forbids further private experiments by medical student West in the school laboratories "after the scientific slaughter of uncounted small animals." HPL summed up and dismissed most of his own childhood teachers and authority figures—and their damp moralizing—with this killing description of Dr. Halsey: "the product of generations of pathetic Puritanism, kindly, conscientious, and sometimes gentle and amiable, yet always narrow, intolerant, custom-ridden, and lacking in perspective."

Warming to the topic, HPL's nameless narrator accused Halsey's type of citizen of "Ptolemaism, Calvinism, anti-Darwinism, anti-Nietzscheism and every sort of Sabbatarianism and sumptuary legislation." (Ptolemy was the ancient Greek scientist who proposed that the universe revolved around the earth; here the word doubtless means a scientific reactionary. Calvinism is the harsh and morally severe Christian doctrinal variation propounded by the 17th century Swiss preacher, Jean Calvin, and is historically associated with the original Puritan settlers of New England. Sabbatarianism means, or meant, the feeling that Sunday, the Sabbath day, should be treated with reverence and as the biblical "day of rest" by all, and that that reverence should be compelled if necessary; which in HPL's time in New England and most other parts of America meant that retail businesses, drinking establishments, and perhaps other facilities were typically closed on Sundays by force of local law. "Sumptuary" laws were regulations prescribing what kinds of clothing were allowed to be worn by different categories of people, or genders.)

Naturally this stalwart New England fossil earned the scorn and contempt of those young Nietzschean materialists, Herbert West and his comrade. And "like most youths," West also indulged in "elaborate daydreams of revenge, triumph, and final magnanimous forgiveness." Dr. Halsey performs mighty and courageous works of healing during the great Arkham typhoid epidemic in the summer of 1904, becoming the hero of the town. Exhausted from his labors, the old doctor dies on August 14, and is buried the next day in a funeral that is necessarily hasty, but is attended by all the Miskatonic students and full of tributes from the grateful citizens of Arkham. West and his comrade spend the afternoon drinking at the Commercial House bar, and then go to exhume Dr. Halsey from his fresh grave and inject his corpse with the reviving solution that night in their apartment, a little after 2:00 a.m. on the morning of the 16th.

Unfortunately, instead of coming back to life with surprise, gratitude, and awed respect for his former lowly medical students (who could then offer their "magnanimous forgiveness"!), the revenant Halsey knocks them both unconscious and escapes. He roams Arkham as a raving homicidal cannibal. As such, that body which once proudly bore the name of Dr. Allan Halsey is captured on the third night afterwards, after no fewer than *seventeen* murders. The cannibal-killer disgusts all who see him by his "nauseous eyes, voiceless simianism, and daemoniac savagery," but most of all because of his incredible resemblance to the late, muchbeloved Dr. Halsey. Confined to Sefton Asylum, the thing is released years later by a band of mysterious marauders. Herbert West's immediate comment on the failure? "Damn it, it wasn't *quite* fresh enough!"

Halsey Street, and the "Halsey Mansion" house, were both close to Hope Street High School, where HPL was once a student.

Modern Americans and Europeans are usually not familiar with typhoid fever, formerly one of the most feared epidemic diseases. Typhoid is contracted by eating or drinking substances contaminated with the bacteria *Salmonella typhi,* and is marked by a sudden and sustained fever, severe headache, nausea, and severe loss of appetite; if left untreated, typhoid proves fatal in about 10% of cases. Antibiotics to cure the disease were not invented until the 1940s. Typhoid epidemics occur in areas where poor sanitation combined with warm weather permits the contamination of water or food supplies by fecal material; at this writing there are still an estimated 17 million cases a year, principally in India and Africa. Typhoid in HPL's time was a near and immediate danger wherever people congregated in the right conditions; during the Boer War in South Africa in the late 1890s, for example, the British Army had some 8,000 soldiers killed in battle and 13,000 killed by typhoid fever. Even closer, a woman who became notorious in the tabloid newspapers of the day as "Typhoid Mary" Mallon was shown to have infected more than fifty New Yorkers in her job as a cook, in 1906, only two years after the fictional Arkham epidemic of 1904, and of course several years before this tale was written.

HANGMAN'S BROOK (DWH): A stream running somewhere to the south of Arkham; in the 1920s, there are only open fields to the other side. On the evening of April 20, Walter Gilman wanders this far from town by nightfall; then he realizes that he is being "drawn" toward a point in the sky between the constellations of Hydra and Argo Navis.

HANWELL ASYLUM (RW): In the tale, an English madhouse where Mr. de la Poer, and "Thornton" the psychic investigator, are confined in adjoining cells in 1923. Hanwell is the name of a former rural English community, now a suburban area in the western part of metropolitan London. At the time there actually was an insane asylum there, which Lovecraft biographer S.T. Joshi suggests HPL probably read of in one of Lord Dunsany's tales, *The Coronation of Mr. Thomas Shap,* in the collection called *The Book of Wonder.*

HARLEY, FRANCIS (RW): "Francis Harley, of Bellview," described as a "gentleman-adventurer" in the early-17th-century Virginia colony, who met fellow-colonist Walter de la Poer and wrote approvingly about him in his journal. The character is fictitious, but Bellview (an Anglicization of "Bellevue"), would presumably have been the name of the owner's Virginia plantation.

HARRIS FAMILY (SH): HPL provided an elaborate and convincing family history for the fictitious owners of the house at 135 Benefit Street, in Providence; a house whose original owner was, in fact, an 18th century gentleman named Stephen Harris. In the tale, "William Harris" who built the house circa 1763, is married to the former Rhoby Dexter. (HPL's maternal grandmother Robie Place Phillips, who died when he was six, shared this old-fashioned name, with the spelling difference.) Their four children were a daughter, Elkanah (b.1755), Abigail (b.1757), William Jr. (b.1759), and Ruth (b.1761). William Harris was a ship's officer and merchant in the West Indies trade, and from 1761 the master of the brig *Prudence*, owned by Nicholas Brown & Co. of Providence. Abigail and Ruth died in April, 1764, followed into death by their father in 1766. Elkanah died in 1768, after which Rhoby became violently insane, shouting for hours in "a coarse and idiomatic form of French," a language she could barely understand, and complaining wildly of a staring thing that bit and chewed at her; and was locked in the upper part of the house for the rest of her life, which ended in 1773. William Harris, Jr., suffered from feebleness during his entire youth, except during the period when he lived away from the house with his cousin Peleg Harris in another part of town. At the age of 16, in 1775, he managed to enlist in the Continental Army and thereafter thrived physically. By 1780, as a captain in a Rhode Island regiment, he married Phebe Hatfield in her home state of New Jersey. He returned home with his new bride upon leaving military service in 1781; her first pregnancy ended in a stillbirth in 1782. "At last thoroughly convinced of the radically unhealthful nature of his abode," Harris moves with his wife to the Golden Ball Inn (a colonial-era hostelry which was still standing in HPL's day), then to a new and better home on Westminster Street. Their son Dutee Harris is born there in 1785. William and Phebe Harris die in the yellow fever epidemic of 1797, an historical event which decimated parts of the northeastern United States. Dutee is thereafter raised by his cousin Rathbone Harris, grows up to become a distinguished fighting sailor during the War of 1812, marries in 1814, and becomes father to a son, Welcome Harris, on September 23, 1815. Welcome Harris dies "gloriously," presumably as an soldier in the Union army, at the battle of Fredericksburg in 1862—at which date his father Dutee was still living—but left behind a son, Archer, and a daughter, Alice. In 1876 Archer Harris moves to a "sumptuous but hideous French-roofed mansion" on Angell Street, and dies in 1916, survived by his sister. (This mansion is generally identified as 276 Angell Street, which was not really built until 1896.) Archer's son and heir, Carrington Harris, is the owner of the long-vacant Shunned House as of June, 1919, the date of the climactic events of this tale. Afterwards, we are told, he cannily installs modern plumbing in the old place and begins to lease it out to tenants again.

HART, ROBERT (CDW): Night watchman at the North Burial Ground in Providence, 1927–28, where he proves himself completely incapable of preventing either grave robberies *or* surreptitious interments.

HARTWELL, DR. (DH): The elderly Dr. Armitage's physician in Arkham, who visits and treats him for exhaustion on September 6, 1928.

HARVARD UNIVERSITY (DH, CDW, TD): The famed university founded in 1636 at Cambridge, Massachusetts. A copy of the Olaus Wormius Latin translation of the *Necronomicon* is in its Widener Library, where Wilbur Whateley ventured in the spring of 1928 in an attempt to see it. It is mentioned that some of the "undecayed" Whateleys and Bishops from the Dunwich region still send their sons to Harvard, or to Miskatonic. Charles Dexter Ward also did historical research at the Widener Library in the 1920s. Daniel Upton of *The Thing on the Doorstep* studied architecture at Harvard.

HASTUR (WD): Originally, Hastur is "the god of shepherds" faithfully worshipped by the naïve and hardworking Haïta in the tale *Haïta the Shepherd* by Ambrose Bierce (1842–1914?), one of the short stories in his 1891 collection *Tales of Soldiers and Civilians*. The tale itself is a gentle—for the ferocious cynic nicknamed "Bitter Bierce"—fable about finding and losing happiness, and Hastur seems to be a very benevolent god to his faithful worshippers. The word was later used in the tale *The Yellow Sign*, by Robert W. Chambers, in the book of loosely connected tales of fright called *The King in Yellow*. As described by HPL in his essay *Supernatural Horror in Literature*, a certain talisman "is indeed the nameless Yellow Sign handed down from the accursed cult of Hastur, from primordial Carcosa, whereof [a mysterious book] treats, and some nightmare memory of which seems to lurk latent and ominous at the back of all men's minds." "Hastur" is one of the names mentioned in passing in the unparalleled fantasy name-dropping of *The Whisperer in Darkness*, having no actual import or significance to that tale.

HATHEG (OG, CU, DQ): A town in Dreamland, the last town before the desert begins on the way to Hatheg-Kla. There are traders based here.

HATHEG-KLA (OG, SHH, DQ): A mountain in Dreamland. "...far in the stony desert beyond Hatheg...[it] rises like a rock statue in a silent temple." It is always misty near the summit, "for mists are the memories of the gods, and [earth's gods] loved Hatheg-Kla when they dwelt on it in the old days," *i.e.*, before moving to Kadath. Sometimes earth's gods return to dance on the peak. Barzai and Atal reach the base of the mountain after a 13 day walk from Hatheg, suggesting that it might be between 100–150 miles distant. Three days of difficult climbing bring them to just below the summit, where they wait for the moon to become clouded over. On the fifth night, the gods came to dance. Barzai races up the slope to the top, beholds earth's gods, and is then swept away into space by their protectors. Atal wakes up the next morning somewhere far down the mountain. Later, a party of men from Hatheg, Ulthar and Nir scale the peak by daylight to look for Barzai's remains, but find only "a curious and cyclopean symbol fifty cubits wide" engraved in the mountain stone as if by a giant chisel; it is a mysterious symbol also found in the *Pnakotic Manuscripts*. (A cubit is the English word for an ancient unit of linear measurement most familiar from the Bible. Defined as the distance from the elbow to the tip of the longest finger of a man, a cubit was obviously not a very exact measuring-unit, but it is commonly converted to modern measures at the ratio of 18 inches or 0.46 meters = one cubit. Therefore "fifty cubits" would be 75 feet wide or 34.5 meters.)

In *The Strange High House in the Mist*, Thomas Olney's host talks timidly of "the dim first age of chaos…when only the other gods came to dance on the peak of Hatheg-Kla." Passing through Ulthar in *The Dream-Quest of Unknown Kadath*, Randolph Carter hears Barzai's story from Atal's own lips, and he hears it again from Nyarlathotep in Kadath.

HATHORNE, JUDGE (DWH): "There was much in the Essex County records about Keziah Mason's trial, and what she had admitted under pressure to the Court of Oyer and Terminer…. She had told Judge Hathorne of lines and curves that could be made to point out directions leading through the walls of space…." John Hathorne (1641–1717), great-great-grandfather of the celebrated 19th century American author Nathaniel Hawthorne, is famous or infamous as one of the associate judges who investigated the Salem witchcraft allegations in 1692. Hawthorne wrote of him (in *The Custom House, Introductory to The Scarlet Letter*) that he "made himself so conspicuous in the martyrdom of the witches, that their blood may fairly be said to have left a stain upon him. So deep a stain, indeed, that his old dry bones, in the Charter Street burial-ground, must still retain it, if they have not crumbled utterly to dust!" The special court over which Hathorne presided in 1692 was formally known as the Court of Oyer and Terminer, a then-current English judicial designation for a trial court able to conduct hearings and render decisions (*oyer* and *terminer* in French).

HAWKINS (CC): This sailor from the *Emma* survives the sea-fight to land on R'lyeh. After the curious sailor Donovan has somehow succeeded in causing the gigantic door of Cthulhu's house to open, "the quick-eared Hawkins thought he heard a nasty, slopping sound down there." A few seconds later great Cthulhu emerges. Hawkins and Rodriguez must be the two men "who perished of pure fright in that accursed instant."

HEISENBERG (DWH): *See* "Mathematicians of Arkham."

HERMES TRISMEGISTUS (CDW, EC): The purported historical author of ancient, complex, alchemical and magical texts. Renaissance-era philosophers and alchemists believed that the writings of "Hermes Trismegistus" were older than those of Plato, and were in fact among the purest and earliest sources of occult learning. Based on certain passages in these texts, Hermes Trismegistus was even sculpted in stone in the great cathedral of Siena, Italy, as a huge old man with a flowing beard, an inspired pagan prophet of the Christian future. The "Hermetic" texts, a vast body of written lore, dealt with both "popular" and "erudite" Hermeticism, including works on astrology, magic, alchemy, occult practices, and Gnostic religion. But in fact there was no such person. The god Hermes was the closest Greek equivalent to Thoth, the Egyptian god of learning and medicine. When ancient Greek civilization encountered Thoth, they added some of his attributes to the ongoing cult of Hermes. Later the honorific title "Trismegistus"—Greek for "thrice-greatest"—was added to the god's other popular titles. The so-called writings of Hermes Trismegistus appear to have been composed by numerous unknown authors writing in the Greek language during the 2nd–4th centuries A.D. The truth about these texts and the nonexistence of the sage Hermes Trismegistus was first demonstrated by the linguistics scholar Isaac Casaubon in a 1614 book. HPL knew this, writing to his friend Willis Conover: "Greek god—Egyptian god—Chaldean philosopher...it's all the same. None of these hypothetical bearers of the name ever existed!" However, the "Hermetic" texts had a long half-life among magicians and esoteric adepts. Hermetic writings are to be found in the libraries of both Joseph Curwen and the "evil clergyman."

HERRERO, MRS., and ESTEBAN (CA): Mrs. Herrero is the slovenly landlady of the narrator's Manhattan tenement, a four-story brownstone building on West 14th Street, built in the 1840s. She comes from Barcelona, Spain. Her son Esteban Herrero does all of Dr. Muñoz's errands for food, laundry, medicines, and chemicals. As Dr. Muñoz's condition becomes more and more extreme, she "turned him over" to the sympathetic narrator, refusing to allow young Esteban to do any more services for the weird invalid.

The building HPL had in mind while writing *Cool Air* was a boarding house at 317 W. 14th Street in Manhattan, between 8th and 9th Avenues; at this writing, it is still standing in what has become a rather prosperous neighborhood. One of his friends lived there during August-September 1925.

HETFIELD, PHEBE (SH): A young lady from Elizabethtown (now Elizabeth), New Jersey. During his stay in New York City, HPL enjoyed visiting Elizabeth, which is still relatively rich in surviving colonial-era architecture. Captain William Harris, Jr. marries her there in 1780. In 1781 (a year which saw the end of the Revolutionary War) she moves to his family home in Providence, suffering a stillbirth in the house the next year. After moving to a new home with her husband, she gives birth to a son, Dutee Harris, who is destined to live long and prosper. Phebe Hetfield Harris and her husband both perish in the terrible yellow fever epidemic which afflicted the United States in 1797. As he did so often, HPL must have derived the name from his readings in local history; although Phebe Hetfield is a fictitious person, a certain Cornelius Hetfield, Sr., was a leading patriot in Elizabethtown during the Revolutionary War, and other local Hetfields were also active on the American side in the conflict; the name "Hetfield," a rare variant of "Hatfield," is too unusual to allow any other reasonable conclusion.

HETTY (SOI): A merchant brig, one of the three vessels owned by Captain Obed Marsh.

HEXHAM (CDW): *See* "Caerleon, Hexham, and Hadrian's Wall."

HIGH PRIEST NOT TO BE DESCRIBED (CE, DQ): The high priest "wears a yellow silken mask over its face and dwells all alone in a prehistoric stone monastery on the cold desert plateau of Leng," praying to the Other Gods and their crawling chaos Nyarlathotep. The dreamer who becomes King Kuranes "barely escapes" from it, as mentioned in *Celephaïs*. Randolph Carter also has a narrow escape in *The Dream-Quest of Unknown Kadath*. Kidnapped by the slant-eyed merchant, he is flown to the monastery, "a squat windowless building, around which a circle of crude monoliths stood," in an arrangement which somehow gave an impression of having "nothing human" about it. Sculpted or painted on the walls of the interior corridors are bas-reliefs and frescoes of historical subjects (like the story-telling walls in the Nameless City, and in the Antarctic lost city of *At the Mountains of Madness*). They recount the history of Leng, how its almost-human inhabitants fought the large purple spiders, and how they later surrendered to the invading moonbeasts in their black galleys. Carter also learns that the deserted city of Sarkomand was their ancient capital. The high priest dwells in darkness, in "a great domed space whose walls were carved with shocking bas-reliefs, and whose center held a gaping circular pit surrounded by six malignly stained stone altars." At one end of this space is a stone dais with five steps, surmounted by a golden throne upon which "sat a lumpish figure robed in yellow silk figured with red [a color combination which HPL also associated with the robes of the demoniacal New Yorkers of the future in *He*] and having a yellow silken mask over its face." The slant-eyed merchant "spoke" to the high priest by a kind of sign-language, and it replied with musical notes played on an ivory flute. "Then the figured silk slipped a trifle from one of the greyish-white paws," and Carter understands that the high priest not to be described is a moonbeast.

HILL, LIEUTENANT ROBERT (HW): A gallant (although fictitious) World War I aviator of the Canadian Army, shot down and killed while flying Major Clapham-Lee to the divisional field hospital at St. Eloi, Belgium.

HILLS OF IMPLAN (DCS): Although far away from Sarnath, these hills are nonetheless a source of young goats for the imperial city's great feasts.

HIMALAYAS (SOT, WD, MM): The highest mountain range in the world, located in India, Tibet, Nepal, and China, which includes Earth's tallest peak, Mount Everest. During his possession by a member of the Great Race, Professor Nathanael Peaslee spent a month in the Himalayas in 1909. The mountains that walled off the abandoned city in Antarctica, as surveyed by Professor Atwood, topped out at from 30,000–34,000 feet high, higher than anything in the Himalayas as Professor Lake points out. (Meanwhile, the mountains some 300 miles farther west of the city, by Professor Dyer's visual estimate, "must have been over 40,000 feet high.") The Mi-Go are usually identified, we are told, as the creatures who are responsible for the legends of the Abominable Snowmen of the Himalayas.

HIRAM (TT): A faithful old servant of the Dudley family, much attached to young Jervas Dudley, who compliments him as "loyal to the last." After his young master's confinement to an asylum, Hiram breaks into the old Hyde family tomb and finds an empty coffin labeled *Jervas*; Jervas Dudley's family promise he will be buried in it after his death.

The biblical Hiram, king of Tyre, was a friend of the Jewish kings David and Solomon, and supplied cedar wood and skilled workmen for the construction of the Temple in Jerusalem (1 Kings 5:1, etc.)

HLANITH (DQ): A vast seaport city on the Cerenarian Sea, at the mouth of the river Oukranos. Its city walls are granite, and its buildings are peaked and gabled. The dull folk of Hlanith are more like waking humans than anyone else in Dreamland, but at least in compensation for their dullness, the artisans are known for especially solid work. Oxcarts clog the city streets and the bazaars are full of yelling merchants. Randolph Carter spends only a day in this unlovely commercial hub, wandering around and asking questions about Inganok in the waterfront taverns; then he sets off on the four-day sailing voyage up the coast to Celephaïs.

HOADLEY, REVEREND ABIJAH (DH): He was "called" to Dunwich in 1747 to become the minister of the Congregational church (probably the same church building which is Dunwich's broken-steepled general store by 1928). Not long after arriving, he preached "a memorable sermon on the close presence of Satan and his imps," which he vowed he could hear from his own parsonage (residence). The sermon was later printed at nearby Springfield, Massachusetts. (In 18th century America, books of collected sermons by noted ministers were among the most popular items in the publishing market, so this would not have been unusual!) Surely by mere coincidence, Reverend Hoadley disappeared forever shortly after preaching this sermon.

The name "Hoadley," English in origin, is a very rare one. But HPL knew of a famous and long-dead New England maker of "grandfather" (long-case) clocks, Silas Hoadley, who may have loaned his surname to the unfortunate fictitious pastor in this tale. Abijah is an Old Testament Hebrew name, such as was once common in New England.

HOFFMANN (RW): A German author (1776–1822) who belongs to the "Romantic" era in European literature. The multitalented Ernst Theodor Amadeus Hoffmann was a judge, opera composer, music critic, and writer. He is best known to posterity for his for often bizarre and vaguely sinister tales, which are full of grotesque and supernatural elements. In HPL's tale, Mr. de la Poer comments that even Hoffmann "could not conceive a scene more wildly incredible, more frenetically repellent, or more Gothically grotesque than the twilit grotto through which we seven staggered," in the great cavern under Exham Priory.

"HOLLAND CHURCHYARD" (TH): A lonely Dutch cemetery in which St. John and his companion, the narrator, dig up a medieval tomb-robber's bones, and steal the jade medallion from his remains. It is a frightening place, suitable for any horror to occur: with grotesquely-shaped trees, overgrown grass, crumbling tombstones, legions of giant bats, night-glowing insects, and everywhere the stench of mold. HPL enjoyed all these gothic details so much, he essentially repeated them in successive paragraphs. Later, St. John's comrade returns alone to the churchyard in Holland, reopens the grave, and finds the lich inside "covered with caked blood and shreds of alien flesh and hair," also glowing eyes and bloody fangs. Then he hears a baying like a hound, and he hastily departs. The "Holland churchyard" was thinly-based on the real cemetery of the old Dutch Reformed Church in Brooklyn, New York (founded in 1662, current building erected in 1796, and located at 890 Flatbush Avenue), which HPL visited with his friend Rheinhart Kleiner on the night of September 16, 1922.

HOLMES, LOWELL and LONGFELLOW (PM): The sinister artist Pickman, in one of his secret paintings, depicted some of the corpse-eating ghouls gathered around a "well-known Boston guidebook," and all pointing at a certain passage while convulsing with laughter. "The title of the picture was, 'Holmes, Lowell, and Longfellow Lie Buried in Mount Auburn.'" Oliver Wendell Holmes (1809–94), not to be confused with his son and namesake who served on the U.S. Supreme Court in the 20th century, was a Harvard professor of anatomy and physiology, with a separate career as a witty and well-known journalistic contributor to magazines and newspapers. James Russell Lowell (1819–91) was one of the most prominent men of letters in 19th century America, as a poet, magazine editor, author and critic. Like Holmes, he served Harvard University for many years as a professor. Henry Wadsworth Longfellow (1807–82), an intellectual comrade in arms of Holmes and Lowell and, like them, a Harvard professor for many years, was additionally one of the most popular of all American poets, although his sentimental and historical-nostalgic poems, enormously popular in their time and ubiquitous in American schools up until the mid-20th century, are now out of fashion and little read. Mount Auburn is a cemetery in Cambridge, Massachusetts, the home of Harvard University, across the Charles River from the city of Boston.

HOLT, CAPTAIN EBENEZER (PH): A fictitious 18th century merchant sailor who was known as "Eb" to his friends and who lived, when not on voyages, in a house in the countryside near Arkham, Massachusetts. Apparently he could read Latin. He served for years on merchant ships out of Salem, Massachusetts, and used to buy and bring home strange things from overseas. In 1768 he did a swap or trade with a rural neighbor, who badly wanted a book that Holt had purchased in a London shop; it was a copy of Pigafetta's *Regnum Congo*. Captain Holt died in the Revolutionary War.

HOMERIC (CDW): The ocean liner that lands Charles Dexter Ward at New York harbor in May, 1926, after he has spent nearly three years (HPL slips up and calls it "nearly four years") away from New England, pursuing mysterious studies in Europe. He next travels by bus to Providence, and HPL's lyrical and evocative description of the sights along the way from Connecticut to the Ward family home on College Hill no doubt precisely mirrors some of HPL's own sense-impressions as he rode a train from the "New York Exile" back to Providence on April 17, 1926. The *Homeric* was a real ocean liner, operated by the White Star Line on the transatlantic route from 1922 until the early 1930s.

HOOPER'S POND (SHH): A fictitious body of water outside of fictitious Kingsport, Massachusetts; in the tale, Thomas Olney passes it on his circuitous walk to the Strange High House.

HOPKINS, DR. CHAD (SH): A Providence physician who attended the "fever victims" dying in the Shunned House in 1804, and made out all four death certificates, noting the relative lack of blood in the bodies of the deceased tenants.

HOPKINS, ESEK (CDW): Sea captain and Providence civic leader (1718–1802), the sailor-brother of Stephen Hopkins. In the tale, Esek is a member of the secret committee of prominent local men who investigate Joseph Curwen in 1770–71. He is also a commander in the raiding party against the Curwen's Pawtuxet Road farm on April 12, 1771, in charge of the "river group." In 1775 the historical Esek Hopkins became the first commander of the "Continental Navy" in the Revolutionary War.

HOPKINS, STEPHEN (CDW): A leading citizen of colonial and early federal Providence (1707–1785), the brother of Esek Hopkins. In 1770, he was the former colonial governor of Rhode Island, a former member of the "Philosophical Society" in Newport (the capital in colonial days), and "a man of very broad perceptions" as HPL says. In the tale, he is a member of the secret committee to investigate Joseph Curwen in 1770–71. The historical Stephen Hopkins was one of the immortal signers of the Declaration of Independence in 1776, as a representative from Rhode Island, and a distant relative of HPL on his mother's side.

HOPPIN, AARON (CDW): In 1771, this man is a supercargo (clerk) employed by Joseph Curwen in his mercantile and shipping business; he is the great-grandson of Daniel Green.

HORSES (SOI, IV, COS, RW): HPL came of age before working horses had entirely disappeared from city streets, let alone from American farms—grandfather Whipple V. Phillips maintained a stable of carriage-horses and a stable boy at his Angell Street home—and horses turn up in some of his tales. Like other lower animals, they are portrayed as being attuned to psychic influences that are imperceptible (at least initially) to human beings. The Innsmouth residents have a very difficult time with their draft horses, who hate them, until they are able to replace equines with trucks and automobiles. The horse of the undertaker, George Birch, in *In the Vault*, understands quickly that there is something radically wrong about the situation in the Peck Valley cemetery's receiving tomb. As the horse's master works to escape from inside the tomb, the beast "whinnied in a tone which may have been encouraging and may have been mocking." Much later it emits "a scream that was too frantic for a neigh" and bolts into the night, taking with it carriage and all. (In HPL's dream-based story fragment, *The Very Old People*, the detail of horses "screaming" also appears to frightening effect.)

The most used and ill-used horses are in *The Colour Out of Space*. Other people's horses shy away from the Gardner farm after the Colour has taken up residence, while Nahum Gardner's own team of four plow-horses all go mad and must be shot. A replacement horse he borrows from Ammi Pierce will not even go near the Gardner place. Finally, Ammi Pierce's cart-horse, Hero, unfortunately tethered outside the Gard-ner home on the climactic night when the Colour (mostly) departed from the Earth, was heard by the terrified men cowering in the farmhouse to make "a sound such as no man before or since ever heard from a horse."

> Every person in that low-pitched sitting room stopped his ears, and Ammi turned away from the window in horror and nausea. Words could not con-vey it—when Ammi looked out again the hapless beast lay huddled inert on the moonlit ground between the splintered shafts of the buggy. That was the last of Hero until they buried him the next day.

In *The Rats in the Walls*, the horse of Sir John Clave was said to have trodden upon a peculiar, whitish creature one night in a field near Exham Priory, some time during the Middle Ages. We understand by the end of the tale that this was an escaped human food-animal from the dreadful subterranean vaults of the castle.

HOUDINI, HARRY (UP): The legendary escape-artist and stage magi-cian (1874–1926), whose real name was Erich Weiss. With his magic shows and incredible feats of escape from handcuffs, straitjackets, chains and sealed containers of all kinds, he became a wealthy and world-famous celebrity, who remains a legend to this day. The struggling new pulp magazine *Weird Tales* made a bid to boost its circulation with first-person yarns of weird adventure "by" the great Houdini; actually, the stories were only based on story-ideas he suggested, and were penned by professional ghostwriters, enabling Houdini to lend his famous name in exchange for a paycheck and little or no work. *Under the Pyramids,* ghosted by HPL in 1923, was one such secret "collaboration."

In the tale, Houdini, while passing through Cairo en route from Europe to Australia by ship in 1910, finds himself being tricked and made a captive by local Arabs, and lowered into "Cyclopean" depths beneath the desert floor of the pyramid-complex of Giza, where he wanders until he sees revived mummies, and even worse undead things from ancient Egypt, gathering for a hideous celebration and feast. (Houdini's 1910 trip for a series of public performances in Australia, via the Suez Canal in Egypt, is historical fact.)

Houdini was pleased by *Under the Pyramids*, and casually befriended the writer when he moved from Providence to New York City in 1924. Houdini made an attempt to help the unemployed author get hired by a newspaper syndicate—but finding a steady job for HPL proved to be the one magic trick even The Great Houdini could not perform, and the prospect led nowhere. He also treated HPL and his wife Sonia to complimentary tickets to one of his famous stage shows. After HPL had moved back to Providence, Houdini paid him $75 to ghostwrite an article attacking astrology—an argument near and dear to HPL's heart. In 1925–26 there was some talk and correspondence about a book which would have been entitled *The Cancer of Superstition*, about "spiritualist" frauds and fake mediums, a subject in which Houdini, a magician of enormous skill, took a profound skeptical interest; he had exposed many false mediums. The book was to have featured Houdini's experiences and ideas, ghostwritten by HPL's Providence crony Clifford M. Eddy, with HPL serving as the editor. The project was stillborn when Houdini died suddenly of peritonitis at the age of 52.

HOUGHTON, DR. (DH): A physician from Aylesbury, Massachusetts, who is summoned to attend Old Whateley's final hours of life on Lammas Night (August 1) 1924; the reference is to Lammas day in the English church calendar.

HOUND, THE (TH): When the narrator and his comrade, St. John, dig up the medieval tomb-robber from his grave in Holland, they hear "the faint deep-toned baying of some gigantic hound which we could neither see nor definitely place." It is unavoidable to think that HPL may have had in mind the nightmare Hound of the Baskervilles, in Arthur Conan Doyle's famed Sherlock Holmes detective story of the same name!

Around the cadaver's neck is an amulet bearing "an oddly conventional-ized figure of a crouching winged hound, or sphinx with a semi-canine face." While sailing back across the English Channel, the two men seem to hear the baying again. Back in their manor house in England, they are troubled by the shadows of some huge creature, and eventually St. John is seized and torn to shreds by...*something*. The baying sounds follow the narrator on a return trip to the Netherlands, where he digs down to the old grave again. He sees that, while the medieval ghoul-man was appar-ently killed by a great hound (the marks of which are still visible on his bones), the remains are now covered with the blood and hair of slain vic-tims, and the corpse begins to *bay* at the narrator, from a mouth filled with fangs. Technically, the word *hound* applies only to dogs bred to hunt other animals.

HOUNDS OF TINDALOS (WD): One of the unearthly subjects dis-coursed about to Professor Wilmarth by the impostor wearing Henry Akeley's borrowed face and clothes. These hounds, and Tindalos, were the fictional creation of HPL's close friend and fellow-author Frank Belknap Long.

HOW, AMITY (CDW): In the tale, a witness interrogated by Judge Gedney on August 8, 1692. She testified that "Joseph C." and "Simon O." (Curwen and Orne) had been among the people who received the devil's mark from "Mr. G.B." (George Burroughs) at a Salem coven meeting. This character is fictitious, but an *Elizabeth* How, of Ipswich, Massachusetts (incidentally, the closest normal town to Innsmouth in *The Shadow Over Innsmouth*) was one of the women hanged for witchcraft at Salem Village on July 19, 1692, and numerous other members of the extended How family appear in the extant Salem documents as suspects, witnesses, or petitioners for redress. The Boston Public Library has the original copy of Elizabeth How's death warrant, ordering her execution under the supervision of George Corwin, the sheriff of Essex County (and a kinsman of Salem judge Jonathan Corwin; a grim reminder that, as HPL sardonically commented while recounting Joseph Curwen's life story in *The Case of Charles Dexter Ward*, "the Curwens or Corwins of Salem needed no introduction in New England").

The "devil's mark" in European witchcraft lore was a permanent physical mark placed by Satan on the flesh of a new witch as soon as the witch had signed Satan's book, perhaps appearing like a birthmark, mole or skin lump. Part of the typical process of investigating a suspected witch was stripping him or her to search for such a mark. Charles W. Upham in the book *Salem Witchcraft* described how this was done:

It was believed that the Devil affixed his mark to the bodies of those in alliance with him, and that the point where this mark was made became callous and dead. The law provided, specifically, the means of detecting and identifying this sign. It required that the prisoner should be subjected to the scrutiny of a jury of the same sex, who would make a minute inspection of the body, shaving the head and handling every part. They would pierce it with pins; and if, as might have been expected, particularly in aged persons, any spot could be found insensible to the torture, or any excrescence, induration, or fixed discoloration, it was looked upon as visible evidence and demonstration of guilt. A physician or "chirurgeon" was required to be present at these examinations. In conducting them, there was liability to great roughness and unfeeling recklessness of treatment; and the whole procedure was barbarous and shocking to every just and delicate sensibility.

The Peabody Essex Museum in Salem contains a dramatic painting of such a judicial inspection, which HPL may well have seen: *Examination of a Witch* (1853), by the American painter Tompkins H. Matteson (1813–84), a specialist in historical subjects who is best remembered today for his patriotic painting *The Spirit of '76*. Joseph Curwen's own devil's mark was presumably the same "great black mole or cicatrice" [a scar or mark left from the healing of a wound] that appears on the chest of Charles Dexter Ward after his body has been, in a sense, taken over by Curwen.

HSAN, SEVEN CRYPTICAL BOOKS OF (OG, DQ): A set of ancient wisdom-texts that Randolph Carter consults at the Temple of the Elder Ones in Ulthar, looking for information about Kadath; he finds little enough. Barzai the Wise was said to have known these books perfectly.

HUITZILOPOCHTLI (TJR): A mysterious outcry which the narrator hears from Juan Romero's lips during the latter's "transition." He later finds the same word in Prescott's *Conquest of Mexico* (a reference to *History of the Conquest of Mexico* (1843), by the American historian William H. Prescott (1796–1859); a classic work of historical writing which describes the 16th century defeat of the mighty Aztec rulers of central Mexico, by the invading Spanish conquistadors and their Mexican tribal allies). Huitzilopochtli was the sun god and chief deity of the Aztecs, whom they worshipped in the form of an idol, with gory and innumerable human sacrifices, until the fall of the Aztec Empire.

HUTCHINS, ED (DH): A Dunwich farmer, and a member of the posse that trailed around behind the Miskatonic University professors.

HUTCHINS, ELAM (DH): In a diary entry dated November 26, 1916, Wilbur Whateley (then "a child of three and a half who looked like a lad of twelve or thirteen") wrote: "Shot Elam Hutchins' collie Jack when he went to bite me, and Elam said he would kill me if he dast [dared to]. I guess he won't." This entry underscores the instinctive hatred of all dogs for Wilbur Whateley, and foreshadows his death a dozen years later in the fangs and claws of the savage Miskatonic University watchdog when a dented pistol cartridge jams in his revolver.

HUTCHINS, WILL (DH): A relative of Ed Hutchins, who also joins the posse on September 15, 1928.

HUTCHINSON, EDWARD (CDW): A friend of Joseph Curwen. He lived at Salem Village, Massachusetts, circa 1687–92, and was often observed having private conversations with Curwen and Simon Orne. Hutchinson lived in a house in the woods where suspicious noises and lights were sometimes heard or seen, and he displayed an unsettling knowledge about long-dead people and long-forgotten events. At the time of the witchcraft trials in 1692, he suddenly left the area, forever. On July 10, 1692, a woman named Hepzibah Lawson swore to Judge Hathorne that "fortie witches and the Blacke Man were wont to meet [in the habit of meeting] in the Woodes behind Mr. Hutchinson's house." Hutchinson's library, seized by the authorities after his disappearance, was full of books which were deemed to be "uncanny," as was an unfinished manuscript written in a cipher which no one could ever decode. Hutchinson eventually resurfaces living under the name of "Baron Ferenczy" in a remote Transylvanian castle, where he hosts the young Charles Dexter Ward for several months during 1925–26. Later still, he corresponds with the revenant Joseph Curwen. Hutchinson was indeed a prominent family name in Salem Village; the Essex County records show that two respected local men, Benjamin and Joseph Hutchinson, were among the official complainants against several of the accused witches in 1692.

HUYSMANS, J.K. (TH, RW): Mentioned in these tales only as a symbol of fastidious moral decadence, Huysmans (1848–1907) was a Belgian author whose popularity flourished during HPL's youth, best known for such works as the then-scandalous novel *A Rebours* ("Against the Grain"), about a wealthy, super-aesthetic, hypersensitive, bachelor European aristocrat, and his efforts to overcome his ever-constant boredom with fantastic surroundings and experiences, with narcotics and with sexual vice.

HYDE FAMILY (TT): An extinct family whose remains and shadows fill "The Tomb" of the title, apparently in the vicinity of Boston, Massachusetts; their former mansion was on the hill above the family tomb. It

is indicated that this colonial American family was founded by Sir Geoffrey Hyde who emigrated from Sussex, England, in 1640. After a catastrophic fire destroyed the mansion sometime in the 18th century, the
remaining members of the family moved to distant places, returning only
for burials over the years. The last of the Hydes had been placed in the
tomb fifty years before the unspecified year in which this tale opens. The
narrator discovers that he is descended from the Hydes on his mother's
side, and that his face is identical to that of a certain long-dead member
of the family. This plot device, more or less, was used by HPL again in
The Case of Charles Dexter Ward.

HYDRA (SOI, DWH): In ancient Greek mythology, Hydra was a
hundred-headed sea monster with poisonous breath, which Hercules
defeated and killed as one of his twelve labors. According to Zadok
Allen in *The Shadow Over Innsmouth*, "Mother Hydra" is worshipped
along with "Father Dagon" by the members of the Esoteric Order of
Dagon, the town's cult. In *The Dreams in the Witch House,* the student
Gilman once finds himself feeling "drawn" to a point in the sky near the
Hydra constellation.

HYPERBOREA (TGSK): A Greek word meaning "farthest north"; it
was the name of the prehistoric sword-and-sorcery country invented by
HPL's writer-friend Clark Ashton Smith. In this tale, the personage who
calls himself "Swami Chandraputra" tells the other people in the room
that the characters on the mysterious parchment found by Randolph
Carter are "R'lyehian," but that even that was "of course, a translation—
there was an Hyperborean original millions of years earlier in the primal
tongue of Tsath-Yo."

HYPNOS (HY): The ancient Greek god of sleep.

I

IB (NC, DCS, MM): In a very long-ago time, Ib was a grey stone city on the shore of a vast lake in the land of Mnar. According to the "brick cylinders of Kadatheron," Ib was inhabited by non-humans, a race of green, voiceless creatures with bulging eyes and flabby lips, and curious ears, who worshipped a sea-green stone idol chiselled in the likeness of Bokrug, the great water-lizard. The inhabitants of Ib were "soft as jelly to the touch" and not good fighters. It was reputed that these inhabitants had all "descended one night from the moon, in a mist; they and the vast still lake and grey stone city Ib." When men came to Mnar, some of the hardiest pushed ahead to the lake and founded their own city of Sarnath, close by Ib. Disliking their strange neighbors, the men of Sarnath massacred every dweller in Ib, and pushed their bodies and the ruins of their city into the lake. One thousand years later, Ib returns from the lake for its revenge. In *The Nameless City*, Ib is referred to as having been built before mankind existed; and in *At the Mountains of Madness*, Professor Dyer calls Ib a "pre-human blasphemy" like the Antarctic lost city he has found.

IBN GHAZI (DH): Wilbur Whateley's diary for November 26, 1916, notes that he can see "that upstairs"—*i.e.*, his brother—when he blows "the powder of Ibn Ghazi" at it. Ibn Ghazi is an Arab male name in form, but the person was fictitious. The name suggests the Arab involvement in alchemy and esoteric subjects centuries ago.

IBN SCHACABAO (CDW, TF): An Arab sage or magician of unspecified date, who is referred to as an authority in a letter from Joseph Curwen to Simon Orne during the 1750s, with the words: "I laste Night sturcke on ye Wordes that bringe up YOGGE-SOTHOTHE, and sawe for ye first Time that face spoke of by Ibn Schacabao in ye —." The same man is cited in the *Necronomicon* for the saying that: "Happy is the tomb where no wizard has lain, and happy the town at night whose wizards are all ashes." "Ibn" means "son of," but "Schacabao" is meaningless in Arabic. Whether HPL had a particular Arabic word or phrase on his mind in creating the name "Schacabao" seems to be unknown.

ILARNEK (QI, DCS, DQ): A city on the river Ai, in Dreamland. Its people are of the dark-complexioned shepherd folk which colonized the land of Mnar. Iranon passes through on his wanderings. A document called "the papyrus of Ilarnek" told how the pre-human inhabitants of Ib discovered fire and used it in worship. Ilarnek paid tribute to the realm of Sarnath; after the city of Sarnath's cataclysmic disappearance, the people of Ilarnek enshrine the recovered idol of Bokrug, and it is worshipped throughout Mnar. In *The Dream-Quest of Unknown Kadath*, it is mentioned that the merchants of Ilarnek trade for onyx from faraway Inganok.

ILEK-VAD (SK, DQ): In Dreamland, "a fabulous town of turrets atop the hollow cliffs of glass overlooking the twilight sea." At the end of *The Silver Key*, it is suggested that the vanished Randolph Carter might have become a king on Ilek-Vad's opal throne. In *The Dream-Quest of Unknown Kadath*, it is said that the king of Ilek-Vad (who is not Randolph Carter!) comes from his "far realm" riding in a golden palanquin, to pray to the god of Oukranos, who sang to him when he dwelled in a cottage by the banks of the river Oukranos. The Kiran temple complex of Ilek-Vad is built all out of jasper, and the Oukranos runs through it. Only the king of Ilek-Vad has entered the temple or seen its priests.

IMAGE DU MONDE (NC): A "delirious" work by one Gauthier de Metz, mentioned by this tale's narrator. Gauthier or Gautier du Metz was a 13th century French priest and poet. His attributed work *L'Image du Monde* (c. 1246), based on an older medieval Latin work by one Honorius Inclusus, is a lengthy poem dealing with Creation, geography, and astronomy, as well as fabulous monsters, and legends of far-off lands. The poem was very popular during the Middle Ages.

INDIANS, AMERICAN (HE, DH, WD, CDW): HPL was rationally unsentimental about the pre-European inhabitants of the Americas. He knew about them basically from his reading, as New England's once-numerous Indian tribes had been wiped out or decimated one or two centuries before his birth. But the first Americans and their lore occur in a few of his tales.

In *He*, the old "squire" had learned the magic of, and then betrayed and poisoned, an unnamed Indian tribe on the island of Manhattan long ago; at the end of the tale, the murdered Indians return for their revenge. HPL's ex-wife Sonia remembered in the 1940s that "in Prospect Park, Brooklyn [in New York City], we used to explore a very tiny hidden cemetery, ancient in point of time, where, it is said, the Indians used to bury their dead.... I wouldn't be at all surprised if Howard had not somewhere among his writings described this very unusual place." He did not—or not in this tale—but the recollection does show him thinking about buried Indians under the soil of modern New York City, obviously a central device of *He*.

Joseph Curwen's only known servants at his Pawtuxet Road farm in the 18th century are an elderly couple, members of the indigenous Narragansett tribe (the major tribe of the Rhode Island area, already reduced to near-extinction by the middle of the 18th century, although a handful survive to this day). In *The Dunwich Horror* it is stated that although some people prefer to believe that the deposits of skulls and bones around certain hilltops near Dunwich were "burial places of the Pocumtucks," scientific inquiries had proved the remains to be those of Caucasians. The Pocumtucks or Pocumtucs were a small tribe inhabiting the Connecticut River valley of western Massachusetts, and were virtually extinct by the late 1700s.

As a professional folklorist in New England, Professor Wilmarth in *The Whisperer in Darkness* is familiar with the legends of the Pennacook tribe about the "hill creatures" of Vermont; that they were from other planets, and only maintained some outposts on Earth. The Pennacooks principally inhabited the Merrimack River valley of southern and central New Hampshire, down into northeastern Massachusetts and up into southern Maine. The Pennacook tribe had disappeared by about the end of the 18th century, as a result of wars and epidemic diseases, with its remnants being absorbed into other tribes.

INGANOK (DQ): A country in Dreamland. It is the name of a cold, twilight land in the far north, and also of its exquisite capital city, constructed from local onyx stone. To the east of Inganok, on the other side of high, inaccessible mountains, is the plateau of Leng. Inganok's principal business is the mining and exportation of onyx. Its inhabitants include many people with strong resemblances to the face carved into the side of Mount Ngranek, an indication of much genetic inheritance from earth's gods, who sported with mortal women in the past. The Inganok folk keep as slaves the descendants of almost-humans who drifted down from Leng. "There is a wonder and strangeness in the city of Inganok," we are told. The city skyline is a vision of onion domes and minarets, made (like even the streets and sidewalks) from the finest onyx, fabulously carved with designs. On a hilltop at the center of town is a 16-angled tower with a flat-topped dome and a belfry. At intervals a bell rings from within the tower, answered by peals of music from horns and viols, and loud chanting. This is the Temple of the Elder Ones, which lies within a walled garden with seven arched gateways, in a round plaza from whence all of Inganok's main streets radiate. Fountains, pools and basins in the park reflect the flames from tripods burning on the tower's high balconies. At certain times of day, a procession of hooded and masked priests, bearing bowls filled with some kind of liquid, moves in and out of the tower and garden. The priests may not even be human, but no one knows, for only Inganok's monarch, the Veiled King, may even enter their temple. The Veiled King's own palace appears to be magnificent, in keeping with the rest of the city; but no one else may enter the palace, either. Hiring a yak, Randolph Carter leaves the capital and rides through rural Inganok for a day before reaching the village of Urg, where he spends two hours gathering information in taverns. Here the caravan route turns west to Selarn, but Carter follows the road which leads north to the onyx quarries. On the third morning of his journey, he reaches the first quarry, and on the fourth day he passes beyond the inhabited part of Inganok.

INGENIOUS MACHINES (BWS, FB, SOT, EC, TGSK): HPL relied rather little on mechanical devices as critical story elements. His characters move through space and time by mental (or extraordinary physical) powers, with perhaps an incantation or a silver key to help move them along. Even the space aliens tend to glide through the interstellar wastes in their bare skins, being creatures of matter different from our own. But in *Beyond the Wall of Sleep*, the narrator had invented a "telepathic radio" which he attached to himself and to Joe Slater. In *From Beyond*, Crawford Tillinghast creates "a detestable electrical machine" connected to a powerful chemical battery. It has a "crowning cluster of glass bulbs," and produces *visible* ultra-violet, in the rays of which, creatures from other dimensions may be seen and may in fact kill you. The narrator fires a bullet into this strange machine, leaving the device "hopelessly shattered." The member of the Great Race who sojourns in Professor Wingate Peaslee's body during 1908–13, finally constructed a table-top machine which no one was allowed to look at, apparently to propel itself back to its starting point, millions of years earlier. The machine was removed from the house before Peaslee's "reawakening," presumably by the unknown person who also telephoned Peaslee's doctor to come to the house and check on him. The narrator of *The Evil Clergyman* carries an undescribed "ray projector" and uses it to beam a violet light on a matchbox-sized object in the clergyman's room, then beams it at the clergyman after he has appeared. And Randolph Carter—while in the body of Zkauba of Yaddith—uses a Yaddith "light envelope" to travel from planet to planet.

INNSMOUTH (SOI, TD, DWH):

> Haow'd ye like to be livin' in a taown like this, with everything a-rottin' and a-dyin', and boarded-up monsters crawlin' an' bleatin' and barkin' an' hoppin' araoun' black cellars an' attics every way ye turn?

So asks Zadok Allen, 96-year-old lifelong resident. Innsmouth is a fictitious Massachusetts seaport, which HPL identified as lying between Newburyport and Arkham (*i.e.*, Salem), not far from the real inland towns of Rowley and Ipswich. In real-life geographical terms, HPL's Innsmouth would occupy approximately the site of the village of Little Neck, Massachusetts, where the Ipswich River flows into the ocean, west of Ipswich and a little north of Cape Ann. However, the model for Innsmouth was the town of Newburyport, Massachusetts, at the mouth of the Merrimack River, where the narrator boarded Joe Sargent's rattletrap bus for his fateful trip on July 15, 1927. In HPL's time (like the narrator, he visited in the summer of 1927), Newburyport was a run-down, decaying old harbor town, which gave him ample inspiration for run-down, decaying Innsmouth. Parts of Innsmouth also seem to be modeled on parts of Gloucester, Massachusetts, another old seaport which HPL visited for the first time in 1927.

In his *faux*-history of Innsmouth, HPL states that it was founded in 1643 at the mouth of the (also fictitious) Manuxet River, and was a noted shipbuilding center before the American Revolution. In the early 19th century, it was still "a seat of great maritime prosperity" and a minor industrial center, owing to the factories which drew power from the flow of the Manuxet. In fact, the mill at "the falls," built in 1806, is the most recent building the narrator sees there in 1928. Innsmouth's decline began with the War of 1812 against Great Britain, an historical event which impoverished much of New England. Many of the town's best men were lost at sea while serving as privateers during that war, or lost in the following years with the merchant ships *Ranger* and *Eliza*, which both sank with all hands. After 1828, the only townsman to persist in the lucrative, but very risky, long-distance East Indies and Pacific trade was Captain Obed Marsh. "Everybody was in a bad way in them days," Zadok Allen tells the narrator. "Trade fallin' off, mills losin' business— even the new ones." As the bus-ticket seller in Newburyport says, also to the narrator: "That was before the big epidemic of 1846, when over half the folks in Innsmouth was carried off. They never did figure out what the trouble was… It surely was bad enough—there was riots over it, and all sorts of ghastly doings that I don't believe ever got outside of town— and it left the place in awful shape. Never came back—there can't be more'n 300 or 400 people livin' there now." In fact, the 1846 disaster was a municipal *coup d'etat* and massacre, staged by Obed Marsh and his supporters against the rest of the town, with the violent assistance of the Deep Ones. These events followed several years during which Marsh, through his Esoteric Order of Dagon, promoted the worship of the Deep Ones in Innsmouth and gathered followers. After the slaughter, Obed

Marsh (succeeded in time by his descendants) took over as a sort of viceroy for the Deep Ones, who dwell in the abyss on the other side of Devil Reef. Innsmouth became a nearly-closed society, where strangers were very unwelcome. The presence of government "draft men"—that is, officials carrying out Civil War military conscription—in 1863 brought about more concealment, but no changes.

It is in *The Shadow Over Innsmouth*, set in an evil, degenerate town that reeks everywhere of fish, is overrun by "fish-men" and people turning into fish-men, worshipping fish-like gods, and all (originally) for the sake of better fishing, that HPL's hatred of fish and fishy smells may have had its fullest expression. This aversion (notable in a coastal New Englander, born and bred, which HPL was), was pungently described by L. Sprague de Camp:

> HPL had a genuine horror of sea food. Any attempt to make him eat it, he said, would cause instant vomiting. When somebody quietly set before him a salad containing sea food, he at once put it aside…. It is no coincidence that the monsters of his later stories resemble combinations of various denizens of an aquarium, given colossal size and malignant intelligence.

In *The Thing on the Doorstep*, Edward Derby's bride, Asenath Waite, comes (rather improbably) from Innsmouth, and she imports her domestic servants from there. She and Edward Derby visit the town during their honeymoon, and she—in Edward's body—apparently returns often thereafter. Asenath's "overprotuberant eyes" are probably a suggestion of the "Innsmouth look." On their drive home to Arkham from Chesuncook, Maine, Derby reveals to Daniel Upton that he now knows "the secret" of Innsmouth blood, and of Asenath's half-human nature. Walter Gilman, in *The Dreams in the Witch House*, while wandering on April 21 in response to the strong urges drawing him northward, walks all the way out of Arkham and eventually finds himself far from the city, in the salt marshes on the narrow road to Innsmouth: "that ancient, half-deserted town which Arkham people were so curiously unwilling to visit." He turns back.

INNSMOUTH, ENGLAND (CE): In this tale, a village on the coast of the southwestern English region of Cornwall. The man who was also King Kuranes stumbled through Innsmouth, seeming to be only a dazed derelict, on his way to drown in the ocean the same day.

INNSMOUTH, MARTYRS OF (SOI): Hiram Gilman, Nick Pierce, Miss Luella Waite, Adoniram Southwick, Henry Garrison—all mentioned by Zadok Allen as young people who disappeared from Innsmouth (and presumably were sacrificed to the Deep Ones) prior to the massacre of 1846. After that time, one wonders whether a steady supply of young persons must have continued to be sacrificed, paralleling the arrangement that Chief Walakea's tribe had with the Deep Ones in Polynesia.

INUTOS (PO, SOT): Squat, yellow-skinned invaders of prehistoric Lomar in the far north; HPL may have been suggesting their "ancestry" of the Inuits. The Inuits, as they call themselves, are the native peoples who exist in the far northern areas from Alaska across to Greenland; the more familiar term "Eskimos" is derived from the Eastern Algonquin word for "eaters of raw meat."

INVADERS, BOOK OF (MB): In HPL's "Irish tale," many readers may be puzzled to find Greek gods or semi-deities turning up on the Emerald Isle. HPL explains that, according to this mysterious book, ancient Greek colonists under the leadership of a certain Partholan once established towns in southern Ireland. The "Book of Invaders" actually exists in the form of the *Leabhar Gabhala*, a 12th century Irish manuscript dealing with Ireland's legendary prehistory. Partholan is the leader of one band of "Invaders."

IPSWICH (SOI): A non-fictitious town in Essex County, Massachusetts. It lies on a scenic route about fifteen miles northwest of Gloucester, and near the mouth of the Ipswich River. In the tale, it is an inland neighbor of Innsmouth. Zadok Allen tells the narrator that Barnabas Marsh, Obed Marsh's grandson who is married to a mortal human female, is now far along in his metamorphosis to fish-hood: "Dun't know haow his poor wife kin feel—she come from Ipswich, an' they nigh [almost] lynched Barnabas when he courted her fifty-odd year' ago."

IRANON (QI): The protagonist of this tale, and an early HPL alter-ego. A "singer of songs," he searches for the city of Aira, where his father was the king, and Iranon the infant prince was rocked in the moonlight by his beautiful mother. He begins his quest as a youth in the valley of Narthos, where he grows up among the humble shepherds there. Then he visits Sinara, Jaren, Stethelos, Thraa, Ilarnek, Kadatheron, Olathoë, and Teloth; in the last-named city he joins up with a traveling-companion, Romnod. Years later, the duo reaches the city of Oonai, where they sojourn for a long time, and Romnod dies of too much good living, overeating and over-drinking. Going on alone, Iranon travels to the land of Cydathria, and beyond the Bnazic Desert. Through all his wanderings he remains eternally youthful, slender and pale, golden-haired, dressed in ragged purple garments. At long last he encounters a squalid old shepherd on a stony slope, next to a quicksand marsh, and asks his eternal question about the whereabouts of Aira. The old man recalls a childhood playmate, known in those parts since the day of his birth, who had always dreamed and talked about such a place before he ran away. His dreams shattered, the long years suddenly visible in his face and frame, disillusioned Iranon takes his own life by walking into the quicksand.

IRED-NAA (DQ): Nyarlathotep says to Randolph Carter at Kadath:

> Steer for that brightest star just south of the zenith—it is Vega, and in two hours you will be just above the terrace of your sunset city.... Look then back to earth, and you will see the deathless altar-flame of Ired-Naa shining from the rook of a temple. That temple is your desiderate sunset city, so steer for it....

Ired-Naa is not further explained. The exceedingly rare English word "desiderate" means "that which it is wished to have or to see," and is rooted in the Latin word for "desire." The bright star called Vega is prominent in northern hemisphere skies during the summer months.

IREM (NC, CC, TGSK): Irem, the City of Pillars, is the work of human hands although weirdly old. The explorer-narrator in the Arabian "Nameless City" of a vanished reptilian race sees a late-period wall painting which depicts "a primitive-looking man, perhaps a pioneer of ancient Irem, torn to pieces by members of the [reptile] race." In *The Call of Cthulhu*, the cult-member Castro thinks that "the centre of the cult lay amid the pathless deserts of Arabia, where Irem, the City of Pillars, dreams hidden and untouched." Nothing else substantiates this tidbit. In *Through the Gates of the Silver Key*, Randolph Carter gives this explanation to his friend Etienne-Laurent de Marigny: the Silver Key "would unlock the successive doors that bar our free march down the mighty corridors of space and time to the very Border which no man has crossed since Shaddad with his terrific genius built and constructed in the land of Arabia Petraea the prodigious domes and uncounted minarets of thousand-pillared Irem." (For what it is worth, "Arabia Petraea"—an ancient Roman-era name for the northwestern part of the Arabian peninsula, from the ancient city of Petra that lies in the region—is also the title of a long and significant book review by Edgar Allan Poe.) Irem (or Iram) is mentioned in the Koran (*surah* 89, "The Dawn"), in which the question is asked: "Have you not heard how God dealt with Ad? The people of the many-columned city of Iram, whose like has never been built in the whole land?" God destroyed the people of Ad for their terrible sins.

HPL may have read this in a translation of the Koran, but more likely came across the name and fame of Irem in some collection of Arabian legends, a species of reading to which he was devoted as a child. Irem was long the subject of fable in Arab lands. Lovecraft biographer S.T.

Joshi points to the discussion of Irem in the 9th edition of the *Encyclopedia Britannica*, which HPL owned and frequently consulted for information.

And in the story-segment called "The City of Many-Columned Iram," in Sir Richard F. Burton's standard translation of the *Tale of a Thousand Nights and a Night* (the so-called "Arabian Nights") which HPL had read, there appear the words: "Wottest thou [*i.e.*, "do you know?"] of any city founded by man which is builded of gold and silver, the pillars whereof are of chrysolite and rubies, and its gravel is pearls and balls of musk and ambergris and saffron?"

ISLES OF NARIEL (DCS): Islands in the Middle Ocean (a sea which does not appear in any other HPL fantasia); the rulers of Sarnath feasted on peacocks imported from the Nariels.

IVES, DR. JOB (SH): Providence physician who tends Abigail and Ruth Harris, children of William Harris, Sr., in April, 1764, and diagnoses their wasting-away deaths as the result of "some infantile fever."

IWANICKI, FATHER (DWH): The parish priest of St. Stanislaus Church in Arkham during the 1920s. Mr. Dombrowski, the landlord of the Witch House, gets a blessed crucifix—the type worn as a pendant to a necklace—from this priest to give to Walter Gilman, who accepts it without interest. But in the climactic scene on Walpurgis Night, an accidental glimpse of this crucifix gives Keziah Mason such a shock that Gilman is able to overpower her and strangle her with the chain. This is the only example in HPL's tales of a traditional holy symbol proving effective in some way. Perhaps we are to understand that Keziah Mason, who after all was a human product of the 17th century, panicked for a fatal moment at the sight of the cross, allowing Gilman to get the advantage.

J

JACKSON, STEPHEN (CDW): Headmaster of the Providence school, opposite the square called Court House Parade, which Eliza Tillinghast attended as a young girl circa 1760.

JAMM, PETER (CDW): Pierre Jammy, a French Dominican friar, published the 13th century writings of Albertus Magnus in France in 1651. A copy of this edition was to be found in Joseph Curwen's mid-18th century library in Rhode Island. "Peter Jamm" is of course an English form of "Pierre Jammy."

JAREN (QI): A city on the frigid Xari River, with onyx walls, downriver from the valley of Narthos where Iranon grew up. Iranon travels to Jaren by barge early in his wanderings. But the soldiers there laugh at him and throw him out.

JENCKES, DANIEL (CDW): A real Providence bookstore owner in colonial times; in the tale, it is said that Joseph Curwen helped him to open his bookstore, and thereafter is his best customer.

JERMYN, SIR ARTHUR (AJ): "If we knew what we are, we should do as Sir Arthur Jermyn did; and Arthur Jermyn soaked himself in oil and set fire to his clothing one night." According to the narrator, Arthur Jermyn was so peculiar-looking that many people with his facial features would have wanted to die; but he has a sweet soul. He is a poet, a dreamer, a scholar, and a First Class Honors graduate—the highest possible rank—of Oxford University. He is the son of Sir Alfred Jermyn and "a music-hall singer of unknown origin." (Music halls were popular forms of working-class entertainment in the 19th and early 20th centuries, featuring a variety of less-than-great singers warbling typically sentimental, comical, or patriotic songs in front of large audiences, on a variety-show bill interspersed with comedians, acrobats, magicians, and so forth. A gentleman's marriage to a music-hall singer in the late Victorian era would have been a social scandal.) After her husband deserted the family, the mother raised her son at Jermyn House, the family seat, although their circumstances were not especially wealthy. In 1911, Sir Arthur makes an expedition to the Belgian Congo (now simply "Congo"), among the Onga and Kaliri tribes. He meets Mwanu, an elderly Kaliri, and hears some significant stories about a lost city and its inhabitants. In 1912 he finds the remains of the lost city Sir Wade described, which—in a constant characteristic of HPL's lost cities—has passageways that "[seemed] to lead down into a system of vaults," perhaps hiding horrors unrevealed on the surface. In June, 1913, back in England, Sir Arthur is informed by a letter from Monsieur Verhaeren, his Belgian contact in the Congo, that a certain stuffed goddess from the lost city had been found in the keeping of the now-peaceful N'bangu tribe. Sir Arthur receives the mummified relic in a box on August 13, 1913, and opens it privately. The box, he instantly understood, contained the withered and battered corpse of his great-great-great-grandmother, "a mummified white ape of some unknown species, less hairy than any recorded variety, and infinitely nearer mankind—quite shockingly so." Then, with a scream, he races out of the room, douses himself with flammable liquid, and sets fire to himself on the moors beyond Jermyn House. His remains were *not* collected and buried, and some of the Royal Anthropological Institute burn the mummy and afterwards refuse to admit that Arthur Jermyn ever existed.

JERMYN FAMILY (AJ): There is a Jermyn Street in a fashionable part of London, which perhaps suggested this unusual family name to HPL. Additionally, a certain Henry Jermyn (c. 1636–1708), Earl of Dover, a gambler, duelist, and lover of many women, was one of the profligate English aristocrats in the circle of the Earl of Rochester (the latter poet-rogue is mentioned in *The Tomb*), and HPL may have come across his name in some published diary or other account of Restoration-era high society. In the tale, the Jermyn males are apparently an English line of baronets, the holders of a title of knighthood inheritable by the eldest son—nothing but hereditary right could explain how the mostly-dreadful series of Jermyns following Sir Wade continue to wear a noble title. The ones described in this story are:

> **SIR WADE:** One of the earliest European explorers of the Congo region. After his second and longest trip to Africa, he returns home with a wife, said to be the daughter of a Portuguese trader in Africa, who is never glimpsed by anyone in England, other than himself; and also with their infant son. Years later he travels to Africa with the wife, and returns alone (it should be remembered that the mere sailing voyage from England to Africa would then have taken some weeks to accomplish). Back home, he talks wildly about a lost city in the jungle, and its half-ape, half-human inhabitants. His "bizarre conjectures on a prehistoric white Congolese civilization" earn him much ridicule when his book, *Observations on the Several Parts of Africa*, is published. Looking after his strange son alone, he spends

more and more time drinking at the Knight's Head tavern and telling shocking stories of Africa to the local folk. In 1765 he is locked up in the lunatic asylum at Huntingdon, England, and seems somehow grateful for this. He dies three years later.

SIR PHILIP: Only child of Sir Wade and the unknown mother who came back with Sir Wade from his second African expedition. Raised after her departure by "a loathsome black woman from Guinea" and then entirely by his father, he grows to be "a highly peculiar person," unsociable, densely stupid and prone to sudden violence; small in stature, but extraordinarily agile and powerful. He scandalously marries his own gamekeeper's daughter in 1780, but almost immediately afterwards enlists as a common sailor in the Royal Navy, which completes this strange knight's social ruination. After the end of "the American war" (*i.e.*, the Revolutionary War, which concluded in 1781), he becomes a sailor on a merchant ship in the African trade, gaining a reputation for amazing strength and climbing ability. He disappears one night when his ship is moored off the Congo coast.

SIR ROBERT: Born circa 1781, the only child of Sir Philip and the gamekeeper's daughter. He is tall and fairly handsome in an exotic way, although his physical proportions seem somehow "odd." He becomes a significant scholar, and a pioneer of the new science of ethnology (the study of different human ethnic groups). Despite the "madness" of his grandfather, Sir Wade, and the badness of his father, Sir Philip, not to mention having a mother from the servant class, his family's remaining respectability and his own academic laurels seem to have made Sir Robert Jermyn socially acceptable, for in 1815 he marries a daughter of the seventh Viscount Brightholme, a higher-ranking aristocrat than himself. They have three children, two of whom are always kept hidden on account of unspecified "deformities." The middle child, Nevil, although presentable in public, is still a trial to his father because of his wild misconduct. Sir Robert eventually makes two long expeditions to the African interior, concentrating on researching the legends of the Onga tribe, from the area his grandfather had explored some sixty years earlier. On October 19, 1852, when he was about 70 years old, Sir Robert receives a visit at Jermyn House from one Samuel Seaton, another English explorer of the Onga country. They speak privately in the library. For some unknown reason, Sir Robert ends the discussion by strangling Mr. Seaton to death, then leaves the library and murders all three of his children. Confined to a madhouse, he refuses to speak a word, and attempts suicide several times. He dies of apoplexy (a stroke) in 1854.

NEVIL: The "singularly repellent" middle child of Sir Robert and his wife; proud and surly in disposition, he elopes with a "vulgar dancer" in 1849, but is allowed to return home the next year after his wife's death, along with their baby son, Alfred. He successfully prevents his father from murdering little Alfred in 1852, but is killed himself. (The fact that his father outlived him, so that he never inherited the title, is why he is only Nevil and not Sir Nevil.)

SIR ALFRED: Presumably raised by guardians; at age 20, he joins a music hall's performing company, later marrying a music-hall singer and fathering a child, Arthur. This was thoroughly shameful and scandalous behavior for an English aristocrat. He abandons his family in 1886 and joins a circus in the United States, becoming a successful gorilla-trainer. One morning in Chicago, while rehearsing a boxing-match act with his gorilla, he loses his temper and violently attacks the animal—behaving almost like an angry gorilla himself—and the beast struggles with and kills him.

SIR ARTHUR: *See* separate entry.

JEVONS (SOT): In *The Shadow Out of Time*, Professor Nathaniel Peaslee's mind is taken over by an alien intelligence one day in 1908 while he is delivering an economics lecture to undergraduates at Miskatonic University. On September 27, 1915, he returns to himself, muttering as if still in mid-lecture:

> "—of the orthodox economists of that period, Jevons typifies the prevailing trend toward scientific correlation. His attempt to link the commercial cycle of prosperity and depression with the physical cycle of the solar spots forms perhaps the apex of—"

William Henry Jevons (1835–82), a brilliant English economist and logician, was the author of *The Theory of Political Economy* (1871) and *The General Mathematical Theory of Political Economy* (1862), as well as other works; his most lasting contribution to economics lies in the development of the marginal utility theory of value. Jevons devoted much of his short life to correlating mountains of scientific and economic data in an attempt to prove that "sun spots" (solar magnetic storms, which tend to appear and disappear in a roughly cyclical time-pattern) affected weather patterns on earth, which in turn affected crop growth, finally resulting in the ups and downs of multi-year business cycles, the latter being a phenomenon he had already done much to help identify.

The sun spot theory once attracted many adherents, but was conclusively disproved long ago.

JEWEL LAKE (TJR): A fictional lake near the Norton Mine, somewhere in the far southwestern United States.

JOB 14:14 (CDW): The only Bible chapter and verse specifically cited in a tale by HPL, who prized the Old Testament's Book of Job as a transcendent work of pessimistic literature. The verse is:

> If a man die, shall he live again? All the days of my appointed time will I wait, till my change doth come.

As asked by Job in the Bible, the answer to the question is "no." But as the text is cited in a letter from Joseph Curwen to Simon Orne, written circa 1750–60, the answer is clearly "maybe"!

In her memories of HPL, his ex-wife Sonia recalled one of his editing clients, who was what is sometimes called a writer of "inspirational" or "self-help" books: "When he wanted a quotation from the Bible or any other source, he would mention a word or two, not knowing what he really wanted, and H.P. would supply the necessary information."

JOHANSEN, GUSTAV (CC): The second mate (third in command after the captain and first mate) on board the schooner *Emma*, out of Auckland, New Zealand, where he lived with his wife on West Street. The only officer to survive the sea-battle with the Cthulhu-cultists of the *Alert*, he takes command of the surviving sailors. He and the sailor William Briden are the only men to escape from R'lyeh (Johansen steering the fleeing steamship directly through Cthulhu's semi-gaseous head), and only Johansen is still alive when the *Alert* is found drifting in the middle of the Pacific Ocean by the freighter *Vigilant*. Johansen is very reticent when giving evidence to a board of inquiry in New Zealand; but he writes all the hideous details in a manuscript written in English, which his widow later hands over to Francis W. Thurston. Johansen and his wife leave New Zealand for his native Oslo, Norway shortly after the board of inquiry, but he dies suddenly following a peculiar accident not long after his return there.

JUPITER (BWS, TGSK): "You and I have drifted to the worlds that reel about red Arcturus, and dwelt in the bodies of the insect-philosophers that crawl proudly over the fourth moon of Jupiter," the narrator of this tale is told by his "brother of light" from outer space, the one who, for a time, was condemned to wear the skin of the mountain-dwelling half-wit Joe Slater. With or without insect-philosophers that "crawl proudly," the fourth moon of Jupiter (Callisto), as well as the first other three, was discovered by Galileo in 1610 and therefore bears a special significance in astronomy, perhaps the reason it occurred to HPL. The discovery of these planetary satellites provided evidence in support of the Copernican theory that the universe did not revolve around the earth. In *Through the Gates of the Silver Key*, Randolph Carter, in the body of Zkauba, passes through our solar system and "learned an untellable secret from the close-glimpsed mists of Jupiter and saw the horror on one of the satellites...."

K

KADATH (OG, MM, DQ): (1) In *The Other Gods*, the place where earth's gods retreat from human curiosity and encroachments, a place on the plateau of Leng. In *The Dream-Quest of Unknown Kadath*, Kadath is described as a vast, immeasurably high palace of unearthly splendor, in the far north of Dreamland. (2) In *At the Mountains of Madness*, Professor Dyer suggests that the lost city in the Antarctic is the basis for all the legends about "Kadath in the cold waste." This is a prime example of HPL's "demythologizing" of his own earlier mythos, a feature of his later works that has been noted by Lovecraft biographer S.T. Joshi and others.

KADATHERON (DCS, QI, DQ): A town in the valley of the river Ai, inhabited by a race of swarthy shepherds, who founded Kadatheron as well as other cities. Iranon passed through this place. It lay on a caravan route to and from the city of Sarnath, bringing wealth to both but particularly the latter. The "brick cylinders of Kadatheron" bear writings that describe the appearance of the inhabitants of Ib, their possible origin, and their worship of Bokrug. It has been suggested that "Sardathrion," a city in Lord Dunsany's fantasy tales, influenced this name-choice from HPL's "Dunsanian" period.

KALIRIS (AJ): A tribe in the Congo River basin of central Africa, neighbors of the Ongas whom some members of the Jermyn family came from England to study. In 1911–12 Sir Arthur Jermyn talks with Mwanu, an aged Kaliri tribesman, and learns some interesting lessons about the lost jungle city from him.

KALOS (TR): One of two fictitious ancient Greek sculptors who live and work together by Mount Maenalus in Arcadia (a district in central Greece). His name is the word for "handsome." Kalos' famous statue of the god Hermes occupies a shrine in the city of Corinth. The reclusive Kalos prefers above all else to meditate on abstract beauty in his peaceful olive grove, while his friend Musides revels in the lusty pleasures to be found in the neighboring city of Tegea. The two men compete to carve a statue of the goddess Tyché for the Tyrant of Syracuse. During the competition Kalos grows ill and dies; although the people who know them suspect nothing, we readers are to understand that Musides has poisoned

Kalos to death. He is buried next to their house, with some olive sprigs placed by his head. A strange olive tree springs up from his grave, which eventually drops a branch on the house, crushing Musides and his prize-winning statue. It may be noted that the Latin tag-line at the beginning of this tale—"Fata viam invenient"—is a proverb, "The fates will find the way." The Greek words at the end of the tale ("Οιδα! Οιδα!—*I know! I know!*") are pronounced "Oida! Oida!" (O-ee-da).

KAMAN-THAH (DQ): One of the two priests in the Cavern of Flame, which is separated from the waking world by the seventy steps of light slumber. Randolph Carter obtains their advice and blessings before proceeding downward to the Gate of Deeper Slumber at the beginning of his dream-quest. Curiously, when his ghoul-escorts through lower Dreamland learn that they would have to pass these priests in order to return to the waking world and thence to the ghoul country, they elect to try the more difficult route via Dylath-Leen and Sarkomand.

KARTHIAN HILLS (QI): A range of hills lying between the cities of Teloth and Oonai.

KEITH (WD): *See* "Anthropologists of the Mi-Go."

KENT (HY): Kent is one of the southernmost counties of England, south of London, a shire very rich in history and beauty. It is in "the tower studio chamber of the old manor-house in hoary Kent" that the narrator and his only friend "with exotic drugs courted terrible and forbidden dreams." After one shocking encounter in the world of dream, they move to a studio in the crowded metropolis of London—for solitude is now unbearable to the author's friend, and he can only find relief in "revelry of the most general and boisterous sort."

KHEM (HD): The word is a variant of the ancient Egyptian name for Egypt, *Khmet*. After many previous events, the Shining Trapezohedron sinks along with Atlantis (here perhaps conceived of as a vanished Mediterranean Sea island), and is dredged up ages afterward by Minoan fishermen from the island of Crete, who sell it to "swarthy merchants from nighted Khem," and thus it winds up in the hands of the reigning Pharaoh.

KHEPHNES (SOT): One of the captive minds encountered by Professor Wingate Peaslee during his stay with the Great Race; he is an Egyptian of the period of the 14th Dynasty, who tells Peaslee "the secret of Nyarlathotep." The 14th Dynasty belongs to a poorly-documented era in the long history of ancient Egypt, known as the Second Intermediate Period; this dynasty ruled Egypt circa 1650 B.C.

KHEPHREN (UP): A non-fictitious Egyptian pharaoh, better known today as Cheops, the Greek form of his name. He reigned circa 2680 B.C., during the so-called Old Kingdom, when the Sphinx and the major pyramids (including the Great Pyramid, his own) are believed to have been erected.

KIEL (TE): A port city in north Germany on the Baltic Sea. It was a major German navy base, important as a submarine station in both world wars.

KILDERRY (MB): The ruined castle and estate which Denys Barry returns from America to reclaim. It is near a (fictitious) village called Ballylough, in Ireland's County Meath. "Kilderry" is, or was, a rural hamlet in County Cavan, and is occasionally encountered as an Irish surname, which is how HPL may have heard it.

KING'S CHURCH (CDW): A non-fictitious Anglican (Episcopalian) church in 18th century Providence; it was renamed "St. John's Church" during the American Revolution. In the tale, in 1738, the new rector of King's Church, Dr. Checkley, calls socially on Joseph Curwen, and leaves feeling very disturbed by the man, a sense of distress that never leaves him afterward. In 1763 or 1764 (by which time Dr. Checkley was dead and a certain Reverend Graves was the incumbent rector), Joseph Curwen and his new wife Eliza become parishioners of King's Church in an apparent compromise between their respective Congregational and Baptist church affiliations. Their only child, Ann, is christened at King's Church in May, 1765. Considering that Joseph Curwen is a black magician, necromancer, murderer, and even worse, contemporary readers may well wonder sometimes at his active public practice of the Christian religion. This is a small example of HPL's steady, sure-handed historical sense. At that time and place, non-attendance at church would still have rendered a gentleman almost a pariah in the community, and Joseph Curwen wants as much as possible to be seen as a pillar, not a pariah, of respectable society. Curwen's religiosity is mere window-dressing, on a par with his frequent examples of civic-minded generosity to local charities and good causes.

It is worth wondering whether, when writing about the grotesque Curwen-Tillinghast nuptials at King's Church, HPL thought about his own marriage to Sonia Greene a few years earlier, in lovely old St. Paul's Chapel in lower Manhattan: an avowed atheist marrying a Jew in an atmosphere of Christian incense, candles, and prayers. Of this event Lovecraft biographer S.T. Joshi suggests that: "the way in which Lovecraft soberly went through an Anglican ceremony at a colonial church indicates that his sense of aesthetics had overwhelmed his rationality."

KINGSPORT (TF, TOM, SHH, DQ, SK, TD, CDW):

> Kingsport with its ancient vanes and steeples, ridgepoles and chimney-pots, wharves and small bridges, willow-trees and graveyards; endless labyrinths of steep, narrow, crooked streets, and dizzy church-tower-crowned central peak...ceaseless mazes of colonial houses piled and scattered at all angles and levels like a child's disordered blocks.

Such is "Kingsport" on the Massachusetts coast. HPL was describing, with only a little embellishment, real places that he knew: preeminently the antique maritime community of Marblehead, Massachusetts, a few miles south of Salem. HPL actually invented Kingsport in the 1920 tale, *The Terrible Old Man*, before he ever laid eyes on Marblehead. But he visited Marblehead during a sightseeing vacation in 1922, and in 1929 penned this still-excited, oft-quoted recollection of that first view:

> Shall I ever forget my first stupefying glance of MARBLEHEAD'S huddled and archaick [*sic*] roofs under the snow in the delirious sunset glory of four p.m., Dec. 17, 1922!!! I did not know until an hour before that I should ever view such a place as Marblehead, and I did not know *until that moment itself* the full extent of the wonder I was to behold. I account that instant—about 4:05 to 4:10 p.m., Dec. 17, 1922—the most powerful single emotional climax during my nearly forty years of existence. In a flash all the past of New England—all the past of Old England—all the past of Anglo-Saxondom and the Western World—swept over me and identified me with the stupendous totality of all things in such a way as it never did before and never will again. That was the high tide of my life.

In *The Festival*, the nameless narrator is called back to Kingsport at Yule-tide (the Christmas season) for the ceremony of his ancestors, and takes part in an eerie procession through the night streets, up to and into the hilltop church, and down into the secret caverns honeycombing the hill. The Terrible Old Man lives in Kingsport, "all alone in a very ancient house on Water Street near the sea," behind a high and ivy-clad stone wall and a weather-stained oaken door. In *The Strange High House in the Mist*, the professor Thomas Olney, from Rhode Island, takes his dull family to spend the summer vacation in Kingsport, to enjoy its cliffs and "crooked alleys," its "hills and antique roofs and spires," its "pleasant hearths and gambrel-roofed taverns." Besides mentioning "spectral" Marblehead in his end-of-the-tale evocation of New England scenes, Nyarlathotep in *The Dream-Quest of Unknown Kadath* praises "antediluvian Kingsport hoary with stacked chimneys and deserted quays and overhanging gables, and the marvel of high cliffs and the milky-misted ocean with tolling buoys beyond." In *The Silver Key* it is mentioned that Randolph Carter drove his automobile past the old white house outside of Arkham where his mother and her ancestors had been born, from which "the distant spires of Kingsport" could be seen on the horizon. A little later, when he has traveled back in time to the 1880s, he looks over toward Kingsport and sees "the old Congregational steeple on Central Hill in Kingsport," before suddenly recalling that the church had been torn down long ago to make room for the Congregational Hospital. In *The Thing on the Doorstep*, it is mentioned that the teenage Asenath Waite was a boarding student at "the Hall School" in Kingsport, presumably a girls' private school. In *The Case of Charles Dexter Ward*, it is mentioned that, when he visited Joseph Curwen's farmhouse circa 1746, John Merritt turned tail at the sight of a disguised copy of the *Necronomicon,* "of which he had heard such monstrous things" whispered some years previously after the exposure of nameless rites at the strange little fishing village of Kingsport, in the Province of Massachusetts-Bay.

KINGSPORT HEAD (MM, SOI): A "head" (in the sense it is used in "Kingsport Head") is a geographical term for a cape or "headland" on a coast. In *At the Mountains of Madness*, Kingsport Head is given as the location of the radio relay station which receives transmissions from the Miskatonic University Expedition in Antarctica. "Wireless" messages from expeditioners in the Antarctic interior are picked up by the ship radio operator on the *Arkham,* moored in McMurdo Sound, and re-transmitted to Kingsport Head by the ship's "powerful apparatus." (For the sake of radio-technology buffs, Professor Dyer mentions that the ship's transmitter uses wavelengths of up to fifty meters.) In *The Shadow Over Innsmouth*, the narrator, while on his bus trip into Innsmouth from Newburyport:

> beheld the outspread valley…where the Manuxet joins the sea just north of the long line of cliffs that culminate in Kingsport Head and veer off toward Cape Ann. On the far, misty horizon I could just make out the dizzy profile of the Head, topped by the queer ancient house of which so many legends are told…. [*i.e.,* "The Strange High House in the Mist"]

KINGSTON-BROWN, NEVIL (SOT): One of the captive minds Professor Peaslee encounters with the Great Race; he is an Australian physicist "who will die in 2518 a.d."

KIRAN (DQ): A place that Randolph Carter passes during his pleasant journey down along the river Oukranos. Kiran is a temple compound of more than an acre in extent, built entirely of the semi-precious stone jasper, with seven pinnacled towers. The Oukranos passes directly under Kiran, but only the king of Ilek-Vad, who makes an annual pilgrimage hither, may enter the temple—or see the priests who serve in it.

KISH (MM): Objects on the slopes of the mountains, on the other side of which lies the lost city in the Antarctic wastes, remind Professor Dyer of "the primal foundations of Kish as dug up by the Oxford-Field Museum Expedition in 1929." Kish was an ancient city of the Sumerian culture, in present-day Iraq; it flourished as much as 4,000 years ago. The Field Museum is a Chicago institution, which worked collaboratively with Oxford University on the referenced expedition.

KLARKASH-TON (WD): Described as a high priest of Atlantis, the preserver of the "Commoriom myth-cycle." Actually a mock-reference to HPL's good friend by correspondence, the poet, fantasy writer, and painter Clark Ashton Smith (1893–1961), of Auburn, California. Smith and HPL were both fairly regular contributors to *Weird Tales* and other pulp magazines, and the so-called "Commoriom myth-cycle" refers to Smith's series of stories about the prehistoric land of "Hyperborea." HPL was fond of rather juvenile wordplays involving the names of the men in his circle of friends, or his own name; for example, he sometimes referred to himself third-person-style as a personage called "Eich-pi-el" (HPL).

KLAUSENBURG (CDW): Former name of the city currently called Cluj-Napoca, in Romania, founded by German immigrants centuries ago; it is often considered as the unofficial "capital" of Transylvania. Early in 1925 Charles Dexter Ward sent his parents a postcard from this place, telling them that he was on his way to visit a certain Baron Ferenczy in that region.

KLED (TGSK, DQ): Down the river Oukranos from the city of Thran lie the perfumed jungles of Kled. Here are found deserted palaces of ivory, kept unharmed and undecayed by the spells of the Elder Ones. Elephant caravans also travel through Kled.

KLENZE, LIEUTENANT (TT): An officer in the German Navy; in 1917, the executive officer (second in command) on board submarine U-29. According to his commanding officer, the severe Prussian aristocrat Graf von Altburg-Ehrenstein, Klenze "was a soft-headed Rhinelander who went mad at troubles a Prussian could bear with ease." (The "Rhineland," the sunny, southwesterly, wine-making region of Germany along the Rhine River and adjacent to France, is stereotypically the part of the country from which come romantic and lovable men, devoted to wine, women, and song; while the now-vanished kingdom of Prussia in the northeast, centered on Berlin, with a colder climate and poorer soil, was the hard cradle of hard militarists such as U-29's commanding officer.) On June 28, 1917, Lieutenant Klenze takes from one of the sailors a carved ivory image found in a drowned victim's coat pocket; he suspects the object of possessing great antiquity and significant artistic merit. Later, as the crew disintegrates psychologically, Klenze chafes under the strain of "trifles" such as the increasingly large pods of dolphins surrounding the cruising submarine, or their drift in a southward current that is not indicated on any of their nautical charts. On July 2 he is required to shoot the sailor Traube, who has agitated among the crew for surrender to a passing U.S. warship. After von Altburg-Ehrenstein shoots the remaining, increasingly mutinous crewmen two days later, Klenze begins drinking heavily and staring for long periods at the ivory carving. As the disabled submarine drifts helplessly and hopelessly under the sea, "the fact of our coming death affected him curiously," as his ironhearted commander von Altburg-Ehrenstein puts it, causing Klenze to pray remorsefully about all the innocent lives he has helped to take during his career as a German submariner. He begins to quote poetry, and to talk of sunken ships. His commander's verdict is not exactly easy to dispute: "I was very sorry for him, for I dislike to see a German suffer; but he was not a good man to die with." On August 12, Lieutenant Klenze appears to go completely insane, and demands to be put out of the U-boat—suicide, under the circumstances—as a measure of repentance for his sins. He urges von Altburg-Ehrenstein to join him and be forgiven as well, but the commander refuses. The same afternoon, Klenze goes into the ocean through the submarine's double-hatch.

KLÜBER (DH): *See* "Cryptographers of Dunwich."

K'N-YAN (WD): A subterranean world below our world, invented by HPL in *The Mound*, a very effective horror story which he ghost-wrote for a client. In his own tale, *The Whisperer in Darkness*, it is mentioned that the Mi-Go from Yuggoth had visited K'n-yan during some of their visits to Earth.

KOENIG (WE): A "division commander" of the Venus Crystal Company. Frederick N. Dwight belonged to Koenig's detachment.

KRANON (CU): The old "burgomaster" (an office corresponding to mayor) of Ulthar, who at first suspects that the caravan of dark-skinned people had taken away all the town's cats, and curses them for it. Then the felines return. Two weeks after the cruel, cat-slaying couple is last seen, Kranon calls on their cottage with the citizens Shang and Thul as his witnesses. They find only two skeletons, picked clean of all flesh.

KURANES, KING (CE, DQ): The identity in Dreamland of a certain Englishman, the last scion of an old family from the very rural region called Cornwall, who winds up poor and alone in London, dreaming gorgeous dreams and using narcotics to heighten and prolong them. After many dream-adventures, now broken and desperate in his outer form but borne along by swelling, splendid visions of another land, the man is seen staggering through the Cornish coastal village of Innsmouth, toward the sea. He is, perhaps, the unidentified drowned man whose body washes up on the shore by Trevor Towers some time later. In *The Dream-Quest of Unknown Kadath*, Randolph Carter finds him as King Kuranes, ruling Celephaïs and the cloud-realm of Serranian in inconceivable beauty and luxury. But Kuranes prefers to retreat to an imitation English manor-house which he has constructed outside of Celephaïs, complete with servants who have been trained to speak—in English, presumably—with provincial English accents. Kuranes gives Carter assistance and advice for his quest.

KYNARATHOLIS, KING (CE): During his dream-searches for Ooth-Nargai and Celephaïs, the man who would be King Kuranes comes across a vast, ruined city in a dead land, "as it had lain since King Kynaratholis came home from his conquests to find the vengeance of the gods." This is a reference to a tale by Lord Dunsany.

KYNARTH (TGSK): Passing through our solar system in a light-beam envelope, Randolph Carter-as-Zkauba "saw Kynarth and Yuggoth on the rim."

KYTHANIL (TGSK): One of the innumerable cosmic facets of "the ultimate, eternal 'Carter' outside space and time" is one of those pre-human "entities which had dwelt in primal Hyperborea and worshipped black, plastic Tsathoggua after flying down from Kythanil, the double planet that once revolved around Arcturus...."

L

LACTANTIUS (TF): Lucius Caecilius Firmianus Lactantius (c. 260–340 A.D.), an early Christian author from North Africa. A quotation from Lactantius is the introduction to this tale: *Efficiunt Daemones, ut quae non sunt, sic tamen quasi sint, conspicienda hominibus exhibeant.* Roughly translated this means: "Demons bring it about that things which do not exist, appear worth looking at, as if they existed."

LAFITTE (CC): The Louisiana swamp residents who send for the urgent help of the New Orleans police on November 1, 1907, are described as "primitive but good-natured descendants of Lafitte's men." Jean Lafitte (1780–1826) was a pirate, principally against Spanish shipping, operating in the Gulf of Mexico from hideouts on the coasts of Louisiana and Texas. In 1814–15, in the late phase of the War of 1812 between the United States and Great Britain, Lafitte and his band of underemployed Louisiana pirates wrote a colorful page in American history when he volunteered their services to the American army under General Andrew Jackson, and helped to defeat a British force at the Battle of New Orleans in 1815.

LAKE, PROFESSOR (MM): A biology professor at Miskatonic University. He is one of the scholar-leaders of the Miskatonic University Expedition. He is brilliant and headstrong; and during the early blasting-and-boring operations at the base camp, it is Lake who finds a "queer triangular, striated marking about a foot in greatest diameter" on some sandstone fragments from a site slightly west of the Queen Alexandra Range, fragments which inspire him to some very serious thinking. On January 6, 1931, Lake is one of the large group that makes an overflight of the South Pole. Lake "doggedly" insists on an expedition to the northwest of the base camp. He theorizes that the peculiar sandstone marking "was the print of some bulky, unknown, and radically unclassifiable organism of considerably advanced evolution," despite the fact that the sandstone chunk in question dated from the Cambrian, or even the Pre-Cambrian, geological epoch, some 500 million to 1 billion years ago. Lake is fired by "wild hopes of revolutionising the entire sciences of biology and geology," and persuades Professor Dyer and the other expedition leaders to allow his sub-expedition. He makes a preliminary sledging and boring trip with Professor Pabodie and five other men between January 11–18, 1931. On January 22, at 4:00 a.m., he sets off with Professor Atwood and a number of other expeditioners in four of the airplanes. Two hours later they land about 300 miles west of the base camp, and quickly drill a shaft, finding slate fragments with more of the odd markings. At 3:00 p.m. the group flies further westward, although the wind is starting to blow a gale. When Professor Dyer objects by radio, "Lake replied curtly that his new specimens made any hazard worth taking. I saw that his excitement had reached the point of mutiny, and that I could do nothing." At 10:05 p.m., Lake reports that his party has reached a mountain range possibly as high as the Himalayas, at approximately latitude 76° 15´ south, longitude 113° 10´ east. One of the planes is forced down by mechanical problems, and Lake establishes his camp on the plateau in the foothills where it lands. Professor Atwood makes surveying measurements of the nearby mountains, showing them to exceed 30,000 feet—higher than Mount Everest. In local boring operations the next day, Lake's team finds a subterranean cave, seven or eight feet deep, but vast and filled with shells and bones from between 30 million and 300 million years ago. That night, excavators discover 600 million-year-old footprints of the unknown species. Before midnight, fourteen intact, inert specimens of the creatures that made the footprints (which Lake calls the "Elder Ones" half-jokingly) are found. He attempts to dissect one specimen at the camp, but is stymied by the abnormal toughness of its flesh, as well as other bizarre qualities. At 4:00 a.m. on January 24, Professor Lake sends his last message. He dies with the rest of his party sometime during that day, and is buried at the site by the rescue party which arrives the next day.

LAMB, CHARLES (DH): Charles Lamb (1775–1834) was an English man of letters, the author of some classic essays on a wide variety of subjects, still read by connoisseurs of the English language and the essay form. An excerpt from one of these pieces, *Witches and Other Night-Fears*, first published in 1823, provides the introduction to this tale.

LANIGAN (HD): The individual (and perhaps a newspaperman) whom the reporter Edwin M. Lillibridge intends to ask for an 1851 photograph of the Starry Wisdom church.

LARSEN (MM): Sailor on the Miskatonic University Expedition. He remains at the McMurdo Sound depot with two other men and the reserve airplane. On January 24, 1931, he flies with the other men to Professor Dyer's base camp, and then on to the Lake-Atwood camp the next morning as part of the rescue party. Larsen was the first man to spot the great range of mountains, in front of which Professor Lake had established his site. By inference, Larsen must have been used to help clean up the ruins and bury the human remains, before returning, with the other rescuers, to the waiting ships.

LAST VOID (TGSK): It is the place—which is not a place, or anyplace—"outside all earths, all universes, and all matter." Randolph Carter arrives at this nirvana for physicists after passing through the Ultimate Gate, and he learns many things from the BEING that he meets there.

LATHI (WS): An "eidolon" (*i.e.*, apparition) that reigns over Thalarion, the City of a Thousand Wonders. The gruesome streets of Thalarion are white with the bones of those men who have looked upon Lathi.

LAWSON, HEPZIBAH (CDW): In the tale it is said that such a woman swore on July 10, 1692, under interrogation by Judge Hathorne during the Salem witch trials, that "fortie Witches and the Blacke Man were wont to meet in the Woodes behind Mr. [Edward] Hutchinson's house." Hepzibah, a Hebrew girl's name meaning "my delight is in her," comes from the Old Testament. In the fictitious Hepzibah Lawson, HPL doubtlessly recalled the name of the Reverend Deodat Lawson, minister at Salem Village from 1684–88, who returned to visit during the witchcraft mania of 1692 and in the same year published a pamphlet entitled *A Brief and True Narrative of Some Remarkable Passages Relating to Sundry Persons Afflicted by Witchcraft at Salem Village*. Reverend Lawson came to believe that his wife and daughter, both of whom died during his years as Salem Village's pastor, had been killed by witchcraft. HPL may also have been thinking of "Hepzibah Pyncheon," a woman in Nathaniel Hawthorne's popular 1850 novel *The House of the Seven Gables*; this important character is the poor and elderly descendant of a witch-hunting Puritan colonial leader.

LEAVITT, ROBERT (HW): In July, 1910, the tow-headed (a now rather quaint phrase meaning yellow-haired, since the plant called "tow" is yellowish in color) Dr. West is finding it difficult to acquire everfresher human corpses to experiment on. One day he tells his faithful comrade that the new body lying in their laboratory is that of a vigorous man, a well-dressed stranger who had arrived that day to do some business or other at the Bolton Worsted Mills; that he had stopped at their clinic to ask for directions; and that he had dropped dead of a sudden heart attack. Furthermore his papers show him to have been named Robert Leavitt, to have been from the distant city of St. Louis, Missouri, and to have had no immediate family anywhere. On July 18, the doctors inject the current version of the resurrection formula into the cadaver, who revives only long enough to shout what must have been his last conscious thoughts or words *before* dying:

"Help! Keep off, you cursed little tow-head fiend! Keep that damned needle away from me!"

LEE'S SWAMP (WD): On his 1928 trip to his friend Vrest Orton's farm in Vermont, HPL met some neighbors named Lee, and helped them to round up a stray cow. "Lee's Swamp" is probably the result. In the tale, it is a marsh in the neighborhood of Henry Akeley's farm, outside of Townshend, Vermont; here there rose the wooded western slope of Dark Mountain, a popular gathering-spot for the Mi-Go.

LEFFERT'S CORNERS (LF): A fictitious village in the Catskills region of New York state, where "affable reporters" gather to chase the big story of an inexplicable massacre at a nearby squatter camp. It is the nearest village to Tempest Mountain, and the narrator joins forces here with one of the visiting newsmen, Arthur Munroe.

LEGRASSE, INSPECTOR JOHN R. (CC): A New Orleans Police Department detective, a "commonplace-looking middle-aged man" who lives at 121 Bienville Street in New Orleans. On November 1 (the ancient All Hallows Day or "Hallowmas" in some Christian churches, the "day of the dead") in 1907, he leads a party of twenty policemen into the swamps south of the city to respond to a "frantic summons" from the Cajun swamp-dwellers about kidnappings and some kind of murderous cult. The policemen raid the cult ceremony, and take a few dozen prisoners. Inspector Legrasse confiscates an odd-looking statuette of a peculiar creature, which the cultists had worshipped. In 1908 the inspector takes the idol to the American Archaeological Association (a fictitious organization) annual convention in St. Louis, Missouri. He shows it to a number of scholars, including Professor Webb, who kept it for some years before returning it to the policeman. Professor George Angell, and later Francis W. Thurston, each visit Inspector Legrasse in the 1920s to hear his story.

LEMDIN, FRED (CDW): A night watchman in Pawtuxet, Rhode Island, who on a mid-June night at about 3:00 a.m. hears in the distance "a phenomenal baying of dogs...mixed with something very like the shrieks of a man in mortal terror and agony."

LEMURIA (HD, CC, MM): The name of a mythical prehistoric continent, like Atlantis. According to *The Haunter of the Dark*, "the first men" lived in Lemuria, and some of them had been familiar with the Shining Trapezohedron. Lemuria was a topic in a book that was once more well known, W. Scott-Eliot's *The Story of Atlantis and the Lost Lemuria*, which HPL enjoyed reading without believing its claims, and which was also part of Professor Angell's reading material in *The Call of Cthulhu—*

in which a prehistoric land sunk beneath the ocean is defined as R'lyeh. Comparing Lemuria with the frightfully ancient Antarctic city, Professor Dyer in *At the Mountains of Madness* calls all such prehistoric human cultures "recent things of today—not even yesterday."

The word "Lemuria" was coined in the 19th century by the English zoologist Philip R. Schlater, with reference to the small semi-apelike creatures known as lemurs (which are thought of as being the type of very primitive primates which preceded the evolution of mankind, and which are found today around the shores of the Indian Ocean, in East Africa, Madagascar, India, and the Malay Archipelago). Darwin's 19th century scientist-defenders sought to explain the wide distribution of lemurs, which could not have crossed the seas, by hypothesizing the existence of a giant land-mass in the ancient Indian Ocean, between present India and Madagascar. (It would not be understood for many years that the continents and proto-continents were mobile, not fixed, over the length of geological time.) Ernst Haeckel, Darwinism's leading advocate in Germany and a favorite pseudo-scientific author of HPL's, carried on to suggest that the reason that no fossil remains of very early man had been found, was that the fossils were all on Lemuria, and Lemuria was now at the bottom of the ocean. Schlater and Haeckel were both wrong in their guesswork; the distribution of lemurs is explainable without the need of a putative land bridge, because of the discovery of plate tectonics or "continental drift"; and early man's fossil remains have been found in East Africa. But as a result of their writings and those of others, the name of "Lemuria" was not altogether unfamiliar to educated readers in the early 20th century. Moreover, Helene Blavatsky, the renowned 19th century mystic, claimed revelation that the civilization of humans on Lemuria had flourished about 150 million years ago.

LENG (TH, CE, WD, MM, DQ): A place mentioned in the *Necronomicon*. L. Sprague de Camp referred to Leng as "a dreamland version of Tibet," and the image is not a bad one. In *Celephaïs*, the dreamer who was King Kuranes finds Leng in Dreamland, calling it a cold desert plateau. Thus it also appears in *The Dream-Quest of Unknown Kadath*, wherein Randolph Carter flies over Leng on a shantak-bird as a captive. Leng is:

> ...a grey barren plain...[with] low huts of granite and bleak stone villages whose tiny windows glowed with pallid light.... Around the feeble fires dark forms were dancing.... Very slowly and awkwardly did those forms leap, and with an insane twisting and bending.... They leaped as though they had hooves instead of feet, and seemed to wear a sort of wig or headpiece with small horns. Of other clothing they had none, but most of them

were quite furry. Behind [them] they had dwarfish tails and when they glanced upward he saw the excessive width of their mouths.

These ungainly creatures are the almost-humans of Leng. Later, in the temple of the high priest not to be described, Carter learns Leng's history from murals of bas-reliefs on the walls. Leng's luckless, almost-human inhabitants fought wars with the "bloated purple spiders of the neighboring vales," and then were invaded by the black galleys from the moon, whose "polypous and amorphous [polyp-like and shapeless]…slippery greyish-white blasphemies" they worship as gods; allowing scores of their biggest and best males to be taken away to the moon each year as tribute, as slaves or for eating. Any Leng-ites who escape and cross the mountains into Inganok are made into slaves by the humans there. Carter also learns that the deserted city of Sarkomand was once Leng's seaport and capital.

After *Celephaïs*, Leng was mentioned next in *The Hound*. The corpse of the medieval grave-robber wears an amulet with an "oddly conventionalised figure of a crouching winged hound…carved in antique Oriental fashion from a piece of green jade." The figure was "the ghastly soul-symbol of the corpse-eating cult of inaccessible Leng, in Central Asia."

In *At the Mountains of Madness*, Professor Dyer's first sight of the Admiralty Range on the coast of Antarctica reminds him of "the evilly fabled plateau of Leng." Later, flying into the unexplored interior to search for the Lake-Atwood party, he speculates:

> I felt, too…how disturbingly this lethal realm corresponded to …Leng in the primal writings. Mythologists have placed Leng in Central Asia; but the racial memory of man—or of his predecessors—is long, and it may well be that certain tales have come down from other lands…earlier than Asia and earlier than any human world we know… Leng, wherever in space or time it may brood, was not a region I would care to be in or near.

As he and Danforth explore the lost city, "the conviction grew upon us that this hideous upland must indeed be the fabled nightmare plateau of Leng which even the mad author of the *Necronomicon* was reluctant to discuss." Professor Dyer eventually wonders (and later decided it was "beyond doubt") whether "Kadath in the Cold Waste" could be the mountains glimpsed 200–300 miles west of the city, which appear to be much more than 40,000 feet high. "Leng" is also among the places written about to Professor Wilmarth, by Henry Akeley, in *The Whisperer in Darkness*; but without providing any further details.

LEONARDO (WD): *See* "Sodoma and Leonardo."

LERION, SLOPES OF (DQ, OG): a hill-region where the river Skai begins its course. Men "have heard the sighs of the gods in the plaintive dawn-winds of Lerion."

LESLIE, CAPTAIN STEPHEN (CDW): Royal Navy officer, commander of the H.M.S. *Cygnet*, an armed schooner which seizes the merchant ship *Fortaleza* in Rhode Island waters in January, 1770, on suspicion of transporting contraband goods; *i.e.*, smuggling.

LEVI, ELIPHAS (CDW): A famed 19th century French occultist, whose real name was Alphonse-Louis Constant (1810–1875). Eliphas Levi was a comprehensive expert on "classical" European magic as well as on wide-ranging occult subjects such as the tarot, pentacles, and the alleged secret doctrines of the medieval Knights Templars. He was the author of influential books whose English-translation titles include *The Doctrine of Transcendental Magic* (1855), *The Ritual of Transcendental Magic* (1856), and *The History of Magic* (1860). In this tale he is referred to as "that cryptic soul who crept through a crack in the forbidden door and glimpsed the frightful vistas of the void beyond."

LIBER DAMNATUS (CDW): "The Damned Book," an otherwise-unnamed book of sorcery mentioned in this tale. In a letter sent circa 1750, Joseph Curwen wrote to Simon/Jedediah Orne:

> I last Night strucke on yᵉ Words that bringe up YOGGE-SOTHOTHE, and sawe for yᵉ firste Time that fface [face] spoke of by Ibn Schacabao in yᵉ ————. And IT said, that yᵉ III Psalme in yᵉ Liber-Damnatus holdes yᵉ Clauicle [*i.e.*, clavicle, key]. With Sunne in V House, Saturne in Trine, drawe yᵉ Pentagram of Fire, and saye yᵉ ninth Uerse [verse] thrice. This Uerse repeate eache Roodemas and Hallow's Eue [Eve]; and yᵉ Thing will breede in yᵉ Outside Spheres.

In mid-October, 1754, Curwen wrote in his journal—later found by Charles Dexter Ward—"Ye Verse from Liber-Damnatus be'g [being] spoke V Roodmasses and IV Hallows-Eves, I am Hopeful yᵉ Thing is breed'g Outside yᵉ Spheres."

LIDDEASON, ELI (SH): A farmer's son from Rehoboth, Massachusetts, a neighboring town to Providence where HPL used to pass some of his time during his youth. Liddeason is one of the domestic servants in the Harris household between 1763–65. He constantly complains of feeling weak, and would have returned to his family farm but for developing a sudden romantic attachment to a new maidservant, Mehitabel Pierce. He dies in 1765.

LILITH (HRH): In non-biblical Jewish legends, Lilith was the *first* wife of Adam, who left him and became an immortal demoness and the mother of many demons; whereupon God created Eve as Adam's second and better helpmeet. The name Lilith is usually thought to come from *lilitu*, a Babylonian and Assyrian word for a female demon or wind-spirit, but possibly earlier traces of the name in the form of a demoness called *Lillake* have been found in a Sumerian tablet of the Gilgamesh epic, dating from circa 2000 B.C.

In the tale, by some series of events that is never explained, Lilith apparently becomes the demonic bride of Robert Suydam, and kills him and his new wife (the former Cornelia Gerritsen) on the first night of their honeymoon voyage. The ancient Chaldean characters spelling the word "Lilith" are visible on the wall of the ship's cabin when the bodies are discovered, but the letters soon fade out of sight. In the climax of this tale, Detective Malone seems to see Lilith, who appears in the aspect of a horrible being, surrounded by her worshippers in a tunnel-complex under the streets of Brooklyn. A "naked phosphorescent thing...swam into sight, scrambled ashore, and climbed up to squat leeringly on a carved golden pedestal...in the blood of stainless childhood the leprous limbs of phosphorescent Lilith were laved [washed]."

LIRANIAN DESERT (QI): The king of Oonai imports some "wild whirling dancers" from hereabouts, who replace Iranon and his sad songs as the court's favorite entertainment.

L'MUR-KATHULOS (WD): One of the many places and things which are mentioned without further explanation in this tale. "Kathulos" was the name of a sorcerer of Atlantis in some sword-and-sorcery tales by HPL's faithful correspondent Robert E. Howard of "Conan the Barbarian" fame. "L'mur" may be a reference to "Lemuria."

LOBON (DCS): One of the trio of gods who are the chiefs of the gods worshipped in Sarnath. Like the other two, Lobon is represented by the idol of a "graceful, bearded" monarch sitting on an ivory throne. *See* "Zo-Kalar" and "Tamash".

LOMAR (PO, SOT, MM, TGSK, DQ): A prehistoric human kingdom or city-state in the far north of the planet, at a time long ago when the climate there was more temperate. In *Polaris*, it is said that Lomar was conquered from the indigenous Gnophkehs, and then lost to the invading yellow-skinned Inutos. In *At the Mountains of Madness*, the coming of the great cold to the polar regions millions of years ago, which finally drove the winged, star-headed Old Ones of Antarctica from the planet's surface, is suggested as the root cause of Lomar's disappearance as well.

During his sojourn with the Great Race, Professor Peaslee meets the captive mind of "a king of Lomar who had ruled that terrible polar land one hundred thousand years before the squat, yellow Inutos came from the west to engulf it."

LOT'S WIFE (MM): Professor Dyer and the graduate student Danforth make the mistake of looking backward as they flee from a shoggoth under the lost Antarctic city. "Unhappy act! Not Orpheus himself, or Lot's wife, paid much more dearly for a backward glance." In the Bible, Lot is the name of the one righteous man in the wicked city of Sodom, allowed by Jehovah to leave the doomed city with his household, all of whom are forbidden to turn back and look upon its utter destruction by the Lord. "But his wife looked back from behind him, and she became a pillar of salt." (Genesis 19:26)

LOW, ZENAS (SH): A "capable Boston man" hired by Mercy Dexter in 1768 to work in the Harris home, since local Providence servants would no longer accept job offers there. When Zenas Low dies in the house in 1772, mad Rhoby Harris "laughed with a shocking delight utterly foreign to her."

LUBBOCK (WD): *See* "Anthropologists of the Mi-Go."

LULLY, RAYMOND (CDW): French form of the name of Blessed Ramón Lull (1235–1315?), a Spanish scholar, mystic, and self-trained philosopher whose esoteric brilliance was such that he was even reputed to have achieved the alchemists' dream of changing base metal into gold. Born into a well-to-do family on the island of Majorca, Lull was a pleasure-loving royal courtier, love poet and married man before a mid-life religious experience turned him toward his eventual career as a Franciscan lay brother and missionary preacher. He mastered Arabic in order to better understand Islam and debate its believers. Along the way he invented a moving paper device designed to answer logical problems mechanically—the remotest ancestor of computer logic?—and the familiar intersecting circles used to demonstrate overlapping qualities, which are now known as "Venn diagrams". His central work *Ars Magna* ("The Great Art") was fundamentally a defense of Christianity, in which he maintained that philosophy (including science) was not divorced from theology and that every article of the Christian faith could be demonstrated perfectly by logic. HPL mentions that Joseph Curwen owns a copy of the "Zetsner" edition of Lull's famous book *Ars Magna et Ultima*; this was first published by Lazare Zetsner or Zetzner at Strasbourg in 1598. The stunning variety of Lull's output is evidenced by the fact that the Roman Catholic church and the Theosophical movement both claim him as one of their own.

LYDIA (TR): Name of an ancient country, famous for its wealth, in what is now northwestern Turkey; by classical Greek times the Lydian kingdom had been reduced to a mere province of the Persian Empire, but its people kept close ties to Greek cities and civilization. In this tale, it is mentioned that the fame of Kalos and Musides extended "from Lydia to Neapolis," or in other words from one end of the ancient Greek cultural space to the other.

LYMAN, DR. (CDW): A psychiatrist who is called in to help treat Charles Dexter Ward's apparent mental illness. This "eminent Boston authority" feels that the onset of Ward's madness occurred "in 1919 or 1920, during the boy's last year at Moses Brown School, when he suddenly turned from the study of the past to the study of the occult, and refused to qualify for college on the grounds that he had individual researches of much greater importance to make." Dr. Lyman regards Ward's letter of February 8, 1928, to Dr. Marinus Willett, as "positive proof of a well developed case of *dementia praecox*" (a now-obsolete term for schizophrenia), but Dr. Willett "frequently quarreled" with Dr. Lyman about this opinion. On Thursday, March 8, 1928, Dr. Lyman (along with Drs. Willett, Peck, and Waite) interviews young Ward in his Pawtuxet bungalow. Afterwards, all the doctors agree that he should be temporarily committed to Dr. Waite's private mental asylum. Some bizarre letters from foreign addresses, sent to Ward's "companion," Dr. Allen, did not receive much attention from Drs. Lyman, Peck, and Waite. They knew, as HPL slyly but pointedly observes, "the tendency of kindred eccentrics and other monomaniacs to band together"!

M

MACHEN, ARTHUR (HRH, DH, WD): A Welsh author of horror and fantasy tales (1863–1947), of whom one critic has written: "Machen's work is a necessity to any connoisseur of fantasy. His favorite subject is the survival in Britain, in caves, cults, and covens, of pagan magic and fertility worship and of the spirits to whom these rites were addressed." HPL considered Arthur Machen to be perhaps the greatest supernatural-horror author of their time, and Machen's tale, *The White People,* to be the second-greatest weird tale of the era. Numerous critics have traced Machen's significant influence on HPL's works. HPL seems never to have thought of himself as being in the same league with Machen or Lord Dunsany, contemporary literary idols during some or all of his own career. In *The Whisperer in Darkness* he alludes directly to "the fantastic lore of lurking 'little people' made popular by the magnificent horror-fiction of Arthur Machen," and the persistence of such malevolent semi-humans—which Lovecraft biographer S.T. Joshi sums up as "a supposedly pre-Aryan race of dwarfish devils who still live covertly in the secret places of the earth and occasionally steal human infants, leaving one of their own behind"—is certainly one of Machen's most notable fictional themes.

A quote from Machen's tale *The Red Hand* leads off *The Horror at Red Hook.* The concepts it voices are key to much of HPL's fiction (and better on the whole than most of Lovecraft's tale):

> There are sacraments of evil as well as of good about us, and we live and move to my belief in an unknown world, a place where there are caves and shadows and dwellers in twilight. It is possible that man may sometimes return on the track of evolution, and it is my belief that an awful lore is not yet dead.

MACHU PICCHU (MM): This is a ruined city of the ancient Inca tribe, in high mountains northwest of Lima, Peru. It is a large complex of massive stonework and terraces, displaying impressive qualities of architecture and of construction technique. Neither the city's dates of occupation or its purpose are well understood, and it clearly had been abandoned and forgotten for centuries before the American explorer Hiram Bingham, a professor at Yale University, discovered the ruins in 1911.

In exploring the lost city he has discovered in Antarctica, Professor Dyer naturally is reminded of Machu Picchu.

MACKENZIE, ROBERT B.F. (SOT): Australian mining engineer who resides at 49 Dampier Street, Pilbarra, Western Australia. In 1932, he discovers a number of large blocks of very old, dressed (artificially shaped and smoothed) stone, some 500 miles east of Pilbarra in the desert. He estimates the location as 100 miles southeast of Joanna Spring, at a point approximately 22° 3′ 14″ south, 125° 0′ 39″ east. He takes photographs of about a dozen of the stone blocks, and provides them to the Western Australia state government in Perth, which, however, takes no action. On May 18, 1934, he writes to Professor Nathanael Peaslee, having heard of him and his strange dreams from the Australian psychologist, Dr. Boyle. In early 1935, Mackenzie makes the very long journey to Arkham, Massachusetts to make the final arrangements for the joint expedition, and then accompanies the Americans back to Australia on the passenger ship S.S. *Lexington*, leaving Boston on March 28, 1935. He has already made the necessary logistical arrangements in Australia. Mackenzie is "a tremendously competent and affable man of about fifty, admirably well-read, and deeply familiar with all the conditions of Australian travel." He leads the expedition which sets out in May, 1935.

MAENALUS, MOUNT (TT, MB): The name of a real mountain referred to in these ancient-Greece fantasies. Mount Maenalus actually lay in the Greek region which was called Arcadia in classical times. It is mentioned in some classical myths which HPL might have read, such as *The Story of Callisto and Arcas* in Book II of Ovid's *Metamorphoses*, in which the goddess Diana is described while hunting on the heights of Maenalus.

MAGAHS (DQ): A species of Dreamland fowl. They are seven-colored, prismatic birds, who live in resin groves near Mount Ngranek. Perhaps HPL was thinking of macaws, a colorful type of earthly tropical bird, when he coined this name.

MAGELLANIC CLOUDS (WD): In the course of a conversation with the fake "Henry Akeley," Professor Wilmarth is able to guess "the secret behind the Magellanic Clouds and globular nebulae." The Large and Small Magellanic Clouds are the two galaxies closest to our own Milky Way galaxy.

MAGNALIA CHRISTI AMERICANA (TU, PM, PH, CDW): "Great Works of Christ in America," by the Puritan minister Cotton Mather (1663–1728), of Boston. HPL inherited a vintage copy of this early-18th-century tome, which he read in his youth, and he referred to it several times in tales. The full title is *Magnalia Christi Americana, or, the Ecclesiastical History of New England, from its First Planting, in the Year 1620, unto the Year of our Lord 1698, in Seven Books*. Mather conceived of his massive book as a comprehensive history of Puritan New England, and took about seven years to write it. In the words of a recent Mather biographer:

> As published in London in 1702, *Magnalia Christi Americana*...was unmistakably a grandly imagined and formidable work, about eight hundred folio pages in double columns, divided in seven substantial books— history of the settlement of New England; lives of the governors; lives of the leading ministers (the longest book); history of Harvard College [Mather's alma mater], with lives of eminent graduates; account of the New England manner of worship; "Remarkables of Divine Providence"; and a history of the invasion of New England churches by heretics...devils, Indians, and others.

The great 19th century American author Nathaniel Hawthorne wrote in his 1851 book of history for children, *Grandfather's Chair*: "The Magnalia is a strange, pedantic history, in which true events and real personages move before the reader with the dreamy aspect which they wore in Cotton Mather's singular mind." The hodgepodge sixth book, "Remarkables of Divine Providence," was the repository for accounts of Salem witchcraft, demonic possession, and other horrors. HPL, in *The Unnamable*, wrote:

> Cotton Mather, in that daemoniac sixth book which no one should read after dark, minced no words as he flung forth his anathema. Stern as a Jewish prophet, and laconically unamazed as none since his day could be....

But the sinister 20th century Boston artist, Richard Pickman, thought that *Magnalia Christi Americana* was only a weak effort at telling the truth. In *The Case of Charles Dexter Ward* Simon/Jedediah Orne writes a word of warning about necromancy and black magic to Joseph Curwen, circa 1750:

> But I would have you Observe what was tolde to us aboute take'g Care whom to calle up, for you are Sensible [aware] what Mr. Mather writ in ye Magnalia of ———— and can judge how truely that Horrendous thing is reported.

MAGNA MATER (HRH, RW): The "Great Mother," worshipped as a fertility deity in ancient Rome and elsewhere.

MAGNUM INNOMINANDUM (WD): A phrase meaning "the great not-to-be-named."

MALAY PRIDE (SOI): A merchant ship owned by one Esdras Martin, of Innsmouth, which makes a South Seas voyage in 1828. After that year, only Captain Obed Marsh persists in the long-distance Pacific trade.

MALKOWSKI, DR. (DWH): A "local practitioner who would repeat no tales," this physician is sent for by Landlord Dombrowski on Walter Gilman's last day alive. He gives the suffering student some sedative drugs, and makes the discovery that both of Gilman's eardrums have been ruptured as if by some tremendous sound. His Polish surname signifies that he practices in the working-class immigrant area of Arkham where the Witch House is located.

MALONE, JAMES F. (HRH): Probably the most unlikely New York City policeman in all of literature, Malone is the hero of this jumbled and unsuccessful tale from the period of HPL's "New York Exile." Lovecraft biographer S.T. Joshi has suggested that HPL may have made the tale's central character a police-department sleuth in hopes of expanding his literary market to include the "detective" pulp magazines: if so, the gambit failed. Detective Malone, 42 years old at the beginning of the tale, was born in a "Georgian" (*i.e.*, 18th or early 19th century) villa in the exclusive Phoenix Park district of Dublin, Ireland; no ordinary Irish-cop stereotype, Malone also attended Dublin University (sometimes known as Trinity College) and was a published author with "many poignant things to his credit in the *Dublin Review*" (which does not exist). Malone's "experiment in police work" was, for such an educated gentleman, "a freak beyond sensible explanation"—and HPL does not supply any sensible explanation for it either—and scoffed at by the intellectual New Yorkers of his acquaintance. In his youth a poet, Malone had experienced "poverty and sorrow and exile," and combines "Celtic" inner vision with keen logic.

Assigned to the Red Hook waterfront area in south Brooklyn, he investigates the cult whose apparent leader, Robert Suydam, he has already "heard of indirectly as a really profound authority on medieval superstition...[he] had once idly meant to look up an out-of-print pamphlet of [Suydam's] on the Kabbalah and the Faustus legend." (These two tossed-away references are obviously a foreshadowing of what Suydam is involved with in Red Hook.) On the night that Malone's investigation comes to a climax in the police raid on the sect of Asiatic devil-worshippers in Red Hook, Malone has a true Lovecraftian hero's ordeal in the "nighted crypts" of a network of underground caverns and chambers. Afterwards he goes on medical leave to the village of Chepachet, Rhode Island, to board on a dairy farm and attempt to recover his mental health.

MALWA (UP): A passenger ship of the once-ubiquitous "P.&O." (or P&O) steamship line which, in the tale, Houdini and his wife take from Marseilles, France to Port Said, Egypt, in January 1910. During the voyage, Houdini humiliates a mediocre magician on board the ship, destroying his own incognito for the rest of his Egyptian vacation, with the most serious consequences for himself. Always known informally (and today legally) as "the P&O," the former Peninsular & Oriental Steam Navigation Company was, in its time, the most wide-ranging shipping company in the world, best known for transporting British subjects to and from every port in the British Empire, including to India by way of the Suez Canal.

MAMMOTH CAVE (BC): The site of one of HPL's earliest short stories (besides some very inconsequential juvenilia), written at the tender age of 15; the narrator becomes lost in this vast cave after wandering away from a guided tour, and encounters another lost human who has descended into bestial savagery and aspect after years of solitary and unlighted cave-living.

The vast cavern-complex of Mammoth Cave lies several miles northwest of Bowling Green, Kentucky, and is now a U.S. national park. Although HPL had never seen Mammoth Cave when he wrote the tale, he carefully described it from his reading, including the relics of the subterranean "consumptive colony" where desperate tuberculosis victims had once encamped in hopes of easier breathing in the pure, cool, cave air. HPL's choice of this spectacular, well-known cave as a story-setting prefigured the many, many other caves, vaults, tunnel systems, subterranean worlds, and buried tombs that this most troglophiliac of fantasy-writers would employ in his mature work.

MANNING, REVEREND JAMES (CDW): A prominent Rhode Island citizen and revolutionary patriot, James Manning (1738–91) was the first president of Rhode Island College, later renamed Brown University.

In 1770–71, Reverend Manning is a member of the secret committee that investigates the activities of Joseph Curwen. As a member of the raiding party in April, 1771, he is assigned to Captain Matthewson's group, which stormed the stone outbuilding. This minister of the Gospel was probably the most psychically disturbed of all the raiders by what he saw that night; but he eases his spiritual anguish with prayer.

MANTON, JOEL (TU): The principal of East High School in Arkham: "born and bred in Boston, and sharing New England's self-satisfied deafness to the delicate overtones of life." Sitting with "Carter" on a tomb in the old Arkham cemetery one afternoon, he joins in speculating on the existence of things that could possibly be termed "unnamable," a concept he denies. When the two men are then attacked by a spectral beast, Manton receives two malignant gorings in the chest, plus cuts and gouges in his back. He is found with Carter the next day in a field beyond Meadow Hill, and brought to St. Mary's Hospital in Arkham to recover. "Joel Manton" was based on HPL's friend Maurice Moe, with whom he shared amiable disputes in which Moe, as a partisan of literary realism, questioned HPL's love of the weird, and the atheist HPL responded with mildly-phrased arguments against Moe's Christian religious beliefs.

MANUXET RIVER (SOI): Fictitious river in Massachusetts, which runs through the town of Innsmouth on its way to the sea, with a few waterfalls; it is the source of hydraulic power for the industrial mills which flourished in Innsmouth during the early 19th century.

MAPLE HILL (LF): A fictitious hill near Tempest Mountain and the devastated squatter camp in the Catskills.

MARKHEIM (WE): An employee of the Venus Crystal Company who is part of the team that finds the remains of Stanfield and Dwight in the invisible labyrinth; he finds a doorway which could have led Stanfield on the path to a swift escape, directly behind the body—"an opening which he overlooked in his exhaustion and despair." The unusual name, Markheim, may have occurred to HPL on the basis of Robert Louis Stevenson's 19th century short story of the same name, which HPL called "a permanent classic" of a certain genre of horror-writing.

MARS (TGSK): Flying through the solar system in a light-beam envelope, Randolph Carter/Zkauba has time to gaze at "the Cyclopean [gigantic and brutish] ruins that sprawl over Mars' ruddy disc."

MARSH, BARNABAS (SOI): The son of Onesiphorus Marsh, and grandson of Obed Marsh; he marries an unsuspecting (and very unfortunate) young woman from nearby Ipswich, Massachusetts, circa 1877. He is still alive in 1927, and the owner of the Marsh Refining Company. He has not been seen in public since about 1917, and although he continues to visit the gold refinery occasionally, it is always in a limousine with curtained windows. Barnabas Marsh was a great dandy in his youth, and is said to continue to wear the "frock-coated finery" popular in his younger years, but *adapted* to certain physical changes. Zadok Allen says that Barnabas Marsh is "about changed" and can no longer shut his eyes; soon he will depart to live under the sea as one of the Deep Ones. The narrator sees him late the same night, leading a search party down the Rowley road: a dreadful figure "clad in a ghoulishly humped black coat and striped trousers, [with] a man's felt hat perched on the shapeless thing that answered for a head."

MARSH, CAPTAIN OBED (SOI): An "old limb of Satan," Zadok Allen called him. In the early 19th century, Obed Marsh is a sea captain and the owner of three merchant sailing-ships, *Columbia, Hetty,* and *Sumatra Queen.* He is the only Innsmouth ship owner to persist in the long-haul East Indies and Pacific trade during the 1830s and 1840s, a round-trip that lasted several months and could be very dangerous. On the evidence of his life and deeds, Obed Marsh is a very intelligent, ambitious, and ruthless man. Zadok says: "never was nobody like Cap'n Obed...he cud read folks like they was books." Zadok also remembers: "I kin mind [I can remember] him a-tellin abaout furren parts [foreign lands], an' calln' all the folk stupid fer goin' to Christian meetin' and bearin' their burdens meek an' lowly. Says they orter [ought to] get better gods like some o' the folk in the Injies [East Indies]—gods as ud [that would] bring 'em good fishin' in return for their sacrifices, an' ud really answer folks's prayers." Some time around 1830, while on a voyage aboard *Sumatra Queen,* he finds an island east of Otaheite (Tahiti) and befriends its tribal chief, Walakea. He eventually learns from Walakea the secret of the islanders' profitable relationship with the Deep Ones. During several subsequent voyages, Captain Marsh brings home golden jewelry from the Deep Ones, and purchases an old mill to refine the gold into ingots that he can sell—the beginning of the Marsh Refining Company, which is still in business when the narrator visits Innsmouth in the 1920s.

He returns to the Pacific island in 1838, and finds that the islanders have been exterminated by their neighbors. This terminates his gold business for the moment and hits his own income very hard, which in turn affects Innsmouth's already-depressed economy. "That's the time Obed he begun a-cursin' at the folks fer bein' dull sheep an' prayin' to a Christian heaven as didn't help 'em none." He organizes the Esoteric Order of Dagon, promising Innsmouthers that this new worship would bring them plenty of fish and gold. More and more people join the Order, and little Zadok Allen witnesses Obed Marsh and others rowing boats out to Devil Reef late at night, chanting and dropping objects—including human sacrifices—into the deep water. Then Marsh "begun to git on his feet agin [again]"; his refinery is always busy, and his daughters wear splendid golden jewelry. What his real desires may have been is left a bit unclear; Zadok recounts:

> Remember, I ain't sayin' Obed was set on hevin' things jest like they was on that Kanaky ["Kanaka," South Seas islander] isle. I dun't think he aimed at fust [at first] to do no mixin' nor raise no younguns [children] to

take to the water an' turn into fishes with eternal life. He wanted them gold things, an' was willin' to pay heavy, an' I guess the *others* was satisfied fer a while.

In 1846, Obed Marsh and 32 of his followers are arrested and jailed by town authorities; two weeks later, the Deep Ones attack the town from the water and free them, with much slaughter of the resisters. The next morning, with dead bodies still lying in the streets of Innsmouth:

Obed he kinder [kind of] takes charge an' says things is goin' to be changed...*others'll* worship with us at meetin'-time [church], an' sarten [certain] haouses hez got to entertain *guests*...*they* wanted to mix like they did with the Kanakys, an' he fer one didn't feel baound to stop 'em. Far gone, was Obed...jest like a crazy man on the subjeck. He says they brung us fish an' treasure, and shud [should] hev what they hankered arter [wanted].

Obed took a second wife in 1846, whom no one ever saw—certainly a Deep One—and had three children by her; two of them are never seen in public either, but the middle daughter looked altogether human, and Obed Marsh, cunning to the last, "got her married off by a trick to an Arkham feller as didn't suspect nothin'." She is the ancestress of the narrator, the resemblance of whose eyes to Obed Marsh's is noticed and commented upon by Zadok Allen. Obed Marsh dies in 1878, but his Deep One descendants are "fishes with eternal life" in old Zadok's phrase.

MARSH, ONESIPHORUS (SOI): The eldest son of Obed Marsh and his first, human wife. Along with the first wife's other children, he was dead by the time of the tale's events in 1927. Onesiphorus Marsh marries "another o' them as wa'n't never seed [was never seen] aoutdoors," Zadok Allen said, referring presumably, to one of the Deep Ones. As a result, his son Barnabas would mutate into a Deep One and be relatively immortal.

MARTENSE FAMILY (LF): Descendants of the Dutch settler Gerrit Martense, who resided in and around the Martense mansion on Tempest Mountain in the Catskills. They were marked by a genetic peculiarity, one eye usually being blue, the other brown. Trained to hate the encroaching English settlers, they live in seclusion, marrying within the family and becoming slow-witted. During the 18th century, some of them descended to merge with the mongrel population of the rural area, while others stuck to the old mansion, "becoming more and more clannish and taciturn, yet developing a nervous responsiveness to the frequent thunderstorms." Passers-by saw lights in the mansion's windows as late as the year 1810, but not thereafter. Investigators who broke into the mansion in 1816 found no inhabitants, but much evidence of the family's continued animalistic degeneration. In 1921, the narrator discovers the descendants of the Martenses: thousands of "dwarfed, deformed hairy devils or apes," "filthy whitish gorilla things with sharp yellow fangs and matted fur," living in caverns burrowed under the district and feeding on the local squatter population or on each other. They are the products of so-called "reverse evolution," a pseudo-Darwinian concept that was believed in or feared by many members of the reading public in HPL's day.

MARTENSE, GERRIT (LF): A wealthy Dutch merchant from New Amsterdam (now New York City), who left that Dutch colony after it came under British rule, and in 1670 built a mansion house on Tempest Mountain in a remote part of the Catskills. Finding the constant summer thunderstorms of the neighborhood "injurious to his head, he fitted up a cellar into which he could retreat from their wildest pandemonium." Thus began the descent underground of the Martense family.

MARTENSE, JAN (LF): Young scion of the Martense family in the mid-18th century. Although the Martenses keep themselves apart from other people, and hate the English colonists in particular, young Jan goes in 1754 to Albany, New York, and enlists in the British royal service for the French and Indian War. He leaves the colonial forces in 1760. After returning to the family home, he is treated with surly suspicion by his Dutch family, and writes to a friend he has made in Albany, Jonathan Gifford, about his plans to move away again. When letters from him cease abruptly in 1762, his Albany friend visits Tempest Mountain and manages to discover Jan Martense's bones, the skull shattered as if by heavy blows. He had presumably been murdered by members of his unforgiving family.

MARTENSE STREET (HRH): A real street in the Flatbush district in the borough of Brooklyn, New York City, five or six blocks from the Lovecraft apartment on Parkside Avenue. Robert Suydam's fictitious house is on Martense Street.

MASON, KEZIAH (DWH): A "mediocre" elderly woman in 1692, in Arkham, Massachusetts. She was the tenant of the oddly-angled room which Walter Gilman rents in the 1920s. Arrested in 1692 as a suspected witch, she gave some strange testimony "under pressure"—a euphemism for severe interrogation, or even torture—then drew some peculiar geometrical angles on the wall of her cell with a "red liquid" and disappeared. She became part of Arkham folklore, said to have been seen repeatedly over the years, and to be responsible for the inexplicable disappearances of small children around Halloween and Walpurgis Night. She appears to Walter Gilman after he has dwelled in the room for a while, along with Brown Jenkin, her familiar. During many nights she leads Gilman to other worlds, introducing him to her master, Nyarlathotep. Later, when she attempts to involve Gilman in the ritual sacrifice of a kidnapped infant, he attacks and strangles her. Her bones are found years later, in 1931, in one of the spaces in the wall formed by the ceiling's angles.

Keziah Mason's unusual first name is from the Old Testament, and refers to the pretty tree called "cassia" in English, a cinnamon relative with fragrant bark and oil. In HPL's favorite book of the Bible, the Book of Job, it is given to the second daughter of Job's new family, after his restoration to health and wealth: "And he called the name of the first Jemima, and the name of the second Keziah...and in all the land were no women found so fair as the daughters of Job."

MATHEMATICIANS OF ARKHAM (DWH): Walter Gilman wanted to live in the Witch House, "where some circumstance had more or less suddenly given a mediocre old woman of the seventeenth century an insight into mathematical depths beyond the utmost modern delvings of Planck, Heisenberg, Einstein, and de Sitter." Max Planck (1858–1947), of Germany, was one of the great modern physicists, a Nobel Prize winner, and described as the "father" of quantum theory, one of the foundational elements of modern physics. Werner Heisenberg (1901–76), also of Germany and also a recipient of the Nobel Prize, did work in the same area of quantum theory, and at the same advanced level, as Max Planck. For Albert Einstein, *see* separate entry. Willem de Sitter (1872–1934), a Dutch astronomer and mathematician, combined astronomy with Einstein's theory of relativity to develop the theory of a constantly expanding universe, an idea that is now generally accepted and familiar.

MATHER, REVEREND COTTON (DWH, TU, PM): Colonial American minister and author (1663–1728):

> ...a figure on horseback, so darkly conspicuous, so sternly triumphant, that [some] mistook him for the visible presence of the [Devil] himself; but it was only his good friend, Cotton Mather, proud of his well-won dignity, as the representative of all the hateful features of his time; the one blood-thirsty man, in whom were concentrated those vices of spirit and errors of opinion that sufficed to madden the whole surrounding multitude.

So wrote Nathaniel Hawthorne (1804–64) in one of his short stories (*Alice Doane's Appeal*, found in Hawthorne's famous 1835 collection *Twice-Told Tales),* almost a century and a half after Cotton Mather played a significant public role during the Salem witchcraft mania. In reality, Mather was not quite so monstrous. A contemporary obituary, for example, called him "perhaps the principal Ornament of this country, and the greatest Scholar that was ever bred in it... [B]esides his universal Learning, his exalted Piety and extensive Charity, his entertaining Wit and singular Goodness of Temper recommended him to all, that were judges of real and distinguishing Merit."

Cotton Mather, pastor from 1685–1728 of Old North Church in Boston and the last major Puritan clergyman of colonial Massachusetts, has passed into American mythology as the black-clad prototype of the strict, stern, condemning preacher. But he was also an avid amateur scientist, a Fellow of the Royal Society for the advancement of scientific knowledge, and, during a 1721–22 epidemic, a vociferous promoter of the new invention of smallpox vaccination, despite enormous public fear and opposition. He wrote prodigiously, and historians are in his debt for much of what is known about New England in the Puritan era that began with the *Mayflower* voyage in 1620 and was already becoming a mere memory by the time of his death. His greatest flaw may have been excessive credulity.

One aspect of Cotton Mather was the stiff-necked zealot who in 1692 almost single-handedly kept a Salem Village crowd from halting the public hanging of George Burroughs, the former village minister, for witchcraft (the event which Hawthorne vaguely alluded to in his tale); but another was the gentle natural-history enthusiast who could write of the humble barnyard pig:

> How surprisingly is the *Head* and *Neck* of the *Swine* adapted for his rooting in the *Earth*.... The strong Snout of the *Swine*, such that he may sufficiently thrust it into the Ground, where his living lies, without hurting his Eyes; and of so sagacious a Scent, that we may employ them to hunt for us and even his *Wallowing in the Mire*, is a wise contrivance for the Suffocation of troublesome Insects!

Mather's reputation from his own time to the present has naturally been tainted by his strong support for the Salem witch trials, and for their so-called "spectral evidence" (testimony by the accusers about wrongful acts done by defendants while they were invisible, except to the accusers). He defended the trials in a 1693 book, *The Wonders of the Invisible World*, although he modified his position years later after most of the accusers had recanted their testimony. History proved Mather wrong in Salem, meanwhile brushing aside the unitary theocratic society or "Christian Israel" that the English Puritans had hoped to build in Massachusetts. Mather himself believed, with reason, that his outspoken contemporary defense of the Salem proceedings later cost him the job he wanted most of all, the presidency of his alma mater, Harvard College.

Late in Reverend Mather's life he met an already rather irreverent, skeptical, and progressive-minded teenager named Benjamin Franklin, still unknown to fame—truly an encounter of old and new mental worlds. Their meeting was, however, a cordial one.

In *The Dreams in the Witch House*, the narrator notes that when in 1692 the accused witch Keziah Mason disappeared from Salem Gaol (jail):

> ...the gaoler had gone mad and babbled of a small, white-fanged furry thing which scuttled out of Keziah's cell, and not even Cotton Mather could explain the curves and angles smeared on the grey stone walls with some red, sticky fluid.

In *The Unnamable*, the narrator Randolph Carter refers to Mather's book *Magnalia Christi Americana* and describes him, in his written accounts of supernatural phenomena, as being "stern as a Jewish prophet, and as laconically unamazed as none since his day could be...."

MATHEWSON, CAPTAIN JAMES (CDW): Master of the ship *Enterprise*, of Providence, in 1770. He is the first person approached by Ezra Weeden to hear Weeden's suspicions about Joseph Curwen. They met in an upper room of a tavern by the docks. Captain Mathewson recruits the other members of the secret committee. In April, 1771, he is the leader of the section of the raiding party that storms the stone outbuilding.

MATSUGAWA (WE): Individual who aerially surveyed the Venusian plateau called Eryx or the Erycinian Highlands, fifty years before the events of this tale. The only Japanese name in any of HPL's tales, adding to the futuristic atmosphere of this straight science-fiction tale.

MAUMEE (SOI): A small town in northern Ohio, now practically a suburb of the neighboring city of Toledo. The narrator spent a month in Maumee recovering from his horrific Innsmouth experiences before returning for his senior year at Oberlin University, also in northern Ohio.

MAUSOLUS (TR): As Kalos is dying, poisoned by the hand of his deceitful friend Musides, the latter sculptor promises the dying man "a sepulchre more lovely than the tomb of Mausolus," but the ever-philosophical Kalos "bade him speak no more of marble glories."

Mausolus (d. 353 B.C.) was the *satrap* (Persian local governor) and effective ruler of Caria, a wealthy province in modern southwestern Turkey. His white marble tomb—the Mausoleum—at his capital city of Halicarnassus was one of the ancient Seven Wonders of the World. It is thought to have been "in the form of an Ionic peristyle set on a lofty and massive base that contained the sarcophagus, and surmounted by a stepped pyramid on whose truncated apex was a marble quadriga, or four-horse chariot." It was decorated with sculpture well in keeping with the general magnificence. Nothing of the Mausoleum remains today, but some of the sculptures are in the British Museum.

MAWSON, SIR DOUGLAS (MM): Australian polar explorer (1882–1958). In the tale, Professor Dyer mentions Mawson's expedition (which took place between 1929–30) in the vicinity of the Antarctic coastal region called Queen Mary Land, as having been in progress at the same time as the Miskatonic University Expedition. Mawson's exploits in Antarctic exploration were numerous; in the 1929–30 expedition, he used a seaplane to aid in his exploration and mapping of unknown areas, a detail which probably helped HPL in conceiving of the fleet of specially-equipped airplanes the Miskatonic explorers use.

MAZUREWICZ, JOE (DWH): A "superstitious loom fixer" (*i.e.*, a fabric-mill equipment repairman) and fellow-tenant of Walter Gilman in the Witch House in Arkham. A member of the Catholic, non-Anglo-Saxon proletariat whose presence in New England HPL tended to resent, he is a good if simple fellow, anxious to help "the young gentleman," Gilman. He lives on the ground floor, and has seen the apparitions of Keziah Mason and Brown Jenkin. For relief from his anxious fears, he prays almost constantly while in the Witch House, with the help of a Rosary and a silver crucifix given him by his priest, Father Iwanicki. He celebrates until late at night on Patriots Day—April 19th, a public holiday in Massachusetts—and when coming home after midnight, he sees a violet light emanating from Gilman's room. A few days later he gives the student a cheap nickel crucifix on a metal chain, blessed by Father Iwanicki. As Walpurgis Night approaches, he and the tenant Desrochers have sympathetic discussions about the poor doomed young gentleman, Gilman. He is finally one of the witnesses to Gilman's slaying by Brown Jenkin, and notices the half-human nature of the rat-like creature's bloody paw-prints.

McGREGOR BOYS (COS): From "Meadow Hill," possibly the one mentioned elsewhere (*see* entry for Meadow Hill) as being outside the town of Arkham. In February, 1883, the two youths shoot a woodchuck near the Nahum Gardner farm. But on picking up the body of their prey, they see that "the proportions of its body seemed altered in a queer way impossible to describe, while its face had taken on an expression which no one ever saw in a woodchuck before." The boys, "genuinely frightened," throw the thing away from them.

McTIGHE (MM): A mechanic on the Miskatonic University Expedition, who is also a qualified pilot. Working as the radio operator at the base camp, he receives and transcribes the urgent bulletins from the Lake-Atwood party. On January 24, 1931, he tries to make radio contact with Professor Lake, but can get no response. On January 25, he is made a member of the search-and-rescue party, and flies the aircraft for part of the way. He sends the last "uncensored" message to the outside world as the plane begins to descend for a landing. Later, he helps to repair two damaged aircraft left at the site.

MEADOW HILL (HW, COS, TU, DWH): A hill located not far outside of Arkham. In *Herbert West—Reanimator,* the duo's first secret laboratory is in "the deserted Chapman farmhouse beyond Meadow Hill." In *The Unnamable*, Randolph Carter tells Joel Manton about the story of an Arkham "post-rider" (letter carrier), circa 1700, "who said he saw an old man chasing and calling to a frightful, loping, nameless thing on Meadow Hill in the thinly moonlit hours before dawn...." One day in February, 1883, in *The Colour Out of Space*, "the McGregor boys from Meadow Hill" go out shooting woodchucks near Nahum Gardner's farm and kill one that badly frightens them when they pick it up to look: "The proportions of its body seemed slightly altered in a queer way impossible to describe, while its face had taken on an expression which no one ever saw in a woodchuck before." In *The Dreams in the Witch House*, Joe Mazurewicz tells Walter Gilman that the Arkham millworkers "were whispering that the Walpurgis-revels would be held in the dark ravine beyond Meadow Hill where the old white stone stands in a place queerly void of all plant-life." The Arkham police raid these revels, but succeed in catching nobody.

MEMNON (NC): "Then suddenly above the desert's far rim came the blazing edge of the sun...and in my fevered state I fancied that from some remote depth there came a crash of musical metal to hail the fiery disc as Memnon hails it from the banks of the Nile." This classical allusion is complex. Memnon was the name of an "Ethiopian" king in early Greek mythology. The Colossi of Memnon are two enormous stone statues built as part of a mortuary temple (now vanished) by the pharaoh Amenhotep III (Greek: Amenophis III) in the 14th century B.C. An earthquake in the 1st century B.C. devastated the temple and created cracks in the stone fabric of the Colossi. As a result of these cracks, each Colossus began to produce vaguely musical sounds at dawn when the rays of the strong Egyptian sun first warmed its night-cooled surface. Thereafter the Greeks dubbed the Colossi "the Oracle of Memnon" and turned them into a pilgrimage site, a cult in which they were joined by

Romans. A Roman emperor of the 3rd century A.D. had the statues "restored" to gain Memnon's favor: after the restoration, the sounds ceased forever, although the statues are still to be seen. In this tale, the "crash of musical metal" which the nameless narrator hears at dawn and at dusk in the Nameless City turns out to be a vast brazen door which opens and shuts for the spirits of the city's reptilian builders at those times.

MENA HOUSE (UP): The hotel in the vicinity of the Giza pyramid-complex, where Houdini and his wife stay during their 1910 sightseeing vacation in Egypt. This famous hotel opened in 1869 for the newly-created tourist trade, and still exists under the same name; it is currently a five-star luxury hotel and casino of great beauty, outside of Cairo and almost in the shadow of the great pyramids.

MENES (CU): The name of a little orphan boy who accompanies a caravan of dark-complexioned "wanderers" from the south, a caravan which passes through the stolid village of Ulthar. His family had died from some plague, leaving him with only a tiny black kitten for company: "and when one is very young, one can find great relief in the lively antics of a black kitten," HPL writes, probably thinking of his beloved childhood pet, a clever black cat. Menes calls down a mighty curse on the wicked cat-killing couple after they apparently slay his pet.

MERCURY (SOT): The closest planet to the sun; "when the earth's span closed," Professor Peaslee learns, the Great Race's transferable minds "would again migrate through time and space—to another stopping-place in the bodies of the bulbous vegetable entities of Mercury."

MERLUZZO, FATHER (HD): A "young, intelligent, and well-educated" Catholic priest of "Santo Spirito Church" in Providence's Federal Hill district. On the night of August 8–9, 1935, he is standing outside the abandoned Starry Wisdom church at 2:35 a.m., with a crowd of frightened, mostly Italian-American residents of the district, when he witnesses the strange events.

MEROË (CU, NC): Meroë was a city of the ancient Kushites, a semi-Egyptianized black people who lived along the remote upper Nile river in present-day Sudan. During the last six centuries of the 1st millennium B.C., the city of Meroë was the capital of the late-Kushite empire also called Meroë. The Kushite religion drew heavily upon that of Egypt, meaning that cats were honored among them.

MERRITT, JOHN (CDW): The non-fictitious John Merritt (1687–1760), was "an elderly English gentleman of literary and scientific leanings," who moved to Providence from Newport, Rhode Island, in 1746. He built his country house in a district called "the Neck," keeps the first coach and liveried (uniformed) servants in town, and owns not only a telescope and a microscope, but a fine library. We are told that he was a friend of Dr. Checkley, the rector of King's Church. In the tale, Mr. Merritt pays a social call on Joseph Curwen and is granted the unique favor of an invitation to that person's Pawtuxet Road farmhouse, where he sees many intriguing books. One of the books is a worn-out copy of a work by Borellus, with the significant passage about "essential Saltes" much underlined.

MICHEL MAUVAIS (TA): In French, *mauvais* means "wicked." A sorcerer who lives near the chateau of the de C family during the Middle Ages, he is strongly suspected of having burnt his wife alive as a human sacrifice, and of being responsible for the many unexplained disappearances of people in the neighborhood. The Count de C came to suspect Michel Mauvais—wrongfully—of having kidnapped his son and heir Geoffrey de C, so he strangled the old wizard to death. For this he and his family are punished for generations by the curse of Michel's son, Charles le Sorcier.

MIDDLE OCEAN (DCS): An ocean mentioned only in this tale, the location of the Isles of Nariel.

MIDIANITES (PH): The unnaturally old Yankee cannibal in this tale tells the nameless narrator, while looking at the drawing of an African cannibal "butcher shop" in a very old book:

> When I read the Scripter [*i.e.,* Holy Scriptures, the Bible] about slayin'— like them Midianites was slew—I kinder think things, but I ain't got no picter of it. Here a body kin see all they [there] is to it—I s'pose 'tis sinful, but ain't we all born an' livin' in sin?

The Midianites were a nomadic tribe of a district in northern Arabia ("the land of Midian") in ancient times, mentioned many times in the Old Testament. They were inveterate enemies of the Israelites. Some of the bloodier passages of the Old Testament deal with wars with and massacres of Midianites by the children of Israel. The old man may have been thinking of the words of Judges 7:25, which describes the aftermath of one battle:

> And they took two princes of the Midianites, Oreb and Zeeb, and they slew Oreb upon the rock Oreb, and Zeeb they slew at the winepress of Zeeb, and pursued Midian, and brought the heads of Oreb and Zeeb to Gideon on the other side [of the] Jordan.

MI-GO (MM, WD): Crab-like creatures from outer space who are responsible for the legends of "abominable snowmen" and other fabled hill-creatures in remote places all around the world. The phrase "Mi-Go," HPL identifies as the word of the "Nepalese hill tribes" for the "'Abominable Snow-Men' who lurk hideously amidst the ice and rock pinnacles of the Himalayan summits." (In the Tibetan language, Mi-Go is indeed the compound word for "man-swift" (fast-moving man), used to describe these legendary creatures.) To look at, the Mi-Go are:

> ...pinkish things about five feet long, with crustaceous bodies bearing vast pairs of dorsal fins or membraneous wings and several sets of articulated limbs, and with a sort of convoluted ellipsoid, covered with multitudes of short antennae, where a head would ordinarily be.

Elsewhere in *The Whisperer in Darkness* they are described as:

> ...a sort of huge, light-red crab with many pairs of legs and with two great bat-like wings in the middle of their back. They sometimes walked on all their legs, and sometimes on the hindmost pair only, using the others to convey large objects.... On one occasion they were spied in considerable numbers, a detachment of them wading along a shallow woodland water-course three abreast in evidently disciplined formation.

The image of the Mi-Go on the march, in the placid New England countryside, is somehow charming. The alien creatures can walk and fly, converse in buzzing tones, and glide through space to (for example) Pluto/Yuggoth, their nearest fully-inhabited planet. They cannot be photographed because their physical composition does not register on photographic film. Dr. Wilmarth is told that these creatures are:

> ...perhaps the most marvellous organic beings in or beyond all space and time—members of a cosmos-wide race of which all other life-forms are merely degenerate variants. They are more vegetable than animal, if these terms can be applied...and have a somewhat fungoid structure; though the presence of a chlorophyll-like substance and a very singular nutritive system differentiate them altogether from true cormophytic fungi. Indeed, the type is composed of a form of matter totally alien to our part of space—with electrons having a wholly different vibration-rate.

They inhabit the most remote hills of Vermont as well as other places in Europe and Asia, mining a type of stone they could not find elsewhere. They leave people alone if not spied upon; but if disturbed, they are ready to respond severely. Henry Akeley in his farm compound is literally besieged by Mi-Go and perhaps their renegade human helpers on many nights, in "Fort Apache"-style gun battles that Lovecraft biographer S.T. Joshi has aptly described as being unintentionally funny. It develops that they have means for detaching human brains from human bodies without ending either life or intelligence, and packing the brains into metal cylinders for transportation to Yuggoth or elsewhere in the universe.

In *At the Mountains of Madness*, it is said that these Mi-Go were half-fungus, half-crustacean creatures who invaded Earth during the Jurassic era, driving the winged, star-headed Old Ones out of all the northern lands.

MILLER, WESLEY P. (WE): Employee of the Venus Crystal Company, supervisor of "Group A," which included Kenton Stanfield. After Stanfield has been out for several days, Miller takes five men and Scouting Plane FR-58 to search for him. They found his body and that of Dwight in the invisible labyrinth on the Erycinian Highland. A practical type, Miller has his men survey the place with the aid of long cords, then dynamite it, only saving some of the material for research. In his cold-blooded report to the company, Miller suggests that the extermination of the Venusians by humans should not be far off.

MILLS (MM): A member of the Miskatonic University Expedition, probably one of the mechanics. He is assigned to the Lake-Atwood group, and with Boudreau and Fowler, finds thirteen of the unidentifiable new specimens in the subterranean cave at about 11:00 p.m. on January 23, 1931. Earlier the same night, he had been sent back to the camp to get electric lights so that digging could continue. He is found dead with the rest of the Lake-Atwood party on January 25.

MINOAN CRETE (MM, HD): Crete is a large island in the southeastern Mediterranean Sea, closer to Egypt than to Europe; it was inhabited by the pre-Greek "Minoan" civilization during the span of time between roughly 3000–1000 B.C. In *At the Mountains of Madness*, Professor Dyer hopes for a long time that "the omnipresence of the five-pointed motif meant only some cultural or religious exaltation of the Archaean natural object [*i.e.*, the winged, star-headed Old One]...as the decorative motifs of Minoan Crete exalted the sacred bull." Then he is compelled to realize that the five-pointedness was not the work of human worshippers in some conceivable past, but the work of the things themselves millions of years ago. In *The Haunter of the Dark* it is said that the Shining Trapezohedron, long after the destruction of Atlantis, was dredged up from the sea by a Minoan fisherman and sold to some Egyptian merchants.

MINOT, JOE (PM): Mutual acquaintance of Richard Upton Pickman and "Thurber," the narrator. He is one of the artsy types who avoid Pickman as his work grows increasingly morbid.

MIRAGE PLANTS (WE): One of the deadliest threats to life on Venus. They have shaggy stalks, spiky leaves, and blossoms that exude a gas which can penetrate any mask, and cause narcotic effects such as shimmering colors, swirling lights, a steady drumming sound in the ears, and loss of balance. Kenton Stanfield comes across one on his trek and is nearly overcome, but "recalling what happened to Bailey three years ago," and also his warning from Anderson, he rushes away from the plant and its aroma.

MIRANDOLA (CDW): Giovanni Pico della Mirandola (1463–94), was a brilliant Renaissance philosopher-humanist, one of the Italian neo-Platonists. He was a prolific author on serious subjects before his early death. The magical incantation which a witness heard being pronounced during the 1771 raid on Joseph Curwen's farmhouse reminds Charles Dexter Ward of something he had seen in Mirandola's writings, denounced by the Italian as "the ultimate horror among black magic's incantations."

MISKATONIC (MM): One of the two ships that carry the Miskatonic University Expedition to and from Antarctica. Her captain is Georg Thorfinnssen, a veteran Antarctic whaler. Like the other ship, the *Arkham*, she is a wooden ex-whaling ship, reinforced for ice conditions and with auxiliary steam power.

MISKATONIC CLUB (TD): Presumably a private and socially exclusive club in Arkham; in the era of the early 20th century such a club would normally have been confined to an all-male membership. It is there that Edward Derby's banker, in an "overexpansive mood," mentions the checks that Derby is regularly sending to his three ex-servants in Innsmouth.

MISKATONIC RIVER (VALLEY) (DWH, SHH, HW, PH, SK, DH): A fictitious river in Massachusetts, first mentioned in *The Picture in the House*. It seems as if it must flow from west to east across the state. The town of Dunwich, in north central Massachusetts, is on the Miskatonic's upper reaches. The river flows through the town of Arkham towards the coast, and enters the sea at Kingsport. The mill town of Bolton is apparently up the river from Arkham, but not far away. In the middle of the river at Arkham is an uninhabited island, with "moss-grown rows of grey standing stones" of "obscure and immemorial" origin. Walter Gilman rows out to this island twice to sketch the angles formed by the rows of stones. On April 19 as he walks across the Garrison Street bridge and looks upstream, he sees Keziah Mason standing on the island, and runs away. On another day, wishing to avoid the sight of the island, he crosses the river by the Peabody Street bridge instead.

HPL made up the name *Miskatonic*, which he described as "simply a jumble of Algonquin roots." (The Algonquins were a small group of tribes in the future northeastern United States, who mistakenly allied with the French against the British and their Iroquois allies; by the 17th century they were already nearly extinct. However, their place-names are still found all over New England.) He must have thought about the Housatonic River, which flows for 130 miles from western Massachusetts through western Connecticut, to Long Island Sound.

MISKATONIC UNIVERSITY (COS, TF, HW, DWH, DH, SOI, TD, WD, SOT, MM): The fictional university located in Arkham, plainly modeled on such great Ivy League institutions as Harvard, Yale, and Providence's Brown University. Its library is world-famous, counting among its holdings one of the few known copies of the *Necronomicon*, as well as other rare books of ancient lore. Miskatonic also has a medical school, from which Herbert West and his comrade graduate in 1904. In the university museum rests the spiky metallic object of completely unknown provenance, donated by a former student, the late Walter Gilman. Brown Jenkin's partly-crushed skeleton, acquired after the demolition of the Witch House, is "still a topic of debate...among the members of Miskatonic's department of comparative anatomy." It is unclear whether Miskatonic has an all-male undergraduate student body, as most similar northeastern universities did in HPL's lifetime. The only female Miskatonic student ever mentioned, Asenath Waite, is already 23 years old when she enrolls there to study medieval metaphysics; perhaps she is a graduate student. She is a member of a certain so-called "Bohemian" group of wild students in the 1920s, which was of course the era of "flaming youth" all over the United States.

Early 20th-century MU professors named in HPL's tales include (with their departments, when known):

Dr. Allan Halsey	Dean of the Medical School
Professor Upton	Mathematics
Professor Albert N. Wilmarth	English
Dr. Henry Armitage	Chief Librarian
Professor Warren Rice	
Dr. Francis Morgan	
Professor Nathaniel N. Peaslee	Political Economy
Professor Wingate Peaslee	Psychology
Professor William Dyer	Geology
Professor Lake	Biology

Professor Pabodie	Engineering
Professor Atwood	Physics
Professor Tyler M. Freeborn	Anthropology
Professor Ferdinand C. Ashley	History
Professor Dexter	Zoology
Professor Ellery	Chemistry

To this list may be added the three unnamed professors from Miskatonic, presumably astronomers, who visit Nahum Gardner's farm in 1882 to investigate the meteorite that has landed there.

MISKATONIC UNIVERSITY EXPEDITION (MM): 1930–31 expedition intended primarily to take bore samples of soil that has been buried beneath the Antarctic icecap for millions of years, in order to study them and thereby learn more about Earth's earliest epochs. Funding came from the Nathaniel Derby Pickman Foundation. The expedition's members included ("p" indicates qualified pilot):

Professor William Dyer (p)
Professor Pabodie
Professor Lake
Professor Atwood

Graduate students: Danforth (p), Gedney, Carroll (p), Ropes (p), Fowler, Moulton (p), Orrendorf or Watkins.

Mechanics: Sherman (p), McTighe (p), Williamson, Mills, Boudreau, Orrendorf or Watkins, and three others. (It is apparent that of Orrendorf and Watkins, one is a graduate student, the other a mechanic; but it seems impossible to tell which is which from the text.)

Sailors: Captain J.B. Douglas, *Arkham*; Captain Georg Thorfinnssen, *Miskatonic*; Larsen, Gunnarssen, and others.

The expedition sails from Boston on September 2, 1930, passing through the Panama Canal, to Samoa, and Hobart, Tasmania. It crosses the Antarctic circle seven weeks later, on October 20. The expeditioners sight the Admiralty Range, mountains on the Antarctic coast, on October 26. They enter McMurdo Sound on November 8 and moor the ships by Mount Erebus, then offload their supplies in a depot established on Ross Island, on November 9. On November 21, they establish the "Southern Base" above Beardmore Glacier, at latitude 86° 7´ south, longitude 174° 23´ east. On January 6, 1931, Dyer, Lake, Pabodie, all of the graduate students, and four of the mechanics, fly over the South Pole in some of the airplanes. On January 11–18, Professors Lake and Pabodie, with five other men, make a preliminary drilling journey to the northwest, followed on the 22nd by Lake and Atwood's flight in that direction with four of the expedition's five aircraft, most of the equipment and sled-dogs, and the following men: Gedney, Carroll, Fowler, Moulton, Orrendorf, Watkins, Mills, Boudreau, and two unnamed mechanics.

The Lake-Atwood party found preserved specimens of the winged, "star-headed," Old Ones, and Professor Lake, the biologist, attempts to dissect one specimen. On January 24, the base camp loses radio contact with the Lake-Atwood party. On January 25, Professors Dyer and Pabodie, together with Danforth, Ropes, Sherman, McTighe, Williamson, and a mechanic—that is, all of the remaining members of the land expedition—fly to the Lake-Atwood campsite to attempt a rescue. They find that all of the men and dogs are dead by violence, except for Gedney and one dog, who are missing along with much equipment. The camp itself looks torn apart by high winds and a desperate fight of some sort. Danforth and Professor Dyer take an airplane up over the nearby mountains while Pabodie and the others repair two of the damaged aircraft, and bury the dead men. Dyer and Danforth discover the lost city of the Old Ones, the bodies of Gedney and the dog, and much else besides, all of which they keep secret from the group and the world.

The expedition is aborted and on January 27 the survivors fly back to the "Southern Base" in three airplanes. On the 28th they return to McMurdo Sound, where the ships are still moored, and begin loading equipment. On February 2, the ships begin the long voyage back to Boston.

MNAR (NC, DCS, MM): A land drained by the river Ai; a froglike race built the city of Ib here in unimaginably remote times.

MONAHAN, WILLIAM J. (HD): Irish-American policeman in Providence, assigned to Central Station and a walking beat on Federal Hill; he is "an officer of the highest reliability." On the night of August 8–9, 1935, he is outside the abandoned Starry Wisdom church with Father Merluzzo, and witnesses amazing events.

MONTAGNY, PIERRE-LOUIS (SOT): One of the captive minds encountered by Professor Peaslee among the Great Race; he is an elderly Frenchman from the time of the reign of Louis XIII (who reigned from 1610–43).

MONT SAINT-MICHEL (PM): This is a tiny island about a mile off the coast of northwestern France, on which was established in 708 an abbey of the Benedictine order of monks. In the ensuing centuries the monks superintended the construction of strong fortifications on the steep and rocky islet, and a spectacular church in the Gothic style, built principally in the 13th century. In this tale, Thurber refers to "the mediaeval chaps who did the gargoyles and chimaeras on Notre Dame and Mont Saint-Michel." "Notre Dame" is certainly a reference to the medieval Cathedral of Notre-Dame de Paris in the French capital, the glorious Gothic construction built between 1163 and the early 14th century.

MOONBEASTS (DQ): These creatures dwell on the moon and form the unseen officers and rowers of the black galleys which sometimes put in at Dylath-Leen, selling fabulous rubies and taking away gold, and black slaves from Parg, "whom they bought by the pound." They use the almost-humans of Leng, costumed to look really human, to deal with people in port and to do menial service elsewhere—or to eat. Kidnapped and flown to the moon on one of the galleys, Randolph Carter is flown to a city of the creatures on the moon, and he is able to really see them:

> ...great greyish-white slippery things which could expand and contract at will, and whose principal shape—though it often changed—was that of a toad without any eyes, but with a curiously vibrating mass of short pink tentacles on the end of its blunt, vague snout.

These creatures dominate and take living tribute from the Lengites, are indifferent to light and darkness, communicate at times by blowing flutes. One of them, clad in robes that conceal its true nature, is the high priest not to be described. On a rock far out in the sea from Sarkomand, in Dreamland, the cruel moonbeasts have a fortress and colony which Carter later is able to attack with the help of night-gaunts and ghouls. Throughout the tale they are Carter's principal opposition in his quest for Kadath; while being held captive on the moon, Carter thinks that "what his fate would be, he did not know; but he felt that he was held for the coming of that frightful soul and messenger of infinity's Other Gods, the crawling chaos Nyarlathotep."

MOON CITY (DQ): After being kidnapped in Dylath-Leen, Randolph Carter is flown in a moonbeast galley to the city of the moonbeasts. It has "thick unpleasant grey towers without windows, noisome wharfs, tiled streets and black doorways and endless rows of windowless buildings," as well as an abundance of moonbeasts and their slaves. He is rescued and carried back from the moon by an army of earthly cats.

MOORE, THOMAS (NC): Irish poet and composer (1779–1852). He was a friend of Percy Bysshe Shelley and Lord Byron, and in the field of historical-narrative poetry he was thought in his time to be the equal of Byron and Sir Walter Scott. HPL's dazed narrator in this tale nervously rattles off ten lines from one of Moore's poems while making a steep, blind descent in the vaults under the Nameless City.

MORGAN, DR. FRANCIS (DH): A "lean, youngish" professor at Miskatonic University in 1927. He visits his colleague Dr. Armitage on September 4, and meets together with Armitage and Professor Rice on two further occasions in the following weeks. Later that month, he travels with Armitage and Rice to Dunwich, and takes part in all of the Horror-eradication efforts.

MORRYSTER (TF): Author of an old book, *Marvells of Science*, which the narrator glimpses in the house on Green Lane in Kingsport.

MOSES BROWN SCHOOL (CDW): An elite private school in HPL's Providence neighborhood, which has been educating young people since 1819. Charles D. Ward graduated in the class of 1920, although without earning high marks. The school is still in existence.

MOST ANCIENT ONE, THE (TGSK): One of the most sage inhabitants of the planet Yaddith; Zkauba consults with him about Zkauba's troubling sense of "possession" by an alien being named Randolph Carter.

MOULTON (MM): A graduate student on the Miskatonic University Expedition. As a trained aviator, he pilots one of the airplanes carrying the Lake-Atwood party. The group's encampment on January 22, 1931, is made at the spot where Moulton's airplane is forced down with mechanical problems. On January 23rd Professor Lake sends Moulton hurrying back from the excavation site with an urgent message for transmission to the base camp; Moulton stays at the radio set (in one of the airplanes) for the rest of the day and night, sending and receiving additional messages. He is found dead with the rest of the Lake-Atwood group on January 25.

MOWRY, SELECTMAN (SOI): A "selectman" (*i.e.*, elected member of the town council) in Innsmouth, circa 1846. The boy Zadok Allen tells him about what he has seen happening on Devil Reef at night, which he has seen from the cupola of his family's house. This information helps lead to the arrest of Obed Marsh and a number of his supporters from the Esoteric Order of Dagon. On the night that the Deep Ones attack the town a couple of weeks later, Zadok's father takes his gun and leaves their house through a window, to find Mowry and try to organize some resistance. He is never seen again, and Selectman Mowry presumably dies on the same terrible night.

MTAL (DCS): A place by the sea where pearls are harvested; the pearls of Mtal, dissolved in vinegar, are one of the gourmet delights offered during the orgiastic feasting that marks what will turn out to be Sarnath's last night of existence.

MTHURA (TGSK): A world in one of the 28 different galaxies which the inhabitants of planet Yaddith can visit in light-beam "envelopes."

MULLER (TT): The "boatswain" (pronounced BO-sun) or senior enlisted man on German submarine U-29 in 1917. To his commander, von Altburg-Ehrenstein, Muller is "an elderly man" and a "superstitious Alsatian swine." As a native of the disputed, mostly Catholic, border province of Alsace (now a part of France), he could have seemed a semi-French mongrel to the proud Prussian captain. It is Muller who swears that when the dead youth was thrown back into the sea, he put his arms and legs into a swimming position and sped away beneath the waves. The next day—June 19th—his talk grows increasingly wild, and he speaks of seeing dead sailors killed in U-29's earlier operations swimming by the portholes, with the drowned youth as their leader. For this kind of talk he is confined in shackles, whipped, and then released after 24 hours. Sometime during the following week, he apparently leaps overboard to die.

MUÑOZ, DR. (CA): The tenant in the apartment one floor above the narrator's apartment, in a building on West 14th Street near Eighth Avenue, Manhattan, in 1923. He is a very reclusive Spaniard, formerly a famous physician in Spain. Dr. Muñoz needs to keep his apartment's temperature at about 55° Fahrenheit—eventually as low as 28°, four degrees below the freezing temperature of water—by means of an "absorption method of ammonia cooling," a primitive precursor of modern air-conditioning, powered by a gasoline-fueled pump. The learned doctor is a perfect Spaniard of an elegant and noble kind, being "short but exquisitely proportioned, and clad in somewhat formal dress of perfect cut and fit. A high-bred face of masterful though not arrogant expression was adorned by a short iron-grey full beard, and an old-fashioned pince-nez." (A "pince-nez"—literally "pinch-nose"—is a pair of metal eyeglasses that fit tightly over the bridge of the nose, with no pieces going back over the ears; pince-nez eyeglasses were rather popular in the early 20th century.) Dr. Muñoz impresses the narrator by his intelligence, courtesy, and medical skill; at the same time, he also feels an inexplicable sense of repugnance. Eventually the doctor confides in the narrator that he has spent his life and his fortune battling against death itself, and that eighteen years in the past he had suffered a great "crisis" through which he had been nursed by Dr. Torres of Valencia,

Spain. As the year 1923 goes on, Dr. Muñoz visibly begins to decline, and to require colder and colder temperatures in his apartment. He writes mysterious letters addressed to certain people in the East Indies, and to a French medical doctor who is thought by the world to be dead. (The narrator, entrusted with these letters for mailing, later chooses to destroy them instead.) In October, Dr. Muñoz's cooling system breaks down on a very warm day, and before it can be repaired, he dissolves after scenes of increasing horror. He had, of course, died during his "crisis" in 1905, and on his last day suffered accelerated putrefaction and dissolution. It is easy to note HPL's debt to Edgar Allan Poe's horror tale *The Facts in the Case of M. Valdemar*, in which the newish science of "mesmerism" (hypnosis), not scientific technology, was the preservative force for a dead man's unnatural survival.

It is mentioned in connection with Dr. Muñoz's 1905 health crisis that the extraordinary "healing" process involved "scenes and processes not welcomed by elderly and conservative Galens." Galen (c. 130–c. 200) was a Greek physician of great skill, and a prolific author on medical and anatomical subjects, who practiced medicine in Rome for most of his adult life. For centuries after his death, until the Renaissance, his surviving works were regarded as virtually supreme authorities on medicine. In the quoted passage, HPL uses "Galens" as an equivalent for "physicians."

MUNROE, ARTHUR (LF): A news reporter whom the narrator befriends in Leffert's Corners, New York; "a dark, lean man of about thirty-five, whose education, taste, intelligence, and temperament all seemed to mark him as one not bound to conventional ideas and experiences." In September and October, 1921, the two men make historical inquiries about the vanished Martense family of sinister local lore, and interview many members of the rural district's "squatter" population. At last, on a tempest-tossed afternoon in mid-October, the two inquirers take refuge in the very same deserted hamlet where the unexplained massacre of the inhabitants took place several weeks before. It was a dark and stormy night, and Munroe takes a seat by the open window of the cabin in which they have found shelter, while the thunder continues to crash outside. After a while, the narrator discovers that something outside has chewed off Arthur Munroe's face, killing him. He buries the dead newsman secretly, letting the world believe that Munroe had simply drifted away.

The odd spelling of the name that is almost invariably given as "Monroe" points us straight in the direction of HPL's boyhood friend Harold B. Munroe. By 1921 Munroe was a deputy sheriff, and in August of that year he took HPL on an automobile excursion through the country districts around Taunton, Massachusetts, where they had played together as boys.

MURRAY, MARGARET (CC, HRH): British anthropologist (1863–1963), the author of the influential book *The Witch-Cult in Western Europe* (1921), which HPL read with interest, and to which he referred in two of his tales. An ardent advocate of rights for women, who had had to overcome tremendous obstacles to become a qualified archaeologist and anthropologist in Victorian England, Murray was perhaps the first academic to claim that the witchcraft-mania and persecution in Europe represented a concerted attack by a new, patriarchal social/ religious establishment on ancient, pre-Aryan, female-centered religions, a claim which, assisted by the modern feminist movement, has taken root in "Wiccan" and New Age-type thinking. (Modern scholars of both genders cast grave doubts both on Murray's methodology and her conclusions.) For his part, HPL responded very eagerly and seriously to the notion of hidden remnants of ancient cults, hiding beneath the surface of modern civilization, certainly a feature of *The Call of Cthulhu* and *The Horror at Red Hook*. In a letter to a friend about his tale, *The Festival*, HPL wrote: "In intimating an alien race I had in mind the survival of some clan of pre-Aryan sorcerers who preserved primitive rites like those of the witch-cult—I had just been reading Miss Murray's *The Witch-Cult in Western Europe*." (This is why the nameless narrator of the tale is self-described as "dark" and of an unspecified but clearly non-Nordic heritage.)

MUSIDES (TR): The fictitious companion and fellow-sculptor of the equally fictitious Kalos. His name is simply an adjective for "of or relating to the muses," the female personifications of the arts of sculpture, painting, history, and so on. Musides' famous statue of the goddess Pallas Athena stood on a pedestal in Athens, near the Parthenon. Unlike Kalos, Musides loves his nightly revels in the nearby town. During a competition to carve the statue of Tyche for the Greek colony of Syracuse on the island of Sicily, Musides shows some signs of jealousy over his friend's excellent work; not long afterward Kalos suddenly sickens and dies, despite Musides' constant nursing. For three more years Musides works on the great statue of Tyche, but on the night before it is to be carried in triumph to Syracuse, a strange olive-tree drops a branch down on the house, crushing it. No trace of Musides or the statue is later found.

MWANU (AJ): An elderly chieftain of the Kaliri tribe in the Congo region; he has "a highly retentive memory, a singular degree of intelligence, and an interest in old legends." Sir Arthur Jermyn meets him during a 1912–13 African expedition, and Mwanu tells him about a grey stone city in the jungle with "hybrid" inhabitants. The N'bangu tribe had conquered the place and wiped out its peculiar inhabitants, Mwanu says, and carried away the city's fetish or idol, a stuffed goddess of some kind. Mwanu also tells Sir Arthur the "very picturesque legend" about a white ape-princess and her marriage to a great white god who had come out of the west—certainly a reference (we understand) to Jermyn's ancestor, the mid-18th century English explorer Sir Wade Jermyn.

N

NAACAL LANGUAGE (TGSK): A purported "primal language" of the "Himalayan priests," studied by Harley Warren. The 20th century author Colonel James Churchward claimed that Naacal was the all-but-forgotten ancient language that he learned from a Hindu priest in India; and that understanding Naacal was his key to perceiving Muvian (*i.e.*, of or pertaining to the alleged lost continent of Mu) traces in religious symbols, myths, and traditions, from many lands. There is no Naacal language known to linguistics.

NADEK, JOSEF (CDW): An evil old man who has lived in a house with the address of Kleinstrasse 11, in the Altstadt, the oldest part of Prague (now the capital of the Czech Republic in central Europe), for more years than anyone can remember in 1928. "Josef Nadek" is, in fact, the undying Simon Orne, Joseph Curwen's old friend from 17th century Salem, Massachusetts. In his last letter to Curwen (dated February 11, 1928), Nadek asks him to obtain and send the "Saltes" of Benjamin Franklin! Charles Dexter Ward visits Nadek from the autumn of 1924 until January, 1925. In the spring of 1928, Nadek's house is mysteriously and completely destroyed, and its inhabitant vanishes without a trace and forever; presumably the work of the mysterious "No. 118."

NAMELESS CITY (NC): Remote in the uninhabited desert of the Arabian peninsula, already a lost and forgotten ruin before the beginnings of ancient Egypt and Babylon, lies the Nameless City. It may be the subject of Abdul Alhazred's inexplicable couplet: "That is not dead that can eternal lie/And with strange aeons even death may die." The narrator of the tale finds the Nameless City while wandering through the desert. Like some other frightful Lovecraftian locales (*e.g.*, R'lyeh), the city's geometry is somehow repellent in itself, indicative of its non-human origin: there were "certain *proportions* and *dimensions* in the ruins which I did not like." The narrator comes to realize that the city's inhabitants had been an tremendously ancient pre-human race of reptile-like beings. Before realization comes, he finds their relics buried out of sight, in tunnels and vaults under the surface city—just like Nathaniel Peaslee in *The Shadow Out of Time*, and quite a few other investigators in HPL's tales. From study of their historical epic wall-paintings—like those of the events of Leng in the temple of the high priest not to be described in *The*

Dream-Quest of Unknown Kadath, or the wall-carvings of the Antarctic city in *At the Mountains of Madness*—the narrator learns the history of the place. At the time he is still imagining that humans and not "grotesque reptiles" had built the city:

> Holding this view, I thought I could trace roughly a wonderful epic of the nameless city; the tale of a mighty sea-coast metropolis that ruled the world before Africa rose out of the waves, and of its struggles as the sea shrank away, and the desert crept into the fertile valley that held it. I saw its wars and triumphs, its troubles and defeats, and afterward its terrible fight against the desert when thousands of its people—here represented in allegory by the grotesque reptiles—were driven to chisel their way down through the rocks in some marvellous manner to another world whereof their prophets had told them. It was all vividly weird and realistic, and its connexion with the awesome descent I had made was unmistakable. I even recognized the passages.

"It was all vividly weird and realistic" is actually a suitable description for the best of HPL's mature fiction, and the effect he set out to create. As the narrator learns, the grotesque reptile-folk were real, not a peculiar allegory—and they are still there, at the bottom of the descent, in an underground world—like the shoggoths under the remains of the lost Antarctic city. He sees that they exactly resemble the curious mummified remains he had earlier pondered about, and believed to be totem-beasts of the humans who must have inhabited the city, when he thought:

> To convey any idea of these monstrosities is impossible. They were of the reptile kind, with body lines suggesting sometimes the crocodile, sometimes the seal, but more often nothing of which either the naturalist or the palaeontologist ever heard. In size they approximated a small man, and their fore legs bore delicate and evidently flexible feet curiously like human hands and fingers. But strangest of all were their heads, which presented a contour violating all known biological principles. To nothing can such things be well compared—in one flash I thought of comparisons as varied as the cat, the bulldog, the mythic Satyr, and the human being. [They had a] colossal and protuberant...forehead, yet the horns and the noselessness and the alligator-like jaw placed the things outside all established categories.... To crown their grotesqueness, most of them were gorgeously enrobed in the costliest of fabrics, and lavishly laden with ornaments of gold, jewels, and unknown shining metals.

NARATH (SK): Presumably a city or palace in Dreamland; in a gibe at "realism" in art and literature, HPL has Randolph Carter politely "not dissent when they [*i.e.,* "realist" authors or critics] told him that the animal pain of a stuck pig or dyspeptic ploughman in real life is a greater thing than the peerless beauty of Narath with its hundred carven gates and domes of chalcedony, which he dimly remembered from his dreams..."

NARAXA RIVER (CE, DQ): A river in Dreamland, which flows through the Valley of Ooth-Nargai, down to the city of Celephaïs.

NARG RIVER (WS): A river in the fabled land of Cathuria, full of colorful fish; it is said to flow beneath the glass floors of the palace of Cathuria.

NARGIS-HEI (DCS): The last monarch of Sarnath, a mighty and powerful emperor of many lands. He commands the gigantic banquet to be held on the 1000th anniversary of the destruction of Ib. That night he meets his doom along with the imperial city and all of its people.

NARRATIVE OF ARTHUR GORDON PYM, THE (MM): Edgar Allan Poe's sole novel-length work, written in 1838; it has a high rank among the most cryptic and bizarre works of weird fantasy; modern critics can still busy themselves arguing what it all really means. Much of the action takes place on a sailing expedition in Antarctic waters, then almost unknown; the explorers first discover a land, called Tsalal, where everything is black, even the teeth of the local people; then after some adventures they find themselves being drawn further and further south into a mysterious realm of whiteness, where even the ocean turns white and milky to the sight. Poe's story has no real ending. *The Narrative of Arthur Gordon Pym*, which brought together two of HPL's favorite youthful interests—Antarctica and the works of Poe—receives due homage in *At the Mountains of Madness*, when the graduate student Danforth expresses "queer notions about unsuspected and forbidden sources to which Poe may have had access when writing his *Arthur Gordon Pym* a century ago." Huge sea-birds in Poe's story shriek "Tekeli-li! Tekeli-li!" So do the blind penguins and the shoggoths in the subterranean caverns beneath the lost city in *At the Mountains of Madness*.

NARTHOS (QI): The rural valley where Iranon passed his childhood and early youth, and to which he finally returns at the end of his life and quest.

NASHT (DQ): One of the two priests in the Cavern of Flame, whom Randolph Carter consults at the beginning of his dream-quest.

NATH-HORTHATH (CE, DQ): A god that is worshipped in a turquoise temple in Celephaïs, by priests who are swathed in orchid blossoms.

N'BANGUS (AJ): A warlike Congo tribe that destroyed the grey stone city in the jungle, slaughtered all of its hybrid inhabitants, and finally carried away in triumph the stuffed white ape-goddess. By 1912, having become peaceful subjects of the Belgian colonial authorities, they are willing to sell this old trophy, and Monsieur Verhaeren acquires it to send to Sir Arthur Jermyn in England.

NEAPOLIS (TR): The name of the southern Italian city of Naples in ancient times, when it was founded as a Greek colony. In this tale, it is mentioned that the fame of Kalos and Musides extended "from Lydia to Neapolis," or in other words from one end of the classical Greek cultural zone to the other.

NECRONOMICON (CDW, DWH, TH, TF, DH, MM, TGSK, TD, SOT): The most familiar and beloved of all the literary inventions of HPL, who provided the following translation in a letter to his friend Harry O. Fischer, in February, 1937: "The name Necronomicon (necros, corpse; nomos, law; eikon, image = An Image [or Picture] of the Law of the Dead) occurred to me in the course of a dream, although the etymology is perfectly sound." In fact, HPL's understanding of classical Greek was small and the etymology is perfectly unsound, but that does not matter. According to his mock-historical essay "The History of the *Necronomicon*," HPL wrote that the book was composed in Arabic (with the Arabic title *Al Azif*) by the mad Arab Abdul Alhazred, who died mysteriously in 738 A.D. *Azif*, according to HPL, meant: "the word used by the Arabs to designate the nocturnal sound (made by insects) suppos'd to be the howling of daemons." HPL did not read or understand Arabic, and got the word from the footnotes in the 18th century English edition of William Beckford's Arabo-Gothic horror novel *Vathek.*

The *Necronomicon* was secretly translated into Greek in about 950 by Theodorus Philetas, a scholar of Constantinople, who gave the book its familiar name; later, in 1050, Patriarch Michael of the Orthodox church in Constantinople ordered the burning of all copies. However, at least one survived to be translated into Latin by the western European scholar Olaus Wormius, in 1228. But in the year 1232, Pope Gregory XI, occupying the same kind of preeminent position in the Catholic Church that Patriarch Michael once did in the Orthodox system, ordered the suppression—that is, the destruction—of both the Greek and Latin translations. Nonetheless an edition of the Wormius translation was printed in Germany during the 15th century, and the Greek version was reprinted in the first half of the 16th century in Italy. A Spanish translation from the Latin appeared in the 1600s, and we learn also of a English version translated by Dr. John Dee, who died in 1608—Wilbur Whateley inherited a copy of this translation in the early 20th century. At some point the original Arabic text was lost forever, and the various editions in western European languages all stem from the sturdy Latin of old Olaus Wormius.

Despite all this past publishing activity, the *Necronomicon* is still an extremely rare book by the early 20th century. There are known copies under lock and key in the libraries of the British Museum, the *Bibliotheque National* in Paris, Harvard University, Miskatonic University, and the University of Buenos Aires in Argentina. A few copies are also known to be in private hands; for example, it is mentioned in the "History of the *Necronomicon*" that the Boston artist Pickman had owned a copy of the book.

In *The Hound*, the grave-robbing aesthetes who have stolen a peculiar amulet from a medieval grave in Holland note that "We read much in Alhazred's *Necronomicon* about its properties, and about the relation of ghouls' souls to the objects it symbolised; and were disturbed by what we read." Previously they had read that the winged-hound shape on the amulet was "the ghastly soul-symbol of the corpse-eating cult of inaccessible Leng, in Central Asia." The shape, according to "the old Arab daemonologist" (*i.e.*, Abdul Alhazred) was "drawn from some obscure supernatural manifestation of the souls of those who vexed and gnawed at the dead." (This passage was, incidentally, the first mention of the *Necronomicon* in Lovecraft's tales.)

The nameless narrator of *The Festival*, while waiting in the ground-floor room of the seventh house on the left in Green Lane, notices among other old books on a table, "worst of all, the unmentionable *Necronomicon* of the mad Arab Abdul Alhazred, in Olaus Wormius' forbidden Latin translation; a book which I had never seen, but of which I had heard monstrous things whispered." The old man from the house takes the book with him for the procession through Kingsport, and in the cavern beneath the hilltop church he holds it over his head at certain times during the ritual, whereupon the throngs of weirdly cloaked figures do "groveling obeisance." Much later, after the narrator has been found on the beach at Orange Point and taken to a hospital, Arkham doctors use their influence to obtain Miskatonic University's well-guarded copy for him to study. This helps him to recall the words that so haunted him when he read them in the house on Green Lane, which he provides a translation for:

> The nethermost caverns...are not for the fathoming of eyes that see; for their marvels are strange and terrific. Cursed be the ground where dead thoughts live new and oddly bodied, and evil the mind that is held by no head. Wisely did Ibn Schacabao say, that happy is the tomb where no wizard has lain, and happy the town at night whose wizards are all ashes. For it is of old rumour that the soul of the devil-bought hastes not from his charnel clay, but fats and instructs *the very worm that gnaws;* till out of corruption horrid life springs, and the dull scavengers of earth wax crafty to vex it and swell monstrous to plague it. Great holes are secretly digged where earth's pores ought to suffice, and things have learnt to walk that ought to crawl.

Walter Gilman, Miskatonic University undergraduate student in *The Dreams in the Witch House*, was barred by the professors from consulting the *Necronomicon* in the library any more, "but all these precautions came rather late in the day, so that Gilman had some terrible hints...to correlate with his abstract formulae on the properties of space and the linkage of dimensions known and unknown." Later he links the "thin, monotonous piping of an unseen flute" in his cosmic dreams with "what he had read in the *Necronomicon* about the mindless entity Azathoth, which rules all time and space from a curiously envisioned black throne at the center of Chaos." Later, the witch Keziah Mason's chanting as she prepared to sacrifice the stolen baby Ladislas Wolejko was "in a language which Gilman could not understand, but which seemed like something guardedly quoted in the *Necronomicon.*"

In *The Case of Charles Dexter Ward*, Joseph Curwen in the 18th century is discovered by his visitor Mr. Merritt to own a copy of the *Necronomicon* disguised as a book called the *Qanoon-E-Islam*. Later, in a letter to Simon Orne, Curwen mentions "I am foll'g [following] out what Borellus saith, and haue [have] Helpe in Abdool Al-Hazred his VII. Booke." His comrade in magic Simon Orne (then known as Jedediah) writes back that "I have not ye Chymicall art to followe Borellus, and owne my Self confounded by ye VII. Booke of ye Necronomicon that you recommende."

In *The Dunwich Horror*, when the Dunwich rustics recall how the hills once shook when Old Whateley "shrieked the dreadful name of *Yog-Sothoth* in the midst of a circle of stones with a great book open in his arms before him," we can be pretty certain what that book was. In the winter of 1927, having failed to obtain the loan of a copy of the *Necronomicon* from any library that owned it, Wilbur Whateley visits the Miskatonic University library in person, bringing his "priceless but imperfect copy of Dr. Dee's English version" and intending to look at the library's Latin translation "with the aim of discovering a certain passage which would have come on the 751st page of his own defective volume"—as his grandfather had instructed him on his deathbed. He dies not long afterwards in an attempt to steal the book by night. Later, Dr. Armitage consults the *Necronomicon* extensively in his striving to undo what the Whateleys had done.

During his ship's approach to the coast of Antarctica in *At the Mountains of Madness*, Professor Dyer finds the scenery peculiarly disturbing:

> Something about the scene reminded me of the strange and disturbing Asian paintings of Nicholas Roerich, and of the still stranger and more disturbing descriptions of the evilly fabled plateau of Leng which occur in the dreaded *Necronomicon* of the mad Arab Abdul Alhazred. I was rather sorry, later on, that I had ever looked into that monstrous book at the college library.

Later we learn that the graduate student Danforth, Dyer's eventual partner in exploring the lost city of the Old Ones, was one of the "the few who have ever dared go completely through that worm-riddled copy of the *Necronomicon*" in the Miskatonic library. The professor also notes that Abdul Alhazred "in his frightful *Necronomicon*" had hinted at the existence of shoggoths, but said they were not to be found on earth "except in the dreams of those who had chewed a certain alkaloidal herb." The book had also hinted that the winged, star-headed things were "the makers and enslavers of [earth] life, and...the originals of the fiendish elder myths" mentioned in the *Necronomicon* and the Pnakotic Manuscripts. In his messages back to the base camp, Professor Lake did more than hint at the same thing.

In *Through the Gates of the Silver Key,* we learn that "a whole chapter in the forbidden *Necronomicon* of the mad Arab Abdul Alhazred had taken on significance" for Randolph Carter, when he finally deciphered the designs engraved on the Silver Key. Carter also remembers what "the monstrous *Necronomicon*" had said about "the Guide," the Most Ancient One, in the void:

> And while there are those...who have dared to seek glimpses beyond the Veil, and to accept HIM as a Guide, they would have been prudent had they avoided commerce with HIM; for it is written in the Book of Thoth how terrific is the price for a single glimpse. Nor may those who pass ever return, for in the Vastnesses transcending our world are Shapes of darkness that seize and bind. The Affair that shambleth about in the night [a translation of *negotium perambulans in tenebris*, a phrase in the Vulgate (the original Latin translation of the Bible), which provided the title of a horror tale by the English author E.F. Benson (1867–1940), which HPL justly admired. The King James Version English translation of the phrase, which occurs in the Bible at Psalms 91:6, is "the pestilence that walketh in darkness," but this is hardly adequate], the Evil that defieth the Elder Sign, the Herd that stand watch at the secret portal each tomb is known to have, and that thrive on that which groweth out of the tenants within—all these Blacknesses are lesser than HE Who guardeth the Gateway; HE Who will guide the rash one beyond all the worlds into the Abyss of unnamable Devourers. For HE is 'UMR AT-TAWIL, The Most Ancient One, which the scribe rendereth as THE PROLONGED OF LIFE.

Professor Nathaniel Peaslee, in discussing the human minds who had returned from time with the Great Race over the millennia, wrote:

> Some minds recalled more than others, and the chance joining of memories had at rare times brought hints of the forbidden past to future ages....
> There probably never was a time when groups or cults did not secretly cherish certain of these hints. In the *Necronomicon* the presence of such a cult among human beings was suggested—a cult that sometimes gave aid to minds voyaging down the aeons from the days of the Great Race.

The existence of such a cult probably explains the "lean, dark, curiously foreign-looking man" who visited Peaslee's Arkham house in an automobile on Friday, September 26, 1913, and no doubt took away the inexplicable machine from the sitting-room table, and the "hesitant, foreign voice" that called from a phone booth at Boston's North Station the next morning, telling Peaslee's physician, Dr. Wilson, to go to Peaslee's house and bring him out of "a faint."

In *The Thing on the Doorstep*, Edward Derby once tells his friend Daniel Upton: "Some people know things about the universe that nobody ought to know, and can do things that nobody ought to be able to do. Today I'd burn that damned *Necronomicon* and all the rest if I were librarian at Miskatonic."

NEGROES, TWO (HW): Cadavers for medical training and research were once very hard to come by, when few people were willing to donate their mortal remains to science. In a situation that was not unknown in real life at the time, the Miskatonic University medical school in 1904 employs private contractors to keep the school discreetly supplied with corpses that won't be missed, snatched from local cemeteries. However, for their own personal experiments, medical student Herbert West and his comrade have to find dead bodies on their own. In referring to the medical school's "two negroes," HPL may have been thinking about "Jess," the memorable African-American corpse-locator for a medical college in Ambrose Bierce's classic tale of the macabre, *One Summer Night.*

NEMED (MB): "Only the wooded hills" buried the ancient Greek city under the moon-bog by the time when "the men of Nemed swept down from Scythia in their thirty ships."

In the fictional Irish "Book of Invaders" (*Leabhar Gabhala*), it is written: "Now Ireland was waste thirty years after the plague-burial of Partholan's people, till Nemed son of Agnoman...of the Greeks of Scythia, reached it."

NEMESIS (TH, HD): According to the nameless narrator of *The Hound:*

> Down unlit and illimitable corridors of eldritch phantasy sweeps the black, shapeless Nemesis that drives me to self-annihilation [*i.e.*, suicide]. May heaven forgive the folly and morbidity which led us both to so monstrous a fate!

In Greek mythology, *Nemesis* was a goddess who personified the revenge of the gods for crimes against sacred law; she was thought to pursue malefactors to their doom. In this tale, the metaphorical "Nemesis" comes in the form of the spectral hound which pursues the grave robber St. John and his companion. The poem-excerpt labeled

"Nemesis" at the beginning of *The Haunter of the Dark* is from a longer poem of that name, written in the early morning hours after Halloween, 1917, by HPL himself.

NEPAL (TGSK): In attempting to translate the "R'lyehian" hieroglyphics copied from a missing parchment scroll, Randolph Carter (hiding out in Boston while trapped in Zkauba's body) "made great strides through a book he imported from Nepal." Nepal is a small country in the Himalaya mountain range between India and China.

NEPHREN-KA (TO, CDW, HD): A fictitious Egyptian pharaoh, associated with some gruesome behavior. In *The Outsider*, the narrator eventually finds his destiny in playing "amongst the catacombs of Nephren-Ka in the sealed and unknown city of Hadoth by the Nile." In *The Case of Charles Dexter Ward*, Mr. Hutchinson (also known as "Count Ferenczy") uses "Nephren-Ka nai Hadoth" as a kind of closing salutation in a 1928 letter to Joseph Curwen. In *The Haunter of the Dark*, it is explained that the pharaoh Nephren-Ka obtained the Shining Trapezohedron, then "built around it a temple with a windowless crypt, and did that which caused his name to be stricken from all monuments and records," neatly explaining why there *isn't* any known pharaoh of this name! The temple was destroyed by the next pharaoh, and the Shining Trapezohedron remained buried under the ruins until the 19th century A.D., when it came into the hands of the American scholar Enoch Bowen. HPL had an abiding interest in ancient Egyptian history, and delighted in making up vaguely Egyptian names, of which "Nyarlathotep" (created in one of his dreams) is probably the most familiar.

NEPTUNE (WD, TGSK): In his journey through the solar system, Randolph Carter in the body of Zkauba "passed close to Neptune and glimpsed the hellish white fungi that spot it." In *The Whisperer in Darkness*, the thing pretending to be Henry W. Akeley tells Dr. Wilmarth that among the cylinders on the shelves include the brains of "two beings from Neptune (God! if you could see the body this type has on its own planet!)."

NEWBURYPORT (SOI): A small seaport in Massachusetts at the mouth of the Merrimack River. HPL visited the town for the first time in 1921. Newburyport was to a large extent the model for "Innsmouth," and the narrator of the tale commences his fateful day-trip to Innsmouth from Newburyport.

NEWBURY STREET (PM): A real avenue in the fashionable Back Bay section of Boston; the artist Pickman has his "official" studio here, although his secret studio where he does the ghoul-portraits is in an old building in North End.

NEWFANE (WD): A Vermont village, some fifteen miles northwest of Brattleboro. It is the last settlement before the wild hills and the Akeley farm; HPL, who visited the community in 1928, called it a "quaint and sightly" place.

NGRANEK (OG, DQ): A very high lava mountain on the island of Oriab, in Dreamland. On one side, some giant hand has carved a face like one of earth's gods. Randolph Carter climbs the forbidden mountain to look upon this wonder, and sees the great face, larger than a large temple: "a god chiseled by the hands of gods." It has long, narrow eyes, long-lobed ears, a thin nose and pointed chin. After he has seen it, Carter is suddenly seized and carried off by one of the guardian night-gaunts who live in caves near the mountain peak.

NHHNGR (DH): *See* "Yr."

NIG (CDW): The "venerable and beloved black cat" in the Ward household. During young Ward's periods of occult chanting in the attic, the feline sometimes "bristled and arched its back perceptibly." On Good Friday, 1927, when Charles Dexter Ward's occult activities climax in the resurrection of Joseph Curwen, Nig's "stiffening form" is later found dead in the basement, "with staring eyes and fear-distorted mouth."

NIGGER-MAN (RW): The favorite of the five cats owned by Mr. de la Poer. His acute and persistent reactions to the spectral rats in the walls led his owner and Captain Norrys to discover the evidence of the subterranean vaults beneath Exham Priory, and the cat accompanies the exploration party into those dark chambers. After several hours, Nigger-Man is found leaping and biting at Mr. de la Poer's neck as he chews on the dead body of Norrys; and in his cell in the insane asylum, Mr. de la Poer laments that the cat has been taken away from him.

Since this cat's name raises more eyebrows today than it does laughter, it should be noted that at the time—the year 1923—most of the American reading public would have thought it an unexceptional name for a black cat; some large percentage of the same reading public would have thought it an unexceptional thing to call a black man. The only pet that HPL ever owned (although he befriended many a prowling feline) really *was* a black cat called Nigger-Man, during his childhood in his grandfather's mansion at 454 Angell Street. In later years, HPL praised this cat as "one of the most fascinating and understanding creatures I've ever seen.... He used to talk in a genuine language... He used to play ball with me—kicking a large rubber sphere back at me...with all four feet as he lay on the floor." This wonderful and sagacious animal some-how vanished in the terrible year of 1904, when HPL's beloved grandfa-ther died and the big old house was sold, propelling the sensitive youth and his mother into the genteel poverty which would persist for the rest of his life.

NIGHT-GAUNTS (DQ): Strange harpies of Dreamland, they are eye-less, faceless, noiseless black beings with smooth, oily, whale-like skins, ugly prehensile claws, membranous bat-wings, and barbed tails. They are cold, damp, and slippery, bizarrely strong, and can fly forever without tiring. Their master is primal Nodens, and their task is to guard certain significant places from curious visitors. They seize intruders and carry them off; if there is resistance, they *tickle* their prey, with subtle strokes, until the resistance ceases. "All they ever do is clutch and fly and tickle; that was the way of the night-gaunts." They carry their captives away to the subterranean abyss of the vale of Pnath, and dump them there among the bone-heaps, the bholes, and the eternal blackness. The ghouls of Dreamland have a sort of partnership with the night-gaunts, and at one point a fleet of the flying creatures carries an army of ghouls to the moonbeasts' rock for battle, then fly the surviving moonbeasts away to the vale of Pnath, a dreadful fate. Afterwards, night-gaunts bear Randolph Carter and his ghouls all the way to Kadath.

HPL explained the night-gaunts thusly, in a letter to a friend:

> When I was 6 or 7 I used to be tormented constantly with a peculiar type of recurrent nightmare in which a monstrous race of entities (called by me "night-gaunts"—I don't know where I got hold of the name) used to snatch me up by the stomach & carry me off through infinite leagues of black air over the towers of dead and horrible cities. They would finally get me into a grey void where I could see the needle-like pinnacles of enormous moun-tains miles below. Then they would let me drop—& as I gained momentum in my Icarus-like plunge I would start awake in such a panic that I hated to think of sleeping again. The "night-gaunts" were black, lean, rubbery things with horns, barbed tails, and *no faces at all*. (Undoubtedly I derived the image from the jumbled memory of Doré drawings (largely the illus-trations to "Paradise Lost") which fascinated me in waking hours.)

NIR (OG, CU, DQ): A town near Ulthar, with one broad main street, in the comfortable lands on the plain of the river Skai. It is on the nearer side of Ulthar and was the furthest that Randolph Carter had traveled in Dreamland, before starting his quest to find Kadath.

NITH (CU): The lean and observant notary (meaning a legal official) of the town of Ulthar.

NITHRA (QI): One of the two rivers flowing through Iranon's longed-for city of Aira; the other river is the Kra, which is smaller than the Nithra.

NITOKRIS (TO, UP): A semi-legendary Egyptian queen, described in the *History* of the Greek traveler/author Herodotus, who wrote during the 5th century B.C. According to a fanciful tale that was already old when Herodotus heard it, Nitokris invited all of her enemies to a feast held in a subterranean chamber; and at a certain point she gave a signal and some barriers were opened to let in the waters of the river Nile to drown her foes. In both of HPL's tales, the narrator sees the "ghoul-queen" Nitokris. (During the 1920s, the pulp magazine *Weird Tales* published a rather clumsily-written tale based on this legend—*The Vengeance of Nitocris*—by a teenager called Tennessee Williams, later to become a famous American playwright. As probably one of the few people who was both familiar with Herodotus and a fairly faithful reader of *Weird Tales*, HPL may well have enjoyed this tale.)

N'KAI (WD): A subterranean world like K'n-yan; both places were invented for *The Mound,* a tale HPL helped a ghost-writing client to create. N'kai is a deep subterranean abyss. In *The Whisperer in the Darkness,* the fake Henry Akeley tells Professor Wilmarth of "black, lightless N'kai. It's from N'kai that frightful Tsathoggua came—you know, the amorphous, toad-like god-creature mentioned in the Pnakotic Manuscripts and the *Necronomicon...*"

"NO. 118" (CDW): During his odyssey in the cellars or catacombs beneath what was once Joseph Curwen's farmhouse on Pawtuxet Road, Dr. Marinus B. Willett finally enters the horrid chamber where Curwen had reconstituted and resurrected "essential Saltes" into wise men of the past, and interrogated them with "savage whips" and torture instruments. Because Curwen (in the form of Charles Dexter Ward) had been interrupted by psychiatrists and committed to a mental hospital while in the middle of his latest operations, there is an open dish of "Saltes" in the room, sitting next to an empty jar tagged "No. 118." While standing in the chamber, Willett idly recites the invocation of the Dragon's Tail, "Ascending Node," and to his horror No. 118 materializes from the dust. No. 118 is a bearded man with intense eyes, and when he departs he leaves Dr. Willett—who has fainted away—a note: *Corvinus necandus est. Cadaver aq forti dissolvendum, nec aliqd retinendum. Tace ut potes.* ("Curwen must be killed. The body must be dissolved in aqua fortis, nor must anything be retained. Keep silence as best you are able." *Aqua fortis*, Latin for "strong water," was what the medieval alchemists called nitric acid, a very powerful acidic compound.) The note is written in the "pointed Saxon minuscules of the eight or ninth century A.D.," suggesting that No. 118 is an English or German sage or wizard of the Dark Ages; that is all we ever learn about him. Within the year, Curwen's collaborators Orne and Hutchinson are mysteriously eradicated along with their homes in Europe. No. 118 is not heard from again. But was No. 118 even the person Joseph Curwen though he would be? As Dr. Willett teased Curwen, quoting from Simon Orne's letter of February 11, 1928: "stones are all changed now in nine grounds [graveyards] out of ten. You are never sure until you question!"

NODENS (SHH, DQ): Nodens is one of the only likable Lovecraft Mythos figures; he seems to be an archaic god of indistinct but great powers. In *The Strange High House in the Mist*, he appears—along with Neptune, the Roman god of the sea, counterpart to the Greeks' Poseidon—from the sea, spectacularly: "upon dolphins' backs was balanced a vast crenulate shell wherein rode the grey and awful form of primal Nodens, Lord of the Great Abyss. Then hoary Nodens reached forth a wizened hand and helped Olney and his host into the vast shell." In *The Dream-Quest of Unknown Kadath*, it is said of the night-gaunts that even the Great Ones fear them, and that their ruler is not the "crawling chaos" Nyarlathotep, but immemorial Nodens. Thus Randolph Carter feels that he can fly a night-gaunt all the way to Kadath. Later, during Carter's wild flight home from Kadath, as he plummeted through space, "archaic Nodens was bellowing his guidance from unhinted deeps," and "raised a howl of triumph" when Carter landed home safely and Nyarlathotep's malign desires were frustrated.

One commentator has observed that "in Celtic mythology, Nodens (also called Nudd or Nuada) is a god of fertility and medicine and a protector of fishermen." The *Larousse World Mythology* notes that this deity, by whatever name, was a member of the *Tuatha de Danann* or Celtic pantheon of pagan Ireland: "certain characteristics of the Roman Jupiter can be found in Nuada."

Most important for HPL, perhaps, is that Arthur Machen mentioned Nodens in his famous tale *The Great God Pan*, as the subject of an inscription at a Roman ruin in Wales, which mysteriously reads: "To the great god Nodens (the god of the Great Deep or Abyss) Flavius Senilis has erected this pillar on account of the marriage which he saw beneath the shade." Machen's fictitious inscription was doubtlessly inspired by a real one found at the English Roman-era temple of Nodens in Lydney Park, Gloucestershire, especially the mosaic-floor inscription which reads: "'For the god Nodens, Titus Flavius Senilis, officer in charge of the supply-depot of the fleet, laid this pavement with money offerings."

NOOSENECK HILL (SH): This is a real district in Rhode Island, with a wonderful name suggesting the noose of a gallows rope. "Mercy [Dexter] should have known better than to hire anyone from the Nooseneck Hill country, for that remote bit of backwoods was then, as now, a seat of the most uncomfortable superstitions." The superstitious domestic servant in question, Ann White, came from "that part of North Kingstown now set off as the township of Exeter." Nooseneck, Rhode Island, a rural village in the southern part of the state, is about ten miles cross-country from the village of Exeter. As HPL mentions in this tale, as late as 1892 some Exeter residents exhumed the body of a young woman—a supposed vampire—and her heart was cut out and burned. The young woman's name was Mercy Brown, and perhaps Mercy Dexter's first name was inspired by hers.

NORRYS, CAPTAIN EDWARD (RW): A "plump" young man, a member of the Norrys family which owns the former lands of the de la Poers in England, along with the ruins of Exham Priory, the one-time family seat of the de la Poers. Captain Norrys, a wartime officer of the Royal Flying Corps (the World War I precursor of the Royal Air Force), meets the American aviator Alfred Delapore in 1917, and tells him some of the colorful legends about the de la Poers and Exham Priory. In December, 1921, Captain Norrys hosts Alfred's father at Anchester, and assists him in gathering plans and information for the renovation of the castle, meanwhile collecting local tales about the family and their home. On July 23 and 24, 1923, after moving into Exham Priory, Mr. de la Poer (formerly Delapore) visits Captain Norrys and complains about rat noises in the restored castle. During his second visit, "stout" Norrys lends Mr. de la Poer some rat traps and "Paris green" (an extremely poisonous, green-colored compound of copper and arsenic, then in use for vermin control). On the 26th, Captain Norrys spends the night at Exham Priory and helps to explore the Roman sub-cellar. The two men travel to London together to recruit a group of expert investigators. On August 7th, the "fat-faced" Norrys joins the other men in penetrating the subterranean caverns full of bones: "used as he was to the trenches" (*i.e.*, to the hideous trench-warfare of the First World War), Norrys is badly shocked by what they find there. At some point he wanders off on his own; hours later, Mr. de la Poer is found crouching in the dark over Norrys' "plump, half-eaten body." This cannibal moment has been prefigured by the stress on Norrys' corpulence, and by an earlier dream of Mr. de la Poer in which the "flabby features" of one of the manlike beasts in the grotto bear a resemblance to Norrys that Mr. de la Poer mentally suppresses.

NORTH BURIAL GROUND (CDW, SH): A cemetery on Branch Avenue in Providence, established in 1700 and now on the National Register of Historic Places. In *The Case of Charles Dexter Ward,* the bodies of John Brown and James Manning, (two leaders of the actions against Joseph Curwen in 1771) are interred here, among many other prominent citizens of old Providence, including Sarah Helen Power Whitman, the local poet courted by Edgar Allan Poe in 1848–49. Human remains from the even older private graveyards on Back Street and elsewhere in the vicinity were transferred there early in the 18th century, *except for* (in *The Shunned House*) the bones of the Roulet family, which remain under the Shunned House when it is constructed. It is mentioned that the fictitious William and Rhoby Dexter Harris were buried at North Burial Ground in 1765 and 1773, respectively. In *The Case of Charles Dexter Ward*, in late March, 1927, young Ward hires four men to dig up Joseph Curwen's lead casket from an unmarked grave at this cemetery, and transport it to his attic. In mid-June of the same year, the grave of Ezra Weeden is excavated and rifled, with unfortunate consequences for the late Ezra. At about 2:00 a.m. on April 11, 1928, Dr. Willett goes to the North Burial Ground and buries Charles Dexter Ward's ashes in the Ward family plot, escaping the usual fruitless pursuit of Robert Hart, night watchman.

NORTH POINT (WS): The cape near Kingsport where Basil Elton, his father, and his grandfather served as lighthouse-keepers.

NORTON MINE (TJR): A gold mine in the fictitious Cactus Mountains, somewhere in the American West.

NOTON, MOUNT (PO): A mountain within sight of the city of Olathoë, in ancient Lomar.

NOVA PERSEI (BWS): A nova or exploded star, which indicates that the alien being once trapped in Joe Slater's body has escaped to outer space to wreak "cataclysmic vengeance" on its cosmic foe. *Nova Persei*, the Perseus Nova (or to give it its scientific designation, GRO J0422+32) does exist and was discovered in 1901 as HPL described. Although the spectacular nova faded in a few weeks, it has given rise to a strange gaseous nebula, known to astronomers as the "Firework Nebula" or "GK Per."

As stated in this tale (in the words of the contemporary astronomer and popular-science author Garrett P. Serviss):

> On February 22, 1901, a marvellous new star was discovered by Dr. Anderson, of Edinburgh, *not very far from Algol*. No star had been visible at that point before. Within twenty-four hours the stranger had become so

bright that it outshone Capella. In a week or two it had visibly faded, and in the course of a few months it was hardly discernable with the naked eye.

"NOYES, MR." (WD): A mysterious person who meets Professor Wilmarth at the Brattleboro, Vermont railroad station on September 12, 1928, stating that he is a friend of Henry Akeley. He is not over middle age, fashionably dressed like a city man, with a small, dark mustache and a cultivated manner of speaking. He drives a powerful automobile with Massachusetts license plates. While driving Wilmarth to the Akeley farm, he seems very curious to learn all that Professor Wilmarth has learned about the situation. That evening, Wilmarth learns that Mr. Noyes is one of the human agents for the Mi-Go, whose voice had been recorded by Akeley in 1915, while Noyes was leading a Sabbat-ritual in the forest. Professor Wilmarth hears Noyes' "suave Bostonian tones" again downstairs that night, talking with two of the Mi-Go; and during his escape he passes Noyes while the latter is sleeping in the living room.

For what it is worth, in 1692 the minister of the First Church, at Salem, Massachusetts, was an early and active participant in the witchcraft investigations of that year; his unusual name was Nicholas Noyes.

NUG-SOTH (SOT): One of the captive minds encountered by Wingate Peaslee, among the Great Race. He is "a magician of the dark conquerors of 16,000 A.D."

NYARLATHOTEP (RW, CDW, DQ, WD, HD, DWH): Azathoth's deputy—although HPL's conception of the character varied over the years—he is the "crawling chaos." The name is vaguely Egyptian; "-hotep" was a frequent suffix to men's names in ancient Egypt, such as that of the famous pyramid architect Imhotep. In the prose poem *Nyarlathotep* (1920), where the pseudo-god was first unveiled in print, HPL hinted that he had been one of the Ethiopian rulers who conquered Egypt some 2700 years ago, and ruled for a few generations as what is known as the 25th Dynasty. The name, HPL wrote, came to him in a dream, a dream in which he read a friend's letter that said: "Don't fail to see Nyarlathotep if he comes to Providence. He is horrible—horrible beyond anything you can imagine—but wonderful. He haunts one for hours afterward.... I am still shuddering at what he showed." In *Nyarlathotep*, Nyarlathotep appears as modern-day "itinerant showman or lecturer" who shows a large public audience cinematic images that drive them all mad.

Mr. de la Poer in *The Rats in the Walls* referred to "grinning caverns of earth's centre where Nyarlathotep, the mad faceless god, howls blindly in the darkness to the piping of two amorphous flute players."

But this description reads more like that of Azathoth. In *The Dreams in the Witch House*, Nyarlathotep appeared as the real Black Man of so much witchcraft lore, the master of Keziah Mason and her familiar, Brown Jenkin. As seen by Gilman and other witnesses, he was "a tall, lean man of dead black colouration [*sic*] but without the slightest sign of negroid features; wholly devoid of either hair or beard, and wearing as his only garment a shapeless robe of some heavy black fabric." Gilman could not see the Black Man's feet, but assumed them to be shod somehow, as clicking sounds were heard when he moved along a floor. (Claws? Cloven hooves?) Trying to escape from the child-kidnapping in Orne's Gangway on the night of April 28, Gilman was "seized and choked" by the Black Man, and awoke in his own bed with dark, livid marks on his throat. At dawn on May Eve, the Arkham police raid "some curious revellers in a ravine beyond Meadow Hill," but all escaped, including one participant described as "a huge negro."

Infinitely variable, Nyarlathotep makes a glamorous appearance in *The Dream-Quest of Unknown Kadath*. After escaping Nyarlathotep's servants, the moonbeasts, Randolph Carter finally meets the deputy of the Other Gods, in Kadath: "a tall, slim figure with the young face of an antique Pharaoh, gay with prismatic robes and crowned with a golden pshent... [Egyptian headdress] whose proud carriage and swart [dark] features had in them the fascination of a dark god or a fallen archangel, and around whose eyes there lurked the languid sparkle of a capricious sense of humor." Nyarlathotep delivers what must be (considering the circumstances, and the source) the most unexpected and unlikely tribute to New England ever voiced:

> There is Providence, quaint and lordly on its seven hills over the blue harbour, with terraces of green leading up to steeples and citadels of living antiquity.... Cool vales in Concord, cobbled lanes in Portsmouth, twilight bends of rustic New-Hampshire roads where giant elms half-hide white farmhouse walls.... Vistas of distant steepled towns and hills beyond hills along the North Shore, hushed stony slopes and low ivied cottages in the lee of huge boulders in Rhode-Island's back country. Scent of the sea and fragrance of the fields; spell of the dark woods and joy of the orchards and gardens at dawn.

Fickle and capricious to the last, he tries to send Carter to his doom while pretending to help him homewards, but seems not overly disappointed when this scheme fails.

The Mi-Go of Yuggoth and Vermont, it is said, worship Nyarlathotep. Their English-language ritual prayers, recorded by Henry Akeley, includes the following phrases: "To Nyarlathotep, Mighty Messenger, must all things be told. Nyarlathotep, Great Messenger, bringer of strange joy to Yuggoth, through the void, Father of the Million Favoured Ones," et cetera. Robert Blake suggests in his journal that The Haunter of the Dark is an avatar of Nyarlathotep, who took the form of man in ancient "Khem" (Egypt).

NYTHON (TGSK): A fictitious triple star, somewhere in space; entities from Yaddith could travel to its solar system in light-beam envelopes.

O

O'BRIEN, KID (HW): Low-quality professional boxer, described as "a lubberly and now quaking youth with a most un-Hibernian hooked nose." In an illegal prize fight in Bolton, Massachusetts, this Jewish boxer—HPL's "hooked nose" reference can probably be understood in no other way—knocks out and accidentally kills Buck ("The Harlem Smoke") Robinson.

OGROTHAN (DQ): A city in Dreamland where dressed onyx blocks from Inganok are popular trade items.

OLATHOË (PO, DQ, QI): A great city built from marble, between the peaks of Noton and Kadiphonek, in the prehistoric northern land of Lomar. In *Polaris*, it is the city under attack by the squat, yellow-skinned, savage Inutos, and defended by General Alos some 26,000 years ago. The men of Olathoë are tall, grey-eyed, and of noble bearing, and consider themselves to be the bravest of all the Lomarian race. Olathoë or Lomar seem to have been the origin-place of the Pnakotic Manuscripts, which an ancient zoog in the enchanted forest tells Randolph Carter have been made by "waking men in forgotten boreal [northern] kingdoms and borne into the land of dreams" when Olathoë was conquered by the yellow hordes and the land of Lomar fell. In *The Quest of Iranon*, Iranon tells Romnod "I...have dwelt long in Olathoë in the land of Lomar."

OLD ONES (CC, DH, MM, SOT, SOI): "Old Ones" is a confusing term to define, partly because HPL used it confusingly. It has at least two completely different uses.

In *The Call of Cthulhu*, the Cthulhu-cultists captured in a police raid near New Orleans in 1907, told interrogators that they worshipped:

> ...the Great Old Ones who lived ages before there were any men, and who came to the young world out of the sky. Those Old Ones were gone now, inside the earth and under the sea; but their dead bodies had told their secrets in dreams to the first men, who formed a cult which had never died.

The half-breed worshipper Castro tells the New Orleans detectives:

> These Great Old Ones...were not composed altogether of flesh and blood. They had shape...but that shape was not made of matter. When the stars

were right, They could plunge from world to world through the sky; but when the stars were wrong, They could not live. But although They no longer lived, They would never really die.

During the winter of 1927–28, in *The Dunwich Horror*, Wilbur Whateley visits the Miskatonic University library to look at its Latin edition of the *Necronomicon*, to locate "a kind of formula or incantation" which should have come on the 751st page of his damaged and imperfect copy of the Dee translation. The passage is devoted to the sinister view of the Old Ones. It is also the longest *Necronomicon* quote in HPL's works:

> Nor is it to be thought, that man is either the oldest or the last of earth's masters, or that the common bulk of life and substance walks alone. The Old Ones were, the Old Ones are, and the Old Ones shall be. Not in the spaces we know, but *between* them, They walk serene and primal, undimensioned and to us unseen. *Yog-Sothoth* knows the gate. *Yog-Sothoth* is the gate. *Yog-Sothoth* is the key and guardian of the gate. Past, present, future, all are one in *Yog-Sothoth*. He knows where the Old Ones broke through of old, and where They shall break through again. He knows where They have trod earth's fields, and where They still tread them, and why no one can behold Them as They tread. By Their smell can men sometimes know Them near, but of Their semblance can no man know, *saving only in the features of those They have begotten on mankind*; and of those are there many sorts, differing in likeness from man's truest eidolon to that shape without sight or substance which is *Them*. They walk unseen and foul in lonely places where the Words have spoken and the Rites howled through at their Seasons. The wind gibbers with Their voices, and the earth mutters with Their consciousness. They bend the forest and crush the city, yet may not forest or city behold the hand that smites. Kadath in the cold waste hath known Them, and what man knows Kadath? The ice desert of the South and the sunken isles of Ocean hold stones whereon Their seal is engraven, but who hath seen the deep frozen city or the sealed tower long garlanded with seaweed and barnacles? Great Cthulhu is Their cousin, yet can he spy Them only dimly. *Iä! Shub-Niggurath!* As a foulness shall ye know Them. Their hand is at your throats, yet ye see Them not; and Their habitation is even one with your guarded threshold. Yog-Sothoth is the key to the gate, whereby the spheres meet. Man rules now where They ruled once; They shall soon rule where man rules now. After summer is winter, and after winter summer. They wait patient and potent, for here shall They rule again.

The Old Ones described in this passage are clearly different in conception from those of *The Call of Cthulhu*. Unlike Cthulhu's tribe, they do not seem to be confined anywhere, but to ramble widely through the universe, although for the moment they cannot "break through" to our world. Cthulhu is demoted to "Their cousin" who cannot even see them clearly.

Yet another vision of "Old Ones" comes in *At the Mountains of Madness*. In this tale, after their preliminary explorations in the Antarctic lost city of primordial age, Professor Dyer and his faithful graduate student Danforth come to a shocking realization about its builders: "They were the Great Old Ones that had filtered down from the stars when earth was young—the beings whose substance an alien evolution had shaped, and whose powers were such as this planet had never bred." These beings are called "the Old Ones" or the "winged, starheaded Old Ones" during the rest of the tale. As such, they are distinguished from two of HPL's earlier alien races; the "land race of beings shaped like octopi and probably corresponding to the fabulous pre-human spawn of Cthulhu," and the "half-fungous, half-crustacean creatures from a planet identifiable as...Pluto" who are remembered in the Himalayas as the "Mi-Go". Professor Dyer notes that the Cthulhu-ites and the Mi-Go seem different and far more alien even than the winged starheads: "They were able to undergo transformations and reintegrations impossible for their adversaries [*i.e.,* the winged starheads], and seem therefore to have originally come from even remoter gulfs of cosmic space."

The Old Ones of *At the Mountains of Madness* are thoughtfully described, both as a species and a civilization. A full-grown specimen is about eight feet long, with a six-foot five-ridged barrel torso with a 3.5 foot central diameter, tapering to one foot diameter at both ends. Incredibly tough-fibered and muscular, the things have seven-foot membraneous wings, five arm-stalks with 25 small tentacles at the end of each ("infinitely delicate, flexible, strong, and accurate...ensuring the utmost skill and dexterity in all artistic and other manual operations") and five powerful legs with a "paddle, fin, or pseudo-foot" on each. On top is a "yellowish five-pointed starfish-shaped apparent head, covered with three-inch wiry cilia of various prismatic colors," with a mouth-stalk and an eye-stalk arranged at each point. They are partly vegetable in nature, and appear to have been capable of breathing with lungs, gills, or even through their skin-pores. They could live on organic or inorganic matter, they reproduced by spores, and their lifespans were very long indeed. They had originally come from outer space, gliding through the ether with their great wings, but through the ages of earth-dwelling they lost the ability for further interstellar travel. Concerning their society, HPL's voice can be heard through Professor Dyer's words: "Being non-pairing and semi-vegetable in structure, the Old Ones had no biological basis for the family phase of mammal life; but seemed to organize large households on the principles of comfortable space-utility and...congenial mental association.... Government was evidently complex and probably socialistic." Evidently complex as well was their superb technology, their predominantly urban culture, their religion, their "highly evolved" intellectual and aesthetic tendencies, their architectural and artistic skills. They had actually created earth-life on the lifeless planet, "using available substances according to long-known methods," making shoggoths and "allow[ing] other cell-groups to develop into other forms of animal or vegetable life for sundry purposes; extirpating any whose presence became troublesome." HPL's firm conviction concerning mankind's unimportance in the universal scheme of things was delicately hinted at, as well:

> It interested us to see in some of the very last and most decadent sculptures a shambling primitive mammal, used sometimes for food and sometimes as an amusing buffoon by the land dwellers, whose vaguely simian and human foreshadowings were unmistakable.

Of all his cosmic creations, one senses that HPL liked the winged, starheaded Old Ones the best. This is seen most clearly near the end of the tale, when Professor Dyer and the graduate student Danforth find the grievously torn bodies of several revived Old Ones, who had slaughtered Dyer's colleagues at their camp but had in turn been slaughtered by shoggoths under the frozen primordial city:

> Poor devils! After all, they were not evil things of their kind. They were the men of another age and another order of being.... They had not even been savages—for what indeed had they done [but defend themselves]? Scientists to the last—what had they done that we would not have done in their place? ...Radiates, vegetables, monstrosities, star-spawn—whatever they had been, they were men!

The winged starheads are also mentioned, but no more, in *The Shadow Out of Time*, where it is noted that the Great Race of that tale sometimes fought wars against "the winged, star-headed Old Ones who centred in the Antarctic." Touchingly, there is also a mention by Professor Nathaniel Peaslee of "the tower where S'gg'ha, the captive mind from the star-headed vegetable carnivores of Antarctica, had chiselled certain pictures on the blank spaces of the walls." In *The Shadow Over Innsmouth*, finally, there is a mention of "Old Ones", of unspecified type, when Zadok Allen tells the narrator how the Deep Ones could wipe out the human race if they had felt it worth the trouble, "that is, any [people] as didn't hev sarten [certain] signs sech as was used onct [once] by the lost Old Ones, whoever they was." A couple of pages later Zadok mentions how the Pacific island tribe that dealt with the Deep Ones had been exterminated by its neighbors from other islands, who also left "little stones strewed about—like charms—with somethin' on 'em like what ye call a swastika naowadays. Prob'ly them was the Old Ones' signs." But as the narrator comments at the end of the tale: "The Deep Ones could never be destroyed, even though the palaeogean [of or pertaining to the prehistoric world] magic of the forgotten Old Ones might sometimes check them."

OLNEY COURT (CDW): A fictitious Providence street on Stampers' Hill, where Joseph Curwen built his new town house on the site of his old place in 1761, a place which HPL describes in a casual display of his familiarity with the architectural idiom of the past:

> The place...had never been a mansion; but was a modest two-and-a-half story wooden town house of the familiar Providence colonial type, with plain peaked roof, large central chimney, and artistically carved doorway with rayed fanlight, triangular pediment, and trim Doric pilasters.

Although falling apart, the house is still standing in the 1920s when Charles Dexter Ward discovers Curwen's portrait there. Olney (rhymes with "pony") is one of the old English-settler family names of Rhode Island. Olney Street is an important thoroughfare in HPL's old neighborhood.

OLNEY, THOMAS (SHH): A philosophy professor at a college "by Narragansett Bay" in Rhode Island. He comes to Kingsport, Massachusetts for a summer vacation with his "stout wife and romping children"; the Strange High House on its distant cliff begins to intrigue him. Bored with his dull and ordinary spouse and progeny, he discusses the odd house with the Terrible Old Man (who even invites him into his cottage) and Granny Orne. On a day in August, Olney walks up to the house, a roundabout journey of several hours. He taps on a window on its landward side, and is admitted for what turns into a night of curious and magnificent scenes, at the end of which he rides off with Neptune and Nodens in a giant seashell borne by dolphins. He walks back into Kingsport the next morning and outwardly goes on with his commonplace way of life; but some part of him, call it his soul, will remain in the Strange High House forever. HPL said that the setting of the tale was suggested by the cliffs over the sea at Magnolia, Massachusetts, a resort which he visited more than once, sometimes with Sonia, who seems to have enjoyed it. The name of Olney was an old one in New England. A certain Thomas Olney, a cobbler from Hertfordshire, England, emigrated to Boston with his family in 1635, later becoming one of the earliest settlers of Providence.

O'MALLEY, FATHER (HD): A Catholic priest in 19th century Providence who learned something about the Starry Wisdom cult, possibly from some ex-member's confession; according to the notes of Edwin Lillibridge, the priest told "of devil-worship with box found in great Egyptian ruins—says they call up something that can't exist in light. Flees a little light, and banished by strong light. Then has to be summoned again."

ONGAS (AJ): Congo tribe which is studied by Sir Robert Jermyn, Samuel Seaton, and eventually Sir Arthur Jermyn; the Onga tribe have legends about a grey stone city in the jungle and its hybrid race of men-apes.

OONAI (QI): The city to which Iranon and Romnod walked after leaving the stern, hardworking city of Teloth. It is on the far side of the Karthian mountains, and apparently it took them years to get there, so that the boy Romnod is a grown man when they finally arrive. Oonai is Teloth's opposite—a place of harsh and glaring lights, a place of dancing and music, full of luxury and revelry, but not much morality. For a time Iranon's plaintive songs are popular with the court, until they grow bored and turn to newer attractions in the form of lively dancers. Romnod drinks and eats himself to death here. The mournful, ascetic Iranon buries Romnod in Oonai and departs, unnoticed and unmissed.

OOTH-NARGAI, VALLEY OF (CE, DQ): A green and lovely river valley leading to the sea and Celephaïs.

OPHIR (CU): An ancient land mentioned in the Bible (for example, in Psalm 45, and 1 Kings 9:28 and 10:11), as being rich in gold, precious stones, and rare woods. Modern biblical scholars suggest that the land of Ophir, if it existed at all, was at the southwest corner of the Arabian peninsula, in present-day Oman; but there are also arguments for Ethiopia. The nameless narrator of *The Cats of Ulthar* describes the cat as "bearer of tales from forgotten cities in Meroë and Ophir."

ORANGE POINT (TF): A place on the sea shore near Kingsport, where the narrator washes up on the beach, unconscious and freezing, after escaping from the "festival."

ORIAB (DQ): A large, inhabited island in Dreamland; Randolph Carter ventures there from Dylath-Leen to visit Mount Ngranek on the island. The merchants of Oriab deal in resin, Baharnian pottery, and carved lava rocks from the lower slopes of Ngranek. While on Oriab, Carter travels on riding-zebras, which he hires or purchases locally.

ORNE FAMILY (SOI): An Arkham, Massachusetts family to which the narrator of this tale—who is a student at the non-fictitious Oberlin University (in Oberlin, Ohio), and from the city of Toledo, Ohio—is related. In his genealogical research he discovers that he is the grandson of Eliza Orne (born in 1867), of Arkham, who married a certain James Williamson, of Ohio, in 1884. Eliza Orne's father Benjamin had married Eliza's mother in 1865 or 1866. Eliza's mother, in turn, was said to have been the orphaned daughter of "Enoch and Lydia Meserve Marsh, of New Hampshire," a girl who was raised in France and supported by funds from an unknown guardian. But strangely, no record of the existence of these supposed parents had ever been found in the state of New Hampshire. Judging only by her looks, some people thought Eliza's mother might have been the illegitimate daughter of some Marsh from Essex County, Massachusetts.

Eliza Orne Williamson, with her curious personal background, and the staring-eyed expression that always frightened her grandson, disappeared without a trace when he was eight years old. It was thought at the time that she had "wandered off" in her grief after the suicide of her oldest son Douglas. (Because the narrator seems likely to be in the Oberlin graduating class of 1928, and was therefore probably born in about 1907, this suicide may well have taken place circa 1915.) In fact, she has undergone "the change" and has gone to live beneath the sea as a Deep One. She appears to the narrator in a dream after the events at Innsmouth, showing that she lives in a phosphorescent palace on the ocean floor. She will never die, and she tells him that this is his destiny as well.

Eliza's mysterious mother was really the normal-looking daughter of Captain Obed Marsh and the female Deep One Pth'thya-lyi. She was married "by a trick to an Arkham feller as didn't suspect nothing," Zadok Allen recalled for the narrator in 1928.

As an historical matter, the Ornes were one of the old-settler families of Salem, Massachusetts, Arkham's real-life counterpart, and a clan that was numerous and prominent in colonial times.

ORNE, GRANNY (SHH): A very old woman in Kingsport, but apparently without the frightful tendencies of her aged neighbor the Terrible Old Man. Questioned by Thomas Olney in her "tiny gambrel-roofed abode in Ship Street," concerning the Strange High House, Granny Orne "croaked over something her grandmother had heard at second-hand, about shapes that flapped out of the eastern mists straight into the narrow single door" of the place—a doorway that opens into thin air on the side of a sheer cliff.

ORNE, SIMON (JEDEDIAH) (CDW): A resident of Salem, Massachusetts in the 17th century; he and Edward Hutchinson are Joseph Curwen's principal associates. Orne is one of those people who received the Devil's Mark from George Burroughs at the same coven meeting as Curwen. Simon Orne lives in Salem until 1720, "when his failure to grow visibly old began to incite attention." He then disappears. Thirty years later, a man who looks like his "double" comes to Salem and claims Simon Orne's property as his own, claiming to be a son of Simon, named "Jedediah Orne." Of course, this is really the ageless Simon Orne. The so-called Jedediah Orne leaves Salem for good, under pressure, in 1771. Orne eventually takes on a new identity in Europe as "Josef Nadek, of Prague." Exactly when he did so is not stated, but by the late 1920s an evil old man, Josef Nadek, has been living in a house in Prague for as long as any living person can remember. Charles Dexter Ward visits him there in 1924. After Joseph Curwen's resurrection, he and Orne eagerly renew their correspondence after a 157-year interruption! Nadek/Orne vanishes later when an inexplicable catastrophe obliterates his house in Prague.

ORPHEUS (MM): Professor Dyer and the graduate student Danforth make the mistake of looking backward as they flee from a shoggoth under the lost Antarctic city. "Unhappy act! Not Orpheus himself, or Lot's wife, paid much more dearly for a backward glance." In Greek mythology, Orpheus was the greatest of musicians and singers, who married the nymph Eurydice. When she unexpectedly died, he was allowed to go into Hades and bring her back, on condition that he not look back at her again until he had led her into the light of the upper world. But he did take a look back, a moment too early, and Eurydice vanished back into Hades forever.

ORRENDORF (MM): A member of the Miskatonic University Expedition. It is unclear from the text whether Orrendorf is a mechanic or a graduate student, although probably the latter. He is part of the Lake-Atwood party, and at 9:45 p.m. on January 23, 1931, he is working in tandem with "Watkins" when they find the "monstrous barrel-shaped fossil of wholly unknown nature," which galvanizes the underground search. He is killed along with the rest of the Lake-Atwood group.

OSBORN (WD): *See* "Anthropologists of the Mi-Go."

OSBURN, JOE (DH): The owner of Dunwich Village's only store; it is in the abandoned church with a broken steeple, at the heart of the miserable village. In February, 1913, the excited Old Whateley, whose daughter Lavinia has just given birth to his grandson Wilbur Whateley, makes a startling prediction to the loungers at Osburn's store. In 1928, Joe Osburn is a member of the posse that accompanies the Miskatonic University professors. Predictably (since Dunwich is said to have been founded by families that left Salem rather hurriedly during the witchcraft mania of 1692), a certain Sarah Osburne or Osburn was one of the first three women arrested in Salem Village that year for suspected witchcraft; she died in jail while awaiting trial. Other members of her family appear in different contexts in the investigation records.

OSLO (CC): The capital of Norway, and the home town of Gustaf Johansen, formerly second mate of the ship *Emma* in the South Pacific. He returns there, a broken man, after his horrible experience in 1925. Francis Wayland Thurston comes to Oslo to speak with Johansen but finds he is too late. HPL mentions local sights, culled from a travel book or encyclopedia—the Egeberg mountain, the Gothenburg dock. The "King Harald Haardrada" ("Harold Stern-Council" in Old Norse) mentioned in this part is King Harald III of Norway (d.1066), the warrior-king who founded Oslo in about 1050. In the early 17th century, by which time Norway had fallen under the rule of the kings of Denmark, the city was rebuilt by the orders of the Danish monarch Christian IV, and renamed after him as "Christiana." Norway became an independent nation again in the early 20th century; the official reinstatement of Oslo's ancient name occurred in 1925; Thurston refers to the change of name.

OUKRANOS (DQ, SK, TGSK): A "singing," willow-fringed river that leads from the enchanted wood to the Cerenarian Sea, passing through garden lands of extraordinary, painterly beauty. "Men walk through [this valley] as through a faery place, and feel greater joy and wonder than they ever afterward remember." Lively and glowing fishes live in this crystal stream, and the lumbering creatures called buopoths come shyly out of the woods to drink from the pure waters. At noon on the first day of his walk down the Oukranos, Randolph Carter passes by Kiran; at dusk he reaches Thran, where he spends the night. The next morning he takes passage on a galleon bound to Celephaïs.

P

PABODIE, PROFESSOR FRANK R. (MM): A professor of engineering at Miskatonic University and one of the leaders of the Miskatonic University Expedition. He is also the inventor of the "remarkable drill" which the expedition planned to use to secure deep rock and soil samples from under the thick Antarctic icecap. HPL described the device with zeal, in a fine display of his genius for descriptive writing:

> Pabodie's drilling apparatus...was unique and radical in its lightness, portability, and capacity to combine the ordinary artesian drill principle with the principle of the small circular rock drill in such a way as to cope quickly with strata of varying hardness. Steel head, jointed rods, gasoline motor, collapsible wooden derrick, dynamiting paraphernalia, cording, rubbish-removal auger, and sectional piping for bores five inches wide and up to 1000 feet deep all formed...no greater load than three seven-dog sledges could carry.

Professor Pabodie also develops fuel-warming and quick-ignition devices for the expedition's aircraft. To cope with the thick ice-sheets covering the land, he works out "a plan for sinking copper electrodes in thick clusters of borings and melting off limited areas of ice with current from a gasoline-driven dynamo." The Miskatonic explorers only have a chance to experiment with this procedure, but the upcoming "Starkweather-Moore" expedition proposes to make extensive use of it. Professor Dyer's announced purpose for writing and publishing the "report" (*i.e.,* the tale), is to dissuade this new expedition from ever using the procedure.

On December 13–15, 1930, Professor Pabodie makes the difficult ascent of Mount Nansen, with the graduate students Gedney and Carroll. On January 6, along with most of the expedition members, he flies over the South Pole. From January 11–18 he makes a preliminary drilling trip in company with Professor Lake and five other men; however, he remains at the base camp with Professor Dyer when Lake and Professor Atwood depart with their sub-party on January 22. On the 25th, Pabodie and Dyer lead the rescue party and discover the wreckage of the Lake-Atwood encampment. While Dyer and Danforth fly over the nearby mountains for some additional exploration, Pabodie and several other men successfully repair two more aircraft for the flight back to base.

Pabodie departs Antarctica with the other survivors, and subsequently publishes some articles about the expedition—not including, of course, any information about the lost city or the nature of the winged, star-headed Old Ones, of which he had no knowledge because Danforth and Professor Dyer had kept silent, even to him.

"Pabodie," like many other Lovecraftian surnames, has New England historical undertones; HPL was probably aware, for example, that Elizabeth Alden Pabodie, the first white female born in the New England colonies, lies buried at the village of Little Compton, Rhode Island. Even closer to home, HPL was apt to have known of William J. Pabodie, a 19th century Providence attorney and man of letters, who was a friend of both Edgar Allan Poe and of Poe's Providence lady-love, Mrs. Whitman.

PALACE OF SEVENTY DELIGHTS (DQ): Kuranes' magnificent palace in the city of Celephaïs, from which he reigns for half of each year.

PALINURUS (TT): Jervas Dudley, in the full flight of his belief that he is Jervas Hyde dying in a burning mansion in the 18th century, exclaims to himself: "*Jervas Hyde* should never share the sad fate of Palinurus!"

Palinurus appears in Virgil's ancient Latin epic the *Aeneid* as the helmsman of the ship that is carrying Aeneas and his companions from fallen Troy to a new life in Italy, where their descendants will found Rome. Poseidon, god of the sea, required the life of one crewman to allow the others to reach land in safety, and chose the noble Palinurus, who fell into the sea by night and was lost in the waves. Washed ashore in a barbaric country, he was killed by the natives and left unburied, so that his soul could not enter Hades and had to wander outside the entrance to the next world.

PAN (TR, DH): The ancient Greek god of woods, fields, and wildlife, and patron of hunters and shepherds, who was worshipped in the form of an ugly but exuberant man with a goat's horns, ears, and legs. Pan's behavior and that of his cult were oftentimes merry and musical, but sometimes more sinister—the word "panic" for overwhelming terror derives from Pan's unpleasant habit of mischievously frightening people who walked through the forest at night. In *The Tree* it is correctly noted that in legend, Pan frequented Mount Maenalus in the Greek region of Arcadia, and in the tale, the local people believe Pan's strange companions, the Panisci, must have something to do with the very oddly-shaped tree that grew in the ruins of a certain villa on the slope of the mountain.

Arthur Machen, the British author whose work HPL treasured, wrote a famous tale of supernatural horror entitled *The Great God Pan* (1894), referred to in *The Dunwich Horror* when Dr. Armitage of Miskatonic

University says to himself, concerning the idiotic Dunwich folk: "God, what simpletons! Shew them Arthur Machen's Great God Pan and they'll think it a common Dunwich scandal!" Since Machen's tale concerned the frightful and tragic results of the mating of Pan with a modern English-woman, HPL could hardly have done more to hint at the similarly hideous cross-breeding at the heart of the Dunwich mystery.

PARACELSUS (CDW, EC): His magnificent full name was Philippus Aureolus Theophrastus Bombast von Hohenheim, and he lived from 1493–1541. This Swiss-German alchemist, humanist, physician and traveler is credited by historians with being the first to introduce the developing modern science of chemistry to the theory and practice of medicine. Among other achievements, Paracelsus (the name he adopted professionally) was the author, in 1530, of the first known clinical description of syphilis. He was the author of some influential books on the natural sciences; many other books of esoteric wisdom were later falsely attributed to him. Books by the famed Paracelsus are mentioned as being in the libraries of both Joseph Curwen and the evil clergyman.

PARADISE LOST (DA): John Milton (1608–74) was one of the greatest poets in the English language; his masterpiece is the epic poem *Paradise Lost*, which deals with the aftermath of Satan's rebellion in heaven, up through the expulsion of Adam and Eve from the Garden of Eden, or as Milton began his great work:

> *Of Man's first disobedience, and the fruit*
> *Of that forbidden tree, whose mortal taste*
> *Brought Death into the world, and all our woe,*
> *With loss of Eden, till one greater Man*
> *Restore us, and regain the blissful seat....*

At one point in *Dagon* the nameless narrator clambers to the edge of a moonlit canyon, his mind full of "curious reminiscences of *Paradise Lost*, and of Satan's hideous climb through the unfashioned realms of darkness." He is probably referring to the passages in Book One of the poem, when Satan first arises from the bottom of the pit of hell (where he has been hurled by God along with the other rebellious angels) and explores his new infernal realm.

PARG (DQ): A land across the river from Dylath-Leen; Parg exports black slaves and ivory carvings. The "fat black men of Parg" are often taken away as cargo from Dylath-Leen, by the galleys of the moonbeasts; it is hinted that the moonbeasts think they make good eating.

PARKER (CC): A sailor on the *Emma* who survives the sea-battle with the *Alert* and transfers to that vessel as the *Emma* begins to sink. Days later, he lands on the risen city of R'lyeh. His fate is cryptic: as the sailors all run away from Cthulhu, Parker slips on one of the algae-covered stones, "and Johansen [swore] that he was swallowed up by an angle of masonry that shouldn't have been there; an angle which was acute, but behaved as if it were obtuse." He is not seen again.

PARKER PLACE (HRH): A squalid side-street ("since re-named") in the Red Hook section of Brooklyn, New York. The foreign devil-cultists dwelt here in crowded tenements that the narrator calls "rookeries," and Robert Suydam leases a basement apartment on Parker Place for his secret activities. During the police raid on this street, some of the buildings collapse, killing half of the policemen and most of the foreign cult-members. The earth below the buildings is found to be honeycombed with tunnels, vaults, and hidden galleries, even a subterranean canal.

PARKS (SK, TGSK): The "cockney" London-born servant of young Randolph Carter's Boston family in the 1880s; he is still alive and working for Carter when his master disappears on October 7, 1928. The old servant died early in 1930. After Randolph Carter's disappearance, Parks testified about a mysterious, aromatic wooden box that Carter had found in an attic, with a silver key and an old scrap of parchment inside.

PARTHOLAN (MB): The peasants of Ballylough and Kilderry object to the draining of the bog for fear of:

> ...secrets that had lain hidden since the plague came to the children of Partholan in the fabulous years before history. In the *Book of Invaders* it is told that these sons of the Greeks were all buried at Tallaght, but old men in Kilderry said that one city was overlooked save by its patron moon-goddess; so that only the wooded hills buried it when the men of Nemed swept down from Scythia in their thirty ships.

And that lost Greek city, naturally, is covered by the bog that Denis Barry wishes to drain and improve. In the medieval Irish *Leabhar Gabhala* or *Book of Invaders*, it is recounted that the Partholanians were the second group of legendary invaders who settled in Ireland, the first to arrive after the biblical Flood. According to the legend, Partholan was the son of King Sera of Greece, and he fled his homeland after murdering his parents in some dispute. After wandering for seven years, he and his followers reached Ireland, where they founded a colony and fought the hostile Fomorians. Some generations later all the Partholanians died of a plague. According to the *Leabhar Gabhala*:

Nine thousand of Partholan's people died in one week on Sean Mhagh Ealta Edair, namely, five thousand men and four thousand women. Whence is named Taimhleacht [Tallaght] Muintire Parthaloin. They had passed three hundred years in Ireland.... Now Ireland was waste thirty years after the plague-burial of Partholan's people, till Nemed son of Agnoman...of the Greeks of Scythia, reached it.

PASCOAG (HRH): A non-fictitious small town in northern Rhode Island with some business and commercial blocks. Thomas Malone walks there from nearby Chepachet one day to buy some magazines, and suffers from a panic attack at the sight of the multi-level buildings.

PAWTUXET ROAD FARM (CDW): An isolated farm and set of buildings owned by Joseph Curwen during the mid-18th century, which he uses for his dreadful experiments on black slaves, runaway soldiers and sailors, and "essential Saltes" stolen from old graves. At that time it lay well outside the city of Providence. The secret committee of prominent citizens, and their armed strongmen, raided the farm in April, 1771, and Curwen to all appearances died in the raid. By the 1920s, the neighborhood of the old Curwen farm lay in the suburbs of ever-expanding Providence, and the subterranean regions lie beneath a certain bungalow-style house which Charles Dexter Ward leased and occupied, along with "Dr. Allen" and the mulatto servant Tony Gomes.

PAWTUXET (CDW): A small, non-fictitious community a few miles south of the city of Providence, where the Seekonk River estuary meets the ocean.

PEABODY, E. LAPHAM (SOI): The curator of the Arkham Historical Society in 1927, when he courteously helps the narrator to establish some facts of regional history and Marsh family history.

PEASLEE FAMILY (SOT): This family consists of Nathaniel Wingate Peaslee, his wife Alice Keezar Peaslee, and their three children: Robert (b. 1898), Wingate (b. 1900), and Hannah (b. 1903). Up until 1908, the family resided together at 27 Crane Street in Arkham. After her husband's "possession" began, Mrs. Peaslee obtained a divorce from him (in 1910), and refused ever to see him again; nor would his children Robert and Hannah.

PEASLEE, PROFESSOR NATHANIEL WINGATE (SOT): The son of Jonathan and Hannah (maiden name Wingate) Peaslee, born circa 1870 and raised on Boardman Street in Haverhill, Massachusetts, a non-fictitious town. Beginning in 1895, Nathaniel Wingate Peaslee is an instructor at Miskatonic University. Having married the former Miss

Alice Keezar in 1896, he became the father of three children in the next seven years.

At 10:30 a.m. on Thursday, May 14, 1908, while lecturing to his Political Economy IV class, he begins to hallucinate, then faints. For the next five years, four months, and eighteen days, he displays a complete amnesia about his own past life, and various signs of a completely different personality than his old self. At the same time his mental abilities become extraordinarily superior to the norm. After the event, his wife always regarded him "with extreme horror and loathing, vowing that I was some utter alien usurping the body of her husband." (She was correct.) Mrs. Peaslee left the family home along with their children, and obtained a divorce without ever seeing her mate again. With his teaching duties suspended, Peaslee apparently visits the Himalayas in 1909, makes a camel journey across Arabia in 1911, and in summer, 1912, charters a ship to take him somewhere to the north of Spitzbergen, a large island north of Europe on the Arctic Circle. Later that year, he spends two weeks alone in a limestone cave-complex in Virginia. During these years, he is observed to study intensively a variety of academic subjects, including certain forbidden texts. Peaslee recovers his prior personality and knowledge under odd circumstances on September 27, 1913. He regains legal custody of son Wingate in 1913–14, but his other children refuse to have any further contact with him. He returns to teaching economics for the 1914–15 school year, then retires from his profession.

His increasingly strange dreams, and visions of another world, lead him to the serious study of psychology. He begins to arrive at a dream-based theory of a "Great Race" of creatures that existed in Earth's remote past. He publishes some articles based on his dream-work and additional research in the *Journal of the American Psychological Society*, during 1928–29. In 1934 he receives a letter concerning an archaeological find reminiscent of his dream-subjects, in the desert of Western Australia. In 1935, he goes on an expedition to the Australian site, accompanied by his son Wingate, by Professors Dyer, Ashley, and Freeborn of Miskatonic University, and by their Australian hosts/guides, Mr. Boyle and Mr. Mackenzie. One night at the site, Professor Peaslee is led into the Lovecraftian hero's typical quest in hidden caverns and tunnels, leading to his understanding that the Great Race was real.

PEASLEE, PROFESSOR WINGATE (SOT): Son of Nathaniel and Alice Peaslee. Born 1900, raised in Arkham where his father is a professor at Miskatonic University. Separated from his father at the age of 8, but reunited with him after Nathaniel's return to normal in 1913. He shares in his father's psychology studies, eventually becoming a psychology professor at Miskatonic. He accompanies his father on the Australian expedition in 1935.

PECK, DARIUS (IV): A resident of Peck Valley, in his nineties, whose body was one of the nine corpses that spent the bitter winter of 1880–81 in the receiving tomb of the town cemetery. His remains are taken out and buried by George Birch on April 14, 1881, after the spring thaw has sufficiently softened the ground.

PECK VALLEY (IV): Fictitious New England village which is the setting of this tale.

"PENDRIFTER, THE" (WD): A Vermont newspaper column which mentions Professor Wilmarth's opinions about the strange creatures reportedly glimpsed in certain Vermont rivers during a period of terrible flooding.

"The Pendrifter" actually was a feature of the Brattleboro *Reformer*, in Brattleboro, Vermont; in this column HPL's friend and host Vrest Orton published a complimentary article about the visiting author on June 16, 1928.

PENNACOOKS (WD): An actual Indian tribe from the Merrimack River region in western New England, more or less extinct since the late 18th century. According to Professor Wilmarth, the Pennacook tribal legends told the most detailed stories about the mysterious hill-dwelling creatures. Their "consistent and picturesque" myths, as Wilmarth puts it, say that "the Winged Ones came from the Great Bear in the sky, and had mines in our earthly hills whence they took a kind of stone they could not get on any other world.... They knew the speech of all kinds of men— Pennacooks, Hurons, men of the Five Nations...." The Hurons were another and much larger Indian tribe of the present day northeastern United States, as were the "men of the Five Nations"—that is, the Iroquois Confederation.

PENTELICUS (HY): The narrator says of his dramatic-looking friend, "his brow was as white as the marble of Pentelicus." The classical Mount Pentelicus is a 3,670 foot (1,120 m) peak in central Greece, northeast of Athens. In ancient times the fine white marble quarried here was used for many Athenian public buildings and for elegant statues.

"PETERS" (PM): A false identity that Richard Pickman used in order to lease his secret studio, in the North End district of Boston.

PETRA (MM): Professor Dyer notices "a fantastic conical monument carved out of the solid rock and roughly resembling such things as the well-known Snake Tomb in the ancient valley of Petra." Petra, in the

Jordanian desert, is an ancient, abandoned city in which many buildings were carved out of the valley's rock walls, some 2000 years ago; it is now one of the major tourist attractions of the Middle East. The Snake Monument is a rock-cut tomb, over which is a carved, coiled snake.

PHAROS (DQ): The great lighthouse or beacon in the harbor of Cele-phaïs. The name is not original with HPL. The "Pharos of Alexandria" was one of the ancient Seven Wonders of the World, the most famous lighthouse of ancient times. Built circa 280 B.C. by the Greek engineer Sostratus of Cnidus, for Pharaoh Ptolemy II, it stood over 440 feet high on the island of Pharos in the great harbor of Alexandria, Egypt. According to ancient writers, the light could be seen from forty miles out in the Mediterranean Sea. The structure was surmounted by a colossal statue of Helios, the sun god. The Pharos was still standing in the 12th century A.D., but eventually collapsed and fell into ruins. To this day, a light-house is *el faro* in the Spanish language.

PHILLIPS, WARD (TGSK): "An elderly eccentric of Providence, Rhode Island," and a longtime correspondent of Randolph Carter. He comes to the meeting at E.-L. de Marigny's apartment to argue that Carter's estate should not be divided among his heirs, as he was "still alive in another time-dimension and might well return someday." The character is of course a mild parody of HoWARD PHILLIPS Lovecraft himself, and his physical description—"lean, grey, long-nosed, clean-shaven, and stoop-shouldered"—is HPL's own.

PHIPPS (PM): The wormy, centuries-old wood panelling in Pickman's secret Boston studio reminds Thurber of the "the days of Andros and Phipps..." Sir William Phips, or Phipps (1651–95) was a most unusual colonial American, born in what is now the state of Maine. After early years of labor as a carpenter and shipbuilder, he discovered a large trea-sure on a sunken Spanish galleon in the Caribbean Sea, which made him a very wealthy man, soon afterwards knighted by the king of England. Afterwards he had a lively and prominent career which included a stint (1692–94) as the first royal governor of the Massachusetts colony.

PHLEGETHON (OG): Barzai's shrieking from the top of Hatheg-Kla seems to Atal like a cry such "as no man ever heard save in the Phleg-ethon of unrelatable nightmares."

In classical mythology, Phlegethon was one of the rivers of Hades, the underworld conceived of by the Greeks and borrowed by the Romans. Its Greek name means "fiery," and it is said to flow with a fire that burns but does not consume those in it.

[NATHANIEL DERBY] PICKMAN FOUNDATION (MM): Organization which provided funding for the Miskatonic University Expedition. A reunion of two of HPL's big names, Derby and Pickman.

PICKMAN, RICHARD UPTON (PM, DQ): Introduced in the tale *Pickman's Model*, he is a 20th century Boston painter; later, a ghoul. Born in Salem, Massachusetts, of an old local family; his great-great-great-great-grandmother was hanged for a witch in 1692, "with Cotton Mather looking sanctimoniously on." His father was still living in Salem as of 1926. In the opinion of his acquaintance Thurber, "Boston never had a greater painter"; his special skill was accurately painting faces. Pickman liked "wild" artistic theories and metaphysical speculations, and even owned a personal copy of the *Necronomicon* (not mentioned in a tale but in HPL's "History of the *Necronomicon*"), but as a painter he was strictly and rigorously *representational*, a strong clue that his ghoul-paintings are not imaginary scenes. He is an expert on local history and architecture, familiar with tunnels, alleys, and secret passageways said to wind through Boston's North End, and takes Thurber there to see the paintings in his secret studio. He painted ghouls, and was himself part-ghoul. He disappears from Boston in 1926.

In *The Dream-Quest of Unknown Kadath*, Randolph Carter, who used to know Pickman as a human being in Boston, meets him again in Dreamland on the Peaks of Thok, where he has become a ghoul chieftain. He is "naked and rubbery, and had acquired so much of the ghoulish physiognomy that [his] human origin was already obscure. But [he] still remembered a little English...." Pickman proves to be a wonderful helper to Carter, first by ordering three ghouls to escort the traveler back to upper Dreamland, later by organizing an army of ghouls and night-gaunts to fight and rout the moonbeasts, and to fly with Carter to unknown Kadath.

In *Pickman's Model*, the artist Pickman maintains an open-to-the-public studio on fashionable Newbury Street, Boston, and a secret studio in a very old North End building, which he rents under the name of Peters from its Italian slumlord owner. The directions to the studio are so tantalizingly precise that millions of readers have probably wondered about trying to find it, by taking a shuttle to the Battery Street station, going along the old waterfront past Constitution Wharf, and turning up one of the cross streets, but not Greenough Lane; then, when in the "dirtiest and oldest alley" ever seen (where one may catch a glimpse of a house with "a peaked roof-line of the almost forgotten pre-gambrel type, though antiquarians tell us there are none left in Boston"), turning left into a narrower, lightless alley, walking for one minute, making an obtuse turn to the right in the dark, and looking for a worm-eaten, ten-paneled oak door. HPL actually had a particular Boston structure in mind, a certain row of very old houses he had once spotted on a ramble in North End. On a 1927 visit to Boston, he took a friend on a walk to show him "Pickman's studio" and was flabbergasted to find that "the actual alley & house of the tale [had been] utterly demolished; a whole crooked line of buildings having been torn down."

PIERCE, AMMI (COS): A "stolid" farmer from west of Arkham, probably born circa 1842; the friend and neighbor of Nahum and Nabby Gardner in 1880. At the time he tells his story to a curious land-surveyor for Arkham's new dam and reservoir, he is a white-bearded, unkempt widower living alone in a tumbledown cottage. However, he speaks like an intelligent man who has had some education. During 1882–83 he witnesses the destruction of the Gardner farm and family at close range; by the end, he is the only neighbor who will still go visit the place. In early November, 1883, he witnesses the death of Nahum Gardner (in perhaps the most frightening, because most understated, single climax in all of HPL's tales) and brings the coroner and some lawmen to the house afterwards. He leads the party away by foot the same evening, as the Colour waxes strong and prepares to leave the Earth. Fifty years later, we are told, he has never returned to the ruins of the Gardner farm, and because of his terrible knowledge, he has "never been quite right since."

Although he is a plain and ordinary Yankee farmer, not a university professor or an esoteric adept, Ammi Pierce seems worthy of being counted among the intrepid, insatiably curious academic or gentlemanly investigators who dominate the Lovecraftian world. His unusual first name is originally found in the Bible, in the Old Testament book of the prophet Hosea, in chapters 1 and 2, when God tells the prophet to name his daughter "Lo-ruhamah," "no mercy," and his son "Lo-ammi," "not my people," "for ye are not my people, and I will not be your God"— because the Hebrews have once again sunk into depravity and sin. But later the Lord will command: "Say ye unto your brethren, Ammi; and to your sisters, Ruhamah." The figurative name Ammi, "my people," according to the sense of the passage, will be a name for restored Israel when the people have repented of their sins, when the children of Israel have become "numerous as the sand of the sea, which cannot be measured nor numbered" and when they are called "the sons of the living God."

The project to construct a great water-reservoir for Boston in the rural Swift River Valley of central Massachusetts (now Quabbin Reservoir, constructed and filled in the 1930s and 1940s) was already on the drawing-boards and the topic of considerable discussion at this time. It possibly suggested the framing device for this tale: the survey for a vast new reservoir for the city of Arkham, requiring the damming of a river and the drowning of some long-settled agricultural districts, including the locale of the former Gardner farm. In a letter to a friend, HPL referred to the 1926 creation of the large Scituate Reservoir, which is fifteen miles west of central Providence, as his inspiration for "the reservoir element" of this tale.

A note on dates: *The Colour Out of Space* was published in 1927. But near the end of the tale, the nameless narrator mentions that "it is over half a century since the horror happened." Since the horror happened very precisely in 1882–83, the statement would logically lead to a present-time date of 1934 or later, seven years or more after the tale was published. HPL did not slip up in counting. In the original 1927 publication of the tale in a pulp magazine, the phrase read: "It is forty-four years now since the horror happened." The alteration was made by HPL himself in about 1934 for a pamphlet-sized republication suggested by a fan, a project which wound up going nowhere.

PIERCE, MRS. AMMI (COS): She was a farm wife and the neighbor and friend of Mrs. Nabby Gardner circa 1880. On the first day that the Miskatonic University scholars came to take a meteor sample in June, 1882, they stopped in at the Pierce place on their homeward way, and it is Mrs. Pierce who first observes that their fragment was slowly shrinking, and had burned out the bottom of their metal pail. On October 19, 1883, she helps her husband Ammi to console Nahum Gardner over the death of his son Thaddeus. Three days later, while she is all alone in her house, Nahum staggers into her kitchen and gives her the alarming news of his son Merwin's disappearance, while she listens "in a clutching fright." She dies at some later date, leaving Ammi Pierce a widower by the time he talks to the surveyor decades later.

PIERCE, MEHITABEL (SH): A maidservant in the William Harris household, hired in 1764 to replace Hannah Bowen, who had died in June of that year. The manservant Eli Liddeason falls in love with the new maid and stays on in the job he had intended to quit, until he dies the following year. Mehitabel Pierce dies in the house in 1768, being replaced by the gossipy Ann White.

PIERRE (TA): The last servant to serve the de C household, he is responsible for raising the orphaned narrator Antoine de C. When Pierre finally dies of old age, his young master buries the faithful-unto-death retainer under the stones of the chateau courtyard.

PIGAFETTA'S *REGNUM CONGO* (PH): HPL described this real book as follows: "It was bound in leather with metal fittings.... It proved to be...Pigafetta's account of the Congo region, written in Latin from the notes of the sailor Lopez and printed at Frankfort in 1598." The book contained "curious illustrations by the brothers de Bry...drawn entirely from imagination and casual descriptions, and represent[ing] negroes with white skins and Caucasian features." The volume seen by the narrator tended to open up to the unwholesome Plate XII, a drawing of a cannibal butcher-shop—the "picture in the house" of the tale's title.

Regnum is the Latin word for "kingdom" or "domain," or more loosely "country," and *Congo* of course refers to the basin of the great Congo River in central Africa. This extremely rare and peculiar-sounding book has been the source of consuming curiosity for many HPL fans from the 1920s to the present day. Lovecraft biographer S.T. Joshi closed the case in his *Lovecraft: A Life*:

> The book was, to be sure, printed in Frankfort in 1598; but its first edition was not in Latin, as [stated in the tale], but in Italian (*Relazione del reame di Congo et della cironvicine contrade*, Rome, 1591); it was subsequently translated into English (1597) and German (1597) prior to its Latin translation; and it was in the German (as well as the Latin) translation that the plates by the brothers De Bry were introduced. Lovecraft appears not to have known any of this because he derived his information on the book entirely from Thomas Henry Huxley's essay "On the History of the Man-like Apes", in *Man's Place in Nature* (1894).... What is more, Lovecraft never consulted the De Bry plates themselves but only some rather inaccurate engravings of them printed in an appendix to Huxley's essay. As a result, Lovecraft makes errors in describing the plates; for example, the old man thinks the natives drawn in them are anomalously white-looking, when in fact this is merely the result of a poor rendering of the plates by Huxley's illustrator. All this is only of interest because it reveals Lovecraft on occasion to have used exactly that "second-hand erudition" for which he later chided Poe.

"Pigafetta" was Filippo Pigafetta (1533–1604), an Italian in the service of the king of Spain. "The sailor Lopez" was Duarte Lopez (or Lopes), a Portuguese trader who sailed to Africa and settled near the mouth of the Congo River in about 1578. In the late 1580s he returned to Spain as ambassador on a diplomatic mission for the local African monarch, bearing letters to the king of Spain and to the Pope (one must recall that in this period Lopez's homeland of Portugal was part of the kingdom of Spain). While in Spain he told everything he could remember to Pigafetta, who turned these recollections into a book in his native Italian, first published in 1591 as stated above. The Italian title means: "Relations concerning the kingdom of Congo and the countries around it." Duarte Lopez returned to the Congo in 1589; nothing more is known of him. The "brothers de Bry" were Johann Theodor de Bry (1561–1623) and Johann Israel de Bry (1570–1611), renowned early illustrators and mapmakers in Germany. The town HPL called "Frankfort" was more properly Frankfurt-am-Main in Western Germany, still a publishing center.

PILBARRA (SOT): A real town in the state of Western Australia, Professor Nathaniel Peaslee receives a letter from a Pilbarra man, Robert Mackenzie, in 1934, which leads him to travel there with his son and some other researchers in 1935, on their way into the Great Sandy Desert.

PILTDOWN MAN (RW, DA): The skulls found in the grisly stockyard beneath Exham Priory in England "were mostly lower than the Piltdown Man in the scale of evolution, but in every case definitely human." With these words HPL fell as another hapless victim of one of the greatest hoaxes in scientific history. In 1912, newspapers reported that an English amateur archaeologist had discovered bone fragments which were the earliest-known human remains, near Piltdown in southern England. Intense excitement and extensive press coverage followed the announcements, and for many years scholars struggled, with increasing difficulty, to fit the mysterious bones into the known archaeological and geological record. Not until 1953, when researchers had access to vastly-improved laboratory dating methods, could scientists conclusively prove that Piltdown Man was an elaborate hoax created by some as-yet-unidentified, but brilliant, prankster. The bone fragments were from a modern ape and a modern human, ingeniously "faked up" to seem as if they came from some Missing Link in the remote past. Writing in 1923, HPL plainly accepted Piltdown Man as probably genuine. The narrator of *Dagon* tells himself that the grotesquely-carved monolith from the ocean floor was "merely" the relic of some primitive tribe "whose last descendant had perished eras before the first ancestor" of Piltdown Man.

PLANCK (DWH): *See* "Mathematicians of Arkham."

PLINY (AJ): In his drunkenness, Sir Wade Jermyn raved to his disbelieving English listeners of the living things that might haunt such a place as the lost city he claimed to have discovered in the Congo River region of central Africa, "creatures half of the jungle and half of the impiously aged city—fabulous creatures which even a Pliny might describe with scepticism."

Gaius Plinius Secundus (c. 23–79), known in English as Pliny the Elder, was a Roman historian and what would later be called a naturalist, a student of what was once generally referred to as "natural history," meaning the study of natural things in the world around us. He famously died during the volcanic eruptions of Mount Vesuvius which buried the Italian towns of Pompeii and Herculaneaum in 79 A.D.; he had gone up close to get a better look. His only surviving work is the *Historia Naturalis*, an encyclopedia-style compendium which covers geography, zoology, botany, and mineralogy, among other things. Pliny readily reported second-hand accounts of fabulous creatures in distant parts of the world, whether he could verify them or not; hence this reference. He visited North Africa and was impressed enough to write the following still-remembered words: *Ex Africa semper aliquid novi*, "there is always something new out of Africa."

PNAKOTIC MANUSCRIPTS (PO, OG, DQ, WD, MM, TGSK, SOT, HD): Often alluded to, but barely described, the Pnakotic Manuscripts are very much a mystery. They seem to have originated in the ancient northern land of Lomar; at one point it is suggested that the last remaining set is in Ulthar. Barzai the Wise was an expert in these texts, some frightful parts of which are too ancient to be read, according to *The Other Gods*. In *At the Mountains of Madness*, Professor Dyer notes that the Great Old Ones "were...above all doubt the originals of the fiendish elder myths which things like the Pnakotic Manuscripts and the *Necronomicon* affrightedly hint about." At a different point he reports that: "A few daring mystics have hinted at a pre-Pleistoscene origin for the fragmentary Pnakotic Manuscripts...." In geological time, the Pleistoscene Epoch was the last to precede our own Holocene Epoch. It is considered to have run from approximately 2,000,000–11,000 years ago, during which time human beings first appeared. The daring mystics, in other words, proposed a non-human origin for the Pnakotic Manuscripts.

PNATH, VALE OF (DCS, DQ, HD): A vast, lightless, subterranean valley in Dreamland, guarded by the night-gaunts. It is filled with huge heaps of bones; the creatures called bholes live there in the eternal night. Randolph Carter is dropped in here by night-gaunts who catch him trespassing on the upper slopes of Mount Ngranek; but escapes by means of a ladder dropped by ghouls on the cliffs above, the Peaks of Thok. In *The Haunter of the Dark,* it is mentioned that one of Robert Blake's short stories was called "In the Vale of Pnath."

POE, EDGAR ALLAN (DA, SH, MM, WD): American author and poet (1809–1849), the inventor of the modern detective story and the only American author of supernatural horror who can be considered HPL's superior. HPL's self-described "God of Fiction" was doubly-treasured because he visited the city of Providence on a number of occasions to court the local poetess Sarah Helen Whitman, an attractive widow who deeply admired his verses. As a bonus, Poe had grown up in Richmond,

Virginia, an attractive southern city that HPL visited in his later years and liked very much for its historical scenery and old-fashioned southern gentility. HPL opens the tale *The Shunned House* with an indubitable statement: that Poe himself must certainly have walked past the "shunned house" (the real 135 Benefit Street), in 1848–49, even if he never noticed it, as it is extremely close to Mrs. Whitman's former home, also on Benefit Street. In *The Whisperer in Darkness*, Dr. Wilmarth's host at the Akeley farmhouse, after describing the "black rivers of pitch" that flow under mysterious bridges on Yuggoth "ought to be enough to make any man a Dante or a Poe if he can keep sane long enough to tell what he has seen." In *The Horror at Red Hook*, Detective Thomas F. Malone tells himself that the story of what happened in Red Hook could not be written: "—for like the book cited by Poe's German authority, *es lässt sich nicht lesen*—it does not permit itself to be read." The phrase occurs in Edgar Allan Poe's tale or fable *The Man of the Crowd;* it was invented by Poe himself and is not even particularly good German.

Poe is also cited in *At the Mountains of Madness*, for his weird Antarctic story *The Narrative of Arthur Gordon Pym*, and for a later poem—the name of which was *Ulalume*—in which he mentioned a polar volcano he called "Yaanek," a peak which the graduate student Danforth identifies with Mount Erebus in Antarctica. The passages dealing with Poe in HPL's masterly essay *Supernatural Horror in Literature* display his familiarity with, and critical insights regarding, the master's works. He began this section with the following tribute:

> In the eighteen-thirties occurred a literary dawn directly affecting not only the history of the weird tale, but that of short fiction as a whole; and indirectly moulding the trends and fortunes of a great European aesthetic school. It is our good fortune as Americans to be able to claim that dawn as our own, for it came in the person of our illustrious and unfortunate fellow-countryman Edgar Allan Poe.... Whatever his limitations, Poe did that which no one else ever did or could have done, and to him we owe the modern horror-story in its perfected state.

POLARIS, the POLE STAR (PO): In *Polaris* the familiar North Star seems to menace and taunt the narrator with visions of an earlier human age, when it lulled him to sleep and led him to fail in his duty as watchman for his endangered city. "The Pole Star, evil and monstrous, leers down from the black vault, winking hideously like an insane watching eye which strives to convey some strange message, yet recalls nothing save that it once had a message to convey." In addition, this tale mentions the constellations of Cassiopeia and Charles's Wain (the Big Dipper), the stars Arcturus and Coma Berenices and Aldebaran.

POLYPHEMUS (DA, UP, CC): Polyphemus is one of the monsters encountered by Ulysses (or "Odysseus") in the ancient Greek epic poem, the *Odyssey*. He is a Cyclops, *i.e.,* a savage, cave-dwelling, man-eating giant with only a single eye, located in the middle of his forehead. The Cyclops captures Ulysses' crew and eats several of the sailors without ceremony or even a pinch of salt, simply picking them up and shoving them into his vast maw to be chewed and swallowed. To the narrator of *Dagon*, the creature that emerges from the water to worship the carved monolith is "vast, Polyphemus-like, and loathsome," with a hideous head and giant, scaly arms. At one point in *Under the Pyramids* Houdini refers to a "yawning Polyphemus-door" deep beneath the earth, to something inside of which, hideous worshippers seem to be tossing hideous offerings. In *The Call of Cthulhu*, when Cthulhu watches Johansen and Briden beginning to escape from R'lyeh on the steamship *Alert*, "the titan Thing from the stars slavered and gibbered like Polypheme cursing the fleeing ship of Odysseus. Then, bolder than the storied Cyclops, great Cthulhu slid greasily into the water and began to pursue...."

PONAPE (SOI): In *The Shadow Over Innsmouth*, Zadok Allen tells the narrator that the "island east of Otaheite" where Captain Obed Marsh first learned of the Deep Ones had "a lot o' stone ruins older'n anybody knew anything abaout, kind o' like them on Ponape, in the Carolines, but with carvins' of faces that looked like the big statues on Easter Island." Ponape, now the state of Pohnpei in the "Federated States of Micronesia," is a small volcanic island in the Caroline Islands in the Pacific Ocean, which has ruins of ancient walls, dykes, and columns, all built with the black basalt rock of the island by pre-modern inhabitants.

PORTA, GIAMBATTISTA (DH): *See* "Cryptographers of Dunwich."

POTTER, WELCOME (CDW): One of Charles Dexter Ward's great-great-grandfathers; in 1785 he married "Ann Tillinghast, daughter of Mrs. Eliza, daughter to Capt. James Tillinghast." In fact, Ann is also the daughter of Joseph Curwen, whose name his wife Eliza legally discarded after his shocking death and posthumous disgrace.

PRE-RAPHAELITES (TH): The Pre-Raphaelite Brotherhood was a group of painters and artists, including such famed men as William Morris and Dante Gabriel Rossetti, who flourished as an artistic movement during the mid-19th century in England. In a reaction to the reigning Victorian dourness, they sought to return to the directness of early Renaissance Italian painting (hence the name of the group, suggesting the prevailing style before the advent of the Italian painter Raphael); the hallmarks of their work are flamboyant colors and sometimes rather sensual themes, with stunning and ethereal female models clad in vaguely medieval or ancient attire.

PRINN, LUDVIG (HD): The purported author of the "hellish" book *De Vermis Mysteriis*; he was a pure creation of HPL's who was loaned to the author's teenage pen-pal Robert Bloch (who described the hideous death of an unnamed but manifestly Lovecraftian sage in a story called *The Shambler From the Stars*), and taken back, so to speak, for this tale in which HPL kills off a Bloch-substitute, tit for tat. There is a very pleasant story about this exchange of hideous fates. Before publishing his own trifle of a weird tale in *Weird Tales*, the nervous young author worried about upsetting his respected older mentor H.P. Lovecraft, by fictionally feeding him to an outer-space monster. But the "gentleman from Providence" set Bloch at ease with this "release":

> This is to certify that Robert Bloch, Esq., of Milwaukee, Wisconsin, U.S.A.—reincarnation of Mijnheer Ludvig Prinn, author of *De Vermis Mysteriis*—is fully authorized to portray, murder, annihilate, disintegrate, transfigure, metamorphose, or otherwise manhandle the undersigned in the tale entitled *The Shambler From the Stars*.
>
> [signed] H.P. Lovecraft

The title "Mijnheer" suggests that Prinn is conceived of as a Dutchman, not a German, as "mijnheer" is the Dutch-language equivalent of "Mister."

PRIOR (TT): The narrator begins to scrawl on the flyleaves of his books witty remarks "which brought up suggestions of Gay [and] Prior," along with other English wits and "rimesters" of the early 18th century. Matthew Prior (1664–1721), poet and diplomat, wrote mostly humorous and gently-satirical verse.

PROSPECT STREET: The "Halsey Mansion" (1801), the model for Charles Dexter Ward's family home, stands at 140 Prospect Street in Providence. HPL's last residence, the "Lewis Mumford House" (1825), which then stood at 66 College Street, was moved to 65 Prospect Street in 1959.

PROSPECT TERRACE (CDW): HPL's own description in this tale, one surely based on earliest memories, cannot be bettered:

> The nurse used to stop and sit on the benches of Prospect Terrace to chat with policemen; and one of the child's first memories was of the great westward sea of hazy roofs and domes and steeples and far hills which he saw one winter afternoon from that great railed embankment, all violet and mystic against a fevered, apocalyptic sunset of reds and golds and purples and curious greens.

Located at the corner of Congdon and Cushing Streets in the College Hill district, Prospect Terrace still offers a panoramic view of central Providence and its environs, facing west in the direction of the sunset.

PROVIDENCE: The capital, and only large city, of the northeastern state of Rhode Island; which is itself the smallest state in the Union, only 1,545 square miles. At the turn of the 20th century the population of Providence was about 120,000 people, and after another century it still hasn't approached 200,000. The initial colonial settlement was founded by Roger Williams in 1636, as a refuge for himself and other religious dissenters unwelcome in the Puritan semi-theocracy of Massachusetts; by contrast, Providence offered genuine religious freedom, promised even to Jews or "Turks" (Muslims). It is ideally positioned as a harbor, at the head of Narragansett Bay, where the Seekonk River flows to the sea. It is the home of Brown University, the Rhode Island School of Design, and other institutions of higher learning. During the 18th and 19th centuries Providence prospered quietly but steadily as a regional center of trade and manufacturing, and amassed a nice collection of architectural highlights, most of which HPL mentions in various tales.

Many a reader from afar may have felt tempted to visit the city of which HPL wrote so ecstatically. The fact is that Providence is a pleasant-enough New England city with some attractive views, and some well-preserved and handsome public and private buildings of the 18th and 19th centuries; but it is hardly a wonder of the world. HPL's Angell Street is attractive along most of its length, in its New England style, but there are probably a hundred other streets up and down in New England that are as attractive or better. It is hard to imagine many objective visitors considering Providence superior (simply as a matter of visual appeal) to Paris, San Francisco, or any of a whole host of other scenic cities or towns of lesser note. Quite a lot of Providence, even the central part that HPL praised so shrilly, is frankly drab and could scarcely have been otherwise in the early 20th century.

To be sure, HPL loved Providence perhaps more than anyone else ever has, as his tales and letters make clear. But after a while one may begin to suspect that if he had been born and raised in Poughkeepsie, New York, or Portland, Oregon, or anywhere else, it would have been all the same to him; he would have loved that place as much instead, and come up with sufficient reasons for doing so. It was a matter of his nature, his dominating love for the first places he knew, the first things he saw.

PROVIDENCE ART CLUB (CC): Henry A. Wilcox is a brilliant but disturbing artist in Providence during the 1920s; the Club, "anxious to preserve its conservatism, had found him quite hopeless." Founded in 1880, the Providence Art Club still exists but it is certainly less conservative today.

PROVIDENCE *BULLETIN*; *JOURNAL*; *TELEGRAM* (HD): Real local papers. The hapless 1890s reporter Edwin M. Lillibridge covered the news "for the old Providence *Telegram.*" On July 17, 1935, the morning newspaper the *Journal* reports that during a power failure on Federal Hill the night before, members of the Italian community had gone almost "mad with fright," and had surrounded the old Starry Wisdom church bearing lighted candles, and complaining about the strange noises from within. That day, some reporters from the evening *Bulletin* go to have a look inside the abandoned church. In her memoirs, HPL's ex-wife Sonia stated that the Providence *Bulletin* was one of her husband's favorite newspapers.

PTH'THYA-L'YI (SOT): One of the Deep Ones, who became Obed Marsh's secret second wife after 1846 and who bore him three children. The older and younger offspring were never seen, but the middle child, a daughter, appeared completely human on the outside and was married off "by a trick" to the unsuspecting Benjamin Orne, of Arkham. The narrator sees Pth'thya-l'yi in a dream; she is his great-great-grandmother. She had lived in the city of Y'ha-nthlei (on the ocean floor where it makes a great descent on the far side of Devil Reef) for 80,000 years before leaving to marry Captain Marsh, and she returned there after the mortal's death. She tells him that the Deep Ones can never be destroyed, but would resurface some day to take "the tribute that Cthulhu craved": a bigger city than Innsmouth, next time. She tells the narrator that when he comes to live with them, he will have to do a penance for his misguided actions, but not a heavy one.

PTOLEMAIS (PH): There were several cities in the ancient Mediterranean world named after the Ptolemaic dynasty in late classical Egypt, or some of its individual members, who all had "Ptolemy" in their names. One city of Ptolemais was an important seaport in the classical-era region of Cyrenaica in North Africa; it is now Tolmeita in the nation of Libya. This Ptolemais was founded in the 3rd century B.C. and named after Ptolemy II Philadelphius, the Greco-Egyptian pharaoh at the time. The city grew to its height of wealth and splendor during the Roman Empire, in the 3rd century A.D. After centuries of barbarian invasions and urban decline, great Ptolemais was finally abandoned by its last inhabitants in the 11th century. Thereafter it lay mostly buried in sand, and known only through classical writings, until 20th century excavations brought the ancient city to light.

Or it may have been the port known to the Greeks and Romans as Ptolemais in Palestine, the "Acre" of the Crusaders, now Akko in the nation of Israel. This Ptolemais is mentioned in the Bible, in Acts 21:7, as having been visited for a day by St. Paul. It is unresolvable from the tale, which Ptolemais HPL may have had in mind. "Ptolemais" is mentioned in an Edgar Allen Poe fiction which HPL had of course previously read: *Shadow—A Parable.*

PURPLE SPIDERS (DQ): They lived in vales near Leng; in ancient times the almost-humans of Leng fought what must have been especially distasteful wars with these giant spiders.

Q

QUANTUM PHYSICS (DWH): Quantum physics, sometimes known as quantum mechanics, is that branch of mathematical physics which deals with the emission and absorption of energy by matter, and with the motion of infinitesimal material particles. Its main theories were developed in the early 20th century by such renowned physicists as Max Planck and Niels Bohr. It is a particularly complex area of science. Niels Bohr once said that anyone who claimed to understand quantum physics had not understood quantum physics! Together with Einstein's theory of relativity, quantum science forms the theoretical basis of modern physics.

As a student at Miskatonic University in the 1920s, Walter Gilman studies this then-new, and very difficult topic of quantum physics, along with "non-Euclidean calculus" and folklore. This proves to be a dangerous mixture.

HPL's youthful progress toward a longed-for career as a professional astronomer ended when he proved to be no better than an average– to below-average student in high school algebra. As he well understood, the ability to master higher mathematics was a pre-condition for advanced studies and academic work in astronomy, and his dream died. Years later he told a friend:

> It was *algebra* which formed the bugbear. Geometry was not so bad. But the whole thing disappointed me bitterly, for I was then intending to pursue *astronomy* as a career, and of course advanced astronomy is simply a mass of mathematics.

But during the rest of his life he took a sophisticated layman's interest in the contemporary progress of the physical sciences. In the tale *Hypnos* he wrote: "One man with Oriental eyes [certainly a reference to the Jew, Albert Einstein] has said that all space and time are relative, and men have laughed. But even that man with Oriental eyes has done no more than suspect. I had wished and tried to do more than suspect...."

HPL may have been more prescient than he could have imagined in *The Dreams in the Witch House*; certainly, some people active in outer-fringe, creative thinking in science are still pondering ways to travel through space and time as well as the witch Keziah Mason ever could. Interstellar travel remains a practical impossibility because of the fantastic amount of energy necessary to propel an object at close to the speed of light; a problem known as "the Einstein barrier." Time travel appears even more inconceivable. However, theoretical subtleties inherent within Einstein's general theory of relativity and quantum mechanics, may hold the answer. If it were possible to physically alter or deform four-dimensional space-time, the argument goes, then a kind of space-time "tunnel" or "gate" could be constructed. In the jargon of contemporary physics, such theoretical tunnels are sometimes called "traversable wormholes." A traversable wormhole would be literally a shortcut through both space and time. If cosmic-scale engineering were a reality, then one could conceivably fabricate traversable wormhole time-travel gates, enter a wormhole in one region of space-time, and emerge in another region of space-time—perhaps extremely distant. The science for this kind of speculative physics is radically complex, involving such esoteric topics as "dark matter" and "imaginary time." Still, it is interesting to compare this unorthodox contemporary research with the descriptions of the space-time travel of Walter Gilman, Keziah Mason, Brown Jenkin, and Nyarlathotep, written in 1931.

QUATREFAGES (WD): *See* "Anthropologists of the Mi-Go."

QUEBEC (MM): While his ship approaches the Antarctic coastline, Professor Dyer notes "the great ice barrier; rising perpendicularly to a height of 200 feet like the rocky coast of cliffs of Quebec." The reference is to the bluff which upholds the "Upper Town" of the city of Quebec, in Canada, a cliff which attains an elevation of 300 feet above the St. Lawrence River.

Among the longest individual works HPL ever wrote was a book-length travelogue entitled *A Description of the Town of Quebeck, in New-France, Lately Added to His Britannic Majesty's Dominions.* This item is a detailed companion to the historic locales of Quebec city; all written, incredibly, in ersatz 18th-century English prose—a dead idiom which HPL had loved and attempted to master (with moderate success) almost from his cradle. This book, which one writer has aptly termed "an impressively scholarly but curious indulgence," monopolized more or less all of HPL's writing time for five months in 1930–31. But it was seemingly never intended for publication, never even typed from HPL's manuscript original, and it moldered like its composer for many years. In 1976, Lovecraft biographer L. Sprague de Camp saw to the book's tardy publication from HPL's manuscript, but it remains a rare curiosity. One sample: "Among the most striking events of [a past era] is the wholesale conversion of redskins by Jesuit missionaries, who work'd over the whole region & branch'd out into unknown inland domains with fanatical zeal & incredible bravery. Learning the Indian tongue, these heroick fathers endur'd every hardship of the wilderness & in many cases suffer'd martyrdom amidst incredible tortures." There are some 75,000 words of this sub-Johnsonian antiquarianism, which certainly proved that HPL could churn out mediocre imitations of Georgian prose in middle age as readily as he could churn out mediocre imitations of Georgian poetry in his younger years. The best thing that can be said about *A Description of the Town of Quebeck* may be, as Lovecraft biographer S.T. Joshi has suggested, that it seems to have given HPL real pleasure to compose, and it was certainly his privilege to write for his own solitary pleasure.

R

RAABE (TE): An engineer on board German submarine U-29 in 1917; he is killed instantly in the boiler-room explosion on June 28, 1917.

RAEBURN (CDW): Sir Henry Raeburn (1756–1823), a Scot, was one of the most talented and successful British portrait-painters of his time. In the tale, he is mentioned as an equal to Cosmo Alexander, the Scot who painted Joseph Curwen's portrait.

RAKUS, TRANSYLVANIA (CDW): The nearest village to the castle of "Count Ferenczy," who is really Edward Hutchinson. Once within the kingdom of Hungary, it becomes part of Romania following the border adjustments after World War I. (One of Hutchinson's letters to Curwen complains rather amusingly that the new Romanian authorities were harder to bribe than the Magyars—*i.e.*, Hungarians—had been.) Charles Dexter Ward sent his parents a postcard from Rakus early in 1925, saying that Count Ferenczy's carriage had just arrived to meet him, and that he was about to depart for the mountain castle.

RANGER (SOI): A merchant ship owned by the Gilman family of Innsmouth. She is lost at sea with all hands, probably during the 1820s, taking many good Innsmouth men down with her and hastening the town's economic and moral decline.

RAYMOND (IV): A resident of the Peck Valley region who was financially ruined by the ever-vengeful Asaph Sawyer, thirty years after the two men had a lawsuit over a property line.

RED HOOK (HRH): A waterfront slum in the borough of Brooklyn, New York City, on the murky shores of Gowanus Bay. Nowadays it is a slum for blacks and Hispanics; in the 1920s it was a slum full of new immigrants from southern Europe and the Middle East and their first-generation American offspring. These poor and darker-skinned New Yorkers were nightmare and anathema to the author, and in the tale, HPL calls Red Hook "a maze of hybrid squalor...a babel of sound and filth...this tangle of material and spiritual putrescence...." The heart of the district is only about a mile and a half straight along Clinton Street from HPL's 1925–26 studio apartment at 169 Clinton Street in the more pleasant district of Brooklyn Heights. The fictional horror at Red Hook is devil worship and infant sacrifice, combined with visitations of the demoness Lilith. The principal culprits are the teeming hordes of Central Asian immigrants in the area, chiefly a Kurdish sect of "Yezidi devil worshippers."

The Horror at Red Hook was written during HPL's 1924–26 "New York Exile," and should not be judged too harshly, although it is not very good. The author was in a delicate mental state as a result of the combined pressures of an unsuitable marriage, prolonged absence from Providence, fruitless searches for appropriate employment, and his disgust at the polyglot ethnicity of New York City, something he could only see as the decadent mongrelization of a formerly "white" American city. Years later, his ex-wife Sonia wrote about the origin of this tale:

> It was on an evening while he and [a few friends] were dining in a restaurant somewhere in Columbia Heights [in Manhattan] that a few rough, rowdyish men entered. He was so annoyed by their churlish behavior that out of this circumstance he wove "The Horror at Red Hook". This one story alone perhaps indicates the hatred he developed for New York in general—a hatred that made him nostalgic for his beloved Providence.

A specific memory of the rowdy churls in the restaurant may lie behind HPL's obsessively thorough description of the horde of "bleareyed and pockmarked young men," foreign-born youths decked out like gangsters in "flashy American clothing," whom the tale's hero, Brooklyn detective Thomas Malone, constantly notices lurking and congregating on street corners, at cafeteria tables, or in the dark around taxi cabs pulled up in front of tightly-shuttered old houses.

REGAN, PATRICK (HD): An Irish-American denizen of 19th century Federal Hill, in Providence. He disappeared mysteriously in 1869, whereupon a crowd of other Irish youths mobbed the Starry Wisdom church, presumably searching for him.

REID, DR. (PM): A mutual acquaintance of Pickman, the artist, and Thurber, the narrator. He is among those so-called "fussy old women" (in Pickman's scornful words) who socially "dropped" or "cut" the increasingly sinister painter in the years or months prior to his disappearance. In Reid's case, the last straw was Pickman's nasty laugh when Mr. Eliot asked him where he found the grotesque faces—ghoul faces—that he painted.

> Reid, you know, had just taken up comparative pathology, and was full of pompous "inside stuff" about the biological or evolutionary significance of this or that mental or physical syndrome. He said Pickman repelled him more and more every day, and almost frightened him toward the last—that

the fellow's features were developing in a way he didn't like, in a way that wasn't human. He had a lot of talk about diet....

Later, Pickman himself curses the absent Dr. Reid for "whispering that I'm a sort of monster bound down the toboggan of reverse evolution." But Reid was right.

REMIGIUS (TF, DH): The author of *Daemonolatreia*, a book on sorcery methods and detection published in France in 1595, which the nameless narrator of *The Festival* glimpses in the house on Green Lane in Kingsport. Dr. Armitage also consults this tome while trying to decide just what could be done about the Dunwich Horror. "Remigius" was the Latinized name of Nicolas Remy (1530–1612), a judge and ducal privy counselor in Lorraine (at that time an independent duchy, and subsequently a part of France). On the title page of his book, Remigius, concerned like any other serious how-to author with proving his credentials, indicated that in 15 years of hard work on the criminal-court bench he had sent 900 witches ("more or less") to their executions. HPL seems likely to have read of Remigius and also the Spanish witch-hunter he called "Delrio" (*see* separate entry) in the ninth chapter of the massive treatise *A History of the Warfare of Science with Theology in Christendom* (1896), by Andrew Dickson White, LL.B., Ph.D., co-founder and former president of Cornell University; the book's very title would have operated like catnip on the young infidel and science buff in Providence.

RICCI, ANGELO (TOM): One of three robbers who attempt to rob the Terrible Old Man in his Kingsport cottage. He and Manuel Silva invade the home, while their accomplice Joe Czanek waits in the getaway car. Ricci is never seen alive after that; presumably his is one of the three mutilated bodies that the tide washes up a day or two later.

RICE, STEPHEN (COS): A rural neighbor of Nahum Gardner and Ammi Pierce. While driving his horse and wagon past the Gardner place one morning in March, 1883, he noted that the newly-sprouted skunk cabbages (a type of wild vegetation, not a food crop) were of abnormal size with bizarre shapes and colors.

RICE, PROFESSOR WARREN (DH): A "stocky, iron-grey" Miskatonic University professor; in the summer of 1927, he is a witness to the death and dissolution of Wilbur Whateley at the university library. Later, he and Dr. Morgan assist Dr. Armitage in eradicating the Dunwich Horror.

RIDER, SIDNEY S. (SH): A Providence antiquarian and book-dealer, Sidney S. Rider (1833–1917) authored the series of "Rhode Island Historical Tracts" circa 1880, and published other works of local history.

In the tale, it is mentioned that the narrator's history-minded kinsman Dr. Elihu Whipple often "broke a lance" (*i.e.*, engaged in friendly debate; from the wooden lances which medieval knights broke on each other's shields and armor in tournaments) with Mr. Rider.

RILEY, SERGEANT (CDW): A city of Providence policeman in 1927, assigned to the police department's Second Station. He gives his opinion that the first nocturnal-digging outrage at North Burial Ground (which was actually Charles Dexter Ward's removal of Joseph Curwen's lead-lined casket from its unmarked grave) was the work of bootleggers seeking a new hiding-place for their illegal liquor. (During the years 1919–33 in the United States—the so-called "Prohibition Era"—the trade in wine, beer, and liquor became a federal crime and illicit smugglers and sellers of alcohol—known as "bootleggers"—made fortunes from millions of citizens who wanted to buy a drink.) The second incident (really the grave-robbing of Ezra Weeden's remains) was something different, the policeman thinks. But when asked by the newspapers for more comments after the mysterious April, 1928 digging in the Ward family plot (when Dr. Willett buried Charles Dexter Ward's remains in secret), Sergeant Riley attributes the activity to bootleggers again.

RIMBAUD (WD): Of his midnight escape by automobile from Henry Akeley's remote farm, Dr. Wilmarth says: "The ride that followed was a piece of delirium out of Poe or Rimbaud or the drawings of Doré." Arthur Rimbaud (1854–91), a Frenchman, was the original modern poet/rebellious youth, living fast, shocking the bourgeoisie, furiously rejecting all authority, and eventually even rejecting poetry as well—he stopped writing poems in about 1875 before turning to what was more or less a life of crime in Asia and Africa. Moreover, he was homosexual or bisexual and didn't care who knew it. Rimbaud's bad-boy glamour, as much as his frenzied and controversial poems ("A Season in Hell" is a characteristic title), made him famous by the time he was in his late teens, and he has served as an icon for successive generations of artistic rebels and would-be rebels ever since. The poet's character (mostly bad), his conduct, and his unconventional poetry were *so* opposite to HPL and his traditional versification that it is surprising to see his name in a Lovecraft tale; but his study of alchemy and occultism, and his manifesto that true artists must cultivate "the derangement of the senses" could have had some appeal.

RINAR (DQ): One of the places where dressed onyx stones from Inganok are prized and traded.

R'LYEH (CC, WD, MM, TGSK): The home of the "Cthulhu-spawn" in remote prehistoric ages; in a great cataclysm it sank beneath the waters of what is now the South Pacific Ocean. But its inhabitants live on in their enormous stone houses, in a kind of suspended animation that will continue for millions of years. The Cthulhu-cultists of our time chant a phrase: *Ph'nglui mglw'nafh Cthulhu R'lyeh wgah'nagl fhtagn*—which their elders say means "something like": *In his house at R'lyeh dead Cthulhu waits dreaming.* The surviving crewmen of the *Emma* go ashore on R'lyeh after it has risen from the ocean floor; only two men survive the landing and their encounter with Cthulhu, and one of them for not long. Glimpsed on their quick entry and quicker exit, R'lyeh is a nightmare place of completely inhuman scale and monstrously large stone buildings, full of surfaces and turns that are inexplicably shaped in "crazily elusive angles" that seem to abnormally defy earthly geometry, and covered with the green sea-algae of ages. Apparently it is returned to the oceanic depths a short time later, but the lasting mental anguish of those few investigators who know about R'lyeh is that it is still down there, and will re-surface eventually to end the world as we know it. R'lyeh is mentioned in passing in *The Whisperer in Darkness* and *At the Mountains of Madness*; in *Through the Gates of the Silver Key* it is mentioned that the mysterious parchment found with the silver key bears hieroglyphic writing in "R'lyehian, which was brought to earth by the spawn of Cthulhu countless cycles ago."

ROBBINS, MARIA (SH): A maidservant in William Harris' household. She is "a faithful and amiable Amazon" from Newport, Rhode Island (the word "Amazon" alluding to unusual strength and endurance for a woman), whom Mercy Dexter hires in 1769 to replace the fired gossip Ann White from Exeter. (Native Providence servants would no longer work at the house.) Maria Robbins was very tough and strong; in 1781 she is still alive, although after a dozen years in the house the former Amazon has become "stooped," "hollow-voiced," and of "disconcerting pallor." She even survives to make the move into a new home with William Harris, Jr. and his wife in 1783. Thereafter she lives at least long enough to be nursemaid to their son Dutee, born in 1785. In his own later years, Dutee Harris recalls that his old nurse Maria Robbins:

> seemed darkly aware of something that might have lent a weird significance to the French ravings of Rhoby Harris, which she had so often heard during the last days of that hapless woman. Maria...had seen Mercy Dexter die. Once she hinted to the child Dutee of a somewhat peculiar circumstance in Mercy's last moments, but he had soon forgotten all about it save that it was something peculiar.

ROBINSON, BUCK ("The Harlem Smoke") (HW): A ridiculous black man in a ridiculous horror story. Still, his turn on the stage is not without interest. Buck Robinson is a poor-quality boxer brought to Bolton, Massachusetts for a secret, illegal prizefight against another wretched boxer, "Kid O'Brien," one night in March, 1905. He takes a bad blow to the head and dies in the ring. According to Dr. West's comrade, the deceased fighter "was a loathsome, gorilla-like thing, with abnormally long arms which I could not help calling fore legs [a fore-shadowing!], and a face that conjured up thoughts of unspeakable Congo secrets and tom-tom poundings under an eerie moon." Dr. West and his comrade are quietly sent for to dispose of the body, and they carry it off—but only for another experiment with their revivifying chemical injections. The shots do not work, absurdly, because of Robinson's race; the "solutions [were] prepared from experience with white specimens only," an example of the racist pseudo-science that many in HPL's time would have accepted without a qualm. So, into a shallow grave goes the erstwhile Harlem Smoke, his fire snuffed out. The next afternoon a five-year-old boy is missing in Bolton. That very night at 3:00 a.m., the two mad scientists hear a "steady rattling at the back door," a very early example of the stealthy latch-rattling that seemed to haunt HPL enough to appear over and over again in his tales. When they open the door, they see "a glassy-eyed, ink-black apparition nearly on all fours [those fore legs!], covered with bits of mould, leaves, and vines, foul with caked blood" and holding in its teeth the torn-off arm of a little white child. Dr. West empties his revolver at the thing, and we may *assume* that this is the end of bad-luck Buck. However, in the last chapter when "the tomb-legions" seize and carry off Dr. West, one of their number is a huge black man, probably all that was left of the man who was Buck Robinson.

ROBINSON, COLLECTOR (CDW): Non-fictitious royal official in the government of the Rhode Island colony, in charge of collecting revenue in the form of duties and taxes of all kinds. In the tale, in 1770, the ship *Fortaleza* is seized for having entered Rhode Island waters without authorization—but carrying only a non-contraband (and non-taxable!) cargo of Egyptian mummies—and Robinson recommends that the ship be set free but forbidden to dock in Rhode Island; his recommendation is followed.

ROCHESTER (TT): "My formerly silent tongue waxed voluble with the easy grace of a Chesterfield or the godless cynicism of a Rochester," reports the narrator in discussing the result of spending night after night in an 18th century family crypt. John Wilmot (1647–80), second Earl of Rochester, packed much experience into few years. The English aristocrat matriculated at Oxford University at the unusual age of 12, and left with a Master of Arts degree at the age of 14—it helped, perhaps, that his uncle, the Earl of Clarendon, was the chancellor of the university. Still in his teens, Rochester became the hero of a sea-battle against the Dutch. His subsequent career was summed up a century later by the stern moralist Dr. Samuel Johnson (a favorite of HPL's), as follows:

> In a course of drunken gaiety and gross sensuality, with intervals of study perhaps yet more criminal, with an avowed contempt of decency and order, a total disregard to every moral, and a resolute denial of every religious observation, he lived worthless and useless, and blazed out his youth and health in lavish voluptuousness.

(The above lines have been quoted at length partly to demonstrate the influence that the English literary prose of the 18th century often had upon HPL's writing style, which reveled in piling well-made clause upon clause.) The Earl of Rochester died at 33, presumably of syphilis. His talented poetry and his one play (entitled *Sodom, or, the Quintessence of Debauchery*) tended toward the obscene and atheistic, and were often banned or condemned.

ROCK WITH NO NAME (DQ): Two days' sailing from Inganok, out in the open sea, is a large, rocky island with no name. It is the fortress of the moonbeasts, with their galleys. Randolph Carter passes the island while sailing from Celephaïs to Inganok: it appears as a great, jagged cliff protruding from the sea, and dull, ceaseless howling can be heard coming from it every night. The captain of Carter's vessel notes that no ship would ever land there. Later on in Leng, from looking at the fresco paintings in the monastery of the high priest not to be described, Carter deduces that this rock was the earth-station of the moonbeasts. When Carter and the ghoul Pickman lead a force of ghouls and night-gaunts to eliminate the shipload of moonbeasts and almost-humans then in Sarko-mand, the three ghouls they have rescued suggest that they now take the moonbeasts' galley and use it to attack and wipe out the colony on the rock. This is done.

On inspection, the rock has steep sides, with bulging-walled dwellings that are queerly-made and windowless, like the houses on the moon which Randolph Carter had previously seen. The island has a small harbor with stone quays, and a town with "towers and aeries and fortresses" carved from the solid rock. Investigating the interiors of the structures, Carter finds many poor prisoners in torture chambers and dungeons, including some even weirder creatures than he has already seen: he puts them all out of their misery. In the homes of the unpleasant moonbeasts, he finds "grotesque stools and benches carven from moon-trees," and walls painted with "nameless and frantic designs." In their temples, carved into chambers high up on the great rock, Carter finds evidence of hideous rites and living sacrifices. There is a cavern-network as well: "a low black passage which Carter followed far into the rock with a torch until he came to a lightless domed hall of vast proportions, whose vaultings were covered with daemoniac carvings...." The other exits from this cave were "a foul and bottomless well" in the floor, and on the far side of the chamber "a small door of strangely wrought bronze." Carter does not feel like investigating any further—time is pressing to find Kadath—and we never learn where the well and the door might have led to.

RODRIGUEZ (CC): He is a Portuguese sailor on the *Emma*. He survives the sea-battle with the *Alert* and transfers to that vessel as the *Emma* sinks. He lands on R'lyeh with his fellow-sailors. At the foot of the great stone monolith which the men had first glimpsed from the sea, Rodriguez finds "the immense carved door with the now-familiar squid-dragon bas-relief," as big a large barn-door; it is the entrance to Cthulhu's house. When Cthulhu emerges from deep within, Rodriguez simply drops dead from terror.

ROERICH, NICHOLAS (MM): Nikolai Konstantinovich Roerich (1874–1947), was a famed painter and theatrical set-designer. Born in St. Petersburg, Russia, he made his name before the Russian Revolution as a painter-designer of spectacular backdrops for prestigious opera and ballet performances, particularly those set in the distant past or in other worlds. In Paris he painted the famous backdrops for the first performance of Igor Stravinsky's groundbreaking modern symphonic music/dance piece, *Le Sacre du Printemps* (*The Rite of Spring*, 1913). After permanently emigrating to the West in the wake of the Russian Revolution, and becoming known as a studio artist, he turned to Buddhism and mysticism, and even traveled to trek and paint in the Himalayas of Tibet and Nepal, far from a swift or easy journey in the 1920s. Roerich's evocative and haunting paintings of vaguely "prehistoric" landscapes became well-known, and were alluded to by HPL in this tale, when the bleak and desolate coast of Antarctica reminds Professor Dyer of the Russian's "Asian" paintings. Later, commenting on the lines of low ramparts visible on the high Antarctic mountains he has discovered, Professor Lake comments: "—like the old Asian castles clinging to steep mountains in Roerich's paintings."

HPL saw some of Roerich's "Himalayan" paintings at the Roerich Museum in New York City in 1930, less than a year before beginning this tale, and wrote privately: "Surely Roerich is one of those rare fantastic souls who have glimpsed the grotesque, terrible secrets outside space

& beyond time, & who have retained some ability to hint at the marvels they may have seen." Lovecraft biographer S.T. Joshi has noted that HPL mentions Roerich six times in *At the Mountains of Madness*, "as if Lovecraft is going out of his way to signal the influence."

ROKOL (DCS): A place at some great distance from the city of Sarnath; her princes travel to the celebration of the 1000th anniversary of the destruction of Ib.

ROMERO, JUAN (TJR): A young Mexican miner, part of the horde of diggers and laborers employed by the Norton Mine in the summer and autumn of 1894, when the narrator also works there. His features "though plainly of the Red Indian type, were yet remarkable for their light colour and refined conformation," and reminiscent of the ancient, noble Aztecs instead of the "common" Mexican or Indian. Except for his noble-Aztec face, there is nothing exceptional about Romero, who is "ignorant and dirty, the orphan child (apparently) of unknown peasants in Old Mexico, and reared by a cattle-thief, who had named him." Romero becomes very interested in the narrator's "Hindoo" ring and its curiously symbolic engravings. They seem to stir some memory deep inside him, and he attaches himself to the narrator as a kind of servant. On the night of October 18–19, deep within a cave at the bottom of the mine and witnessed only by the narrator, Juan Romero undergoes his Aztec "transition."

The Transition of Juan Romero is neither very frightening nor very good. Lovecraft disliked it, and it was never published until 1944, seven years after his death. But, written in 1919 when HPL was still developing his mature style, it offers foretastes of many themes that would be hallmarks: caverns and subterranean worlds; "racial memory"; the stock Lovecraftian narrator-protagonist, well-bred, bookish, solitary, often reduced from past prosperity, given to observation more than action, and prone to fainting when the scene needs to change; the ever-recurring "gibbous moon"; astronomy; an abyss that appears and then disappears, replaced by seemingly solid rock; and much more. Also, as HPL's only "western" tale (except for *The Mound* and *The Curse Of Yig*, ghostwritten years later for a paying client from Oklahoma), it demonstrates the capable way that the author—who at this time had never even ventured out of his own corner of New England—could soak up "local color" from reading and nimbly employ it in his own fiction.

ROMNOD (QI): A youth from the dull, granite-built city of Teloth. On the day that the wandering minstrel Iranon is expelled from Teloth for unwillingness to take on "gainful employment" as an apprentice shoemaker, little Romnod is a sad-eyed boy watching the sluggish river Zuro, hoping to see green, budding branches washed down the river from someplace more attractive. He joins Iranon and travels with him for years, singing together and living off the land, until they reach the fabulous city of Oonai. By now a young man, Romnod takes heartily to the city's luxurious way of life, feasting, drinking, and reveling until he has turned red-faced and coarse, sodden and obese. "Then one night the red and fattened Romnod snorted heavily amidst the poppied silks of his banquet couch and died writhing, while Iranon, pale and slender" lived on. The ascetic and long-lived Iranon buries his ex-comrade's bloated body under a pile of green, budding branches, symbols of Romnod's lost youthful beauty and idealism. It may be noted that HPL's tall and almost-gaunt natural physique was important enough to him to carefully preserve with long walks and very moderate eating habits, reinforced by his poverty, lifelong abstinence from alcohol, and instinctively monkish ways. Ironically he would die of natural causes at 47 years of age, regardless of a lifetime of self-denial and ascetic moderation.

ROODMAS; CANDLEMAS (DH, CDW): In one of the several pompous and verbose mutterings to himself that are one of this story's unfortunate means of carrying the plot forward, Dr. Armitage asks: "Born on Candlemas—nine months after May-Eve of 1912.... What walked on the mountains that May-Night? What Roodmas horror fastened itself on the world in half-human flesh and blood?" Roodmas, the old English name for the religious day which celebrates the finding of the True Cross (the "Rood" or "Holy Rood"—a word akin to rod and reed), is celebrated in some churches on May 3. Dr. Armitage is talking about Wilbur Whately, his conception and his birth on Candlemas day (February 2). In *The Case of Charles Dexter Ward*, Joseph Curwen in 1754 speaks of the verse from the "Liber-Damnatus" that he must repeat for several Roodmasses and Hallows-Eves (Halloweens) in a row.

ROPES (MM): A graduate student member of the Miskatonic University Expedition, and one of the team's airplane pilots. Ropes and Danforth are the graduate students who remain with Professor Dyer and his colleague Pabodie, and then go with the professors on the rescue mission for the Lake-Atwood party on January 25, 1931. Ropes takes over the aircraft controls to make the difficult landing. He assists Professor Pabodie and the other men in repairing aircraft while Dyer and Danforth go on their aerial reconnaissance. Ropes returns to the United States subsequently with the other survivors.

ROSA, SALVATOR (COS): An Italian baroque painter and etcher (1615–73). He is famed for his highly romantic or "sublime" landscapes. They tend to be picturesque, somewhat eerie scenes of wild nature, in which any human figures appear small and isolated. In *The Colour Out of Space,* the nameless narrator writes of the haunted countryside near the old Gardner homestead, full of long-abandoned farmhouses and too-thick woods: "Upon everything was...a touch of the unreal and the grotesque... This was no region to sleep in. It was too much like a landscape of Salvator Rosa."

ROULET FAMILY (SH): A family of French *Huguenots* (the often-persecuted Protestant dissenters from the official Catholic faith of France), originally from the town of Caude, in France. They settled in East Greenwich, Rhode Island in 1686, but became unpopular there and were expelled from the community in 1696. Having been given permission by the authorities of Providence to settle in that larger town, they lease a small tract of land in the "Throckmorton lot" in 1697, and construct a one-story dwelling with an attic—and a private family graveyard in the back. The contemporary members of the Roulet family were slaughtered by an angry Providence mob some 35 years later during the 1730s. Later, when Back Street (subsequently Benefit Street) is cut through and partly straightened between 1747–58, the Roulet graves are not transferred to North Burial Ground along with the remains from all the other old family burying-places; and the "shunned house" is built right on top of them in 1763, after their location has been forgotten.

The narrator recalls reading an account of the reputed werewolf "Jacques Roulet, of Caude" in France, who was condemned to death as a lycanthrope in 1598 but was later reprieved and put in a madhouse. Dr. Whipple suggested to him that *something* about the Roulet graves was the bad influence in the house; not a ghost—HPL did not believe in ghosts and neither do his investigators—but "an alien nucleus of substance or energy, formless or otherwise, kept alive by imperceptible or immaterial subtractions from the life-force...of...living things into which it penetrate[d]." Such a thing, we are told, "was surely not a physical or biochemical impossibility in the light of a newer science which include[d] the theories of relativity and intra-atomic action." Here, of course, HPL was tossing out the whole apparatus of traditional ghosts, vampires, shape-shifters, and other occult frighteners, while concocting a more-or-less scientific or "mechanistic" horror to suit his own rationalist and materialist beliefs. The narrator asks rhetorically, had "kinetic patterns in the morbid brain" of Paul Roulet "continued to function in some multiple-dimensioned space along the original lines of force?"

The case of Jacques Roulet is well-known and still appears to this day in popular accounts of "werewolves." In his time, HPL could have read the story in a number of sources, such as John Fiske's fine book *Myths and Myth-Makers: Old Tales and Superstitions Interpreted by Compara-*

tive Mythology (1872), a copy of which was in HPL's personal library. Discussing the origins of the werewolf legend, Fiske wrote:

> In the year 1598, "in a wild and unfrequented spot near Caude, some countrymen came one day upon the corpse of a boy of fifteen, horribly mutilated and bespattered with blood. As the men approached, two wolves, which had been rending the body, bounded away into the thicket. The men gave chase immediately, following their bloody tracks till they lost them; when, suddenly crouching among the bushes, his teeth chattering with fear, they found a man half naked, with long hair and beard, and with his hands dyed in blood. His nails were long as claws, and were clotted with fresh gore and shreds of human flesh." [Citation omitted] This man, Jacques Roulet, was a poor, half-witted creature under the dominion of a cannibal appetite. He was employed in tearing to pieces the corpse of the boy when these countrymen came up. Whether there were any wolves in the case, except what the excited imaginations of the men may have conjured up, I will not presume to determine; but it is certain that Roulet supposed himself to be a wolf, and killed and ate several persons under the influence of the delusion. He was sentenced to death, but the parliament [*parlement*, similar to a court of appeals] of Paris reversed the sentence, and charitably shut him up in a madhouse.

ROULET, ETIENNE (SH): The head of the Roulet family when they moved to Providence in 1696. Swarthy, and "less apt at agriculture than at reading queer books and drawing queer diagrams," he gets a job as a clerk in the warehouse at Pardon Tillinghast's wharf. He is already dead by the time of the riot that exterminated the Roulet family in the 1730s.

ROULET, PAUL (SH): The son of Etienne: "a surly fellow whose erratic conduct had probably provoked the riot which wiped out the family." Some people in Providence said his prayers "were neither uttered at the proper time nor directed toward the proper object."

ROUND HILL (WD): A fictitious wooded hill one and a half miles east of the Akeley place near Townshend, Vermont. Here, Henry Akeley found the "black stone." It is "a notorious haunted spot"; later, Professor Wilmarth could find no one in the area, other than Mr. Akeley, who had ever dared to explore it. Wilmarth learns that the principal earthly outpost of the Mi-Go is *inside* Round Hill, and that this lair is "a very cosmopolitan place," as one disembodied brain puts it, because of all the disembodied brains from all over the galaxy that are stored here in metal cylinders.

ROUND MOUNTAIN (DH): A fictitious mountain close to Dunwich village.

ROWLEY (SOI): A small, non-fictitious Massachusetts village south of Newburyport; it is said to lie further inland from "Innsmouth." The narrator escapes from Innsmouth at night by following a set of abandoned branch-railroad tracks to Rowley, while his pursuers fruitlessly hunt for him on the Rowley road. The next morning in Rowley, he had a meal and buys some new clothing, then catches the evening train to Arkham.

RUE D'AUSEIL (MEZ): A little street in a great, but unnamed, French city, where the narrator lives in a tenement block owned by a certain Monsieur Blandot. Rue d'Auseil is gloomy and mysterious, so mysterious in fact that the narrator cannot even find it again after he has moved away; in subsequent consultations with city maps of all historical periods, and long searches on foot, he can not "find the house, the street, or even the locality, where during the last months of my impoverished life as a student of metaphysics at the university, I heard the music of Erich Zann." Even though he recalled the street as being less than half an hour's walk from the university, "I have never met a person who has seen the Rue d'Auseil." It lay on one side of a dark, stench-ridden river, bordered by shadowy old warehouses and factories. It was unreasonably narrow and steep, "almost a cliff, closed to all vehicles, consisting in several places of flights of steps, and ending at the top in a lofty ivied wall." Rue d'Auseil is paved partly with stone slabs, partly with cobblestones, and partly with packed soil. The houses are medieval and lean in all directions, sometimes bending into each other across the way and blocking out all light beneath them; there are aerial bridges built between some others. The inhabitants are all silent and very old. Only one window in the entire street—the one in Erich Zann's attic flat—allows a view of the rest of the city.

RUSSELL FAMILY (CDW): In the 1760s this non-fictitious family owned a shop at the Sign of the Golden Eagle in Providence. According to the tale, they depended almost entirely on Joseph Curwen to sell them the merchandise they retailed to the public. This pseudo-fact is dropped into the tale to suggest the great wealth and influence of Curwen in the town.

RUTLAND *HERALD* (WD): A real Vermont newspaper; in the tale, it prints "half a page of extracts from letters on both sides" of the dispute over the existence of mysterious hill-creatures; the letters are seen by Henry Akeley, who mentions them in his May 5, 1928 letter to Professor Wilmarth of Miskatonic University.

S

SADUCISMUS TRIUMPHATUS (TF): The book whose longer title is *Saducismus Triumphatus: Or, Full and Plain Evidence Concerning Witches and Apparitions*, by the English philosopher Joseph Glanvill (1636–80; he was a member of the 17th century intellectual movement now labeled as the Cambridge Platonists), is among the handful of peculiar old books that the narrator notices in the house on Green Lane. It was first published in 1681, in London, and contains many accounts of modern hauntings and witchcraft personally known to Glanvill, his friends and colleagues.

The "Sadducees" of New Testament times (see, *e.g.*, Matthew 3:7 and 16:1–12) were a Jewish sect that denied the existence of an afterlife, the resurrection of the dead, and the existence of angels and spirits; their principal opponents within Judaism were the more numerous and better-known-to-us Pharisees, who affirmed these things. The Sadducees, whose most prominent representatives included the ancient high-priestly families of Israel, completely disappeared from Jewish history after the destruction of the Temple in Jerusalem in 73 A.D. However, "Sadducism" in 17th century Christian theological jargon was a euphemism for agnostic or atheistic tendencies, which could begin with the denial of the reality of spirits, angels, and demons. The learned and science-minded Joseph Glanvill himself "was both a preeminent demonologist and a member of the Royal Society (for the advancement of scientific learning), which he urged to investigate apparitions and demons," according to a biographer. The Latin title means: "Sadducism Defeated." Although HPL may never have known it, Cotton Mather (*see* separate entry) kept a copy of *Saducismus Triumphatus* in his personal library.

SALEM; SALEM WITCH TRIALS (TF, DWH, CDW, DH, PM, SK, TGSK):

> For six months in 1692 a pack of young girls, mostly teenagers, were all-powerful in Massachusetts.... These girls were very ordinary young people, some of them daughters of farmers in an obscure village, some of them servingmaids. A few had been taught by their parents to spell out their Bibles; others were illiterate. Yet ministers and magistrates who read [the Bible] in Greek and Hebrew and corresponded in Latin, hung on their words as if they were Holy Gospel. For a time the Great and General Court

[the colonial legislature] conducted little business except that which concerned what came to be called "the visionary girls."

So did Marion Starkey begin her novel *The Visionary Girls*, a thinly-fictionalized companion to her classic history of Salem witchcraft, *The Devil in Massachusetts*.

The so-called Salem witch trials began not in the Massachusetts town that is still known as Salem, but in nearby Salem Village (later renamed Danvers), at the time a rural community of 500–600 people some miles north of Boston. But the disturbance would spread to a number of neighboring towns before running its course. Originally a group of girls and unmarried young women from this Puritan farming village, including the minister's own daughter, began to meet to have their fortunes told by a Indian slave-woman imported from a Caribbean island. Little by little, their secret meetings (fortune-telling was a criminal offense, and they would all have been punished severely by their families for engaging in the practice so alien to Puritan beliefs) turned into what today would be called a form of collective hysteria, a psychological condition not recognized or understood in the 17th century. Shrieking, gasping, barking like dogs, complaining of being vexed and pinched by invisible tormentors, the girls appeared to be plainly bewitched to the assortment of farmers, housewives, rural magistrates, and village ministers who saw them. The search for witches began, using time-honored methods and know-how used in the mother country, England. Names were named, and eventually hundreds of men and women in Salem and neighboring towns were jailed on suspicion of communicating with the Devil.

As the mania grew in scope and ferocity, a picture seemed to emerge of an immense conspiracy consisting of at least 300–500 witches and warlocks sworn to evil, all local people who for the most part led apparently blameless lives, and all leagued in secret against the Christian religion, good government, and their unsuspecting neighbors. Many suspects fed the conspiracy theory by confessing eagerly to crimes and coven meetings which could only have been imaginary; but the lives of "confessors" were spared. There were criminal trials for the more recalcitrant—in a special court which sat from May–October 1692—and nineteen men and women were eventually convicted and hanged. Within a short time the mania burned itself out, the surviving accused persons were quietly pardoned and released in 1693, and within a few more years opinion in the colony had swung to the belief that the entire affair had been a grievous mistake. By 1711 an official commission was doling out compensation payments to the families of the victims, and some of the "visionary girls" had stood up in their churches to express regrets and humble apologies for the fatal effects of their delusions.

Modern scholars, depending on their areas of interest, have tended to focus more on gender or socioeconomic issues, rather than spiritual explanations, for what went wrong in Salem in 1692 (or for that matter, in the incomparably larger massacre of so-called "witches" in western Europe during the 16th and 17th centuries). Closer in time and perhaps in religious feeling to the Salem persecutors, however, the Salem clergyman Charles W. Upham, in his classic *Salem Witchcraft* (1867), said the most that can really be said in expiation of the mania from the point of view which would have made the most sense to the actual participants, that of religion. Uncomfortably, his explanation could be applied, with some changed words, to the irreligious Nazi and Communist slaughterers of the bloody 20th century:

> The men of the day and scene we are now to contemplate, however deluded, to whatever extremities carried, were controlled by fixed, absolute, sharply defined, and, in themselves, great ideas. They believed in God. They also believed in the Devil. They bowed in an adoration that penetrated their inmost souls, before the one as a being of infinite holiness: they regarded the other as a being of an all but infinite power of evil. They feared and worshipped God. They hated and defied the Devil. They believed that Satan was waging war against Jehovah, and that the conflict was for the dominion of the world, for the establishment or the overthrow of the Church of Christ. The battle, they fully believed, could have no other issue than the salvation or the ruin of the souls of men. This was not, with them, a mere technical, verbal creed. It was a deep-seated conviction, held earnestly with a clear and distinct apprehension of its import, by every individual mind. For this warfare, they put on the whole armor of faith, rallied to the banner of the Most High, and met Satan face to face. In this one great idea, a stern, determined, unflinching, all-sacrificing people concentrated their strength.

The Salem witch hunts have a central place in HPL's fiction. On one level, HPL seems to enjoy referring to Salem witchcraft for its local color and instant sinister evocations. Essex County, Massachusetts, in which Salem Village/Danvers is to be found, also became the apparent locale of fictional Kingsport, Arkham, and Innsmouth. The anonymous narrator of *The Festival*, along with Richard Upton Pickman, Randolph Carter, and the founding families of Dunwich, all have ancestors who were hanged as witches or who fled the Salem area in advance of the mass arrests of summer, 1692. Pickman even mentions that his great-great-great-great-grandmother was hanged then, "with Cotton Mather looking sanctimoniously on." (Historically considered, this could only have been Martha Carrier, of Andover, Massachusetts, the sole woman in a group of convicted witches who were hanged on August 19, 1692, the only occasion on which Reverend Mather was present for a Salem execution. Mather referred to her glancingly in his subsequent book as "a rampant Hag"; she was much-hated by her neighbors and insolent to the judges. Carrier was identified by many witnesses as George Burroughs' female partner at the head of the witch-conspiracy; her own children testified that the Devil had promised to make her the queen of hell!) In this regard, a Salem-witch pedigree for a character is merely authorial shorthand to suggest a sinister family background. But in *The Case of Charles Dexter Ward* (in which Joseph Curwen's personal involvement, including his reception of the Devil's Mark from "Mr. G.B." at Salem, is stressed) and *The Dreams in the Witch House*, HPL did something more daring by posing the question: what if there really *had* been a conspiracy of the evilly adept; only not the straightforward Satanic conspiracy imagined by the magistrates, but something deeper, more frightening if possible, and moreover beyond their powers to understand or even suspect?

SALTONSTALL STREET (DWH, TD, WD): Mentioned as one of the more prosperous residential streets in Arkham; the worker, Joe Mazurewicz, complains that the fine folk on Saltonstall Street and similar places don't know what really happens in town on Halloween and Walpurgis-night. Saltonstall is one of the old New England settler names, and a certain Nathaniel Saltonstall (1639–1707) was a judge from Haverhill, Massachusetts who sat on the panel that convicted several of the Salem witches in July, 1692. He protested against the quality of the prosecution evidence, and refused to take part in any further proceedings—only to be later accused of being a witch himself. Edward Derby's friend Daniel Upton lives on Saltonstall Street, as did Professor Wilmarth (at no. 118).

SANSU (OG): The last man (before Barzai) to scale the summit of Hatheg-Kla; he is "written of with fright in the mouldy Pnakotic Manuscripts." It is said there that he had "found naught but wordless ice and rock when he climbed Hatheg-Kla in the youth of the world."

SARGENT, JOE (SOI): Innsmouth resident and the operator of the daily bus running between Newburyport, Innsmouth, and Arkham. It is the only public carrier going in or out of Innsmouth, and apparently is used very little. He is:

> a thin, stoop-shouldered man not much under six feet tall, dressed in shabby blue civilian clothes and wearing a frayed grey golf cap. His age was perhaps thirty-five, but the odd, deep creases in the sides of his neck made him seem older.... He had a narrow head, bulging, watery blue eyes that never seemed to wink, a flat nose, a receding forehead and chin, and singularly undeveloped ears. His long, thick lip and coarse-pored, greyish cheeks seemed almost beardless...; and in places the surface seemed

queerly irregular, as if peeling from some cutaneous disease. His hands were large and heavily veined.... As he walked toward the bus I observed his shambling gait and saw that his feet were inordinately immense.

The person whom the narrator has described at such length is, in fact, a classic example of what he will come to call "the Innsmouth look." The slovenly rural bus-driver, who in addition to his questionably human appearance, also seems somehow greasy and fishy-smelling, is on his way to turning into a Deep One who will enjoy immortality in a glowing city beneath the sea. In the tale, the narrator takes Joe Sargent's bus into Innsmouth. But that evening, when he wants very much to leave the place again, the bus is unavailable due to "mechanical problems."

SARGENT, MOSES and ABIGAIL (TD): A repellent pair of servants in the Arkham household of Edward and Asenath Derby, imported from Asenath's home town of Innsmouth. Edward Derby fires them both after Asenath "left him," but he continues to mail them checks, apparently as hush-money. "Sargent" is one of the pedigree names of old Massachusetts; a certain Peter Sargent was one of the Salem witchcraft judges in 1692.

SARKIS, PLATEAU OF (PO): The region in Lomar where the city of Olathoë was, 26,000 years ago.

SARKOMAND (DQ): This town was the ancient capital and seaport of the almost-humans of Leng. By the time Randolph Carter sees it, Sarkomand is an abandoned and dead city whose empty piers are lapped by oily black waves. The moonbeasts' galleys moor here to pick up their tributes from Leng. There is a gateway to the city, leading to a tunnel which goes all the way down to the ghoul district in lower Dreamland. When Carter has made his difficult way to Sarkomand and sees a shipload of moonbeasts torturing the three captured ghouls, his former guides, he hurries down to the ghoul land and brings back a large rescue force. With their newly-captured galley, Carter, the ghouls, and the night-gaunts set forth to attack the rock with no name, far out in the sea. There is an ancient, once-mighty Central Asian city of Samarcand; perhaps HPL thought of it when he made up the name of "Sarkomand."

SARNATH (DCS, NC, QI): A city in the land of Mnar, founded by the dark-haired shepherd people who colonized Mnar and established this and several other cities. Sarnath was at the edge of this region, and was neighbor to the much older city of Ib, inhabited by a race of intelligent froglike beings. Proud and confident in their youthful power, Sarnath's warriors attacked and destroyed Ib, slaughtering all of the non-humans and pushing their bodies and the very stones of their city into the large adjoining lake.

After another thousand years have passed, Sarnath has become inconceivably magnificent and opulent, "the wonder of the world and the pride of all mankind," an imperial city to which many other cities bear tribute, seeming to combine all the best features of ancient Babylon, Jerusalem, Rome, and the most fabulous fantasy-city ever invented by Lord Dunsany's fertile pen. The population at this time is fifty million people. Sarnath's chief gods are Zo-Kalar, Tamash, and Lobon; its greatest king was named Zokkar; and its last king is the ill-fated Nargis-Hei. During the unequalled festivities for the 1000th "feast of the destroying of Ib," the long-dead Ibites rise up, along with the actual lake waters, and drown and exterminate Sarnath. Curious travelers coming to see the aftermath find nothing on the former site of Sarnath but a marshy shoreline. The minstrel Iranon passes by this forlorn swamp during his early wanderings. And the dreamy modern-day narrator of *The Nameless City*, seeing the mighty outlines of a desert metropolis, recalls "Sarnath the Doomed, that stood in the land of Mnar when mankind was young."

SATURN, CATS OF (DQ): These cats are the only creatures feared by Earth's cats; they are said to be large and "peculiar" in some unspecified ways. The cats of Saturn are in league with the moonbeasts, and are notoriously hostile to earthly cats.

SAWYER, ASAPH (IV): A Peck Valley resident who dies during the winter of 1880–81, of a "malignant fever." Asaph Sawyer was known far and wide for his own malignant, vengeful nature. For example, he financially ruined his neighbor Mr. Raymond, merely for spite, thirty years after the two men were adversaries in a lawsuit over a property line; and once he stepped on and crushed a puppy that snapped at him. When Sawyer dies, George Birch the village undertaker puts him in a too-short casket originally built for little old Matthew Fenner, secretly sawing Sawyer's feet off at the ankles to make the body fit. The dead man gets his appropriate revenge on Birch. The name "Sawyer" itself is the old English word for one who wields a saw-blade to cut wood; it is an added joke in this darkly humorous tale in a New England village setting.

SAWYER, EARL (DH): A Dunwich farmer who sold many head of cattle to Old Whateley in the years after Lavinia Whateley gave birth to the child of an unknown father. In 1917, Earl Sawyer acts as a guide to out-of-town visitors, principally newspaper reporters, interested in the local oddities. He is the "common-law husband" of Dunwich woman Mamie Bishop. (In old English law—the "common law" used and adapted in most American states—a man and woman who lived together openly and monogamously as husband and wife for a certain period of years might be considered as married in a form of law, even without a license and official ceremony to create the union. Common law marriage was however formally abolished in almost all the states during the 20th century.) HPL's intention in stating that Earl Sawyer and Mamie Bishop are a common-law married couple is probably to suggest the lowered moral standards prevalent in the decaying and isolated community of Dunwich.

SAWYER, SALLY and CHAUNCEY (DH): In 1928, Sally Sawyer, presumably some kinswoman of the farmer Earl Sawyer, is the house-keeper at Seth Bishop's farm near Dunwich, the closest farm to Old Whateley's place. Her son Chauncey lives there as well. On September 10, Chauncey (who had heard strange noises the night before) is out early, but comes running home soon afterwards. He tells his mother that the Whateley farm was "all blowed up," with huge tracks in the mud around it; and that Seth Bishop's cattle have all been killed or carried away by something. Mrs. Sawyer relays the information to Mrs. George Corey over the telephone, along with her own shrewd suspicions that the late Wilbur Whateley was somehow at the bottom of this, and that what-ever the thing was that had slaughtered the cattle, it had gone to a lair in Cold Spring Glen. Several nights later, the subscribers along the party-line telephone used by Seth Bishop are all awakened by Sally Sawyer, who (in words and tones of increasing terror) describes the onslaught of some great invisible monster on the farmyard, until they all hear her final screams.

SCHMIDT (TE): A sailor on the imperial German navy submarine U-29 in 1917. He is instantly killed in the catastrophic boiler-room explosion on June 28.

SCHOOL OF DESIGN (SH): The famous Rhode Island School of Design in Providence, an art college, has a miniature painting of Rhoby Dexter Harris in its museum.

SCORESBY, WILLIAM (MM): A renowned English explorer of Arctic waters (1789–1857). Captain Scoresby sailed about the 70th degree of north latitude, an important feat at the time; his writings about his voyages were informative and inspirational to many. He charted Greenland's eastern coast, including Scoresby Land and Scoresby Sound, which have been named in his honor. In the tale, Professor Dyer men-tions wild mirages "observed and drawn by the Arctic whaler Scoresby in 1820," while struggling to comprehend an immense Arctic mirage of a gigantic city built "according to no human architecture."

SCOTT-ELLIOTT, W. (CC): A non-fictitious member of the Theosophist movement of the 19th and 20th centuries, and the author of a very popular book speculating about lost, sunken civilizations of prehistoric times: *The Story of Atlantis and the Lost Lemuria* (1896 and 1925), as well as other books on the same general theme. HPL thoroughly enjoyed reading the book, without believing it. Mr. Scott-Elliot claimed specific knowledge of events in the remote past by means of "astral clairvoyance" from "Theosophical Masters," and wrote of a giant Lemurian continent that stretched from Africa out into the present Pacific Ocean. In a 1926 letter to Clark Ashton Smith, HPL wrote:

> I've also been digesting something of vast interest as background or source-material—which has belatedly introduced me to a cycle of myth with which I have reason to believe you are particularly familiar—i.e., the Atlantis-Lemuria tales, as developed by modern occultists and the sophical charlatans. Really, some of these hints about the lost "City of the Golden Gates" & the shapeless monsters of archaic Lemuria are ineffably pregnant with fantastic suggestion; I only wish I could get hold of more of the stuff. What I have read is *The Story of Atlantis & The Lost Lemuria* by W. Scott Elliott. [sic]

SEATON, SAMUEL (AJ): British explorer of Africa who calls on Sir Robert Jermyn at Jermyn House in England on October 19, 1852, bringing with him notes of investigations among the Onga tribe in the Congo. Their private conversation was never known, but Sir Robert ends the meeting by strangling the explorer and then killing all of his own offspring.

SEFTON ASYLUM (HW): Mental hospital where the cannibal monster who once was Allan Halsey, M.D., is confined from 1904–20. He is finally released by a weird group of intruders, led by a man in military uniform with a peculiar, waxy head. A couple of asylum attendants are killed during the breakout. There is no town of Sefton in Massachusetts, although there is one in England which perhaps provided HPL with this name.

SELARN (DQ): A town or district in the land of Inganok; after departing the village of Urg, Randolph Carter does not continue west to Selarn on the great caravan road, but heads north on the quarry road instead.

SEMPRONIUS BLAESUS, TITUS (SOT): A captive mind encountered by Professor Nathaniel Peaslee while he was with the Great Race; it is said that Sempronius Blaesus was a Roman *quaestor* (an urban magistrate) during the period of the dictatorship of Sulla (1st century B.C.), but the character is fictitious.

SENTINEL HILL (DH): One of the hills outside of Dunwich; Wilbur Whateley climbs it at regular intervals to conduct secret rituals, at first with and later without his mother Lavinia. The Miskatonic University professors confront and destroy the Dunwich Horror on this hilltop, while it calls out for its father, Yog-Sothoth. Wilbraham Mountain outside of Wilbraham, Massachusetts, is thought to have been the "model" for Sentinel Hill.

SEPHIROTH and SAMAEL (HRH): Two names invoked in rituals by the Brooklyn devil-worshippers; "Sephiroth" refers to the spheres on the Kabbalistic Tree of Life.

SERRANIAN (CE, DQ): A city in the clouds over Dreamland. King Kuranes has the additional title of "Lord of the Sky around Serranian." He first visits Serranian in *Celephaïs*, traveling from that city by a flying galley. Serranian is built of pink marble, "on that ethereal coast where the west wind flows into the sky." As king of Celephaïs, Kuranes alternates his royal court between the two cities.

SERVISS, PROFESSOR GARRETT P. (BWS): An American author (1851–1929) of books on popular science and of what would later be called "science fiction." In this tale he is mentioned for publishing a report on the 1901 first observation of *Nova Persei*.

Professor Serviss wrote early science-fiction novels such as *The Moon Metal* (1900), and astronomy-for-the-masses books including *Astronomy in a Nutshell* and *Pleasures of the Telescope*. From the last-named book come the following words which the devoted amateur astronomer HPL must have read and agreed with:

> If the pure and elevated pleasure to be derived from the possession and use of a good telescope...were generally known, I am certain that no instrument of science would be more commonly found in the homes of intelligent people.

In 1898, Professor Serviss published a novel entitled *Edison's Conquest of Mars* as a personal "sequel" to H.G. Wells' 1897 Martian-invasion classic *The War of the Worlds*. In the Serviss novel, American scientists reverse-engineer the Martians' devices, travel to Mars, and fight the Martians on their own turf! Among the warriors of science who accompany Thomas Edison's expedition are the physicists Lord Kelvin, Lord Rayleigh, and Professor Roentgen, as well as Professor Serviss himself. It could scarcely be doubted that HPL, an inveterate sci-fi reader for most of his life, would have read and enjoyed some of the yarns of Garrett P. Serviss. In 1909 Serviss published the tale *A Columbus of Space* in *All-Story Magazine*, a publication which HPL read religiously in his youth. It dealt with a uranium-powered flight to Venus; maybe HPL thought of it in passing while co-authoring *In the Walls of Eryx*.

A certain Garrett Serviss of the U.S.A. won the silver medal in the high jump event at the 1904 Olympic Games in St. Louis, Missouri. At 53 years of age Professor Serviss was probably not the same man, but the name is a most unusual one; perhaps the astronomer's high-flying son?

S'GG'HA (SOT): One of the captive minds encountered by Professor Nathaniel Peaslee among the Great Race; it is one of the winged, star-headed beings of prehistoric Antarctica, one of the creatures from *At the Mountains of Madness*.

SHACKLETON, AMUNDSEN, SCOTT and BYRD (MM): The 1930–31 Miskatonic University Expedition intended to operate mostly in the mountain ranges and the plateau south of the Ross Sea in Antarctica, previously explored "in varying degree" by these men. This refers to the well-known expeditions earlier in the 20th century led by Ernest Shackleton (1874–1922); Roald Amundsen (1872–1928), who in 1911 became the first human to reach the South Pole; Robert Falcon Scott (1868–1912); and Richard Byrd (1888–1957). They were not the only Antarctic exploration leaders, but they were the best known. Richard Byrd in 1929 pioneered the technique of aerial exploration from the security of a Ross Sea-area base camp—he called his "Little America"—just as the Miskatonic University Expedition intended to do. *At the Mountains of Madness* was written in 1931, which would have allowed time for HPL to read and digest the news reports.

SHADDAD (TGSK): In prehistory, we are told, Shaddad "with his terrific genius built and concealed in the sands of Arabia Petraea the prodigious domes and uncounted minarets of pillared Irem." Only Shaddad had crossed the border of space and time, before Randolph Carter did it again. According to Arab legends, Shaddad was the son of King Ad and the grandson of Noah.

SHAKESPEARE, WILLIAM (BWS): England's bard, the sweet singer of Avon (1564–1616), enters the Lovecraft canon with one line that is used as the introduction to *Beyond the Wall of Sleep*:

> I have an exposition of sleep come upon me.

The line comes from Act IV, Scene 1, of the comedy *A Midsummer Night's Dream*, and is spoken by Bottom while he has been transformed with an ass's head. (*See* also the entry "Blasted Heath.")

SHAGGAI (HD): A distant planet mentioned in Robert Blake's disjointed final journal-entry on August 9, 1935; the young man writes that he "remembered" Shaggai. "Shaggai" is listed as one of the five stories he had written earlier.

SHANG (CU): The blacksmith of the town of Ulthar (HPL invented a name that sounds like metal striking on metal); he is selected to be a witness when the headman Kranon breaks down the cottage door of the evil, cat-slaying old couple.

SHANTAKS (DQ): There is a range of vast mountains in between Leng and Kadath. In the mountain chasms dwell the shantaks, horse-headed birds that are larger than elephants, with slippery scales on their bodies instead of feathers. The "slant-eyed merchant" forces Randolph Carter to fly with him over Leng on a shantak, to the temple of the high priest not to be described. Later, Nyarlathotep gives Carter another shantak in order to fly from Kadath to his "dream city," and also to use it to lure earth's gods back home:

> Easier even than the way of dim memory is the way I will prepare for you. There comes hither a monstrous shantak...[you must] land amongst [earth's gods] with the shantak, and let them see and touch that noisome and hippocephalic [horse-headed] bird.... And the shantak will talk to them after the manner of shantaks.

With a rousing cry of *Hei! Aa-shanta 'nygh!* to the bird, Nyarlathotep sends it off in flight with Carter on board. During the flight through space, Carter realizes that ever-treacherous Nyarlathotep has actually directed him towards doom, so he leaps off the shantak into space.

SHEPHERD'S HOTEL (UP): This is clearly a mistake for "Shepheard's Hotel." The very peculiar spelling of "Shepheard" has confused many a person; even the renowned English author Rudyard Kipling, who should have known better, got it wrong (as "Shepherd's", like HPL) in his 1890 novel *The Light That Failed*. Shepheard's was and is a deluxe Cairo hotel originally built for the monied European tourist trade in the latter part of the 19th century. An image of the Shepheard's Hotel crowd in 1873 comes from the delightful book *A Thousand Miles Up the Nile*, by the Victorian lady traveler Mrs. Amelia B. Edwards:

> It is the traveller's lot to dine at many *table-d'hôtes* [hotel dining-tables] in the course of many wanderings; but it seldom befalls him to make one of a more miscellaneous gathering than that which overfills the great dining-room at Shepheard's Hotel in Cairo during the beginning and height of the regular Egyptian season. Here assemble daily some two to three hundred persons of all ranks, nationalities, and pursuits; half of whom are Anglo-Indians [*i.e.*, British colonials of the Indian Empire] homeward or outward bound, European residents [of Cairo], or visitors established in Cairo for

the winter. The other half, it may be taken for granted, are going up the Nile.

Except for changes in sartorial fashion over a couple of generations, the scene would not have been all that different when, as presented in the tale, Harry Houdini and his wife stay here during an Egyptian sightseeing vacation in 1910.

SHINING TRAPEZOHEDRON (HD): Resembling a sphere, and only four inches across, it is on closer inspection "a nearly black, red-striated polyhedron with many irregular flat surfaces; either a very remarkable crystal of some sort, or an artificial object of carved and highly polished mineral matter." By staring into it, one will receive strange visions, but also awaken the Haunter of the Dark, a being that possesses all knowledge but demands sacrificial tributes. Robert Blake calls the Shining Trapezohedron a window on all time and space. He learns from the Aklo-language journal he discovers, that the thing was fashioned on the planet Yuggoth, then brought to earth, where it was worshipped by the "crinoid things of Antarctica" who made the odd golden box it rests in, tens of millions of years ago. Later it was "salvaged from their ruins by the serpent-men of Valusia, and peered at aeons later in Lemuria by the first human beings." Eventually it reached Atlantis, and later still it sank with Atlantis. Long afterwards it was dredged up from the sea by a Minoan fisherman (here we enter historical time; the Minoan culture flourished on the Mediterranean island of Crete during the second millennium B.C.), and sold to some Egyptian merchants. In Egypt it became the object of a cult instituted by a certain Pharaoh Nephren-Ka, then it was lost in the sands of the desert after the cult was brought to an end. Professor Enoch Bowen brings it from Egypt to his home in Providence, in 1844, and founds the Starry Wisdom cult to give proper worship to the Shining Trapezohedron. After Robert Blake's death in 1935, a certain Dr. Dexter drops box and all into the deepest channel of Narragansett Bay.

SHIP STREET (TOM, SHH): The back garden gate of the Terrible Old Man's house opens onto Ship Street, where the robber Joe Czanek waited one night in a getaway car. This street is also the home of Granny Orne, who lives in a ladylike "tiny gambrel-roofed abode in Ship Street...all covered with moss and ivy," where she sat and talked with Thomas Olney about the Strange High House in the Mist. One rather enjoys thinking of the Terrible Old Man and gentle old Granny Orne as Ship Street back-fence neighbors, and wishes that we knew if they spent time together talking about the days of old.

SHIPPEN, DR. (CDW): A non-fictitious, influential citizen of Philadelphia in late colonial times. In the tale, it is mentioned that "the Pennsylvania Historical Society also had some curious letters by Dr. Shippen regarding the presence of an unwholesome character in Philadelphia," presumably letters dating from 1770–71 and presumably dealing with some confederate of Curwen, Orne, and Hutchinson, the necromancers. This "Dr. Shippen" is in all likelihood a reference to Dr. William Shippen, Jr. (1712–1801), a leading man of old Philadelphia who ranks among the founders of both the University of Pennsylvania and Princeton University, and who served as a delegate in the Continental Congress during the American Revolution. The Shippens were one of the most prominent families in that place and time, and the wealthy, well-connected, and public-spirited Dr. Shippen would have been a natural center of influence for dealing with a local situation that might have been revealed to him by letters from—perhaps—members of the secret anti-Curwen committee in Providence.

SHOGGOTHS (MM, SOI, WD, TD): The natural history of shoggoths receives a very full description in *At the Mountains of Madness*. Shoggoths were originally created by the winged, star-headed Old Ones of prehistoric Antarctica, out of inorganic matter, for employment as unthinking beasts of burden. Later on they became able to reproduce themselves amoeba-like, by fission. They were:

> multicellular protoplasmic masses capable of moulding their tissues into all sorts of temporary organs under hypnotic influence and thereby forming ideal slaves to perform the heavy work of the community.

Abdul Alhazred referred to shoggoths in the *Necronomicon*, although he denied that they had ever really existed except in narcotics-fueled dreams.

Shoggoths, like their Old Ones creators and masters, could live equally well on land or under water. In appearance, they were:

> shapeless entities composed of a viscous jelly which looked like an agglutination of bubbles, and each averaged about fifteen feet in diameter when a sphere. They had, however, a constantly shifting shape and volume, throwing out temporary developments or forming apparent organs of sight, hearing and speech in imitation of their masters....

Eventually they acquired a modicum of intelligence and independent conduct, and then rose up in a revolt against their masters. The shoggoths were violently subdued in their first slave-rebellion. We learn at the end of the Antarctic tale that they must again have risen up against their masters after the movement of the population from the surface city to the "sea-cavern city," this time successfully:

> Formless protoplasm able to mock and reflect all forms and organs and processes—viscous agglutinations of bubbling cells—rubbery fifteen-foot spheroids infinitely plastic and ductile—slaves of suggestions, builders of cities—more and more sullen, more and more intelligent, more and more amphibious, more and more imitative—Great God! What madness made even those blasphemous Old Ones willing to use and carve those things?
>
> ...We...looked and understood what must have triumphed and survived down there in the Cyclopean water-city of that nighted, penguin-fringed abyss....

In their relationship to the Old Ones, the shoggoths are reminiscent of the "Morlocks" in H.G. Wells' famous science-fiction novel *The Time Machine* (1895). In this parable, the Morlocks are the industrial workers of the distant future, subterranean machine-tenders whose physiology gradually evolves into something inhuman, and who eventually turn the tables to become the masters and eaters of the beautiful, surface-dwelling Eloi, the descendants of the upper class.

In *The Thing on the Doorstep* Edward Derby tells Daniel Upton that he saw a shoggoth, 6000 steps down in the "pit of the shoggoths" in northern Maine, where Ephraim Waite's coven met. In *The Shadow Over Innsmouth* Zadok Allen hints to the inquisitive young visitor that when the Deep Ones are finally ready to wipe the surface-dwellers off the planet, shoggoths will be part of the attack. To return to *At the Mountains of Madness*, when Professor Dyer and the graduate student Danforth flee from a shoggoth beneath the lost Antarctic city of the Old Ones, Danforth catches a backward glimpse of the thing and partially loses his sanity. In this tale it is said that the shoggoths constantly cry *Tekeli-li! Tekeli-li!* in piping or whistling tones.

SHONHI (TGSK): This is one of the many other planets of the twenty-eight galaxies to which dwellers on Yaddith may travel in "light-beam envelopes."

SHUNNED HOUSE (SH): HPL provided one of his trademark architectural word-pictures in the tale itself:

> The house was—and for that matter still is—of a kind to attract the attention of the curious. Originally a farm or semi-farm building, it followed the average New England colonial lines of the middle eighteenth century—the prosperous peaked-roof sort, with two stories and dormerless attic, and with the Georgian doorway and interior paneling dictated by the progress of taste at that time. It faced south, with one gable end buried to the lower windows in the eastward rising hill, and the other exposed to the foundations toward the street. Its construction, over a century and a half ago, had followed the grading and straightening of the road in that especial vicinity; for Benefit Street—at first called Back Street—was laid out as a lane wind-

ing amongst the graveyards of the first settlers, and straightened only when the removal of the bodies to the North Burial Ground made it decently possible to cut through the old family plots.

The house was built for the family of Captain William Harris in 1763. After years of ill-health and many deaths of family members and household servants, the surviving Harrises move out in 1782. Later they rent quarters in the house to tenants. After four tenants die in 1804, the town council orders the then-owner, Rathbone Harris, to fumigate the place with sulphur, tar and gum camphor, thinking a recent fever epidemic was responsible. But as years go by tenants continue to die; for example Mrs. Stafford in 1815 and Eleazar Durfee in 1845, and some unnamed victims in 1860–61, in a series of "anemia" deaths, preceded by progressive madness in which the patient would craftily attempt the lives of relatives by making incisions in their necks and wrists. After this the house became unrentable and it sat vacant for many years, the focus of neighborhood legend. On June 25, 1919, the narrator and his uncle Dr. Whipple spend the night in the cellar of the house to investigate the problem, and Dr. Whipple does not come out alive, or come out at all for that matter. The next day, June 26, the narrator returns to the cellar with digging tools and some "carboys" (large containers) of acid, with which he finally kills the vampirish thing buried under the house. Afterwards the current Harris owner is able to refurbish the house and put it on the rental market.

The real house which was the model for the Shunned House is at 135 Benefit Street. It is privately owned and not open to uninvited visitors, but from the street one can see the gable, the rising hill to the rear, and, of course, the exposed wall of the fateful cellar.

SHUB-NIGGURATH (DWH, TD, WD): An especially poorly-defined deity in the mythos; it seems to be worshipped as a fertility principle. Familiar to readers for the ritual outcry: "Iä! Shub-Niggurath! The Black Goat of the Woods with a Thousand Young!" (Memorably burlesqued by one critic as *Iä! Shub-Niggurath! We want a touchdown!*) Although readers may automatically think of "Shub-Niggurath" as being "the Black Goat, etc.," the connection is not explicit and may or may not exist.

In Lord Dunsany's idyllic fantasy, *Idle Days on the Yann,* a story in his 1910 collection *A Dreamer's Tales,* the narrator passing through a jungle feels moved to pray: "So I bethought me…of Sheol Nugganoth, whom the men of the jungle have long since deserted, who is now unworshipped and alone; and to him I prayed." We probably need look no further for the remote origin of the name Shub-Niggurath.

It has also been conjectured that "Shub" was a humorous wordplay, a transposition of the letters in the name of one David Van Bush (1882–1959), who was for several years HPL's best client for literary revision and ghostwriting. Van Bush was an energetic, charismatic author and lecturer on self-help and the power of positive thinking—his catch-phrase was "the new gospel of dynamic psychology"—who has been long since forgotten except in HPL's life story, but who was apparently quite a success in his day. In private to his own friends, HPL called Mr. Van Bush "a damned fool," and he regarded his client's brand of upbeat inspirational writing for the masses with amused contempt. But to his credit: of all of HPL's clients, David Van Bush paid the best and the most promptly. This busy self-help guru clearly recognized writing talent where he saw it, and was willing to pay well for it; not a bad quality.

Some of the short books that HPL may well have revised or ghosted for Mr. Van Bush include *Poems of Mastery and Love Verse* (1922); *The Power of Visualization: How to Make Your Dreams Come True*; and even, hard to imagine, *Psychology of Sex: How to Make Love and Marry* (1924); perhaps Sonia may have offered suggestions for the last-named book, as she and HPL married one another that year. The possibility exists that America's modern master of supernatural horror worked over this bit of Van Bush verse, apparently inspired by broken-down cars, from the book *Grit and Gumption* (1921)—and there would be many other such books and verses:

> *Don't have a face so glum and long*
> *You look like a baboon*
> *But have a grin upon your chin*
> *Like that upon the moon.*
> *So with a smile meet ev'ry foe;*
> *Just boost 'er up and make 'er go!*

SIDRAK (QI): A mountain across the bridge from Teloth. Briars grow here which rip Iranon's cloak.

SIFICLIGHS (WE): A Venusian creature, perhaps like a worm, that scavenges on carrion. They are a nuisance to be crushed underfoot (or for Venusians, under a "suction disc.") Sificlighs feed on the body of the prospector Dwight.

SIGN OF KOTH (DQ, CDW): A symbol of great mystic power. Randolph Carter spies it in lower Dreamland, at the center of the Gug city. There was a tower, taller than all the rest, "above whose colossal doorway was fixed a monstrous symbol in bas-relief which made one shudder without knowing its meaning." The huge stone steps in this tower lead all the way to upper Dreamland. In *The Case of Charles Dexter Ward*, Dr. Willett, while exploring the catacombs under the Pawtuxet bungalow, finds the room where Curwen practiced his dark alchemy. Over the door he sees a crudely-etched symbol, chiseled into the stone lintel:

> It was only a symbol, but it filled him with vague spiritual dread; for a morbid, dreaming friend of his had once drawn it on paper and told him a few of the things it means in the dark abyss of sleep. It was the sign of Koth, that dreamers see fixed above the archway of a certain black tower standing alone in twilight.

SIME (CC, PM): Sidney Herbert Sime (1867–1941), a British artist, drew illustrations for certain books by Lord Dunsany and Arthur Machen, two of HPL's favorite fantasy or horror authors. In *Pickman's Model*, Thurber tells Eliot: "There's something these [artists with a talent for the weird] catch—beyond life—that they're able to make us catch for a second. Doré had it. Sime has it. Angarola of Chicago has it."

SIMPSON, GOODMAN (TO): The Boston undertaker who stole the silver-buckled shoes, silken hose, and satin breeches from the corpse of Squire Brewster before his burial in 1711. In old New England society, "Goodman" was a form of address equivalent to "Mr.", not the man's first name. It may be recalled that HPL's inspiration for this tale was the site of a crumbling tombstone from the year 1711, on a 1917 walk through Swan Point Cemetery in Providence.

SINARA (QI): The first place that Iranon visits after leaving the valley of Narthos where he had grown up. It is on the "southern slope," on the river Xari, and is an abode of "smiling dromedary-men in the market-place." The prim Iranon finds the songs of the dromedary-drivers to be "drunken and ribald," and leaves the town quickly.

SIX KINGDOMS (DQ): The men in Dylath-Leen tell Randolph Carter that the shoes of the merchants from the black galleys—who are really almost-humans from Leng—"were the shortest and queerest ever seen in the Six Kingdoms," but just which kingdoms make up the Six Kingdoms is left unstated.

SKAI RIVER (CU, OG, DQ, SHH, SK): A river in the pleasant part of upper Dreamland that dreamers travel through first. Its source is in the Slopes of Lerion, and the pretty towns of Hatheg, Nir and Ulthar lie in its plain. Fertile farmlands, inhabited by peaceful farmers in thatched cottages, line the river on both banks. A great stone bridge crosses the Skai at one point; 1300 years before Randolph Carter crosses the span, its masons had sealed a living human sacrifice into its central pier. Six days of walking along the Skai from Ulthar, through the countryside full of peak-roofed houses and octagonal windmills, brings the traveler to the Southern Sea and the crowded port city of Dylath-Leen. Across the river, here, lay a country called Parg, the source for black slaves.

SKORAHS (WE): A small, wriggling, ground-dwelling Venusian carnivore with a superb sense of smell.

SLATER, JOE (BWS):

> His appearance was that of a typical denizen of the Catskill Mountain region.... Though well above the middle stature, and of somewhat brawny frame, he was given an absurd appearance of harmless stupidity by the pale, sleepy, blueness of his small watery eyes, the scantiness of his neglected and never-shaven growth of yellow beard, and the listless drooping of his nether lip.

Judging from Slater's baldness and decayed teeth, an insane-asylum doctor feels that the patient is about 40 years old. An illiterate hunter, trapper, and vagabond from the Catskills region of upstate New York, Joe Slater was always prone to long sleep and to strange dreams. Then, one day, he has a very bad nightmare, awakens and kills his companion Peter Slater, while shrieking that he will "jump high in the air and burn his way through anything that stopped him." Captured by lawmen and tried for the murder, Joe Slater is judged not guilty by reason of insanity, and committed to the state mental hospital where the tale's narrator works. As the narrator gradually comes to believe from his close study of the inmate, Slater's remarkable dreams—breathtaking visions that seem very inexplicable coming from such a low-quality human intelligence as that of Slater—are a manifestation of the truth. In the course of a cosmic feud, the personality of a highly-developed alien being has been trapped inside the living body of an inbred, decrepit, almost witless earthling. By means of a "telepathic radio" of his own invention, the narrator is able to communicate with this "brother of light" on the night of February 22, 1901, before it takes flight from Slater's dead body and pursues its revenge in another galaxy. HPL took the name from a 1919 newspaper article about the Catskills, which mentioned a family of rustics called Slater or Slahter. (For what it may also be worth, HPL attended Slater Avenue Elementary School in Providence during his on-again, off-again formal education; he was not the average primary-school boy, and seems to have been a trial to the female principal and teachers. The school building he knew in the 1890s was torn down long ago.)

SLATER, PETER (BWS): Catskills squatter who is brutally slain by Joe Slater during a "fit of madness," leading to Joe's commitment to the state hospital for the insane.

SLOCUM, PETER (CDW): An elderly resident of the Providence suburb of Pawtuxet, near the site of Joseph Curwen's 18th century farm; Charles Dexter Ward interviews him in about 1919. Slocum recollects a peculiar rumor known to his own grandfather: that a week after the April, 1771 raid on the Curwen place, "a charred, distorted body" was found in a neighboring field, a body which "was neither thoroughly human nor wholly allied to any animal which Pawtuxet folk had ever seen or read about." This seems likely to have been one of the hybrid creations of Curwen's dark arts, some of which Dr. Willett finds still living in the caverns under the Pawtuxet bungalow.

SMITH, CLARK ASHTON (PM, MM): One of HPL's best pen-pal friends, the poet, painter, and author Clark Ashton Smith (1893–1961) of Auburn, California, received direct mention in these tales, a unique honor for anyone in HPL's circle of friends. In *Pickman's Model*, the narrator Thurber refers to "the trans-Saturnian landscapes and lunar fungi that Clark Ashton Smith uses to freeze the blood." In *At the Mountains of Madness*, in a message to the base camp from his forward position, Professor Lake reports that the unknown winged creatures they have discovered, seemingly dead and preserved from millions of years ago, "have such uncanny resemblance to certain creatures of primal myth that suggestion of ancient existence outside antarctic becomes inevitable. Dyer and Pabodie have read *Necronomicon* and seen Clark Ashton Smith's nightmare paintings based on text, and will understand when I speak of Elder Things supposed to have created all earth-life as a jest or mistake."

SMITH, ELEAZAR (CDW): The drinking-crony of young Ezra Weeden in 1760s Providence; Weeden hires him to keep watch on Joseph Curwen and the Pawtuxet Road farmhouse during the periods when Weeden is away at sea. Smith keeps a "none too coherent" diary, which Charles Dexter Ward is lucky enough to find in the possession of some of Smith's descendants 160 years later. Smith accompanies Weeden to the meeting with Captain Mathewson at which Weeden lays out his suspicions regarding Curwen. Later, Smith serves as a member of the April 12, 1771 raiding party at Curwen's farm; in charge of the reserve group, he misses the main part of the action, except for hearing some frightening sounds such as roarings, cries, and explosions, and even thunderous words coming from the "upper air." Smith's diary is "the only written record which has survived from that expedition."

SMITH, PRESERVED (SH): A manservant in the William Harris household, probably hired as the replacement for Eli Liddeason, who died in 1765. In 1768 Smith quits his job "without coherent explanation—or at least, with only some wild tales and a complaint that he disliked the smell of the place." He complains that something "sucked his breath" at night.

"SNAKE-DEN" (SK, TGSK): A cave in the hills outside of Arkham, near the old Carter farmstead. The Snake-Den is rumored to have been used for ritual ceremonies by the 17th century wizard Edward Carter, and the country folk shun it. The cave is deep—"far deeper that anyone but Randolph [Carter] suspected, for the boy had found a fissure in the farthermost black corner that led to a loftier grotto beyond; a haunting sepulchral place whose granite walls held a curious illusion of conscious artifice." The inner sanctum contains a pylon carved from the living rock. (For similar cave-within-a-cave treatments, compare the vaults of *The Rats in the Walls* and the temple on the rock of the moonbeasts in *The Dream-Quest of Unknown Kadath*.) In October, 1883, nine-year-old Randolph Carter spends part of a day alone in the Snake-Den with the silver key he had brought along from home, during which time he seems to have experienced some strange revelations: "Something occurred to heighten his imagination." When Carter disappears on October 7, 1927, a handkerchief found near the Snake-Den raises local fears. And when returning from Yaddith in the lobsterish body of Zkauba, Carter initially hides his light-beam envelope in the cave.

There is a Snake Den State Park a few miles outside of Providence; the park was not established until 1969, but the name is an old local appellation.

SNIRETH-KO (DQ): A dreamer of great prowess; with the exception of Randolph Carter, who came later, he was perhaps the only fully-human being to have seen the dark side of the moon (not glimpsed by astronauts until some thirty years after HPL's death).

S'NGAC (DQ): This entity is a violet gaseous substance; as Randolph Carter is falling through voids of space at the end of this tale, S'ngac points the way he must take to return home safely. This may have been the same intriguing vapor that Kuranes met in *Celephaïs*:

> Hasheesh [*i.e.*, hashish] helped a great deal, and once sent him to a part of space where form does not exist, but where glowing gases study the secrets of existence. And a violet-coloured gas told him that this part of space was outside what he had called infinity. The gas had not heard of planets and organisms before, but identified Kuranes merely as one from the infinity where matter, energy, and gravitation exist.

SOAMES (AJ): The butler at Jermyn House in 1913, when Sir Arthur Jermyn burnt himself to death.

SODOMA and LEONARDO (WD): Driving in the hills of Vermont on a sunlit day, Dr. Wilmarth admires such beauty of wooded heights as he had never seen before "save in the magic vistas that sometimes form the backgrounds of Italian primitives. Sodoma and Leonardo conceived such expanses, but only in the distance, and through the vaultings of Renaissance arcades. We were now burrowing bodily through the midst of the picture...."

"Sodoma" is "Il Sodoma," whose real name was Giovanni Antonio Bazzi (c. 1477–1549). From northern Italy, he spent most of his career in Rome and Siena. Leonardo refers to Leonardo da Vinci (1452–1519), the Italian painter and sculptor, one of the greatest artists of all time.

SOUTHERN SEA (WS, DQ): A calm sea in Dreamland, much traveled by pretty galleys and sailing ships. Basil Elton sails thither on the White Ship, passing Zar, Thalarion, and Xura, and stopping for a season at Sona-Nyl. Dylath-Leen is another and more normal harbor city on this sea; there Randolph Carter is kidnapped and placed aboard a black galley bound for the moon. While traveling on the galley, he passes the four places seen by Elton on his earlier voyage. There is at a certain point a mysterious sunken city, clearly visible from the surface; Carter sees it on his second, voluntary voyage out of Dylath-Leen. Far out in the Southern Sea is the large, balmy island of Oriab.

SONA-NYL (WS, DQ): On the coast of the Southern Sea in Dreamland; it is the Land of Fancy, splendid in every way. Basil Elton sojourns here for many days, before yielding to the fatal urge to sail on in search of legendary Cathuria. Randolph Carter passes Sona-Nyl without being able to stop.

SPITZBERGEN (SOT): A non-fictitious, large, forbidding island—its name is German for "sharp mountains"—in the Arctic Sea, near 80° latitude, some 600 miles east of northern Greenland. Professor Nathaniel Peaslee travels near it on a mysterious voyage during his body's "possession" by a mind from the Great Race.

"SQUIRE, THE" (HE): While wandering the night streets of the Greenwich Village section of Manhattan (as HPL often did when he lived in New York City), the narrator meets a man wearing a cloak and wide-brimmed hat of an archaic style: he is "very slight, thin almost to cadaverousness," with a soft and hollow-sounding voice. Introducing himself as a fellow antiquarian, he leads the author through older and older streets, to a small estate sheltered behind an ivy-covered wall, in "a little back court off Perry Street." Under his cloak, he proves to be clad in "full mid-Georgian costume from queued [*i.e.*, long-braided] hair and neck ruffles to knee breeches, silk hose...and buckled shoes." Speaking to the narrator, he claims to be the last survivor of an old family, dressed in this fashion for the sake of historical whimsy. Speaking in a more and more pronouncedly 18th century English fashion, he tells of his "ancestor," "the Squire," an Oxford graduate who also studied at the University of Paris, and who learned secrets of time-travel from some local Indians of Manhattan circa 1768, before poisoning them all to death. Ill-advisedly, the stranger shows the narrator a vision of Manhattan in the future; the narrator's screams of panic at the hideous scene of dancing mongrel-race humans somehow attract the vengeful spirits of all those murdered Indians. The old man "shriveled and blackened as he lurched near and strove to rend me with vulturine talons," almost the same image as the dissolution of Dr. Whipple in *The Shunned House*, then dissolves to a mere "head with eyes" still impotently glaring, which is carried off by the undead avengers—just like Dr. West's head at the end of *Herbert West—Reanimator*. Other tales in which frightful old men survive for unnaturally long years include *The Picture in the House, The Terrible Old Man,* and *The Case of Charles Dexter Ward.*

ST. ELOI (HW): The non-fictitious Saint-Eloi is a tiny hamlet in Belgium a few miles from the French border, northeast of the French city of Reims (more usually spelled Rheims). The entire region around St. Eloi was the scene of constant fighting in the First World War. In the tale, it is where Dr. West and his comrade, while serving as Canadian Army surgeons in 1915, are assigned to a divisional hospital near the battlefront. Here, in a secret laboratory, they experiment with the remains of many fallen soldiers, including those of Major Sir Eric Moreland Clapham-Lee, M.D., D.S.O.

ST. JOHN (TH): The central protagonist in this horror tale; he is a decadent English hyper-aesthete, living with a friend who shares his peculiar tastes, in a lonely manor house. "St. John" is a family name, his first name is not mentioned. Bored with successive levels of romantic decadence, St. John and his comrade turn to grave-robbing and to decorating their secret subterranean chamber with cadavers and bones, etc., all described with hyper-Lovecraftian bombast. At length, St. John and his comrade venture to Holland to rob the grave of a famous medieval graverobber, and they steal from his skeleton the winged-dog jade amulet of "the ancient corpse-eating cult of Leng, in Central Asia." From that moment on, the mysterious hound pursues them. On September 24 of the unnamed year, at night, the narrator hears a knock at his chamber door; thinking it to be St. John, he bids his friend enter, but is answered only by shrill laughter from out in the hallway. On September 28, St. John and the narrator are disturbed in their underground secret museum of horrors, by a "low, cautious" scratching at the door. On the 29th of October they find "a series of footprints utterly impossible to describe" in soft earth below a window of the manor library. Finally on November 18, St. John, while incautiously walking home on the moors from the "dismal railway station" after dark, is seized and ripped to shreds by it. The following night his friend buries him in one of the manor's decayed gardens, mumbling over the body "one of the devilish rituals he had loved in life."

ST. JOHN'S CEMETERY (SH, CDW): The narrator of *The Shunned House* places an urn here in memory of his grandfather, Dr. Elihu Whipple. The Gothic Revival-style church (now the cathedral of St. John) on North Main Street, an Episcopalian house of worship dating from 1811, is one of Providence's treasures. HPL loved to sit up until long after midnight on the tombs in its picturesque old churchyard, in:

> ...the place that Poe loved—the hidden grove of giant willows on the hill, where tombs and headstones huddle quietly between the hoary bulk of the church and the houses and back walls of Benefit Street.

On at least one occasion HPL brought along a young lady to enjoy the midnight-cemetery atmosphere, which she appreciated far less than he did.

ST. MARY'S HOSPITAL (TF, TU): A hospital in Kingsport; the narrator of *The Festival*, and Mr. Carter and his friend Joel Manton from *The Unnamable*, all awaken here after nocturnal misadventures.

ST. STANISLAUS' CHURCH (DWH): A Catholic parish in Arkham, presumably serving working-class Polish-Americans. One parishioner is the Witch House tenant Joe Mazurewicz, who obtains some crucifixes blessed by Father Iwanicki. He gives one to Walter Gilman, on a cheap metal chain which Gilman later puts to practical use in strangling Keziah Mason. After the horrible discoveries during the demolition of the Witch House in 1931, the workmen on the project light "candles of gratitude in St. Stanislaus' Church because of the shrill, ghostly tittering [of Brown Jenkin] they felt they would never hear again." HPL was probably thinking of the Church of St. Stanislaus Kostka, a Polish parish in the Catholic diocese of Providence, founded in 1905.

STAFFORD (SH): A "gentle old lady" tenant in the house, who died there in 1815; before her death she became "transfigured in a horrible way, glaring glassily and attempting to bite the throat of the attending physician." The circumstances are reported in the April 12, 1815 edition of the *Providence Gazette and Country-Journal*.

STAHL (CDW): Presumably a reference to Georg Ernst Stahl (1660–1734), a German physician, chemist, and professor. He was arguably the most influential chemist of the early 18th century, and some book or books authored by him—perhaps including his important collection *Opusculum Chymico-Physico-Medicum* (1715)—are among those "philosophical, mathematical, and scientific works" glimpsed by Mr. John Merritt in Joseph Curwen's Providence library, circa 1746.

STANFIELD, KENTON J. (WE): An employee of the Venus Crystal Company; his home address given as 5317 Marshall Street, Richmond, Virginia (one of HPL's favorite cities as a tourist). Working as a crystal prospector, he undertakes a solo mission to Eryx, or the Erycinian Highland. Along the way he slays three attacking Venusians and almost falls victim to a mirage-plant. He enters the invisible structure to retrieve a huge crystal from the body of the prospector Dwight, then cannot relocate his point of entrance. His fruitless attempts to find his way out of the labyrinth, while beset by increasing weakness and depression, make up most of the balance of the tale. The other theme is the Venusian-loathing Stanfield's own ironic development of respect for the Venusians who have trapped him in the maze, and whom he watches through the labyrinth's transparent walls as they gather around to watch him. At the start of his doomed mission he harbors the typical prejudices of a young foot-soldier in any colonial enterprise against strange and potentially dangerous natives. He urges the Venusians' total extermination at the beginning of his journal, a diary which he maintains to the last possible moment. Days later, knowing that death is near, he writes: "As the end approaches, I feel more kindly toward the things. In the scale of cosmic entity who can say which species stands higher, or more nearly approaches a space-wide organic norm—theirs or mine." Stanfield's supervisor notes at the end of the tale that the prospector's remains will be buried in the Company graveyard on Venus, and hints that the extermination of the Venusians for the sake of unhindered crystal-gathering is not far off.

Surely it must have been HPL's idea to give the protagonist of this tale a name with the same initials and rhythm as that of his teenage admirer and co-author, Kenneth J. Sterling (1920–95). This exceptional high school student, a resident of Providence, was a zealous science-fiction fan who already had a few published pulp-magazine sci-fi tales to his credit. Ultimately young Sterling chose a career as a medical doctor over a career as a writer, but *In the Walls of Eryx* means that he will be remembered for as long as HPL is remembered. The name "Kenton" is not a common one.

STARKWEATHER-MOORE EXPEDITION (MM): A proposed Antarctic expedition, with plans for large-scale blasting, melting, and drilling, which Professor Dyer says he hopes to prevent by publishing his true story.

STARRY WISDOM (HD): The name of a "disliked and unorthodox" religious cult founded in Providence in 1844 by Professor Enoch Bowen, after his return from Egypt. Starry Wisdom occupies a "huge, dark church" of weathered and grimy stone (HPL, a formidable self-taught expert on New England architectural styles, cannot resist elaborating that the church's architecture "was that earliest experimental form of Gothic revival which preceded the stately Upjohn period and held over some of the outlines and proportions of the Georgian age. Perhaps it was reared around 1810 or 1815") on Federal Hill, formerly the property of a Free-Will Baptist congregation. We learn something of the cult's history, as Robert Blake gets a synopsis from a talkative Irish-American policeman in the neighborhood, and does other research. By the end of 1845 Starry Wisdom counted 97 members, which had risen to 200 or more by the war year of 1863—not counting men away in the army. The late 19th century newspaper reporter Edwin M. Lillibridge learned of three disappearances of local people in 1846, seven more in 1848, one—that of a certain Patrick Regan—in 1869, and six more in 1876, all blamed on the cult. Under severe pressure thereafter from the authorities and the local community, the cultists closed their church in April, 1877, and by the end of the year some 181 members had moved out of Providence. the cultists abandon the site under pressure from the authorities and the local community. On finding a way into the locked church building, Blake finds no sign of anyone—except for Lillibridge, whose old bones are on the floor of the chamber in the steeple—having been inside for almost sixty years. The stained-glass windows in the sanctuary are blasphemous parodies of those to be seen in a proper Christian church, and the altar cross is no cross, but an Egyptian *ankh* symbol. In the vestry rooms Blake discovers books of forbidden lore, and a journal written in the esoteric Aklo language. In the steeple, instead of a church bell, Blake finds the Shining Trapezohedron. No latter-day members of Starry Wisdom turn up in the tale, leading one always to wonder where the membership dispersed to after 1877.

The Starry Wisdom church building was based on a real house of worship which used to loom large on the landscape of Federal Hill, St. John's Catholic Church on Atwells Avenue (not to be confused with St. John's Episcopal Church on College Hill, in HPL's neighborhood), built in 1871. The old church was demolished in the early 1990s, after the parish was abolished.

STEELE (CDW): In the tale, it is remarked that it was "not wholesome" that Charles Dexter Ward (or that which purports to be him) in the 20th century should know so much about how in 1762 the actors at the theater in Providence "cut the text of Steele's *Conscious Lover* so badly that one was almost glad the Baptist-ridden legislature closed the theater a fortnight later." Besides another backhand slap at the Baptist faith of HPL's early upbringing, this sentence seems to contain a small error. Sir John Steele (1672–1729), British journalist, essayist, and playwright, authored the romantic comedy *The Conscious Lovers* (not *Lover*) in 1722.

STETHELOS (QI): A place "below the great cataract." It is one of the many places that Iranon tells Romnod about visiting.

STOWACKI, PETE (DWH): A working-class denizen of Arkham, and the boyfriend of Anastasia Wolejko; he refuses to protect her two-year-old son, Ladislas, on Walpurgis-night because he wants the child—presumably not his own—"out of the way," and therefore doesn't care if Keziah Mason and Brown Jenkin take him.

"STRANGE DAYS, THE" (COS): A phrase used in Arkham and its environs for the period between March, 1882, when the meteorite landed on the Nahum Gardner farm outside of town, until November, 1883, when whatever it was that came that night seemed to go away again. People avoided talking about the strange days.

STRANGE HIGH HOUSE, THE (SHH): A mysterious cottage on a towering ocean cliff outside of Kingsport, Massachusetts. The summer-vacationer, Professor Olney, hikes up to it one day and spends a very memorable night there. One side of the house is built flush with the edge of the sheer cliff over the sea; curiously, its only door opens into empty air. The oldest people in Kingsport, such as the Terrible Old Man, know almost nothing about the place except that it has always been there. Professor Olney gains his admittance through a rear window on the landward side.

STREET, THE (TS): In an unnamed New England city, a street passes through centuries of American history while transforming from colonial forest pathway, to elegant avenue of the early Republic, to squalid early-20th-century ghetto teeming with swarthy Bolshevik bomb-throwers, who are described so as to leave no doubt of their Jewish, Russian, or similar suspect origins. These Marxist malcontents congregate along the Street in such dens as the Rifkin School of Modern Economics, Petrovich's Bakery, and the Liberty Café. At their command, "millions of brainless, besotted beasts would stretch forth their noisome talons from the slums of a thousand cities, burning, slaying, and destroying until the land of our fathers should be no more." But just before the Reds can give the order for their followers to rise up in violent revolution—on the Fourth of July!—the Street's ancient buildings collapse on their heads, killing them all and averting the bloody communist revolt. In the air above the smoking ruins, a pair of visionary passers-by seem to see an image of the Street, looking the way it looked during its finest 19th-century days as a pleasant thoroughfare for true and free Americans. The reader is to understand that the Street itself engineered the collapse of the buildings along its route to snuff out the revolutionary leaders.

The Street, which Lovecraft biographer S.T. Joshi has described as perhaps the single worst story HPL ever wrote, is typically consigned to the hell of "Early Tales" in the back pages of collections, an embarrassment to critics and fans alike. It is hardly a real story so much as a "wild, paranoid, racist fantasy," which only shows "how spectacularly awful Lovecraft can be when riding one of his hobby-horses, in particular his stereotyped lament on the decline of New England at the hands of foreigners," to quote Joshi. It may also be noted that the Street is an obvious precursor of "Parker Place" in *The Horror at Red Hook*, another collapsible warren of old buildings crowded with alien menaces to society, invented by HPL in another period of socio-political paranoia.

For contemporary readers, the piece has to be put into its increasingly-remote historical context. *The Street* was composed late in 1919, in the era of the bloody and horrific Russian Revolution and civil war between Soviet and anti-Soviet forces (followed by copycat uprisings of socialist radicals in a number of European locales), and also of the "Palmer Raids" to which it even vaguely alludes: the national crackdown on leftist radicals, particularly foreign-born communists, which was supervised by U.S. Attorney General Alexander M. Palmer during 1919–20. Some three thousand allegedly subversive aliens were rounded up for deportation during this first American "red scare," although all but a few hundred were eventually released when the hysteria had died down. In a 1920 magazine article entitled *The Case Against the Reds*, Attorney General Palmer outlined his theory of the Bolshevik menace in America, sounding almost like HPL in this tale:

> Like a prairie-fire, the blaze of revolution was sweeping over every American institution of law and order a year ago. It was eating its way into the homes of the American workmen, its sharp tongues of revolutionary heat were licking the altars of the churches, leaping into the belfry of the school bell, crawling into the sacred corners of American homes, seeking to replace marriage vows with libertine laws, burning up the foundations of society.

On the other side, suspected anarchists set off bombs in eight American cities in 1919, including one which partially destroyed Palmer's house in Washington, D.C. For his specific inspiration, HPL pointed to a long strike (he called it a "mutiny") by the Boston police in September–October 1919, which led to their replacement in the city streets by rifle-carrying National Guard soldiers, who appeared to his fevered imagination as "symbols of the strife that lies ahead in civilization's struggle with the monster of unrest and bolshevism." *The Street* does reflect in full measure HPL's arch-conservative political stance at the time of its writing; fifteen years later the artist was earnestly advocating something he called "fascistic socialism" as the ideal or utopian form of government.

STREET OF THE PILLARS (DQ): The main boulevard of the city of Celephaïs, in Dreamland. It leads from the harbor to the Temple of Nath-Horthath, where Randolph Carter consults with one of the high priests.

SUMNER'S POND (HW): A small lake in or near the town of Arkham; the medical student, West, and his comrade, perform one of their early human-reanimation experiments on the corpse of a "brawny young workman" who has drowned in the pond.

SURREY (CE): A small and lovely county in England, south of London; its terrain was and remains predominately wooded or agricultural. Kuranes and his escort "rode majestically through the downs of Surrey" en route from London to his ancestral region.

SUYDAM, ROBERT (HRH): A "lettered recluse of ancient Dutch family," still hanging on during the 1920s in the "spacious but ill-preserved" family mansion on Martense Street in the urban Flatbush district of Brooklyn, New York, a home built by his grandfather when Flatbush "was little more than a pleasant group of Colonial cottages surrounding the steepled and ivy-clad Reformed Church with its iron-railed yard of Netherlandish gravestones." (The same old cemetery, which HPL had thoroughly investigated during his New York sojourn, was also the inspiration for the Dutch graveyard in *The Hound*.) About sixty years of age, Suydam has spent most of his life in the mansion, surrounded by "ponderous, archaic and vaguely repellent" books, except for eight youthful years in Europe. He is a profound expert on medieval superstitions, witchcraft, and the Kabbalah, the Jewish body of mystical teachings of rabbinical origin, often based on an esoteric interpretation of the Hebrew Scriptures. Already known as a "queer, corpulent old fellow [with] unkempt white hair, stubbly beard, shiny black clothes, and gold-headed cane," his appearance and manners turn even worse when he rents a basement apartment in squalid Parker Place, in Brooklyn's Red Hook waterfront section, and begins to consort with Central Asian rowdies and take part in ceremonial rites.

At the time when "a wave of kidnappings and disappearances" shocks New York, the fat, aging, and unkempt scholar begins to grow slender, more youthful, with the energy and "buoyancy" of a much younger man. (One apprehends that human sacrifice somehow lies at the back of his renewed vigor and health. Most of the kidnapping victims are "young children of the lowest classes.") He returns to polite society, hosts large and elegant parties, and finally marries a very respectable young lady, Cornelia Gerritsen. On the first night of their honeymoon voyage on a transatlantic liner, both are mysteriously slain in their stateroom, and a tramp steamer with a crew of loathsome foreigners sails alongside the big ship, carrying "papers" permitting them to claim Suydam's body in the event of his death. In catacombs and crypts under Parker Place, the police detective Malone witnesses Suydam's corpse being brought before Lilith, and then sees the cadaver come horribly to life, to turn on its former cohorts in evil. At the end of it all, "Robert Suydam sleeps beside his bride in Greenwood Cemetery…. The Suydams hope that posterity may recall him only as a gentle recluse who dabbled in harmless magic and folklore."

SWAN POINT CEMETERY (CDW): Swan Point Cemetery—which is listed in the National Register of Historic Places—lies off Blackstone Boulevard, well to the east of downtown Providence, but relatively close to the site of HPL's boyhood home and to the rest of his beloved College Hill neighborhood. HPL was buried here on March 18, 1937, in the Phillips family plot on Avenue B, next to the graves of his mother and father. In *The Case of Charles Dexter Ward*, the author mentioned his future resting-place as one of the Providence cemeteries that Ward was quickly able to rule out as a place where Joseph Curwen's body might have been buried in 1771. It may also be noted that HPL wrote in a letter about visiting Swan Point Cemetery one day in June, 1917, with one of his aunts, and seeing a crumbling slate headstone with the date of 1711. The fantasy of being able to talk with the man of the 18th century who was buried there, inspired him to write *The Tomb* on the same night.

SYDNEY *BULLETIN* (CC): A real Australian newspaper; in the tale, it recounts the tale of the *Emma*'s crew on April 18, 1925. The story includes a picture of an image like Cthulhu's idols. The article catches the eye of Francis Thurston when he sees the newspaper page by the merest chance, lining a storage shelf in a museum in Paterson, New Jersey. Soon afterwards Thurston is en route to Australia to continue his investigation.

Francis Thurston's visit to a "learned friend"—who happens to be the curator of a museum in humble Paterson, N.J.—is a tip of the hat to HPL's good friend James F. Morton (1870–1941), an erudite, mildly eccentric gentleman who was one of HPL's amateur-publishing cronies in the early 1920s, and who by 1925 had landed the salaried position of curator at the new municipal museum of Paterson. During 1925–26 it appeared that HPL might become Morton's paid assistant at the institution—HPL thought seriously about it, "being a born museum curator if any man ever was," as L. Sprague de Camp wrote—but funding for the post did not become available.

SYLVIUS (CDW): Presumably a reference to Franciscus Sylvius (Franciscus de Boe) (1614–72), a Dutch scientist who was professor of medicine at the University of Leiden for many years. Sylvius was one of the most prominent of the early modern chemists and physiologists, and may have established the earliest university chemistry laboratory. His writings are among those "philosophical, mathematical, and scientific works" glimpsed by Mr. John Merritt in Joseph Curwen's Providence library, circa 1746.

SYMBOLISTS (TH): An avant-garde artistic movement that flourished in the last years of the 19th century. Symbolist poets such as Charles Baudelaire, Stephane Mallarme, Arthur Rimbaud and Paul Verlaine—all Frenchmen—sought to express ideas, values and feelings through symbols and suggestions, rather than direct statements, as with the previous generation of bluntly realist authors. The Symbolists sought to interpret reality through imagination, and also to discard established formal rules of versification. The two decadent protagonists of *The Hound* have already passed through a phase of Symbolist enthusiasm long before beginning their career of aesthetic grave-robbing.

SYRACUSE (TR): A powerful Greek city-state of ancient times, founded by Greek colonists in the 8th century B.C. on the island of Sicily near the site of the modern Italian city of Siracusa. In the tale, Syracuse's "tyrant" or dictator announces that he will purchase a statue of Tyché from either the sculptor Kalos or his companion-sculptor Musides, triggering the competition between the two artists which leads to the death of both. Syracuse had several rulers in her history who were referred to as "tyrants" (a word which, unlike in modern usage, did not then necessarily imply cruel or unjust rule). Since a character in the tale refers to the tomb of Mausolus, which was built circa 352 B.C., the tyrant in question was probably Dionysius II, whose "reign" was from approximately 353–344 B.C. (if HPL thought the matter through that far).

T

TABLETS OF NHING (TGSK): Suffering from persistent, recurrent dreams which include "an entity of absurd, outlandish race called 'Randolph Carter' on a world of the future not yet born," the wizard Zkauba on the planet Yaddith felt "he must rest and reflect, and consult the Tablets of Nhing for advice on what to do. Climbing a metal wall in a lane off the main concourse, he entered his apartment and approached the rack of tablets."

TAMASH (DCS): One of the three "graceful, bearded gods" who are the chief member's of Sarnath's pantheon. *See* "Zo-Kalar" and "Lobon".

TANARIAN HILLS (CE, DQ): A range which screens the valley of Ooth-Nargai, in which lies Celephaïs.

TARAN-ISH (DCS): Sarnath's high priest in the year that the men of Sarnath exterminated the non-human inhabitants of neighboring Ib. On the night of this victory, Ib's idol of Bokrug is placed in the temple of Sarnath; the next morning it has disappeared, and Taran-Ish is dead. He has scrawled the symbol for DOOM on a chrysolite altar.

TARTARUS (HRH, CC): When the reanimated corpse of Robert Suydam pushes Lilith's carved golden pedestal (the "necromantic importance" of which is "evidently great") into the subterranean pool under Brooklyn, "it sank heavily below to undreamable gulfs of lower Tartarus." While drifting through great storms on the *Alert*, in *The Call of Cthulhu*, Second Mate Johansen seems to hear a chorus that includes "...the green, bat-winged, mocking imps of Tartarus." Tartarus in Greek mythology was the lowest part of the underworld, where the most wicked people were condemned to misery after their deaths.

TARTARY (TGSK): Not to be confused with "Tartarus," Tartary is an archaic English word for the vast, ill-defined area of Central Asia from which came the Tartar tribesmen, warriors on horseback, centuries ago. The "tall, uncertainly coloured mitres" on the Shapes outside the Ultimate Gate are "strangely suggestive of those on certain nameless figures chiselled by a forgotten sculptor along the living cliffs of a high, forbidden mountain in Tartary...."

TAYLOR; WEGENER; JOLY (MM): Frank B. Taylor (1860–1938), Alfred L. Wegener (1880–1930) and John Joly (1857–1933) were all scientists whose work (most prominently that of Wegener in his 1915 book *The Origin of Continents and Oceans*) went into creating the theory of plate tectonics, better known as "continental drift," the concept of the gradual movement of continental plates around the surface of the earth over immense eons of time. The continental drift theory was still ignored, dismissed, or ridiculed by the majority of geologists in 1931 when HPL gave it a favorable mention in *At the Mountains of Madness*; it did not become a generally accepted doctrine until the 1960s.

TCHO-TCHOS (SOT): All that Professor Nathaniel Peaslee can do with these creatures is to label them "wholly abominable." These pre-human inhabitants of earth first saw the light of print in August Derleth and Mark Schorer's 1932 story "Lair of the Star-Spawn" in *Weird Tales.*

TEGEA (TR): An ancient, non-fictitious Greek city-state of middling power and importance. In the tale, Tegea is the nearby city to the home shared by the sculptors Kalos and Musides. The latter artist is also fond of the "urban gaieties" offered in Tegea, his steady distraction from the hard work of producing profound art, like his austere and always-serious housemate Kalos. The unnamed "men of Tegea" are witnesses to many of the events in this minor tale (one is almost tempted to write: "just like a Greek chorus").

TELOTH (QI): A somber, granite city by the sluggish river Zuro, which Iranon visited one day. Its men are dark and stern, and live in square houses. As a civic leader tells Iranon: "All in Teloth must toil, for that is the law…. The gods of Teloth have said that toil is good. Our gods have promised us a haven of light beyond death, where there is rest without end, and crystal coldness." They give the wandering minstrel Iranon leave to stay in the city for one night, after which he must take up gainful employment or depart. He leaves the next morning, taking the youth Romnod with him. In this early tale, one gets a hint of the youthful HPL justifying his failure to go out and begin a career like his contemporaries in bourgeois Providence.

TEMPEST MOUNTAIN (LF): A fictional mountain which HPL locates in the Catskill Mountains of New York. As its name suggests, the mountain's environs are notorious for violent and prolonged thunderstorms. In around 1670, Gerrit Martense builds his mansion at Tempest Mountain, which becomes the dwelling place for centuries of Martenses, above, and eventually below, the ground.

TEMPLE OF THE ELDER ONES (DQ): A surpassingly magnificent temple in the city of Inganok. It is in a plaza at the center of the city, from which all the main streets radiate. The temple boasts sixteen carved sides, a flattened dome, and a lofty, pinnacled bell-tower. It is surrounded by a wall with seven open gateways, and inside the wall is a beautiful garden, filled with onyx fountains and tiled pathways leading past the shrines of lesser gods. When the great bell rings, columns of black-masked and hooded priests bearing steaming bowls, and walking with peculiar strides, issue from the temple's seven doorways and proceed into the lodges of the seven gates. The Veiled King is the only non-priest permitted to enter the temple.

TEMPLE OF THE HIGH PRIEST NOT TO BE DESCRIBED: *See* "High Priest Not To Be Described."

TERRA NOVA (WE): Latin for "New Earth," it is the earthlings' base on the planet Venus and planetary headquarters of the Venus Crystal Company. The company graveyard there is the final resting-place for the hapless prospectors Kenton Stanfield and Frederick Dwight.

TERRIBLE OLD MAN, THE (TOM, SHH): A tall, lean, old man with long white hair and beard, and yellow eyes, who lives on Water Street in Kingsport. He is thought to conceal a large fortune somewhere in his house, for he pays for his purchases with Spanish gold and silver coins of the 18th century. People also say that he was a clipper-ship captain in the East India trade (which flourished in the first half of the 19th century!); but he is "so old that no one [could] remember when he was young, and so taciturn that few [know] his real name." His ancient house has gnarled old trees and curiously-painted stones in the front yard. On a table in a ground-floor room are "many peculiar bottles, in each [of which] a small piece of lead [hung] suspended pendulum-wise from a string." He talks to these bottles individually, using such sailor-like names as Long Tom, Spanish Joe, and Mate Ellis, and the pendulums seem to vibrate in response. In *The Strange High House in the Mist* we read of the T.O.M. in a milder mood than in the tale that bears his name, in which he bests three young would-be robbers. He speaks to Thomas Olney about the house up on the high cliff, and says that "these things were the same when his grandfather was a boy, and that must have been inconceivable ages ago when Belcher or Shirley or Pownall or Bernard was Governor of His Majesty's Province of the Massachusetts-Bay." He also "wheeze[d] a tale" handed down from his father, about "lightning that shot one night up from [the house] to the clouds of higher heaven...."

THAGWEED (DQ): A substance which the men of Dylath-Leen smoke in order to endure the stench from the black galleys when south winds blow it up from the direction of the docks.

THALARION (WS, DQ): A port on the Southern Sea, passed by Basil Elton and later by Randolph Carter. It is an inconceivably vast place, and its spires seem to reach into the heavens, and yet it is somehow repellent to both of them. It is the "City of a Thousand Wonders," into which "many have passed but none returned. Therein walk only daemons and mad things that are no longer men." Other features of Thalarion include the eidolon Lathi and the great gate called Akariel.

THAYER STREET (CC): The Providence street where Henry Wilcox's physician, Dr. Tobey, has his medical practice.

THEODOTIDES (SOT): A captive mind encountered by Nathaniel Peaslee during his time with the Great Race; he is a "Graeco-Bactrian official"—that is, a Greek or part-Greek, but living in Central Asia—of circa 200 B.C. This was during the "Hellenistic" era when Greeks and Greek-style culture were spread far and wide in the wake of the conquests of Alexander the Great.

THEOSOPHISTS (CC): The newspaper clipping service hired by George Gammell Angell provides him with a news item from California, 1928, which "describes a theosophist colony as donning white robes en masse for some 'glorious fulfillment' which never arrives." At about the same time "a widely known architect with leanings toward theosophy and occultism, went violently insane...and expired several months later after incessant screamings to be saved from some escaped denizen of hell." It is also noted that the captive Cthulhu-cultist Castro "remembered bits of hideous legend that paled the speculations of theosophists and made man and the world seem recent and transient indeed." Some readers have probably wondered who these "theosophist" people were.

In general, "theosophy" (from Greek, "divine wisdom") is an ancient philosophical system which, under many names, has claimed insight into the nature of God through spiritual knowledge and metaphysical or mystical speculation, and taught a pathway to the Godhead through contemplation of the infinite and a recognition that evil comes from the human obsession for obtaining worldly goods and desires. The Kabbalists and Gnostics of old European vintage may be classified as types of theosophists in this broad sense. Classical Western theosophy lent itself beautifully to amalgamation with Eastern religions, a process which began to occur in the second half of the 19th century as Hinduism and Buddhism became better understood in the western world. In cooking up this "colony," HPL was probably thinking specifically of the Theosophical Society, which was founded in New York City in 1875 by the extraordinary Russian mystic and traveler, Helena Blavatsky, and a number of her associates. The Theosophical Society's intermingling of Eastern and Western spirituality and its other inclusionary practices, although common today in Europe and the Americas, were radical departures from the religious norm both at the time and for many years thereafter. The Society's objects were (and still are):

1. To form the nucleus of a universal brotherhood of humanity, without distinction of race, creed, sex, caste, or color;

2. The study of ancient and modern religions, philosophies and sciences, and the demonstration of the importance of such study; and

3. The investigation of the unexplained laws of nature and the psychical powers latent in man.

In the words of one American scholar in the 1980s:

> The Theosophical Society became the most widely influential organization for the public promotion of occult teaching in modern times.... The Society is historically important for popularizing ideas of reincarnation and karma, secret masters, and Tibet as the land of ageless wisdom...for encouraging the comparative study of religion; and for persuading many that the essential teachings of the great religions are one.

Scholarship has documented Theosophical Society membership or influence in a number of major poets or authors who were among Lovecraft's contemporaries, including William Butler Yeats, James Joyce, Jack London, E.M. Forster, D.H. Lawrence, T.S. Eliot, Thornton Wilder, and L. Frank Baum, an American member of the Society whose children's classic *The Wizard of Oz* (1900) it has been said, "can be regarded as Theosophical allegory, pervaded by Theosophical ideas from beginning to end." Nicholas Roerich, whose weird paintings HPL adored, freely acknowledged the theosophical influence on his artwork and revered the memory of his countrywoman Madame Blavatsky.

The godless HPL was certainly not a Theosophist or even a good candidate for membership, but he gave a nod to the movement near the beginning of *The Call of Cthulhu*:

> Theosophists have guessed at the awesome grandeur of the cosmic cycle wherein our world and human race form transient incidents. They have hinted at strange survivals in terms which would freeze the blood if not masked by a bland optimism.

THESEUS (TO): In ancient Greek mythology, the folk hero Theseus was the son of King Aegeus of Athens, who left him as an infant with his mother, on a remote farm. Before departing, the mighty Aegeus placed a sword and a pair of sandals beneath an enormous stone, telling the mother that if and when the boy ever grew strong enough to push the stone away, he should bring the sword and sandals to Athens to claim his royal birthright—which Theseus eventually did when he had become a young man. In *The Tomb,* the narrator compares himself to Theseus as he waits for the ability to open and enter the Hyde family's tomb..

THICKNESSE (DH): *See* "Cryptographers of Dunwich."

THOMAS, ISAIAH (PH): In the house with the picture (in *The Picture in the House)*, the nameless narrator notices an 18th century copy of *Pilgrim's Progress*, "illustrated with grotesque woodcuts and printed by the almanack-maker Isaiah Thomas." *The Pilgrim's Progress* by John Bunyan (1628–1688) is a 17th century allegorical narrative of a Christian's journey from the evil world to the Heavenly City; for probably two centuries there was no more popular book (except for the Bible itself) among English-speaking Protestants such as the colonists of New England. Isaiah Thomas (1749–1831) was a printer in Worcester, Massachusetts, and a patriot and soldier in the American Revolution.

A popular almanac in the 18th or 19th century was usually an annual collection of calendar information, astronomical charts, miscellaneous facts and statistics, articles, humor, moral proverbs, weather predictions, and other material of general appeal; they were once very common especially in rural homes that could afford few books.

THON and THAL (DQ): Twin beacons of the harbor of Baharna, on the island of Oriab.

THORABONIA (DQ): A country in Dreamland. Randolph Carter, while still in Celephaïs, gets information about Leng and Inganok from a Thorabonian sailor.

THORFINNSSEN, CAPTAIN GEORGE (MM): The captain of the *Miskatonic*, one of the two vessels that carry the Miskatonic University Expedition to and from Antarctica. He is "a veteran sailor in Antarctic waters."

THORNTON (RW): One of the team of British experts collected in London by Mr. de la Poer and Captain Norrys to investigate the understructures of Exham Priory. He is a psychic investigator. When the subterranean cavern is first breached, Thornton faints into the arms of the man standing behind him; later, in the cavern, he faints again; finally, we learn, he is confined as a madman in Hanwell Asylum, in the cell adjoining that of Mr. de la Poer.

THOTH, BOOK OF (TGSK): A book of old forgotten lore mentioned in the *Necronomicon* by Abdul Alhazred. "It is written in the Book of Thoth how terrific is the price of a single glimpse" of 'Umr at-Tawil, the guide at the gate.

L. Sprague de Camp writes that the "real" Book of Thoth "first appeared in an ancient Egyptian tale [that is] known from a Ptolemaic papyrus but probably much older. According to this [Egyptian tale], this book of mighty spells was originally penned by the Egyptian ibis-headed god of wisdom, Tehuti or Thoth. When the papyrus was published early in [the 20th] century, fantasy writers seized upon the *Book of Thoth* as a prop for their stories."

THRAA (QI, DCS, DQ): A city in the land of Mnar.

THRAN (DQ, SK, TGSK): A magnificent city in Dreamland, on the splendid river Oukranos. Its alabaster walls are lofty beyond belief, slope inwardly toward the top, and most marvelous, "are wrought in one solid piece by what means no man knows." The walls have one hundred gates and two hundred turrets. Behind them, in the city, are a thousand gilded spires, all far higher than the sheltering walls. On the riverbank are marble wharves "with ornate galleons...riding gently at anchor." To gain permission to enter Thran, a dreamer like Randolph Carter must tell the sentry "three dreams beyond belief." On his dream-quest, Carter spends a night in Thran, and buys his passage out on a galleon bound down the Oukranos and over the Cerenarian Sea to Celephaïs.

THROCKMORTON, JOHN (SH): A non-fictitious Providence pioneer (born before 1627, d. 1687) from Norwich, England. He was the original owner of the large tract of land, on a portion of which the fictitious William Harris built his house in the 18th century.

THUL (CU): A stonecutter in the town of Ulthar; he accompanies the burgomaster Kranon as an official witness when Kranon breaks into the house of the wicked old couple.

THURAI (OG): A snow-capped mountain where earth's gods used to dwell and play before they moved to Kadath, and where men have felt the tears of the gods of earth, "as they try to play in the olden way on remembered slopes."

THURBER (PM): The narrator of *Pickman's Model* is addressed several times by Pickman as "Thurber." He keeps up an acquaintance with Pickman after most of the artist's previous acquaintances have dropped him; he listens with interest to Pickman's increasingly strange hints and stories; and he finally receives the unique favor of a trip to Pickman's secret studio in the North End, where he sees Pickman's scariest works and then, most frightening of all, a *photograph* of a ghoul. After this experience he also drops Pickman, and before much longer Pickman drops out of sight, permanently. Thurber is apparently a member of the Boston Art Club together with "Eliot," the mute cipher to whom he recounts the tale in 14 pages of uninterrupted narration mingled with the second-hand rantings of the absent Pickman. Thurber says at one point to Eliot, "I guess you saw enough of me in France to know I'm not easily knocked out." This could only be a reference to combat service during World War I, which the United States entered in 1917–18. Paradoxically for such a dedicated and witty conversationalist as HPL, dialogue was not his strong suit as a writer; he understood this and kept real conversation to a minimum in his fiction.

THURSTON, FRANCIS WAYLAND (CC): A Bostonian who is the grand-nephew, sole heir and executor of the estate of the late Professor George Gammell Angell of Brown University in Providence. While curiously investigating some odd papers and images found among Professor Angell's property, starting in 1927, Mr. Thurston becomes the man who knew too much about Cthulhu and the Cthulhu-cult, dooming himself— as he realizes. Thurston is one of HPL's most active and effective characters. Like many other protagonists, he is a Lovecraftian alter-ego, but one blessed with a substantial private income. His opening words in the tale—"The most merciful thing in the world, I think, is the inability of the human mind to correlate all its contents"—are properly regarded as one of the best sentences that the great sentence-maker HPL ever put on paper. Thurston, unfortunately, is a driven correlator, and what he correlates—"an old newspaper item and a dead professor's notes," as he puts it—give him an insight into ultimate horrors that he would have been better off not having. Thurston pursues the case from Providence to New Orleans, to New Jersey, to Australia and Norway, and back home in despair to New England, there to arrange his thoughts on paper and to await his own inevitable murder.

TILLINGHAST, MISS ANN (CDW): The only child of Joseph Curwen and his bride Eliza, maiden name Tillinghast; born on May 7, 1765, and christened at King's Church by the Reverend John Graves. She becomes Ann Tillinghast, instead of Curwen, in 1772 when her mother legally recovers her maiden name as part of the attempted eradication of traces of Joseph Curwen from the community. In 1785, Ann Tillinghast marries Welcome Potter, Charles Dexter Ward's maternal great-great-grandfather; obviously this makes Ward a descendant of Joseph Curwen. The narrator notes that Curwen welcomed the birth of this daughter, his only child, "with a fervour greatly out of keeping with his usual coldness"; it was really because she would presumably have offspring and descendants, one of whom could someday reanimate the dead Curwen, as Charles Dexter Ward eventually does.

TILLINGHAST, CRAWFORD (FB): An obsessed mad scientist in the classic mode, an acquaintance of the narrator of this early tale.

> That Crawford Tillinghast should ever have studied science and philosophy was a mistake. These things should be left to the frigid and impersonal investigator, for they offer two equally tragic alternatives to the man of feeling and action; despair if he should fail in his quest, and terrors unutterable and unimaginable if he should succeed.

In the large attic of his house on Benevolent Street in Providence he constructs a device—"a detestable electrical machine, glowing with a sickly, sinister, violet luminosity.... In reply to my question Tillinghast mumbled that this permanent glow was not electrical in any sense I could understand"—that renders ultra-violet rays visible to the naked eye, and can make visible the frightful-looking creatures from parallel dimensions that exist in the air, so to speak, all around us, through the medium of the body's pineal gland. Sadly, his years of toil and frustration and rejection, crowned by vindicating success, have turned him fanatical and heartless. He rants to his former friend, "I have seen beyond the bounds of infinity and drawn down daemons from the stars... I have harnessed the shadows that stride from world to world to sow death and madness.... Space belongs to me, do you hear?" He cares not that some of "his pets," as he terms them, "the things that devour and dissolve," disintegrated all of his domestic servants when a housekeeper disobeyed orders and switched on an electric light in the house below, attracting their presence. Tillinghast dies of a sudden apoplexy (a stroke) just as the terrified narrator puts a bullet through his mysterious machine to end the display of other-dimensional monsters. "[The coroner] told me that I had undoubtedly been hypnotised by the vindictive and homicidal madman.... What prevents me from believing the doctor is this one simple fact—that the police never found the bodies of those servants whom they say Crawford Tillinghast murdered."

In the character of "Crawford Tillinghast," HPL united the names of two leading Providence families in colonial times. In fact, a Mr. Crawford and a Mr. Tillinghast each owned property on opposite sides of Benevolent Street in the 18th century, raising the possibility of what Lovecraft biographer S.T. Joshi aptly called "an extraordinarily obscure historical in-joke" hidden in the mad scientist's name.

In Crawford Tillinghast's attic laboratory there is a trace of HPL's youthful experience, as described by his ex-wife Sonia, who would have heard it from his lips or those of his aunts:

> While H.P. was intensely interested in astronomy he studied also physics and chemistry. The basement of 598 [Angell Street, HPL's home from 1904–24] was constructed and equipped as a chemical laboratory, with all sorts of vials and philtres and test-tubes as well as whatever chemicals he was able to acquire for his studies. With these he would experiment endlessly.

TILLINGHAST, CAPTAIN DUTEE (CDW): One of Joseph Curwen's "best and oldest sea-captains, a widower of high birth and unblemished standing," presumably a (fictitious) collateral relative of the wealthy merchant Tillinghasts of colonial Providence. He resided on Power's Lane Hill in Providence. Unfortunately he has little money, and is completely under Curwen's domination. After a "terrible interview" with his employer, he consents to give his only daughter Eliza in marriage to the sinister old man, in 1763. Captain Tillinghast is a good crony of Captain Abraham Whipple, the tough sea-dog who led the secret raid on Joseph Curwen's farm in 1771, and although the facts are at first hidden from him, he learns enough from Whipple to demand, in 1772, that his daughter and granddaughter change their name from Curwen to Tillinghast, and to cause the burning of Curwen's library and papers and the obliteration of the inscription of his name on the slate slab above his grave.

TILLINGHAST, ELIZA (CDW): The daughter of Captain Dutee Tillinghast: a young lady who is blessed "with every conceivable advantage except prospects as an heiress." A maiden with no expectations of a substantial wedding dowry or inheritance was typically doomed to go unclaimed by any suitor in the 18th century marriage market. This is what makes her the available target of Joseph Curwen, as well as the fact that her father is one of Curwen's frightened employees. Probably born in 1744, Eliza Tillinghast attended Stephen Jackson's school in Providence, and had learned all of the domestic arts from her mother before that parent's death from smallpox in 1757. A sampler she stitched in 1753 at the age of 9 was in the collection of the Rhode Island Historical Society in the 1920s. After her mother's death she began to keep her father's house, with the help of a black housemaid. Eliza became engaged at age 18 to Ezra Weeden, a young sailor who clearly must have loved her as a person. But the engagement was broken when her father agreed instead to marry her to the wealthy Joseph Curwen—who was then known to be approximately 100 years old! The peculiar wedding took place in the Baptist Church on March 7, 1763, some seventy years after the bridegroom had first moved to Providence and gone into business, "in the presence of one of the most distinguished assemblages which the town could boast." As announced in the Providence *Gazette*:

> Monday evening last, Mr. Joseph Curwen, of this Town, Merchant, was married to Miss Eliza Tillinghast, Daughter of Captain Dutee Tillinghast, a young lady who has real merit, added to a beautiful Person, to grace the connubial State and perpetuate its Felicity.

Charles Dexter Ward, reading this old newspaper item in the 1920s, "observ[ed] with amusement the meaningless urbanity of the language," given what he already knew about his ancestor Curwen's increasingly sinister reputation in Providence by the time of the marriage. However, "in his treatment of his wife, the strange bridegroom astonished both her and the community by displaying an extreme graciousness and consideration" toward her. He did require marital relations, which resulted in the birth of their daughter Ann. Eliza lived in Curwen's Olney Court town house in Providence, and never visited the Pawtuxet Road farm where he spent so much of his time. Following Curwen's death in 1771, and at her father's insistence, the widow was granted a legal restoration of her maiden name of Tillinghast, on the grounds that "her Husband's name was become a publick Reproach by Reason of what was knowne after his Decease; the which confirming an antient common Rumour, tho' not to be credited by a loyall Wife till so proven as to be wholely past doubting." Known after 1772 by the odd title "Mrs. Tillinghast," she sold Curwen's Olney Court house and lived in her father's house in Power's Lane until her death in 1817.

(PARDON) TILLINGHAST'S WHARF (SH): Described as lying near the end of Town Street in 17th century Providence. Etienne Roulet got a job there as a warehouse clerk after he and his family settled in Providence in 1686.

TILTON, MISS ANNA (SOI): In this tale, the curator of the Newburyport Historical Society in 1927. Before he visits Innsmouth, the narrator calls on this "ancient gentlewoman," who shows him one of the Society's treasures: a peculiar golden tiara, thought to be of East Asian or "Indo-Chinese" (Southeast Asian) provenance. It had been pawned in 1873 by a drunken Innsmouth man who was "shortly afterward killed in a brawl," whereupon the Society had purchased it from the pawnbroker. The Marsh family from Innsmouth had made steady and lucrative offers to buy the tiara ever since, but the Society had steadily refused to sell it. Miss Tilton tells the narrator a little more hearsay about Innsmouth—a place she had never seen, although she lived but a few miles away—and

Innsmouth's cult, the Esoteric Order of Dagon, which she calls "undoubtedly a debased, quasi-pagan thing imported from the East a century before."

TOBEY, DR. (CC): Henry Wilcox's physician in 1925. Professor Angell talks with him frequently in late March that year, to learn the topics of Wilcox's dreams and ravings.

TOBEY, WILLIAM (LF): One of the "faithful and muscular men" who accompany the narrator on his overnight stay in the half-ruined Gerrit Martense mansion, and who disappears from his side as the trio slept in the same bed, never to be seen or heard of again.

TOWER OF MILIN (QI): A tower in the city of Teloth; Iranon sings in the public square in front of the tower.

TORRES, DR. (CA): An elderly medical doctor of Valencia, Spain. He was Dr. Muñoz's collaborator in life-extension experiments, and nursed him through a great, unspecified crisis in 1905. Torres died after that; later, it is said that the shock of what he had to do to preserve (actually, to restore) life in Muñoz's body, was the death of him.

TOWNSHEND (WD) A non-fictitious village in southern Vermont, not far from Bellow's Falls. When Professor Wilmarth flees through the night from the Akeley farmhouse, he winds up in Townshend; it is the nearest settlement.

TRAUBE (TE): A German navy sailor aboard submarine U-29 in 1917. On July 2, when the crippled sub drifts near an American warship, he urges the "un-German act" of surrender "with especial violence," until he is summarily executed with a bullet by Lieutenant Klenze, the second in command.

TRASK, DR. (RW): One of the experts Mr. de la Poer and Captain Norrys bring to investigate the subterranean levels of Exham Priory. An anthropologist, Dr. Trask finds the skulls there to be "a degraded mixture which utterly baffled him." In a prehistoric stone construction far back in the cavern, he discovers "skulls which were slightly more human than a gorilla's, and which bore indescribable ideographic carvings."

TREVOR, LADY MARGARET (RW): A Cornish noblewoman who married into the de la Poer family during the Middle Ages; her husband was Godfrey, the second son of the fifth baron. She seems to have entered enthusiastically into the family cult, for she "became a favorite bane of children all over the countryside, and the daemon heroine of a particularly horrible ballad not yet extinct near the Welsh border." Trevor is a reasonably common family name in the region of extreme south-western England called Cornwall, where names beginning with "Tre-" were derived from the ancient and now-extinct local language, Cornish.

TREVOR TOWERS (CE, DQ): An ivy-covered mansion belonging to a certain wealthy, fat, and boorish brewer (*i.e.*, a beer manufacturer), where he "enjoys the purchased atmosphere of extinct nobility," near a village which HPL calls Innsmouth and locates in the English duchy of Cornwall. The corpse of the English derelict who was also King Kuranes washes up on the rocky beach below the stately home, although his other self has gone on to claim his kingdom in Dreamland. Trevor Towers was the man's ancestral family home; in *The Dream-Quest of Unknown Kadath* it is noted that Kuranes has built a replica of a Cornish mansion to dwell in outside his fantastically beautiful city of Celephaïs, "and tried to think that it was ancient Trevor Towers, where he was born and where thirteen generations of his forefathers had first seen the light."

TRIMALCHIO, BANQUET OF (RW): This refers to a scene in the Roman episodic and comic tale *Satyricon*, by Petronius Arbiter (c. 27–66), who was a leading courtier during the reign of the Roman emperor Nero in the 1st century A.D. In the *Satyricon*, "Trimalchio," a tremen-dously wealthy and equally vulgar ex-slave, hosts a large number of friends and acquaintances at an elaborate but thoroughly piggish dinner-party, which is hilariously depicted as the epitome of crude overabun-dance and grossness. After moving into Exham Priory, Mr. de la Poer dreams of an unspeakable feast, which he compares to the *cena Trimal-chionis*.

TRITHEMIUS (EC, CDW, DH): Johannes Trithemius (1462–1516) was an alchemist, humanist, and author. A Catholic monk, he served as the abbot of the Benedictine monastery at Sponheim (or Spanheim), and later of the monastery at Würzberg, both in Germany. He was also an expert on cryptography and the occult arts. The books of this real "renaissance man" appear on the shelves in Joseph Curwen's library and in the collection of the evil clergyman. *See also* "Cryptographers of Dunwich."

TSAN-CHAN (BWS, SOT): An evil empire that will exist in Earth's future. The alien in Joe Slater's body tells the narrator of *Beyond the Wall of Sleep* that Tsan-Chan will come "three thousand years hence." In *The Shadow Out of Time*, Professor Nathaniel Peaslee meets the captive mind of Yiang-Li, a philosopher from cruel Tsan-Chan, "which is to come in 5000 A.D." The name of the empire and the philosopher suggest a Chinese menace.

TSATHOGGUA (WD, SOT, MM, TGSK): According to Professor Nathaniel Peaslee in *The Shadow Out of Time*, Tsathoggua was worshipped by the "furry pre-human Hyperboreans," three of whom Peaslee met as fellow captive minds among the Great Race. In *Through the Gates of the Silver Key*, Tsathoggua is described as "black and plastic" (*i.e.*, not quite solid but flowing and able to change shape), and the Hyperborean worshippers are said to have flown here from Kythanil, a double-planet that once revolved around the star Arcturus. In *At the Mountains of Madness*, Professor Dyer mentions (referring to Tsathoggua) "Hyperborean legends of formless star-spawn associated with that semi-entity." (What is a semi-entity, exactly?) He also notes that "a few daring mystics have hinted at a pre-Pleistocene origin for the fragmentary Pnakotic Manuscripts, and have suggested that the devotees of Tsathoggua were as alien to mankind as Tsathoggua itself." And in *The Whisperer in Darkness*, the false Henry Akeley tells Professor Wilmarth about Tsathoggua, saying: "It's from N'kai that frightful Tsathoggua came—you know, the amorphous, toad-like god-creature mentioned in the Pnakotic Manuscripts and the *Necronomicon* and the Commorion myth-cycle preserved by the Atlantean high-priest Klarkash-Ton."

Tsathoggua, the "black, furry toad-god," was another borrowed bad angel in the Lovecraft Mythos, the creation of HPL's friend Clark Ashton Smith ("Klarkash-Ton") for a 1931 *Weird Tales* magazine story entitled *The Tale of Satampra Zeiros*. In mid-1935, when HPL's young California pen-pal Helen Sully was feeling blue, HPL sent her an encouraging letter comparing her youth, versatility and beauty to his own advanced age (he was 45) and failings, and concluded: "For Tsathoggua's sake cheer up!"

TSATH-YO (TGSK): Worlds beyond worlds beyond worlds deep in Lovecraftian cosmology: it is explained that the mysterious writing on the parchment found together with the silver key is "not Naacal but R'lyehian…. It is, of course, a translation—there was a Hyperborean original millions of years earlier in the primal tongue of Tsath-Yo."

TUKAHS (WE): Flying creatures native to Venus, but on the other continent from that on which was the narrator, Kenton J. Stanfield. Perhaps HPL was thinking of toucans, a tropical bird-type, just as the "magahs" of Mount Ngranek in *The Dream-Quest of Unknown Kadath* evoke the thought of macaws.

TULANE UNIVERSITY (CC): Non-fictitious New Orleans university where Inspector Legrasse first took the Cthulhu idol captured in a swamp raid in 1907. The learned professors at Tulane were unable to help him with any information about it.

TUPPER (SOT): An Australian miner who meets Professor Nathaniel Peaslee at 11 p.m. on July 17, 1935, as Peaslee walks out of the expedition camp. Tupper watches him swiftly walking away toward the northwest.

TURBA PHILOSOPHORUM (CDW): Meaning "assembly of philosophers," this is the title of a renowned and ancient, non-fictitious book on alchemy. In the tale, Mr. Merritt glimpses a copy in Joseph Curwen's farmhouse in 1746. The *Turba Philosophorum*, which dates back as far as 12th century Europe, is presented in the form of 72 "dictums" pronounced by a series of experts to the titular assembly of "philosophers," or alchemists, who operate as a kind of Greek chorus. It is worth quoting from to convey the true flavor of antique alchemy:

> Custos saith:- I am surprised, O all ye Turba! at the very great force and nature of this water, for when it has entered into the said body, it turns it first into earth, and next into powder, to test the perfection of which, take it in the hand, and if ye find it impalpable as water, it is then most excellent; otherwise, repeat the cooking until it is brought to the required condition. And know that if ye use any substance other than our copper, and rule not with our water, it will profit you nothing. If, on the other hand, ye rule our copper with our water, ye shall find all that has been promised by us.
>
> But the Turba answereth:- Father, the envious created no little obscurity when they commanded us to take lead and white quicksilver, and to rule the same with dew and the sun till it becomes a coin-like stone.
>
> Then he: They meant our copper and our permanent water, when they thus directed you to cook in a gentle fire, and affirmed that there should be produced the said coin-like stone, concerning which the wise have also observed, that Nature rejoices in Nature, by reason of the affinity which they know to exist between the two bodies, that is to say, copper and permanent water. Therefore, the nature of these two is one, for between them there is a mixed affinity, without which they would not so swiftly unite, and be held together so that they may become one.
>
> Saith the Turba:- Why do the envious direct us to take the copper which we have now made, and roasted until it has become gold!

TYCHÉ (TR): The Tyrant of Syracuse calls for the great sculptors Kalos and Musides each to carve a statue of Tyché, with the winning statue to be lodged in a place of honor and pilgrimage in his city. Tyché (pronounced "Ty-KAY)," a lower-level goddess of Greek mythology, was the deity of fortune, chance or luck. She was usually depicted as a lovely young woman holding a rudder, symbolizing her guiding and conducting the affairs of the world; sometimes she was depicted holding a ball, to represent the variability of fortune, which could go in any direction like a rolling ball. Notably for this story, from 485 B.C. onward a large district of the city of Syracuse was called Tyché in honor of a temple of the goddess there.

TYRE (CC): Henry A. Wilcox says of his dream-inspired clay tablet: "It is new indeed, for I made it last night in a dream of strange cities; and dreams are older than brooding Tyre, or the contemplative Sphinx, or garden-girdled Babylon." Tyre, a community mentioned many times in the Bible, was a wealthy Phoenician island-city off the coast of modern Lebanon, and an important place as early as 1400 B.C.

U

U-29 (TE): *Unterseeboot* (U-boat, submarine) number 29 of the World War I German navy. (Presumably HPL chose the number randomly; the historical submarine U-29 had no similar adventures.) Her home port is Wilhelmshaven in north Germany, and in summer, 1917, she is on patrol in the North Atlantic, preying on Allied merchant ships. Her crew of fifteen men consists of:

Lieutenant-Commander K.-H. von Altburg-Ehrenstein	Captain
Lieutenant Klenze	First Officer
Muller	Boatswain
Raabe	Engineer
Schneider	Engineer
Bohm	Sailor
Schmidt	Sailor
Zimmer	Sailor
Traube	Sailor
"six remaining pigs"	Sailors

Confronted by the overwhelming might of the British surface fleet, and suffering from the effects of the British naval blockade preventing goods from abroad to enter German ports, the German high command in World War I (fought between 1914–18) used submarines to try to even the score. Unfortunately for Germany's war hopes, "unlimited" submarine warfare—the no-warning sinking of civilian ships bound for England, most notably the ocean liner *Lusitania* in 1915, with more than a hundred American civilian passengers among the lost—was a propaganda disaster, and perhaps the biggest single factor in eventually provoking the United States to enter the war against Germany. In making a German U-boat's utterly heartless and ruthless commander the villain of this tale, and consigning him at the end to some unspeakable fate, HPL was adding his own, rather unique tone and style to the chorus of Anglo-American fury. As a lover of his romanticized image of Britain, he was deeply in favor of the British cause, and enraged that it took the United States until 1917 to declare war on Germany.

The entire tale takes place in and around the submarine. The submarine vessels of that era were very small and primitive compared to modern subs. They needed to remain on the surface for some hours at least every couple of days, to recharge their electric batteries and to ventilate the hull in the open air. Forced to remain submerged for a longer period, they would eventually run out of electricity and oxygen. (Modern nuclear submarines, by contrast, can travel for months at a time without surfacing.) Submersion also drastically reduced speed. Nor could they communicate over long distances—U-29 is only able to send a message back to Germany by radioing it to a homeward-bound submarine that is passing by. Since submarines spent so much time cruising on the surface, they had tiny, flat upper decks like a surface ship's, and deck guns; on such a deck and with such a gun, the early action of *The Temple* takes place.

Ironically, HPL's vision of the U-boat service in the German navy was not too accurate from the human point of view. In contrast to the German army, which indeed had more than its share of very competent but supremely arrogant aristocratic officers (who would have tended to regard service on a tin-can submarine as degrading) the navy was built on middle-class officers with engineering and mathematical skills rather than pedigrees. On submarines, in particular—where small crews of hand-picked officers and men live and work close-up for weeks on end and share one common fate if their vessel is destroyed, relations tended—and still tend—to be somewhat informal and comradely within the necessary limits of naval discipline. However, HPL wanted to combine the two worst features of the German armed forces, from the crude propagandistic inventory: the cruel and frightful Prussian officer, and the silent, evasive U-boat, assassin of the high seas.

U-61 (TE): German submarine, homeward bound to the German port of Kiel, to which U-29 radioed the news of her sinking of the freighter *Victory*. It was U-29's last contact with the world we know.

UGRATS (WE): An organism, possibly a carnivorous plant, on Venus. Kenton J. Stanfield mentions "slashing" at ugrats as he tried to make his way through the land.

ULTHAR (CU, OG, DQ): A town in Dreamland, beyond the river Skai. It is one of the first settlements, being just on the far side of the enchanted forest and the Gate of Deeper Slumber. In Ulthar, no one may kill a cat; *The Cats of Ulthar* explains the origins of this law. There is a temple in Ulthar, dedicated to the Elder Ones. Barzai the Wise, the sage of *The Other Gods*, long dwelt there, studying the Seven Cryptical Books of Hsan, and the Pnakotic Manuscripts. His young disciple was Atal, son of the village innkeeper. Barzai was the man who advised the town fathers to enact the law strictly prohibiting any harm to cats. When visited by Randolph Carter in *The Dream-Quest of Unknown Kadath*, Atal is 300 years old. Ulthar is very pleasant to behold, with "old peaked roofs and overhanging upper stories and numberless chimney-pots and narrow hill streets," and overrun by sleek and graceful cats. Carter spends a night in Ulthar after consulting with Atal and his old books, befriending a little black kitten during his stay. Later, the grandfather of this Ultharian kitten leads an army of cats to rescue Carter from a bad predicament on the moon.

ULTIMATE GATE (TGSK): A "titanic arch," a cryptical entryway to the Last Void, "which is outside all earths, all universes, and all matter."

ULYSSES (MM): Flying away from the lost Antarctic city and hearing "the wind's strange piping"—which reminds him of the penguins of the abyss and the shoggoths—Professor Dyer wishes "that I had wax-stopped ears like Ulysses' men off the Sirens' coast to keep that disturbing wind-piping from my consciousness."

Ulysses, or Odysseus, is the craftiest of the Greek warriors in the Trojan War recounted in Homer's *Iliad*. In the *Odyssey*, which tells of Ulysses' adventurous journey home by ship, he at one point passes the land of the Sirens, demonic beautiful women whose irresistibly lovely singing lures ships' crews to doom against the jagged rocks of the coast. He avoids this doom by having his crewmen plug their ears with soft wax.

'UMR AT-TAWIL (TGSK): Arabic for the "Prolonged of Life," he is the frightful Guide and Guardian of the Ultimate Gate. He "had been an entity of earth millions of years before, when man was undreamed of, and when forgotten shapes moved on a steaming planet building strange cities among whose last, crumbling ruins the earliest mammals were to play," and was "nothing less than that which all the world has feared since Lomar rose out of the sea and the Winged Ones came to earth to teach the Elder Lore to man." His name was given to him by the Arab scribes from whose work Abdul Alhazred derived a chapter in the *Necronomicon* and reflects co-author E. Hoffman Price's interest in the Arabic language.

UNAUSSPRECHLICHEN KULTEN (DWH, TD, SOT, HD): A book of mystery by an author called Friedrich Wilhelm von Junzt. The made-up title was intended to mean "Unspeakable Cults" although the German is not correct. The book and its author were brain-children of HPL's friend and fellow-author Robert E. Howard. In several tales, *Unaussprechlichen Kulten* is mentioned in passing as a volume of frightful and hidden information, consulted by Walter Gilman, Professor Nathaniel Peaslee (and his Great Race alter-ego), the Starry Wisdom cultists, and Edward P. Derby.

UNDERWATER CITIES (DA, TE, MB, DCS, DQ, SOI, CC, MM, SOT, SK, TGSK): Underwater cities, sometimes lavishly described, figure in several tales.

The nameless narrator of *Dagon*, adrift in a lifeboat somewhere in the Pacific Ocean, finds himself one morning on an uncharted land that seems to have risen from the sea floor overnight. After walking for two days, he comes upon a gigantic obelisk whose strange carvings appear to belong to an ancient and non-human civilization. Later, after his escape and rescue, he "cannot think of the deep sea without shuddering at the nameless things that may at this very moment be crawling and floundering on its slimy bed, worshipping their ancient stone idols and carving their own detestable likenesses on submarine obelisks of water-soaked granite."

Lieutenant Commander von Altburg-Ehrenstein, protagonist of *The Temple*, descends in his disabled submarine until reaching the Atlantic Ocean floor and the marble ruins of "a large city at the bottom of a narrow valley, with numerous isolated temples and villas on the steep slopes above.... At the bottom of that valley a river once had flowed, for as I examined the scene more closely I beheld the remains of stone and marble bridges and sea-walls, and terraces and embankments once green and beautiful."

In *The Moon-Bog*, the nameless narrator comes to Kilderry, Ireland, and learns immediately of the local legend of "an imagined city of stone deep down below the swampy surface" of the bog. He laughs at the tale—for a while. This plot-angle is reminiscent of how the stones of the city of Ib were pushed into the adjacent lake by the triumphant warriors of the young city of Sarnath, in *The Doom That Came to Sarnath*.

In *The Dream-Quest of Unknown Kadath*, when Randolph Carter sails as a passenger aboard a merchant ship bound from Dylath-Leen to the island city of Baharna, he notices the sailors growing "nervous" on the fifth day of the voyage. The captain explains that the ship is "about to pass over the weedy walls and broken columns of a sunken city too old for memory, and that when the water was clear one could see so many moving shadows in that deep place that simple folk disliked it." That night, in bright moonlight, Carter peers over the ship's side and sees in the depths:

> ...the dome of a great temple, and in front of it an avenue of unnatural sphinxes leading to what was one a public square. Dolphins sported merrily in and out of the ruins...one could clearly mark the lines of ancient climbing streets and the washed-down walls of myriad little houses.
>
> Then the suburbs appeared, and finally a great lone building on a hill.... It was dark and low and covered four sides of a square, with a tower at each corner, a paved court in the centre, and small curious round windows all over it.

It appears to Carter as though "some phosphorescent fish" must be what causes the windows to have a "shining" appearance, but we know better. Finally he notices a monolith in the courtyard; bound to it, upside down, is a dead sailor in the silk robes of Oriab. This presumably confirms the captain's earlier admission that many ships had disappeared mysteriously in that part of the sea. Carter is happy when a fresh wind carries their ship away from the underwater city.

In *The Shadow Over Innsmouth*, Zadok Allen tells the narrator of how Captain Obed Marsh found out from the Polynesian chieftain Walakea ("Nobody but Obed ud ever a [would ever have] believed the old yeller [yellow] devil, but the Cap'n cud read folks like they was books. Heh, heh!") about the Deep Ones who "had all kinds o' cities on the sea-bottom." It was by a chance raising of part of one of their cities to the Pacific Ocean's surface, through some submarine eruption, that the Deep Ones—who had known of the surface dwellers ages earlier, "but lost track o' the upper world arter [after] a time"—became acquainted with Walakea's island tribe and through it, to Captain Marsh from Innsmouth. After surviving his terrible night in Innsmouth, the narrator, while employed by an Midwestern insurance company during the winter of 1930–31 and deliberately "buried in routine as deeply as possible," begins to dream of "great watery spaces," of "wandering through "titanic sunken porticos and labyrinths of weedy Cyclopean walls," and of "praying monstrously at...evil sea-bottom temples." Eventually his grandmother comes to him in a dream, and also "that which had been her grandmother." They tell him of the underwater city of Y'ha-nthlei, tens of thousands of years old, off the coast from Innsmouth and Devil Reef—and of his own destiny there.

In *The Call of Cthulhu*, old Castro tells Professor Angell of how the city of R'lyeh (*see* separate entry), metropolis of the Great Old Ones (also called Old Ones and Great Ones) of the race of Cthulhu, was built on dry land in the present-day Pacific Ocean millions of years ago, but became an underwater city—with its inhabitants in suspended animation—when the land sank beneath the waves in some distant prehistoric cataclysm.

While investigating the lost Antarctic city in *At the Mountains of Madness*, Professor Dyer and the intrepid graduate student Danforth learn from their perusal of wall-carvings that the Old Ones (confusingly, the same phrase that is sometimes applied in *The Call of Cthulhu* to the race of Cthulhu, a very different type of creature) had first arrived on earth at a time when water still covered the entire globe, settling first in the Antarctic Ocean; the Antarctic region remaining, forever after, their "sacred" heartland.

> They had lived under the sea a good deal, building fantastic cities and fighting terrific battles with nameless adversaries by means of intricate devices employing unknown principles of energy.... It was under the sea, at first for food and later for other purposes, that they first created earth-life—using available substances according to long-known methods.... With the aid of the shoggoths, whose expansions could be made to lift prodigious weights, the small, low cities under the sea grew to vast and imposing labyrinths of stone not unlike those which later rose on land.

Their cities existed both in shallow waters and at the lower depths, since "even the terrific pressures of the deepest sea-bottoms appeared powerless to harm" the incredibly durable, semi-vegetable Old Ones. Phosphorescent organisms provided all the light they needed.

During wars against the "Cthulhu spawn" who landed on earth millions of years after the Great Old Ones, the latter were driven "for a time wholly back under the sea—a colossal blow in view of the increasing land settlements." Later, after the spawn of Cthulhu were sunk in the catastrophe which drowned R'lyeh, the Old Ones' cities "dotted all the land and water areas of the globe." However, "the steady trend down the ages was from water to land, a movement encouraged by the rise of new land masses, though the ocean was never wholly deserted." Their other problem was that while the dinosaurs which the Old Ones had created for heavy work on land were "highly tractable," the "shoggoths of the sea" upon which all successful submarine living depended, "reproducing by fission and acquiring a dangerous degree of accidental intelligence, presented for a time a formidable problem." The shoggoths seem to have mounted a slave rebellion "toward the middle of the Permian Age, perhaps 150 million years ago," when they had to be re-subjugated in war by the "marine Old Ones." With "the coming of the great cold" to the polar regions, some 500,000 to a million years ago, the Old Ones had built their last underwater city, in the "neighboring black abyss of subterrene waters" close to their great Antarctic metropolis, and migrated to it as ice gradually covered the land. There in the depths, eventually, the shoggoths rose up again and this time exterminated their masters.

In *The Shadow Out of Time*, Professor Nathaniel Peaslee is rewarded for good service to the Great Race with "increased library and travel opportunities." A very Lovecraftian reward! During such travel he once "was taken under the ocean in a gigantic submarine vessel with searchlights.... I saw...the ruins of incredible sunken cities...."

In both *The Silver Key* and *Through the Gates of the Silver Key*, a submarine community is hinted at in identical words which call Ilek-Vad "that fabulous town of turrets atop the hollow cliffs of glass overlooking the twilight sea wherein the bearded and finny Gnorri build their singular labyrinths." We learn no more about the amazing maze-makers.

UPDIKE, MRS. (FB): The "thick-witted housekeeper"—according to her irritated employer—in the household of Crawford Tillinghast, mad scientist of Providence. He warned her, he tells the narrator, not to switch on the downstairs electric lights while he was operating his secret machine in the attic, but she apparently did. Later Tillinghast found "those empty heaps of clothes around the house" where the unfortunate servants had been standing, including the clothing of Mrs. Updike next to the front hall light-switch.

UPHAM, PROFESSOR (DWH): A mathematics professor at Miskatonic University, circa 1927–28. Walter Gilman was one of his students. As Gilman's "dreams" increased in their power, the young student developed "an intuitive knack for solving Riemannian equations" and "astonished" Professor Upham by his comprehension of "fourth-dimensional and other problems which had floored the rest of the class." In this class, Gilman expounded on his theory that "given [sufficient] mathematical knowledge, [one might] step deliberately from the earth to any other celestial body which might lie at one of an infinity of specific points in the cosmos." Upham also admired Gilman's "demonstration of the kinship of higher mathematics to certain phases of magical lore." It seems likely that in this tale, based on the historical facts of the Salem witchcraft mania of 1692, the name of HPL's "Professor Upham" was inspired by that of Charles W. Upham (1802–76), the Salem minister who authored *Salem Witchcraft, With an Account of Salem Village, and a History of Opinions on Witchcraft and Kindred Subjects*(1867), probably the best 19th century book on the topic.

UPTON, DANIEL (TD): The best friend of Edward Pickman Derby, and narrator of this tale. As the wife-troubled Derby is in many ways a Lovecraftian self-image, so Upton is the sort of steady male friend that HPL always counted on. Possibly born in about 1883, Upton was eight years older than Derby, but the latter boy was so intellectually precocious that they had been friends since Upton's sixteenth year. Upton left Arkham to study architecture at Harvard and in a Boston architectural firm, but returned to open his own studio on Saltonstall Street in Arkham. He married, and fathered a son—Edward Derby Upton—who eventually went to Harvard as well. He joined the Army during the First World War and attended the officer candidate school at Plattsburg, New York, but did not get overseas to Europe before the war ended (on November 11, 1918).

Daniel Upton had heard some strange things about Asenath Waite from one of her boarding-school classmates, the daughter of an old friend. Moreover, he had seen her father Ephraim Waite in Arkham more than once in the past, and had "hated his wolfish, saturnine face." Nonetheless, he attended Edward Derby's wedding to Asenath, and remained loyal to his boyhood companion. In the fourth year of the marriage, he drove to the remote village of Chesuncook, Maine, at the request of the town marshal, to take Derby home from custody. While traveling back to Massachusetts in the car, Upton learns more about the strange marital relationship; and when a personality transference takes place in front of his eyes—Asenath reasserting psychic control—he realizes that "this man, for all my lifelong knowledge of Edward Pickman Derby, was a stranger—an intrusion of some sort from the black abyss"; shades of Alice Peaslee's reaction to her possessed husband in *The Shadow Out of Time*. Upton aids and shelters Edward Derby after Asenath's alleged departure, and when Derby seems to suffer a nervous breakdown, arranges for his confinement in Arkham Sanitarium, becoming his legal guardian. A few weeks later he is visited by the "thing on the doorstep"—Edward, his mind trapped in Asenath's dead, decaying body—and then goes over to the asylum and shoots the "Edward" there six times in the head.

In HPL's youth he was befriended by a certain Professor Winslow Upton, a Brown University astronomer and family friend, who allowed him to have the run of the then-new Ladd Observatory on the university campus. HPL also used the name in *Pickman's Model*, for the sinister artist Richard Upton Pickman.

UPTON, EDWARD DERBY (TD): The only child of Daniel Upton, born when the father's friend Edward Derby was twenty years old, and named after him.

URG (DQ): A small village in Inganok, one day's walk north on the quarry road from the city of Inganok. Here the main caravan route turns west to Selarn. Randolph Carter arrives in Urg at 10 o'clock one morning, and spends two hours picking up information in taverns before continuing northward on his own.

USHER, RODERICK (HD): A character in Edgar Allan Poe's moody masterpiece, *The Fall of the House of Usher*, which HPL in his essay *Supernatural Horror in Literature* called a story in which could be found "those very summits of artistry whereby Poe takes his place at the head of fictional miniaturists." In HPL's tale, Robert Blake alludes to Roderick Usher in his final, frenzied notes. In Poe's tale, Roderick Usher waited nervously in his chamber as he sensed his "dead" twin sister leaving her casket and coming toward him. Likewise, on the last night of his life, Blake waits nervously and watches the Starry Wisdom church from his window, while feeling an Usher-like sensation of oneness with the thing in the church, trying to escape: "I am it and it is I...I want to get out."

UZULDAROUM (MM): The name of a "Hyperborean" fantasy-city invented by HPL correspondent Clark Ashton Smith in one of his own stories, *The Tale of Satampra Zeiros*. Professor Dyer says that compared to the horrifying antiquity of the Antarctic lost city he has found, Uzuldaroum, Commoriom and other such places "are recent things of today—not even of yesterday."

V

VALUSIA (SOT, MM, HD): A prehistoric, indeed prehuman realm on earth. In the abandoned Antarctic city, Professor Dyer noticed maps of the globe during the Carboniferous geological epoch of a hundred million years ago, showing Europe ("then the Valusia of hellish primal legend") as still connected to Africa and the Americas. Elsewhere he calls Valusia "a whispered pre-human blasphemy" on a par with "R'lyeh, Ib in the land of Mnar, and the Nameless City in Arabia Deserta"—a real Lovecraftian trio. Professor Nathaniel Peaslee, while in mental captivity among the Great Race, encounters a mind from "the reptile people of fabled Valusia." In *The Haunter of the Dark*, Robert Blake provides a rough chronology while considering the Shining Trapezohedron's frighteningly long history, noting that "it was treasured...by the crinoid things of Antarctica, salvaged from their ruins by the serpent-men of Valusia, and peered at aeons later in Lemuria by the first human beings." Valusia and her scaly natives were concepts borrowed from the "King Kull" series of sword-and-sorcery tales by HPL's friend Robert E. Howard.

VAN HELMONT (CDW): Presumably a reference to Jean Baptiste van Helmont (1579–1644), a Belgian physician and chemist who was the first scientist to realize that there were gases other than "air," and who identified four such gases: carbon dioxide, carbon monoxide, nitrous oxide, and methane. Van Helmont also tried to apply information from the chemistry laboratory to the treatment of human ills. His writings are among those "philosophical, mathematical, and scientific works" glimpsed by Mr. John Merritt in Joseph Curwen's Providence library, circa 1746.

VEILED KING (DQ): The king of Inganok, who is never seen without a face-covering veil. We never learn what is beneath the veil.

VENUS; VENUSIANS (WE, SOT): In *In the Walls of Eryx*, a "straight" science-fiction story (co-written with a much younger fan/friend, Kenneth J. Sterling), HPL operated on the then-popular belief that our cloud-covered neighbor planet, Venus (which is "only" 26 million miles/ 42 million kilometers away at its nearest), would prove to have a climate and composition not terribly unlike that of our own world, and that humans could dwell there someday, perhaps with breathing-apparatus for a different atmosphere, as in this tale. Kenton J. Stanfield mentions in his unbelievably wordy journal (for a prospector caught in a life-or-death situation) that humans had first landed on Venus seventy-two years before his present time. The Lovecraft-Sterling Venus is a rather damp place, with water, jungles full of exotic flora and fauna, creeping vines and many insects. The air is toxic to humans, but only after about thirty seconds of exposure. The planet is populated by a tentacled race of intelligent Venusians. The reality is otherwise, as revealed by unmanned space probes launched since the 1960s; Venus is a completely uninhabitable world, with a storm-ravaged atmosphere composed almost entirely of carbon dioxide, atmospheric pressure about 100 times that of Earth, and a barren, waterless surface with a temperature of about 890° Fahrenheit (475° Celsius).

HPL's Venusians are scaled-down versions of some of his other Others, with the stock resemblance to some kind of vast, ambulatory squid. Stanfield calls them "man-lizards." They average seven feet in height, with flat heads, green and slimy skins, stumpy bodies, and "suction discs" instead of feet. A major peculiarity is the set of "four long, ropy, pectoral tentacles," which they use in lieu of hands and—by gestures—for speech. As Stanfield learns to his cost, they have a kind of sardonic humor as well. They worship the crystals which the Venus Crystal Company seeks to exploit, and conduct a low-technology warfare against the crystal-hunters from Earth, using swords, poison darts, and nuisance tactics such as cutting water pipelines. Once a hater of the Venusians, the dying Stanfield ironically abandons his prejudices as he sits trapped in the invisible maze:

> As the end approaches I feel more kindly toward the things. In the scale of cosmic entity who can say which species stands higher, or more nearly approaches a space-wide organic norm—theirs or mine?

Some critics have noted that this tale coincided with HPL's late-life mellowing on some (not all) ethnic and social distinctions much closer to home than Venus. Certainly we are not meant to sympathize with the Crystal Company boss Wesley Miller who later predicts a day when the Earthlings—not a word used in HPL's story, but one that seems appropriate for this old-school science fiction—will "bring across enough troops to wipe out the natives altogether."

In *The Shadow Out of Time*, during his years as a coddled mental-captive of the Great Race, Professor Peaslee encounters "a mind from the planet we know as Venus, which would live incalculable epochs to come."

VENUS CRYSTAL COMPANY (WE): The well-organized and well-equipped Earth company that searches for crystals on Venus—crystals which can be converted into abundant energy for power-supply on Earth. The desirable crystals can be found on the surface of the planet, and the company employs prospectors to journey over the planet by foot and airplane. The company has a base on Venus at Terra Nova ("New Earth"). In addition to prospectors it has a support staff that includes managers and equipment specialists.

VERHAEREN (AJ): In 1912, when the central African nation currently called "Congo" was a colony of Belgium, the fictitious Verhaeren is the Belgian representative at a Congo River trading post. He tells Sir Arthur Jermyn that he can probably locate and obtain the stuffed white ape-goddess from the N'Bangu tribe. In June, 1913, Sir Arthur receives a letter in England from Monsieur Verhaeren, announcing the finding of the mummified relic; the letter is backed up by a locket found on the idol, a locket which bears some European coat-of-arms. The stuffed thing arrives at Jermyn House in a crate on August 3, 1913. In his letter, Verhaeren "expressed a humorous wonder" as to how the mummy's face would strike Sir Arthur when he saw it; this proves to be a sinister foreshadowing.

VERMONT (WD): HPL's "Vermont story," *The Whisperer in Darkness*, owes its fine sense of scene partly to a fortnight that HPL spent in this small inland state during June, 1928, visiting his friend Vrest Orton. Not coincidentally, Orton lived in a remote farmhouse in the vicinity of Brattleboro, built in the 1820s by a certain Samuel *Akeley*. In the tale, Professor Wilmarth is quite precise about the sightings of odd bodies floating in Vermont's flooded rivers during 1927; he mentions the Winooski River near Montpelier, the West River in Wyndham County, beyond Newfane, and the Passumpsic River in Caledonia Country, above Lyndonville.

VICTORY (TE): A British freighter bound from New York to Liverpool, sunk by the German submarine U-29 on the afternoon of June 18, 1917, at latitude 45° 16′ north, longitude 28° 34′ west. The *Victory* went down by the bow (*i.e.,* she sank front end first); the Germans allow her crew to board lifeboats while they film them doing so. They then stop filming, sink the lifeboats with the submarine's deck gun, and submerge.

VIGILANT (1) (CC): A freighter owned by the Morrison Company of Sydney, Australia, which meets the drifting steam-yacht *Alert* in the South Pacific at latitude 34°17′ south, longitude 152° 17′ west, on April 12, 1925, and tows her to Sydney, arriving on April 18. *Vigilant* had left

Valparaiso, Chile on March 25, and had been "driven considerably south of her course by exceptionally heavy seas and monster waves" on April 2, causing her to eventually cross paths with the *Alert.* This was the storm during which, presumably, R'lyeh sank back beneath the ocean.

VIGILANT (2) (SH): In the tale, a privateer ship aboard which Dutee Harris served with distinction under "Captain Cahoone" during the War of 1812, from which he returned home to Providence unharmed in 1814. Such a ship actually existed, but it was a "revenue cutter," not a privateer. A privateer was essentially a licensed pirate in time of war—a private citizen commissioned by a government at war with another, to prey upon the civilian shipping of the enemy. Privateersmen went into action under their national flag, received a large share of all the enemy ships and cargo they could capture, and by the laws of naval warfare, were not subject to punishment as ordinary pirates if captured themselves. The United States, with a comparatively small national navy, made extensive use of New England-based privateers during the two wars against Great Britain, the Revolutionary War and the War of 1812. By contrast, a revenue cutter was a small, fast, and very maneuverable warship typically used to patrol the coastline of a nation in search of smugglers seeking to avoid import taxes ("revenue") on valuable cargo. The U.S. Revenue Cutter Service was the ancestor of the U.S. Coast Guard, which still calls its patrol ships "cutters." The historical *Vigilant* which sailed in Rhode Island waters under a Captain Cahoone was built in Newport in 1812 specifically as a revenue cutter, did heroic work during the War of 1812, and continued in service until 1845, when it was sold to a private owner and passed out of history. From 1812 until 1832 or later it was commanded by Captain Cahoone. The ship was of 70 tons, 40 feet in length, and carried four cannon plus smaller weapons.

VIOLET-COLOURED GAS (CE): When the man who was King Kuranes was smoking hashish in London, before his money ran out and he could no longer purchase hashish, he was once mentally transported to "a part of space where form does not exist, but where glowing gases study the secrets of existence. And a violet-coloured gas told him that this part of space was outside what he had called infinity. The gas had not heard of planets and organisms before, but identified Kuranes merely as one from the infinity where matter, energy and gravitation exist."

VIRGIL (TT): *The Tomb* begins with an untranslated quote from the greatest of the Roman poets, Publius Virgilius Maro (70–19 B.C.), known in English as Virgil: *Sedibus ut saltem placidis in morte quiescam.* It is found at Book VI, line 371 of the *Aeneid*, Virgil's epic poem of the mythological coming to Italy of Trojan warriors, survivors of the fall of Troy, whose descendants would found the city of Rome. In their context the Latin words mean roughly: "—that I may find peace and rest at last in death." They are the end of a speech by the soul of the dead Trojan warrior, Palinurus, to the witch called the Sibyl of Cumae, who has guided the poem's hero Aeneas to the waiting area outside of Hades, the underworld of the dead. Palinurus was the steersman on Aeneas' ship, and he seeks the help of the living to have his body buried, so his soul can finally cross over the river Styx on Charon's boat, and enter Hades.

VIRGINIA CAVES (SOT): Late in 1912, the being from the Great Race that possessed Professor Peaslee's body "spent weeks alone beyond the limits of previous or subsequent exploration in the vast limestone cavern systems of western Virginia."

(GRAF) VON ALTBURG-EHRENSTEIN, KARL-HEINRICH (TE): As of 1917, this narrator is a Lieutenant Commander in the Imperial German Navy, and the captain of submarine U-29 on patrol in the Atlantic. Graf (Count) von Altburg-Ehrenstein is presented as a completely frightful Prussian *Junker*, or member of the militaristic aristocracy of the old kingdom of Prussia in northern Germany: the conceited and sneering quintessence of Allied anti-German propaganda in World War I. In the captain's log of events which constitutes the framework of this story, he is given to making references to "my iron German will," "the unjust war of aggression which the English pig-dogs are making on the Fatherland," etc., etc. In other respects he has qualities which HPL could have admired (in an American or Englishman!), being an extremely competent naval officer, highly educated, "rational" and materialistic *á la* Lovecraft in his personal philosophy, and very interested in science and history for their own sakes. Sometimes his words even read exactly like those of HPL at his most obnoxiously rationalistic in amateur-journal debates of the same period, as when he writes in his log: "It is only the inferior thinker who hastens to explain the singular and the complex by the primitive short cut of supernaturalism." At the tale's end, alone in his disabled U-boat at the bottom of the Atlantic Ocean, he is stoically engaged in setting down his precise recollections for posterity, finding a bottle in which to float them to the surface, and then preparing to take his last walk (with a deep-sea diving suit) into the mysterious temple on the ocean floor. Men have died less well.

The passionately pro-English HPL was a willing victim of the Allied propaganda campaign in the First World War (1914–18), passionately in favor of Great Britain as against Germany, passionately angry at pacifist objectors to the conflict, and passionately impatient with the American delay in entering the war on Britain's side, an event which finally took place in April, 1917. After the U.S. declaration of war he even attempted to enlist in the Rhode Island National Guard, although he was ultimately rejected for service by some obscure combination of real invalidism and his mother's urgent protests and string-pulling through the family doctor concerning her son's "nervous condition"; later he was apparently classified as physically or psychologically unfit for the regular army draft. (The United States had the luxury of picking and choosing its soldiers; as a citizen of any of the European combatant nations, HPL would probably have been in uniform years earlier.) He was not really cut out to be a soldier. Germany's "unrestricted submarine warfare," a response to the crippling and illegal blockade of German ports by the British navy, led to a number of sinkings of merchant ships or liners with loss of life among British and American civilian passengers, making German U-boats and their commanders into targets of hatred and reproach.

VON JUNZT, FRIEDRICH WILHELM (DWH, TD, SOT, HD): The fictitious German author of the fictitious *Unaussprechlichen Kulten*.

VON MARTEN (DH): *See* "Cryptographers of Dunwich."

VOONITHS (DQ): "Amphibious terrors" on the island of Oriab, which live in pools of water and howl at night; but even they do not dare to approach Mount Ngranek.

VOORISH SIGN (DH): Wilbur Whateley's diary for November 26, 1916, notes that he could see the thing upstairs "a little" when he made "the Voorish sign." The concept came from Arthur Machen's *The White People*, a tale of supernatural horror which HPL justly admired. Later, Professor Armitage exclaims rather verbosely: "What simpletons! Shew [*sic*] them Arthur Machen's Great God Pan and they'll think it a common Dunwich scandal!" This is another homage, in this case to Machen's effective and influential horror tale *The Great God Pan*.

W

WAITE, ASENATH (TD): *See* "Derby, Asenath Waite."

WAITE, DR. (CDW): A fictitious Providence psychiatrist, one of several medical men whom Mr. Ward hires to examine and treat his "disturbed" son Charles. Dr. Waite is one of the group that talks with Charles—by now only a shell for the undying mind of Joseph Curwen—in the Pawtuxet bungalow. He also owns and operates a private insane asylum on Conanicut Island in Narragansett Bay, not far from Providence. Here Ward/Curwen disappears forever from his room following an interview with Dr. Marinus B. Willett; a presumed escape which becomes "one of the unsolved wonders of Dr. Waite's hospital," as the only exit except for the door to the hallway is a window overlooking a sheer drop of sixty feet.

WAITE, EPHRAIM (TD): He used to live "in a half-decayed mansion in Washington Street, Innsmouth, and those who had seen the place (Arkham folk avoid going to Innsmouth whenever they can) declared that the attic windows were always boarded.... The old man was said to have been a prodigious magic student in his day." Daniel Upton had seen him once or twice on the streets of Arkham and "hated his wolfish, saturnine face with its tangle of iron-grey beard." Ephraim Waite belonged to a coven that met in a deep cavern in the remote forests of Maine; his coven name was "Kamog". In his old age he took a wife, "an unknown wife who always went veiled." Perhaps she was one of the Deep Ones. By this wife, he had one child, a daughter named Asenath, small, dark, with vaguely protuberant eyes. Ephraim was supposed to have died shriekingly insane, locked in an attic, "under rather queer circumstances." In fact, he used his power of mind-transference to take over Asenath's fresh young body and expel her mind to his dying old shape. Then, as Asenath, he sought out a husband like Edward Derby, with a combination of youth, good health, keen intelligence, male gender, and weak willpower, whom he could gradually supplant, so as to end the process with the brain and body of a man again. Thus for increasing periods of time, Edward's mind is possessed by Asenath (who is really Ephraim), while the Edward-mind is consigned to his wife's body—and eventually, to his wife's *dead* body.

WAITE FAMILY (SOI): One of the prominent families of Innsmouth, with many members over the years; in the 1840s, a certain Luella Waite is kidnapped and sacrificed to the Deep Ones. In the early 20th century, Edward Derby keeps hearing "whispers" among the Waites he meets about the strange madness and death of Ephraim Waite.

WAKEFUL (CDW): On October 16, 1754, Joseph Curwen writes in his diary that:

> My Sloope [a type of sailing ship] the *Wakeful* this Day putt in from London with XX [twenty] newe Men pick'd up in ye Indies, Spaniards from Martineco [the Caribbean island of Martinique] and 2 Dutch Men from Surinam. Ye Dutch Men are like to Desert from have'g [having] hearde Somewhat ill of these Ventures, but I will see to ye Inducing of them to Staye.

This passage serves to remind the reader that Joseph Curwen's reputation in Providence has become so sinister, and the problem of sailors disappearing forever while running shore errands for Curwen has become so chronic, that his ships are manned by either strangers from the West Indies or else men over whom he can exert some kind of pressure, such as a debt or a mortgage or blackmail.

WALAKEA (SOI): A "kanaka" (an old term for Pacific islanders) whom Obed Marsh meets during a South Seas voyage in the 1820s or 1830s. The narrator learned about him in 1928 from Zadok Allen, town drunk of Innsmouth. He was chief of an island east of "Otaheite" (Tahiti), which featured carved stone ruins on the land and a permanent surplus of fish in the water. Captain Marsh wormed the true facts out of Walakea ("Nobody but Obed ud ever a [would ever have] believed the old yeller devil, but the Cap'n cud read folks like they was books," remarks Zadok). The facts were that in exchange for a certain number of youthful human sacrifices each year, the Deep Ones brought the islanders gold, and endless supplies of fish for catching. Most of the island families had intermarried with the Deep Ones before Marsh's visit, so that natives would disappear—from the surface world—before ever reaching old age. Only Walakea's family, and a few others that would marry with people from neighboring islands, were still purely human. Obed Marsh returned to the island on subsequent voyages, and Walakea eventually gave him a "lead thingumajig" which he could drop into the sea anywhere in the world where there were nests to summon Deep Ones. In 1838, Captain Marsh visited the island once again, only to find that warriors from neighboring islands had wiped out Walakea's entire hybrid tribe, erased all signs of habitation, and denied that anybody had ever lived on the island.

WALDRON, DR. (DWH): The campus physician at Miskatonic University in the 1920s. He examined the ailing student Walter Gilman, and unilaterally cut Gilman's course load for the rest of the semester, hoping to lessen his strain.

WALLACE, ADMIRAL (CDW): The non-fictitious commander of the British customs fleet in Rhode Island waters in 1770.

WALLACE, DR. (SOI): As of 1927, the pastor of Asbury Methodist Episcopal Church in Arkham; he is the clergyman of the Arkham youth who manages the chain-store grocery in Innsmouth, and we learn that he strenuously warns the young man not to attend any church in that town.

WALPURGIS-NIGHT (DWH): Saint Walburga (died c. 779) or Walpurgis was an 8th century English missionary nun who was the superior of the important German convent of Hildesheim. Her feast day in the calendar of the Catholic Church falls on May 1. Since ancient times in Scandinavia and Germany the night of April 30—Walpurgis Night—was celebrated as the beginning of summer, with bonfires and quaint rituals. Particularly in Germany, *Walpurgisnacht* or Walpurgis-night was traditionally feared as the night when witches held their celebrations and met with their master the Devil, like All Hallows' Eve (Halloween) six months later. In this tale, Walpurgis-night is always a bad night in Arkham, and it is for a Walpurgis-night sacrifice that Keziah Mason, the Black Man, and Brown Jenkin, with Walter Gilman in tow, kidnap the infant Ladislas Wolejko.

WAMPS, WEB-FOOTED (DQ): They spawn in dead cities, and in the graveyards of upper Dreamland they function just as do the ghouls in the cemeteries of the waking world. On the island of Oriab, Randolph Carter ignores the warnings of the local people and camps one night in certain "nameless ancient ruins" on the far shore of Lake Yath. Once during the night, he feels "the wings of some insect" brushing his face. In the morning he saw that all the blood has been drained from his tethered riding-zebra, that his pack has been opened and several "shiny knick-knacks" taken away, and that "all around on the dusty soil were great webbed footprints." He has been visited by wamps, and on his way out of the ruins he shudderingly notices a low archway "with steps leading down in the darkness farther than he could peer."

WANTASTIQUET (WD): A low mountain in western New Hampshire. On September 12, 1928, while riding on the northbound train along the western bank of the Connecticut River, south of Brattleboro, Vermont, Dr. Wilmarth is able to look over the river into New Hampshire and see "the approaching slope of steep Wantastiquet, about which singular old legends cluster." HPL and his Vermont friend Arthur Goodenough climbed Wantastiquet together on June 14, 1928.

WARD, CHARLES DEXTER (CDW): The son of Mr. and Mrs. Theodore H. Ward, of Providence. Born in April, 1902, his delivery was performed by Marinus Willett, M.D., who would play a large role in his later life. Ward grows up in the College Hill section of Providence, near Brown University, like his creator HPL; and, like HPL, he grows up to be a youth who is tall, slim, and fair, "with studious eyes and a slight stoop, dressed somewhat carelessly, and giving a dominant impression of harmless awkwardness rather than attractiveness." Also like his creator, he was "always a scholar and an antiquarian," "an antiquarian from infancy, no doubt gaining his taste from the venerable town around him, and from the relics of the past which filled every corner of his parents' old mansion...on the crest of the hill." He share's HPL's zest for long walks through every corner of the old parts of Providence. And, other than for his adoring but useless mother, the fair sex plays no role in his life, either.

Ward attends Moses Brown School (*see* separate entry), graduating "none too brilliantly" in 1920. By that time he has already begun his researches into the life of Joseph Curwen, and he refuses to attend college. Between 1920–23 there comes "a three-year period of intensive occult study and graveyard searching," which unsurprisingly causes him to become "recognized as an eccentric." After turning 21 in April, 1923, and having inherited some money from his maternal grandfather, Ward sails from Boston to Liverpool on a White Star liner, in June. His European travels—very rare for Americans at that time—lead him first to London, where he apparently studies in the British Museum; and next to Paris, in June, 1924, from whence he writes home about "a special search among rare manuscripts in the library of an unnamed private collector." By October, 1924, he is in Prague, where he meets a "very aged man," presumably the one going by the name of "Josef Nadek." In January, 1925, he passes through Vienna on his way to Klausenburg in Transylvania, thence to the mountain castle of "Baron Ferenczy." In May, 1926, he returns to Providence.

For the next several months he "applies himself diligently to the strange books he had brought home, and to equally strange delvings within his quarters," *i.e.*, his private workroom in the garret of the Ward mansion. After increasingly strange behavior during the early months of 1927, Charles Dexter Ward's "researches" come to a climax on April 15, 1927, Good Friday, when he brings back to life Joseph Curwen, dead since 1771. During the next twelve months young Ward's behavior, whether alone or in company with his new friend "Dr. Allen," becomes increasingly bizarre, until the point when we realize that he has been murdered and his body recreated from "Saltes" by the evil revenant Joseph Curwen. He is then a strange 26-year-old indeed:

> His organic processes shewed [*sic*] a certain queerness of proportion which nothing in medical experience can parallel. Respiration and heart action had a baffling lack of symmetry...digestion was incredibly prolonged and minimized, and neural reactions to standard stimuli bore no relation at all to anything heretofore recorded, either normal or pathological. The skin had a morbid chill and dryness, and the cellular structure of the tissue seemed exaggeratedly coarse and loosely knit.

At this point he is confined in a private mental institution for observation. On April 13, 1928, before he can successfully talk his way out of confinement, Joseph Curwen—wearing the skin of Charles Dexter Ward like a suit of second-hand clothes—has his last interview with Marinus B. Willett, an interview he does not survive. That doctor has previously penned this "epitaph" for the real Charles: "he was never a fiend or even truly a madman, but only an eager, studious, and curious boy whose love of mystery and of the past was his undoing. He stumbled on things no mortal ought ever to know, and reached back through the years as no one ever should reach; and something came out of those years to engulf him."

WARD, THEODORE HOWLAND (CDW): The father of Charles Dexter Ward, a "trim, blue-eyed, clean-shaven gentleman." He is a wealthy capitalist who owns mills in the community of Riverpoint, south of Providence, and lives with his family in "a great Georgian mansion" with a "double-bayed brick façade." (Lovecraft scholars agree that the model for this house is the historic Halsey Mansion at 140 Prospect Street in the College Hill district.) Mr. Ward is a generous, patient father, who tolerates and supports his son's increasingly strange interests and behavior as long as he reasonably can, and then hires a team of learned physicians when his son's reason appears to be lost. He has known Dr. Marinus B. Willett since boyhood, and accompanies the doctor to the Pawtuxet bungalow on April 6, 1928, and is so sickened and disoriented by the "noxious blast" of "mephitic air" when the cellar manhole cover is lifted, that Dr. Willett sends him home. The next day, at about noon, Mr. Ward returns to the bungalow and discovers Willett unconscious but unharmed on a bed in an upstairs room. He and Dr. Willett are the only two people who ever understand the details of Joseph Curwen's undying evil and Charles Dexter Ward's well-meaning part in it.

WARD, MRS. THEODORE H. (CDW): A loving and indulgent mother, from beginning to end she never understands anything about what her son Charles was doing. However, she has the good instinct when the 18th century portrait of her distant ancestor Joseph Curwen is discovered in the house in Olney Court, to think it looks like it would be better to burn it than keep it. She faints with fright at the weird chants and sounds emanating from the attic as (unbeknownst to her) her son works his spells to resurrect Joseph Curwen on the fateful Good Friday, 1927. In early July of that year, on Dr. Willett's advice, her husband sends her on a vacation of indefinite length to the seaside resort of Atlantic City, New Jersey, and she exits from the story.

WARREN, HARLEY (SRC, TGSK): Friend of Randolph Carter, and a devoted student of mystical lore. He owned a "vast collection of strange, rare books on forbidden subjects." With Carter, he visits a very old cemetery in the southern United States late one night, and opens an ancient tomb which proves to have steps leading far down into the earth. Warren descends alone into the black depths, carrying a telephone handset and a long wire. After more than a quarter of an hour, he telephones back some frantic comments about what he is seeing. Carter's answering screams on the telephone line are eventually answered by someone else's voice, saying: "You fool, Warren is DEAD."

In *Through the Gates of the Silver Key*, the late Harley Warren is referred to as "a South Carolina mystic whose studies in the primal Naacal language of the Himalayan priests had led to such outrageous conclusions." It is further explained that the tomb-adventure took place in December, 1919, and that the mysterious book Warren carried with him had come from India earlier that year; in its script, all the letters descended from horizontal word-bars.

WATCHTOWER OF THAPNEN (PO): A tower by the city of Olathoë in ancient Lomar; here the narrator is ordered to keep watch for the invading Inutos who were trying to surprise the town by capturing "the narrow pass behind the peak Noton," and to light a beacon-fire if he sees them. In the topmost chamber of the tower, however, he is lulled by the Pole Star "fluttering as if alive, and leering like a fiend and tempter," which sings him to sleep.

WATER STREET (TOM, SHH): The Kingsport street where Granny Orne lives, and onto which the Terrible Old Man's back gate opens.

WATERMAN STREET (CC): The street where Henry Wilcox's family lives in Providence; the artist's own apartment is elsewhere in town. He is brought to Waterman Street on the night of March 22–23, 1925, in a feverish delirium.

WATKINS (MM): A member of the Miskatonic University Expedition, 1930–31. It is uncertain whether he is a graduate student or one of the mechanics. He becomes part of the Lake-Atwood party, and at 9:45 p.m. on January 23, 1931, while working underground in the cavern of an ancient riverbed, he and Orrendorf "found [a] monstrous barrel-shaped fossil of wholly unknown nature"—the first of the winged, star-headed Old Ones to be discovered. He is found dead with the rest of the Lake-Atwood group on January 25, and buried.

WEBB, PROFESSOR WILLIAM CHANNING (CC): In the tale, a professor of anthropology at Princeton University, and a noted explorer. He attends the American Archaeological Society annual convention in St. Louis in 1908. In 1860, Professor Webb had traveled through Iceland and Greenland in search of "Runic inscriptions" (*i.e.*, rune-letters possibly left by the Scandinavian settlers of those places), and had encountered a "tribe or cult" of degenerate Eskimos "high up on the West Greenland coast." He observed the carved fetish-doll they worshipped, and copied their chant phonetically. While comparing accounts with Inspector Legrasse at the convention, Webb demonstrates that the Greenland worshippers inexplicably venerated the same form of idol, with the same chant, as the cult-members who met in the swamps of southern Louisiana. Professor Webb borrows the small Cthulhu statuette from Inspector Legrasse, but upon his death it is returned to the policeman.

WEEDEN, EZRA (CDW): A merchant seaman from Providence, a man "of a quiet and ordinarily mild disposition," who becomes the 18th century nemesis of Joseph Curwen. While in his early 20s and serving as second mate—an officer two ranks below the captain—of the Crawford-owned merchant ship *Enterprise*, he is engaged to Miss Eliza Tillinghast. However, her father orders her to end the engagement, as he is compelled to marry her to his own employer, Joseph Curwen. From that point (1763) onwards, Weeden is committed to revenge. Like a dogged private eye in another kind of story, he stalks his proud and unsuspecting quarry, "systematically studying" Curwen and all his doings, observing his wharves and warehouses by night, and keeping as close an eye as he dared on the Pawtuxet Road farm. Ezra Weeden "had a vindictive persistence which the bulk of the practical townsfolk and farmers lacked; and subjected Curwen's affairs to a scrutiny such as they had never had before." So little by little he gathers proof that Curwen is importing some very strange things, and that the frightful old man is doing some even stranger things in secret. Finally, with the help of his friend Eleazar Smith, he puts together enough information to interest some of the prominent older men who run Providence, and who form a secret committee to deal with the unspecific but definite menace that Curwen seems to present. Weeden is a member of the raiding party on the farmhouse on April 12, 1771; he lived for another 53 years and was buried in North Burial Ground.

WEEDEN, HAZARD (CDW): In 1927, a living descendant of Ezra Weeden, and a resident of 598 Angell Street in Providence (which was HPL's own address that year; "Hazard" was the name of an old Rhode Island family, which figured in HPL's maternal pedigree). When Ezra Weeden's grave is desecrated and his remains stolen in June, 1927, Hazard recalls for the press "a family legend according to which Ezra Weeden was involved in some very peculiar circumstances...shortly before the Revolution; but of any modern feud or mystery he is frankly ignorant."

WELLS: *See* "Caves, Caverns, Wells and Abysses."

WENTWORTH, GOVERNOR (WD): Dr. Wilmarth mentions "the Scotch-Irish element of New Hampshire, and their kindred who had settled in Vermont on Governor Wentworth's colonial grants...." This refers to Benning Wentworth (1696–1770), royal governor from 1741–67 of the colony of New Hampshire, in which he had been born. The "New-Hampshire Grants" were enormous land grants made by him to settlers to the west of the Connecticut River, in the future state of Vermont. One may note that Henry Akeley's middle name is Wentworth.

WEST, DR. BENJAMIN (CDW): An 18th century resident of Providence, a medical doctor "whose pamphlet on the late transit of Venus [an astronomy topic] proved him a scholar and a keen thinker." He is one of the first men whom Captain Mathewson approached with Ezra Weeden's surmises about Joseph Curwen, and he joins the secret committee.

WEST, DR. HERBERT (HW): A surgeon who attended Miskatonic University's medical school (Class of 1904), in Arkham; helped to treat the sick and dying during the great Arkham typhus epidemic of '04, and then set up a small general practice with a medical school classmate, in the industrial town of Bolton, Massachusetts. After the outbreak of World War I in 1914, he and his partner obtain medical officers' commissions in the Canadian Army (historically, numerous Americans who wished to fight in the First and Second World Wars before their own country did, managed to do so by going over the border and enlisting in Canada's armed forces). They are assigned to serve in military field hospitals close to the fighting in Europe. The two comrades return at war's end in 1918, to open up a prosperous medical practice in Boston, but Dr. West disappears forever in 1921.

Herbert West, an atheist and materialist, while still in medical school set about trying to identify the purely chemical basis of "life," and thereby learn how to reverse the process of death. In medical school his fierce pursuit of this vision led him to slaughter countless laboratory animals, until the faculty barred him from the lab. Undaunted, he began to work on his own with freshly-dead human corpses, and on at least one occasion—in Bolton—with a stranger he had murdered in his desperation for useful specimens; this pretty much sums up what plot and story-line this tale has. West's chemical solutions do work up to a point—but produce only momentary resurrections or homicidal maniacs. The obsessed doctor is eventually dismembered in his subterranean Boston laboratory by a gang of dead victims led by another of his experimental subjects, his former friend the late Major Sir Eric Moreland Clapham-Lee, M.D. Herbert West was "small, slender, spectacled," with yellow hair and pale blue eyes (generally blazing with determination).

WHATELEY, CURTIS (DH): A Dunwich farmer who is one of the "undecayed Whateleys," and the son of the farmer Zechariah. He sells two Alderney cows to Old Whateley in February, 1913, within a month after Lavinia Whateley's delivery of her son Wilbur. Old Whateley, and later Wilbur, never afterward ceased to purchase cattle from local farmers; but never seemed to have many cattle on their land, all the same. In 1928, when the professors from Miskatonic University come to investigate the Horror, Curtis Whateley joins the posse which follows them around. He looks on through a telescope as the three academic men make the monster become visible, and he gives a horrified description to the other yokels, before fainting away.

WHATELEY FAMILY (DH): The Whateley clan of north-central Massachusetts has a first-rate Lovecraftian pedigree, being descended from ancestors who originally fled to remote Dunwich in 1692 to avoid the Salem witchcraft trials. HPL separated the numerous latter-day descendants of those pioneers into "decayed" and "undecayed" branches. Several Whateleys figure in this tale. "Whately," a variant spelling of the same name, is the name of a real village in the putative neighborhood of the fictitious Dunwich; it lies about halfway between the towns of Northampton and Greenfield, Massachusetts.

Less explicitly in this tale than in *The Lurking Fear, Beyond the Wall of Sleep*, and (for that matter) *The Shadow Over Innsmouth*, HPL made fictional use of a theme which was the subject of much debate and research in the United States during his formative years: the potential physical and moral degeneration of isolated rural populations over the span of several generations. In this tale, while commenting on the decadent Dunwichers' general propensity to "woefully low" intelligence, and "overt viciousness…[leading to] half-hidden murders, incests, and deeds of almost unimaginable violence and perversity," the narrator adds that elements of certain old families like the Whateleys had "kept somewhat above the general decay; though many branches are sunk into the sordid populace so deeply that only their names remain as a key to the origin they disgrace."

WHATELEY, LAVINIA (DH): A countrywoman in Dunwich township circa 1878–1926. As of 1913 she was a "somewhat deformed, unattractive albino woman of thirty-five," living with her fearsome father, Old Whateley. She is fond of "wild and grandiose daydreams"; "a lone creature given to wandering amidst thunderstorms in the hills," and uselessly trying to read her father's old sorcery books. Her mother died mysteriously when Lavinia was only 12. On February 2, 1913, Lavinia Whateley gave birth to Wilbur, son of an unknown father, and—we learn—to another child who will not be seen in public for many years to come. At first, Lavinia carries her precocious baby on her hill-walks; but he, growing and maturing with unnatural rapidity, soon learns to walk and then to run up the hills quite well on his own. As the years pass, Wilbur treats Lavinia with increasing contempt, finally forbidding her to accompany him to the hills on the annual events of Halloween and May-Eve. She begins to tell one of her few local woman friends that she feels afraid of her son. On Halloween, 1926, she disappears forever, probably as a human sacrifice.

WHATELEY, "OLD" (DH): A decrepit rustic wizard in Dunwich, described as a "grey, unshaven old man," "aged and half insane," living in a tumbledown old farmhouse; he is the father of Lavinia Whateley, grandfather of Wilbur Whateley and his always-hidden brother. His sinister reputation attaches him to the practice of black magic and to the "unexplained death by violence of Mrs. Whateley when Lavinia was twelve years old." A week after grandson Wilbur's birth, "Wizard Whateley"—his other appellation—rode his sled into Dunwich Village, almost beside himself with excitement, and told the loiterers at Osburne's general store:

> I dun't keer what folks think—ef Lavinny's boy looked like his pa, he wouldn't look like nothin' ye expeck. Ye needn't think the only folks is the folks hereabouts. Lavinny's read some, an' has seed some things the most o' ye only tell abaout. I calc'late her man is as good a husban' as ye kin find this side of Aylesbury; an' ef ye knowed as much abaout the hills as I dew, ye wouldn't ast no better church weddin' nor her'n. Let me tell ye suthin—some day yew folks'll hear a child o' Lavinny's a-callin' its father's name on the top o' Sentinel Hill!

Old Whateley appears to have originated the scheme for something that was to be carried out by his grandchildren, the secret progeny of Yog-Sothoth, for "letting in" something from "outside" the planet, which would then wipe out the human race. He died in old age, on Lammas Night (August 1), 1924, leaving the plan in Wilbur's hands. When close to death, Old Whateley commented wryly on the whippoorwill birds which, according to local belief, gathered to catch the souls of dying people if they can: "I expeck them an' the souls they hunts fer hev some pretty tough tussles sometimes." His words may deliberately echo the title of one of Ambrose Bierce's most effective tales of the macabre, certainly known to HPL: *A Tough Tussle*. The world Lammas comes from the English "loaf-mass," *i.e.*, the celebration at the time of the earliest harvest of wheat in northern climes. It is one of the four "great Sabbaths" of witchcraft; the others are Candlemas (February 2); May Eve or "Walpurgis night" (April 30); and Halloween (October 31). In this context it may be mentioned that Wilbur Whateley was born on Candlemas ("which the people of Dunwich curiously observe under another name"), February 2, 1913, nine months after May Eve of 1912, a night of weird noises in the air, when Lavinia Whateley presumably became with child; Lavinia, the dimwitted "twisted albino," who would disappear forever on Halloween night in 1926, probably sacrificed on Sentinel Hill by her son Wilbur.

WHATELEY, SAWYER (DH): The local "squire"; also, the chairman of the Dunwich-area draft board in the war year of 1917, when he "had hard work finding a quota of young Dunwich men fit even to be sent to development camp." A "development camp" was a step below the normal army basic-training camp, geared to simply making men physically and mentally fit to be trained as soldiers, so this indicates that the social, medical, and educational level of Dunwich was extremely low. In response to such "signs of wholesale regional decadence," the government sent an investigating team, newspaper reporters from Arkham and Boston descended on the wretched community, and the peculiar household of "Old Whateley" was even written about in the so-called "Sunday supplements"—what we would currently call newspaper magazines.

WHATELEY, WILBUR (DH): The son of Lavinia Whateley and an unknown father, discovered at the end to have been Yog-Sothoth. Born on February 2, 1913, his weird physical giantism and his mental precociousness make him notorious in the Dunwich region. He is schooled by his grandfather in the occult knowledge found in, among other texts, the *Necronomicon*—of which they own a copy of the Dee translation, in poor condition. He corresponds widely with other experts in this branch of learning, including Professor Armitage at Miskatonic University. Wilbur Whateley is killed by an enormous and savage guard-dog in September, 1928, while trying to break into the Miskatonic library to steal, or at least consult its unmutilated copy of the *Necronomicon*. His body is revealed to be horribly half-human, or to put it another way, inhuman from the waistline down; but within a few minutes after his death, the remains melt away into thin air.

WHATELEY, ZEBULON (DH): An elderly man in 1928, a member of a branch of the Whateleys that "hovered halfway between soundness and decadence." After the obliteration of the Frye farm, he makes "darkly wild suggestions about rites that ought to be practiced on the hilltops"— in fact, exactly what the Miskatonic University professors will ultimately do. His branch of the clan was "traditionalistic," we are told, and "his memories of chantings in the great stone circles [on the hilltops] were not altogether connected with Wilbur and [Wilbur's] grandfather." Zebulon Whateley was also one of the loungers in Osborn's general store on the occasion in 1913 when the excited Old Whateley told the crowd that someday they would hear a child of Lavinia's calling its father on the top of Sentinel Hill. Zebulon accompanies the posse following Professor Armitage in 1928.

WHATELEY, ZECHARIAH (DH): One of the "undecayed Whateleys," the father of Curtis. He is described as "old" in 1913, when he led the first two cows of many over to Old Whateley's farm. The Horror-brother, we eventually understand, was eating all those cows over the years as it grew larger.

WHEELER, HENRY (DH): A Dunwich man, who joins the posse in 1928. He looks on from a safe distance, along with the other rustic men, as the three Miskatonic professors deal with the monster. After the telescope falls from fainting Curtis Whateley's hands, "only Henry Wheeler" thought to pick it up and brush off the mud. Afterwards he shares it with Earl Sawyer.

WHIPPLE, CAPTAIN ABRAHAM (SH, CDW): A non-fictitious Providence sailor (1733–1819). A successful privateer captain during the French and Indian War (known as the Seven Years' War in Europe, it ended in 1763), Captain Whipple is best-known in American history for commanding the capture and burning of the British tax-collecting ship *Gaspee* in Rhode Island's Narragansett Bay in 1772, one of the increasing violent and defiant incidents that were the immediate precursors to the American Revolution. He later became one of the first American naval heroes for his exploits as an navy captain during the Revolutionary War.

This bold man of action looms large in the "historical" section of *The Case of Charles Dexter Ward*, after being called in by the fine gentlemen of the secret committee to lead the raiding party of tough sailors armed with muskets and harpoons that attacks Joseph Curwen's farm on April 12, 1771. Whipple's own team storms the main farmhouse, and brave Captain Whipple is one of the most badly-wounded men that night. In later years the tough old sea-dog is heard now and then to say: "Pox on that _____ [referring to Curwen], but he had no business to laugh while he screamed. 'Twas as though the damn'd _____ had summ'at [something] up his sleeve. For half a crown [an insignificant amount of coin money; it is like saying "for two cents" in modern American idiom] I'd burn his _____ house." Captain Whipple never did burn down Curwen's old townhouse in Providence, and generations later, young Charles Dexter Ward finds Curwen's portrait and papers hidden there for him to find.

Abraham Whipple was one of HPL's maternal ancestors; and his grandfather's name was Whipple V. Phillips. HPL's ex-wife Sonia remembered in 1948 that Captain Whipple's portrait, which she had been shown somewhere, "looked exactly as H.P. might have appeared in 1775."

WHIPPLE, DR. ELIHU (SH): The narrator's much-loved and honored uncle; a medical doctor and Providence antiquarian. He was "a bachelor; a white-haired, clean-shaven, old-fashioned gentleman," living in a Georgian-era house on North Court Street with only one manservant. His grandfather was a cousin of Captain Abraham Whipple, we are told. He is an intellectual with interests outside of the medical field; it is mentioned that he had made "interminable translations...from anthropological and antiquarian articles in the *Revue des Deux Mondes*" (the "Review of Two Worlds," a French scholarly publication founded in the 19th century). Out of curiosity, Dr. Whipple had collected much material about the history of the Shunned House, material that he shared with his nephew. On June 25, 1919, at the age of 81, he accompanies his much younger nephew for a night in the cellar of the terrible house. Unfortunately, he is seized upon by the starving, buried entity that was the true "vampire" of the dwelling, and seems to dissolve "to an abhorrent plasticity...[that] with blackening and decaying features leered and gibbered at me, and reached out dripping claws to rend me in the fury which this horror had brought." As Dr. Whipple melts down, his face takes on the outlines of many faces, one after another: "He was at once a devil and a multitude, a charnel-house and a pageant." Then, "toward the last...it seemed as though the shifting features fought against themselves, and strove to form contours like my uncle's kindly face. I like to think that he existed at that moment, and that he tried to bid me farewell." As the narrator leaves the cellar by the street door, "a thin stream of grease follow[ed] me through the door to the rain-drenched sidewalk." (Like the end of Mrs. Nahum Gardner in *The Colour Out of Space*, this big-finish demise is strongly reminiscent of the ending of Arthur Machen's horror-tale *The Novel of the White Powder*—and of HPL's own short-story *He*.) Later, the narrator erects an urn to his uncle's memory in the "church-yard" or cemetery of St. John's, in Providence.

The character of Dr. Whipple was based in part on Dr. Franklin Chase Clark (1847–1915), a medical doctor married to one of HPL's maternal aunts. This favorite uncle was wise about more than his own profession. He was, moreover, a talented writer not only on medical subjects, but also about regional history and genealogy; late in life he was elected to the Rhode Island Historical Society. He was of considerable encourage-ment and assistance to HPL in the latter's earliest reading and writing projects.

WHITE, ANN (SH): A "morose" domestic servant employed in the William Harris household. Mercy Dexter hired her in 1768 to replace a previous maid, Mehitabel Pierce, who had died. Ann White came from "that part of North Kingstown now set off as the township of Exeter" in rural Rhode Island. Of this district, the narrator notes that as late as 1892, the corpse of a local person—it was, in historical fact, a young woman—was dug up as a suspected vampire, and her heart burned; "and one may imagine the point of view of the same section in 1768." Ann White proved to be a terrible gossip concerning events inside the house, and flatly refused to go down into its cellar. She "promulgated" the idea of a vampire buried under the house, and her "dogged insistence on a search under the cellar [was] prominent in bringing about her discharge," which took place after only a few months of employment. Maria Robbins replaced her. But Ann White was right.

WHITE SHIP, THE (WS): Basil Elton sees the White Ship from his vantage point in the North Point lighthouse, ever coming from the south when the moon is full. One night he walks out across the water to board her. She carries sails and also banks of rowing-oars, and her captain is a robed and bearded man. Together he and Elton sail to the south and beyond our everyday world, passing the harbors of Zar, Thalarion, and Xura, before stopping in gorgeous Sona-Nyl. At Elton's urging but against the captain's better judgment, they sail the White Ship onward through the Basalt Pillars of the West in search of Cathuria, but the ship goes over the great waterfall at the end of the world instead. Awakening on the beach at North Point, Elton finds "a single shattered spar [a pole or length of wood used to support a sail on a ship], of a whiteness greater than that of the wave-tips or of the mountain snow."

WHITMARSH, DR. (SH): *See* "Chase and Whitmarsh, Drs."

WILCOX, HENRY ANTHONY (CC): The youngest son of an excellent Providence family. In the Lovecraftian cosmos, he is the type of person most likely to be receptive to occult messages, being thin, dark, neurotic-looking, and "psychically hypersensitive." Wilcox studies sculpture at the famous Rhode Island School of Design, at 2 College Street, another of HPL's neighborhood landmarks. This precocious genius lives in an apartment in the "Fleur-de-Lys" building nearby to the school. On March 1, 1925, he calls on Dr. Angell to discuss a bas-relief sculpture he had made after a strange dream of "great Cyclopean cities of titan blocks and sky-flung monoliths, all dripping with green ooze." The bas-relief reminds Dr. Angell of the sculpture seized by the New Orleans police after the raid on the Cthulhu-cultists in a Louisiana swamp in 1908. For the next few weeks, Dr. Angell records Wilcox's vivid dreams, until March 23rd, when the young artist collapses into a feverish delirium. After he returns to normal on April 2, his dreams are ordinary and of no further interest to the professor.

WILDE, OSCAR (CDW): The brilliant Anglo-Irish playwright, author, and wit (1854–1900), creator of stage comedies such as *The Importance of Being Earnest*, and stories such as *The Canterville Ghost*, popular successes in their time which remain charming and entertaining after more than a century. Following his public exposure as a homosexual in the course of a famous series of London trials in the 1890s, Wilde was sentenced to prison for two years and became a despised social outcast. Describing the veil of silence and denial that descended over the memory of Joseph Curwen in Providence after April, 1771, HPL wrote that "it can be compared in spirit to the hush that lay on Oscar Wilde's name for a decade after his disgrace."

WILHELMSHAVEN (TE): A north German seaport, apparently the home port of submarine U-29. The submarine had begun its journey back to Wilhelmshaven about two hours before an engine-room explosion crippled the vessel at 2:00 p.m. on June 28, 1917.

WILKES (MM): An Antarctic explorer mentioned in the tale; he was Charles Wilkes (1798–1877), a U.S. Navy officer who commanded an 1838–1842 American scientific expedition which sailed to South America, Antarctica, the South Pacific, the Pacific coastline of North America, and thence around the world. Wilkes Land on the Antarctic coast is named after him.

WILLETT, MARINUS BICKNELL (CDW): A Providence physician, and the Ward family doctor. He eventually takes the leading role in investigating the events surrounding Charles Dexter Ward's "madness" and inexplicable behavior. In one of the most memorable long passages in all of Lovecraft's works, he explores the unsuspected subterranean realm of Joseph Curwen, and its horrible contents. At length, he has the final confrontation with Joseph Curwen—wearing the body of Charles Dexter Ward—which ends in the destruction of the evil alchemist.

WILLIAMS STREET (CC): The Providence street where Professor George Angell lived. He collapsed and died while walking back there from the Newport ferry landing.

WILLIAMSON FAMILY (SOI): Some of the maternal relations of the unnamed narrator, who is by his own description an Ohio man and a student at Oberlin College, in Ohio. He is the grandson of James Williamson of Ohio, who married Eliza Orne, the daughter of Benjamin Orne and a certain Miss Marsh, in Arkham in 1867 (sixty years before the modern-day events of this tale). The Williamson family lived in the city of Cleveland, Ohio. The narrator's grandmother, Eliza Orne Williamson, who somehow always seemed "strange and almost terrifying" to him as a child, disappeared when he was eight years old. This occurred after her son Douglas shot himself to death following a visit he had made to Arkham; on internal evidence, this suicide probably took place in about 1915. The vanished grandmother Eliza and the narrator's late Uncle Douglas had both had a "staring, unwinking" expression that the narrator hated as a child. Eliza's other son, Walter Williamson, the narrator's other uncle, was normal-looking, but Walter's son Lawrence (the narrator's cousin) was said to be "very peculiar" and had been committed to a sanitarium—or "madhouse"—in Canton, Ohio. The narrator's own late mother was Eliza's third child; apparently without having been affected by them herself, she had passed Eliza's Deep One genes on to him, so that he can transform and become immortal beneath the sea. (*See* "Orne Family".)

WILMARTH, PROFESSOR ALBERT N. (WD, MM): A professor in the English department at Miskatonic University, who is a specialist in comparative folklore. He lives at 118 Saltonstall Street in Arkham. He carries on a lengthy and detailed correspondence with Henry Akeley of Vermont, concerning the alleged hill-creatures, and finally makes a visit to Akeley's farm, only to flee in terror several hours after arrival. In *At* *the Mountains of Madness*, Professor Dyer mentions having had conversations with Professor Wilmarth, back in Arkham.

WILSON, DR. (SOT): An Arkham physician who is summoned to Dr. Nathaniel Peaslee's home at 6:00 a.m. on September 27, 1913, by a "hesitant, foreign" voice calling from what is later determined to have been a pay telephone at North Station in Boston. He finds Peaslee unconscious in the sitting room, and helps him back to full awareness.

WINGED, STAR-HEADED OLD ONES (MM, SOT, HD): *see* "Old Ones."

WINSON, REVEREND SAMUEL, JR. (CDW): The Baptist minister who marries Joseph Curwen and Eliza Tillinghast on March 7, 1763. His Baptist church was the bride's "home" congregation.

WITCH HOUSE (DWH): A very old, rather large, gable-roofed house in Arkham, where the accused witch Keziah Mason lived in the late 1600s. By the 1920s it has become a working-class boarding house, owned by a Mr. Dombrowski and inhabited by Polish-American and French-Canadian proletarians. Two Miskatonic University students dwell there as well: Frank Elwood, who is simply too poor to live anyplace else; and Walter Gilman, who is fascinated by the old legend of Keziah, and succeeds in getting her own old room, with its gables and curious interior angles. What seems like a persistent rat infestation is one problem in the Witch House; another is the spectral presence of Keziah Mason and her familiar creature Brown Jenkin, who are occasionally glimpsed on the premises. The Witch House is finally abandoned after Walter Gilman's horrific death, and condemned as a habitation by a municipal building inspector. In March, 1931, gale-force winds collapse the roof and the great chimney, and the building is pulled down in the following December. The demolition crew finds dreadful things in the wreckage of the attic spaces behind the slanting walls of Keziah's garret, including the bones of hundreds of small children, of a bent old woman, and of a monstrous, "diseased" rat; these are the remains of Keziah Mason, Brown Jenkin, and the children who were their sacrificial victims over a time span of some 250 years.

Arkham's Witch House was based on the actual "Witch House" (1642) at the corner of Essex Street and North Street in Salem, Massachusetts. A witch did not dwell there; ironically, this was the home of Judge Jonathan Corwin, Judge Hathorne's assistant in the 1692 Salem witch trials. Over 200 suspected witches were interrogated by the judges in this house. In the tale, tt was built in 1675, with the overhanging gables, heavy timbers, and small-paned windows of contemporary

Anglo-American home design. It has long been a local tourist attraction, and HPL saw the place more than once. Tourists nowadays are generally not allowed into the attic room, which has unsafe flooring and is only accessible by a trap door. But HPL may have been able to venture in. For ordinary structural reasons, the room has odd angles and inward-sloping walls, creating large areas of "dead space" behind the plaster, presumably the inspiration for Keziah's chamber.

WOLEJKO, ANASTASIA and LADISLAS (DWH): Anastasia Wolejko—whose name indicates her origins as an eastern European immigrant or child of immigrants, the "new Americans" of the early 20th century—is a "clod-like laundry worker" who lives in a rented room in Orne's Gangway, Arkham. Ladislas is her 2-year-old son. The boy disappears on the night of April 28–29, shortly before Walpurgis-night or May Eve. Walter Gilman reads a newspaper account of the mystery on April 29:

> She had, she said, seen Brown Jenkin about the place now and then ever since early in March, and knew from its grimacings and titterings that little Ladislas must be marked for sacrifice at the awful Sabbat on Walpurgis-Night.

On the night of the Sabbat, little Ladislas is surely the naked infant boy whom Walter Gilman prevented Keziah Mason from slaying with her ritual knife, only to find that Brown Jenkin has killed the child anyway by chewing open a vein in the boy's wrist. Ladislas Wolejko's bones presumably would have been among the many found along with Keziah Mason's in the garret rubble when the Witch House was razed in December, 1931, among the "several things that made the workmen pause and call in the police."

WONDERS OF THE INVISIBLE WORLD (PM): A lengthy book by the Reverend Cotton Mather (1663–1728), dating from just after of the Salem witch trials, and dealing with them and with other occult and moral issues. In HPL's tale, the ghoulish and sinister artist Pickman calls it "puerile" (childish) and scornfully claims that Mather knew about other things that he was too afraid to put in the book. Cotton Mather's stalwart defense of "spectral evidence" in the witch trials cost his later reputation dearly. The book was published at Boston in 1693, with the full title:

> The Wonders of the Invisible World. Observations As well Historical as Theological, upon the Nature, the Number, and the Operations of the Devils. Accompany'd with: I. Some Accounts of the Grievous Molestations, by Dæmons and Witchcrafts, which have lately annoy'd the Countrey; and the Trials of some eminent Malefactors Executed upon occasion

thereof: with several Remarkable Curiosities therein occurring. II. Some Counsils, Directing a due Improvement of the terrible things, lately done, by the Unusual and Amazing Range of Evil Spirits, in Our Neighbourhood: and the methods to prevent the Wrongs which those Evil Angels may intend against all sorts of people among us; especially in Accusations of the Innocent. III. Some Conjectures upon the great Events, likely to befall the World in General, and New-England in Particular; as also upon the Advances of the time, when we shall see Better Dayes. IV. A short Narrative of a late Outrage committed by a knot of Witches in Swedeland [Sweden], very much Resembling, and so far Explaining, That under which our parts of America have laboured! V. The Devil Discovered: In a Brief Discourse upon those Temptations, which are the more Ordinary Devices of the Wicked One.

WOODVILLE, JAMES (SOT): One of the captive minds encountered by Nathaniel Peaslee among the Great Race; he is an English gentleman from the county of Suffolk, in the time of Oliver Cromwell's Puritan government (circa 1649–58).

WORMIUS, OLAUS (TF, DH): In HPL's mock-historicizing about the history of the *Necronomicon*, Olaus Wormius is named as the medieval translator of the forbidden book into Latin, circa 1228, working from the Greek translation of the Arabic original text.

There was a real Olaus Wormius (whose birth name was Ole Wurm); however, he lived from 1558–1654. He was a Danish physician, a professor of medicine at the University of Copenhagen, and a literary antiquarian of renown. HPL's chronological howler, as Lovecraft biographer S.T. Joshi has shown, came from a simple error in understanding a passing comment about Wormius contained in (of all things) an 18th century English book on ancient Gothic poetry.

X

XARI (QI): "Frigid" river in the valley of Narthos; during his wanderings, Iranon once sails down the Xari to reach Jaren.

XURA (WS, DQ): On the Southern Sea, Xura is the "Land of Pleasures Unattained." At first glance, from a ship out at sea such as those in which Basil Elton and Randolph Carter become passengers, Xura is lovely to behold, with sunlit groves and arbors. Sailors can even hear bursts of song and peals of faint, delicious laughter. But when the wind shifts and comes out to sea from the land of Xura, "the air [is] filled with the lethal, charnel odour of plague-stricken towns and uncovered cemeteries."

Y

YAANEK, MOUNT (MM): An Antarctic peak mentioned in "Ulalume," a poem by Edgar Allan Poe; HPL, using the graduate student Danforth as his mouthpiece, identifies Yaanek with Mount Erebus, a real mountain on the frozen continent, which is near McMurdo Sound where the Miskatonic University Expedition drops anchor and sets up a base camp.

YADDITH (TGSK, HD): A distant planet. After passing "through the gates," Randolph Carter's personality becomes lodged in another "Carter-facet": Zkauba, a wizard on Yaddith. The planet is populated principally by such as Zkauba, "clawed, snouted beings...rugose, partly squamous, and curiously articulated in a fashion mainly insect-like yet not without a caricaturish resemblance to the human form." They have several claws and live extremely long lives. Their city is "a labyrinth of inexplicably fashioned metal under a blaze of diverse solar color," and they can travel to twenty-eight other galaxies in "light-beam envelopes." Yaddith is honeycombed beneath its surface with the tunnels of burrowing and hostile creatures, the bholes, who will one day overcome the best spells of the surface-dwellers, emerge from their caverns, and conquer the planet. In a chronological sense, Yaddith seems to precede the existence of mankind by eons of time; however, Randolph Carter spends a very long time there, while comparatively little time, a year or two, passes on Earth.

In *The Haunter of the Dark*, Robert Blake writes in his death-diary: "Everything depends on lightning. Yaddith grant it will keep up!"

YATH, LAKE OF (DQ): A lake on the large island of Oriab. One side of the town of Baharna slopes downward toward the lake, and the captain of the ship that brings Randolph Carter to Oriab lives in a house on the lake's nearer shore, where Carter spends several nights. On the far side of the lake are "the vast clay-brick ruins of a primal city whose name is not mentioned." Camping amid those ruins, Carter is beset by wamps.

YELLOW SIGN (WD): One of the "names and terms" which Henry W. Akeley mentions in a very long letter describing things he has overheard or inferred during his study of the mysterious beings in the Vermont hills. Dr. Wilmarth, the recipient of the letter, had already heard of it in "the most hideous of connexions."

In a subsequent letter dated September 6, 1928, which purports to be from Henry Akeley, Dr. Wilmarth is further informed:

> There is a whole secret cult of evil men (a man of your mystical erudition .
> will understand me when I link them with Hastur and the Yellow Sign)
> devoted to the purpose of tracking [the fungi from Yuggoth, or Mi-Go]
> down and injuring them on behalf of monstrous powers from other dimen-
> sions.

Given that the very letter is a fraud designed to lure Dr. Wilmarth to the Akeley farm with the photographs and recordings he has been previously sent, this information may be a lie.

The Yellow Sign is, or was, a graphic symbol of unspecified appearance but great power, alluded to in a collection of grotesque short stories which HPL had read and admired in youth, *The King in Yellow* (1895), by the American author Robert W. Chambers (1859–1933). In *The Repairer of Reputations*, the first tale in the collection, the Yellow Sign is embroidered on the robes of the would-be emperor; its precise nature and appearance go unexplained. It may be noted that Chambers presented the Yellow Sign of his invention as the token of the god Hastur of the lost city of Carcosa; two names he had in turn lifted from the fantastic fiction of the slightly earlier American master of the weird, Ambrose Bierce (1842–1914?), namely the short stories *Haïta the Shepherd* (in which Hastur is "the god of shepherds") and *An Inhabitant of Carcosa*.

YEZIDIS (HRH): According to the narrator of *The Horror at Red Hook*, they are foreigners from Asia, devil-worshippers and human-sacrificers, who remain malevolently active while living as illegal aliens in New York City. HPL describes the Yezidis as swarthy, "Mongoloid" and mis-shapen.

The real Yezidis are members of a small religious group comprising a subset of the Kurds, a Muslim ethnic group of many millions that principally inhabit the connected mountainous regions of Turkey, Armenia, and Iraq. L. Sprague de Camp explained that "the real Kurds...are big, ruddy, wholly [Caucasian] men, and the Yezidis are a peaceable, well-behaved sect despite their peculiar theology." But HPL was something less than an expert on Central Asian peoples, and in 1925, as today, a suspense writer in search of a "story hook" could always get one from the sinister subject of "devil worship."

For the many readers of this tale who must have wondered about those obscure "Yezidi devil worshippers" over the years, there follows a short explanation. The Yezidi, or Yazidi, religion combines elements of Zoroastrian, Manichaean, Jewish, Islamic, and so-called Nestorian Christian concepts and practices in an understandably unique mixture. Although the Yazidi sect has existed for centuries, there are thought to be fewer than 100,000 left today, spread across the Kurdish areas between Mosul, in northern Iraq, and the Caucasus Mountains to the north. To the extent possible, Yezidis dwell in a sectarian world apart from their overwhelmingly Muslim neighbors. In the Yezidi theology, Satan (*Sheitan*) repented of his sin of pride, and was then pardoned by God and reinstated as chief of the angels, or *Malak Taus*, the Peacock Angel. Malak Taus is the ruler of the world, which God has created but takes no further interest in for the present. Therefore Malak Taus is the being worshipped and propitiated by the Yezidis and their hereditary priesthood; but not by any means with human sacrifices. To Western visitors hearing garbled and imperfect explanations of Yezidi beliefs, however, the Sheitan/Malak Taus story was enough to produce the fallacy of Yezidi "devil worshippers" in mass-market travel books published prior to the year when HPL wrote this tale.

Y'HA-NTHLEI (SOI): A luminous city of the Deep Ones, at the bottom of the unmeasured depths of the oceanic trench that begins on the far side of Devil Reef, in Innsmouth harbor. The city was damaged, but not destroyed, when a U.S. Navy submarine fired torpedoes downward toward the ocean floor in 1927–28. Pth'thya-l'yi, Obed Marsh's Deep One consort, returned here after the mortal's death; she had previously dwelt there for 80,000 years.

YHE (SOT): Purportedly a vanished prehistoric land in the Pacific; Nathaniel Peaslee, while among the Great Race, met the mind of an "archimage"—a senior wizard—from Yhe.

YIAN (WD): An unexplained reference in this tale, but compare "Yian-Ho."

YIANG-LI (SOT): One of the captive minds encountered by Nathaniel Peaslee among the Great Race; he is a philosopher from the empire of Tsan-Chan, which is to come in what would be the historic future viewed from Peaslee's own human lifetime.

YIAN-HO (TGSK): A "dreadful and forbidden city," the "hidden legacy" of Leng. There was a Hindu yogi who claimed to have been the only living human to have seen it. It is suggested that it was this yogi who sent to Etienne-Laurent de Marigny of New Orleans the tall, coffin-shaped clock "with four hands and hieroglyphed dial, whose crazy ticking followed no known rhythm of earth."

YIG (WD): Henry Akeley's simulacrum tells Professor Wilmarth about "Yig, the Father of Serpents." This was a salute from HPL to his "revisions" client Zealia B. Reed and her published story, *The Curse of Yig*— or rather, a salute to himself, since he had for all intents and purposes written the tale based on her initial idea. In HPL's words to a friend, "this story is well-nigh a piece of original composition on my part, since all I had to go on was a synopsis of notes.... All the plot & motivation in the present tale are my own." As summed up by one Lovecraft expert, Darrell Schweitzer, "a pioneer couple [in the American West] run afoul of the snake-god Yig when the wife kills a nest of baby [rattlesnakes]. Yig customarily deals with malefactors by turning them into snakes, after suitable torture." In this tale the wife ends up accidentally killing her husband in the dark with an axe.

YITH (SOT): According to hints in the Eltdown Shards, this is the "obscure, trans-galactic world" from which the Great Race came to Earth, hundreds of millions of years ago.

YOGASH THE BLACK (DQ): Nyarlathotep, in making his ceremonious entrance at Kadath, is escorted by "twin columns of giant black slaves with loin-cloths of iridescent silk. Upon their heads were strapped vast helmet-like torches of glittering metal...in their right hands were crystal wands whose tips were carved into leering chimaeras, while their left hands grasped long, thin silver trumpets." One of this awe-inspiring group, whom Nyarlathotep names as Yogash the Black, helps Randolph Carter to mount a shantak for his flight away from Kadath.

YOG-SOTHOTH (CDW, DH, WD, MM, TGSK, HD): "I really believe that *Yog-Sothoth* is a basically immature conception, & unfitted for really serious literature."—HPL to his friend Frank Belknap Long, 1931. In another personal letter he alluded humorously to his invented pantheon or pseudomythology as "this Cthulhuism and Yog-Sothothery of mine." But despite the author's misgivings, Yog-Sothoth remains one of the more memorable entities of Lovecraft's imagination.

Yog-Sothoth's first mention comes in *The Case of Charles Dexter Ward* (1927) in a letter from Joseph Curwen to Simon Orne written "not much later than 1750":

> I last Night strucke on ye Words that bringe up YOGGE-SOTHOTHE, and sawe for ye firste Time that fface [face] spoke of by Ibn Schacabao in y^e ————. And IT said, that ye III Psalme in ye Liber-Damnatus holdes ye Clauicle [*i.e.*, clavicle, key]. With Sunne in V House, Saturne in Trine, drawe ye Pentagram of Fire, and saye ye ninth Uerse [verse] thrice. This Uerse repeate eache Roodemas and Hallow's Eue [Eve]; and ye Thing will breede in ye Outside Spheres.

And in a diary in the caverns under the Pawtuxet bungalow in 1928, Dr. Willett finds a recent journal in Curwen's hand with the cryptic entry: "Rais'd *Yog-Sothoth* thrice and was ye next day delivered."

On April 15, 1927, it being Good Friday, Charles Dexter Ward's mother listens through his door and hears him chanting "syllables that sounded like 'Yi-nash-Yog-Sothoth-he-lgeb-fi-throdog'—ending in a 'Yah!' whose maniacal force mounted in an ear-splitting crescendo." This can only be the "Dragon's Head" formula which Dr. Willett chants on April 5, 1928, in the catacombs below the Pawtuxet bungalow (having seen it inscribed on a wall there), namely "Y'AI 'NG'NGAH, *YOG-SOTHOTH* H'EE—L'GEB F'AI THRODOG *UAAAH!*" His repeating of this formula causes the "Saltes" of No. 118 to convert from dull-green powder into some powerful wizard of ancient times. Later, in Dr. Waite's asylum Dr. Willett attacks Curwen with the Dragon's Tail formula, almost the reverse of the other: "OGTHROD AI'F GEB'L—EE'H *YOG-SOTHOTH* 'NGAH'NG AI'Y *ZHRO!*" to spectacular effect:

> At the very first word from Willett's mouth the previously commenced formula of the patient stopped short. Unable to speak, the monster made wild motions with his arms until they too were arrested. When the awful name of *Yog-Sothoth* was uttered, the hideous change began. It was not merely a *dissolution*, but rather a *transformation* or *recapitulation*; and Willett shut his eyes lest he faint before the rest of the incantation could be pronounced.

Simon Orne closes his February 11, 1928 letter to Joseph Curwen with the cheery salutation, "Yogg-Sothoth Neblod Zin."

In *The Dunwich Horror*, it is said that the Dunwichers spice all conjectures about Wilbur Whateley "with references to the bygone magic of Old Whateley, and how the hills once shook when he shrieked the dreadful name of *Yog-Sothoth* in the midst of a circle of stones with a great book open in his arms before him." On his deathbed in 1924, Old Whateley tells Wilbur: "Open up the gates to Yog-Sothoth with the long chant that ye'll find on page 751 [of the *Necronomicon*]...ef it [the Horror] gits aout afore ye opens to Yog-Sothoth, it's all over an' no use." When consulted, the relevant formula in the *Necronomicon* includes the passage:

> *Yog-Sothoth* knows the gate. *Yog-Sothoth* is the gate. *Yog-Sothoth* is the key and guardian of the gate. Past, present, future, all are one in *Yog-Sothoth*. He knows where the Old Ones broke through of old, and where they shall break through again.... *Yog-Sothoth* is the key to the gate, where the spheres meet.

Dying on the floor of the genealogy reading-room of the Miskatonic University library in the early morning of August 3, 1928, the monstrous half-human thing that was called Wilbur Whateley is heard to murmur *"N'gai, n'gha'ghaa, bugg-shoggog, y'hah; Yog-Sothoth, Yog-Sothoth..."* On September 15, 1928, as Wilbur's fraternal-twin brother the Horror is being dispatched from our universe, it cries out in terror: *"Eh-ya-ya-ya-yahaah—e'yayayayaaaa... ngh'aaaaa... ngh'aaaa... h'yuh... h'yuh...* HELP! HELP!... *ff—ff—ff*—FATHER! FATHER! YOG-SOTHOTH!" A few minutes later an explanation delivered by Dr. Armitage to the assembled Dunwich rustics makes it more clear that both Wilbur and his brother had been the children of Yog-Sothoth and Lavinia Whateley.

In his letter of May 5, 1928, to Dr. Wilmarth, Henry Akeley of *The Whisperer in Darkness* writes: "I suppose you know all about all the fearful myths antedating the coming of man to the earth—the Yog-Sothoth and Cthulhu cycles—which are hinted at in the *Necronomicon*."

In *At the Mountains of Madness*, "Yog-Sothoth" is one of the series of names or concepts which the temporarily maddened Danforth babbles as Professor Dyer pilots the escape plane. In *The Haunter of the Dark*, Robert Blake's last scrawled entry in his diary as he looks out from his apartment window in the direction of the old Starry Wisdom church reads: "I see it—coming here—hell-wind—titan blur—black wings— Yog-Sothoth save me—the three-lobed burning eye...."

Yog-Sothoth makes a big exit in *Through the Gates of the Silver Key*, one of HPL's last tales, co-authored with E. Hoffman Price in 1932–33. Having passed through the Ultimate Gate, Randolph Carter—or whatever we ought to call the transmogrified "quasi-Carter," at that point—gradually senses a being of matchless power and knowledge:

> It was an All-in-One and One-in-All of limitless being and self—not merely a thing of one Space-Time continuum, but allied to the ultimate animating essence of existence's whole unbounded sweep—the last, utter sweep which has no confines and which outreaches fancy and mathematics alike. It was perhaps that which certain secret cults have whispered of as YOG-SOTHOTH, and which has been a deity under other names; that which the crustaceans of Yuggoth worship as the Beyond-One, and which the vaporous brains of the spiral nebulae know by an untranslatable Sign— yet in a flash the Carter-facet realised how slight and fractional all these conceptions are.

YOTH (WD): A "red-litten" secret world under the Earth's surface.

YR (DH): "I shall have to learn all the angles of the planes and all the formulas between the Yr and the Nhhngr," Wilbur Whateley wrote in his diary on November 26, 1916. These unpronounceables were invented by HPL, left unexplained, and never appear again in any of his tales. The same is true of "the Dho formula" and "the Dho-Hna formula," also found in this diary entry.

YUCATAN (TT): The Yucatan peninsula is a large land-formation that juts out from the Atlantic coast of Mexico. The sealed glass bottle containing the last journal of the submarine commander Karl Heinrich von Altburg-Ehrenstein washes ashore in Yucatan, having drifted westward across most of the Atlantic Ocean.

YUGGOTH (WD, HD, TGSK): The "secret name" of Pluto, the planet which was discovered at the far edge of our solar system in 1930. The Mi-Go, those part-crustacean, part-fungoid aliens who infest Vermont's remote hills, come from Yuggoth. *Fungi From Yuggoth* is also the name of a cycle of poems by HPL. In *The Whisperer in Darkness* we obtain our best glimpse of Yuggoth:

> There are mighty cities on Yuggoth—great tiers of terraced towers built of black stone.... The sun shines there no brighter than a star, but the beings need no light. They have other, subtler senses, and put no windows in their great houses and temples. Light even hurts and hampers and confuses them, for it does not exist at all in the black cosmos outside time and space, where they came from originally. To visit Yuggoth would drive any weak man mad...the black rivers of pitch that flow under those mysterious Cyclopean bridges—things built by some elder race extinct and forgotten before the beings came to Yuggoth....

Concerning the name of this place and other names with vaguely scriptural sounds, HPL once wrote to a friend:

> To a large extent they are designed to suggest—either closely or remotely—certain names in actual history or folklore which have weird or sinister associations connected with them. Thus "Yuggoth" has a sort of Arabic or Hebraic cast, to suggest certain words passed down in antiquity in the magical formulae contained in Moorish & Jewish manuscripts.

Z

ZANN, ERICH (MEZ): An elderly, German-speaking foreigner in the unnamed French city where this tale unfolds. A professional viol-player, Zann performs in a cheap theater orchestra by day (harkening back to the pre-motion picture, pre-recorded music era of live matinee plays and vaudeville performances, during the 19th century and the first few decades of the 20th), and by night retreats to his fifth-floor garret room in Monsieur Blandot's tenement building on the Rue d'Auseil, there to play upon his viol the fantastic and entrancing melodies of his own composition. He is surprised and displeased to learn that the starving-student narrator has been listening to his playing from the floor below, and persuades the younger man to move down to the third floor, paying the increase in rent himself. But the student continues to listen secretly from a stairwell landing. Zann's demeanor and music both grow increasingly frantic, until the climactic night when the student knocks on Zann's door and is admitted to hear and see his last performance. Never very popular with readers, *The Music of Erich Zann* was nonetheless HPL's personal second-favorite of all his tales, according to some autobiographical notes he set down in about 1933. HPL seems to have enjoyed the music of the viol, a older and somewhat larger cousin of the violin, with deeper tones and a more limited range: in *Hypnos* the nameless narrator wrote of his extraordinary friend: "his voice was music—the music of deep viols and crystalline spheres."

In youth HPL learned to play the violin, but gave it up. His relationship to music persisted tenuously in his later life. Apparently he had a nice, tenor voice when persuaded to sing; we have it on the authority of his ex-wife Sonia that "his singing voice, while not strong, was very sweet." There is a certain comical consistency with the willful anti-modernism of HPL's thoughts and behavior during most of his life, in Sonia's next words: "He would sing none of the modern songs, only the more favored ones of about a half century ago or more."

ZAR (WS, DQ): A land on the coast of the Southern Sea. From out at sea, Zar displays "lordly terraces of verdure, tree-studded, and shewing [*sic*] here and there the gleaming white roofs and colonnades of strange temples." In Zar "dwell all the dreams and thoughts of beauty that come to men once and are then forgotten." Basil Elton and Randolph Carter, on their respective voyages, sail past Zar, for it is known that whoever lands there can never again return to his native shore. Once a ship that Randolph Carter is traveling aboard encounters a passing "ship with violet sails bound for Zar, in the land of forgotten dreams, with bulbs of strange coloured lilies for cargo."

[BEN] ZARIATNATMIK (CDW): The name seems to be a Hebrew one, garbled by a 17th century American colonial writer. Simon/Jedediah Orne writes mysteriously to Joseph Curwen circa 1750, "I was frighted [frightened] when I read of your know'g what Ben Zariatnatmik hadde in his ebony Boxe, for I was conscious who must have tolde you." On April 15, 1927, Charles Dexter Ward for some two hours chants a "formula" which ends "Almonsin, Gibor, Jehosua, Evam, Zariatnatmik, veni, veni, veni."

ZATH (CU): The coroner of Ulthar, who long disputes with Nith the notary about what was the real cause of the cruel old couple's shocking deaths.

ZENIG OF APHORAT (DQ): A person who tried to visit Kadath without permission, at some time before Randolph Carter's quest: "his skull is now set in a ring on the little finger of one whom I need not name," Nyarlathotep tells Carter.

ZIMMER (TE): A sailor on German submarine U-29 in 1917. He is one of the crewmen who search the clothing of the drowned young victim found clinging to the deck railing on June 18, 1917. Some say that the corpse's eyes opened and gazed directly at Zimmer, steadily and mockingly. On the evening of June 19, he leads a delegation of sailors which requests the two officers to throw into the sea the carved ivory image found on the youth's body. The request is denied. During the week following June 20, Zimmer and Boatswain Muller disappear, presumably suicides in the ocean "as a result of the fears which had seemed to harass them."

ZIN (DQ): The dark vaults of Zin, in the Great Abyss of lower Dreamland, are the dwelling-places of the ghasts. Periodically, gugs enter Zin on hunting expeditions for ghasts, or gangs of ghasts emerge in hopes of picking off a tasty gug sentry.

ZKAUBA (TGSK): A wizard of the dominant race on planet Yaddith. He begins to have troublesome dreams about "an alien of absurd, outlandish race called 'Randolph Carter' on a world of the future not yet born." Meditation leads this sage to the answer:

Nevermore could he know the peace of being one entity. For all time and space he was two: Zkauba the Wizard of Yaddith, disgusted with the thought of the repellent earth-mammal Carter that he was to be and had been, and Randolph Carter, of Boston on the earth, shivering with fright at the clawed, snouted thing which he had once been, and had become again.

Zkauba's ordinary work was to "weave spells" to keep his planet's tunneling bholes under control and trapped beneath the surface; he is an important creature on Yaddith. At times the Randolph Carter mind is able to take over Zkauba's body, and during one of these episodes he succeeds in returning to earth in 1930, and feigning human shape as "Swami Chandraputra." At the end of the tale, however, the Zkauba-mind seems to regain control, and the being disappears into de Marigny's weird clock, perhaps never to be seen again on Earth.

ZOBNA; ZOBNARIAN FATHERS (PO): Zobna was the more-northerly land that the prehistoric men of Lomar inhabited before coming to Lomar, "until the advance of the great ice-sheet." The fainting narrator of *Polaris* is a student of the "wisdom of the Zobnarian Fathers" in Olathoë.

ZOHAR (CDW): The medieval book of Jewish Kabbala lore and magic. *Zohar*, which means "The Radiance" or "Book of Splendor" in Hebrew, consists of a series of mystical commentaries on the Torah (the first five books of the Bible), written in the Aramaic language, purportedly written by a Jewish rabbi in the 2nd century A.D., and rediscovered by a certain Jew in Spain during the 13th century. (A majority of scholars today believe that it was composed in literary Aramaic by the medieval Spanish-Jewish "discoverer," perhaps drawing on older source material that is now lost.) It has been called "the greatest classic of Jewish mysticism." In the tale, Joseph Curwen has a copy of the *Zohar* among his other esoteric books in the 18th century.

ZOKAAR (DCS): A great early king of Sarnath; at his command, the city's famous gardens were created.

ZO-KALAR (DCS): One of Sarnath's trio of principal gods, bearded and man-like in appearance. *See* "Lobon" and "Tamash".

ZOOGS (DQ): Creatures which inhabit the enchanted forest near the entrance to Dreamland from the waking world. They are small, brown, and ground-dwelling, with large eyes; and difficult to observe because of their small size and skill at hiding. Not completely trustworthy, zoogs have been known to devour unwary dreamers; but Randolph Carter had often made treaties with them. The zoogs can make a very potent wine, a flask of which they give to Carter when he passes through their forest in search of Kadath. Some zoogs follow him uninvitedly, however, but only as far as Ulthar, where they disappear, presumably eaten by cats of the town. Much later on, when Carter reemerges from in the wood through the trap door from lower Dreamland, he overhears the zoogs making a plan to attack the cats for revenge. Carter swiftly fetches a feline army, which surrounds and captures the zoogs and forces them to make peace.

ZURO (QI): A sluggish river that flows through the city of Teloth; Romnod often sits by its banks looking into the water, until he leaves Teloth with Iranon.

Appendix

Caves, Caverns, Wells & Abysses

HPL was something special in his obsession with caves, caverns, and abysses, but hardly alone at the time in using them fictionally, and his debt to other writers would be an interesting topic. Arthur Machen's malevolent "Little People" under British hills are one source, but there could be others. For example, in *The Coming Race* (1871) by the best-selling British novelist Edward Bulwer-Lytton (*see* separate entry under "Bulwer"), a man lost down a mineshaft encounters the Vril-ya, a superior race of taller and wiser humanoids with incredible powers, in a subterranean world. The Vril-ya intend one day to move to the surface and "supplant all the inferior races now existing therein." He had probably read H.G. Wells' popular *The First Men in the Moon* (1901), wherein humans encounter the "Selenites" who dwell in labyrinths of tunnels and caverns beneath the lunar surface. It is not impossible that he had read *Underground Man* by the French sociologist Gabriel Tarde, which appeared in English translation in 1905; this future fantasy describes a well-adapted race of "neo-troglodytes," humans who retreated to a deep underground existence after the sun suddenly cools off, deep-freezing the Earth's surface and everything on it, getting power from the earth's molten core and sending splendid tunnels under the continents and the solidly-frozen oceans. The progress of scientific knowledge seems to have made this variety of sub-surface fantasy almost obsolete.

HPL would be 37 years old before he got into a cave. It happened when he and some friends visited a forest place called the Bear's Den near Athol, Massachusetts, on June 28, 1928. Lovecraft wrote soon afterwards:

> There is a deep forest gorge there…. Above the tumbling stream rise high rock precipices crusted with strange lichens & honeycombed with alluring caves. Of the latter several extend far into the hillside, though too narrowly to admit a human being beyond a few yards. I entered the largest specimen—it being the first time I was ever in a real cave, notwithstanding the vast amount I have written concerning such things.

This was a very small tribute to a very small cave. It would be different when HPL entered the kind of big cave he had so often imagined.

The locale was "Endless Caverns" in New Market, Virginia, a popular tourist attraction; the time was a few weeks later in the summer of 1928. His ecstatic report of a guided tour in Endless Caverns is worthy of the most "abysmal" of his fiction:

> For over an hour I was led spellbound through illimitable gulfs and chasms of elfin beauty and daemonic mystery—here and there lighted with wondrous effect by concealed lamps, and in other places displaying awesome grottoes and abysses of unconquered night; black bottomless shafts and galleries where hidden winds and waters course eternally out of this world and all possible worlds of mankind, down, down, to the sunless secrets of the gnomes and night-gaunts, and the worlds where web-winged monsters and fabulous gargoyles reign in undisputed horror....
>
> As deep gave way to deep, gallery to gallery, and chamber to chamber, I felt transported to the strangest regions of nocturnal fancy. Grotesque formations leered on every hand, and the ever-sinking level appris'd me of the stupendous depth I was attaining. Glimpses of far black vistas beyond the radius of the lights—sheer drops of incalculable depth to unknown chasms, or arcades beckoning laterally to mysteries yet untasted by human eye—brought my soul close to the frightful and obscure frontiers of the material world, and conjured up suspicions of vague and unhallowed dimensions whose formless beings lurk ever close to the visible world of man's five senses. Buried æras—submerged civilizations—subterraneous universes and unsuspected orders of beings and influences that haunt the sightless depths—all these flitted thro' an imagination confronted by the actual presence of soundless and eternal night.

In his short autobiographical sketch, *Some Notes on a Non-Entity*, written in the early 1930s, HPL wrote that the earliest piece of fiction he could recall writing was "a tale of a hideous cave perpetrated at the age of seven and entitled 'The Noble Eavesdropper'." Elsewhere he once mentioned that this first of all his tales featured "a boy who overheard some horrible conclave of subterranean beings in a cave." Nothing more is known of *The Noble Eavesdropper*, but what *is* known is certainly emblematic of HPL's abiding fascination with caves, caverns and abysses high and low, on land, sea and, in a certain sense, in air.

A story called *The Secret Cave or John Lees adventure* [sic], written when HPL was eight or nine years old, features two children, ten-year-old John Lee and his two-year-old sister Alice. With their mother away from the house:

> ...the younger Lees went down cellar & began to rummage among the rubbish little alice leaned against the wall watching John. As John was

making a boat of barrel staves the Little girl gave a piercing cry as the bricks behind her crumbled away he rushed up to her & Lifted her out screaming loudly as soon as her screams subsided she said "the wall went away" John went up & saw that there was a passage he said to the little girl "lets come & see what this is" "Yes" she said the entered the place they could stand up it the passage was farther than they could see they John went back upstairs & went to the kitchen drawer & got 2 candles & some matches & then they went back to the cellar passage. the two once more entered there was plastering on the walls ceiling & floor nothing was visible but a box this was for a seat nevertheless they examined it & found it to contain nothing the walked on farther & pretty soon the plastering left off & they were in a cave Little alice was frightened at first but at her brothers assurance that it was "all right" she allayed her fears. soon they came to a small box which John took up & carried within pretty soon they came on a *boat* in it were two oars he dragged it with difficulty along with him soon they found the passage came to an abrupt stop he pulled the obstacle away & to his dismay water rushed in in torrents....

In what remains of this tiny story, John is able to swim but his sister drowns, John uses the boat to reach the cellar again, and the box proves to contain "a *solid gold* chunk worth about $10,000 enough to pay for any thing but the death of his sister." Besides the early appearance of the cave-theme, *The Secret Cave* is proof positive that at one time even HPL wrote like a child, albeit a very bright child.

In *The Mystery of the Grave-Yard or "A Dead Man's Revenge," A Detective Story*, written according to a note by HPL "in late 1898 or early 1899," the tale begins with a group of people in the village of "Mainville," all "standing around the Burns' Tomb":

> Joseph Burns was dead. (When dying, he had given the following strange orders:—"Before you put my body in the tomb, drop this ball onto the floor, at a spot marked 'A'." He then handed a small golden ball to the rector.) ... After The funeral services were finished, Mr Dobson (the rector) said, "My friends, I will now gratify the last wishes of the deceased. So saying, he descended into the tomb. (to lay the ball on the spot marked "A") Soon the funeral party began to be impatient, and after a time Mr. Cha's. Greene (the Lawyer) descended to make a search. Soon he came up with a frightened face, and said, "Mr Dobson is *not there*"!

There ensue several more "chapters" of approximately equal length to the first, until Dobson turns up again, unharmed. He reveals that before the time when he escaped:

"When I went down into the tomb," Said Dobson, "Everything was darkness, and I could see nothing. but Finally I discerned the letter "A" printed in white on the onyx floor, I dropped the ball on the Letter, and immediately a trap-door opened and a man sprang up...and he pulled me down into a brilliantly lighted, palatial apartment where I have Lived until today."

Then HPL grew several years older. His next surviving "early tale," the 1905 story entitled *The Beast in the Cave*, besides being written with adult-level competence, takes place entirely within "Mammoth Cave"—presumably the famous one in the U.S. state of Kentucky. Here the nameless narrator becomes separated from his tour group and wanders helplessly in the darkness until he encounters and kills a kind of white, degenerate, savage beast—which turns out to have been a man who had become lost in the cave-complex at some much earlier date.

The last of the line of the Counts de C—— in *The Alchemist*, while delving in the lower levels of one of the most dilapidated of the ancient turrets of his deserted castle, suddenly observes "a small trap-door with a ring, which lay directly beneath my feet."

> Pausing, I succeeded with difficulty in raising it, whereupon there was revealed a black aperture, exhaling noxious fumes which caused my torch to sputter, and disclosing in the unsteady glare the top of a flight of stone steps...I commenced my descent. The steps were many, and led to a narrow stone-flagged passage which I knew must be far underground.

In a subterranean chamber he encounters the deathless and malevolent alchemist Charles le Sorcier.

In *The Tomb*, the narrator Jervas Dudley in Massachusetts comes to know of "a vault...of ancient granite, weathered and discolored.... Excavated back into the hillside, the structure is visible only at the entrance." This sepulchre, the tomb of the extinct Hyde family, fascinates Jervas until (with the aid of an ancient key, conveniently found in his family's attic) he seems to himself to be able to enter "the vault on the abandoned slope," and travel into its black depths, continuing:

> A spell was upon me, and my heart leaped with an exultation I can but ill describe. As I closed the door behind me and descended the dripping steps by the light of my lone candle, I seemed to know the way; and though the

candle sputtered with the stifling reek of the place, I felt singularly at home in the musty, charnel-house air.

Later, he prowls the ruins of the 18th century Hyde mansion, near his home:

A favorite haunt of mine during the day was the ruined cellar of the mansion that had burned down.... On one occasion I startled a villager by leading him confidently to a shallow sub-cellar, of whose existence I seemed to know despite the fact that it had been unseen and forgotten for many generations.

In *Dagon*, the nameless narrator adrift in a lifeboat in the Pacific Ocean finds himself aground on a huge, muddy land that seems to have suddenly risen from the bottom of the sea. After making his way across the hideous and fish-reeking plain for many hours, he climbs a high mound:

...and looked down the other side into an immeasurable pit or canyon, whose black recesses the moon had not yet soared high enough to illumine. I felt myself on the edge of the world; peering over the rim into a fathomless chaos of eternal night. Through my terror ran curious reminiscences of *Paradise Lost*, and of Satan's hideous climb through the unfashioned realms of darkness.... As the moon climbed higher in the sky, I began to see that the slopes of the valley were not quite so perpendicular as I had imagined... Urged on by an impulse which I cannot definitely analyse, I scrambled with difficulty down the rocks and stood on the gentler slope beneath, gazing into the Stygian [*i.e.*, as deep and dark as hell itself] deeps where no light had yet penetrated.

A short while later, in this "abyss which had yawned at the bottom of the sea since the world was young," to his horror he spies a giant, carved monolith, and then the nightmarish sea-creature that seems to worship the monolith. "I think I went mad then."

The nameless narrator of *The Transition of Juan Romero*, which takes place in and around a vast underground gold mine, reports that the mining operation originally began with "a cavern of gold, lying deep below a mountain lake," following which "additional grottoes" full of gold had been located, so that miners now toiled day and night "in the numerous passages and rock hollows. The Superintendent, a Mr. Arthur, often [speculated] on the probable extent of the chain of caves." After a powerful blast of explosives in the deepest part of the mine, "a new abyss yawned indefinitely below the site of the blast; an abyss so monstrous that no handy line might fathom it, nor any lamp illuminate it."

> Baffled, the excavators sought a conference with the Superintendent, who ordered great lengths of rope to be taken to the pit, and spliced and lowered till a bottom might be discovered. Shortly afterward the pale-faced workmen apprised the Superintendent of their failure. Firmly though respectfully they signified their refusal to revisit the chasm, or indeed to work further in the mine until it was sealed. Something beyond their experience was evidently confronting them, for as far as they could ascertain, the void below was infinite.

The narrator's co-worker, Juan Romero, had been found as an apparent orphan child in Mexico in a hut "close to a rather unusual rock fissure," a rock fissure which had been closed by a subsequent avalanche. On the night following the discovery of the great abyss, Romero is impelled to enter the mine and find his way down ladder after ladder to the newly-opened cavern, with the narrator in hot pursuit. Finally the narrator reaches the abyss in the earth "which was now redly aglow, and which had evidently swallowed up the unfortunate Romero...[and was] now a pandemonium of flickering flame and hideous uproar." In the conclusion of the tale we learn that the "void" or "gulf" at the bottom of the mine now seems to have become, or returned to being, solid rock as far as drills can detect.

The central action of *The Statement of Randolph Carter* revolves around the descent into earth's depths by Randolph Carter's friend, Harley Warren. When the two men have pried up a certain immense granite slab in a forgotten rural cemetery in a "deep, damp hollow," they reveal "a black aperture, from which rushed an effluence of miasmal gases so nauseous that we started back in horror," and "the top of a flight of stone steps, dripping...and bordered by moist walls encrusted with nitre." Warren descends the steps for a very long time to "the innermost depths of that damnable open sepulchre," and what he sees down there is both horrible and not described, and he never comes back.

The German submarine commander in *The Temple*, alone at the bottom of the sea, discovers a mighty sunken city of tremendous antiquity, perhaps the fabled Atlantis. Chief among the structures he observes is the magnificent façade of a great building, "evidently a temple, hollowed from the solid rock.... It is palpably a part of the valley wall, though how the vast interior was ever excavated I cannot imagine. Perhaps a cavern or series of caverns furnished the nucleus." Although he cannot see inside the darkness of the great doorway, the interior of the temple "drew me more and more, [but] I feared its aqueous abysses with a blind and mounting terror." Later he sees "a flickering radiance, as if from an altar-flame far within" coming from inside the temple, and fancies "that I discerned objects in the temple—objects both stationary and moving—and seemed to hear again the unreal chant." As the tale ends, while still telling himself that he is hearing and seeing only illusions, he has donned his deep-sea diving apparatus and, like a true Lovecraftian hero, is on his way straight into the big cave: "I shall die calmly, like a German, in the black and forgotten depths.... I will...walk boldly up the steps into that primal shrine; that silent secret of unfathomed waters and uncounted years."

In *Facts Concerning the Late Arthur Jermyn and His Family*, the 18th century British explorer Sir Wade Jermyn, on foot in the Congo region of central Africa, locates "the gigantic walls and pillars of a forgotten city, and [the] silent, stone steps leading interminably down into the darkness of abysmal treasure-vaults and inconceivable catacombs." Early in 1912, his descendant Sir Arthur Jermyn ventures into the jungle and finds "what was left of" the lost city after its destruction by the N'bangu tribe.

> Its size must have been exaggerated, yet the stones lying about proved that it was no mere negro village. Unfortunately no carvings could be found, and the small size of the expedition prevented operations toward clearing the one visible passageway that seemed to lead down into the system of vaults which Sir Wade had mentioned.

We never do find out what might have been in those subterranean vaults found by Sir Wade and Sir Arthur.

In dreams, Kuranes of *Celephaïs* finds himself led through a village like his old ancestral village, "toward the channel cliffs, and...to the end of things—to the precipice and the abyss where all the village and all the world fell abruptly into the unechoing emptiness of infinity, and where even the sky ahead was empty and unlit...." At the end of his life

Kuranes plunges into the abyss that "was now a seething chaos of roseate and cerulean [*i.e.*, brilliant reds and blues] splendour," and falls through clouds and ether to his dream city.

The nameless searcher of *The Nameless City* discovers a low cliff face, hewn into which "were the unmistakable facades of several small, squat rock houses or temples," which prove to be cavern-temples undoubtedly used for worship by the unknown creatures who built the city. He investigates the interiors of these sand-choked hollows, finding altars and relics. By night he detects a strong night-wind coming from "the black orifice of a temple" larger than the rest, "presumably a natural cavern." Perceiving by his torchlight a small doorway chiseled from the rock at the back of the temple, "the opening to those remoter abysses whence the sudden wind had blown," he discovers "a black tunnel with the roof arching low over a rough flight of very small, numerous, and steeply descending steps." Naturally he goes down the mysterious stairway, traveling seemingly for miles underground, until he comes to an enormous cavern where he can only kneel or advance with a "creeping run." Growing phosphorescence shows him that: "This hall was no relic of crudity like the temples in the city above, but a monument of the most magnificent and exotic art." Further below he discovers a great brass gateway which leads to a "an illimitable void of uniform radiance," an infinity of subterranean effulgence," a "luminous abyss," into which the dawn wind now seems to be blowing *from* the surface world. He never passes this gateway, but he sees or senses what does: "the crawling reptiles of the nameless city," or at any event the furious "wind-wraiths" into which they have turned during uncountable ages of time.

The creature who narrates *The Outsider* speaks of being raised in a dank and sunless castle, all by himself, surrounded by towering black trees and all the suggestions of death: "To me there was nothing grotesque in the bones and skeletons that strowed some of the stone crypts deep down among the foundations." After a young lifetime of this he can stand no more, and climbs a great black tower, higher than any other, only (like Randolph Carter in the tower in the gugs' city in *The Dream-Quest of Unknown Kadath*) to find at the top a stone barrier, and after investigation "a slab [which] was the trap-door of an aperture leading to a level stone surface of greater circumference than the lower tower, no doubt the floor of some...observation chamber." Instead of that, upon raising the trap-door and passing through the "aperture," he finds himself inside a tomb, in a graveyard, and we (and he) come to realize that his entire remembered existence has been subterranean. Later he returns to the tomb:

> ...and went down the steps [and] found the stone trap-door immovable; but I was not sorry, for I had hated the antique castle and the trees. Now I ride with the mocking and friendly ghouls on the night-wind, and play by day among the catacombs of Nephren-Ka in the sealed and unknown valley of Hadoth by the Nile. I know that light is not for me, save that of the moon over the rock tombs of Neb, nor any gaiety save in the unnamed feasts of Nitokris beneath the Great Pyramid; yet in my new wildness and freedom I almost welcome the bitterness of alienage.
>
> For although nepenthe has calmed me, I know always that I am an outsider; a stranger in this century and among those who are still men.

Barzai the Wise in *The Other Gods* seems to be sucked into a hole in the heavens that seems analogous to a cave. From just below the peak of Hatheg-Kla, Barzai's disciple Atal hears him crying out: "Go back!... Do not see!... Do not see!... The vengeance of the infinite abysses... That cursed, that damnable pit...Merciful gods of earth, *I am falling into the sky!*"

In *Herbert West—Reanimator*, Dr. West and his comrade, during their years of medical practice in Bolton, use "a secret laboratory we had fitted up in the cellar." Years later in Boston, they install a secret laboratory in "a sub-cellar secretly constructed by imported workmen." Their house is across a street from one of Boston's oldest cemeteries, and the delving workmen strike "some exceedingly ancient masonry," "far too deep to correspond with any known sepulchre" in the graveyard. "After a number of calculations West decided that it represented some secret chamber beneath the tomb of the Averills [family], where the last interment had been made in 1768." One of its walls becomes a wall of the new sub-cellar. On the night of West's destruction, the old tomb-wall begins to open as "a small black aperture" with the smell of "the charnel bowels of a putrescent earth." West's dead victims emerge to dismember him and then to carry the fragments back "into that subterranean vault of fabulous abominations."

St. John and his companion, the nameless narrator of *The Hound*, having given up on modern art and poetry and turned to grave-robbing for thrills, prepare a "nameless museum" in their large stone house.

> It was a secret room, far, far underground, where huge winged daemons carven of basalt and onyx vomited from wide grinning mouths weird green and orange light, and hidden, pneumatic pipes ruffled into kaleidoscopic dances of death the lines of red charnel things hand in hand woven in voluminous black hangings. Through these pipes came at will the odours our moods most craved; sometimes the smell of pale funeral lilies, sometimes the narcotic incense of imagined Eastern shrines of the kingly dead, and sometimes—how I shudder to recall it—the frightful, soul-upheaving stenches of the uncovered grave.

The nameless narrator of *The Lurking Fear* is for a long time unable to comprehend how whatever is killing the upstate New York yokels in the Catskill Mountains—climaxing in the massacre of some 75 residents of a village of squatters on one night in the summer of 1921—is able to move about the countryside without being observed or detected, or leaving any trail. His puzzlement continues although he has noticed the "curious mounds and hummocks" in the rotten soil around Tempest Mountain. But on the night of November 21, 1921, he finds himself digging in the grave of Jan Martense when "at a monstrous depth" the ground gives way and he is in a "small horizontal tunnel which led away indefinitely in both directions." He scrambles into this earthen tunnel to see what he may find:

> What language can describe the spectacle of a man lost in infinitely abysmal earth; pawing, twisting, wheezing; scrambling madly through sunken convolutions of immemorial blackness...I became one with the moles and grubs of nighted depths.

On a subsequent night he runs through the dark to the cellar of the ruined Martense mansion, "digging unreasonably" in all parts of this hole. "And then I recall how I laughed when I stumbled on the passageway; the hole at the base of the old chimney...." From a place of concealment he watches as there came:

> ...from that opening beneath the chimney a burst of multitudinous and leprous life—a loathsome night-spawned flood of organic corruption....

> Seething, stewing, surging, bubbling like serpents' slime it rolled up and out of that yawning hole, spreading like a septic contagion and streaming from the cellar at every point of egress....

"It" is a horde of thousands of "dwarfed, deformed, hairy devils or apes," the reverse-evolution products of the troglodytic and cannibalistic Martense clan. The movement to beneath the earth's surface clearly had its origin in the 17th century, when the wealthy Martense who built the mansion began to retreat to the cellar to escape the sound and flashes of Tempest Mountain's frequent thunderstorms. Although the narrator later sends "a gang of men" to dynamite the Martense mansion and seal all the mound-burrows, his fear still lurks:

> The thing will haunt me, for who can say the extermination is complete, and that analogous phenomena do not exist all over the world? Who can, with my knowledge, think of the earth's unknown caverns without a nightmare dread of future possibilities? I cannot see a well or a subway entrance without shuddering...why cannot the doctors give me something to make me sleep, or truly calm my brain when it thunders?

In *The Rats in the Walls*, the entire tale is built on getting the protagonist into a vast cavern and driving him mad there. At first we learn that the foundation of Exham Priory was "a very singular thing, being merged on one side with the solid limestone of the precipice from whose brink the priory overlooked a desolate valley...." On the night of July 24, 1923, Mr. de la Poer is harassed by a dream of the most horrible sort, in which "I seemed to be looking down from an immense height upon a twilit grotto, knee-deep with filth.... [A] stinking abyss...." That night he hears the rats in the walls—which shouldn't be there at all—"engaged in one stupendous migration from inconceivable heights to some depth conceivably, or inconceivably, below." And all the cats in the place congregate yowlingly "before the closed door to the sub-cellar." That sub-cellar, a "vault built by Roman hands" and still containing a Roman altar, is thought to be the lowest part of the castle. Then they realize that there is another level beneath it:

> The discovery that some vault deeper than the deepest known masonry of the Romans underlay this accursed pile—some vault unsuspected by the curious antiquarians of three centuries—would have been sufficient to excite us without any background of the sinister. As it was, the fascination became twofold....

With a team of academic experts and one "psychic investigator" (who faints and then goes mad, while the tougher-fibered scholars do not), Mr. de la Poer and his neighbor Captain Norrys succeed in finding the way to the lower level, in the supposedly "solid limestone" of the foundation.

> Through a nearly square opening in the tiled floor [under the altar in the Roman vault]…[they descended to] a twilit grotto of enormous height, stretching away farther than any eye could see; a subterraneous world of limitless mystery and horrible suggestion….
>
> …
>
> Having grasped to some slight degree the frightful revelations of this twilit area…we turned to that apparently boundless depth of midnight cavern where no ray of light from the [natural fissures in the] cliff could penetrate. We shall never know what sightless Stygian worlds yawn beyond the little distance we went, for it was decided that such secrets are not good for mankind. But there was plenty to engross us close at hand, for we had not gone far before the searchlights shewed [*sic*] that accursed infinity of pits in which the rats had feasted….
>
> God, those carrion black pits of sawed, picked bones and opened skulls! Those nightmare chasms choked with the pithecanthropoid, Celtic, Roman, and English bones of countless unhallowed centuries! Some of them were full, and none could say how deep they had once been. Others were still bottomless to our searchlight, and peopled by unnamable fancies.

In *The Festival*, a bizarre midnight procession through the streets of Kingsport, with the nameless narrator in the crowd, ends in the great white church at the top of a high hill in the middle of town, where the creatures file into the sanctuary—and then go "to the trap-door of the vaults which yawned loathsomely open just before the pulpit, and were now squirming noiselessly in. I followed dumbly down the footworn steps and into the dank, suffocating crypt." The line of worshippers goes further and further down a stone spiral staircase that seems to be endless:

> It was a silent, shocking descent, and I observed after a horrible interval that the walls and steps were changing in nature, as if chiselled out of the solid rock…. After more aeons of descent I saw some side passages or burrows leading from unknown recesses of blackness to this shaft of nighted mystery. Soon they became excessively numerous, like impious catacombs of nameless menace…. I knew we must have passed down through the mountain and beneath the earth of Kingsport itself, and I shivered that a town should be so aged and maggoty with subterranean evil.
>
> The downward journey ends with a broadening of the passage to reveal "the boundless vista of an inner world—a vast fungous shore litten by a

belching column of sick greenish flame and washed by a wide oily river that flowed from abysses frightful and unsuspected to join the blackest gulfs of immemorial ocean."

All the important action of *Under the Pyramids* takes place—needless to say?—under the pyramids. After foreshadowing remarks in the earlier part of the tale about possible subterranean passages beneath the great Sphinx (including the intriguing "I would give much, in view of my experience, and of certain Bedouin whisperings...to know what has developed in connexion with a certain well in a transverse gallery where statues of the Pharaoh were found in curious juxtaposition to the statues of baboons"), Houdini finds himself being involuntarily lowered at the end of a rope through some kind of trap-door in the desert floor. His horror increases; the drop is too long; nothing should be as deep as the hole he is descending into. Finally waking on some kind of rock floor, he feels the rope let go from the top, and the cord beginning to fall and pile around him. Just as the shaft felt too deep, the rope is equally too long:

> I have said that the falling rope was piling up around and about me. Now I saw that it was *continuing to pile*, as no rope of normal length could possibly do. It gained in momentum and became an avalanche of hemp, accumulating mountainously on the floor, and half burying me beneath its swiftly multiplying coils. Soon I was completely engulfed and gasping for breath as the increasing convolutions submerged and stifled me. My senses tottered again.... It was not merely that I was tortured beyond human endurance—not merely that the life and breath seemed to be crushed out of me—it was the knowledge of *what those unnatural lengths of rope implied*, and the consciousness of what unknown and incalculable gulfs of inner earth must at this moment be surrounding me. My endless descent and swinging flight through goblin space, then, must have been real; and even now I must be lying helpless in some nameless cavern toward the core of the planet.

Later still, somehow freed from all that rope, and while trying to find some way out of this underground world, Houdini tripped at the top of an unseen stairway "and was precipitated headlong down a black flight of huge stone stairs into a gulf of hideousness unrelieved." Down at the bottom is a chamber of staggering height and extent, and in the chamber there is yet another hole, a doorway of some kind, so vast that "an ordinary house would have been lost in it, and any average public building could easily have been moved in and out." In that hole is the most frightening thing that Houdini will see.

"But after all, the attic was not the most terrible part of the house. It was the dank, humid cellar which somehow exerted the strongest repulsion on us, even though it was wholly above ground on the street side...." So HPL introduces the locus of life-sucking infestation in *The Shunned House*. In that cellar the nameless narrator and his uncle spend a night to try to solve the mystery of so many strange deaths in the building over the years, and the older, physically-weaker man is literally dissolved and melted by the malevolent and hungry being that is buried in the soil under the cellar.

The cellar of *The Shunned House* turns out to be the place where the mysterious vampirish entity is strongest; pointedly, we are told that:

> For example, the servant gossip was practically unanimous in attributing to the fungous and malodorous *cellar* of the house a vast supremacy in evil influence. There had been servants—Ann White especially—who would not use the cellar kitchen....

It is in the course of two subsequent visits to the cellar—which, owing to the architecture of the house, is partly dug into the slope to the rear, partly at ground level with a door opening to the sidewalk—that the nameless narrator first loses his uncle, then destroys the monstrous being buried deep beneath the cellar's dirt floor.

The Horror at Red Hook begins to move underground near the opening when Robert Suydam rents "a squalid basement flat in the Red Hook district, where he spent nearly every night, receiving odd delegations of mixed rowdies and foreigners, and apparently conducting some kind of ceremonial service...." Eventually he leases three entire apartment houses on the street called Parker Place. Meanwhile, the authorities learn vaguely that illegal aliens are being brought into Red Hook from ships in New York harbor "by stealth on moonless nights in rowboats which stole under a certain wharf and followed a hidden canal to a secret subterranean pool beneath a house." Investigating a missing-child case, Detective Malone has occasion to search the "old stone church and dance-hall" in Red Hook, "and he explored the basement with particular assiduity before he left."

On the June evening that follows the mid-day wedding of Robert Suydam and Cornelia Gerritsen, and at about the time of the honeymoon couple's weird deaths on a Europe-bound ocean liner, Malone takes part around midnight in a police raid on Parker Place and its environs, surprising "unbelievable throngs of mixed foreigners in figured robes, mitres, and other inexplicable devices," who hurl objects "hastily down unexpected shafts" to hide them from the policemen. Malone goes to Suydam's original basement flat, which has all the trappings of an alchemist's or wizard's den, and then attempts to break down a locked door leading down to a cellar below the basement apartment. As he strikes the old door, it cracks open from:

> the *other* side, whence poured a howling tumult of ice-cold wind with all the stenches of the bottomless pit, and whence reached a sucking force not of earth or heaven, which, coiling sentiently around the paralysed detective, dragged him through the aperture and down unmeasured spaces....

After passing through what seem to be "nighted crypts" and "titan arcades," he finds himself in a vast, luminous "crypt" where "dark, sticky water" washes against onyx piers and the hideous Lilith swims up out of the mirk. No one else ever sees these things that Malone has seen, but it is indisputable that he is later found "by the edge of a night-black pool," that is "deep below the house of Robert Suydam"—the Red Hook house, that is. And elsewhere the police learn:

> the canal to [Suydam's] house was but one of several subterranean channels and tunnels in the neighbourhood. There was a tunnel from this house to a crypt beneath the dance-hall church; a crypt [containing] a vast arched chapel with wooden benches and a strangely-figured altar. The walls were lined with small cells, in seventeen of which—hideous to relate—solitary prisoners in a state of complete idiocy were found chained, including four mothers with infants of disturbingly strange appearance. These infants died soon after exposure to the light; a circumstance with the doctors thought rather merciful.

The police note that at one place under Suydam's house the underground canal sank "into a well too deep for dredging." Although the well was "choked up at the mouth and cemented over when the cellars of the new homes were made.... Malone often speculates on what lies beneath." Meanwhile the police eventually learn that there are "rumours of new canals running underground" and that "the filled-up crypt has been dug out again, and for no simply explainable purpose."

In *He*, at a certain point while following his odd guide (the Squire) through the midnight streets of the Greenwich Village section of New York City, the narrator squeezes through cracks, tiptoes through corridors, clambers over brick walls, and "once crawled on hands and knees

through a low, arched passage of stone whose immense length and tor-
turous twistings effaced at last every hint of geographical location I had
managed to preserve." This is a man-made cavern. Later in the tale, when
the guide has been reduced by old magic to "a head with eyes...emitting
feeble little spits of immortal malice," the shapeless inky substance
(which must be the vengeful murdered Indians of the 18th century, having taken the Squire's head), sweeps past the narrator in "an awful torrent
of blackness.... It was seeking the door to the cellar, and when it found
it, it vanished therein."

In *In the Vault*, the receiving-tomb of the Peck Valley Cemetery
where George Birch gets his just deserts is a sort of cavern, being partly
underground at the rear: it is described as "the side-hill vault," *i.e.*, a
vault built into the side of a hill. "The vault had been dug from a hillside,
so that the narrow ventilation funnel in the top ran through several feet of
earth...." In a story that is so explicitly stated to take place on Good
Friday, HPL seems to be setting up a macabre parallel between George
Birch struggling to get out of this above-ground, dug-out tomb, and the
familiar image of Jesus Christ's resurrection from his similar place of
burial.

In *The Call of Cthulhu*, the New Orleans police detachment which
enters the swamps on November 1, 1907, visited a region where the local
squatters whispered of a hidden lake "in which dwelt a huge, formless
white polypous thing with luminous eyes," and of the "bat-winged devils
[which] flew up out of caverns in inner earth to worship it at midnight."
In his account to the Vice-Admiralty inquiry in Sydney, Australia,
Second Mate Johansen testified in a "queerly reticent" manner that six of
the *Emma*'s sailors died on the unknown island by "falling into a rock
chasm."

The unlucky sailors who come ashore at R'lyeh on March 23, 1925,
had found "an immense carved door," seeming to their disoriented eyes
like a trap-door or slanting outside cellar-door of gigantic size, which
they innocently succeeded in opening on some sort of counterweight-
system:

> The aperture was black with a darkness almost material. That tenebrous-
> ness was indeed a *positive quality*; for it obscured such parts of the inner
> walls as ought to have been revealed, and actually burst forth like smoke

from its aeon-long imprisonment, visibly darkening the sun as it slunk away into the shrunken and gibbous sky on flapping membraneous wings. The odour arising from the newly opened depths was intolerable, and at length the quick-eared Hawkins thought he heard a nasty, slopping sound down there. Everyone listened, and everyone was listening still when It lumbered slobberingly into sight and gropingly squeezed Its gelatinous green immensity through the black doorway....

Pickman's Model is a celebration of caverns, which revisits and improves upon *The Lurking Fear*'s central concept of reverse-evolution cannibals moving about in tunnels unsuspected by the surface dwellers: in this case, the corpse-eating ghouls (who also appear in *The Dream-Quest of Unknown Kadath*).

"There was something [in Pickman's secret studio]—and now I can't use the subway or (and you may as well have your laugh at this, too) go down into cellars any more," says the narrator, Thurber, to his friend Eliot near the beginning of the tale. Pickman had once told Thurber:

> Look here, do you know the whole North End [of Boston] once had a set of tunnels that kept certain people in touch with each other's houses, and the burying-ground, and the sea?... Why, man, out of ten surviving houses built before 1700 and not moved since I'll wager that in eight I can shew [*sic*] you something queer in the cellar. There's hardly a month that you don't read of workmen finding bricked-up arches and wells leading nowhere in this or that old place as it comes down....

When he sees Pickman's paintings set in modern times, Thurber feels some cause for alarm:

> Gad, how that man could paint! There was a study [*i.e.*, a painting] called "Subway Accident," in which a flock of the vile things were clambering up from some unknown catacomb through a crack in the floor of the Boylston Street subway [station] and attacking a crowd of people on the platform.... Then there were any number of cellar views, with monsters creeping in through holes and rifts in the masonry and grinning as they squatted behind barrels or furnaces and waited for their first victim to descend the stairs.
>
> One disgusting canvas seemed to depict a vast cross-section of Beacon Hill [a Boston district], with ant-like armies of the mephitic monsters squeezing themselves through burrows that honeycombed the ground.

The studio where Pickman paints these paintings, which he stores in a decaying and very old building he has rented in the North End, is in fact in the cellar of the place.

My host was now leading the way down cellar [*sic*] to his actual studio.... As we reached the bottom of the damp stairs he turned his flashlight to a corner of the large open space at hand, revealing the circular brick curb of what was evidently a great well in the earthen floor. We walked nearer, and I saw that it must be five feet across, with walls a good foot thick and some six inches above the ground level—solid work of the seventeenth century, or I was much mistaken. That, Pickman said, was the kind of thing he had been talking about—an aperture of the network of tunnels that used to undermine the hill. I noticed idly that it did not seem to be bricked up, and that a heavy disc of wood formed the apparent cover.

After Randolph Carter has seemingly gone back in time to himself as a young boy on a pleasant ordinary day at his uncle's farm in autumn, 1883, he takes *The Silver Key* with him to:

The strange cave in the forest slope, the dreaded "snake-den" which country folk shunned.... It was deep; far deeper than anyone but Randolph suspected, for the boy had found a fissure in the farthermost black corner that led to a loftier grotto beyond—a haunting sepulchral place whose granite walls held a curious illusion of conscious artifice. On this occasion he crawled in as usual, lighting his way with matches...and edging through the final crevice with an eagerness hard to explain even to himself.

During his day with the keeper of *The Strange High House in the Mist*, Thomas Olney hears from his host "how the Kings of Atlantis fought with the slippery blasphemies that wriggled out of rifts in ocean's floor." While climbing to the house from Kingsport, Professor Olney had at one point been able to "just make out the ancient graveyard by the Congregational Hospital, beneath which rumour said some terrible caves or burrows lurked."

All of Dreamland in *The Dream-Quest of Unknown Kadath* may be thought of as a metaphysical cavern, in that Randolph Carter descends by seventy steps of lighter slumber to reach the cavern-temple called the Cavern of Flame, then down another seven hundred steps to the Gate of Deeper Slumber. Before ascending Mount Ngranek, Carter hears talk of "caves in that mountain, which might be empty and alone with elder darkness, or might—if legend spoke truly—hold horrors of a form not to be surmised." Once he is high up on the mountainside, he perceives "curious cracks and caves.... Some of these were above him and some beneath him, all opening on sheerly perpendicular cliffs and all wholly unreachable by the feet of man." Darkness falls with Carter on a high and difficult cliff, with "a cave's dark mouth just out of reach above him." In the darkness, the night-gaunts appear to seize him and carry him "into that cliffside cavern and through monstrous labyrinths beyond," and fly downward until they come to "that inner world of subterrene horror," the Vale of Pnath.

He escapes and reaches upper Dreamland again only with the aid of the ghouls. The escape route in the twilit lower abyss takes the party through "endless burrows" and past the "the sheer perpendicular cliff at whose base an immense and forbidding cavern yawned...the entrance to the unhallowed vaults of Zin" where the ghasts dwell. Much later, when he has been captured in Inganok, he is taken to the temple of the high priest not to be described; it is stone, with no windows, and Carter is prodded through "mazes of narrow winding corridors"; it is a cave built by hands. The high priest is found in "a great domed space...whose centre held a gaping circular pit surrounded by six malignly stained stone altars in a ring." Attempting to escape, Carter shoves one of his captors into "that gaping well which rumour holds to reach down to the hellish Vaults of Zin," and races wildly through the pitch-black labyrinths of the monastery. As he persists, "the vault-like smell and incrustations on the greasy walls and floor alike warned him that he was burrowing deep in Leng's unwholesome table-land." And then he falls "dizzily downward in the dark through a burrow which must have been well-nigh vertical. He falls out of a cavern entrance in the ruined and deserted ancient city of Sarkomand.

Later he reaches the rock of the moon-beasts, out in the ocean, and with some ghouls roams curiously through the deserted "towers and eyries and fortresses chiselled from the solid stone.... Frightful were the secrets uncovered in those evil and windowless crypts...":

> The upper parts of the rock held more temples than private homes, and in numerous hewn chambers were found terrible carven altars.... From the rear of one great temple stretched a low black passage which Carter followed far into the rock with a torch till he came to a lightless domed hall of vast proportions...in whose centre yawned a foul and bottomless well like that in the hideous monastery of Leng.... On the distant shadowy side, beyond the noisome well, he thought he discerned a small door of strangely wrought bronze; but for some reason he felt an unaccountable dread of opening it or even approaching it, and hastened back through the cavern....

Watching Joseph Curwen's Pawtuxet road farm from concealment in the late 1760s, in *The Case of Charles Dexter Ward*, Ezra Weeden and his cohort Eleazar Smith "became early convinced that a great series of tunnels and catacombs...underlay the farm." Their later observations confirm them in the suspicion that there are "regions below" the house:

> Faint cries and groans unmistakably came up now and then from what appeared to be the solid earth in places far from any structure; whilst hidden in the bushes along the river-bank in the rear, where the high ground sloped steeply down to the valley of the Pawtuxet, there was found an arched oaken door in a frame of heavy masonry, which was obviously an entrance to caverns within the hill.

Before and during the raid on Joseph Curwen's farmhouse on the night of April 12–13, 1771, Captain Abraham Whipple, "whose belief in the existence of catacombs was absolute," makes careful plans for disposing some of the raiding party to enter any caverns they discover, and fight whatever enemy might be found there.

In the summer of 1927, Charles Dexter Ward purchases an old bungalow in Pawtuxet, Rhode Island, "a squalid little wooden edifice with a concrete garage, perched high on the sparsely settled bank of the [Seekonk] river slightly above Rhodes." Soon enough afterwards, the local people start to talk of "muffled shouting, declamation, rhythmic chanting, and screaming supposed to come from some very deep cellar below the place." Later inquiries carried out by Dr. Willett and Charles' father bring up rumors of "deeper and more spreading crypts" somewhere under the bungalow.

On April 6, 1928, Dr. Willett and the senior Mr. Ward go into the cellar of the Pawtuxet bungalow (which, needless to say, had been built by chance roughly over the site of Joseph Curwen's 18th century subterranean complex), and there find a hidden concrete manhole of recent date, leading downward. Upon taking off the cover, Dr. Willett sees "a sheer cylindrical drop with concrete walls and an iron ladder; after which the hole appeared to strike a flight of old stone steps which must originally have emerged to earth somewhat south of the present building." Below the ground, in an "underground world of nightmare labyrinths," the doctor finds old offices, storerooms, cells for captives, a laboratory, torture devices and implements, even "a circle of pillars grouped like the monoliths of Stonehenge, with a large carved altar on a base of three steps in the centre...." He finds worse than that, too.

In *The Colour Out of Space*, the Colour takes shelter eventually in the well in the barnyard of Nahum Gardner's farm. In 1883, "Thaddeus went mad in September, after a visit to the well. He had gone with a pail and had come back empty-handed, shrieking and waving his arms, and sometimes lapsing into an inane titter or a whisper about 'the moving colours down there.'" Later, Merwin Gardner simply disappears one night when he goes out to the well for water. When Ammi Pierce visits the Gardner farm two weeks later, and asks where the other boy, Zenas, is, Nahum Gardner answers madly: "In the well—he lives in the well—" A few minutes later, before he crumbles to dust, Gardner tells Pierce: "...the colour...it burns...cold an' wet, but it burns...it lived in the well...."

When Ammi Pierce returns to the Gardner farm in the afternoon with three Arkham policemen, the coroner, the medical examiner, and an Arkham veterinarian, the authorities insisted on searching the fatal well:

> ...Ammi had to wait trembling while pail after pail of rank water was hauled up and splashed on the soaking ground outside. The men sniffed in disgust at the fluid, and toward the last held their noses against the foetor they were uncovering. It was not so long a job as they had feared it would be, since the water was phenomenally low. There is no need to speak exactly of what they found. Merwin and Zenas were both there, in part, although the vestiges were mainly skeletal. There were also a small deer and a large dog in about the same state, and a number of bones of smaller animals. The ooze and slime at the bottom seemed inexplicably porous and bubbling, and a man who descended on hand-holds with a long pole found that he could sink the wooden shaft to any depth in the mud of the floor without meeting any solid obstruction.

That night Pierce and the men from Arkham are involuntary witnesses to the Colour's departure into what the nameless narrator later calls "the deep skyey voids above." Decades later when the nameless narrator wades through the ruins of the Gardner farmyard, surveying for the new Arkham reservoir, he spies "the yawning black man of [the] abandoned well whose stagnant vapours played strange tricks with the hues of the sunlight."

Dr. Albert N. Wilmarth, near the outset of *The Whisperer in Darkness*, mentions the rumors of "certain caves of problematical depth in the sides of the [Vermont] hills; with mouths closed by boulders in a manner scarcely accidental...." Later, Henry W. Akeley sends him a photograph of such a suspicious, blocked cave-mouth. When he visits Akeley's farm at last, Dr. Wilmarth learns from a disembodied human brain in a metal cylinder, attached to a kind of speaking-machine, that the Mi-Go have an outpost underneath Round Hill not far from the Akeley place, where it and the brains of other human and non-human entities are stored in transit.

Scouting the Antarctic interior from an airplane on January 22, 1931, in *At the Mountains of Madness*, Professor Lake reports a mountain range with peaks higher than any others known on earth, and that "close flying shews [shows] many cave mouths, some unusually regular in outline, square or semicircular." A day or two later, Lake's boring team "struck a cave"—a covered-up and dry prehistoric river—from at least thirty million years ago. Through "a jagged aperture perhaps five feet across and three feet thick, they discover a "subterrene secret" that is a "hollowed layer not more than seven or eight feet deep, but extend[ing] off indefinitely in all directions and [which] had a fresh, slightly moving air which suggested its membership in an extensive subterranean system." In this cave, besides much "normal" fossil material, they find the preserved bodies of a number of the winged, star-headed anomalies from, apparently, thirty million years ago.

Later, in the lost city of the winged, star-headed Old Ones, Professor Dyer recounts that: "The best of the maps and diagrams were on the walls of a frightful abyss below even the ancient ground level—a cavern perhaps 200 feet square and sixty feet high, which had almost undoubtedly been an educational centre of some sort."

The endless wall-carvings inform them of a "sea-cavern city" to which the inhabitants of the surface city had retreated with the coming of the great cold, millions of years ago. Professor Danforth and the graduate student Dyer pick up the challenge like proper Lovecraftian heroes:

> ...our study of the decadent sculptures brought about a change in our immediate objective. This of course had to do with the chiselled avenues to the black inner world, of whose existence we had not known before, but which we were now eager to find and traverse. From the evident scale of the carvings we deduced that a steeply descending walk of about a mile through either of the neighbouring tunnels would bring us to the brink of the dizzy sunless cliffs above the great abyss; down whose side adequate paths, improved by the Old Ones, led to the rocky shore of the hidden and nighted ocean. To behold this fabulous gulf in stark reality was a lure which seemed impossible of resistance once we knew of the thing....

After much exploring the men locate the tunnel-mouth:

> Then the corridor ended in a prodigious open space which made us gasp involuntarily—a perfect inverted hemisphere, obviously deep underground; fully an hundred feet in diameter and fifty feet high, with low archways opening around all parts of the circumference but one, and that one yawning cavernously with a black arched aperture which broke the symmetry of the vault to a height of nearly fifteen feet. It was the entrance to the great abyss.... The black tunnel yawned indefinitely off at a steep descending grade.... From that cryptical mouth we fancied a current of slightly warmer air and perhaps even a suspicion of vapour proceeded....

"Doubtless it was suicidally foolish to venture into that tunnel under the known conditions, but the lure of the unplumbed is stronger in certain persons than most suspect," dryly comments Professor Dyer, and venture in they do. Finding their way through the black depths with their flashlights, they encounter steep descents, an increasing number of inexplicable side-galleries "honeycombing" the earth, and a vast artificial cavern with a smooth and level rock floor. Eventually they find a shoggoth, one of many that must be living in the abyss, and flee to the surface.

Significantly, when the narrator of *The Shadow Over Innsmouth* first sees the mysterious town, while riding in Joe Sargent's bus, he passes an old church that has "a disproportionately high basement with shuttered windows":

> The door of the church basement was open, revealing a rectangle of blackness inside. And as I looked, a certain object crossed or seemed to cross that dark rectangle, burning into my brain a momentary conception of nightmare which was all the maddening because analysis could not shew [*sic*] a single nightmarish quality in it.... Clearly, as I realised a moment later, it was the pastor; clad in some peculiar vestments....

In *The Dreams in the Witch House* the student Walter Gilman spends many a night dreaming dreams:

> ...consist[ing] largely in plunges through limitless abysses of inexplicably colored twilight and bafflingly disordered sound; abysses whose material and gravitational properties, and whose relation to his own entity, he could not even begin to explain.... The abysses were by no means vacant, being crowded with indescribably angled masses of alien-hued substance, some of which appeared to be organic while others seemed inorganic.... All the

objects—organic and inorganic alike—were totally beyond description or even comprehension.

In *Through the Gates of the Silver Key* the child Randolph Carter is at first back in that cave, the place people always associate with the old wizard Edmund Carter. "In another moment he had wriggled through the weed-choked fissure at the farthest end, and was in the vast, unknown inner grotto whose ultimate rock wall seemed half like a monstrous and consciously shapen pylon." After many incredible experiences out of this world and time, he manages to return to the area of the cave, and for a time he hides his light-beam envelope there. On the planet Yaddith, the wizard Zkauba, whose body Randolph Carter shares, has the job of casting spells to keep the bholes from breaking out of their subterranean tunnels and laying waste to the surface world. "There were hideous struggles with the bleached, viscous bholes in the primal tunnels that honeycombed the planet."

In *The Thing on the Doorstep*, after a couple of years of marriage Edward Derby tells his oldest friend, Daniel Upton, some shocking things about "terrible meetings in strange places, of Cyclopean ruins in the heart of the Maine woods beneath which vast staircases lead down to abysses of nighted secrets...." Some time later, when Upton has been called to retrieve his friend from a cell in the village of Chesuncook, Maine, where he had inexplicably emerged from the forest like a "draggled madman," Derby tells him of:

> The pit of the shoggoths! Down the six thousand steps...the unholy pit where the black realm begins and the watcher guards the gate....

Later Derby shoots his wife Asenath—who is really Ephraim Waite in his daughter's body—and buries the corpse in a "remote cellar storeroom" of their mansion. Some weeks afterwards Derby found himself "choked in the dark—in Asenath's rotting carcass down there in the cellar under the boxes where I put it."

In the marvelous *The Shadow Out of Time,* after Professor Nathaniel Wingate Peaslee of Miskatonic University has had his strange transformation in 1908, he:

> ...spent weeks alone beyond the limits of previous or subsequent exploration in the vast limestone cavern systems of western Virginia—black labyrinths so complex that no retracing of my steps could even be considered.

After 1915, as his interior visions of the years he had spent as a captive of the Great Race begin to emerge in his dreams, he sees the sights he had witnessed in their midst 150,000,000 years before, including "multiple levels of black vaults below [certain structures], and never-opened trap-doors, sealed down with metal bands and holding dim suggestions of some special peril." He learns later that these sealed trap-doors, for which the Great Race have a special fear, concerns the "horrible elder race of half-polypous, utterly alien entities...only partly material—as we understand matter" who had preceded the Great Race in tenanting Earth, and who had been driven "down to those caverns of inner earth which they had already joined to their abodes and begun to inhabit." It was known that one day the elder things would have the strength and numbers to erupt to the surface solely to take vengeance on the Great Race—before returning to "earth's inner abysses" which they seemed to really prefer. In other words, they could still be down there. In other dreams Peaslee revisits the Great Race's central archives, "in a colossal subterranean structure near the city's centre."

Late on the night of July 17–18, 1935, Peaslee leaves his expedition's camp in the Australian desert and finds his way alone through the shockingly ancient ruins to discover—like Mr. de la Poer in *The Rats in the Walls*—a "faint, insidious stream of cool air trickling upward," which tells him of "a hidden gulf of great size beneath the disordered blocks on the surface."

> I wrenched aside one titan fragment of stone and then another, till there welled up a strong draught [draft] whose dampness contrasted oddly with the desert's dry air. A black rift began to yawn, and at length...the leprous moonlight blazed on an aperture of ample width to admit me.... [There was] a gulf of impenetrable blackness at whose upper edge were signs of gigantic, stress-heaved vaulting....
>
> In retrospect, the barest idea of a sudden, lone descent into such a doubtful abyss—and at a time when one's whereabouts were unknown to any living soul—seems like the utter apex of insanity. Perhaps it was—yet that night I embarked without hesitancy upon such a descent.

Of course, he does. During the ensuing passages he explores, or re-explores, buried structures he had known while his mind was held captive by the Great Race in the age of dinosaurs, and finds one of those trap-doors...open....

It may be stretching a point to call the invisible labyrinth of *In the Walls of Eryx* a kind of exposed cave, functionally, but the similarity to being lost in a complex underground cavern is there, for in both situations the trapped individual's sense of sight is materially diminished in value. The tale's protagonist, Stanfield, also notes that there are no higher life-forms on Venus than the "man-lizards": "unless those holes in the Dionaean Plateau hide something."

MORE LOVECRAFTIAN BOOKS

THE PSEUDONOMICON
by Phil Hine

What is *The Pseudonomicon*?
It's Cthulhu Mythos.
It's Cthulhu Madness!
It's a Cthulhu Pathworking!!

First published in a very limited
edition in1994, and reprinted only
once since, *The Pseudonomicon*
has been extremely difficult to find.
By special arrangement with Dagon
Productions, we have brought it
back in this revised and expanded
edition.
ISBN 1-56184-195-1

THE INFERNAL TEXTS: NOX & LIBER KOTH
by Stephen Sennitt

NOX includes 22 Infernal Texts from
the Order of Nine Angles, the
Werewolf Order, and the Esoteric
Order of Dagon by such notables as
Phil Hine, Anton Long and Stephen
Sennitt.

Liber Koth is a book of invocations. It
utilizes Lovecraftian symbology
including Yog-Sothoth, Nyarlathotep,
Cthulhu, Tsathogua and others.
ISBN 1-56184-234-6

FROM TIMOTHY LEARY, Ph.D.

NEUROPOLITIQUE

A New Vision of Neuropolitics
With Robert Anton Wilson &
George Koopman

The first version of *Neuropolitics* was written between 1973-1976 when Dr. Leary was in prison. Several chapters were composed during solitary confinement. Leary explores the role of the dissident/ philosopher and offers a multitude of brilliant observations on our past, present and, especially, our future. One of his best. Updated and rewritten for the 90's.

ISBN 1-56184-012-2

INFO-PSYCHOLOGY

A Revision of Exo-Psychology

"The Info-Worlds our species will discover, create, explore and in- habit in the immeditate future will not be reached from launch pads alone, but also through our per- sonal computer screens."

Dr. Leary explores the *real* issues of our time: Space Migration, Intelligence Increase and Life Extension in this "Manual On The Use Of The Human Nervous System According To The Instruc- tions Of The Manufacturers".

ISBN 1-56184-105-6

FROM ROBERT ANTON WILSON

COSMIC TRIGGER I
Final Secret of the Illuminati

The book that made it all happen! Explores Sirius, Synchronicities, and Secret Societies. Wilson has been called "One of the leading thinkers of the Modern Age."

"A 21st Century Renaissance Man. ...funny, optimistic and wise..."
—*The Denver Post*

ISBN 1-56184-003-3

COSMIC TRIGGER II
Down to Earth

In this, the second book of the *Cosmic Trigger* trilogy, Wilson explores the incredible Illuminati-based synchronicities that have taken place since his ground-breaking masterpiece was first published.
Second Revised Edition!

"Hilarious... multi-dimensional... a laugh a paragraph." —*The Los Angeles Times*

ISBN 1-56184-011-4

COSMIC TRIGGER III
My Life After Death

Wilson's observations about the premature announcement of his death, plus religious fanatics, secret societies, quantum physics, black magic, pompous scientists, Orson Welles, Madonna and the Vagina of Nuit.

"A SUPER-GENIUS... He has written everything I was afraid to write."
—Dr. John Lilly, psychologist

ISBN 1-56184-112-9

FROM ROBERT ANTON WILSON

PROMETHEUS RISING

Readers have been known to get angry, cry, laugh, even change their entire lives. Practical techniques to break free of one's 'reality tunnels'. A very important book, now in its *eighth* printing.

"*Prometheus Rising* is one of that rare category of modern works which intuits the next stage of human evolution... Wilson is one of the leading thinkers of the Modern age."
　　　—Barbara Marx Hubbard

ISBN 1-56184-056-4

QUANTUM PSYCHOLOGY
How Brain Software Programs You & Your World

The book for the 21st Century. Picks up where *Prometheus Rising* left off. Some say it's materialistic, others call it scientific and still others insist it's mystical. It's all of these—and none.

Second Revised Edition!

"Here is a Genius with a Gee!"
　　—Brian Aldiss, *The Guardian*
"What great physicist hides behind the mask of Wilson?"
　　　　　—*New Scientist*

ISBN 1-56184-071-8

POST MODERN LOGIC

What are the strange connections among the Christian coalition, Aristotelian logic, the foreign policy of the U.S. government, the Knights Templar, the attacks of September 11, 2001, and the confiscation of the author's apartment?

This is an extraordinary book. It's history. It's philosophy. It's an introduction to new discoveries which contribute to understanding the Templars and their Anglo-American roots. Marvelously exciting, delightful to read, with dash, vibrancy and simplicity that compels the reader. One of the most provocative works in post modern history.

ISBN 1-56184-167-6

FUZZY SETS

Fuzzy Sets forces us to look at reality in a different, more expansive and meaningful way. This enthusiastically and carefully argued account will convince any reader that The Devil is back as a serious discussion partner—disguised as the law of excluded middle in Aristotelian Logic. What's more, it's readable, lyrical and even gripping. On the one hand, a majestic analysis and reconstruction of an apparently difficult subject; on the other, a stunning portrait of the power of vagueness.

"An avant-garde work."
— Radio Free Europe

ISBN 1-56184-146-3

New Falcon Publications

Invites You to Visit Our Website:
http://www.newfalcon.com

At the Falcon website you can:

- Browse the online catalog of all of our great titles
- Find out what's available and what's out of stock
- Get special discounts
- Order our titles through our secure online server
- Find products not available anywhere else including:
    - One of a kind and limited availability products
    - Special packages
    - Special pricing
- Get free gifts
- Join our email list for advance notice of New Releases and Special Offers
- Find out about book signings and author events
- Send email to our authors (including the elusive Dr. Christopher Hyatt!)
- Read excerpts of many of our titles
- Find links to our author's websites
- Discover links to other weird and wonderful sites
- And much, much more

Get online today at http://www.newfalcon.com